GUIDE TO AMERICAN CINEMA, 1930–1965

Reference Guides to the World's Cinema

Guide to the Cinema of Spain
Marvin D'Lugo

Guide to American Cinema, 1965–1995
Daniel Curran

A Guide to African Cinema
Sharon A. Russell

GUIDE TO AMERICAN CINEMA, 1930–1965

THOMAS WHISSEN

Reference Guides to the World's Cinema
Pierre L. Horn, Series Adviser

GREENWOOD PRESS
Westport, Connecticut • London

Library of Congress Cataloging-in-Publication Data

Whissen, Thomas R.
   Guide to American cinema, 1930–1965 / Thomas Whissen.
      p.   cm. — (Reference guides to the world's cinema, ISSN
   1090–8234)
   Includes bibliographical references and index.
   ISBN 0–313–29487–9 (alk. paper)
   1. Motion pictures—United States—History.   I. Title.
   II. Series.
   PN1993.5.U6W46   1998
   791.43'75'0973—dc21   97–46520

British Library Cataloguing in Publication Data is available.

Library of Congress Catalog Card Number: 97–46520
ISBN: 0–313–29487–9
ISSN: 1090–8234

First published in 1998

Greenwood Press, 88 Post Road West, Westport, CT 06881
An imprint of Greenwood Publishing Group, Inc.

Printed in the United States of America

The paper used in this book complies with the
Permanent Paper Standard issued by the National
Information Standards Organization (Z39.48–1984).

10 9 8 7 6 5 4 3 2 1

CONTENTS

SERIES FOREWORD

For the first time, on December 28, 1895, at the Grand Café in Paris, France, the inventors of the *Cinématographe*, Auguste and Louis Lumière, showed a series of eleven two-minute silent shorts to a public of thirty-five people each paying the high entry fee of one gold Franc. From that moment, a new era had begun, for the Lumière brothers not only were successful in their commercial venture, but they also unknowingly created a new visual medium quickly to become, throughout the world, the half-popular entertainment, half-sophisticated art of the cinema. Eventually, the contribution of each member of the profession, especially that of the director and performers, took on enormous importance. A century later, the situation remains very much the same.

The purpose of Greenwood's *Reference Guides to the World's Cinema* is to give a representative idea of what each country or region has to offer to the evolution, development, and richness of film. At the same time, because each volume seeks to present a balance between the interests of the general public and those of students and scholars of the medium, the choices are by necessity selective (although as comprehensive as possible) and often reflect the author's own idiosyncracies.

André Malraux, the French novelist and essayist, wrote about the cinema and filmmakers: "The desire to build up a world apart and self-contained, existing in its own right . . . represents humanization in the deepest, certainly the most enigmatic, sense of the word." On the other hand, then, every *Guide* explores this observation by offering discussions, written in a jargon-free style, of the motion-picture art and its practitioners, and on the other provides much-needed information, seldom available in English, including filmographies, awards and honors, and ad hoc bibliographies.

Pierre L. Horn
Wright State University

PREFACE

Given such an abundance of memorable films and film personalities, there is no way, in a book of this length, to be exhaustive. Forced to be selective, I used the following criteria in choosing who and what should and should not be included:

1. *Amount and availability of bibliographical material*. With few exceptions, I did not include entries on works or persons about whom little or nothing has been written. A lack of bibliography suggests a lack of continuing interest, and this book is for those who wish to do further research into a particular film, actor, or director. Therefore, although I have been selective in my choice of bibliographical entries, I have been as complete as possible in most cases, especially where interest in the entry runs high: for example, *Psycho*, James Dean, Marilyn Monroe, Orson Welles.

2. *Number and quality of awards*. Awards are not always the best indication of merit, but they do indicate a level of professional appreciation that cannot be overlooked. Nothing, however, beats reputation. Cary Grant received no awards during his career, yet a roster of Hollywood's greats is unimaginable without him. James Stewart was largely ignored, yet there are those who think he was so very great that his "acting" went unnoticed. Others like Spencer Tracy and Henry Fonda made it all seem so easy that when they did win an award, it was compensation for a lifetime of neglect, while Luise Rainer made two pictures, won Oscars back to back, and was heard from no more.

3. *Notoriety*. Although Marilyn Monroe and James Dean and Judy Garland did possess fantastic talent, it didn't hurt that they made headlines and that they died young. Others like Jean Harlow or Mary Astor are also remembered as being mixed up in scandals. And Elizabeth Taylor built her reputation on a sequence of scandals.

4. *Test of time*. Regardless of their initial reception, some contenders had to be eliminated because they had not withstood the test of time. Movies like *Cavalcade* have dated badly, as have some of the famous comedies of the 1930s. However, personalities like Laurel and Hardy or the Marx Brothers have become such legends that they are included even if their once-celebrated humor has lost much of its charm. The early taste for film biographies resulted in films that seem mostly dated and dull today (*Abe Lincoln in Illinois, The Life of Disraeli, Alexander Graham Bell*). And the western wore itself out, as did the musical, although within those two genres are many gems. Similarly, some reputations have faded. Acclaimed actresses like Norma Shearer, Luise Rainer, or Shirley Booth no longer spark much interest, even among movie buffs. And once popular actresses such as Teresa Wright, Joan Caulfield, or Ruth Roman have long since lost their luster.

5. *Critical acclaim*. What critics think has also played its part in helping me make choices. While I disagree with critics as much as they disagree with each other, if there is a substantial body of considered opinion for or against a film, and if later opinion supports or refutes the originals, I have felt compelled to include that film, especially if the film originally suffered from critical neglect.

6. *Cult favorites*. Some films deserved inclusion because they have become cult classics, meaning that they have remained popular among a group of dedicated fans vocal enough to draw continued attention to them. *Out of the Past* and *Invasion of the Body Snatchers*, for example, are films that, while they may be of little interest to some viewers, may be of intense interest to others.

7. *Personal favorites*. While writing this book, I retreated farther and farther from imposing my taste on the selection process. One by one, some of my personal favorites found their way to the "cutting room floor," while others I've never particularly cared for remained. Still, I must admit that I have tried only halfheartedly to maintain strict neutrality. There simply are some films (*Shane, Citizen Kane, On the Waterfront*) that I find overrated, as there are some actors and actresses about whom I have mixed feelings. (I like the Katharine Hepburn of the 1950s but not the 1930s or the 1960s, and I happen to be an unrepentant Doris Day fan—talk about naturally brilliant but underrated talent!) Although I don't think I have included any movie for personal reasons alone, I admit to not having kept my biases entirely in check.

INTRODUCTION

The first thirty-five years of talking pictures (1930–1965) are often referred to as Hollywood's ''golden age.'' Those were the years when everything about sound pictures was new, and the challenge attracted the best talents from all the arts from all over the world: novelists like F. Scott Fitzgerald and William Faulkner; illustrious stage actors like the Barrymores and Helen Hayes; distinguished composers like Erich Korngold, Franz Waxman, and Max Steiner; popular songwriters like Irving Berlin, Harold Arlen, Jerome Kern, and the Gershwins; renowned foreign directors like Frank Capra, Ernst Lubitsch, Billy Wilder, and Michael Curtiz; not to mention prestigious costume and set designers, makeup artists, cameramen, and playwrights. Into this mix came ambitious home-grown talent so phenomenal that no school of acting has been able to distill the unique magic of such luminaries as Gary Cooper, James Stewart, Clark Gable, Cary Grant, Katharine Hepburn, Bette Davis, Joan Crawford, and Rosalind Russell. And the movies they made could be vastly entertaining without assaulting the ears or insulting the intelligence.

Perhaps the miracle of *Gone with the Wind* best illustrates this period's claim to greatness. In 1939, sound was only ten years old, color was still to a degree experimental, budgets were limited, and there were myriad minor restrictions imposed on filmmaking at the time, the most obvious being the production code that had to be bypassed somehow if Rhett Butler were to be able to speak his ''famous last words.'' To squeeze a thousand-page blockbuster best-seller into a three-and-three-quarter-hour movie (itself a point of controversy) and to hope to satisfy those millions of avid readers who would savage anything that didn't measure up was a formidable undertaking. That what emerged not only pleased but excited the book's fans was a miracle. Look closely and you will glimpse the magic that was filmmaking at the time. Notice the fast pacing, the natural acting, the narrative thrust, the brilliantly appropriate but never intrusive music. It's a movie that's not afraid to underscore its point, yet there is never even a hint of parody. Movies back then took themselves seriously. Imagine today trying to emote in a barren field over a shriveled carrot. Movies then did not wink or smirk. Today they can rarely keep from making fun of themselves—in spite of themselves.

The year 1965 was a watershed year in many ways. The early part of the decade saw the passing of many great world figures, while the last half saw the emergence of what we now casually refer to as "The Sixties." It also marked the collapse of the studio system (which had been teetering since 1950) and the beginning of a totally new era of independent filmmaking that wrought havoc with the studios. By then the impact of television on movie attendance was clear and permanent, and movies had to relax all kinds of standards and dumb down a lot of pictures to get (largely younger) audiences into the theater. (Before 1965, movies were unrated—believe it or not!) It also marked the end of the movie palace and the rise of the multiplex. The impact of this change is obvious even in the careers of persons who span both sides of the 1965 line. Look at the films of Paul Newman or Robert Mitchum before and after. To compare the periods, think of the Audrey Hepburn or Grace Kelly of the 1950s as opposed to Sharon Stone or Madonna of the 1990s.

While modern movies may seem to be emerging at last from the shadows of the past and developing a respectable new cinema, that shadow is a long one, and although they cannot help it, movies still owe a tremendous debt to the past—and especially those richly creative and brilliantly innovative decades of the 1930s and 1940s. *King Kong* set the standard for special effects, while *Frankenstein* and especially *Bride of Frankenstein* not only spawned the "sequel" but also set the standard for both horror and spoof of horror. There's a direct line from *Bride of Frankenstein* to *The Rocky Horror Picture Show*. There's also a direct line from gangster films like *Public Enemy* and *Little Caesar* to *The Godfather* and *Goodfellas*; from *Gun Crazy* to *Natural Born Killers*; from the Saturday matinee serials to the Indiana Jones chronicles. Parallels can be drawn in all genres—westerns, science fiction, war—with the possible exception of musicals, although the success of *Evita* may be a sign. And while directors such as Orson Welles, Billy Wilder, and Alfred Hitchcock have disciple directors like Brian DePalma and Blake Edwards, the screwball comedies of Howard Hawks inspired Peter Bogdanovitch, and the epics of Cecil B. DeMille and John Ford lead directly to those of Steven Spielberg and George Lucas. Even film noir, a sort of "accidental" creation of the 1940s (Bette Davis quipped that Jack Warner was just too cheap to turn up the lights), finds its echo in films like Kenneth Branagh's *Dead Again* and Roman Polanski's *Chinatown*.

A word must be said about the famous (or, if you prefer, infamous) studio system. For all that was wrong with it, particularly the stranglehold it allowed studio heads to have over everything from people to scripts, it had a lot going for it. It left nothing to chance. Talent wasn't just sought; it was created—and cultivated. Only a studio could take the time and money to turn a Rita Casino—with her low brow and peasant look—into Rita Hayworth, sex goddess of the mid-40s. Only a studio could take the time and money to nurture the natural talents of a Gary Cooper or Clark Gable. And considering the years it took to develop a Humphrey Bogart or Spencer Tracy into bankable stars, it is unlikely that either would have made it on his own today. True, the studios put their contract players through the hoops, but it's an exercise that can pay off.

The studio system in its heyday, when studios controlled distribution, could afford to produce quality pictures that, while they might lose money, brought prestige to the studio. These pictures could not have been made had it not been for the lower-budget, popular features that drew in the crowds. Moviemaking has always been a business (deals are still cut in New York City), and the moviemakers of the golden age never forgot this. Egos were sacrificed to the almighty budget and the tyranny of the box office. The story goes that when the eminent playwright George Bernard Shaw was discussing the filming of his plays with director Gabriel Pascal, Shaw, at one point, said, "The trouble with you, sir, is that you are interested in art, while I am interested in money." Pascal did film *Pygmalion* and *Major Barbara* on modest budgets and with gratifying success, but the financial fiasco of *Caesar and Cleopatra* virtually ended his career. With the collapse of the studio system in the early 50s, unleashed egos often led to financial fiascos like *Cleopatra* and *Hello, Dolly*, pictures that effectively sank their host studio. In 1997, another effect manifested itself: the decline of the studio picture in favor of independent productions at Oscar time. Whereas studio pictures had traditionally dominated, if not monopolized, the Academy Awards presentations, only one picture was a studio production when awards time rolled around. Perhaps now the dust of the collapsed studio system has finally settled, and movies can enter an exciting and productive new age.

A

ABBOTT AND COSTELLO. Actors. Bud Abbott was born William A. Abbott on October 2, 1895, in Asbury Park, New Jersey; he died on April 24, 1974. Lou Costello was born Louis Francis Costello on March 6, 1906, in Paterson, New Jersey; he died on March 3, 1959. Abbott and Costello became the most successful comedy team of the 1940s and were always among the top ten moneymakers. Abbott grew up on Coney Island and didn't have much luck breaking into show business until one day in 1931, while working as a cashier at a Brooklyn theater, he was asked to substitute for comedian Lou Costello's ailing straightman. After the team split up in 1957, Abbott tried without much success to resume his stage and TV career alone and with another partner. Abbott spent his last years in poverty in a nursing home. He died of cancer in 1974.

Lou Costello worked as a newsboy, soda fountain clerk, salesman, and prizefighter before going to Hollywood in the late 1920s in an attempt to break into films. About the only film work he could find was as a laborer on the MGM and Warner lots and eventually some stunt assignments and extra work (in, among others, the 1927 Laurel and Hardy comedy *The Battle of the Century*). So he went into vaudeville and burlesque instead until he teamed up with Bud Abbott in 1931. After the team split up in 1957, Costello appeared without his partner in one film, *The Thirty Foot Bride of Candy Rock*, just before his death of a heart attack at age fifty-three.

Not long after they joined forces in 1931, they were headliners on the vaudeville and burlesque circuit, with tall, lean Abbott playing straightman to short, pudgy funnyman Costello. They broke into radio in 1938 and the following year starred in the Broadway revue *Streets of Paris*. Their first film, *One Night in the Tropics*, was hardly noticed, but their next, *Buck Privates*, grossed $10 million and firmly established the team. Although their popularity among moviegoers declined during the 1950s, the team won over new generations of fans with a TV series and endless reruns of their old movies. In 1957, after more than thirty broad slapstick films and some success on television, the two broke up. Their reputation as a comedy team has not survived well, but their most famous routine, ''Who's on First?'' originally performed on film in *The Naughty Nineties*, is enshrined on a plaque in baseball's Hall of Fame.

Filmography: One Night in the Tropics (1940); Buck Privates, In the Navy, Hold That G-host, Keep 'Em Flying (1941); Ride 'Em Cowboy, Rio Rita, Pardon My Sarong, Who Done It? (1942); It Ain't Hay, Hit the Ice (1943); In Society, Lost in a Harem (1944); Here Come the Co-eds, The Naughty Nineties, Abbott and Costello in Hollywood (1945); Little Giant, The Time of Their Lives (1946); Buck Privates Come Home, The Wistful Widow of Wagon Gap (1947); The Noose Hangs High, Abbott and Costello Meet Frankenstein, Mexican Hayride (1948); Africa Screams, Abbott and Costello Meet the Killer Boris Karloff (1949); Abbott and Costello in the Foreign Legion (1950); Abbott and Costello Meet the Invisible Man, Comin' Round the Mountain (1951); Jack and the Beanstalk, Lost in Alaska, Abbott and Costello Meet Captain Kidd (1952); Abbott and Costello Go to Mars, Abbott and Costello Meet Dr. Jekyll and Mr. Hyde (1953); Abbott and Costello Meet the Keystone Kops, Abbott and Costello Meet the Mummy (1955); Dance with Me Henry (1956); The World of Abbott and Costello (compilation, 1965); Entertaining the Troops (archival footage, 1989).

Selected Bibliography

Costello, Chris, with Raymond Strait. *Lou's on First: A Biography*. New York: St. Martin's Press, 1981.

Cox, Stephen. *The Official Abbott & Costello Scrapbook*. Chicago: Contemporary Books, 1990.

Furmanek, Bob, and Ron Palumbo. *Abbott and Costello in Hollywood*. New York: Perigee Books, 1991.

Mulholland, Jim. *The Abbott and Costello Book*. New York: Popular Library, 1975.

Thomas, Bob. *Bud & Lou: The Abbott & Costello Story*. Philadelphia: Lippincott, 1977.

ABBOTT AND COSTELLO MEET FRANKENSTEIN (1948), comedy. Directed by Charles Barton; with Bud Abbott, Lou Costello, Lon Chaney, Jr., Bela Lugosi, Lenore Aubert, and Glenn Strange; screenplay by Robert Olees, Frederic I. Rinaldo, and John Grant.

''Jeepers! The creepers are after somebody—and guess who! More howls than you can shake a shiver at!!!'' went the blurb for this lively spoof of Universal's roster of monsters. The film was tailor-made for this team's brand of comedy. Combined with thrills, it provided the kind of mix reminiscent of the Bob Hope classic *The Cat and the Canary*. This all-time great horror-comedy, probably the Abbott and Costello film that survives best, still works beautifully mainly because the monsters play it straight. This was the first, and certainly the best, of the horror spoofs this comic duo made. In it they take on the studio's infamous bogeymen, including the Frankenstein Monster, the Wolf Man, and Dracula, in a romp that is both funny and scary.

Selected Bibliography

Byron, Stuart, and Elisabeth Weis, eds. *The National Society of Film Critics on Movie Comedy*. New York: Grossman Publishers, 1977.

Furmanek, Bob, and Ron Palumbo. *Abbott and Costello in Hollywood*. New York: Perigee Books, 1991.

ADAM'S RIB (1949), comedy. Directed by George Cukor; with Spencer Tracy, Katharine Hepburn, Judy Holliday, Tom Ewell, David Wayne, Jean Hagen, Hope Emerson, Polly Moran, Marvin Kaplan, Paula Raymond, and Tommy Noonan; screenplay by Ruth Gordon and Garson Kanin.

Ruth Gordon and Garson Kanin were nominated for Academy Awards for writing the screenplay for this smart, sophisticated comedy about husband and wife lawyers on opposing sides of the same murder case. Generally considered one of Hollywood's greatest comedies about the battle of the sexes, this sixth Metro teaming of Tracy and Hepburn contains superb performances from the leads and excellent support from a cast of relative newcomers such as Judy Holliday, Tom Ewell, David Wayne, and Jean Hagen. Holliday gives the definitive portrayal of the dumb Brooklyn blond, while Cukor's deliberate staginess adds the right touch to this stylized production. Although it has not escaped the label of "period piece," it is for that very reason that *Adam's Rib* remains a treat, for there is nothing like a movie caught in the amber of time to prove that "the more things change, the more they stay the same." (The film was remade in Bulgaria in 1956 as the story of a woman who rebels against tradition after her conversion to Marxism-Leninism!) Later it became a TV series.

Selected Bibliography

Deschner, Donald. *The Complete Films of Spencer Tracy*. Secaucus, NJ: Citadel, 1968.

Latham, Caroline. *Katharine Hepburn: Her Films & Stage Career*. New York: Proteus, 1982.

Sennett, Ted. *Great Hollywood Movies*. New York: Abradale Press, 1986.

ADVENTURES OF ROBIN HOOD, THE (1938), adventure. Directed by Michael Curtiz; with Errol Flynn, Olivia de Havilland, Basil Rathbone, Claude Rains, Patric Knowles, Eugene Pallette, Alan Hale, Herbert Mundin, Una O'Connor, Melville Cooper, and Ian Hunter; screenplay by Norman Reilly Raine and Seton I. Miller.

"Only the rainbow can duplicate its brilliance!" ran the blurb for this classic mix of fairy tale, epic, adventure story, and light opera. This is motion picture pageantry at its best. Every actor seems born to the part, especially Errol Flynn in the title role. Warners surrounded him with a lavish production and a superb supporting cast, the result of which is simply one of the greatest adventure films in cinematic history. The film is done in the grand manner of silent epics, the screen filled with swordplay (and horseplay) and some extraordinarily exciting hand-to-hand battles between Normans and Saxons. There is a great sense of fun to this picture, but the film never draws undue attention to itself, for one is always assured that the clowning about is merely a warming-up exercise for the serious business ahead. In short, this film comes as close as any film has to transferring to the screen the rowdy, independent, warmly human spirit of the original story. Unfortunately, many of the actors found that their archetypal roles forever overshadowed their subsequent film appearances, a curse that continues to afflict the stars of larger-than-life epic films.

Awards: Academy Awards: Original Score (Erich Wolfgang Korngold), Interior Decoration (Carl Jules Weyl), Editing (Ralph Dawson); Academy Award Nomination: Best Picture.

Selected Bibliography:

Sennett, Ted. *Great Hollywood Movies*. New York: Abradale Press, 1986.
Vermilye, Jerry. *The Films of the Thirties*. New York: Citadel Press, 1990.

AFRICAN QUEEN, THE (1951), comedy/adventure. Directed by John Huston; with Katharine Hepburn, Humphrey Bogart, Robert Morley, Peter Bull, Theodore Bikel, and Walter Gotell; screenplay by James Agee and John Huston.

An inspired piece of casting brought Humphrey Bogart and Katharine Hepburn together in this story of a trader and a missionary attempting a perilous escape from the Germans down an African river in 1915. *The African Queen* is a comedy, a love story, and a tale of adventure, and it is one of the most charming and entertaining movies ever made. Bogart and Hepburn work together with an effortlessness and a sense of fun that make their unlikely love affair—a puritanical spinster and a gin-soaked riverboat captain—seem not only inevitable but fitting. This film is so entertaining that it is easy to overlook the fact that it is perhaps not quite the classic it is cracked up to be. Bogart is wonderfully hammy, while Hepburn is at her hand-at-the-throat best. Those who complain that the pairing of the two is too far-fetched to take seriously forget that such a pairing is only a step away from the Hepburn-Tracy pairing or even the Astaire-Rogers. If opposites can attract, then surely extreme opposites can attract even more. And it is clear from the beginning that while Bogart is sorely in need of being taken care of, Hepburn is sorely in need of being loosened up. It's pointless to call this an unlikely story when unlikely stories are what great movies are made of.

Awards: Academy Award: Best Actor (Bogart); Academy Award Nominations: Best Director, Actress (Hepburn), Screenplay.

Selected Bibliography

Hepburn, Katharine. *The Making of "The African Queen," or, How I Went to Africa with Bogart, Bacall, and Huston and Almost Lost My Mind*. New York: Knopf, 1987.
Sennett, Ted. *Great Hollywood Movies*. New York: Abradale Press, 1986.
Viertel, Peter. *White Hunter, Black Heart*. New York: Dell, 1987.

ALDRICH, ROBERT. Producer and director. Born on August 9, 1918, in Cranston, Rhode Island; died on December 5, 1983, in Los Angeles. Educated at the

University of Virginia (law and economics). Aldrich went to Hollywood in 1941 and worked his way up from production clerk at RKO. He was a script clerk, then assistant to several directors (including Dmytryk, Milestone, Renoir, Wellmann, Polonsky, Fleischer, Losey, and Chaplin), then production manager, and next associate producer. At the same time, he started writing and directing episodes for TV series (*The Doctor, China Smith*). Aldrich gained much of his dynamic quality from his TV experience and from working as assistant on such films as *The Southerner, G.I. Joe, Force of Evil*, and *Limelight*. In 1953 he directed his first feature film, *The Big Leaguer*, but it was only in his third film, *Apache*, that his assured grasp of genre and his liberal sensibilities came to the fore in a sympathetic but never maudlin portrait of an Indian alienated from both white America and his own people. It was in *Kiss Me Deadly* that Aldrich first displayed his unique style, a style characterized by feverish motion within shots, rapid editing, and an underlying mood of violence and incipient chaos, creating an impression of inconsistency. In 1954 he established his own production company, Associates and Aldrich, and thereafter produced many of his own films. The financial success of *The Dirty Dozen* in 1967 prompted him to acquire his own studio, but ensuing difficulties forced him to sell it in 1973. By aggressively confronting controversial social and political issues and taking uncompromising positions, Aldrich challenged both the studio system and audience expectations.

Filmography: The Big Leaguer (1953); World for Ransom [also co-prod.], Apache, Vera Cruz (1954); Kiss Me Deadly [also prod.], The Big Knife [also prod.] (1955); Autumn Leaves, Attack! [also prod.] (1956); The Garment Jungle [replaced by Vincent Sherman, who got sole screen credit] (1957); Ten Seconds to Hell [also co-sc.] (1959); The Last Sunset, Sodoma e Gemorra/Sodom and Gomorrah [co-dir. with Sergio Leone: It./Fr./U.S.] (1961); What Ever Happened to Baby Jane? [also prod.] (1962); 4 for Texas [also prod., co-sc.] (1963); Hush . . . Hush Sweet Charlotte [also prod.] (1965); The Flight of the Phoenix [also prod.] (1966); The Dirty Dozen (1967); The Legend of Lylah Clare [also prod.], The Killing of Sister George [also prod.] (1968); What Ever Happened to Aunt Alice? [prod. only] (1969); Too Late the Hero [also prod., co-story, co-sc.] (1970); The Grissom Gang [also prod.] (1971); Ulzana's Raid (1972); Emperor of the North Pole (1973); The Longest Yard (1974); Hustle [also prod.] (1975); Twilight's Last Gleaming [U.S./Ger.], The Choirboys (1977); The Frisco Kid (1979); . . . All the Marbles, The Angry Hills (1981).

Honors: Venice Film Festival: Silver Prize Winner (*The Big Knife*, 1955); Venice Film Festival: Italian Critics Award (*Attack!* 1956); Berlin Film Festival: Award of Merit (*Autumn Leaves*, 1956). Served for a time as president of the Directors Guild of America.

Selected Bibliography

Andrew, Geoff. *The Film Handbook*. London: Longman, 1989.
Combs, Richard, ed. *Robert Aldrich*. London: British Film Institute, 1978.

ALL ABOUT EVE (1950), comedy/drama. Directed by Joseph L. Mankiewicz; with Bette Davis, Anne Baxter, George Sanders, Celeste Holm, Gary Merrill,

Thelma Ritter, Marilyn Monroe, Hugh Marlowe, and Gregory Ratoff; screenplay by Joseph L. Mankiewicz.

A sophisticated but cynical look at life in and around the theater, brimming with great parts all played to perfection by some great performers. Bette Davis is flawless as an aging star who takes in (and is taken in by) an adoring fan (Baxter) only to discover too late that the young woman is taking over her life. The dialogue throughout is witty and urbane, especially in the mouth of George Sanders, and wonderfully earthy and stinging when spoken by Thelma Ritter. And Marilyn Monroe's presence, laughed off then but seen now in the light of her later career, reveals a real talent for bimbo-with-a-brain comedy that became her trademark. Originally, critics were stingy with their praise for this delightful concoction, arguing that the whole thing was too peculiarly remote from life to be convincing. There were some, however, who saw that the very archness of the film, its staginess, its superficiality, its brittleness were what gave it its unique flavor, its reminder that the world of the theater is all smoke and mirrors and that actors are the mere ghosts of humanity. Time has been on the side of this film, and modern critics hail it as one of the best pictures of all time, praising it as the best picture ever made about the New York stage. Its bad taste and its vulgarity have come to be seen as necessary ingredients in the re-creation of the artificial world of the theater. For film buffs, *All about Eve* has become a treasure trove of trivia: George Sanders referring to Marilyn Monroe as "a product of the Copacabana school of acting"; Thelma Ritter reacting to Anne Baxter's sob story ("Everything but the hound dogs yapping at her rear end"); and, of course, Bette Davis, in top form ("Fasten your seat belts; it's going to be a bumpy night") playing—well—herself. And she never played herself better. In an ironic twist, Davis later replaced the ailing Baxter in the TV series *Hotel*.

Awards: Academy Awards: Best Picture, Supporting Actor (Sanders), Director, Screenplay, Sound Recording; Golden Globe Award: Screenplay; Directors Guild of America: Quarterly Award and Annual Award; New York Film Critics Circle Award: Picture; British Academy Award: Best Film (Mankiewicz); Academy Award Nominations: Best Actress (Baxter, Davis), Supporting Actress (Holm), B&W Cinematography, Art Direction, Editing, Original Music Score.

Selected Bibliography

Pascall, Jeremy. *Fifty Years of the Movies*. New York: Exeter Books, 1981.
Ringgold, Gene. *Bette Davis: Her Films and Career*. Secaucus, NJ: Citadel Press, 1985.
Sennett, Ted. *Great Hollywood Movies*. New York: Abradale Press, 1986.

ALL QUIET ON THE WESTERN FRONT (1930), war. Directed by Lewis Milestone; with Lew Ayres, Louis Wolheim, John Wray, Slim Summerville, Russell Gleason, Ben Alexander, and Beryl Mercer; screenplay by Maxwell Anderson, Del Andrews, and George Abbott

This screen version of Erich Maria Remarque's eloquent, pacifist novel is a cinematic experience as overwhelming today as it was when the film first appeared, one of the earliest talking pictures. Time has not dimmed its power, or its poignancy, one bit. It has been praised as one of the greatest pacifist films ever made, unrivaled in its graphic portrayal of the brutality of war and its refusal to stoop to cheap sentimentalism. *The Big Parade* (1925) had been the only film of the silent era that attempted to chronicle World War I, and while it offered some harrowing moments, its happy ending was pure fantasy. *All Quiet on the Western Front*, on the other hand, presents the true horrors of war in all their monstrous forms. This film is devastating in its impact, so riveting and realistic that it is impossible to forget. The world had never seen anything like this film, and reactions to it were intense. In Germany, the outraged Nazis labeled it anti-German. Joseph Goebbels, later the Nazi propaganda minister, not only denounced the film in rabid speeches and led pickets in front of the few theaters daring to show the film, but also ordered storm troopers to riot inside the Berlin theaters showing the film. The Nazis also punished the author, Erich Maria Remarque, who had fought on the Western Front and had been wounded five times. Hounded by the Nazis, he finally left Germany. Shortly thereafter, his bank accounts were confiscated and all his books burned in public. Producer Carl Laemmle, Jr., called press conferences in which he declared that the film was designed to establish goodwill toward Germany and its people, not to condemn either, and that its antiwar theme would help to curb future wars. His words fell on the deaf ears of those who were too busy planning future wars to tolerate attempts to curb them. Miraculously, there is no hint of cynicism beneath the straightforward portrayal of war in this picture. In fact, the film unfolds in what is almost a documentary style, leaving viewers repelled by war, not resigned to it. The fact that military leaders in countries planning aggressive acts were decidedly uncomfortable with the film attests to this fact. Ultimately, it is the universality of the film's theme that makes the film a classic. Although the soldiers are German, the film does not take sides. Instead, its soldiers could be the soldiers of any army, and their fate the fate of anyone.

Awards: Academy Awards: Best Picture, Director; Academy Award Nominations: Best Writing, Cinematography; *Photoplay* Medal of Honor.

Selected Bibliography

Guttmacher, Peter. *Legendary War Movies*. New York: MetroBooks, 1996.
Quirk, Lawrence J. *The Great War Films: From "The Birth of a Nation" to Today*. Secaucus, NJ: Carol Publishers, 1994.

ALL THE KING'S MEN (1949), drama. Directed by Robert Rossen; with Broderick Crawford, Joanne Dru, John Ireland, Mercedes McCambridge, John Derek, Shepperd Strudwick, and Anne Seymour; screenplay by Robert Rossen.

All the King's Men is a fine adaptation of Robert Penn Warren's Pulitzer novel about the rise and fall of a southern demagogue named Willie Stark (Crawford). The story is a thinly disguised portrait of Huey Long, the Louisiana state governor and U.S. senator who was assassinated in 1935 after a career ruined by an uncontrollable lust for power. The thesis of the story is basically that power corrupts. Stark starts out with a relentless sense of purpose and a stubborn honesty but then inexorably succumbs to the temptation to seize power and abuse it. His rise and fall are seen through the eyes of an admiring press agent (Ireland), who narrates the story of how he gradually became disenchanted with Stark as he saw firsthand exactly what was going on. Ultimately, it is the press agent who becomes the assassin. Mercedes McCambridge, with her spooky, vibratoless voice, makes a strong impression in her Academy Award–winning role as Stark's hard-boiled secretary in this, her first, film.

Awards: Academy Awards: Best Picture, Actor (Crawford), Supporting Actress (McCambridge); Golden Globe Awards: Best Picture, Actor (Crawford), Supporting Actress (McCambridge), Director, Most Promising Newcomer [female] (McCambridge); Directors Guild of America: Annual Award (Rossen); New York Film Critics Circle Award: Best Picture, Actor (Crawford); Academy Award Nominations: Best Supporting Actor (Ireland), Screenplay, Editing.

Selected Bibliography

Sennett, Ted. *Great Hollywood Movies*. New York: Abradale Press, 1986.
Thomas, Tony. *The Films of the Forties*. Secaucus, NJ: Citadel Press, 1975.

ALLYSON, JUNE. Actress. Born Ella Geisman on October 7, 1917, in the Bronx, New York. June Allyson began her career as a Broadway showgirl, but in the 1930s she was also featured in several two-reel film shorts. She played a leading role in the Broadway musical *Best Foot Forward* in 1941, then went on to play the same part in the screen version two years later. The word *pert* was coined for people like June Allyson. She literally sparkled on screen, and she had a twinkling smile that immediately endeared her to audiences. This diminutive actress had a surprisingly husky voice that was likely to crack under stress, an asset she put to good advantage in mushy romantic roles as well as roles in which she played the brave and noble wife confronting misfortune. During the 1940s she was a favorite performer in many MGM musicals, usually playing the girl next door. During the 1950s she switched to dramas and was often typecast as the devoted wife behind the successful husband. In 1955, however, she played against type, turning in a spine-chilling performance as a spiteful, bitchy wife in José Ferrer's *The Shrike*. Since 1960 she has occasionally ventured out of retirement for TV, stage, nightclub, film, and commercial appearances. She is the widow of actor-director Dick Powell.

Filmography: Best Foot Forward, Thousands Cheer, Girl Crazy (1943); Two Girls and a Sailor, Meet the People (1944); Music for Millions, Her Highness and the Bellboy (1945); The Sailor Takes a Wife, Two Sisters from Boston, Till the Clouds Roll By, The Secret Heart (1946); High Barbaree, Good News (1947); The Bride Goes Wild, The Three Musketeers, Words and Music (1948); Little Women, The Stratton Story (1949); The Reformer and the Redhead, Right Cross (1950); Too Young to Kiss (1951); The Girl in White (1952); Battle Circus, Remains to Be Seen (1953); The Glenn Miller Story, Executive Suite, Woman's World (1954); Strategic Air Command, The Shrike, The McConnell Story (1955); The Opposite Sex, You Can't Run Away from It (1956); Interlude, My Man Godfrey (1957); Stranger in My Arms (1959); They Only Kill Their Masters (1972); Blackout [Can./Fr.] (1978).

AMECHE, DON. Actor. Born Dominic Felix Amici on May 31, 1908, in Kenosha, Wisconsin; died on December 6, 1993. Educated at Columbia (Loras) College, Marquette, Georgetown, and University of Wisconsin (law). Ameche made his stage debut in stock while still a student at the University of Wisconsin, and for several years, he was a radio personality. He entered films in 1935 and quickly became one of the busiest stars at 20th Century–Fox. In over forty films he played leading roles, usually typecast as the young man-about-town with a shine on his shoes and a twinkle in his eyes. However, the film he is most closely identified with is *The Story of Alexander Graham Bell* in which he played the role of the renowned inventor so seriously that for years thereafter it was a running joke to credit Ameche with the invention of the telephone. His talent for light comedy was best displayed in Ernst Lubitsch's *Heaven Can Wait*. In 1975 he was reunited with his frequent screen partner, Alice Faye, in a national tour of the musical *Good News*. After a long absence from the screen, he made a sentimental comeback in the 1980s, turning in award-winning performances in *Cocoon* and *Things Change*.

Filmography: Clive of India, Dante's Inferno (1935); Sins of Man, Ramona, Ladies in Love (1936); One in a Million, Love Is News, Fifty Roads to Town, You Can't Have Everything, Love under Fire (1937); In Old Chicago, Happy Landing, Josette, Alexander's Ragtime Band, Gateway (1938); The Three Musketeers [as D'Artagnan], Midnight, The Story of Alexander Graham Bell [title role], Hollywood Cavalcade (1939); Swanee River [as Stephen Foster], Lillian Russell, Four Sons, Down Argentine Way (1940); That Night in Rio, Moon over Miami, Kiss the Boys Goodbye, The Feminine Touch, Confirm or Deny (1941); The Magnificent Dope, Girl Trouble (1942); Something to Shout About, Heaven Can Wait, Happy Land (1943); Wing and a Prayer, Greenwich Village (1944); It's in the Bag, Guest Wife (1945); So Goes My Love (1946); That's My Man (1947); Sleep My Love (1948); Slightly French (1949); Phantom Caravan (1954); Fire One (1955); A Fever in the Blood (1961); Rings around the World [doc.], Picture Mommy Dead (1966); Suppose They Gave a War and Nobody Came, The Boatniks (1970); Won Ton Ton—The Dog Who Saved Hollywood (1975); Trading Places (1983); Cocoon (1985); Harry and the Hendersons (1987); Coming to America, Things Change, Cocoon: the Return (1988); Oddball Hall (1990); Oscar (1991); Folks! (1992).

Honors: Academy Award: Best Supporting Actor (*Cocoon*, 1985); Venice Film Festival Award: Best Actor [with Joe Mantegna] (*Things Change*, 1988).

AMERICAN IN PARIS, AN (1951), musical. Directed by Vincente Minnelli; with Gene Kelly, Leslie Caron, Oscar Levant, Georges Guetary, Nina Foch, and Eugene Borden; screenplay by Alan Jay Lerner.

An American in Paris is the film that forever identified MGM as the studio for musicals. It could also be argued that it is the musical that foreshadowed the demise of the genre a decade later. Those who admire this film find everything about it superb, from Vincente Minnelli's direction to the lushly orchestrated Gershwin brothers standards, twenty-two in all, and there is no arguing with the quality of the Gershwin score. The highlight of the film is Kelly's fantasy ballet, a seventeen-minute sequence not equaled in musicals before or since. Ambitious as it was to undertake, the ballet today seems overlong and pretentious. (In the opening scene, the dancers all appear to be suffering from lower-back pain.) This number anticipates the overly ambitious production numbers that become oppressive in Kelly's 1969 film version of *Hello, Dolly*, the film that finally did the film musical in. *Singin' in the Rain*, released in 1952, didn't do nearly as well on its initial release, but by the 1960s, it was routinely considered the greatest of all Hollywood musicals, while *An American in Paris* was remembered with more respect than enthusiasm. The difference is clear. *Singin' in the Rain* has a spontaneity about it and a sense of humor, unlike the pompous *An American in Paris*, which takes itself far too seriously. Even so, the movie has many qualities of its own such as the numbers set in everyday Parisian settings that are endlessly inventive in their use of props and locations. But the movie also has scenes that are simply inexplicable, like the café scene in which Levant realizes he and Kelly are both in love with the same girl, and Levant starts lighting a handful of cigarettes while simultaneously trying to drink coffee. It's hard to believe it was ever considered funny. Uneven as it is, this picture deserves to be seen for the Kelly dance sequences (including the still impressive if flawed closing ballet), the Gershwin songs, the bright locations, and the opportunity to enjoy the whimsical charm of the inimitable Oscar Levant.

Awards: Academy Awards: Best Picture, Story and Screenplay, Cinematography/Color (Alfred Gilks, John Alton), Art Direction/Color (Cedric Gibbons, Preston Ames), Musical Scoring (Johnny Green, Saul Chaplin), Costumes/Color (Walter Plunkett, Irene Sharaff), Special Award (Kelly); Golden Globe Award: Best Picture (Comedy/Musical); Academy Award Nominations: Best Director, Editing.

Selected Bibliography

Fordin, Hugh. *The World of Entertainment!: Hollywood's Greatest Musicals*. Garden City, NY: Doubleday, 1975.

Thomas, Tony. *Song and Dance Man: The Films of Gene Kelly*. Secaucus, NJ: Citadel Press, 1974.

ANASTASIA (1956), drama. Directed by Anatole Litvak; with Ingrid Bergman, Yul Brynner, Helen Hayes, and Akim Tamiroff; screenplay by Arthur Laurents.

"The most amazing conspiracy the world has ever known, and love as it never happened to a man and woman before!" In spite of this sort of hype, *Anastasia* is a memorable cinematic achievement, a wonderfully moving and entertaining motion picture from start to finish. Inspired casting makes this film exceptional, especially Ingrid Bergman, who turns in a great performance, well deserving of the Oscar she received. Yul Brynner as the tough Russian exile General Bounine is excellent, and Helen Hayes brings great dignity to her role as the Empress before whose withering interrogation Anastasia triumphs. The story asks us to decide whether Anastasia is an impostor or really the grand duchess of Russia, the only surviving daughter of the last czar. It is a tribute to Bergman's powerful performance that she convinces us, at least within the confines of the movie, that she is, indeed, the only surviving member of the Romanoff family. Her transformation from an emotionally disturbed itinerant to a regal woman born to greatness is a wonder to behold.

Awards: Academy Award, Golden Globe Award, New York Film Critics Circle Award: Best Actress (Bergman); Academy Award Nomination: Musical Score.

Selected Bibliography

Quirk, Lawrence J. *The Complete Films of Ingrid Bergman*. New York: Carol, 1989.

ANATOMY OF A MURDER (1959), drama. Directed by Otto Preminger; with James Stewart, Lee Remick, Ben Gazzara, Arthur O'Connell, Eve Arden, Kathryn Grant, George C. Scott, Orson Bean, and Murray Hamilton; screenplay by Wendell Mayes.

"Last year's number one best seller. This year's (we hope) number one motion picture!" ran the cautious blurb for this classic courtroom drama, which was daring when released. Produced in a slick, terse film noir style, it is the story of the efforts of a small-town lawyer to defend an army sergeant accused of murdering the bartender who, it is claimed, raped his wife. Wendell Mayes's screenplay is outstanding in the way it introduces, in swift, brief strokes, a large number of diverse characters and sets them in motion. Preminger's direction is measured and assured, particularly in the way he illuminates the crucial ambiguities in the characters and offers an objective appraisal of the mechanics of the legal process. It has been pointed out that the film lacks the confidence in the law usually found in courtroom dramas, and this has led critics to wonder if it was this probing cynicism and not the frank language that created the controversy at the time of the film's release. The complex roles in this challenging film are handled with great skill. Ben Gazzara is particularly effective as the insensitive, arrogant defendant, while Stewart and Scott square off as opposing lawyers in the kind of courtroom bantering that is fun to watch just for its own sake. Scott is so sure of himself that it is deeply satisfying to see Stewart, with his "gee-whiz" style, ultimately triumph over him.

Awards: New York Film Critics Circle Award, Venice Film Festival Award: Best Actor (Stewart); Academy Award Nominations: Best Actor (Stewart), Supporting Actor (O'Connell, Scott), Screenplay, B&W Cinematography, Editing.

Selected Bibliography

Jones, Ken D., Arthur F. McClure, and Alfred E. Twomey. *The Films of James Stewart*. New York: Castle Books, 1970.
Pratley, Gerald. *The Cinema of Otto Preminger*. New York: A. S. Barnes, 1971.

ANDREWS, DANA. Actor. Born Carver Dana Andrews on January 1, 1909, Collins, Mississippi; died on December 17, 1992. Educated at Sam Houston

State Teachers College. Andrews, who started out as a bookkeeper for Gulf Oil, got bitten by the acting bug, quit his job, and hitchhiked to Los Angeles, hoping for a film career. Like so many other hopefuls, Andrews had to wait a long time for his first break. Meanwhile, he pumped gas and attended the Pasadena Playhouse while making the rounds of stage companies and film studios. In 1940 he managed to be signed by Sam Goldwyn and began playing secondary roles in Goldwyn and Fox films. His roles steadily improved, and in 1943, he was critically acclaimed for his sensitive performance as the victim of a lynching mob in William Wellman's *The Ox-Bow Incident*. His career reached its peak in the mid-1940s in such films as the classic film noir *Laura*, in which he was convincing and sympathetic as the hard-boiled detective who reveals a soft spot for the woman whose murder he is investigating, and in *The Best Years of Our Lives*, in which he spoke for a generation of returning World War II veterans in his moving performance as the GI who returns to a world in which he feels he no longer has a part. Andrews is too easily dismissed as a star of the second rank when, if you look at his impressive credentials, you will see that he, like Glenn Ford and others, turned in such natural, dependable performances that he has been too easily taken for granted. His so-called wooden features were perfect for a camera that disdains histrionics, and his deep, warm voice inspired confidence and trust. From the 1960s through the 1980s Andrews remained a competent leading man and supporting player and had the opportunity to display his impressive versatility. He also appeared in many television productions, even starring in the daytime TV soap opera *Bright Promise* for three years.

Filmography: Lucky Cisco Kid, Sailor's Lady, The Westerner, Kit Carson (1940); Tobacco Road, Belle Starr, Swamp Water (1941); Ball of Fire, Berlin Correspondent (1942); Crash Dive, The Ox-Bow Incident, The North Star/Armored Attack (1943); Up in Arms, The Purple Heart, Wing and a Prayer, Laura (1944); State Fair, Fallen Angel (1945); A Walk in the Sun, Canyon Passage, The Best Years of Our Lives (1946); Boomerang, Night Song, Daisy Kenyon (1947); The Iron Curtain, Deep Waters, No Minor Vices (1948); Britannia Mews/The Forbidden Street, Sword in the Desert (1949); My Foolish Heart, Where the Sidewalk Ends, Edge of Doom (1950); Sealed Cargo, The Frogmen, I Want You (1951); Assignment Paris (1952); Elephant Walk, Duel in the Jungle, Three Hours to Kill (1954); Smoke Signal, Strange Lady in Town (1955); Comanche, While the City Sleeps, Beyond a Reasonable Doubt (1956); Night of the Demon/Curse of the Demon, Spring Reunion, Zero Hour (1957); The Fearmakers, Enchanted Island (1958); The Crowded Sky (1960); Madison Avenue (1962); In Harm's Way, The Satan Bug, Crack in the World, Brainstorm, Town Tamer, The Loved One, Battle of the Bulge, Berlino—Appuntamento per le Spie/Spy in Your Eye [It.] (1965); Johnny Reno (1966); Il Cobra/The Cobra [It./Sp.], Hot Rods to Hell, The Frozen Dead (1967); I Diamanti che Nessuno Voleva Rubare [It.], The Devil's Brigade (1968); Innocent Bystanders (1972); Airport 1975 (1974); Take a Hard Ride (1975); The Last Tycoon (1976); Born Again (1978); Good Guys Wear Black, The Pilot (1979); Prince Jack (1984).

ANNA KARENINA (1935), drama. Directed by Clarence Brown; with Greta Garbo, Frederic March, Freddie Bartholomew, Maureen O'Sullivan, May Robson, and Basil Rathbone; screenplay by Clemence Dane, Salka Viertel, and S. N. Behrman.

Anna Karenina is a remake of the John Gilbert silent movie *Love* (1927), which also starred Garbo in the title role. Under Clarence Brown's direction, this splendid, moody Greta Garbo vehicle tells the classic Tolstoy tale with great sensitivity. Tolstoy's tragic love story makes an excellent Garbo vehicle, with fine support from March as her lover, Rathbone as her husband, and Bartholomew as her adoring son. Admirers of this film credit its success to the surprising mixture of the trademark MGM gloss, the legendary aloofness of Garbo, and the puzzling complexities of Tolstoy. In fact, many consider Garbo's performance as Tolstoy's complex and tortured heroine to be among her finest. Less enthusiastic critics find the picture well staged but ultimately exasperating, suggesting that it is not Garbo's performance but Garbo's personality that audiences respond to. Such an observation, of course, merely reinforces the notion that personality is what makes an actor a star. Garbo is there not merely to interpret Anna, to turn herself into Anna; she is there to turn Anna into Garbo. As with all great stars, Garbo must always be Garbo regardless of the part she is playing, for she is there, above all, to be gazed upon.

Awards: New York Film Critics Circle Award: Best Actress (Garbo); Venice Film Festival Award: Best Foreign Film.

Selected Bibliography

Conway, Michael, Dion McGregor, and Mark Ricci. *The Films of Greta Garbo*. New York: Bonanza Books, 1963.
Sennett, Ted. *Great Hollywood Movies*. New York: Abradale Press, 1986.

APARTMENT, THE (1960), comedy/drama. Directed by Billy Wilder; with Jack Lemmon, Shirley MacLaine, Fred MacMurray, Ray Walston, Jack Kruschen, Edie Adams, David Lewis, and Joan Shawlee; screenplay by Billy Wilder and I.A.L. Diamond.

"Billy Wilder grew a rose in a garbage pail" was Jack Lemmon's comment on this superior comedy-drama that presents a cynical yet sympathetic view of romantic and corporate success at the beginning of the 1960s. In it Lemmon attempts to climb the corporate ladder by loaning his apartment key to various executives, but his scheme backfires when he falls for his boss's latest girlfriend. The movie was controversial at the time, and it left many critics wondering what attitude to take. Some found it lacking in either style or taste and were upset by its annoying swings between pathos and slapstick without reason or transition, while others wondered how Wilder could apply the label comedy to a film that involves such things as pimping, a suicide attempt, and a whole host of ethically questionable activities. Defenders of *The Apartment* praise Wilder for having the audacity to ridicule American businessmen who value success over morality and trample ethics with complete impunity. However, both sides agree that Lemmon is perfect as the wheedling scumbag with just enough conscience left to block his descent into corruption. And this was clearly MacLaine's first good part, a part she plays in the style that became her trademark—forlorn, neurotic, bubble-headed, winsome, and totally disarming—the hooker with a heart. MacMurray turns in his best "against-type" performance since he played another heel in *Double Indemnity*. For Wilder, this was another landmark film, and his deft touch is visible in every scene, keeping things under control and on target.

Awards: Academy Awards: Best Picture, Director, Original Story & Screenplay, B&W Art Direction, Editing; Golden Globe Awards: Best Picture/Comedy, Actor/Comedy (Lemmon), Actress/Comedy (MacLaine); Directors Guild of America Award: Best Director; New York Film Critics Circle Awards: Best Picture, Director, Screenplay (Wilder, I.A.L. Diamond); British Academy Awards: Best Film, Actor/Foreign (Lemmon), Actress/Foreign (MacLaine); Venice Film Festival Award: Best Actress (MacLaine); Academy Award Nominations: Best Actor (Lemmon), Actress (MacLaine), Supporting Actor (Kruschen), B&W Cinematography, Sound.

Selected Bibliography

Seidman, Steve. *The Film Career of Billy Wilder*. Boston: G. K. Hall, 1977.
Sennett, Ted. *Great Hollywood Movies*. New York: Abradale Press, 1986.

ARNOLD, EDWARD. Actor. Born Guenther Edward Arnold Schneider on February 18, 1890, New York City; died on April 26, 1956. Arnold was a renowned character actor in dozens of films. He grew up on New York's Lower East Side, where he made his first amateur stage appearance as Lorenzo in *The Merchant of Venice*. In 1907 he appeared with Ethel Barrymore in *Dream of a Summer Night*. In 1915 he went to work for Essanay studio in Chicago as a cowboy star, appearing in over 50 silent two-reel action pictures. He also played supporting roles in a number of dramas and comedies before returning to the stage in 1919. In 1932 he returned to the screen to become one of Hollywood's most versatile character actors, specializing in portraying men of sometimes dubious influence—judges, senators, uncompromising businessmen—or lovable curmudgeons. To a whole generation of filmgoers, Arnold was the embodiment of the fat, cigar-smoking, sleazy, unscrupulous robber baron whose very presence in a movie said more than a dozen pages of dialogue. Arnold appeared in over 150 pictures, a presence so familiar to moviegoers that he was all too easily taken for granted. He is best remembered for his leading roles in Frank Capra's *You Can't Take It with You* and *Mr. Smith Goes to Washington*. Arnold has come to be one of the icons of the golden age of American cinema. He has had many imitators, but he remains inimitable. Not surprisingly for the age, he never won any awards, but he did become president of the Screen Actors Guild—an attainment his "fans" would be convinced was a result of smoke-filled backroom politicking.

Filmography: Misleading Lady, Vultures of Society, The Return of Eve (1916); The Slacker's Heart (1917); Phil-for-Short, A Broadway Saint (1919); The Cost (1920); Okay America!, Three on a Match, Afraid to Talk/Merry-Go-Round, Rasputin and the Empress

(1932); Whistling in the Dark, The White Sister, The Barbarian, Jennie Gerhardt, Her Bodyguard, The Secret of the Blue Room, I'm No Angel, Roman Scandals, The Life of Jimmy Dolan (1933); Madame Spy, Sadie McKee, Unknown Blonde, Thirty Day Princess, Hide-Out, Million Dollar Ransom, The President Vanishes, Wednesday's Child (1934); Biography of a Bachelor Girl, Cardinal Richelieu [as Louis XIII], The Glass Key, Diamond Jim [as "Diamond" Jim Brady], Crime and Punishment [as Inspector Porfiry Petrovich], Remember Last Night? (1935); Sutter's Gold, Meet Nero Wolfe [title role], Come and Get It (1936); John Meade's Woman, Easy Living, The Toast of New York [as Tycoon Jim Fisk], Blossoms on Broadway (1937); The Crowd Roars, You Can't Take It with You (1938); Idiot's Delight, Let Freedom Ring, Man about Town, Mr. Smith Goes to Washington (1939); The Earl of Chicago, Slightly Honorable, Lillian Russell [again as "Diamond" Jim Brady], Johnny Apollo (1940); Meet John Doe, The Penalty, The Lady from Cheyenne, All That Money Can Buy [as Daniel Webster], Nothing But the Truth, Design for Scandal (1941); Johnny Eager, Eyes in the Night, The War against Mrs. Hadley (1942); The Youngest Profession (1943); Standing Room Only, Janie, Kismet, Mrs. Parkington (1944); Main Street after Dark, The Hidden Eye, Week-End at the Waldorf (1945); Ziegfeld Follies, Janie Gets Married, Three Wise Fools, No Leave No Love (1946); The Mighty McGurk, Dear Ruth, My Brother Talks to Horses, The Hucksters (1947); Three Daring Daughters, Big City, Wallflower (1948); Command Decision, John Loves Mary, Take Me Out to the Ball Game, Big Jack (1949); Dear Wife, The Yellow Cab Man, Annie Get Your Gun, The Skipper Surprised His Wife (1950); Dear Brat (1951); Belles on Their Toes (1952); City That Never Sleeps, Man of Conflict (1953); Living It Up (1954); The Houston Story, The Ambassador's Daughter, Miami Exposé (1956).

Selected Bibliography

Arnold, Edward, with Frances Fisher Dubuc. *Lorenzo Goes to Hollywood: The Autobiography of Edward Arnold*. New York: Liveright, 1940.

ARTHUR, JEAN. Actress. Born Gladys Georgianna Greene on October 17, 1905, in New York City; died on June 19, 1991. Arthur quit school at age fifteen to become a model, then an actress, making her screen debut in 1923 in a small role in John Ford's *Cameo Kirby*. For the next few years, she played routine ingenue and leading lady parts in numerous low-budget westerns and some comedy shorts. It is one of those puzzling Hollywood paradoxes that Arthur, who was glib and carefree and relaxed on screen, could be unbearably moody and temperamental off screen, one of those actresses often labeled as "difficult." She was possessed of a crippling inferiority complex, and rumor has it that her removal from the starring role in *Temple of Venus* back in 1923 had left her close to suicide. Nevertheless, she persisted, meanwhile battling her own demons as well as her co-workers. Arthur had an unusual cracked, husky voice, not unlike June Allyson's, which became an asset with the advent of sound, and she was given better parts in better films. Even so, she was not happy with the direction her film career was taking, and she quit films briefly for an unsuccessful try at Broadway. When she returned to films, she got a break in John Ford's *The Whole Town's Talking* in which she first had a chance to demonstrate her flair for light comedy. After that she was usually cast as the perky, oddball, somewhat vague heroine of screwball comedies. She became a leading box office attraction and reached the peak of her popularity in Frank Capra's social comedies of the late 1930s. She was nominated for an Oscar for her performance in George Stevens's *The More the Merrier* in 1943. Stevens considered her "one of the greatest comediennes the screen has ever seen," and Capra described her as "my favorite actress." In the mid-1940s, she was released from her contract commitments at Columbia following a prolonged and ugly fight with Harry Cohn. After that she returned only twice to the screen, making her last appearance in Stevens's classic western *Shane* in 1953. In 1950 she appeared in a Broadway production of *Peter Pan*, and in 1956 she starred in a short-lived TV series, *The Jean Arthur Show*, in which she played a lawyer. She later taught drama at Vassar and other colleges and made occasional stage appearances.

Filmography: [sound only]: The Canary Murder Case, Stairs of Sand, The Greene Murder Case, The Mysterious Dr. Fu Manchu, The Saturday Night Kid, Half-Way to Heaven (1929); Street of Chance, Young Eagles, Paramount on Parade, The Return of Dr. Fu Manchu, Danger Lights, The Silver Horde (1930); The Gang Buster, Virtuous Husband, The Lawyer's Secret, Ex-Bad Boy (1931); Get That Venus, The Past of Mary Holmes (1933); Whirlpool, The Defense Rests, The Most Precious Thing in Life (1934); The Whole Town's Talking, Public Hero No. 1, Party Wire, Diamond Jim, The Public Menace, If You Could Only Cook (1935); Mr. Deeds Goes to Town, The Ex-Mrs. Bradford, Adventure in Manhattan, More Than a Secretary (1936); The Plainsman [as Calamity Jane], History Is Made at Night, Easy Living (1937); You Can't Take It with You (1938); Only Angels Have Wings, Mr. Smith Goes to Washington (1939); Too Many Husbands, Arizona (1940); The Devil and Miss Jones (1941); The Talk of the Town (1942); The More the Merrier, A Lady Takes a Chance (1943); The Impatient Years (1944); A Foreign Affair (1948); Shane (1953).

Honors: Academy Award Nomination: Best Actress (*The More the Merrier*, 1943).

ARZNER, DOROTHY. Director. Born on January 3, 1900, in San Francisco; died on October 1, 1979. Educated at the University of Southern California (premedicine). One of the few American women directors of the studio era (and the only major one), she met many important movie personalities while waiting tables in her father's Hollywood café. She drove an ambulance during World War I and then went to work for a newspaper. William DeMille hired her in 1919 as a stenographer in the script department of Famous Players. Soon thereafter, she was promoted to script clerk and film cutter and then to film editor. Her editing of the bullfight scenes in *Blood and Sand* (1922, starring Valentino) so impressed director James Cruze that he asked her to take over the editing of his epic western *The Covered Wagon* (1923). She went on to write a number of scripts, both independently and collaboratively, including Cruze's *Old Ironsides* (1926). In 1927, Paramount gave Arzner her first directing assignment, *Fashions for Women*. From then on, she continued to direct films until 1943. During World War II she produced Wac (Women's Army Corps) training films. After a bout with pneumonia, Arzner officially retired in the mid-1940s, but she continued to be involved with cinema for many years. During the 1960s, she taught film at the Pasadena Playhouse and the University of California at Los Angeles (Francis Ford Coppola was one of her students) and produced Pepsi commercials for her friend Joan Crawford. With the rise in feminist consciousness in the 1970s, interest in her films revived, although they did not actually have demonstrable ties to women's liberation.

Filmography: [feature films]: Fashions for Women, Ten Modern Commandments, Get Your Man (1927); Manhattan Cocktail (1928); The Wild Party (1929); Sarah and Son, Paramount on Parade [co-dir., with many others], Anybody's Woman (1930); Honor among Lovers, Working Girls (1931); Merrily We Go to Hell (1932); Christopher Strong (1933); Nana (1934); Craig's Wife (1936); The Bride Wore Red (1937); Dance, Girl, Dance (1940); First Comes Courage (1943).

Honors: In 1975 Arzner was paid a special tribute by the Directors Guild of America, of which she was the first woman member.

Selected Bibliography

Andrew, Geoff. *The Film Handbook*. (Directors) London: Longman, 1989.

Cook, Pam, and Philip Dodd, eds. *Women and Film: A Sight and Sound Reader*. Philadelphia: Temple University Press, 1993.

Mayne, Judith. *Directed by Dorothy Arzner*. Bloomington: Indiana University Press, 1994.

ASTAIRE, FRED. Actor, dancer. Born Frederick Austerlitz on May 10, 1899, in Omaha, Nebraska; died on June 22, 1987. At the age of seven Astaire started touring the vaudeville circuit with his sister Adele as a dancing partner. Some sources maintain that they appeared in 1915 in the Mary Pickford film *Franchon the Cricket*. They made their Broadway debut in 1917 in the musical *Over the Top*, and the following year they had their first big success in *The Passing Show of 1918*. From then on, they were perennial favorites with both Broadway and London audiences in such hit shows as *Lady Be Good* (1924), *Smiles* (1930), and *The Band Wagon* (1931). In 1931 Adele married, and the partnership was dissolved. When Astaire was given a Hollywood screen test shortly thereafter, his performance received the famous verdict: "Can't act. Slightly bald. Can dance a little." Nevertheless, he landed a small part opposite Joan Crawford in *Dancing Lady* (1933). In 1934, Astaire was paired with newcomer Ginger Rogers, a partnership that continued through ten highly successful films and produced some of the most memorable moments in screen history. When Rogers turned to dramatic roles, Astaire continued to dominate the musical film scene with such partners as Judy Garland, Lucille Bremer, Rita Hayworth, Eleanor Powell, Cyd Charisse, Vera Ellen, Jane Powell, and Audrey Hepburn. In 1946 Astaire announced his retirement, but two years later he replaced the ailing Gene Kelly as Judy Garland's partner in *Easter Parade* and made a triumphant comeback. After that he continued to dance in films for another ten years and to act for another thirty. Fred Astaire's ingenuity left its mark not only on movie musicals to come but on the art of dancing itself. Mikhail Baryshnikov, for example, has often expressed his debt to the art of Fred Astaire. His films always included solo dance numbers in which he skillfully improvised in his free, easygoing style, a style that combined relaxed exuberance with sophistication in what entertainers like to call a "class act." He also introduced many famous songs that had been written especially for him and that he sang in a distinctive but pleasing style that has come to be highly regarded by musician and musical scholar Michael Feinstein. Astaire later turned in impressive performances in straight dramatic roles including *On the Beach* (1959) and *The Towering Inferno* (1974), for which he was nominated for an Oscar as Best Supporting Actor.

Filmography: Dancing Lady, Flying Down to Rio (1933); The Gay Divorcee (1934); Roberta, Top Hat (1935); Follow the Fleet, Swing Time (1936); Shall We Dance, A Damsel in Distress (1937); Carefree (1938); The Story of Vernon and Irene Castle (1939); Broadway Melody of 1940, Second Chorus (1940); You'll Never Get Rich (1941); You Were Never Lovelier, Holiday Inn (1942); The Sky's the Limit (1943); Yolanda and the Thief (1945); Ziegfeld Follies, Blue Skies (1946); Easter Parade (1948); The Barkleys of Broadway (1949); Three Little Words, Let's Dance (1950); Royal Wedding (1951); The Belle of New York (1952); The Band Wagon (1953); Daddy Long Legs (1955); Funny Face, Silk Stockings (1957); On the Beach (1959); The Pleasure of His Company (1961); The Notorious Landlady (1962); Finian's Rainbow (1968); Midas Run (1969); That's Entertainment [on-camera co-narr.], The Towering Inferno (1974); The Amazing Dobermans, Un Taxi mauve/The Purple Taxi [Fr./It./Ire.] (1977); Ghost Story (1981); George Stevens: A Filmmaker's Journey [doc.; on-camera commentary] (1985).

Honors: Academy Award: Special Award for his contribution to films (1949); American Film Institute's Life Achievement Award (1981).

Selected Bibliography

Mueller, John E. *Astaire Dancing: The Musical Films*. New York: Knopf, 1985.
Pickard, Roy. *Fred Astaire*. New York: Crescent Books, 1985.
Satchell, Tim. *Astaire: The Biography*. London: Hutchinson, 1987.

ASTOR, MARY. Actress. Born Lucille Vasconcellos Langhanke on May 3, 1906, in Quincy, Illinois; died on September 25, 1987. Astor was a star of both silent and sound films. Pressured by her father, a strong-willed German immigrant, she entered a beauty contest at age fourteen and films at fifteen. She played an assortment of minor roles until she happened to get cast as John Barrymore's leading lady in *Beau Brummel* in 1924. She was an overnight success, and she remained a leading screen personality through the 1940s. She became the darling of the tabloids and the gossip columnists with her much-publicized off-screen behavior, which included a stormy love affair with John Barrymore, four marriages, a bout with alcoholism, and an attempted suicide. Her first husband, director Kenneth Hawks (brother of Howard Hawks), died in a 1930 plane crash while on a filming assignment. When she divorced her second husband, a physician, in 1936, she found herself in a messy custody battle over her daughter during which her diary was introduced into court. In it she had listed indiscretions that embarrassed quite a few in the film community. She also confessed to having had a secret affair with playwright George S. Kaufman, an affair that became Hollywood's most publicized scandal of the 1930s and almost ruined her career. However, she was soon back on the screen playing what she played best: a cool, sophisticated but often bitchy woman-of-the-world (e.g., *The Maltese Falcon*). One glaring exception was her surprisingly convincing role as the perfect wife and mother (of Judy Garland and others) in *Meet Me in St. Louis*. After 1949, her film appearances were limited to an occasional character role. A heart condition kept her off the screen after 1965. Her latter years were spent in confinement in the Motion Picture Country Home. She authored two autobiographies, *My Story* (1959) and *A Life on Film* (1971) and several reasonably successful novels.

Filmography: Sentimental Tommy [bit, cut from final print], The Beggar Maid [two-reel art film] (1921); The Young Painter [two-reel art film], The Man Who Played God, John Smith (1922); Second Fiddle, Success, The Bright Shawl, Hollywood [cameo], The Marriage Maker, Puritan Passions, The Rapids, Woman-Proof (1923); The Fighting Coward, Beau Brummel, The Fighting American, Unguarded Women, The Price of a Party, Inez from Hollywood (1924); Oh Doctor!, Enticement, Playing with Souls, Don Q Son of Zorro, The Pace That Thrills, Scarlet Saint (1925); High Steppers, The Wise Guy, Don Juan, Forever After (1926); The Sea Tiger, The Rough Riders, The Sunset Derby, Rose of the Golden West, No Place to Go, Two Arabian Knights (1927); Sailors' Wives, Dressed to Kill, Three-Ring Marriage, Heart to Heart, Dry Martini, Romance of the Underworld (1928); New Year's Eve, The Woman from Hell (1929); Ladies Love Brutes, The Runaway Bride, Holiday, The Lash/Adios (1930); The Royal Bed, Behind Office Doors, The Sin Ship, Other Men's Women, White Shoulders, Smart Woman (1931); Men of Chance, The Lost Squadron, A Successful Calamity, Those We Love, Red Dust (1932); The Little Giant, Jennie Gerhardt, The World Changes, The Kennel Murder Case, Convention City (1933); Easy to Love, Upper World, Return of the Terror, The Man with Two Faces, The Case of the Howling Dog (1934); I Am a Thief, Red Hot Tires, Straight from the Heart, Dinky, Page Miss Glory, Man of Iron (1935); The Murder of Dr. Harrigan, And So They Were Married, Trapped by Television, Dodsworth, Lady from Nowhere (1936); The Prisoner of Zenda, The Hurricane (1937); Paradise for Three, No Time to Marry, There's Always a Woman, Woman against Woman, Listen Darling (1938); Midnight (1939); Turnabout, Brigham Young (1940); The Great Lie, The Maltese Falcon (1941); In This Our Life [unbilled cameo], Across the Pacific, The Palm Beach Story (1942); Thousands Cheer, Young Ideas (1943); Blonde Fever, Meet Me in St. Louis (1944); Claudia and David (1946); Fiesta, Cynthia, Desert Fury, Cass Timberlane (1947); Act of Violence, Little Women, Any Number Can Play (1949); A Kiss before Dying, The Power and the Prize (1956); The Devil's Hairpin (1957); This Happy Feeling (1958); Stranger in My Arms (1959); Return to Peyton Place (1961); Youngblood Hawke (1964); Hush . . . Hush Sweet Charlotte (1965).

Honors: Academy Award: Best Supporting Actress (*The Maltese Falcon*, 1941).

Selected Bibliography

Astor, Mary. *A Life on Film*. New York: Delacorte, 1971.
———. *My Story: An Autobiography*. Garden City, NY: Doubleday, 1959.

AUNTIE MAME (1958), comedy. Directed by Morton Da Costa; with Rosalind Russell, Forrest Tucker, Coral Browne, Fred Clark, Roger Smith, Patric Knowles, Peggy Cass, Joanna Barnes, Pippa Scott, Lee Patrick, Willard Waterman, and Connie Gilchrist; screenplay by Betty Comden and Adolph Green.

This is a colorful and highly entertaining film version of Patrick Dennis's novel about his eccentric aunt. "Life is a banquet," she is fond of saying, "and most poor suckers are starving to death." This is a part Rosalind Russell was born to play, and it is fitting that it came toward the end of a career studded with memorable comedic performances (*The Women, His Girl Friday, My Sister Eileen*), for it expresses brilliantly that side of a talent that was large enough also to include superb dramatic parts. The movie has been faulted for being episodic, but it is precisely this quality that gives it the depth that is always present in good comedy. This is a story that takes place in the 1920s and 1930s when the country was moving from the jazz age into the depression and then on to World War II. In the foreground stands Mame Dennis, survivor. This gives Russell the chance to display Mame's eccentric pluck, her talent for preserving illusions, her skill at manipulating people into doing what's best for themselves (and, of course, for her). Above all is her marvelous wit, a wit Russell is better at handling than any actress of her time. An arched eyebrow or a cocked head can speak volumes, and when she actually does speak, her voice, just tinged with sarcasm, can charm the innocent and beguile the unsuspecting. Much of the fun, of course, lies in the fact that Auntie Mame's antics are seen through the eyes of her orphaned nephew, Patrick, whom she "educates" with a vengeance, relishing every moment of this chance to teach him how to live. He is a bit of a prig, which makes the relationship even more interesting, especially when he brings home a hopelessly shallow society girl, inspiring Mame to new heights in her endeavors to nip this romance in the bud. The party scene in which she pulls this off is the highlight of a film studded with memorable scenes. Three years after this film came out, *Breakfast at Tiffany's* was released, prompting one film buff to say that Auntie Mame is really Holly Golightly without the angst.

Awards: Golden Globe Awards: Best Picture [comedy], Best Actress [comedy/musical] (Russell); Academy Award Nominations: Best Picture, Actress (Russell), Supporting Actress (Cass), Cinematography, Art Direction, Editing.

Selected Bibliography

Byron, Stuart, and Elizabeth Weis, eds. *The National Society of Film Critics on Movie Comedy*. New York: Grossman Publishers, 1977.
Russell, Rosalind, and Chris Chase. *Life Is a Banquet*. New York: Random House, 1977.

B

BACALL, LAUREN. Actress. Born Betty Joan Perske on September 16, 1924, in the Bronx, New York. Educated at Julia Richman High School, Manhattan. Bacall studied dancing for thirteen years, trained briefly at the American Academy of Dramatic Arts, and played minor roles in several unsuccessful Broadway plays before turning to modeling. In 1943, Mrs. Howard Hawks saw her photograph on the cover of *Harper's Bazaar* and told her Hollywood producer-director husband of her discovery. Within a month Bacall, only nineteen, had a Hollywood contract and a role opposite Humphrey Bogart in *To Have and Have Not*. She stole the show. Critics raved about her sultry personality, her vitality, her elegance, her feline shrewdness, her self-confidence, her husky voice. Studio publicity dubbed her ''The Look,'' because of the suggestive, come-on twinkle in her eye, and she was on her way to stardom at Warner Bros. In 1945 she married Bogart, with whom she later appeared in three more films, *The Big Sleep*, *Dark Passage*, and *Key Largo*. When Bogart fell ill of cancer, she nursed him devotedly until his death in 1957. Meanwhile, she had been battling with the studio for better parts and was frequently suspended and even fined for turning down scripts. After she finally bought her freedom, she landed a few relatively better parts at other studios, but in general, her career started to lose its momentum. In the late 1960s she returned to Broadway, appearing with great success in *Cactus Flower*. In 1970 she won the Tony Award for her performance in Broadway's *Applause*, a musical remake of the film *All about Eve* in which she played the Bette Davis part. She triumphed again on Broadway in 1981 in *Woman of the Year*. She returned to the screen in 1974 after an eight-year absence, making usually only cameo appearances in movies of very uneven quality. Looking back at the Bacall of a film like *Young Man with a Horn*, one is struck by the fact that even then, only six years after her debut film, she was already beginning to parody herself—the sultriness, the slink, the cigarette, the neurotic behavior and waspish remarks. There is also a latent mannish quality that she put to good use in her bitchier roles, but it is what kept her from hitting a peak and holding it. Her character in *Young Man with a Horn* seems sexually ambivalent, to say the least, and once you suspect that to be the case, you begin to understand a personality that seems otherwise too capriciously complex, as if she's feinting to avoid being found out. It's a quality she shares with Patricia Neal, whose part in *The Fountainhead* she might have played with unexpected depth. In 1996 she was finally nominated for, but did not win, an Oscar for Best Supporting Actress in *The Mirror Has Two Faces*.

Filmography: To Have and Have Not (1944); Confidential Agent (1945); Two Guys from Milwaukee [cameo], The Big Sleep (1946); Dark Passage (1947); Key Largo (1948); Young Man with a Horn, Bright Leaf (1950); How to Marry a Millionaire (1953); Woman's World (1954); The Cobweb, Blood Alley (1955); Written on the Wind, Designing Woman (1957); The Gift of Love (1958); North West Frontier/Flame over India (1959); Shock Treatment (1964); Sex and the Single Girl (1965); Harper (1966); Murder on the Orient Express (1974); The Shootist (1976); H.E.A.L.T.H. (1979); The Fan (1981); Appointment with Death, Mr. North (1988); Tree of Hands (1989); Misery (1990); A Star for Two, All I Want for Christmas (1991); The Portrait (1993); Ready to Wear (1995); The Mirror Has Two Faces (1996).

Honors: Golden Globes: Cecile B. DeMille Award (1992); Academy Award Nomination: Best Supporting Actress (*The Mirror Has Two Faces*, 1996).

Selected Bibliography

Bacall, Lauren. *By Myself*. New York: Knopf, 1979.
Quirk, Lawrence J. *Lauren Bacall: Her Films and Career*. Secaucus, NJ: Citadel, 1986.
Royce, Brenda Scott. *Lauren Bacall: A Bio-Bibliography*. Westport, CT: Greenwood, 1992.

BAND WAGON, THE (1953), musical. Directed by Vincente Minnelli; with Fred Astaire, Cyd Charisse, Oscar Levant, Nanette Fabray, and Jack Buchanan; screenplay by Betty Comden and Adolph Green.

The timeless plot of this "let's-put-on-a-musical" musical takes on added meaning given the similarity between Astaire and the character he plays: an aging film star dancer whose career is on the slide. Astaire's career wasn't exactly on the slide at the time, but he was rather refreshingly admitting that, but for the grace of God, the story really could be his. He was fifty-four when the picture was made, and in a few years, he would retire from films except for a character part or two. It's the show's musical numbers that rescue it from banality, although some of them have lost their luster through repeated retrospectives. The two numbers that retain their vitality are the languorous "Dancing in the Dark" pas de deux and the steamy "Girl Hunt" ballet, both featuring the astonishingly sensuous dancing of Cyd Charisse. Otherwise, the numbers showcase the formidable talents of songwriters Arthur Schwartz and Howard Dietz and are ably performed by Astaire, Charisse, Nanette Fabray, Jack Buchanan, and the acerbic Oscar Levant. Film buffs delight in equating the characters in the film with their real-life counterparts. Buchanan, the jack of all show business trade, is supposed to be either José Ferrer or Orson Welles, and Fabray and Levant play at being Betty Comden and Adolph Green, the screenwriters of this picture. *The Band Wagon* is still a gem, but like all musicals that followed *Singin' in the Rain*, it suffers in comparison.

Awards: Academy Award Nominations: Best Story & Screenplay, Color Costume Design, Scoring of a Musical Picture.

Selected Bibliography

Fordin, Hugh. *The World of Entertainment!: Hollywood's Greatest Musicals*. Garden City, NY: Doubleday, 1975.
Mueller, John E. *Astaire Dancing: The Musical Films*. New York: Knopf, 1985.

BANK DICK, THE (1940), comedy. Directed by Eddie Cline; with W. C. Fields, Cora Witherspoon, Una Merkel, Evelyn Del Rio, Jessie Ralph, Grady Sutton, Franklin Pangborn, Shemp Howard, Russell Hicks, and Reed Hadley; screenplay by "Mahatma Kane Jeeves" [W. C. Fields].

The Bank Dick, written by Fields himself, is about a town drunk who becomes a bank guard. The whole film is an excuse to showcase Fields's repertoire of comedy routines, many of them from earlier pictures, but it includes a lot of new material, too. Fields is the town drunk who is forever forcing himself onto people. One day, quite by accident, he becomes the "hero" of a bank robbery and is rewarded with the job of bank guard. When he accidentally becomes the hero of a second bank robbery, Fields is given both the reward money and a fat contract as a film director. At times imitating Charlie Chaplin, Fields shines under the direction of Eddie Cline, who honed his skills in the style of the Keystone Kop comedies. Although it is now a period piece, the film still has considerable charm. It works on its own terms. Some critics complain about the makeshift story and stock characters, but it is generally considered the best of Fields's later comedies and a classic of American comedy.

Selected Bibliography

Deschner, Donald. *The Complete Films of W. C. Fields*. New York: Carol, 1989.
McCaffrey, Donald W. *The Golden Age of Sound Comedy: Comic Films and Comedians of the 30s*. South Brunswick, NJ: A. S. Barnes, 1973.

BAXTER, ANN. Actress. Born on May 7, 1923, in Michigan City, Indiana; died on December 12, 1985. The granddaughter of architect Frank Lloyd Wright, Ann Baxter was raised in Bronxville, New York, and attended private schools in New York City. When she was only eleven she began studying under the legendary Maria Ouspenskaya, and at thirteen she made her Broadway debut in *Seen but Not Heard*. Her success in Broadway roles led to her screen debut in 1940. In the right part and with the right directors, she could exhibit a combination of charm and determination that gave her performances a sense of mystery and apprehension as if any moment she might reveal a dark side. This elusive quality helped her win a Best Supporting Actress Oscar for *The Razor's Edge* in which she portrayed a sweet, sensitive woman hardened and then destroyed by grief and deceit. She was nominated for another Academy Award in *All about Eve* for her portrayal of the shrewd, ambitious, but outwardly sweet young actress who plays on the insecurities of the temperamental Margo Channing played by Bette Davis. Baxter was respected by, and worked for, some of Hollywood's top directors including Welles, Wilder, Milestone, Wellman, Hitchcock, Lang, and Mankiewicz. In 1961, fed up with the lack of good parts, she turned her back on Hollywood and went with her second husband, Randolph Galt, to live for several years on a cattle station in the Australian outback in primitive, isolated conditions. She told of this experience and the disillusioning effect it had on her in *Intermission: A True Story* (1976), a book highly acclaimed by the critics. In 1971 she took over the role of Margo Channing from Lauren Bacall in the Broadway production of *Applause*, a musical based on *All about Eve*. In an ironic bit of role reversal not uncommon in the world of theater, Baxter now found herself playing the part of the very woman she had schemed to replace in the film version. In 1983, in another ironic twist, Baxter replaced an ailing Davis in the TV series *Hotel*. She stayed with the show until her death of a stroke at sixty-two.

Filmography: Twenty-Mule Team, The Great Profile (1940); Charley's Aunt, Swamp Water (1941); The Magnificent Ambersons, The Pied Piper (1942); Crash Dive, Five Graves to Cairo, The North Star/Armored Attack (1943); The Sullivans, The Eve of St. Mark, Guest in the House, Sunday Dinner for a Soldier (1944); A Royal Scandal (1945); Smoky, Angel on My Shoulder, The Razor's Edge (1946); Mother Wore Tights [offscreen narrator], Blaze of Noon (1947); Homecoming, The Walls of Jericho, The Luck of the Irish (1948); Yellow Sky, You're My Everything (1949); A Ticket to Tomahawk, All about Eve (1950); Follow the Sun (1951); The Outcasts of Poker Flat, My Wife's Best Friend, O. Henry's Full House (1952); I Confess, The Blue Gardenia (1953); Carnival Story (1954); Bedevilled, One Desire (1955); Three Violent People (1957); Chase a Crooked Shadow (1958); Summer of the Seventeenth Doll/Season of Passion (1959); Cimarron (1960); Mix Me a Person, Walk on the Wild Side (1962); The Family Jewels [cameo] (1965); Las Siete Magnificas/The Tall Women (1966); The Busy Body (1967); Fool's Paradise, The Late Liz (1971); Little Mo [orig. for TV] (1978); Jane Austen in Manhattan (1980).

Honors: Academy Award, Golden Globe Award: Best Supporting Actress (*The Razor's Edge*, 1946); Academy Award Nomination: Best Actress (*All about Eve*, 1950).

Selected Bibliography

Baxter, Anne. *Intermission: A True Tale*. New York: Ballantine, 1978.
Fowler, Karin J. *Anne Ba*. *r: A Bio-Bibliography*. New York: Greenwood, 1991.

BECKET (1964), drama. Directed by Peter Glenville; with Richard Burton, Peter O'Toole, John Gielgud, Donald Wolfit, Martita Hunt, Pamela Brown, and Felix Aylmer; screenplay by Edward Anhalt.

Becket is an absorbing motion picture that owes much of its fascination to the presence of Richard Burton and Peter O'Toole in the roles of Becket and Henry II. Critics sometimes like to pretend that stars do not matter; it's the part that counts. But the truth is that one is constantly aware that one is watching two men who are supreme products and victims of the celebrity curse of the mid-twentieth century. First there is Burton for whom greatness remained elusive as he succumbed to the seductions of superstar fame. Then there is O'Toole whose career was over before it really got started. The image of the self-destructive celebrity, O'Toole exploded onto the screen as *Lawrence of Arabia*, and after that, nothing he would ever do could quite measure up. Nevertheless, it is a well-written, well-directed, and well-acted film with stunning visuals to propel the story along. There is also a palpable homoerotic undercurrent that seems to achieve much of its effect from O'Toole's epicene features and body language and Burton's smooth, caressing voice with that ever-so-subtle slur. This undercurrent owes much to the screenplay, which was adapted from Jean Anouilh's original stage script. The modern psychology of Anouilh lends fascination to these twelfth-century goings-on by investing them with special motivational insights rare in costume drama. The basic story is, of course, based on the actual murder on December 29, 1170, in the cathedral of Canterbury of its archbishop, Becket, by barons from the entourage of Henry II, great-grandson of William the Conquerer. For fictional purposes, Becket and the King had been old roustabouts together. O'Toole is a sad, lonely monarch whose only satisfying companionship has been provided by Becket. When Becket finally rises to the position of Archbishop of Canterbury and comes in conflict with Henry, his murder seems motivated more by jealousy than by policy. Although *Becket* is lavishly filmed, it remains stagy and static and lacking in action that could have livened it up. One critic called the film "handsome, respectable and boring." Today we could say that it is the sort of film that fares much better on the History Channel than on the big screen, for it is not only a pivotal piece of history but extraordinary drama, as T. S. Eliot realized so well in his *Murder in the Cathedral*.

Awards: Academy Award: Best Adapted Screenplay; Golden Globe Award, National Board of Review: Best Picture (drama); Academy Award Nominations: Best Picture, Director, Actor (Burton, O'Toole), Supporting Actor (Gielgud), Color Cinematography, Color Costume Design, Color Art Direction, Editing, Original Music Score, Sound.

Selected Bibliography

Freedland, Michael. *Peter O'Toole: A Biography*. New York: St. Martin's, 1982.
Steverson, Tyrone. *Richard Burton: A Bio-Bibliography*. Westport, CT: Greenwood, 1992.

BEN-HUR (1959), historical/religious. Directed by William Wyler; with Charlton Heston, Jack Hawkins, Stephen Boyd, Haya Harareet, Hugh Griffith, Martha Scott, Sam Jaffe, Cathy O'Donnell, and Finlay Currie; screenplay by Karl Tunberg.

Based on the novel by General Lew Wallace, this epic film tells the story of the proud Jew Ben-Hur (Heston) and his boyhood friend Messala (Boyd) who become enemies because of Messala's blind allegiance to Rome. The film moves along at a stately pace, enlivened here and there by some outstanding scenes such as the galley-slave sequence and the climactic chariot race, still a classic among film buffs. Though writer Karl Tunberg receives lone credit for the script, a host of others contributed in one form or another, including such literary luminaries as Maxwell Anderson, S. N. Behrman, Gore Vidal, and Christopher Fry. In fact, Fry remained in Rome as consultant throughout the sequences filmed there. Although it is well nigh impossible to single out which threads were woven by which writer, the overall effort was worthwhile, resulting in three and one-half hours of unforgettable film. Director Wyler tells the story in human, understated terms, calling it later "Hollywood's first intimate epic."

Awards: Academy Awards: Best Picture, Director, Actor (Heston), Supporting Actor (Griffith), Cinematography (Robert L. Surtees), Score (Miklos Rozsa), Costumes (Elizabeth Haffenden), Editing, Sound, Special Effects; Golden Globe Awards: Best Picture, Director, Supporting Actor (Boyd), Special Award for Directing the Chariot Race (Andrew Marton); Directors Guild of America Award: Direction; New York Film Critics Circle Awards: Best Picture, Supporting Actor (Griffith); British Academy Award: Best Film.

Selected Bibliography

Anderegg, Michael A. *William Wyler*. Boston: Twayne, 1979.
Crowther, Bruce. *Charlton Heston: The Epic Presence*. London: Columbus Books, 1986.
Smith, Gary A. *Epic Films: Cast, Credits, and Commentary on Over 250 Historical Spectacular Movies*. Jefferson, NC: McFarland, 1991.

BENNETT, JOAN. Actress. Born on February 27, 1910, in Palisades, New Jersey; died on December 7, 1990. Educated at a Connecticut boarding school and a finishing school in Versailles, France. Bennett, the sister of screen actresses Barbara and Constance Bennett, made her stage debut with her father in *Jarnegan* in 1928, the same year she went to Hollywood to play a minor role in the film *Power*. The following year she played opposite Ronald Colman in *Bulldog Drummond* and became a star. Throughout the 1930s she appeared in many starring roles, but it wasn't until she married producer Walter Wanger in 1940 that she really hit her stride. Under his supervision, she made some of her best films, particularly the four directed by Fritz Lang: *Man Hunt*, *The Woman in the Window*, *Scarlet Street*, and *The Secret beyond the Door*. Bennett was born a blond, but turned brunette for a film in 1938, which caused her to resemble Hedy Lamarr. (In the song "Let's Not Talk About Love," Danny Kaye sings: "Let's talk of Lamarr, that Hedy's so fair; why does she let Joan Bennett wear all her old hair?") Ironically, Joan Bennett's second husband, Gene Markey, later married Miss Lamarr. Bennett could play widely varied roles with equal ease, from that of the selfish schemer in *The Woman in the Window* to the lightweight mother in *Father of the Bride*, opposite Spencer Tracy. She seemed to enjoy playing sensual, mercenary, ambitious women like Macomber's wife (the archetypal Hemingway bitch) in the splendid film version of Hemingway's *The Short, Happy Life of Francis Macomber* in which she "accidentally" shoots her husband (Robert Preston) while on safari and seduces the guide (Gregory Peck). Her portrayal of the desperate mother under the threat of a blackmailer in Max Ophüls's *The Reckless Moment* is nothing short of brilliant. Bennett appeared in several stage plays in the 1950s and early 1960s. From 1966 to 1971 she starred in the TV daytime soap-shocker serial *Dark Shadows* and in 1970 headed its cast in an offshoot feature film.

Filmography: The Valley of Decision [bit] (1916); The Eternal City [bit] (1923); Power (1928); Bulldog Drummond, Three Live Ghosts, Disraeli, The Mississippi Gambler (1929); Puttin' on the Ritz, Crazy That Way, Moby Dick, Maybe It's Love, Scotland Yard (1930); Doctor's Wives, Many a Slip, Hush Money (1931); She Wanted a Millionaire, Careless Lady/The Trial of Vivienne Ware, Week-Ends Only, Wild Girl, Me and My Gal (1932); Arizona to Broadway, Little Women [as Amy] (1933); The Pursuit of Happiness (1934); The Man Who Reclaimed His Head, Private Worlds, Mississippi, Two for Tonight, She Couldn't Take It, The Man Who Broke the Bank at Monte Carlo (1935); 13 Hours by Air, Big Brown Eyes, Two in a Crowd, Wedding Present (1936); Vogues of 1938 (1937); I Met My Love Again, The Texans, Artists and Models Abroad (1938); Trade Winds, The Man in the Iron Mask [as Queen Maria Theresa], The Housekeeper's Daughter (1939); Green Hell, The House across the Bay, The Man I Married, The Son of Monte Cristo (1940); Man Hunt, She Knew All the Answers, Wild Geese Calling, Confirm or Deny (1941); Twin Beds, The Wife Takes a Flyer, Girl Trouble (1942); Margin for Error (1943); The Woman in the Window (1944); Nob Hill (1945); Scarlet Street, Colonel Effingham's Raid (1946); The Macomber Affair, The Woman on the Beach (1947); Secret beyond the Door, Hollow Triumph/The Scar (1948); The Reckless Moment (1949); Father of the Bride, For Heaven's Sake (1950); Father's Little Dividend, The Guy Who Came Back (1951); Highway Dragnet (1954); We're No Angels (1955); There's Always Tomorrow, Navy Wife (1956); Desire in the Dust (1960); House of Dark Shadows (1970); Gidget Gets Married [TV movie], The Eyes of Charles Sand [TV movie] (1972); Inn of the Damned [unreleased] (1974); Suspiria [It.] (1977).

Selected Bibliography

Bennett, Joan, and Lois Kibbee. *The Bennett Playbill*. New York: Holt, Rinehart and Winston, 1970.

BERGMAN, INGRID. Actress. Born on August 29, 1915, in Stockholm, Sweden; died on August 29, 1982. Educated at Stockholm's Royal Dramatic Theater School. From the beginning, Bergman was given leading roles in Swedish films and quickly became the most promising young actress on the Swedish screen. After her appearance in Gustaf Molander's *Intermezzo* in 1936, David O. Selznick invited her to Hollywood to star opposite Leslie Howard in a 1939 American version of the film. The following year, she made her Broadway debut in *Liliom*. Her natural radiance and vitality helped her achieve a popularity that increased with every film she made, particularly such landmark films as *Casablanca*, *For Whom the Bell Tolls*, *Gaslight*, *Notorious*, and *Joan of Arc*. Her screen image as a wholesome, almost saintly woman was shattered in 1949 when she deserted her husband and her daughter Pia for Italian director Roberto Rossellini. Their union, which produced a son and twin girls (one is film actress Isabella Rossellini), almost ruined them professionally. The films he directed with her, even the much-heralded *Stromboli*, were neither critical nor commercial successes. Attacks by religious groups and women's clubs and even politicians barred her from American films for seven years. She seemed destined for oblivion when, in 1956, her career was revived with her appearance first in Renoir's film *Elena et les Hommes/Paris Does Strange Things* and then in *Anastasia*. The Oscar she won for *Anastasia* was Hollywood's way of forgiving her "sins." After her marriage to Rossellini was annulled in 1958, she married Swedish stage producer Lars Schmidt. They divorced in 1975. Suffering from cancer the last eight years of her life, Bergman continued to appear in films and on television. She won a third Oscar (this time for Best Supporting Actress) for her role as a simple-minded nurse in *Murder on the Orient Express*. Her complex role as a concert pianist in Ingmar Bergman's *Autumn Sonata* turned out to be her last feature film. Her final role was a portrait of Israel's Prime Minister Golda Meir in the TV movie *A Woman Called Golda* (1981).

Filmography: [in Sweden]: The Count from the Monk's Bridge (1934); Ocean Breakers/ The Surf, Swedenhielms, Walpurgis Night (1935); On the Sunny Side, Intermezzo (1936); Die Vier Gesellen [Ger.], Dollar, A Woman's Face, One Single Night (1938); A Night in June (1940). [in the United States]: Intermezzo: A Love Story (1939); Adam Had Four Sons, Rage in Heaven, Dr. Jekyll and Mr. Hyde (1941); Casablanca, Swedes in America [two-reel doc.], For Whom the Bell Tolls (1943); Gaslight (1944); Spellbound, Saratoga Trunk, The Bells of St. Mary's (1945); Notorious (1946); Arch of Triumph, Joan of Arc (1948). [in the United Kingdom]: Under Capricorn (1949); [in Italy]: Stromboli (1949); Europa '51/The Greatest Love (1952); Siamo Donne/We the Women, Viaggio in Italia/The Lonely Woman (1953); Giovanna d'Arco al Rogo/Joan at the Stake (1954). [internationally]: Angst/LaPaura/Fear (1954); Elena et les Hommes/Paris Does Strange Things, Anastasia (1956); Indiscreet, The Inn of the Sixth Happiness (1958); Goodbye Again/Aimez-vous Brahms? (1961); Der Besuch/The Visit, The Yellow Rolls-Royce (1964); Stimulantia (1967); Cactus Flower (1969); A Walk in the Spring Rain (1970); From the Mixed-Up Files of Mrs. Basil E. Frankweiler (1973); Murder on the Orient Express (1974); A Matter of Time (1976); Herbstsonate/Autumn Sonata (1978).

Honors: Academy Award Nomination: Best Actress (*For Whom the Bell Tolls*, 1943); Academy Award, Golden Globe Award: Best Actress (*Gaslight*, 1944); Golden Globe Award (*The Bells of St. Mary's*, 1945); New York Film Critics Circle Award (*The Bells of St. Mary's* and *Spellbound*, 1945); *Photoplay* Gold Medal Award: Most Popular Female Star (1946); *Photoplay* Gold Medal Award: Most Popular Female Star (1947); *Photoplay* Gold Medal Award: Most Popular Female Star (1948); Academy Award, Golden Globe Award, New York Film Critics Circle Award: Best Actress (*Anastasia*, 1956); Academy Award, British Academy Award: Best Supporting Actress (*Murder on the Orient Express*, 1974); New York Film Critics Circle Award, National Society of Film Critics Award, National Board of Review Award, Academy Award Nomination: Best Actress (*Autumn Sonata*, 1978).

Selected Bibliography

Bergman, Ingrid, and Alan Burgess. *My Story*. New York: Delacorte Press, 1980.

Leamer, Laurence. *As Time Goes By: The Life of Ingrid Bergman*. New York: Harper & Row, 1986.

Quirk, Lawrence J. *The Complete Films of Ingrid Bergman*. New York: Carol Communications, 1989.

Taylor, John Russell. *Ingrid Bergman*. New York: St. Martin's, 1983.

BERKELEY, BUSBY. Choreographer, director. Born William Berkeley Enos on November 29, 1895, in Los Angeles; died on March 14, 1976. Berkeley was the son of a stage director and a stage and film actress and acquired his nickname from Amy Busby, a Broadway star at the turn of the century. The family moved to New York when he was three, and when he was five, he made his first stage appearance. Later he attended a military academy and then worked for a shoe company. After serving as a field artillery lieutenant in World War I, he began playing bit parts on Broadway and directing in stock. By the end of the 1920s he had become one of Broadway's top dance directors, with twenty-one musicals to his credit. In 1930 Samuel Goldwyn brought him to Hollywood to choreograph the musical numbers of several Eddie Cantor movies as well as Mary Pickford's only musical film, *Kiki*. It was at Warner Bros., however, that Berkeley established himself as one of the most creative dance directors in film history. Starting in 1933, he was responsible for innovative dance sequences that continue to dazzle movie audiences. Given the great technical facilities available at the studio, he was able to provide audiences with breathtaking production numbers in a lavish style that managed to envelop strident sexuality in a cocoon of artistic whimsy. *Elegant eroticism* best describes his style, a style that had a lasting effect on the American musical film. "Nothing succeeds like excess," said Oscar Wilde, and nobody understood this principle better than Berkeley. At every turn, impeccable taste flirted with gaudy vulgarity. Only Berkeley seemed to know where to draw the line, which was somewhere between the phony machismo of *Seven Brides for Seven Brothers* and the campy excess of *Can't Stop the Music* (in which even the screen credits are gaudy rip-offs of Berkeley's style). Each of his lavish numbers employed masses of nubile maidens in a spectacular array of rhythmic movement. One film critic describes one of Berkeley's most notable routines as "kaleidoscopic patterns of female flesh, dissolving into artichokes, exploding stars, snowflakes, and the expanding leaves of water lilies." It has been said that Berkeley was more a dance director than a choreographer since his girls didn't really dance; they moved in ways that created patterns that only the camera could appreciate. In fact, his use of the camera became progressively more inventive with each movie as he introduced such inventions as the monorail to give his camera greater mobility and devised a technique of filming from directly above, a technique that has become known as the "Berkeley top shot." When he moved from directing musical numbers to directing entire films, he had only mixed success, as with *Gold Diggers of*

1935, *Babes in Arms*, and *For Me and My Gal*. He directed his last film in 1949, after which he staged musical numbers for films of others through the mid-1950s. By the early 1960s the movie musical had so declined that Berkeley retired. However, after some of his earlier films had been rereleased in the late 1960s, there was a resurgence of interest in Berkeley's career. He made numerous appearances on campuses, on speaking tours, and on TV. In 1970 he played a cameo part in the film *The Phynx*.

Filmography: [as choreographer]: Whoopee (1930); Kiki, Palmy Days, Flying High (1931); Night World, Bird of Paradise, The Kid from Spain (1932); 42nd Street, Gold Diggers of 1933, Footlight Parade, Roman Scandals (1933); Wonder Bar, Fashions of 1934, Twenty Million Sweethearts, Dames (1934); Go into Your Dance, In Caliente, Stars over Broadway (1935); Gold Diggers of 1937 (1936); The Singing Marine, Varsity Show (1937); Gold Diggers in Paris (1938); Broadway Serenade (1939); Ziegfeld Girl, Lady Be Good, Born to Sing (1941); Girl Crazy (1943); Two Weeks with Love (1950); Call Me Mister, Two Tickets to Broadway (1951); Million Dollar Mermaid (1952); Small Town Girl, Easy to Love (1953); Rose Marie (1954); Billy Rose's Jumbo (1962). [as director]: She Had to Say Yes [co-dir. with George Amy] (1933); Gold Diggers of 1935 (1935); Stage Struck (1936); The Go-Getter, Hollywood Hotel (1937); Men Are Such Fools, Garden of the Moon, Comet Over Broadway (1938); They Made Me a Criminal, Babes in Arms, Fast and Furious (1939); Strike Up the Band, Forty Little Mothers (1940); Blonde Inspiration, Babes on Broadway (1941); For Me and My Gal (1942); The Gang's All Here (1943); Cinderella Jones (1946); Take Me Out to the Ball Game (1949).

Honors: Academy Award Nomination: Dance Direction (*Gold Diggers of 1935*, 1935); Academy Award Nomination: Dance Direction (*Gold Diggers of 1937*, 1936); Academy Award Nomination: Dance Direction (*Varsity Show*, 1937).

Selected Bibliography

Pike, Bob, and Dave Martin. *The Genius of Busby Berkeley*. Reseda, CA: CFS Books, 1973.

Rubin, Martin. *Showstoppers: Busby Berkeley and the Tradition of Spectacle*. New York: Columbia University Press, 1993.

Thomas, Tony, and Jim Terry, with Busby Berkeley. *The Busby Berkeley Book*. Greenwich, CT: New York Graphic Society, 1973.

BEST YEARS OF OUR LIVES, THE (1946), drama. Directed by William Wyler; with Fredric March, Myrna Loy, Teresa Wright, Dana Andrews, Virginia Mayo, Harold Russell, Hoagy Carmichael, Gladys George, and Steve Cochran; screenplay by Robert E. Sherwood.

"I don't care if it doesn't make a nickel," Samuel Goldwyn reportedly declared in a famous Goldwynism regarding this classic film. "I just want every man, woman, and child in America to see it." "Three wonderful loves in the best picture of the year!" was the blurb that introduced this heartwarming slice-of-life drama to postwar audiences. This film tells the story of three veterans returning home after World War II and their problems with readjusting to civilian life. Robert Sherwood's script from MacKinlay Kantor's book captured the mood of postwar America. Sensitively directed by William Wyler, the film presents with great care the various adjustment challenges these servicemen face. The performances are uniformly strong. Dana Andrews, often considered wooden, is perfect as Virginia Mayo's disillusioned war-hero husband. Fredric March is sympathetic as the middle-aged veteran who feels too old to start over and too young to give up. Myrna Loy, as his compassionate wife, is flawless. It is in her fleeting expressions of sympathy and worry and love that we see March's anguish mirrored. Critics were unanimous in praising amputee Harold Russell who, with no acting training whatsoever, played his role with understatement, feeling, and heroic humor. At the time of its release, critics were generally unreserved in their admiration for a movie so in tune with the times and so wonderfully evocative and moving. Later critics, while calling the film one of Wyler's finest, find it not quite the masterpiece it was once thought to be. Today it seems overlong, with the professional polish of the studio system all too much in evidence. Ultimately, it is a splendid example of 1940s-style filmmaking on a theme just a tad too topical to be truly timeless. Of interest to later viewers is its disturbing undercurrent of discontent, barely perceptible at the time but apparent now in the way the film exposes fears about the brave new postwar world that the film's characters seem to be trying desperately to deny. One gets the nagging feeling that as far as these characters are concerned, the best years of their lives might already be behind them.

Awards: Academy Awards: Best Picture, Director, Actor (March), Supporting Actor (Russell), Screenplay, Scoring of a Dramatic Picture (Hugo Friedhofer), Editing, Special Award (Russell); Golden Globe Awards: Best Picture, Award for Non-Professional Acting (Russell); New York Film Critics Circle Awards: Best Picture, Director; Academy Award Nomination: Best Sound.

Selected Bibliography

Anderegg, Michael A. *William Wyler*. Boston: Twayne, 1979.
Levy, Emanuel. *Small-Town America in Film: The Decline and Fall of Community*. New York: Continuum, 1991.

BIG SLEEP, THE (1946), mystery thriller. Directed by Howard Hawks; with Humphrey Bogart, Lauren Bacall, John Ridgely, Martha Vickers, Louis Jean Heydt, Regis Toomey, Peggy Knudsen, Dorothy Malone, Bob Steele, and Elisha Cook, Jr.; screenplay by William Faulkner, Jules Furthman, and Leigh Brackett.

This classic mystery thriller, from Raymond Chandler's first novel, is so convoluted even Chandler himself didn't know who committed one of the murders. But the film is so filled with crackling dialogue, tense action, and incredible film noir atmosphere that no one has ever cared. Howard Hawks, whose direction is brilliant, admitted that neither the author, the writer, nor he himself knew "whodunit." Maybe it's this "riddle of reality" that makes the film so compelling, mirroring as it does the fragmentation of reality in which some pieces are missing and others don't quite fit.

The Big Sleep is the story of Philip Marlowe, a private eye who is hired by the eccentric Sternwood family to protect the younger daughter. Murder and mayhem follow in sinister settings and complicated sequences that are better appreciated viscerally than logically. It's a film to absorb, not figure out. Hawks punctuates long stretches of pure action with short scenes of fast dialogue, a technique that increases the suspense, especially in the last half of the picture. Several scriptwriters worked on the screenplay including William Faulkner who, when given permission to "write at home," turned up, after a frantic search, in his hometown of Oxford, Mississippi. *The Big Sleep* is considered to be one of the finest noir thrillers ever made, and although the plot may be virtually incomprehensible at times, what matters most is the film's sultry mood, its brilliant dialogue, and its flawless performances.

Selected Bibliography

Mast, Gerald. *Howard Hawks, Storyteller*. New York: Oxford University Press, 1982.
McCarty, Clifford. *The Complete Films of Humphrey Bogart*. Secaucus, NJ: Citadel Press, 1965.
Royce, Brenda Scott. *Lauren Bacall: A Bio-Bibliography*. Westport, CT: Greenwood Press, 1992.
Tuska, Jon. *Dark Cinema*. Westport, CT: Greenwood Press, 1984.

BLACKBOARD JUNGLE, THE (1955), drama. Directed by Richard Brooks; with Glenn Ford, Anne Francis, Vic Morrow, Louis Calhern, Sidney Poitier, Richard Kiley, Warner Anderson, Margaret Hayes, Emile Meyer, John Hoyt, Rafael Campos, and Paul Mazursky; screenplay by Richard Brooks.

Director Richard Brooks adapted his screenplay from Evan Hunter's novel of a teacher's harrowing experiences in an inner-city vocational school. This was the first film to feature rock music, in this case Bill Haley's "Rock around the Clock," which is played over the opening credits. The movie was a shocker for its time and was blamed for provoking violence. Its notoriety (and popularity) increased when American ambassador to Italy Clare Booth Luce managed to get it withdrawn from the Venice Film Festival. The film is about contempt for authority, but throughout there is the hope that a solution can be found for this problem. The hero (Ford) is an idealistic teacher who persists in his efforts to reach the few salvageable students from among the many hostile ones who are out to make his life hell. To his dismay, his fellow teachers are mostly apathetic or cowardly or both. Ford's success was not written into the original story. Some critics complained that the movie pulled its punches, but most praised it for going as far as it went. Sidney Poitier gives a standout performance as a racially troubled youth bursting with conflicting emotions of rage and hope. The controversy that raged at the time of the film's release has long since abated, but the film remains a disturbing exposé of conditions that, if anything, have only worsened. Beyond that, there is much to be admired in the sheer professional surface of a movie that was made in less than three months. The casting is uniformly good, the music is varied and exciting, and the tension in the classrooms is palpable. This movie was released the same year as *Rebel without a*

Cause, and one could say that in *The Blackboard Jungle* the "rebel without a cause" meets the "teacher with a mission."

Awards: Academy Award Nominations: Best Screenplay, B&W Cinematography, B&W Art Direction, Editing.

Selected Bibliography

Ford, Glenn, and Margaret Redfield. *Glenn Ford, RFD Beverly Hills*. Old Tappan, NJ: Hewitt House, 1970.

Keyser, Lester J., and Andre H. Ruszkows. *The Cinema of Sidney Poitier: The Black Man's Changing Role on the American Screen*. South Brunswick, NJ: A. S. Barnes, 1980.

BODY AND SOUL (1947), drama. Directed by Robert Rossen; with John Garfield, Lilli Palmer, Hazel Brooks, Anne Revere, William Conrad, Joseph Pevney, and Canada Lee; screenplay by Abraham Polonsky.

Hollywood has turned out a lot of boxing films, but none can compare with this classic story of boxer Garfield working his way up by devious means to become world champion. No punches are pulled in showing how boxers often turn to the ring after growing up on the streets where they become proficient with their fists. Pool rooms and beer halls are realistically employed to capture the sordidness of the boxing world. But beneath the surface the script resonates with the corrupting power of money. In fact, given its director, screenwriter, and star (all of whom had tangled with the House Un-American Activities Committee), it is easy to agree with those critics who saw this film as a socialist morality play about Capital and the Little Man disguised as noir anxiety. In fact, in the tradition of film noir, the whole film is one lone prefight flashback. Fortunately, Garfield's aggressive performance rescues the script from seeming too stagy and episodic. John Garfield, under Rossen's brilliant direction, is superb in the role of the corrupted boxer, giving a dynamic performance that saves the film from being just another predictable ring saga. Critics praised the authentic depression-era flavor, finding its ermine and vermin depiction of the whole spectrum of society refreshingly unsentimental and thus strikingly realistic.

Awards: Academy Award: Best Editing (Francis Lyon, Robert Parrish); Academy Award Nominations: Best Actor (Garfield), Original Screenplay.

Selected Bibliography

Casty, Alan. *The Films of Robert Rossen*. New York: MOMA, 1969. [Distributed by New York Graphic Society, Greenwich, CT]

Swindell, Larry. *Body and Soul: The Story of John Garfield*. New York: Morrow, 1975.

BOGART, HUMPHREY. Actor. Born on January 23, 1899, in New York City; died on January 14, 1957. Educated at Phillips Academy, Andover, Massachusetts, in preparation for medical studies at Yale. Bogart was expelled from Phillips Academy because of discipline problems, and shortly thereafter, when the

United States entered World War I in 1917, Bogart joined the navy. He was wounded during a naval battle, resulting in the scarred and partly paralyzed upper lip that gave him his tight-set mouth and trademark lisp. After his discharge, Bogart found work in the theater, beginning as an office boy and working his way up to road company manager and then stage manager. He also did various odd jobs around the film studios of World Film Corporation. While on the road, Bogart tried his hand at acting, playing romantic or juvenile roles, without much initial success. The redoubtable Alexander Wolcott, reviewing an early Bogart play, described Bogart's acting as "what is usually and mercifully described as inadequate." In 1930 Bogart went to Hollywood and made his film debut in a ten-minute short, *Broadway's Like That*. After that he played second-lead roles in a dreary succession of forgettable feature films for various studios and production companies. His film career on a treadmill, Bogart returned to Broadway, where he found himself in more forgettable parts until he got a break playing the role of the hapless gangster Duke Mantee in Robert E. Sherwood's *The Petrified Forest*. When Warner Bros. decided to film the play, they wanted Edward G. Robinson for the part, but Leslie Howard, the lead in the play, threatened to back out unless the role was given to Bogart. The studio relented, and *The Petrified Forest* put Bogart well on the road to film stardom. Over the next few years, Bogart found himself stuck again, this time typecast as a gangster in more than two dozen films. Finally, however, in 1941, Bogart got the break that led to the "Bogey" legend. Under the direction of John Huston, who had written the screenplay for *High Sierra*, Bogart gave a riveting performance as the callous private eye Sam Spade in the film noir classic *The Maltese Falcon*. Bogart remained immensely popular in such films as *Casablanca*, *The Big Sleep*, and *Key Largo*. It was on the set of *To Have and Have Not* that he met and fell in love with his co-star Lauren Bacall, whom he later married. She was his fourth wife. In 1947 he formed his own company, Santana Pictures, and in the following year, he played the greedy, paranoid prospector in *The Treasure of the Sierra Madre*, the first of a number of roles that revealed an astounding versatility, including *The African Queen* and *The Caine Mutiny*. Shortly after the release of his last film, *The Harder They Fall*, in March 1956, Bogart underwent an operation for cancer of the esophagus. He died in his sleep at his Hollywood home on January 14, 1957. The image of Bogart as the brooding loner, independent and cynical, inspired a cult that has continued since the 1960s. The favorite film of this cult is *Casablanca*, and when its members gather together to view this film for the umpteenth time, they often respond to the soundtrack the way fans respond to *The Rocky Horror Picture Show*, cheering and jeering and mouthing familiar lines in unison. What they see in Bogart is the antihero, that element that has endeared audiences to such film icons as James Cagney, Marlon Brando, and James Dean and spawned a generation of antihero wannabes like Matt Dillon, Johnny Depp, and Sean Penn.

Filmography: Broadway's Like That [short], A Devil with Women, Up the River (1930); Body and Soul, Bad Sister, Women of All Nations, A Holy Terror (1931); Love Affair,

Big City Blues, Three on a Match (1932); Midnight (1934); The Petrified Forest, Bullets or Ballots, Two against the World, China Clipper, Isle of Fury (1936); Black Legion, The Great O'Malley, Marked Woman, Kid Galahad, San Quentin, Dead End, Stand-In (1937); Swing Your Lady, Crime School, Men Are Such Fools, The Amazing Dr. Clitterhouse, Racket Busters, Angels with Dirty Faces (1938); King of the Underworld, The Oklahoma Kid, Dark Victory, You Can't Get Away with Murder, The Roaring Twenties, The Return of Doctor X, Invisible Stripes (1939); Virginia City, It All Came True, Brother Orchid, They Drive by Night (1940); High Sierra, The Wagons Roll at Night, The Maltese Falcon (1941); All Through the Night, The Big Shot, In This Our Life [cameo], Across the Pacific (1942); Casablanca, Action in the North Atlantic, Thank Your Lucky Stars, Sahara (1943); Passage to Marseille (1944); To Have and Have Not, Conflict (1945); Two Guys from Milwaukee [cameo], The Big Sleep (1946); Dead Reckoning, The Two Mrs. Carrolls, Dark Passage (1947); Always Together [cameo], The Treasure of the Sierra Madre, Key Largo (1948); It's a Great Feeling [cameo], Knock on Any Door, Tokyo Joe (1949); Chain Lightning, In a Lonely Place (1950); The Enforcer, Sirocco, The African Queen (1951); Road to Bali [cameo], Deadline—U.S.A. (1952); Love Lottery [cameo], Battle Circus (1953); Beat the Devil, The Caine Mutiny, Sabrina, The Barefoot Contessa (1954); We're No Angels, The Left Hand of God, The Desperate Hours (1955); The Harder They Fall (1956).

Honors: Academy Award Nomination: Best Actor (*Casablanca*, 1943); Academy Award: Best Actor (*The African Queen*, 1951); Academy Award Nomination: Best Actor (*The Caine Mutiny*, 1954).

Selected Bibliography

Hyams, Joe. *Bogie: The Biography of Humphrey Bogart*. New York: New American Library, 1966.

McCarty, Clifford. *The Complete Films of Humphrey Bogart*. Secaucus, NJ: Citadel Press, 1965.

Pettigrew, Terence. *Bogart: A Definitive Study of His Film Career*. New York: Proteus, 1981.

BOOMERANG! (1947), drama. Directed by Elia Kazan; with Dana Andrews, Jane Wyatt, Lee J. Cobb, Arthur Kennedy, Sam Levene, Robert Keith, Taylor Holmes, Ed Begley, Karl Malden, Cara Williams, and Barry Kelley; screenplay by Richard Murphy.

Boomerang! is a gripping, real-life melodrama, based on an as-yet-unsolved murder of a priest in Bridgeport, Connecticut. Told in semidocumentary style, it was one of the first movies to be filmed on location (Stamford, Connecticut). Dana Andrews, in one of his best film roles, heads a convincing cast including outstanding performances by Arthur Kennedy and Lee J. Cobb. Kennedy plays the tramp who is the state's only suspect, and Cobb is the chief detective who tries to carry out his duties while being hounded by both the press and the politicians to get quick results. Andrews is the man who tries to defend the accused tramp against those who want a hasty conviction. Kazan introduces a dramatic trick at the end, uncovering a villain known only to the audience. Thus justice is not done. It was this sort of Sophoclean irony that Kazan would be-

come famous for and that makes *Boomerang!* a movie milestone. The film has
been admired for its study of integrity against a background of political corruption that is all the more shocking when presented in the understated style of a
documentary. Critics praise the film as an exposé of the petty politics and pervasive dishonesty surprisingly commonplace beneath the folksy veneer of a typical American city. This was to become a commonplace theme in films to follow.

Awards: Academy Award Nomination: Best Screenplay.

Selected Bibliography

Pauly, Thomas H. *An American Odyssey: Elia Kazan and American Culture*. Philadel-
    phia: Temple University Press, 1983.
Thomas, Tony. *The Films of the Forties*. Secaucus, NJ: Citadel Press, 1975.

BORZAGE, FRANK. Director. Born on April 23, 1893, in Salt Lake City, Utah;
died on June 19, 1962. After a brief stint in a silver mine at the age of thirteen,
Borzage joined a touring stage company as an extra and then a juvenile lead.
He arrived in Hollywood in 1912, where he appeared in numerous westerns,
then went on to play heavies and leads in dozens of films produced by Thomas
Ince, the man who gave Borzage his first chance to direct. By 1916 he was
directing films for Universal, mostly quickie melodramas and westerns in which
he also starred. His first important film, *Humoresque* (1920), exhibited the romantic elements that would become his trademark in years to come. Borzage
was an unabashed sentimentalist who was responsible for some of the screen's
most beautiful love stories. He was a pioneer in the use of the soft focus, a
technique he combined with a fluid camera movement to give to his lovers an
unearthly aura that contrasted sharply with the harsh reality of the world around
them. Although he was disdained by some critics as a "gushy sentimentalist,"
Borzage was, in fact, a very original artist with a very consistent style. His
reputation reached its peak in the late silent and early sound era when he won
Academy Awards as the best director for *Seventh Heaven* (1927) and *Bad Girl*
(1931). Borzage's films of the 1940s and 1950s were the least interesting of his
career, with the possible exception of *I've Always Loved You*, a blatantly romanticized account of a young woman torn between the charm of the pastoral
life and the glamour of life as one of the world's leading concert pianists. The
story unfolds like a dream and is filled with those touches that make movies
"movies." Lush sets and gorgeous music may have been anachronistic in the
late 1940s, but this is pure Borzage, and as such, deserves special recognition,
if only for having the nerve to put Rachmaninoff's Second Piano Concerto,
Wagner's "Liebestod," Chopin's "Ballade in G Minor," and Beethoven's "Sonata Appassionata" together in the same movie. Borzage was a more versatile
director than he has been given credit for. He had an original and unmistakable
touch that is present not just in his romantic films but also in his films with
keen social and political content and commentary.

Filmography: [since 1927]: *Seventh Heaven* (1927); *Street Angel* (1928); The River, Lucky Star, They Had to See Paris (1929); Song o' My Heart, Liliom (1930); Doctors' Wives, Young as You Feel, Bad Girl (1931); After Tomorrow, Young America, A Farewell to Arms (1932); Secrets [remake of 1924 film], Man's Castle (1933); No Greater Glory, Little Man What Now?, Flirtation Walk (1934); Living on Velvet, Stranded, Shipmates Forever (1935); Desire, Hearts Divided (1936); Green Light, History Is Made at Night, Big City (1937); Mannequin, Three Comrades, The Shining Hour (1938); Disputed Passage (1939); Strange Cargo, The Mortal Storm (1940); Flight Command, Smilin' Through (1941); The Vanishing Virginian, Seven Sweethearts (1942); Stage Door Canteen, His Butler's Sister (1943); Till We Meet Again (1944); The Spanish Main (1945); I've Always Loved You, Magnificent Doll (1946); That's My Man (1947); Moonrise (1949); China Doll (1958); The Big Fisherman (1959).

Honors: Academy Award: Dramatic Direction (*Seventh Heaven*, 1927–1928); Academy Award: Best Director (*Bad Girl*, 1932); Directors Guild of America: D. W. Griffith Award (1960).

Selected Bibliography

Canham, Kingsley. *The Hollywood Professionals*. New York: A. S. Barnes, 1973.
Lamster, Frederick. *Souls Made Great Through Love and Adversity: The Film Work of Frank Borzage*. Metuchen, NJ: Scarecrow Press, 1981.

BOYER, CHARLES. Actor. Born on August 28, 1897, in Figeac, France; died on August 26, 1978. Educated at the Sorbonne (philosophy) and the Paris Conservatory (drama). Although he made both his stage and his film debut in 1920, Boyer remained a stage actor throughout the 1920s. In 1931, after two years of vainly attempting to succeed in Hollywood, he returned to France, but he came back to Hollywood in 1934, was a success in Frank Borzage's *Liliom*, and stayed on for the rest of his career. He quickly emerged as one of Hollywood's "great lovers," the personification of suave Gallic charm. In spite of the perception of him as a "professional Frenchman," Boyer resisted self-parody and consistently turned in professional performances in a variety of characters from debonair dandies to vicious villains, playing opposite Hollywood's most glamorous female stars from Garbo to Bergman. During World War II, Boyer worked hard at improving Franco-American cultural relations, receiving a special Academy Award in 1942 for establishing the French Research Foundation in Los Angeles. Beginning in the early 1950s, Boyer appeared in films on both sides of the Atlantic, in parts that were more "mature." He also made occasional stage appearances, most memorably in Shaw's *Don Juan in Hell*. In 1951 he was a co-founder, along with Dick Powell and David Niven, of Four Star Television and starred in many of the company's TV productions throughout the 1950s and 1960s. Boyer had been married to British-born actress Patricia Paterson for forty-four years when she died in 1978. Two days later, and just two days before his eighty-first birthday, Boyer took his own life with an overdose of barbiturates. Their only child, Michael, had committed suicide in 1965.

Filmography: L'Homme du Large (1920); Chantelouve (1921); Le Grillon du Foyer (1922); L'Esclave (1923); La Ronde infernale (1927); Le Capitaine Fracasse, Le Procès du Mary Dugan [French version of The Trial of Mary Dugan] (1929); Revolte dans la Prison [French version of The Big House], La Bacarolle d'Amour [French version of Brand in der Oper/Bacarole] (1930); Tumultes [French version of Stürme der Leidenschaft], The Magnificent Lie (1931); The Man from Yesterday, Red-Headed Woman, F.P. 1 ne répond plus [French version of F.P. 1 Antwortet Nicht] (1932); Moi et l'Impératrice [French version of Ich und die Kaiserin], The Only Girl/Heart Song [English version of Ich und die Kaiserin], L'Epervier/Les Amoureux (1933); La Bataille [and English version, The Battle], Liliom (1934); Le Bonheur, Private Worlds, Break of Hearts, Shanghai (1935); Mayerling [as Archduke Rudolph of Austria], The Garden of Allah (1936); History Is Made at Night, Conquest/Maria Walewska [as Napoleon], Tovarich (1937); Algiers [as Pepe le Moko], Orage (1938); Love Affair, When Tomorrow Comes (1939); All This and Heaven Too (1940); Back Street, Hold Back the Dawn, Appointment for Love (1941); Tales of Manhattan (1942); Untel Père et Fils/The Heart of a Nation [narrator only; made in France in 1940 but completed and narration added in the U.S., where it was first shown], The Constant Nymph, Flesh and Fantasy (1943); Gaslight, Together Again (1944); Confidential Agent (1945); Cluny Brown (1946); A Woman's Vengeance, Arch of Triumph (1948); The Thirteenth Letter, The First Legion (1951); The Happy Time (1952); Thunder in the East, Madame de . . . / The Earrings of Madame De (1953); Nana, The Cobweb (1955); La Fortuna di Essere Donna/Lucky to Be a Woman, Paris-Palace Hôtel/Paris Hotel, Around the World in 80 Days (1956); Une Parisienne (1957); Maxime, The Buccaneer (1958); Fanny (1961); The Four Horsemen of the Apocalypse, Les Démonds de Minuit, Adorable Julia (1962); Love Is a Ball (1963); A Very Special Favor (1965); How to Steal a Million, Paris brûle-t-il?/Is Paris Burning? (1966); Casino Royale, Barefoot in the Park (1967); Le Rouble à Deux Faces/The Day the Hot Line Got Hot (1968); The April Fools, The Madwoman of Chaillot (1969); Lost Horizon (1972); L'Empire d'Alexandre/Stavisky (1974); A Matter of Time (1976).

Honors: Academy Award Nomination: Best Actor (*Conquest*, 1937); Academy Award Nomination: Best Actor (*Algiers*, 1938); Academy Award: Special Award for establishing the French Research Foundation in Los Angeles as a source of reference for the industry (1942); Academy Award Nomination: Best Actor (*Fanny*, 1961); New York Film Critics Circle Award: Best Supporting Actor, Cannes Film Festival: Special Mention (*Stavisky*, 1974).

Selected Bibliography

Swindell, Larry. *Charles Boyer: The Reluctant Lover.* Garden City, NY: Doubleday, 1983.

BRANDO, MARLON. Actor. Born on April 3, 1924, in Omaha, Nebraska. Educated at the New School for Social Research, Actor's Studio. Following a season of summer stock on Long Island, Brando made his Broadway debut in 1944 as Nels in *I Remember Mama*. Two years later he appeared in two other Broadway plays, *Truckline Cafe* and *Candida*, and in Ben Hecht's salute to Israel, *A Flag Is Born*, which starred Paul Muni. In 1947, Brando forever changed stage (and later screen) acting with his galvanizing performance as the coarse, ill-mannered hunk Stanley Kowalski in Tennessee Williams's *A Streetcar Named Desire*. Brando had studied "the [Stanislavsky] Method" under Stella Adler and Lee Strasberg, and he brought every trick he had learned to his acting. It has been ironically noted that Brando, who detested traditional acting styles, developed an acting style that was just as mannered as Laurence Olivier's could ever be. One trick he learned was how to upstage his fellow actors, a trick he pulled off so well in *Streetcar* that he managed to make Stanley, not Blanche, the center of attention. Brando instinctively sensed Williams's basic awe of the masculine in Stanley and knew that through Blanche, Williams was flirting with Stanley's raw, "rough trade" sexuality. It's a level Brando also exploited in *The Fugitive Kind*, *Reflections in a Golden Eye*, and even *The Wild Ones* where the sexual fusion of biker and bike is powerfully revealed. In his autobiography, *Songs My Mother Taught Me*, Brando makes such a point of being a superstud with women and such a fuss about doubts about his sexuality that critics have wondered if perhaps the gentleman "doth protest too much." At any rate, Brando was an exciting new screen personality, and he immediately acquired cult status, a continuing phenomenon primarily among those who either ignore or forgive some of his latter-day film fiascos. Brando did prove, however, that he could act in movies as various as *Julius Caesar* (in which he did Marc Antony in a voice he could have borrowed from Olivier), *Viva Zapata!* (in which he flirted with stereotype), and *The Godfather* (in which he altered his appearance to, indeed, become the Mafia don he portrayed so brilliantly). Throughout the 1950s Brando remained an artistic and social force, the point man of the rebellious trio that included James Dean and Montgomery Clift. In the 1960s, Brando played in a slew of unsuccessful movies that considerably damaged his professional and personal image. Then came *The Godfather*, for which he won an Academy Award, followed by yet another Oscar nomination along with universal acclaim for his study of middle-age sexuality in Bernardo Bertolucci's *Last Tango in Paris*, a shocker way ahead of its time that only put a further spin on the suspicion of Brando as the grand manipulator. As Brando approached 300 pounds, he limited his screen appearances to undemanding cameos and roles that hid much of his girth in the scenery but for which he could command astronomical fees (*Apocalypse Now*, *Superman*). It was self-exploitation of the most bizarre sort. After a long absence, he returned to the screen in 1989 and received yet another Oscar nomination, this time as Best Supporting Actor in *A Dry White Season*. Many consider him the greatest actor the American screen has ever known, an accolade most actors have to die to earn (Dean, Monroe, Clift). Brando's later life has been marred by domestic tragedy. In the meantime, Brando himself has become increasingly reclusive and eccentric in the fashion of so many late twentieth-century celebrities.

Filmography: The Men (1950); A Streetcar Named Desire (1951); Viva Zapata! (1952); Julius Caesar [as Marc Antony] 1953; The Wild One, On the Waterfront, Désirée [as Napoleon] (1954); Guys and Dolls (1955); The Teahouse of the August Moon (1956); Sayonara (1957); The Young Lions (1958); The Fugitive Kind (1960); One-Eyed Jacks [also dir.] (1961); Mutiny on the Bounty (1962); The Ugly American (1963); Bedtime Story (1964); Morituri/The Saboteur—Code Name Morituri (1965); The Chase, The Appaloosa (1966); The Countess from Hong Kong, Reflections in a Golden Eye (1967);

Candy (1968); The Night of the Following Day, Queimada/Burn! [It./Fr.] (1969); The Night Comers (U.K.) (1971); The Godfather, Ultimo Tango a Parigi/Last Tango in Paris [It.] (1972); The Missouri Breaks (1976); Superman (1978); Raoni [doc.; narr.; Fr./Braz.], Apocalypse Now (1979); The Formula (1980); A Dry White Season (1989); The Freshman (1990); Christopher Columbus, The Discovery (1992).

Honors: Academy Award Nomination: Best Actor (*A Streetcar Named Desire*, 1951); British Academy Award, Cannes Film Festival, Academy Award Nomination: Best Actor (*Viva Zapata!*, 1952); British Academy Award, Academy Award Nomination: Best Actor (*Julius Caesar*, 1953); Academy Award, Golden Globe Award, New York Film Critics Circle Award, British Academy Award: Best Actor (*On the Waterfront*, 1954); Golden Globe Award: World Film Favorite (1955); Academy Award Nomination: Best Actor (*Sayonara*, 1957); Academy Award, Golden Globe Award: Best Actor (*The Godfather*, 1972); New York Film Critics Circle Award, National Society of Film Critics Award, Academy Award Nomination: Best Actor (*Last Tango in Paris*, 1972); Golden Globe Award: World Film Favorite (1973); Academy Award Nomination: Best Supporting Actor (*A Dry White Season*, 1989).

Selected Bibliography

Blye, Nellie. *Brando, Marlon: Larger Than Life*. New York: Pinnacle Books, 1994.
Manso, Peter. *Brando*. New York: Hyperion, 1994.
Ryan, Paul. *Marlon Brando: A Portrait*. New York: Carroll & Graf, 1994.

BREAKFAST AT TIFFANY'S (1961), drama. Directed by Blake Edwards; with Audrey Hepburn, George Peppard, Patricia Neal, Buddy Ebsen, Mickey Rooney, Martin Balsam, and John McGiver; screenplay by George Axelrod.

This film is a charming adaptation of the Truman Capote story about a small-town girl who comes to New York and learns how to survive in the big city without totally selling out. It is as much a slice of the 1950s as Fitzgerald's stories are of the 1920s, and the film evokes that "age of innocence" in all its heartbreaking simplicity. The marvelous cocktail party scene is tops, certainly one of the best screen parties of the era, a flawless 1950s set piece. Perhaps Hepburn gives Holly more class than she really has, but at the same time she does manage to capture Holly's innate sense of style. Holly manages to be both independent and elegant, no easy act to pull off, and with it all she reveals a touching vulnerability. The tacked-on Hollywood happy ending may offend some, but movie conventions are not like literary ones. Movies like this are more like fairy tales or operettas, melodramas that demand an upbeat ending, especially when that ending has the elfin Audrey Hepburn searching for her cat in the rain and ending up in George Peppard's arms. In a way it doesn't violate the original story since it seems unlikely that anything much will come of a romance between what can only be described as a high-class hooker and a gigolo. Martin Balsam as Holly's agent offers a significant insight into his client's personality halfway through the film when he describes her thus: "She's a phony, all right," he says, "but a real phony." With this movie a new kind of woman made her first significant appearance on the screen. Hepburn stands as a precursor of the liberated woman who would appear in the films of the late 1960s. The film's musical score by Henry Mancini is brilliantly appropriate, particularly the haunting ''Moon River'' (lyrics by the great Johnny Mercer), a song with just enough folksy flavor to remind us of Holly's country roots.

Awards: Academy Awards: Dramatic or Comedy Score (Mancini), Song (''Moon River''); Academy Award Nominations: Actress (Hepburn), Screenplay, Art Direction.

Selected Bibliography

Hofstede, David. *Audrey Hepburn: A Bio-Bibliography*. Westport, CT: Greenwood Press, 1994.

Lehman, Peter, and William Luhr. *Blake Edwards*. Athens: Ohio University Press, 1981.

BRENT, GEORGE. Actor. Born George Brendan Nolan on March 15, 1904, in Shannonsbridge, Ireland; died on May 26, 1979. Brent first came to America at age eleven to stay with relatives after his parents' death but later returned to Ireland, where he played bit parts and walk-ons in Abbey Theatre productions. His subversive activities during the Irish Rebellion forced him to flee the country, and he was smuggled aboard a freighter bound for Canada. He toured with a Canadian stock company for two years before heading for New York to begin his stage career. After appearing in a number of Broadway productions in the late 1920s, he went to Hollywood, where he enjoyed a twenty-year-long film career as a gallant, romantic leading man. He was the consummate gentleman, dapper, suave, and sporting a trademark pencil-thin mustache. He projected a sort of restrained virility opposite such leading ladies as Greta Garbo, Ginger Rogers, Barbara Stanwyck, Myrna Loy, Olivia de Havilland, and especially Bette Davis, with whom he appeared in a succession of eleven Warner Bros. dramas in the late 1930s and early 1940s. He retired from the screen in the early 1950s to run a horse-breeding ranch but returned for an isolated appearance in 1978. Another underrated talent, Brent is only now being appreciated as what might be called the physical counterpart of the tuxedo, a somber study in black and white meant to show off the attributes of the gentleman's lady. A perfect example is *Dark Victory*, in which Brent's understated presence allows Bette Davis to dissemble, chatter, lie, beg, as well as become hysterical, contrite, and ultimately sympathetic. Much like Herbert Marshall and Paul Henreid, Brent knew perfectly how to use his subtle talents so as to focus attention on his co-stars' more flamboyant ones.

Filmography: Under Suspicion, Once a Sinner, Fair Warning, The Lightning Warrior [serial], Charlie Chan Carries on, Ex-Bad Boy, Homicide Squad (1931); So Big, The Rich Are Always with Us, Week-End Marriage, Miss Pinkerton, The Purchase Price, The Crash, They Call It Sin (1932); Luxury Liner, 42nd Street, The Keyhole, Lilly Turner, Baby Face, Private Detective 62, Female, From Headquarters (1933); Stamboul Quest, Housewife, Desirable, The Painted Veil (1934); The Right to Live, Living on Velvet, Stranded, Front Page Woman, The Goose and the Gander, Special Agent, In Person (1935); Snowed Under, The Golden Arrow, The Case against Mrs. Ames, Give Me Your Heart, More Than a Secretary (1936); God's Country and the Woman, Mountain Justice, The Go-Getter, Submarine D-1 (1937); Gold Is Where You Find It, Jezebel, Racket Busters, Secrets of an Actress (1938); Wings of the Navy, Dark Victory, The Old Maid, The Rains Came (1939); The Fighting 69th, Adventure in Diamonds, Till We Meet Again, The Man Who Talked Too Much, South of Suez (1940); Honeymoon for Three, The Great Lie, They Dare Not Love, International Lady (1941); Twin Beds, In This Our Life, The Gay Sisters, You Can't Escape Forever, Silver Queen (1942); Experiment Perilous (1944); The Affairs of Susan (1945); My Reputation, The Spiral Staircase, Tomorrow Is Forever, Lover Come Back, Temptation (1946); Slave Girl, The Corpse Came C.O.D., Out of the Blue, Christmas Eve (1947); Luxury Liner, Angel on the Amazon (1948); Red Canyon, Illegal Entry, The Kid from Cleveland, Bride for Sale (1949); FBI Girl (1951); The Last Page, Montana Belle (1952); Tangier Incident, Mexican Manhunt (1953); Death of a Scoundrel [bit] (1956); Born Again (1978).

BRIDE OF FRANKENSTEIN (1935), drama/horror. Directed by James Whale; with Boris Karloff, Colin Clive, Valerie Hobson, Ernest Thesiger, Elsa Lanchester, Una O'Connor, E. E. Clive, Gavin Gordon, Douglas Walton, O. P. Heggie, Dwight Frye, and John Carradine; screenplay by John L. Balderston and William Hurlbut.

Director James Whale displays a devilish sense of humor in this macabre masterpiece. Many find this sequel to *Frankenstein* even better because of the thread of dry wit that runs through it, heightening the horror by contrast. Horror that takes itself seriously becomes unintentionally comic, whereas horror that allows room for a bit of nervous laughter, some whistling, and a little gallows humor softens an audience up for the shocks. Elsa Lanchester is so good playing the bride (and doing a brief preamble as Mary Shelley herself) that one wishes less time had been given to the monster and more to her. There's bitter (yet comic) irony in the fact that the bride, created to love the monster no one else will, is just as horrified by him as everyone else. Karloff, forever associated with the role of the monster, manages to invest the character with some subtleties of emotion that are surprisingly real and touching.

Awards: Academy Award Nomination: Best Sound.

Selected Bibliography

Grant, Barry Keith. *Planks of Reason*. Metuchen, NJ: Scarecrow, 1988.
Vermilye, Jerry. *The Films of the Thirties*. New York: Citadel Press, 1990.

BRINGING UP BABY (1938), comedy. Directed by Howard Hawks; with Cary Grant, Katharine Hepburn, Charlie Ruggles, May Robson, Barry Fitzgerald, Walter Catlett, Fritz Feld, and Ward Bond; screenplay by Dudley Nichols and Hagar Wilde, from Wilde's original story.

This is Hepburn's one and only screwball comedy, and it defines the genre. Cary Grant, who became the master of the art of screwball, is a perfect match for Hepburn in this zany, mind-boggling romp. Director Howard Hawks obviously refused to include one sane character in this film, allowing his penchant for the absurd to run wild. Somehow he manages to keep all this silliness in such delicate balance that reality is never allowed to intrude. In the manner of great art, it creates its own fully realized, self-enclosed world and seduces you into becoming part of it. This picture was the inspiration for Peter Bogdanovich's comedy *What's Up Doc?*

Selected Bibliography

Deschner, Donald. *The Complete Films of Cary Grant*. Secaucus, NJ: Citadel, 1991.

Dickens, Homer. *The Films of Katharine Hepburn*. New York: Citadel Press, 1971.

Poague, Leland A. *Howard Hawks*. Boston: Twayne Publishers, 1982.

Sikov, Ed. *Screwball: Hollywood's Madcap Romantic Comedies*. New York: Crown, 1989.

BURTON, RICHARD. Born Richard Walter Jenkins, Jr., on November 10, 1925, in Pontrhydfen, South Wales; died on August 5, 1984. Educated at Oxford University. Thanks to the tutelage of Philip Burton, his schoolmaster and mentor, Richard Burton won a scholarship to Oxford. In gratitude he took Burton's name as his own professional one. He made his acting debut in Liverpool in 1943 and went with the company to London the following year. From 1944 to 1947 he served with the Royal Air Force as a navigator. He returned to the stage in 1948, the same year he made his debut in British films in *The Last Days of Dolwyn*. Burton's performance in the London production of Christopher Fry's *The Lady's Not for Burning* in 1949 and the New York one in 1950 earned him wide critical acclaim, and soon he was alternating stage and film roles in both England and America. In 1952 he made his first American film, *My Cousin Rachel*, a romantic period piece by Daphne du Maurier, which led to his being typecast in period pieces in his next three films, including *The Robe*, the first movie in CinemaScope. In 1953 he played Hamlet with the Old Vic Company at the Edinburgh Festival and stayed on with that company in several Shakespearean productions. Soon he had established a reputation as one of the preeminent actors of his day. In an impressive departure, he sang the role of King Arthur in the Broadway musical *Camelot* in 1960. Burton reached his peak about that time with continuing successes both on stage and on screen. But starting with the fiasco of *Cleopatra*, the film that filled the coffers of Elizabeth Taylor while it bankrupted 20th Century–Fox, Burton's liaison with Taylor seems, in retrospect, to have been tantamount to selling out. As his fame and fortune increased, his self-respect started to suffer, and soon he found that it was easier to appear in a Taylor film and be assured of a following than it was to take risks as a stage actor and try an occasional stretch. He found himself on a downward spiral from esteemed actor to adored movie star. When Burton came to New York in 1964 to play Hamlet in the John Gielgud production, large crowds ganged up at the stage door like groupies hounding a rock star. As his reputation as an actor tarnished, he was fast becoming a superstar, a new category that emerged in the 1960s, made up primarily of people who are famous for being famous. For several years Burton and Taylor commanded astronomical salaries as they made one flop after the other. The one exception was *Who's*

Afraid of Virginia Woolf?, for which, in a bitter, ironic twist, Taylor, with limited talent, won an Academy Award and Burton didn't (wags say Taylor was merely playing herself), a victory that must have galled Burton, to say the least. In fact, Burton never did win an Academy Award, while Taylor won two. It was to Burton's credit that he managed to redeem himself with such films as *Becket* and *The Spy Who Came in from the Cold*. In the 1970s, the Burtons divorced, reconciled, separated, remarried, and divorced again. Burton spent his last years drinking heavily and working in pictures simply for the money. There was horror in his eyes and desperation in his face. His most tragic role was playing himself, and he played it with a vengeance right up to the bitter end.

Filmography: The Last Days of Dolwyn/Dolwyn, Now Barabbas Was a Robber (1949); Waterfront, The Woman with No Name/Her Panelled Door (1950); Green Grow the Rushes (1951); My Cousin Rachel (1952); The Desert Rats, The Robe (1953); Prince of Players [as Edwin Booth], The Rains of Ranchipur (1955); Alexander the Great [title role] (1956); Sea Wife, Amère Victoire/Bitter Victory (1957); Look Back in Anger (1959); The Bramble Bush, Ice Palace (1960); The Longest Day (1962); Cleopatra [as Marc Antony], The V.I.P.s (1963); Becket [as Thomas à Becket], The Night of the Iguana, Hamlet [filmed Broadway play] (1964); What's New Pussycat? [cameo], The Sandpiper, The Spy Who Came in from the Cold (1965); Who's Afraid of Virginia Woolf? (1966); The Taming of the Shrew [as Petruchio], Doctor Faustus [as Faust; also co-dir. with Nevill Coghill, co-prod.], The Comedians (1967); Boom!, Candy (1968); Where Eagles Dare, Staircase, Anne of the Thousand Days [as King Henry VIII] (1969); Raid on Rommel, Villain (1971); Hammersmith Is Out, Sutjeska [as Marshal Tito], Bluebeard [title role], The Assassination of Trotsky [as Trotsky] (1972); Divorce His Divorce Hers [three-hr., two-pt. TV drama], Rapresaglia/Massacre in Rome (1973); Il Viaggio/ The Voyage, The Klansmen (1974); Jackpot (1975); Exorcist II: The Heretic, Equus (1977); The Medusa Touch, The Wild Geese, California Suite [cameo] (1978); Sergeant Steiner/Breakthrough (1979); Circle of Two (1980); Absolution [release delayed from 1978] (1981); Wagner [title role; orig. for TV] (1983); 1984 (1984).

Honors: Academy Award Nomination: Best Supporting Actor (*My Cousin Rachel*, 1952); Golden Globe Award: Most Promising Newcomer (1952); Academy Award Nomination: Best Actor (*The Robe*, 1953); Academy Award Nomination: Best Actor (*Becket*, 1964); Academy Award Nomination: Best Actor (*The Spy Who Came in from the Cold*, 1965); British Academy Award (*Who's Afraid of Virginia Woolf?*, *The Spy Who Came in from the Cold*, 1966); Academy Award Nomination: Best Actor (*Who's Afraid of Virginia Woolf?*, 1966); Academy Award Nomination: Best Actor (*Anne of the Thousand Days*, 1969); Golden Globe Award, Academy Award Nomination: Best Actor (*Equus*, 1977).

Selected Bibliography
Alpert, Hollis. *Burton*. New York: G. P. Putnam's Sons, 1986.
Junor, Penny. *Burton: The Man behind the Myth*. New York: St. Martin's, 1985.
Steverson, Tyrone. *Richard Burton: A Bio-Bibliography*. Westport, CT: Greenwood Press, 1992.

C

CABIN IN THE SKY (1943), musical/dance. Directed by Vincente Minnelli; with Eddie "Rochester" Anderson, Lena Horne, Ethel Waters, Louis Armstrong, Rex Ingram, Duke Ellington and His Orchestra, The Hall Johnson Choir; screenplay by Joseph Schrank.

A superb black cast highlights this musical fable in which the forces of good and evil vie for the soul of Little Joe (Anderson). This was Vincente Minnelli's first film, and it was here that he introduced his fresh and exciting approach to musical drama. It is certainly one of the best musicals ever made in this country, and it gets better with time because audiences can now enjoy legendary artists who were just then getting their start, including Ethel Waters, Lena Horne, Eddie "Rochester" Anderson, and Duke Ellington. Critics accuse the film of perpetuating stereotypes, but that is hardly surprising given the period in which it was made. Although the picture was shot in sepia, it did not diminish the luster of Minnelli's visual flair. And in spite of some romantic tensions generated by Minnelli's interest in Horne and some jealousy on the part of Waters, the performances are thoroughly professional. In fact, instead of subduing Waters, Minnelli allows her to steal the show, delivering her songs with easy assurance, particularly "Taking a Chance on Love" and the Oscar-nominated "Happiness Is Just a Thing Called Joe," two timeless ballads. The music and lyrics in this film deserve special attention because they are the product of some of the finest talent of this century, including composer Vernon Duke ("April in Paris"), composer Harold Arlen ("Over the Rainbow"), and E. Y. Harburg, who wrote the lyrics for both those great songs.

Selected Bibliography

Miller, Frank. *Movies We Love: 100 Collectible Classics*. Atlanta, GA: Turner Publishing, 1996.

Minnelli, Vincente. *I Remember It Well*. Garden City, NJ: Doubleday, 1974.
Palmer, Leslie. *Lena Horne*. Danbury, CT: Grolier, 1990.

CAGNEY, JAMES. Actor. Born on July 17, 1899, in New York City; died on March 30,1986. Educated at Columbia University. Cagney grew up on the Lower East Side of New York where he worked as a waiter, a pool room racker, and even a female impersonator to help support his family. He married young, and together he and his wife toured in vaudeville, eventually landing parts in Broadway shows in the late 1920s. It was while appearing with Joan Blondell in *Penny Arcade* in 1930 that Cagney was invited to Hollywood in 1930 (along with Blondell) to appear in the film version, *Sinner's Holiday*. This was followed by *The Public Enemy*, the role that made him famous overnight and established his reputation for ruthlessness. However, beneath that callous, cocky exterior, audiences perceived the smart, sensitive side that was to surface in many memorable performances. Cagney was not at all the prototype of the matinee idol that dominated the screen in the 1930s. Instead, he was short, with a square jaw and a feistiness that set the stage for a long succession of short, tough, but tender antiheroes from Alan Ladd to James Dean to Sean Penn. What set Cagney apart from his imitators as well as his rivals was an astonishing versatility that allowed him to play parts as diverse as the psychopathic killer in *White Heat*, the "gimp" in *Love Me or Leave Me*, Lon Chaney in *Man of a Thousand Faces*, Bottom in *A Midsummer Night's Dream*, and the singer/dancer/composer George M. Cohan in *Yankee Doodle Dandy*—and play them all convincingly. In 1942 he formed Cagney Productions with his brother William, a former actor who produced several of Cagney's movies. Cagney directed one film, *Short Cut to Hell* (1957), a so-so remake of *This Gun for Hire*. After twenty years of retirement, Cagney was lured back to Hollywood to play the small but crucial role of a police inspector in the film *Ragtime*. Cagney's comeback was so enthusiastically welcomed that he was encouraged to ignore some serious medical problems and play the lead role as a crotchety ex-boxer in a made-for-TV movie, *Terrible Joe Moran*, in 1984. Two years later, on Easter Sunday, he died of cardiac arrest on his farm. "America lost one of her finest artists," eulogized Cagney's old friend President Ronald Reagan.

Filmography: Sinner's Holiday, Doorway to Hell (1930); Other Men's Women, The Millionaire, The Public Enemy, Smart Money, Blonde Crazy (1931); Taxi, The Crowd Roars, Winner Take All (1932); Hard to Handle, Picture Snatcher, The Mayor of Hell, Footlight Parade, Lady Killer (1933); Jimmy the Gent, He Was Her Man, Here Comes the Navy, The St. Louis Kid (1934); Devil Dogs of the Air, G-Men, The Irish in Us, Frisco Kid, A Great Guy (1936); Something to Sing About (1937); Boy Meets Girl, Angels with Dirty Faces (1938); The Oklahoma Kid, Each Dawn I Die, The Roaring Twenties (1939); The Fighting 69th, Torrid Zone, City for Conquest (1940); The Strawberry Blonde, The Bride Came C.O.D. (1941); Captains of the Clouds, Yankee Doodle Dandy [as George M. Cohan] (1942); Johnny Come Lately (1943); Blood on the Sun (1945); 13 Rue Madeleine (1947); The Time of Your Life (1948); White Heat (1949);

Starlift [cameo], Come Fill the Cup (1951); What Price Glory (1952); A Lion Is in the Streets (1953); Run for Cover, Love Me or Leave Me, The Seven Little Foys [as George M. Cohan], Mister Roberts (1955); Tribute to a Bad Man, These Wilder Years (1956); Short Cut to Hell [dir. only; appears briefly in prologue], Man of a Thousand Faces [as Lon Chaney] (1957); Never Steal Anything Small, Shake Hands with the Devil (1959); The Gallant Hours [as Admiral "Bull" Halsey] (1960); One Two Three (1961); Ragtime (1981); Terrible Joe Moran [for TV] (1984).

Honors: New York Film Critics Circle Award, Academy Award Nomination: Best Actor (*Angels with Dirty Faces*, 1938); Academy Award, New York Film Critics Circle Award: Best Actor (*Yankee Doodle Dandy*, 1942); Academy Award Nomination: Best Actor (*Love Me or Leave Me*, 1955); American Film Institute Life Achievement Award (1974).

Selected Bibliography

Cagney, James. *Cagney by Cagney*. Garden City, NY: Doubleday, 1976.
Dickens, Homer. *The Complete Films of James Cagney*. Secaucus, NJ: Carol, 1989.
McCabe, John. *Cagney*. New York: Knopf, 1997.
Warren, Doug, with James Cagney. *James Cagney: The Authorized Biography*. New York: St. Martin's, 1983.

CAINE MUTINY, THE (1954), drama. Directed by Edward Dmytryk; with Humphrey Bogart, José Ferrer, Van Johnson, Robert Francis, May Wynn, Fred MacMurray, E. G. Marshall, Lee Marvin, Tom Tully, and Claude Akins; screenplay by Stanely Roberts and Michael Blankfort

"As big as the Ocean!" screamed the blurb for this faithful and absorbing screen adaptation of the Herman Wouk novel. *The Caine Mutiny* is the story of a war-weary destroyer-minesweeper and its crew under the despotic authority of Captain Queeg, a psychotic perfectionist who does everything "by the book" in a desperate attempt to conceal a debilitating inferiority complex. Fred MacMurray is Lt. Keefer (playing against type again as he did in *Double Indemnity* and later in *The Apartment*), the officer who spots the crack in Queeg's armor and becomes the instigator of the mutiny. An accumulation of trival incidents builds until finally, in the midst of a violent storm when the ship is in extreme danger, Maryk (Van Johnson) relieves Queeg of his command, citing Navy Article 184, which permits the executive officer to take command under certain emergency conditions. Critical reaction to the movie remains mixed. While some critics think Bogart looks ill and that his poor health limits his performance, others consider it the best of his career. It is an astonishing stretch for him as an actor, and he rises to the occasion, arousing pity and fear as he descends into madness before our very eyes. For most critics the scenes with Bogart disintegrating on the witness stand have become part of American folklore. Bogart was later asked how he managed to capture so completely the paranoid personality of Queeg. "Simple," he quipped, "everybody knows I'm nuts, anyway." While some critics feel that Dmytryk was trying to redeem himself, after having named names during the House Un-American Activities Committee witch-hunt trials, by being as balanced and as fair as possible, others feel he went so far to assure that fair play be seen to be done regarding the characters' various motivations that he ended up with a film that gets bogged down in stodgy liberalism.

Awards: Academy Award Nominations: Best Picture, Actor (Bogart), Supporting Actor (Tom Tully), Screenplay, Editing, Scoring of a Dramatic Picture, Sound.

Selected Bibliography

McCarty, Clifford. *The Complete Films of Humphrey Bogart*. Secaucus, NJ: Citadel Press, 1965.
Spoto, Donald. *Stanley Kramer: Film Maker*. New York: Putnam, 1978.

CALAMITY JANE (1953), musical/western. Directed by David Butler; with Doris Day, Howard Keel, Allyn McLerie, Philip Carey, Dick Wesson, and Paul Harvey; screenplay by James O'Hanlon.

One of the pleasures of seeing *Calamity Jane* a generation or more after its release is its totally innocent disregard for political correctness. Although feminists have rallied around the Doris Day of the later comedies, they are shocked by a picture like *Calamity Jane* that argues for traditional concepts of femininity. Day is told in no uncertain terms to stop dressing and acting like a man—in short, to clean up her act—and the minute she gets gussied up in a party dress and a bouncy hairdo, she has all the local swains lining up to sign her dance card. What's more, this is the way she wins Keel. But it gets worse. When Day first takes Allyn McLerie in as a roommate, Day's cabin looks like the Joad shack in *The Grapes of Wrath*. But McLerie, the picture of femininity, teaches Day something about "a woman's touch" and unlocks in Day some latent feminine instinct that soon has Day helping McLerie turn the cabin into "the enchanted cottage." The scene in which Dick Wesson in drag tries to palm himself off as a hot chorus girl to a passel of scruffy prospectors tramples on a number of modern sensibilities, and one can only guess at how today's radicals would receive Howard Keel dressed as a squaw and carrying a papoose. When it first came out, the picture was criticized for being, of all things, unrealistic, as if anyone cares. Given a movie that announces its intentions from the start with Doris Day standing on top of a speeding stage coach, cracking a whip, and singing her heart out, who can be surprised by the high-spirited hokum that follows? On the contrary, there are scenes to relish, including Day's first encounter with McLerie in Chicago, Day's brilliant song-and-dance rendition of "Just Blew in from the Windy City," and her sudden transformation into a charming riding-school ingenue as she steps out into a fresh spring morning and sings "Secret Love." The musical score is superior to most musical scores, either on stage or on film, in sheer number, to begin with—eleven—and each a gem. Not only is the music memorable, but the lyrics are nothing short of inspired. Just listen to the Day-Keel duet "I Can Do Without You" and compare it with Irving Berlin's "Anything You Can Do" from *Annie Get Your Gun*. It's certainly just as good—and maybe even a bit better. Many critics have praised the movie and particularly the score, finding its sassiness and its musical score superior even to *Annie Get Your Gun*. It was said that this film was compensation to Day for not getting the lead in *Annie Get Your Gun*, a role she richly deserved. Perhaps that explains why the movie was (and still is) politely ignored. Nobody wants to admit that a casting mistake had been made.

Awards: Academy Award: Best Song (''Secret Love''); Academy Award Nomination: Best Musical Direction (Ray Heindorf).

Selected Bibliography

Altman, Rick. *The American Film Musical*. Bloomington: Indiana University Press, 1987.
Young, Christopher. *The Films of Doris Day*. Secaucus, NJ: Citadel, 1977.

CAPRA, FRANK. Director. Born on May 18, 1897, in Bisaquino, Sicily; died on September 3, 1991. Educated at the California Institute of Technology (chemical engineering). Unable to find work in his profession, Capra roamed around the West, selling books and mining stocks door to door and playing poker for a living. In 1922, flat broke, he talked his way into directing a one-reel film adaptation of a Rudyard Kipling ballad, *Fultah Fisher's Boarding House*, for a small San Francisco–based company for $75. In order to learn more about film-making, Capra worked as an apprentice at a film lab in exchange for room and board. Later he worked for comedy director Bob Eddy and as gag writer for Hal Roach and Mack Sennett comedies. Out of work by 1927, he went to New York and managed to land a job directing *For the Love of Mike*, a film featuring Claudette Colbert in her screen debut. The film flopped and Capra returned to Hollywood where he ground out two-reel comedies for Sennett. The turning point in his career came when he was offered a contract to direct for Harry Cohn and Columbia Pictures. The result was a decade of successes that turned Columbia into a major studio and Capra into a leading Hollywood director. In his string of hits, Capra presented the recurrent theme of an idealistic young man up against impossible odds but able at last to thwart the evil schemes of opportunistic cynics. Films like *It Happened One Night*, *Mr. Deeds Goes to Town*, *You Can't Take It with You*, and *Mr. Smith Goes to Washington* all exhibited a fundamental faith in the essential goodness of the common man and the inevitable triumph of honesty and justice over selfishness and deceit. Critics called it ''Capra-corn,'' but audiences ate it up—and still do as evidenced by the cult status of *It's a Wonderful Life*. Capra was ably supported by leads like James Stewart, Gary Cooper, and Barbara Stanwyck, who projected a wholesome blend of ordinary earnestness and individuality, Edward Arnold and Thomas Mitchell, who provided the corruption or sleaziness needed to ignite the drama, along with the formidable talent of screenwriter Robert Riskin (*American Madness*, *It Happened One Night*, *Mr. Deeds Goes to Town*), who helped to define the Capra film and the screwball comedy form. During World War II, Capra directed a much-heralded army documentary series, *Why We Fight*. After the war, he formed his own production company, Liberty Films, whose first film was *It's a Wonderful Life*. At the time of its release, it was not a box office success. The formula that suited a depression audience looking for simple answers did not appeal to restless postwar audiences with a more realistic attitude. Capra was slow to adjust to the changing times, and his reputation faded during the 1940s and 1950s. Feelings run high about Frank Capra. While some dismiss him as idealistic and simplistic, others detect a threat of exploitation running through his depression-era films. After all, Capra was a man of his times, and maybe what shocks us is to realize that he knew it and deliberately exploited it. Like Borzage, he outlived his times, but at his height he did what the public wanted, and he did it with consummate skill. When all is said and done, films like *It Happened One Night*, *Lost Horizon*, and *Arsenic and Old Lace* are simply too inspired to be dismissed easily.

Filmography: Fultah Fisher's Boarding House [short] (1922); Tramp Tramp Tramp [co-dir., co-sc.], The Strong Man (1926); Long Pants, His First Flame [co-sc. only], For the Love of Mike (1927); That Certain Thing, So This Is Love, The Matinee Idol, The Way of the Strong, Say It with Sables [also co-story], Submarine, The Power of the Press (1928); The Younger Generation, The Donovan Affair, Flight [also dial.] (1929); Ladies of Leisure, Rain or Shine (1930); Dirigible, The Miracle Woman, Platinum Blonde (1931); Forbidden [also story], American Madness (1932); The Bitter Tea of General Yen, Lady for a Day (1933); It Happened One Night, Broadway Bill (1934); Mr. Deeds Goes to Town [also prod.] (1936); Lost Horizon [also prod.] (1937); You Can't Take It with You [also prod.] (1938); Mr. Smith Goes to Washington [also prod.] (1939); Meet John Doe [also prod.] (1941); Prelude to War [doc.], The Nazis Strike [doc.; co-dir. with Anatole Litvak] (1942); Divide and Conquer [doc.; co-dir. with Litvak], Battle of Britain [doc.; co-dir.], Battle of Russia [doc.; prod. only], Battle of China [doc.; co-dir. with Litvak]) (1943); The Negro Soldier [doc.], War Comes to America [doc.; prod. only], Tunisian Victory [doc.; co-dir. with Roy Boulting], Arsenic and Old Lace (1944); Know Your Enemy: Japan [doc.; co-dir. with Joris Ivens], Two Down and One to Go [doc.] (1945); It's a Wonderful Life [also prod., co-sc.] (1946); State of the Union [also co-prod.] (1948); Riding High [also prod.] (1950); Here Comes the Groom [also prod.] (1951); A Hole in the Head [also prod.] (1959); Pocketful of Miracles [also prod.] (1961).

Honors: Academy Award Nomination: Best Director (*Lady for a Day*, 1932–1933); Academy Award: Best Director (*It Happened One Night*, 1934); Academy Award: Best Director (*Mr. Deeds Goes to Town*, 1936); Academy Award: Best Director (*You Can't Take It with You*, 1938); Academy Award Nomination: Best Director (*Mr. Smith Goes to Washington*, 1939); New York Film Critics Circle: Special Award (*Why We Fight* series, 1943); Golden Globe Award, Academy Award Nomination: Best Director (*It's a Wonderful Life*, 1946); Directors Guild of America: D. W. Griffith Award (1958); American Film Institute Life Achievement Award (1982).

Selected Bibliography

McBride, Joseph. *Frank Capra: The Catastrophe of Success*. New York: Simon & Schuster, 1992.

Scherle, Victor, and William Turner Levy, eds. *The Complete Films of Frank Capra*. New York: Carol Publishing Group, 1992.

Wolfe, Charles. *Frank Capra: A Guide to References and Resources*. Boston: G. K. Hall, 1987.

CAPTAINS COURAGEOUS (1937), drama. Directed by Victor Fleming; with Spencer Tracy, Freddie Bartholomew, Melvyn Douglas, Lionel Barrymore, Mickey Rooney, John Carradine, Walter Kingsford, Charley Grapewin, and Christian Rub; screenplay by John Lee Mahin, Marc Connelly, and Dale Van Every.

Rudyard Kipling wrote this story during a visit to America a few years before the film was made, and it's a film that does credit to its original. In the story, a Portuguese fisherman rescues a spoiled orphan who's fallen off a cruise ship and, within three months, turns the boy's obnoxious character inside out. As improbable as the promise sounds, this is another good example of the magic Hollywood works when it puts bigger-than-life actors into the mix. Spencer Tracy is so good that he even has you believing he really is a curly headed, salty Portuguese sailor, while Lionel Barrymore only has to grin and snort to become that part he plays so well, the lovable old curmudgeon. Bartholomew, whose name appears above Tracy's and Barrymore's in screen credits, is wonderfully convincing as he makes the transition from a brat to a lovable child, for he has that special, natural (and transient) talent found in only a few child actors. Critics look upon it as a good example of the prestige picture of the 1930s, a well-made sea movie, robust and energetic, but showing, unfortunately, the unmistakable signs of having been made on a sound stage. It has been said that Tracy hated his role during the making of the film. He didn't want to sing, he didn't want to have his hair curled, and he despised his accent. In short, he was convinced that he was doing the worst job of his life. As it turned out, he won the Oscar that year for Best Actor, proof that those with real talent are often unaware of the extent of their natural gift.

Awards: Academy Award: Best Actor (Tracy); Academy Award Nominations: Best Picture, Screenplay, Editing.

Selected Bibliography

Deschner, Donald. *The Complete Films of Spencer Tracy*. Secaucus, NJ: Citadel, 1968.
Miller, Frank. *Movies We Love: 100 Collectible Classics*. Atlanta, GA: Turner Publishing, 1996.

CASABLANCA (1942), drama. Directed by Michael Curtiz; with Humphrey Bogart, Ingrid Bergman, Paul Henreid, Claude Rains, Conrad Veidt, Peter Lorre, Sydney Greenstreet, Dooley Wison, Marcel Dalio, S. Z. Sakall, and Joy Page; screenplay by Julius and Philip Epstein and Howard Koch.

A classic film, a cult film, a legend, a myth, an icon, with the perfect blend of romance, cynicism, intrigue, humor, and sentiment that somehow just happened in the making and that no amount of analysis can ever quite explain. This is a movie that has transcended the ordinary categories. It has outlived the Bogart cult, survived colorization, and won audiences who were born long after it was made. Even when first released, the film produced immediate nostalgia for the world that existed (or seemed to have) between the two world wars, a civilized, urbane time, the values of which could not coexist with the rise of fascism. For millions it has become *the* Ultimate Movie. Sardonic nighclub owner Bogart finds old flame Bergman and her husband, an underground leader on the run, in Casablanca during World War II. Bogart's club, Rick's, is the symbolic setting where enemies glare over drinks and patriots fight with warring anthems. This is one of those movies that are unimaginable with any other cast. Thus, when fans discuss it, they shake their heads over the improbable contenders for the leads (Ronald Reagan, Ann Sheridan, and Dennis Morgan, among others). Bogart seems equally at ease as a world-weary nightclub operator and as a lover, and Bergman, torn between love and duty, is totally sympathetic and believable. Henreid is well cast and does an excellent job, too. Claude Rains is in top form as the dapper chief of police, Conrad Veidt is wonderfully menacing as Major Strasser, and Sydney Greenstreet and Peter Lorre add their own inimitable touches. Even the minor roles are faultlessly performed, lending the picture a unity and honesty and uncanny sense of reality seldom seen on the screen. The film is a favorite of critics and film buffs alike, permanently ensconced among the all-time ten best. Much of this adulation is due to the fact that the film has an intense wartime nostalgia that hasn't dated as much as most wartime films, plus the fact that the dialogue, much of it apparently made up as the movie was being made, has become history. Thus, it has also been branded an accidental classic, one of those rare instances in which everything goes wrong until the whole thing coalesces at the last moment. Cautious critics, while still placing it among their favorites, like to point out that it is a picture that has to be taken on its own terms—that is, not too seriously. Although it has been endlessly scrutinized, it does not really bear close scrutiny. A close look reveals that the sum of its parts is greater than the whole. Roger Ebert (in *Roger Ebert's Book of Film*) sums up the case for *Casablanca* this way: "There are greater movies. More profound movies. Movies of greater artistic vision or artistic originality or political significance. There are other titles we would put above it on our lists of the best films of all time. But when it comes right down to the movies we treasure the most, when we are—let us imagine—confiding the secrets of our heart to someone we think we may be able to trust, the conversation sooner or later comes around to the same seven words: 'I really love *Casablanca*.' 'I do too.' "

Awards: Academy Awards: Best Picture, Adapted Screenplay; Academy Award Nominations: Actor (Bogart), Supporting Actor (Rains), Cinematography, Score, Editing.

Selected Bibliography

Kinnard, Roy, and R. J. Vitone. *The American Films of Michael Curtiz*. Metuchen, NJ: Scarecrow Press, 1986.

Koch, Howard. *"Casablanca": Script and Legend*. Woodstock, NY: Overlook Press, 1973.

Leamer, Laurence. *As Time Goes By: The Life of Ingrid Bergman*. New York: Harper & Row, 1986.

Pettigrew, Terence. *Bogart: A Definitive Study of His Film Career*. New York: Proteus, 1981.

CAT ON A HOT TIN ROOF (1958), drama. Directed by Richard Brooks; with Elizabeth Taylor, Paul Newman, Burl Ives, Jack Carson, Judith Anderson, Madeleine Sherwood, and Larry Gates; screenplay by Richard Brooks and James Poe.

Tennessee Williams's classic study of "mendacity" comes somewhat laundered in this screen version, but it still packs a punch, particularly given its outstanding cast. The story concerns a family's reaction to the imminent death of its patriarch (Ives). His son (Newman) is the only member of the family who does not work overtime to ingratiate himself. Newman is particularly good in this difficult, sensitive role, made even more difficult by the fact that all references to his character's homosexuality were excised from the film version, leaving him to convince audiences that he is not just a wimp but a man wrestling with a fundamental identity crisis. Newman managed enough between-the-lines innuendos to get the point across, thereby giving even more depth to his performance. Elizabeth Taylor is flawless as his beautiful, puzzled wife who doesn't quite know what to make of the situation. The ongoing drama in Taylor's personal life at the time added depth to her performance. One can sense the apprehension and desperation beneath her cool, provocative exterior. And Burl Ives so becomes Big Daddy that he had trouble thereafter shaking the image. All in all it is a glossy drama in the best MGM tradition while at the same time an impressive attempt to bring the complexities of Tennessee Williams's bizarre world as honestly as possible to the screen.

Awards: Academy Award Nominations: Best Picture, Actor (Newman), Actress (Taylor), Director, Screenplay, Cinematography.

Selected Bibliography

D'Arcy, Susan. *The Films of Elizabeth Taylor*. New York: Beaufort, 1982.
Miller, Frank. *Movies We Love: 100 Collectible Classics*. Atlanta, GA: Turner Publishing, 1996.

CITIZEN KANE (1941), drama. Directed by Orson Welles; with Orson Welles, Joseph Cotten, Everett Sloane, Agnes Moorehead, Dorothy Comingore, Ray Collins, George Coulouris, Ruth Warrick, William Alland, Paul Stewart, and Erskine Sanford; screenplay by Orson Welles and Herman J. Mankiewicz.

This was Orson Welles's first film and is generally considered to be his best— as well as one of the best films of all times. Welles was twenty-five when he directed, starred in, and pretty well wrote this landmark film. It was initially a critical but not a commercial success, but as its reputation spread, it more than repaid its initial investment. Meanwhile, although it has assumed classic/cult status, the jury is still out on whether Welles was a wunderkind, enfant terrible, or just a precocious young con artist possessed of more than his share of charm, chicanery, and chutzpah. It cannot be denied that this film broke all the rules and invented some new ones, as it purported to tell the story of the rise and fall of a powerful publisher so obviously based on William Randolph Hearst that only a Welles could deny it and keep a straight face. Enemies in the Hearst camp protested vehemently, including influential columnist Louella Parsons and Hearst's mistress, Marian Davies. Attempts were made to buy Welles off and to prevent distribution of the film. About the only one on the Hearst side who seemed to be enjoying the whole show (including the movie) was the seventy-nine-year-old Hearst himself, or so the story goes. Every comment ever made about this picture is fraught with contradictions. While some praise its originality and invention, others find it brilliant but cold. "We murder to dissect," a poet once said, and in the gutting of Kane, the man turned out to lack both heart and soul. So ruthlessly is he exposed to the analyst's knife that he becomes an empty shell, lacking human emotion to a degree unimaginable in any human being other than perhaps a serial killer. Thus, the final scene in which the secret of "rosebud" is revealed comes across as almost absurdly sentimental, somewhat like contemporary attempts to blame a lifetime of sociopathic behavior on the exhumation of a repressed memory. The story is all surface, a dazzling array of tricks meant to blind us to its hollowness, but ultimately it is a heart of coldness, not darkness, that leaves us puzzled, vaguely dissatisfied, and possibly fooled into thinking that our uncertainty is a sign of its brilliance. Part of the problem lies in the conception of Kane as a man who lacked for nothing except a feeling of human sympathy and tolerance. It is, then, a story of spiritual failure, and Welles seems so intent on revealing Kane's spiritual bankruptcy that the human side of him is undeveloped. Thus, he is never a truly whole person. Roger Ebert, probably the most knowledgeable critic of the film, comments (in *Ebert's Book of Film*) that "reading the many accounts of *Citizen Kane* is a little like seeing the movie: The witnesses all have opinions, but often they disagree, and sometimes they simply throw up their hands in exasperation. And the movie stands there before them, a towering achievement that cannot be explained yet cannot be ignored." There is no doubt that the film has influenced countless filmmakers. It is the consensus among film scholars that *Kane* is the epitome of filmmaking, and they are convinced that Welles will be forever remembered as one of the greatest practitioners of cinematic art. Certainly it is a landmark film with its quick cuts, its imaginative dissolves, and above all, Gregg Toland's deep focus photography. Some think that Toland's photography is the key to the success of the film, since above all the visual motion is what a "moving picture" is all about.

Awards: Academy Award: Best Screenplay; New York Film Critics Circle Award: Best Picture; Academy Award Nominations: Best Picture, Director, Actor (Welles), B&W Cinematography, Art Direction/Set Direction (black and white), Sound, Score, Editing.

Selected Bibliography

Brady, Frank. *Citizen Welles: A Biography of Orson Welles*. New York: Scribner's, 1989.
Carringer, Robert. *The Making of Citizen Kane*. Berkeley: University of California Press, 1985.
Gottesman, Ronald. *Focus on Citizen Kane*. Englewood Cliffs, NJ: Prentice-Hall, 1971.
Kael, Pauline, with Herman J. Mankiewicz and Orson Welles. *The Citizen Kane Book: Raising Kane*. Boston: Little, Brown, 1971.

CITY LIGHTS (1931), comedy/melodrama. Directed by Charles Chaplin; with Charlie Chaplin, Virginia Cherrill, Harry Myers, Hank Mann, and Florence Lee; screenplay by Charles Chaplin.

This classic Chaplin film mixes wry humor with blatant pathos as it recounts the story of the Little Tramp's love for a blind flower girl and his roller-coaster relationship with a drunken millionaire. Critics who like this film find it eloquent, moving, and funny, while other critics object to its excessive sentimentality. Sentimental it is, but much of the sentimentality is prevented from going over the edge by massive doses of slapstick and Chaplin's sensitive acting. Ultimately, it is a film that has brilliant moments scattered within a slipshod structure. Also of interest is the occasional comic use of sound in this otherwise silent film. Chaplin's decision to release *City Lights* as a silent film is what, according to some critics, makes it his greatest work. Chaplin was the master of silent film technique, and when he did eventually venture into sound, it was at the expense of his greatest comic gifts. Although there is an abundance of great comedy throughout the story, it is the film's ending that stands alone in the annals of cinema. When the Little Tramp returns from prison where he was sent for allegedly stealing money to pay for a sight-restoring operation for the flower girl, he finds that she has regained her sight and now has her own flower shop. As he gazes through the shop window at her, a couple of boys begin to make fun of him, and the girl looks on, amused by the expression of adoration on his face. "I've made a conquest," she says to her grandmother. Then, taking pity on him, she steps outside and hands him a flower and a coin. "You?" her title card reads. The vagabond forces a smile and nods his head. "You can see now?" he asks. "Yes, I can see now." Neither of them knows what to say. He looks at her timidly, not daring to hope, yet not daring not to. As he gazes into her eyes, the camera moves in to what for him was a rarity in Chaplin films, a closeup. The scene fades.

Selected Bibliography

Gehring, Wes D. *Charlie Chaplin: A Bio-Bibliography*. Westport, CT: Greenwood Press, 1983.
Lyons, Timothy J. *Charlie Chaplin: A Guide to References and Resources*. Boston: G. K. Hall, 1979.
McDonald, Gerald D., Michael Conway, and Mark Ricci. *The Films of Charlie Chaplin*. New York: Cadillac, 1965.

CLIFT, MONTGOMERY. Actor. Born Edward Montgomery Clift on October 17, 1920, in Omaha, Nebraska; died on July 23, 1966. Clift made his debut in summer stock at age fourteen and before long was appearing on Broadway in increasingly important roles opposite such formidable luminaries as Tallulah Bankhead and Broadway's brightest couple, Alfred Lunt and Lynn Fontanne. He was among the founding members of the Actors Studio in 1947. He was eventually lured to Hollywood, where he made his screen debut in 1948 in Fred Zinnemann's *The Search*, a neglected masterpiece for which he received an Academy Award nomination. Actually, *The Search* was Clift's second picture. A year before, he had starred opposite John Wayne in *Red River*, but the release was delayed. *Red River* brought him to the attention of filmgoers who responded to this lean, handsome, intense young man whose electrifying presence seemed to, as David Thomson puts it, "compel John Wayne into thinking about his part." His success in these films gave Clift the clout to choose parts that seemed to be made for him: the flawed lover in *The Heiress*, the doomed hero in *A Place in the Sun*, the rebellious soldier in *From Here to Eternity*, the retarded victim of Nazi brutality in *Judgment at Nuremberg*. Clift received a total of four Academy Award nominations, but he never won. After a near-fatal car accident in 1957 during the filming of *Raintree County*, Clift lost both his looks and his nerve and ended his career playing parts that exploited his insecurities. During the production of *Freud* (1962), in which he played the title role, he was operated on for the removal of cataracts in both eyes. His concentration was so destroyed by this time that the film had to be shot in ten- to fifteen-second bursts to accommodate his failing memory. Trapped in a hopeless cycle of drugs, alcohol, and sex, he gave a final embarrassing performance in the Raoul film *L'Espion* (*The Defector*) and died shortly thereafter of a heart attack at the age of forty-five. David Thomson calls Clift "the sainted Mess in that trio of American actors who loomed in the 1950s—Brando, Clift, and Dean (two of them born in Omaha)." One could say of images that Dean died before he had time to tarnish his, Clift hung on just long enough to do damage to his, but Brando has survived long enough to ruin his almost entirely.

Filmography: The Search, Red River (1948); The Heiress (1949); The Big Lift (1950); A Place in the Sun (1951); I Confess, From Here to Eternity, Stazione Termini/Indiscretion of an American Wife [It.] (1953); Raintree County (1957); The Young Lions (1958); Lonelyhearts, Suddenly Last Summer (1959); Wild River (1960); The Misfits, Judgment at Nuremberg (1961); Freud [title role] (1962); L'Espion/The Defector [Fr./Ger.] (1966).

Honors: Academy Award Nomination: Best Actor (*The Search*, 1948); Academy Award Nomination: Best Actor (*A Place in the Sun*, 1951); Academy Award Nomination: Best Actor (*From Here to Eternity*, 1953); Academy Award Nomination: Best Supporting Actor (*Judgment at Nuremberg*, 1961).

Selected Bibliography

Bosworth, Patricia. *Montgomery Clift: A Biography*. New York: Harcourt Brace Jovanovich, 1978.

Hoskyns, Barney. *Montgomery Clift: Beautiful Loser*. New York: Grove Weidenfeld, 1992.
Kalfatovic, Mary C. *Montgomery Clift: A Bio-Bibliography*. Westport, CT: Greenwood Press, 1994.

COLBERT, CLAUDETTE. Actress. Born Claudette Lily Chauchoin on September 13, 1903 or 1905 (depending on the source), in Paris; died on July 30, 1996. Educated at Washington Irving High School and the Art Students League (fashion design). Colbert made her stage debut in 1923 and her film debut in 1927, but she continued in ingenue roles on Broadway until her screen career started in earnest in 1929 with the advent of sound. She always had a memorable, melodious voice that seemed as appropriate for fluffy comedy as for sultry melodrama. After proving that she had looks and talent in two Cecil B. DeMille epics, *The Sign of the Cross* and *Cleopatra*, she accepted, with trepidation, the role of the screwball heiress in Capra's *It Happened One Night* and, to her surprise, won an Academy Award for her performance. After that, she leaned toward comedies, although she did take on an occasional serious role such as the one in the tear-jerker *Imitation of Life* in 1934. It is evidence of her remarkable versatility that she played in such diverse films as *Cleopatra*, *Imitation of Life*, and *It Happened One Night* all in the same year. Colbert remained a popular Hollywood star through the mid-1950s, after which she occasionally returned to the stage. Colbert herself wondered if her willingness to do comedy didn't ultimately hurt her career image. Nothing dates like comedy, and much of what she did—critics notwithstanding—has not held up. *Without Reservations* is nerve-racking, *The Palm Beach Story* seems silly and frenzied, and even *It Happened One Night* has to be enjoyed as a period piece. So she had a point. She was a great dramatic actress, perhaps nowhere better than in *Three Came Home* in which she plays an abused inmate of a Japanese prisoner-of-war camp with incredible feeling. Her dignity, her quiet strength, her sustaining love, her righteous indignation combined to make her character one of the screen's great leading ladies.

Filmography: For the Love of Mike (1927); The Hole in the Wall, The Lady Lies (1929); L'Enigmatique M. Parkes [French-language version of Slightly Scarlet], The Big Pond [and French-language version, La Grande Mare], Young Man of Manhattan, Manslaughter (1930); Honor among Lovers, The Smiling Lieutenant, Secrets of a Secretary, His Woman (1931); The Wiser Sex, The Misleading Lady, The Man from Yesterday, The Phantom President, The Sign of the Cross (1932); Tonight Is Ours, I Cover the Waterfront, Three-Cornered Moon, Torch Singer (1933); Four Frightened People, It Happened One Night, Cleopatra, Imitation of Life (1934); The Gilded Lily, Private Worlds, She Married Her Boss, The Bride Comes Home (1935); Under Two Flags (1936); Maid of Salem, I Met Him in Paris, Tovarich (1937); Bluebeard's Eighth Wife (1938); Zaza, Midnight, It's a Wonderful World, Drums along the Mohawk (1939); Boom Town, Arise My Love (1940); Skylark (1941); Remember the Day, The Palm Beach Story (1942); So Proudly We Hail, No Time for Love (1943); Since You Went Away (1944); Practically Yours, Guest Wife (1945); Tomorrow Is Forever, Without Reservations, The Secret

Heart (1946); The Egg and I (1947); Sleep My Love (1948); Family Honeymoon, Bride for Sale (1949); Three Came Home, The Secret Fury (1950); Thunder on the Hill, Let's Make It Legal (1951); The Planter's Wife/Outpost in Malaya (1952); Daughters of Destiny (1953); Royal Affairs in Versailles (1954); Texas Lady (1955); Parrish (1961).

Honors: Academy Award: Best Actress (*It Happened One Night*, 1934); Academy Award Nomination: Best Actress (*Private Worlds*, 1935); Academy Award Nomination: Best Actress (*Since You Went Away*, 1944); Film Society of Lincoln Center Tribute (1984).

Selected Bibliography

Everson, William K. *Claudette Colbert*. New York: Pyramid Publications, 1976.
Gehring, Wes D. *Screwball Comedy: Defining a Film Genre*. Muncie, IN: Ball State University Press, 1983.
Quirk, Lawrence J. *Claudette Colbert: An Illustrated Biography*. New York: Crown, 1985.

COLMAN, RONALD. Actor. Born on February 9, 1891, in Richmond, England; died on May 19, 1958. Starting at sixteen, Colman worked as an office boy for the British Steamship Company for five years, participating meanwhile in amateur dramatics. He was wounded in France during World War I and sent home, where he turned to the stage in 1916. He played bit parts in a few short British films until he began appearing in features in 1918. In 1920 he immigrated to the United States, where Lillian Gish spotted him in a play and chose him to be her leading man in *The White Sister*. Colman, one of the few screen actors to make the transition from silent to sound films, quickly developed into one of Hollywood's most popular romantic stars and the essence of the aristocratic hero. The best silent-film performance was in *Beau Geste*. His sound picture achievements include *Arrowsmith*, *A Tale of Two Cities*, *Lost Horizon*, and *If I Were King*. He was nominated for Oscars for both *Bulldog Drummond* and *Condemned* in 1929 and *Random Harvest* in 1942. Finally, toward the end of his career, he received an Academy Award for his performance in *A Double Life* in the challenging role of an actor so obsessed with the part he is playing on stage (in this case, Othello) that he finds it increasingly difficult to separate his stage persona from his own personality. (Playing dual parts was not new to Colman, who is remembered for similar roles in *The Prisoner of Zenda* and *A Tale of Two Cities*.) Colman campaigned hard for the award, and critics generally agree that it was probably bestowed primarily for sentimental reasons. His voice was so distinctive that mimics loved to impersonate him. Perhaps that is the reason even those who do not remember him find his final speech from *A Tale of Two Cities* curiously familiar (" 'Tis a far, far better thing that I do . . .''). After his retirement, Colman and his wife appeared on radio in a successful series about a professor and his wife called *The Halls of Ivy*.

Filmography: The Toilers, A Daughter of Eve, Sheba, Snow in the Desert (1919); A Son of David, Anna the Adventuress, The Black Spider (1920); Handcuffs or Kisses (1921); The White Sister (1923); The Eternal City, $20 a Week, Tarnish, Romola (1924); Her Night of Romance, A Thief in Paradise, His Supreme Moment, The Sporting Venus,

Her Sister from Paris, The Dark Angel, Stella Dallas, Lady Windemere's Fan (1925); Kiki, Beau Geste [title role], The Winning of Barbara Worth (1926); The Night of Love, The Magic Flame (1927); Two Lovers (1928); The Rescue, Bulldog Drummond [title role], Comdemned (1929); Raffles (1930); The Devil to Pay, The Unholy Garden, Arrowsmith [title role] (1931); Cynara (1932); The Masquerader (1933); Bulldog Drummond Strikes Back [again as Drummond] (1934); Clive of India [as Baron Robert Clive], The Man Who Broke the Bank at Monte Carlo, A Tale of Two Cities [as Sydney Carton] (1935); Under Two Flags (1936); Lost Horizon, The Prisoner of Zenda [dual role] (1937); If I Were King [as François Villon] (1938); The Light That Failed, Lucky Partners (1940); My Life with Caroline (1941); The Talk of the Town, Random Harvest (1942); Kismet (1944); The Late George Apley [title role], A Double Life (1947); Champagne for Caesar (1950); Around the World in 80 Days [cameo] (1956); The Story of Mankind [as the Spirit of Man] (1957).

Honors: Academy Award Nomination: Best Actor (*Bulldog Drummond* and *Condemned*, 1929–1930); Academy Award Nomination: Best Actor (*Random Harvest*, 1942); Academy Award, Golden Globe Award: Best Actor (*A Double Life*, 1947).

Selected Bibliography

Quirk, Lawrence J. *The Films of Ronald Colman*. Secaucus, NJ: Citadel, 1977.
Smith, R. Dixon. *Ronald Colman, Gentleman of the Cinema: A Biography and Filmography*. Jefferson, NC: McFarland, 1991.

COOPER, GARY. Actor. Born Frank James Cooper on May 7, 1901, in Helena, Montana; died on May 13, 1961. Educated at Wesleyan and Grinnell Colleges (agriculture). Upon graduation, Cooper worked for a while as a guide at Yellowstone National Park, meanwhile submitting political cartoons to his hometown newspaper, the Helena *Independent*. In 1924 Cooper set out for California, where he hoped to become a cartoonist for a Los Angeles newspaper, but he wound up as a salesman instead. In 1925, he was introduced by friends to Hollywood casting directors and began playing cowboy extras in westerns. His big break came in 1926 when he was cast as a last-minute replacement for the second lead in Goldwyn's *The Winning of Barbara Worth*, starring Ronald Colman and Vilma Banky. The film was a huge success, and it set Cooper on the path that led to his becoming one of Hollywood's all-time great stars. There was a quality about Cooper that seemed to be the antithesis of what Hollywood stars were supposed to be like. He had neither the polished mannerisms of a Ronald Colman nor the studied uneasiness of a James Stewart. In fact, he really did seem to be, as someone once said, "caught in the headlights," almost embarrassed to be acting so naturally—or what seemed naturally. Cooper was tall and handsome, with a shy smile and a hesitant delivery that made him attractive to both men and women. Viewers often responded sympathetically to this charmer who seemed always on the verge of forgetting his lines. To his many fans the world over, he came to personify the strong, silent American, a man of action and few words. At first he was taken lightly by the critics, but by the mid-1930s he was generally accepted as a capable performer, although the doubt lingered about whether he was really an actor or just playing himself. What surprised everyone was the way his slightly awkward mannerisms and delayed reactions proved to be perfect assets for screen comedy, as demonstrated so well in Howard Hawks's *Ball of Fire* in which he plays a stuffy professor opposite the earthy Barbara Stanwyck. He was nominated for an Academy Award for both *Mr. Deeds Goes to Town* and *The Pride of the Yankees*, and he won Academy Awards for both *Sergeant York* and *High Noon*. James Stewart accepted the *High Noon* award in Cooper's behalf with tears in his eyes, for he had just learned that Cooper was suffering from incurable cancer. Baffled by his genius, critics have tried to cut him down to size by using his style against him. They fail to see that the laconic hero of *For Whom the Bell Tolls* is the same loner as the sheriff in *High Noon* or the rugged individualist of *The Fountainhead*. Much maligned as that film has been, it would be hard to imagine anyone else playing the part of the fiercely independent Howard Roark. ''*The Fountainhead* is a beautiful film, with Cooper as the 'creative force' revealed in an architect,'' says David Thomson. Cooper is perhaps best remembered as the ultimate American in *Meet John Doe* and *Sergeant York*. There *are*, after all, roles that no one else could really play (Clark Gable as Rhett Butler, Bette Davis as Margot Channing, Yul Brynner as the King of Siam, James Cagney as George M. Cohan, and James Stewart as George Bailey). More than any other Hollywood star, Gary Cooper has played roles that are indelibly his, roles that we cannot imagine anyone else playing.

Filmography: [excluding some thirty appearances as an extra]: The Winning of Barbara Worth (1926); It, Children of Divorce, Arizona Bound, Wings, Nevada, The Last Outlaw (1927); Beau Sabreur, The Legion of the Condemned, Doomsday, Half a Bride, Lilac Time, The First Kiss, The Shopworn Angel (1928); Wolf Song, Betrayal, The Virginian (1929); Only the Brave, Paramount on Parade, The Texan, Seven Days Leave, A Man from Wyoming, The Spoilers, Morocco (1930); Fighting Caravans, City Streets, I Take This Woman, His Woman (1931); Make Me a Star [cameo], Devil and the Deep, If I Had a Million, A Farewell to Arms (1932); Today We Live, One Sunday Afternoon, Design for Living, Alice in Wonderland [as the White Knight] (1933); Operator 13, Now and Forever (1934); The Wedding Night, The Lives of a Bengal Lancer, Peter Ibbetson [title role] (1935); Desire, Mr. Deeds Goes to Town, Hollywood Boulevard [cameo], The General Died at Dawn (1936); The Plainsman [as Wild Bill Hickok], Souls at Sea (1937); The Adventures of Marco Polo [title role], Bluebeard's Eighth Wife, The Cowboy and the Lady (1938); Beau Geste [title role], The Real Glory (1939); The Westerner, North West Mounted Police (1940); Meet John Doe, Sergeant York [title role] (1941); Ball of Fire, The Pride of the Yankees [as Lou Gehrig] (1942); For Whom the Bell Tolls (1943); The Story of Dr. Wassell [title role], Casanova Brown (1944); Along Came Jones [also prod.], Saratoga Trunk (1945); Cloak and Dagger (1946); Unconquered, Variety Girl [cameo] (1947); Good Sam (1948); The Fountainhead, It's a Great Feeling [cameo], Task Force (1949); Bright Leaf, Dallas (1950); You're in the Navy Now/USS Teakettle, Starlift [cameo], Distant Drums, It's a Big Country (1951); High Noon, Springfield Rifle (1952); Return to Paradise, Blowing Wild (1953); Garden of Evil, Vera Cruz (1954); The Court-Martial of Billy Mitchell [as Gen. Billy Mitchell] (1955); Friendly Persuasion

(1956); Love in the Afternoon (1957); Ten North Frederick, Man of the West (1958); The Hanging Tree, Alias Jesse James [cameo], They Came to Cordura, The Wreck of the Mary Deare (1959); The Naked Edge (1961).

Honors: Academy Award Nomination: Best Actor (*Mr. Deeds Goes to Town*, 1936); Academy Award, New York Film Critics Circle Award: Best Actor (*Sergeant York*, 1941; Academy Award Nomination: Best Actor (*The Pride of the Yankees*, 1942); Academy Award Nomination: Best Actor (*For Whom the Bell Tolls*, 1943); Academy Award, Golden Globe Award: Best Actor (*High Noon*, 1952); *Photoplay* Gold Medal Award: Most Popular Male Star (1952); Academy Award: Special Award (1960).

Selected Bibliography

Kaminsky, Stuart M. *Coop: The Life and Legend of Gary Cooper*. New York: St. Martin's, 1980.
Swindell, Larry. *The Last Hero: A Biography of Gary Cooper*. Garden City, NY: Doubleday, 1980.

COTTEN, JOSEPH. Actor. Born on May 15, 1905, in Petersburg, Virginia; died on February 6, 1994. Educated at Hickman School of Expression (Washington, D.C.). While he was struggling to support himself as an actor, Cotten worked as a salesman and as a part-time drama critic for the *Miami Herald*. In 1930 David Belasco hired him as understudy and assistant stage manager, and soon he was appearing on Broadway. In 1937 he joined Orson Welles's Mercury Theater, leaving in 1939 to play the lead opposite Katharine Hepburn on stage in *The Philadelphia Story*. He made his screen debut in 1938 in *Too Much Johnson*, a forty-minute farce made by Welles for insertion into an aborted stage production. In 1941 Welles brought him to Hollywood to play leading roles in Welles's first three feature films: *Citizen Kane*, *The Magnificent Ambersons*, and *Journey into Fear*. His low-key style and rich voice also made him a perfect choice for the sinister but beguiling lead in Hitchcock's *Shadow of a Doubt* and for the baffled lead in Carol Reed's *The Third Man*. During the 1940s and 1950s he played romantic leads in several films. He was especially memorable in three films he made opposite Jennifer Jones: *Love Letters*, a much underrated film; *Portrait of Jenny*, something of a cult classic; and *Duel in the Sun*, one of David Selznick's most spectacular failures. In some ways he was an ''actor's actor'' and thus never achieved superstardom. Even so, his appearances in *Citizen Kane* and *Shadow of a Doubt* ensure his place in screen history. His career declined sharply in the late 1950s, when he began appearing in a great number of inferior productions. He hosted several TV shows in the late 1950s and early 1960s including the well-remembered TV series ''Hollywood and the Stars.''

Filmography: Citizen Kane, Lydia (1941); The Magnificent Ambersons, Journey into Fear [also co-sc.] (1942); Shadow of a Doubt, Hers to Hold (1943); Gaslight, Since You Went Away (1944); I'll Be Seeing You, Love Letters (1945); Duel in the Sun (1946); The Farmer's Daughter (1947); Portrait of Jennie (1948); Under Capricorn, Beyond the Forest, The Third Man (1949); Gone to Earth/The Wild Heart [narr. only]; Two Flags West, Walk Softly Stranger (1950); September Affair, Half Angel, Peking Express, The

Man with a Cloak (1951); Othello, Untamed Frontier, The Steel Trap (1952); Niagara, A Blueprint for Murder, Egypt by Three [narr. only] (1953); Von Himmel gefallen/ Special Delivery (1955); The Bottom of the Bottle, The Killer Is Loose (1956); The Halliday Brand (1957); Touch of Evil [cameo], From the Earth to the Moon (1958); The Angel Wore Red/La Sposa Bella (1960); The Last Sunset (1961); Hush . . . , Hush, Sweet Charlotte, The Great Sioux Massacre (1965); The Oscar, The Money Trap, Gli Uomini del Passo Pesanti/The Tramplers (1966); I Crudeli/The Hell Benders, Brighty of the Grand Canyon, Jack of Diamonds, Some May Live (1967); Petulia, Un Giorno di Fuoco/ Days of Fire/Gangster '70 [It.], Comanche Blanco/White Comanche (1968); Latitude Zero, E Vene l'Ora della Vendetta/Hour of Vengeance (1969); The Grasshopper, Tora! Tora! Tora! (1970); The Abominable Dr. Phibes, La Figlia di Frankenstein/Lady Frankenstein (1971); Lo Scopone Scientifico/The Scientific Card Player, Gli Orrori del Castello di Norinberga/Baron Blood, Doomsday Voyage (1972); Sooylent Green, A Delicate Balance (1973); F for Fake (1974); Il Giustiziere sfida la Città/Syndicate Sadists, Timber Tramps (1975); Sussuri nel Buio/Twilight's Last Gleaming, Airport '77 (1977); The Wild Geese, L'Ordre et la Sécurité du Monde, Caravans (1978); L'Isola degli Uomini Pesci/ Island of the Fishmen/The Island of Mutations/Screamers, S.O.S., Concorde/The Concorde Affair, Trauma (1979); Guyana, Cult of the Damned/Guyana, Crime of the Century, The Survivor, The Hearse (1980); Delusion, Heaven's Gate (1981); The House Where Evil Dwells (1982).

Honors: Venice Film Festival International Grand Prize: Best Actor (*Portrait of Jennie*, 1949).

Selected Bibliography

Cotten, Joseph. *Vanity Will Get You Somewhere*. San Francisco: Mercury House, 1987.

COURT JESTER, THE (1956), comedy. Directed by Norman Panama and Melvin Frank; with Danny Kaye, Glynis Johns, Basil Rathbone, Angela Lansbury, Cecil Parker, Mildred Natwick, Robert Middleton, and John Carradine; screenplay by Norman Panama and Melvin Frank.

"The vessel with the pestle has the pellet with the poison, but the chalice from the palace has the brew that is true." Or is it: "The flagon with the dragon"? This is surely Danny Kaye's best film. In it he gets to do all those things he was famous for and do them with consistent style and restraint. It's a silly role that he actually manages to dignify by seeming at all times the comic but pathetic victim of circumstances wildly out of control. *The Court Jester* has all the ingredients for a delightful spoof of costumed swashbucklers with Danny as the phony jester who finds himself involved in romance, court intrigue, and a deadly joust. The delightfully complicated comic situations are superbly performed—the timing is perfect—and the comedy is both broad and sophisticated. Directors Norman Panama and Melvin Frank drag in virtually every time-honored and timeworn medieval drama cliché for Kaye and cast to replay for laughs. Added to this is a tuneful musical score of Sylvia Fine–Sammy Cahn songs, five of which were specifically designed to suit Danny Kaye's unique talent. It's *Singin' in the Rain* in a suit of armor. The cast is uniformly good, featuring such outstanding talent as Glynis Johns and Basil Rathbone. But it is

Mildred Natwick, the princess's evil-eyed and quick-tongued maid, who will remain forever in the memories of fans of this film, for it is she who first utters the devilish ''vessel with the pestle'' jingle that Kaye echoes, then garbles. Other Kaye films have dated badly, and modern audiences have trouble understanding the wild enthusiasm that greeted his celluloid antics. But *The Court Jester* shows Kaye at his best and in so doing becomes one of those films you cannot imagine anybody else starring in.

Selected Bibliography

Byron, Stuart, and Elisabeth Weis, eds. *The National Society of Film Critics on Movie Comedy*. New York: Grossman Publishers, 1977.

Freedland, Michael. *The Secret Life of Danny Kaye*. New York: St. Martin's, 1985.

Gottfried, Martin. *Nobody's Fool: The Lives of Danny Kaye*. New York: Simon & Schuster, 1994.

CRAWFORD, JOAN. Actress. Born Lucille Fay Le Sueur, on March 23, 1904, in San Antonio, Texas; died on May 10, 1977. Joan Crawford is a synonym for ''movie star,'' especially the movie star of Hollywood's golden age. Her life was a Hollywood legend—and a cliché—a story that sounds like one only Hollywood could invent and that nobody would seriously believe. She came from a broken Texas family, a lower-class working girl with unquenchable thirst for social power and the unstoppable ambition to attain it. Shrewdly aware that she could climb to the top of the heap only in the make-believe world of the Hollywood dream factory, she did everything she could to beat out the competition, including dancing the Charleston in a contest (and winning) even though her dancing talents were, to put it charitably, modest. But Crawford always had grit, and she was constantly reinventing herself: a flapper in the 1920s, a face-to-the-wind working girl in the 1930s, a tough, glamorous, independent career woman in the 1940s and 1950s, and finally the horror queen of the 1960s. Above all else, Joan Crawford, who got her name in a publicity contest, was a survivor, with a career spanning five decades—and ending with her as director of Pepsi-Cola upon the death of her husband, chief executive officer Alfred Steele. Few could match her for a combination of driving ambition, hard work, and remarkable adaptability. Along the way, she was periodically ''box office poison,'' only to surprise everybody with another—and usually bigger—comeback. Her most remarkable feat, after she was dismissed by MGM as a has-been in 1943, was to surface at Warner Bros. two years later in an Academy Award–winning role in *Mildred Pierce*. It boggles the mind, and if it were a movie plot, audiences would laugh. (Unless, maybe, it starred Crawford herself.) A bizarre epilogue to this story started with the publication two years after her death of *Mommie Dearest*, a scathing account by her adopted daughter Christina of Crawford as the coat-hanger-wielding Mother from Hell. The book distorted the memory of this larger-than-life personality and spawned a cottage industry of biographical postmortems, mostly embittered, ranging from Gary Crosby's indictment of father Bing to Maria Riva's reviling of her mother, Marlene Dietrich.

Bette Davis's daughter even had the gall to publish her tell-all tome while Davis was still alive—just to see mommie squirm. But even in Hollywood, there is poetic justice. When Faye Dunaway played the part of Crawford in the film version of *Mommie Dearest*, her career suffered and rightly so, for audiences saw through the caricature to the truth, that the only one who could possibly play Crawford convincingly was Crawford. After all, she had been doing it—and doing it to perfection—all her life. Only in Hollywood.

Filmography: Lady of the Night, Proud Flesh, Pretty Ladies, Old Clothes, The Only Thing, Sally Irene and Mary (1925); The Boob, Tramp Tramp Tramp, Paris (1926); The Taxi Dancer, Winners of the Wilderness, The Understanding Heart, The Unknown, Twelve Miles Out, Spring Fever (1927); West Point, Rose Marie, Across to Singapore, The Law of the Range, Four Walls, Our Dancing Daughters, Dream of Love (1928); The Duke Steps Out, The Hollywood Revue of 1929, Our Modern Maidens, Untamed (1929); Montana Moon, Our Blushing Brides, Paid (1930); Dance Fools Dance, Laughing Sinners, This Modern Age, Possessed (1931); Grand Hotel, Letty Lynton, Rain (1932); Today We Live, Dancing Lady (1933); Sadie McKee, Chained, Forsaking All Others (1934); No More Ladies, I Live My Life (1935); The Gorgeous Hussy, Love on the Run (1936); The Last of Mrs. Cheyney, The Bride Wore Red (1937); Mannequin, The Shining Hour (1938); Ice Follies of 1939, The Women (1939); Strange Cargo, Susan and God (1940); A Woman's Face, When Ladies Meet (1941); They All Kissed the Bride, Reunion in France (1942); Above Suspicion (1943); Hollywood Canteen (1944); Mildred Pierce (1945); Humoresque (1946); Possessed, Daisy Kenyon (1947); Flamingo Road, It's a Great Feeling [cameo] (1949); The Damned Don't Cry, Harriet Craig (1950); Goodbye My Fancy (1951); This Woman Is Dangerous, Sudden Fear (1952); Torch Song (1953); Johnny Guitar (1954); Female on the Beach, Queen Bee (1955); Autumn Leaves (1956); The Story of Esther Costello (1957); The Best of Everything (1959); What Ever Happened to Baby Jane? (1962); The Caretakers (1963); Straight-Jacket (1964); I Saw What You Did (1965); Berserk (1967); Trog (1970).

Honors: Academy Award, National Board of Review Award: Best Actress (*Mildred Pierce*, 1945); Academy Award Nomination: Best Actress (*Possessed*, 1947); Academy Award Nomination: Best Actress (*Sudden Fear*, 1952); Golden Globes: Cecil B. DeMille Award (1969).

Selected Bibliography

Guiles, Fred Lawrence. *Joan Crawford: The Last Word*. Secaucus, NJ: Carol Publishing Group, 1985.
Quirk, Lawrence J. *The Complete Films of Joan Crawford*. Secaucus, NJ: Citadel Press, 1988.
Walker, Alexander. *Joan Crawford, the Ultimate Star*. New York: Harper & Row, 1983.

CROSBY, BING. Actor. Born Harry Lillis Crosby on May 2, 1903, in Tacoma, Washington; died on October 14, 1977. Educated at Gonzaga University (Spokane). Crosby started out as a vocalist-drummer with a small combo while he was still attending college. By 1926 he was singing with the Paul Whiteman band, and in 1930 he made his film debut in *King of Jazz* as a member of the Whiteman band. He adopted the professional name of "Bing Crosby," reportedly borrowing the "Bing" from his favorite comic strip, "The Bingville Bugle." Crosby went solo in 1931, appearing in nightclubs and in eight Mack Sennett shorts. It was at this time that he also signed a recording contract. Soon he was the star of his own radio show (theme song "Where the Blue of the Night"), and his records began selling by the millions. Although he possessed more talent than his critics are willing to give him credit for, Crosby was also the classic case of the right man at the right time. He was meant for talking pictures and for radio, two media that came into being in the late 1920s. And although recordings had been around for a while, their sales skyrocketed once audiences could hear singers over the radio or see them in movie musicals. Crosby was indisputably the most popular singer of the 1930s and well into the 1940s. Now that the dust has settled on the battle of the great crooners of the twentieth century, Crosby is being reappraised most favorably. Once dismissed simply because he was from an earlier generation, he is now being listened to for what he does, not for who he was. Louis Armstrong was among the first to recognize his incredible timing, and jazz musicians have long since marveled at his phrasing. The trouble with Crosby is that he was too laid back for his own good. He downplayed his talents and made what he did seem so effortless that he almost hid his talents beneath a pipe-smoking, cardigan-clad exterior that became his trademark—one that he worked hard to perfect. Crosby turned in some powerful screen performances, from the down-to-earth priest in *Going My Way*, for which he received an Academy Award, to the embittered failure in *The Country Girl*, for which he was nominated for an Academy Award. After a decade of mostly light comedies, Crosby joined with Bob Hope and Dorothy Lamour to make a series of what came to be known as "Road" pictures that were both enormously popular and enormously profitable. Second in wealth only to Bob Hope among show people, his fortune was at one time estimated at anywhere between $200 and $400 million. He was executive producer of the film *Final Chapter—Walking Tall* (1977). He died of a heart attack at seventy-three while pursuing his favorite pastime, playing golf. After his death, an unflattering portrait of the star as a selfish and callous manipulator emerged in a critical biography entitled *Bing Crosby—The Hollow Man* (1981) by Donald Shepherd and Robert F. Slatzer. An account of verbal and physical abuse was included in a "Mommie Dearest"–type confessional memoir, *Going My Own Way* (1983), by son Gary Crosby. When Bing's youngest son by Dixie Lee, Lindsay Crosby, shot himself to death in 1989 because he ran out of money to support his family, it was revealed that the star had stipulated in his will that none of his sons could touch a trust fund he had left them before reaching age sixty-five. Oh, well, whether Santa or Scrooge, all is forgiven (or at least forgotten) when Bing sings "White Christmas."

Filmography: King of Jazz (1930); Reaching for the Moon (1931); The Big Broadcast (1932); College Humor, Too Much Harmony, Going Hollywood (1933); We're Not Dressing, She Loves Me Not, Here's My Heart (1934); Mississippi, The Big Broadcast of 1936, Two for Tonight (1935); Anything Goes, Rhythm on the Range, Pennies from

Heaven (1936); Waikiki Wedding, Double or Nothing (1937); Dr. Rhythm, Sing You
Sinners (1938); Paris Honeymoon, East Side of Heaven, The Star Maker (1939); Road
to Singapore, If I Had My Way, Rhythm on the River (1940); Road to Zanzibar, Birth
of the Blues (1941); Holiday Inn, Road to Morocco, Star Spangled Rhythm (1942); Dixie
(1943); Going My Way, Here Come the Waves (1944); Duffy's Tavern, The Bells of
St. Mary's (1945); Road to Utopia, Blue Skies (1946); Variety Girl, Welcome Stranger,
Road to Rio (1947); The Emperor Waltz (1948); A Connecticut Yankee in King Arthur's
Court, Top o' the Morning (1949); Riding High, Mr. Music (1950); Here Comes the
Groom (1951); Just for You, Road to Bali (1952); Little Boy Lost (1953); White Christ-
mas, The Country Girl (1954); Anything Goes, High Society (1956); Man on Fire (1957);
Say One for Me (1959); Let's Make Love, High time, Pepe (1960); Road to Hong Kong
(1962); Robin and the 7 Hoods (1964); Stagecoach (1966); That's Entertainment [on-
screen narrator] (1974).

Honors: Academy Award, *Photoplay* Gold Medal Award: Best Actor (*Going My Way*,
1944); *Photoplay* Gold Medal Award: Most Popular Male Star, Academy Award Nomination: Best Actor (*The Bells of St. Mary's*, 1945); *Photoplay* Gold Medal Award: Most
Popular Male Star (1946); *Photoplay* Gold Medal Award: Most Popular Male Star
(1947); *Photoplay* Gold Medal Award: Most Popular Male Star (1948); National Board
of Review Award, Academy Award Nomination: Best Actor (*The Country Girl*, 1954);
Golden Globes: Cecil B. DeMille Award (1959).

Selected Bibliography

Barnes, Ken. *The Crosby Years*. New York: St. Martin's, 1980.
Bookbinder, Robert. *The Films of Bing Crosby*. Secaucus, NJ: Citadel Press, 1977.
Osterholm, J. Roger. *Bing Crosby: A Bio-Bibliography*. Westport, CT: Greenwood Press,
     1994.

CUKOR, GEORGE. Director. Born on July 7, 1899, in New York City; died on
January 24, 1983. Cukor was attracted to the theater in his teens. At twenty he
was stage manager for a Chicago company and at twenty-one resident director
of a stock company in Rochester, New York. By the time he was twenty-seven,
he was directing such stars as Ethel Barrymore, Jeanne Eagels, and Laurette
Taylor on Broadway. In 1929 he left Broadway for Hollywood, one of many
drawn by the switch from silent to sound pictures. He started out as a dialogue
director, his first assignments being to coach the actors of Lewis Milestone's
All Quiet on the Western Front. In 1931, after having co-directed three films
for Paramount, he made his debut as solo director with *Tarnished Lady*, starring
Tallulah Bankhead. But when he was fired by producer Ernst Lubitsch, who
took director's credit for the film, Cukor followed his friend David O. Selznick
to RKO and later to MGM, where their professional association resulted in such
memorable films as *Bill of Divorcement*, *Dinner at Eight*, and *Little Women*.
Their relationship ended in 1938 when Selznick fired Cukor from the set of
Gone with the Wind only ten days after the start of production. It was said that
Clark Gable felt uncomfortable with Cukor because Cukor, known as a
"woman's director," was favoring Vivien Leigh. It may have had more to do
with the fact that Cukor was gay, and stars like Gable, for whatever reason,

were uncomfortable around him. The truth is that Cukor was much more than a ''woman's director,'' having coaxed brilliant performances out of such masculine icons as Robert Taylor, Cary Grant, James Stewart, and Spencer Tracy. Some say Cukor sulked after being fired from *Gone with the Wind*, but it is probably closer to the truth to say that he was relieved, that he had grown tired of directing dozens of screen tests, but those closer to him knew that an epic was really not his style. He did, however, leave his imprint on Vivien Leigh, for it is his Scarlett who shines through the film. He is also credited with the successes of such stars as Greta Garbo, Katharine Hepburn, Norma Shearer, and Joan Crawford. Cukor suffered a slump in the 1940s, but he bounced back later with two Tracy-Hepburn comedies, a couple of Judy Holliday vehicles, and *A Star Is Born*, thought by many to be among his finest films and one of Judy Garland's most brilliant performances. Cukor did not write his own material, but he selected his material with great care. When Cukor received an Academy Award for the direction of *My Fair Lady*, many felt it was more like a lifetime achievement award than for a picture that could have been better. He continued directing intermittently into his eighties.

Filmography: [as co-dir.]: Grumpy, The Virtuous Sin, The Royal Family of Broadway (1930). [as dir.]: Tarnished Lady, Girls about Town (1931); One Hour with You [co-dir. with Lubitsch; credited to Lubitsch], What Price Hollywood, A Bill of Divorcement, Rockabye (1932); Our Betters, Dinner at Eight, Little Women (1933); David Copperfield (1935); Sylvia Scarlett, Romeo and Juliet (1936); Camille (1937); Holiday, Zaza (1938); Gone with the Wind [replaced by Victor Fleming; uncredited], The Women (1939); The Philadelphia Story, Susan and God (1940); A Woman's Face, Two-Faced Woman (1941); Her Cardboard Lover (1942); Keeper of the Flame (1943); Resistance and Ohm's Law [doc. for Army Signal Corps], Gaslight, Winged Victory (1944); Desire Me [co-dir. with Mervyn LeRoy, neither credited], A Double Life (1947); Edward My Son, Adam's Rib (1949); Born Yesterday, A Life of Her Own (1950); The Model and the Marriage Broker, The Marrying Kind, Pat and Mike (1952); The Actress (1953); It Should Happen to You, A Star Is Born (1954); Bhowani Junction (1956); Les Girls, Wild Is the Wind (1957); Heller in Pink Tights, Song without End [completed for the deceased Charles Vidor; declined screen credit], Let's Make Love (1960); Something's Got to Give [unfinished], The Chapman Report (1962); My Fair Lady (1964); Justine [replaced Joseph Strick] (1969); Travels with My Aunt (1973); The Blue Bird (1976); The Corn Is Green [TV movie] (1979); Rich and Famous (1981).

Honors: Academy Award Nomination: Best Director (*Little Women*, 1932–1933); Academy Award Nomination: Best Director (*The Philadelphia Story*, 1940); Academy Award Nomination: Best Director (*A Double Life*, 1947); Academy Award Nomination (*Born Yesterday*, 1950); Academy Award, Golden Globe Award, Directors Guild of America Award: Best Director (*My Fair Lady*, 1964); Film Society of Lincoln Center Tribute (1978); Directors Guild of America: D. W. Griffith Award (1980).

Selected Bibliography

Levy, Emanuel. *George Cukor: Master of Elegance: Hollywood's Legendary Director and His Stars*. New York: Morrow, 1994.

McGilligan, Patrick. *George Cukor, a Double Life: A Biography of the Gentleman Director*. New York: St. Martin's, 1991.
Phillips, Gene D. *George Cukor*. Boston: Twayne Publishers, 1982.

CURTIZ, MICHAEL. Director. Born Miháli Kertész, on December 24, 1888, in Budapest; died on April 11, 1962, in Los Angeles. Educated at Markoszy University and the Royal Academy of Theater and Art, Budapest. Curtiz's own life was so much like a movie that one wonders if somewhere in his peregrinations fiction replaced reality. His father was an architect, his mother an opera singer, and it is said he made his first appearance on the stage at age eleven in an opera starring his mother. At seventeen he ran away from home to join a traveling circus and the following year made his professional stage debut in Budapest. He entered Hungarian films in 1912 as an actor and within a few months began directing. Shortly thereafter, he spent some time in Copenhagen learning film technique at the Nordisk studios and assisting August Blom on the epic *Atlantis* (1913). During World War I, he served briefly with a Hungarian army film crew. In 1917 Curtiz was appointed production director at Budapest's largest studio, Phönix Films. When the Hungarian film industry was nationalized in 1917, Curtiz sought political asylum in Austria and Germany, where he began to acquire an international reputation as a director. Several of his lavish epics made a strong impression on the Hollywood studio heads. In 1926 Harry Warner brought Curtiz to Hollywood where for the next twenty-five years he directed well over 100 films for Warner Bros. Many critics dismissed him as merely a skilled technician who served his studio well by subordinating his personality to the demands of the system. The truth is that, as with others caught up in the studio system (especially those with unbreakable contracts), he knew the only way to get good pictures was by doing whatever pictures came his way. Therefore, he consented to direct many routine pictures in order to get such gems as *Casablanca*, *Yankee Doodle Dandy*, *Mildred Pierce*, and all those Errol Flynn swashbucklers. Curtiz worked in every film genre imaginable—social drama, musical comedy, westerns, sea sagas, swashbuckling romances, gangster and prison melodramas, horror films, mystery thrillers. Some wise critics even wondered if, after all, Curtiz hadn't somehow managed to make the studio system subservient to him. Apparently Curtiz was a virtual dictator on the set, ruling everyone with an iron hand and hated by all, but it was a technique by which he elicited some brilliant performances in a host of memorable films. Perhaps those who responded best to his tyranny were those who realized that there was a velvet glove on that iron fist.

Filmography: [United States only]: The Third Degree, A Million Bid, The Desired Woman, Good Time Charley (1927); Tenderloin (1928); Noah's Ark, The Glad Rag Doll, Madonna of Avenue A, The Gamblers, Hearts in Exile (1929); Mammy, Under a Texas Moon, The Matrimonial Bed, Bright Lights, A Soldier's Plaything, River's End (1930); God's Gift to Women, The Mad Genius (1931); The Woman from Monte Carlo, Alias the Doctor [co-dir. with Lloyd Bacon], The Strange Love of Molly Louvain, Doctor

X, Cabin in the Cotton (1932); 20,000 Years in Sing Sing, The Mystery of the Wax Museum, The Keyhole, Private Detective 62, Goodbye Again, The Kennel Murder Case, Female (1933); Mandalay, Jimmy the Gent, The Key/High Peril, British Agent (1934); Black Fury, The Case of the Curious Bride, Front Page Woman, Little Big Shot, Captain Blood (1935); The Walking Dead, The Charge of the Light Brigade (1936); Stolen Holiday, Mountain Justice, Kid Galahad/The Battling Bellhop, The Perfect Specimen (1937); Gold Is Where You Find It, The Adventures of Robin Hood [co-dir. with William Keighley], Four's a Crowd, Four Daughters, Angels with Dirty Faces (1938); Sons of Liberty [short], Dodge City, Daughters Courageous, The Private Lives of Elizabeth and Essex/Elizabeth the Queen, Four Wives (1939); Virginia City, The Sea Hawk, Santa Fe Trail (1940); The Sea Wolf, Dive Bomber (1941); Captains of the Clouds, Yankee Doodle Dandy (1942); Casablanca, Mission to Moscow, This Is the Army (1943); Passage to Marseille, Janie (1944); Roughly Speaking, Mildred Pierce (1945); Night and Day (1946); Life with Father, The Unsuspected (1947); Romance on the High Seas (1948); My Dream Is Yours [also prod.], Flamingo Road, The Lady Takes a Sailor (1949); Bright Leaf, Young Man with a Horn, The Breaking Point (1950); Force of Arms, Jim Thorpe—All-American (1951); I'll See You in My Dreams, The Story of Will Rogers (1952); The Jazz Singer, Trouble along the Way (1953); The Boy from Oklahoma, The Egyptian, White Christmas (1954); We're No Angels (1955); The Vagabond King, The Scarlet Hour [also prod.], The Best Things in Life Are Free (1956); The Helen Morgan Story (1957), King Creole, The Proud Rebel (1958); The Hangman, The Man in the Net (1959); The Adventures of Huckleberry Finn, A Breath of Scandal (1960); Francis of Assisi, The Comancheros (1961).

Honors: Academy Award Nomination: Best Director (*Angels with Dirty Faces* and *Four Daughters*, 1938); Academy Award: Short/Two-Reel (*Sons of Liberty*, 1939); Academy Award Nomination: Best Director (*Yankee Doodle Dandy*, 1942); Academy Award: Best Director (*Casablanca*, 1943).

Selected Bibliography

Kinnard, Roy, and R. J. Vitone. *The American Films of Michael Curtiz*. Metuchen, NJ: Scarecrow Press, 1986.

Robertson, James C. *The Casablanca Man: The Cinema of Michael Curtiz*. New York: Routledge, 1993.

D

DAVID COPPERFIELD (1935), drama. Directed by George Cukor; with Freddie Bartholomew, Frank Lawton, W. C. Fields, Lionel Barrymore, Madge Evans, Roland Young, Basil Rathbone, Edna May Oliver, Maureen O'Sullivan, Lewis Stone, Lennox Pawle, Elsa Lanchester, Una O'Connor, and Arthur Treacher; screenplay by Howard Estabrook and Hugh Walpole (who also portrays the vicar).

Critics were quick to acclaim the excellent casting of this film. A host of renowned actors in roles they seem born to play makes this adaptation of the Charles Dickens classic novel an unforgettable experience. It is still hard to imagine anyone but W. C. Fields as Mr. Micawber or, for that matter, anyone but Basil Rathbone as Mr. Murdstone or Edna May Oliver as Aunt Betsey. And the incomparable Freddy Bartholomew, in his prime as the leading child actor of his day (after Shirley Temple), easily assumes the mantle of the world's most famous orphan. Add to these the redoubtable Lionel Barrymore along with Elsa Lanchester (the bride of Frankenstein) and you have a rare film treat. Critics generally agree that this inimitable film is one of those rare things: a blend of Art and Hollywood that actually works. Even though half the characters in the panoramic Dickens novel do not appear in the film, the whole, vast panorama spectacle of the book is somehow conveyed. Other versions of this film have been attempted, but none has yet surpassed this unique original.

Awards: Academy Award Nominations: Best Picture, Editing.

Selected Bibliography

Deschner, Donald. *The Complete Films of W. C. Fields*. New York: Carol, 1989.
Kotsilibas-Davis, James. *The Barrymores: The Royal Family in Hollywood*. New York: Crown, 1981.

Levy, Emanuel. *George Cukor: Master of Elegance: Hollywood's Legendary Director and His Stars*. New York: Morrow, 1994.

DAVIS, BETTE. Actress. Born Ruth Elizabeth Davis on April 5, 1908, in Lowell, Massachusetts; died on October 6, 1989. Davis was attracted to acting in high school, but her road to success was by no means an easy one. She knew she lacked the physical attributes of an ingenue, so she focused on the art of acting, eventually giving performances of such intensity that she created a unique type of actress using mannerisms now associated only with her. She didn't pass her first screen test at Goldwyn in 1930, but later that year she managed to get a contract from Universal in spite of the raised eyebrows of some studio officials. Refusing to accept failure, Davis acquired a flawless understanding of what the camera can do. In this way she could mesmerize an audience into accepting her own image of herself. Her early roles were often supporting or routine, but in 1934, she fought for the right to loan out to RKO for *Of Human Bondage*. Her performance in that film opened doors to better parts, and before long, she acquired a reputation as one of Hollywood's most accomplished actresses. In 1935 she won her first Oscar, for *Dangerous*, and the following year, she had a good part in *The Petrified Forest*. The roles that followed, however, were mediocre, and in rebellion, she fled to England; but Warners issued an injunction, and Davis sued—and lost. However, her little courtroom drama showed them the feisty side of Bette Davis, and in the years that followed, she broadened her range by playing a variety of juicy roles, a great many of them as a strong-willed woman who remains fiercely independent in a male-dominated world. She gained a reputation for playing bitchy, ambitious women. In fact, she became just about the only real superstar who made it to the top playing women who, when crossed, get even by using any means available. Men and women alike admired her nerve and sympathized with her thirst for revenge. She was riding high through most of the 1940s, but toward the end, her career began to wane. *All about Eve* (1950) was supposed to be the film that would revitalize her career, but it proved to be too hard an act to follow, and her career faded to the point where she eventually found herself advertising in the trade press for roles. In the early 1960s, there were signs that her career might be jump-started by the two roles she played in two neo-Gothic Hollywood horror films, *What Ever Happened to Baby Jane?* and *Hush . . . , Hush, Sweet Charlotte*, but by then she was becoming too much an embarrassing parody of herself. The rest of her career was mixed, with some of her best performances being given in made-for-TV dramas. Even so, she had been around for sixty years and remains the only actress ever to receive ten Academy Award nominations.

Filmography: Bad Sister, Seed, Waterloo Bridge (1931); Way Back Home, The Menace, Hell's House, The Man Who Played God, So Big, The Rich Are Always with Us, The Dark Horse, Cabin in the Cotton, Three on a Match (1932); 20,000 Years in Sing Sing, Parachute Jumper, The Working Man, Ex-Lady, Bureau of Missing Persons (1933); Fashions of 1934, The Big Shakedown, Jimmy the Gent, Fog over Frisco, Of Human Bondage, Housewife (1934); Bordertown, The Girl from Tenth Avenue, Front Page Woman,

Special Agent, Dangerous (1935); The Petrified Forest, The Golden Arrow, Satan Met a Lady (1936); Marked Woman, Kid Galahad, That Certain Woman, It's Love I'm After (1937); Jezebel, The Sisters (1938); Dark Victory, Juarez, The Old Maid, The Private Lives of Elizabeth and Essex (1939); All This and Heaven Too, The Letter (1940); The Great Lie, The Bride Came C.O.D., The Little Foxes, The Man Who Came to Dinner (1941); In This Our Life, Now Voyager (1942); Watch on the Rhine, Thank Your Lucky Stars, Old Acquaintance (1943); Mr. Skeffington, Hollywood Canteen (1944); The Corn Is Green (1945); A Stolen Life, Deception (1946); Winter Meeting, June Bride (1948); Beyond the Forest (1949); All About Eve (1950); Another Man's Poison, Payment on Demand (1951); Phone Call from a Stranger, The Star (1952); The Virgin Queen (1955); Storm Center, The Catered Affair (1956); John Paul Jones [cameo, as Catherine the Great], The Scapegoat (1959); A Pocketful of Miracles (1961); What Ever Happened to Baby Jane? (1962); La Noia/The Empty Canvas [It.], Dead Ringer, Where Love Has Gone (1964); Hush . . . , Hush, Sweet Charlotte, The Nanny (1965); The Anniversary (1967); Connecting Rooms (1970); Bunny O'Hare (1971); Madame Sin [TV film, shown in theaters abroad], Lo Scopone scientifico/The Scientific Cardplayer (1972); Burnt Offerings (1976); Return from Witch Mountain, Death on the Nile (1978); The Watcher in the Woods (1980); The Whales of August (1987); Wicked Stepmother (1989).

Honors: Academy Award: Best Actress (*Dangerous*, 1935); Venice Film Festival Award: Best Actress (*Marked Woman* and *Kid Galahad*, 1937); Academy Award: Best Actress (*Jezebel*, 1938); Academy Award Nomination: Best Actress (*Dark Victory*, 1939); Academy Award Nomination: Best Actress (*The Letter*, 1940); Academy Award Nomination: Best Actress (*The Little Foxes*, 1941); Academy Award Nomination: Best Actress (*Now, Voyager*, 1942); Academy Award Nomination: Best Actress (*Mr. Skeffington*, 1944); New York Film Critics Circle Award, Academy Award Nomination: Best Actress (*All About Eve*, 1950); Cannes Film Festival: Best Actress (*All About Eve*, 1951); Academy Award Nomination: Best Actress (*The Star*, 1952); *Photoplay* Gold Medal Award: Most Popular Female Star, Academy Award Nomination: Best Actress (*What Ever Happened to Baby Jane?* (1962); Golden Globes: Cecil B. DeMille Award (1973); American Film Institute Life Achievement Award [fifth recipient, first woman] (1977); French Film Industry (César, 1987); Film Society of Lincoln Center Tribute, San Sebastian Film Festival: Life Achievement Tribute (1989). Not long before her death, she said, "You know what they'll write on my tombstone? 'She did it the hard way.' "

Selected Bibliography

Leaming, Barbara. *Bette Davis: A Biography*. New York: Simon & Schuster, 1992.

Quirk, Lawrence J. *Fasten Your Seat Belts: The Passionate Life of Bette Davis*. New York: W. Morrow, 1990.

Riese, Randall. *All About Bette: Her Life from A-Z*. Chicago: Contemporary Books, 1993.

Robinson, Jeffrey. *Bette Davis: Her Film to Stage Career*. New York: Proteus, 1982.

Spada, James. *More Than a Woman: An Intimate Biography of Bette Davis*. New York: Bantam Books, 1993.

DAY, DORIS. Actress, singer. Born Doris von Kappelhoff on April 3, 1924, in Cincinnati, Ohio. Doris Day's career is a story Hollywood is probably too embarrassed to film because it reads like a story only Hollywood could concoct. She started out as a dancer, but an auto accident at fifteen cut short those ambitions, so she turned to singing. She sang on radio and in clubs and took her stage name from one of her songs, "Day by Day." In the early 1940s she was a featured vocalist with the Bob Crosby and Les Brown bands, and by the middle of the decade, she was a highly successful recording star, her breakthrough hit being "Sentimental Journey" right at the end of the war. She entered films in 1948 as a last-minute replacement for Betty Hutton in the Warner Bros. musical *Romance on the High Seas* and promptly became an audience favorite as the wholesome heroine of light musicals and occasional dramas. She was particularly impressive as the sympathetic singer who sticks by doomed trumpeter Kirk Douglas in *Young Man with a Horn*, holding her own against the formidable Lauren Bacall, whose trademark sultriness couldn't hold a candle to Day's sunny personality. By the early 1950s, she was one of the most popular female stars in the United States and one of the highest paid. In the late 1950s and early 1960s she was the virginal heroine of a series of sophisticated bedroom farces, mostly at Universal, opposite such attractive leading men as Rock Hudson and Cary Grant. The films typically suggested a vague aura of timid sexuality, but Day remained pure and wholesome to the last fadeout (which prompted Oscar Levant to quip: "I knew Doris Day before she became a virgin"—a quip that amused her). A victim of 1960s backlash, she became the scapegoat of the sexual revolution and was perceived as some sort of moral dinosaur. She was even mocked in the high school musical *Grease*. Later critics have reappraised her as a savvy reincarnation of the shrewd woman of Jane Austen's day who knew that the way to land the man (and his fortune) was to get him to the altar first. "Virtue rewarded," they called it, and wise women know that it has always paid off. In her book *Doris Day: Her Own Story* (1975), Day revealed that behind the happy face and bright smile was a victim of abuse and fraud. Her first husband was a psychopath, and her third, Marty Melcher, either mismanaged or embezzled her entire life's earnings of $20 million and left her flat broke, a fact she discovered upon his sudden death. After suffering a nervous breakdown, she make a comeback as a TV star with *The Doris Day Show* (1968–1973). Ironically, she did the show because she had been committed to do it by Melcher, without her knowledge. In 1974 she was awarded more than $22 million in damages from her former lawyer, the one who had helped Melcher manage her business and wipe out her fortune. After more than a decade's hiatus, she returned to the spotlight in 1985–1986 as the host of a cable TV show, *Doris Day and Friends*. The mid-1990s saw a revival of interest in and appreciation of her contribution to film history. Many people feel that *Calamity Jane* is far superior to *Annie Get Your Gun*, at least as a film musical. It was Day's favorite and showed her off at both her tomboyish and glamorous best. Day worked with most of the top Hollywood leading men, including Kirk Douglas, James Stewart, Cary Grant, Clark Gable, Rex Harrison, Frank Sinatra, James Cagney, Rock Hudson, and even Ronald Reagan. Alfred Hitchcock, who favored cool blonds, cast her as the lead in *The Man Who Knew Too Much*, in which she introduced "Che Será Será," the song that was to become her theme song.

Doris Day will be remembered not only as a fine actress and singer but also as a great comedienne in the tradition of Carole Lombard and Marilyn Monroe (whom she replaced, by the way, in *Something's Got to Give*, later retitled *Move Over, Darling*).

Filmography: Romance on the High Seas (1948); My Dream Is Yours, It's a Great Feeling (1949); Young Man with a Horn, Tea for Two, The West Point Story (1950); Storm Warning, Lullaby of Broadway, On Moonlight Bay, I'll See You in My Dreams, Starlift [cameo] (1951); The Winning Team, April in Paris (1952); By the Light of the Silvery Moon, Calamity Jane (1953); Lucky Me (1954); Young at Heart, Love Me or Leave Me (1955); The Man Who Knew Too Much, Julie (1956); The Pajama Game (1957); Teacher's Pet, Tunnel of Love (1958); It Happened to Jane, Pillow Talk (1959); Please Don't Eat the Daisies, Midnight Lace (1960); Lover Come Back, That Touch of Mink, Jumbo (1962); The Thrill of It All, Move Over Darling (1963); Send Me No Flowers (1964); Do Not Disturb (1965); The Glass-Bottom Boat (1966); Caprice (1967); The Ballad of Josie, Where Were You When the Lights Went Out?, With Six You Get Eggroll (1968).

Honors: *Photoplay* Gold Medal Award: Most Popular Female Star (*Lullaby of Broadway*, 1951); Golden Globe Award: World Film Favorite (1957); Golden Globe Award: World Film Favorite (1959); *Photoplay* Gold Medal Award: Most Popular Female Star (1959); Academy Award Nomination: Best Actress (*Pillow Talk*, 1959); Golden Globe Award: World Film Favorite (1962); Golden Globes: Cecil B. DeMille Award (1988).

Selected Bibliography

Braun, Eric. *Doris Day*. London: Weidenfeld & Nicolson, 1991.
Day, Doris, with A. E. Hotchner. *Doris Day: Her Own Story*. New York: Morrow, 1976.
Young, Christopher. *The Films of Doris Day*. Secaucus, NJ: Citadel, 1977.

DAY THE EARTH STOOD STILL, THE (1951), science-fiction/drama. Directed by Robert Wise; with Michael Rennie, Patricia Neal, Hugh Marlowe, Sam Jaffe, Billy Gray, Frances Bavier, and Lock Martin; screenplay by Edmund North.

"From out of space—a warning and an ultimatum!" ran the blurb for this legendary Cold War cautionary tale. The film continues to be praised both as a classic sci-fi flick and as a serious statement about the dark side of human nature. And while its special effects now seem dated, it doesn't matter because it is not gimmicks that are the focus of this picture but the Messianic figure of Michael Rennie, the dignified alien who comes to warn Earth to change its warlike ways or risk annihilation. Rennie is the kind but stern savior whose unique perspective on earthlings gives the picture much of its wry charm. This is one of the more literate sci-fi pictures with an excellent screenplay by Edmund North from the story "Farewell to the Master" by Harry Bates. Ironic suspense is added by having authorities search frantically for the escaped alien while the alien secretly pursues his mission of mercy. The scenes in which the fugitive alien learns about life on Earth while living incognito in a boardinghouse with a young widow and her son are particularly effective. Reinforcing the film's eerie atmosphere and sense of menace is Bernard Hermann's haunting score.

Awards: Golden Globe Award: Best Film Promoting International Understanding.

Selected Bibliography

Brosnan, John. *Future Tense: The Cinema of Science Fiction.* New York: St. Martin's Press, 1978.

Menville, Douglas Alver. *A Historical and Critical Survey of the Science Fiction Film.* New York: Arno Press, 1975.

Parish, James Robert, and Michael Pitts. *The Great Science Fiction Pictures.* Metuchen, NJ: Scarecrow Press, 1977.

DEAN, JAMES. Actor. Born James Byron Dean on February 8, 1931, in Marion, Indiana; died on September 30, 1955, in an auto crash near Salinas, California. Educated at Santa Monica Junior College and the University of California at Los Angeles. Dean began acting with James Whitmore's little theater group, appearing in occasional TV commercials, and playing bit parts in several films. In 1951 he went to New York where, after some tough times, he got a part in Broadway's *See the Jaguar.* He later sat in on classes at the Actors Studio, got bit parts in TV dramas, and then appeared on Broadway again, this time as the cunning Arab boy in Gide's *The Immoralist* (1954), a role that cast the shadow of sexual ambiguity over his career and life. This role led to a screen test at Warners and probably the shortest and most spectacular career of any film star in history. In just over one year, and in only three films, Dean became a widely admired screen personality, a personification of restless American youth of the mid-1950s, and the embodiment of the title of one of his films, *Rebel without a Cause.* Dean had just completed *Giant* when he was killed in a highway crash while driving his Porsche Spider to Salinas to compete in a racing event. His early death ignited a flood of adulation that has only increased over time. Unlike Clift, who burned out in public, or Brando, who became a caricature of himself, Dean died at a moment that leaves him fixed in time as forever young, forever alienated, forever out of reach. Many of his fans refused to accept his death, and a James Dean cult developed into a mass mystique of a kind that had surrounded the personality of no other star since Valentino. Not even the Elvis cult is of the purity and intensity of the Dean cult. And much of this is due to the purity and intensity of Dean's performances. Whether by method or madness, Dean brought his characters so powerfully to life and saw life through his myopic squint with such tortured honesty that audiences felt they were in the presence of an almost mystical force. That the adulation shows no sign of abating can be seen in the proliferation of books about Dean and in the mass gatherings at his grave in Park Cemetery in Fairmount, Indiana, on the anniversary of his death. A biography by former roommate James Bast was made into a TV movie, *James Dean* (1976), starring Stephen McHattie in the title role. There have also been several documentaries, including *The James Dean Story* (1957), directed by George W. George and Robert Altman. Echoes of the Dean worship resonate in Altman's *Come Back to the Five and Dime, Jimmy Dean, Jimmy Dean* (1982) and James Bridges's *September 30, 1955* (1978). The latter film's title represents the date of the star's death.

Filmography: Sailor Beware [bit], Fixed Bayonets [bit] (1951); Has Anybody Seen My Gal? [bit] (1952); Trouble along the Way [bit] (1953); East of Eden, Rebel without a Cause (1955); Giant (1956).

Honors: Golden Globe Award: Posthumous Award for Best Dramatic Actor (*East of Eden*, 1955); Golden Globe Award: World Film Favorite, Academy Award Nomination: Best Actor (*Giant*, 1956).

Selected Bibliography

Adams, Leigh, and Keith Burns. *James Dean: Behind the Scene*. New York: Carol Publishing Group, 1990.

Alexander, Paul. *Boulevard of Broken Dreams: The Life, Times, and Legend of James Dean*. New York: Viking, 1994.

Hyams, Joe, with Jay Hyams. *James Dean: Little Boy Lost*. New York: Warner Books, 1992.

Riese, Randall. *The Unabridged James Dean: His Life and Legacy from A to Z*. Chicago: Contemporary Books, 1991.

Spoto, Donald. *Rebel: The Life and Legend of James Dean*. New York: HarperCollins, 1996.

DEFIANT ONES, THE (1958), drama. Directed by Stanley Kramer; with Tony Curtis, Sidney Poitier, Theodore Bikel, Charles McGraw, Cara Williams, and Lon Chaney, Jr.; screenplay by Harold Jacob Smith and Nathan E. Douglas (blacklisted actor-writer Nedrick Young).

This story of two escaped convicts (one black, one white) shackled together as they flee from police in the South is flawlessly done. Nevertheless, it is shackled to a message that renders it predictable and therefore not entirely satisfying. The message is that what keeps people apart is their "lack of communication." Only communicate, and respect and comradeship will follow, not to mention love. A more idealistic generation bought into this idealism. The civil rights movement was gaining momentum in 1958, and illusions of racial harmony danced in the heads of freedom fighters who sought simple solutions to ingrained wickedness. This led the film's detractors to view it as a typical piece of liberal pleading couched in a much-too-obvious metaphor for racial hatred. The suspense of the manhunt in the swamps notwithstanding, the film, they felt, never really overcomes the dead weight of Kramer's message. Noel Coward spoke wisely when he said, "If you want to send a message, use Western Union." However, supporters of the film credit Stanley Kramer's direction for giving the picture action, compassion, even suspense in spite of the film's predictability. Some even go so far as to consider this film Kramer's best picture, pointing to the way it combines powerful subject matter with exciting action and strong acting. But even they feel a bit uncomfortable with Kramer's transparent singleness of purpose.

Awards: Academy Awards: Best Original Screenplay, B&W Cinematography (Sam Leavitt); Golden Globe Award, New York Film Critics Circle Award: Best Picture; Berlin Film Festival Award: Best Actor (Poitier); British Academy Award: Best Actor/Foreign

(Poitier); Academy Award Nominations: Best Picture, Director, Actor (Curtis, Poitier), Supporting Actor (Bikel), Supporting Actress (Cara Williams), Editing (Frederick Knudson).

Selected Bibliography

Keyser, Lester J., and Andre H. Ruszkows. *The Cinema of Sidney Poitier: The Black Man's Changing Role on the American Screen*. South Brunswick, NJ: A. S. Barnes, 1980.

Spoto, Donald. *Stanley Kramer: Film Maker*. New York: Putnam, 1978.

DE HAVILLAND, OLIVIA. Actress. Born on July 1, 1916, in Tokyo. Educated at Notre Dame Convent (Belmont, California) and Mills College. De Havilland's parents, a British patent attorney and a former actress, divorced when she was three, and her mother brought her and her younger sister, Joan Fontaine, to California. In 1933, while only a freshman in college, she appeared in a local production of *A Midsummer Night's Dream* and was chosen by Max Reinhardt to play Hernia in both his stage and screen versions of the play. Warners signed her to a seven-year contract and proceeded to cast her in one costume drama after the other, invariably as a sweet, delicate heroine dominated usually by Errol Flynn, opposite whom she made a slew of pictures. She fought for the role of Melanie in *Gone with the Wind* (as a loan-out to Selznick), and it earned her an Oscar nomination and the attention of Warners. However, they still insisted on putting her in undemanding roles, and she rebelled and was put on suspension. As a result, when Warners refused to release her from her contract at the end of seven years, she sued and, after a prolonged court battle, won. It was a landmark decision that changed the relationship between studios and contract players forever. Most actors welcomed it and thanked her for it, but some commentators on Hollywood history have cited the decision as the death blow to the studio system that, with all its faults, had produced so much enduring cinema. After a three-year absence from the screen, de Havilland returned in triumph, winning her first Academy Award in 1946 for her deeply felt performance in *To Each His Own*. She won another best actress Oscar in 1949 for *The Heiress*, giving one of the screen's truly great performances. Having claimed her true place in the cinematic firmament, she seemed to lose interest in film, returning for a time to the stage and then making a handful of indifferent films, mostly abroad, and a few TV movies. Her performances have always been polished, but her passion for the craft seemed to wane, especially after her divorce from novelist Marcus Goodrich and her marriage to Pierre Galante, then editor of *Paris Match*.

Filmography: A Midsummer Night's Dream, Alibi Ike, The Irish in Us, Captain Blood (1935); Anthony Adverse, The Charge of the Light Brigade (1936); Call It a Day, The Great Garrick, It's Love I'm After (1937); Gold Is Where You Find It, The Adventures of Robin Hood, Four's a Crowd, Hard to Get (1938); Wings of the Navy, Dodge City, The Private Lives of Elizabeth and Essex, Gone with the Wind (1939); Raffles, My Love Came Back, Santa Fe Trail (1940); Strawberry Blonde, Hold Back the Dawn, They Died with Their Boots On (1941); The Male Animal, In This Our Life (1942); Thank Your Lucky Stars [cameo], Princess O'Rourke, Government Girl (1943); Devotion [made in 1943, released in 1946], The Well-Groomed Bride, To Each His Own, The Dark Mirror (1946); The Snake Pit (1948); The Heiress (1949); My Cousin Rachel (1953); That Lady, Not as a Stranger (1955); The Ambassador's Daughter (1956); The Proud Rebel (1958); Libel (1959); The Light in the Piazza (1962); Lady in a Cage (1964); Hush . . . , Hush, Sweet Charlotte (1965); The Adventurers (1970); Pope Joan (1972); The Fifth Musketeer/ Behind the Iron Mask, Airport '77 (1977); The Swarm (1978).

Honors: Academy Award Nomination: Best Supporting Actress (*Gone with the Wind*, 1939); Academy Award Nomination: Best Actress (*Hold Back the Dawn*, 1941); Academy Award: Best Actress (*To Each His Own*, 1946); National Board of Review Award, New York Film Critics Circle Award, Academy Award Nomination: Best Actress (*The Snake Pit*, 1948); Academy Award, Golden Globe Award, New York Film Critics Circle Award: Best Actress (*The Heiress*, 1949); Venice Film Festival: International Grand Prize: Best Actress (*The Snake Pit*, 1949).

Selected Bibliography

Higham, Charles. *Sisters: The Story of Olivia de Havilland and Joan Fontaine*. New York: Coward-McCann, 1984.
Kass, Judith M. *Olivia de Havilland*. New York: Pyramid, 1976.
Thomas, Tony. *The Films of Olivia de Havilland*. Secaucus, NJ: Citadel Press, 1983.

DEMILLE, CECIL B. Director, producer, screenwriter. Born Cecil Blount DeMille on August 12, 1881, in Ashfield, Massachusetts; died on January 21, 1959. Educated at Pennsylvania Military College and New York's Academy of Dramatic Arts. DeMille, whose mother was an actress, made his acting debut on Broadway in 1900, and for more than ten years, he worked in his mother's company as both actor and general manager while collaborating with his brother on a series of relatively successful plays. In 1913 he entered into a partnership with vaudeville musician Jesse L. Lasky and glove salesman Samuel Goldfish (later Goldwyn). They formed a motion picture firm, the Jesse L. Lasky Feature Play Company, and traveled to Hollywood to produce what would become DeMille's first feature film, *The Squaw Man* (1914). It was a great success and established DeMille as a director on the go. The Lasky company became Paramount Pictures, and DeMille remained there for the rest of his long and illustrious career. His epics attracted such attention that Hollywood was soon becoming the focus of the film industry. In fact, some historians even call DeMille ''the founder of Hollywood.'' His was the first director's name to become a household word, and throughout his career, only Hitchcock rivaled him as a director whose name above the title was more of a box office draw than the names below. A born showman with a knack for anticipating public taste and catering to its changing moods, DeMille assembled his own roster of stars and put them in lavish productions full of sex and violence but always with a moral frame and a poetically just ending. DeMille was a master storyteller who was conventional in the way he developed his plots. Because he was, above all, an enormously successful entertainer, he was loathed by the jealous who scorned his films as simple-minded and vulgar. DeMille produced and directed a total of seventy films and participated in the production of many more. From 1936 to 1945, DeMille hosted and directed *Lux Radio Theatre*, a popular weekly radio show devoted to adaptations of feature films and starring all the luminaries of the silver screen. He also made occasional film appearances, most notably in *Sunset Boulevard*.

Filmography: [as director-producer]: The Squaw Man, Brewster's Millions, The Master Mind, The Only Son, The Man on the Box, The Call of the North, The Virginian, What's His Name, Rose of the Rancho, The Ghost Breaker (1914); The Girl of the Golden West, After Five, The Warrens of Virginia, The Unafraid, The Captive, The Wild Goose Chase, The Arab, Chimmie Fadden, Kindling, Carmen, Chimmie Fadden Out West, The Cheat (1915); The Golden Chance, Temptation, The Trail of the Lonesome Pine, The Heart of Nora Flynn, Maria Rosa, The Dream Girl, Joan the Woman, Romance of the Redwoods, The Little American, The Woman God Forgot, The Devil Stone (1917); The Whispering Chorus, Old Wives for New, You Can't Have Everything, Till I Come Back to You, The Squaw Man [remake] (1918); Don't Change Your Husband, For Better for Worse, Male and Female (1919); Why Change Your Wife?, Something to Think About (1920); Forbidden Fruit, The Affairs of Anatol, Fool's Paradise (1921); Saturday Night, Man-slaughter (1922); Adam's Rib, The Ten Commandments (1923); Triumph, Feet of Clay (1924); The Golden Bed, The Road to Yesterday (1925); The Volga Boatman (1926); The King of Kings (1927); The Godless Girl, Dynamite (1929); Madame Satan (1930); The Squaw Man [second remake] (1931); The Sign of the Cross (1932); This Day and Age (1933); Four Frightened People, Cleopatra (1934); The Crusades (1935); The Plains-man (1937); The Buccaneer (1938); Union Pacific (1939); North West Mounted Police (1940); Reap the Wild Wind (1942); The Story of Dr. Wassell (1944); Unconquered (1947); Samson and Delilah (1949); The Greatest Show on Earth (1952); The Ten Commandments [remake] (1956).

Honors: Academy Award: Special Award (1949); Golden Globe Award: Cecil B. DeMille Award (1951); Golden Globe Award, Academy Award Nomination: Best Director (*The Greatest Show on Earth*, 1952); Academy Award: Irving G. Thalberg Award (1952); Directors Guild of America: D. W. Griffith Award (1952).

Selected Bibliography

DeMille, Cecil B. *The Autobiography of Cecil B. DeMille*. New York: Garland, 1985.
Higashi, Sumiko. *Cecil B. DeMille: A Guide to References and Resources*. Boston: G. K. Hall, 1985.
Higham, Charles. *Cecil B. DeMille*. New York: Da Capo Press, 1980.
Ringgold, Gene, and DeWitt Bodeen. *The Films of Cecil B. DeMille*. New York: Citadel Press, 1969.

DESTRY RIDES AGAIN (1939), western. Directed by George Marshall; with James Stewart, Marlene Dietrich, Charles Winninger, Brian Donlevy, Una Merkel, Mischa Auer, Allen Jenkins, Irene Hervey, Jack Carson, Billy Gilbert, and Samuel S. Hinds; screenplay by Felix Jackson, Gertrude Purcell, and Henry Myers.

"They make the fighting sinful West blaze into action before your eyes!" So promised the blurb that announced this irresistible western satire starring the most unlikely duo in film history: stuttering, nice-guy James Stewart and rowdy, femme fatale Marlene Dietrich. Dietrich's rendition of "See What the Boys in the Back Room Will Have" has become an unforgettable part of film history. Prior to this film, Dietrich had been labeled "box office poison." *Destry* changed all that, and overnight she was welcomed back enthusiastically by audiences skeptical of sultry women with exotic accents. In a part she was reluctant to play, she now reinvented herself as a bawdy, tempestuous wench—but one with a heart of gold. And as if that wasn't enough, what clinched it was the fact that she dies a heroine's death. It was one of those turning-point stories that Hollywood history is made up of, and it didn't hurt Stewart either. He needed to have some of his good-guy image slightly tarnished. What is remarkable about the film itself is the way it combines humor, romance, suspense, and action so seamlessly, leading one critic to label it "just plain, good entertainment." Legend has it that Lord Beaverbrooks once said that Marlene Dietrich standing on a bar in black net stockings, belting out "See What the Boys in the Back Room Will Have" "was a greater work of art than the Venus de Milo." What astute critics noticed was that Dietrich possessed the rarest of civilized virtues, irony, the very quality that makes her role as Frenchy classic. Ultimately, it is the only quality that makes a sex goddess appeal to a general audience. Mae West had it almost to a fault, but Marilyn Monroe had it to an extent scarcely appreciated until it was too late. Marlene now seems to be the one who made the best use of it throughout her long career as film star and cabaret entertainer.

Selected Bibliography

Dickens, Homer. *The Complete Films of Marlene Dietrich*. Secaucus, NJ: Carol, 1992.
Parish, James Robert, and Michael R. Pitts. *The Great Western Pictures*. Metuchen, NJ: Scarecrow Press, 1976.
Sennett, Ted. *Hollywood's Golden Year, 1939*. New York: St. Martin's Press, 1989.

DIETRICH, MARLENE. Actress. Born Maria Magdalene Dietrich on December 27, 1901, in Schöneger (Berlin); died on March 6, 1992. It is next to impossible to encapsulate anything approaching the essence of Marlene Dietrich in a brief (or even a long) biography. She was so many things: seductress, saloon singer, bawd, trickster, heart-of-gold whore, vulnerable heroine, comedienne. In short, the essence of the film star: a chameleon, shifting shadows on the screen, constantly reinvented, a product of lights and makeup and camera angles, a self-parody, a riddle wrapped in an enigma. Like Marilyn Monroe, she had no true identity. She was whatever "they" or she turned her into. She "became" the screen image, and this is what accounted for her success in spite of her detractors who could see nothing special in her—at first. Although she became an accomplished performer, she was truly the creation of the camera. Even her later performances were in-person re-creations of her screen personas. People came to see an illusion, and no one knew better how to give it to them. In her later years, she would be corseted more severely than Scarlett O'Hara, her skin stretched by rubber bands tied to her hair, her face a cosmetic mask. (Much later she actually held a mask of herself before her face if she had to confront anyone.) She knew her provocativeness was manufactured, and she was savvy enough to project this irony in her performances. Even her frozen features actually communicated a sense of drollery. *Destry Rides Again* is pointed to as the best example of her sense of humor, but listen to the (incredible) recording she made in the early 1950s with Rosemary Clooney of "He's Too Old to Cut the Mustard," and you will understand the wondrous comedic talent of this woman. Like Garbo, she knew that to retain the sense of mystery surrounding her (mystery behind which there was no burning secret), she only had to remain aloof. And this she could do even in a crowd. She was least forthcoming when she was beyond camera range. But there is another facet that continues to fascinate: her androgyny. Reminiscent of *Victor/Victoria*, she sometimes seemed to be a female impersonator and was known to perform in gay clubs in Paris. Like Judy Garland, she could wear top hat and tails and feel right at home. And impersonators of them both are almost always men dressed as women dressed as men. In fact, there was always something bisexual about her, including her fifty-one-year marriage to Rudolf Sieber, the father of her only child and the husband from whom she lived apart during most of the marriage. And, of course, no biography of a star of the golden age would be complete without a Mommy-dearest number being done by an ungrateful (or maybe just plain humorless) child. In this case, it was Dietrich's only child, daughter Maria Riva, who, after her mother died at the age of ninety-one (the best guess), took her swipes at her illustrious mother. Probably what she says is true, but it's hard to know which rules apply to people who are truly larger than life yet at the same time emptier than life. Particulars, speculations, fabrications about her early (and later) life abound and can be found in numerous biographies. The Svengali influence of Josef von Sternberg is a source of endless fascination and speculation. It's probably true to say that he "made" her and that, after an ungrateful backlash, she always tried to re-create what he had created. Modern film audiences coming upon *The Blue Angel* for the first time are stunned to see how pudgy (and darkhaired) Marlene is—and, in a way, how vulgar and reedy voiced. It's hard to see the hollow-cheeked, svelte, blond, husky-voiced bombshell of a few years later. Yet *The Blue Angel* launched her reputation as a femme fatale singing a siren's song among the denizens of the demimonde. And the six von Sternberg American films that followed established the legend that was to remain quintessentially "Dietrich" for the rest of her life. She made many good films later on—and managed to look stunningly young and beautiful in all of them—but the image that remains is exotic, aloof, and dangerous. Two later, smaller roles stand out in her filmography: *Witness for the Prosecution*, in which she pulls off a trick only great actresses can pull; and *Judgment at*

Nuremberg, in which she is perfect as the self-deceived wife of a Nazi war criminal and the essence of postwar German blindness.

Filmography: [in Germany]: Der kleine Napoleon/So sind die Männer/Napoleons kleiner Bruder, Tragödie der Liebe/Tragedy of Love, Der Mensch am Wege (1923); Der Sprung ins Leben (1924); Die Freudlose Gasse/The Street of Sorrow [unbilled extra] (1925); Manon Lescaut, Eine Dubarry von heute/A Modern Du Barry, Kopf hoch Charly!, Madame wünscht keine Kinder/Madame Wants No Children (1926); Der Juxbaron, Sein grösster Bluff, Cafe Electric/Wenn ein Weib den Weg verliert/Die Liebesbörse (1927); Prinzessin Olala/The Art of Love (1928); Ich küsse ihre Hand Madame/I Kiss Your Hand Madame, Die Frau nach der man sich sehnt/Three Loves, Das Schiff der verlorenen Menschen/The Ship of Lost Men, Gefahren der Brautzeit (1929); Der blaue Engel/The Blue Angel (1930). [in the United States]: Morocco (1930); Dishonored (1931); Shanghai Express, Blonde Venus (1932); Song of Songs (1933); The Scarlet Empress [as Catherine the Great] (1934); The Devil Is a Woman (1935); Desire, The Garden of Allah (1936); Knight without Armor, Angel (1937); Destry Rides Again (1939); Seven Sinners (1940); The Flame of New Orleans, Manpower (1941); The Lady Is Willing, The Spoilers, Pittsburgh (1942); Follow the Boys [cameo in magic act, being sawed in half by Orson Welles], Kismet (1944); Martin Roumagnac/The Room Upstairs [Fr.] (1946); Golden Earrings (1947); A Foreign Affair (1948); Jigsaw [cameo] (1949); Stage Fright (1950); No Highway/No Highway in the Sky (1951); Rancho Notorious (1952); Around the World in 80 Days [cameo] (1956); Montecarlo/The Monte Carlo Story [It.] (1957); Witness for the Prosecution/Touch of Evil [cameo] (1958); Judgment at Nuremberg (1961); Black Fox [doc.; narr.] (1962); Paris When It Sizzles [cameo] (1964); Schöne Gigolo— arme Gigolo/Just a Gigolo (1979); Marlene [voice only] (1984).

Honors: Academy Award Nomination: Best Actress (*Morocco*, 1930–1931). She was awarded the Medal of Freedom for ''meeting a gruelling schedule of performances under battle conditions despite risk to her life.'' For similar reasons she was also named Chevalier of the French Legion of Honor.

Selected Bibliography

Bach, Steven. *Marlene Dietrich: Life and Legend*. New York: Morrow, 1992.
Dickens, Homer. *The Complete Films of Marlene Dietrich*. Secaucus, NJ: Carol, 1992.
Spoto, Donald. *Blue Angel: The Life of Marlene Dietrich*. New York: Doubleday, 1992.

DINNER AT EIGHT (1933), comedy/drama. Directed by George Cukor; with Marie Dressler, John Barrymore, Wallace Beery, Jean Harlow, Lionel Barrymore, Lee Tracy, Edmund Lowe, Billie Burke, Madge Evans, Jean Hersholt, Karen Morley, Phillips Holmes, and May Robson; screenplay by Frances Marion, Herman J. Mankiewicz, and Donald Ogden Stewart.

This screen version of the highly successful George Kaufman–Edna Ferber play is studded with legendary talent and bravura performances. Harlow shines as a comedienne, but it is Dressler as the acerbic dowager who steals the show. Some critics complained that there were too many famous faces and too little time to absorb the plot, but once you remember that the first rule of the theater is to check your brains at the box office, you can sit back and enjoy a dazzling parade of stars whose separate stories do lead to a final and very satisfactory conclusion. In *Dinner at Eight*, director George Cukor, known for his long takes, carefully pieces together the vignettes of his subjects, all of whom act their roles as if born to play them. The critics were ecstatic. Most considered the film an improvement over the play, particularly the last scene, written by Donald Ogden Smith. As Harlow and Dressler prepare to go in to dinner, Harlow mentions that she's been reading a book. "A book!" says Dressler, taken aback. "It's a screwy sort of book," says Harlow, "all about the future. This man thinks that someday machines will take the place of every known profession." "My dear," says Dressler dryly, "that's something you need never worry about." Years later, when Donald Ogden Smith received an Academy Award for the screenplay of *The Philadelphia Story*, he was quoted as saying, "I have no one to thank. I did it all myself."

Selected Bibliography

Kotsilibas-Davis, James. *The Barrymores: The Royal Family in Hollywood.* New York: Crown, 1981.

Levy, Emanuel. *George Cukor: Master of Elegance: Hollywood's Legendary Director and His Stars.* New York: Morrow, 1994.

Stenn, David. *Bombshell: The Life and Death of Jean Harlow.* New York: Doubleday, 1993.

DMYTRYK, EDWARD. Director. Born on September 4, 1908, in Grand Forks, Canada, to Ukrainian immigrants. Dmytryk's childhood was miserable after his mother died and his father moved to San Francisco and remarried. He escaped his abusive family at fifteen by running off to Hollywood, where he worked for Paramount, first as a messenger boy and later as assistant in various phases of production. From 1930 to 1939 he was film editor, counting among his credits the noted *Ruggles of Red Gap*. During this period, he directed only one film, *The Hawk*, but his career as director officially dates from 1939 when he began making mostly low-budget formula films. The first film he made that brought him any attention was *Hitler's Children*, an antifascist drama that still holds up today. Next he directed two classic suspense thrillers, *Murder My Sweet* (from Raymond Chandler's *Farewell My Lovely*) and *Cornered*, both starring Dick Powell. Dmytryk won high praise from film critics for *Crossfire*, Hollywood's first serious attempt to deal with the subject of anti-Semitism (the subject of the original novel, homosexuality, was still too controversial at that time). It is an honest, engrossing film and features a standout performance by Robert Ryan as a psychopathic bigot. That same year Dmytryk was investigated and found guilty of Communist affiliations (he joined the Communist Party in 1945) by the House Un-American Activities Committee, and as one of the Hollywood Ten he was sentenced to one year in jail. Upon his release, he went into self-imposed exile in England, where he directed three films, including the socially aware *Give Us This Day*. In 1951 he returned to the United States, and this time he named names and helped incriminate several of his former colleagues. As a result of his testimony, his name was immediately removed from the industry's blacklist.

After his reinstatement, he made a promising comeback with such noteworthy films as *Sniper*, *The Caine Mutiny*, and *Broken Lance*, but after that, his work never measured up, and he sort of faded away. In the late 1970s Dmytryk taught film at the University of Texas at Austin and in 1981 was appointed a professor of film at the University of Southern California.

Filmography: The Hawk (1935); Television Spy (1939); Emergency Squad, Golden Gloves, Mystery Sea Raider, Her First Romance (1940); The Devil Commands, Under Age, Sweetheart of the Campus, The Blonde from Singapore, Secrets of the Lone Wolf, Confessions of Boston Blackie (1941); Counter-Espionage, Seven Miles, From Alcatraz (1942); Hitler's Children, The Falcon Strikes Back, Captive Wild Woman, Behind the Rising Sun (1943); Tender Comrade, Murder My Sweet/Farewell My Lovely (1944): Back to Bataan, Cornered (1945); Till the End of Time (1946); Crossfire, So Well Remembered (1947); Obsession/The Hidden Room, Give Us This Day/Salt to the Devil (1949); Mutiny, The Sniper, Eight Iron Men (1952); The Juggler (1953); The Caine Mutiny, Broken Lance, The End of the Affair (1954); Soldier of Fortune, The Left Hand of God (1955); The Mountain [also prod.] (1956); Raintree County (1957); The Young Lions (1958); Warlock [also prod.], The Blue Angel (1959); Cronache di un Convento/ The Reluctant Saint [also prod.; It./U.S.], Walk on the Wild Side (1962); The Carpetbaggers, Where Love Has Gone (1964); Mirage (1965); Alvarez Kelly (1966); Lo Sbarco di Anzio/Anzio [It.], Shalako (1968); Bluebeard (1972); The Human Factor (1975); He Is My Brother (1976).

Honors: Cannes Film Festival Award for the Most Socially Minded Film, Academy Award Nomination: Best Director (*Crossfire*, 1947).

Selected Bibliography

Dmytryk, Edward. *It's a Hell of a Life But Not a Bad Living*. New York: New York Times Books, 1978.
Sennett, Ted. *Great Movie Directors*. New York: Harry N. Abrams, 1986.

DOCTOR ZHIVAGO (1965), drama/war. Directed by David Lean; with Omar Sharif, Julie Christie, Geraldine Chaplin, Tom Courtenay, Alec Guinness, Siobhan McKenna, Ralph Richardson, Rod Steiger, Rita Tushingham, Adrienne Corri, Geoffrey Keen, Jeffrey Rockland, Lucy Westmore, Klaus Kinski, Jack MacGowran, Tarek Sharif, and Peter Madden; screenplay by Robert Bolt.

That Lean was even able to get a workable film narrative out of this sprawling, intense, introspective novel is something of a miracle. Critics remain mixed over his success, agreeing that while it is a sumptuous epic, it does lean toward melodrama and tends to drag a little. Lean was a visual director, veering more and more during his career toward photography. Thus, this is a movie one doesn't sift through but sinks into. It is a winter dream set against the nightmare of the Russian Revolution. Sharif gives a creditable performance as Russian poet/doctor Zhivago, but much of his appeal depends on his dark, moist eyes and melancholy face. Sharif is an orphan who later marries aristocratic Chaplin but falls in love with earthy Julie Christie. The film, which spans several decades, features stirring crowd scenes and gorgeous romantic vistas, all set to the lush romantic music of Maurice Jarre. It's a very good movie but not the masterpiece it has been made out to be. The screenplay is uneven, and so much of the Pasternak novel is left out that the narrative flounders, and the film loses much of its momentum. Even Jarre's score, which gained so much popularity at the time, now seems repetitive and—well—jarring. Although the Lara theme hit the top of the charts when the movie first came out, today it seems manufactured and trite. Just compare it with the other ''Laura'' theme from the 1944 movie starring Gene Tierney, and the difference between a melodic tune and a classic melody becomes clear. Some critics praised it (with faint damnation) by calling it stately and respectable. Nevertheless, *Doctor Zhivago* became an enormously popular success and did much to leave an indelible impression on the minds of those kept in ignorance about Russian history or just what had been going on behind the iron curtain. In other words, the film took on a life of its own—baffling even those who made it—probably because it does all the things a movie is expected to do and does them according to the old MGM dictum: ''Do it big, do it right, and give it class.''

Awards: Academy Awards: Best Screenplay, Original Score (Jarre), Cinematography (Young), Art Direction (Box, Marsh), Costumes (Dalton); Golden Globe Awards: Best Picture, Actor (Sharif), Director; Academy Award Nominations: Best Supporting Actor (Courtenay), Director, Sound, Editing.

Selected Bibliography

Brownlow, Kevin. *David Lean: A Biography*. New York: St. Martin's Press, 1996.
Kael, Pauline. *Kiss Kiss, Bang Bang*. New York: Bantam, 1968.

DODSWORTH (1936), drama. Directed by William Wyler; with Walter Huston, Ruth Chatterton, Paul Lukas, Mary Astor, David Niven, Gregory Gaye, Maria Ouspenskaya, Spring Byington, and Grant Mitchell; screenplay by Sidney Howard.

Sidney Howard adapted his stage play from the Sinclair Lewis novel, and it is his play that is transferred faithfully to the screen under the expert care of master director William Wyler. It is the story of a middle-aged American industrialist who retires to Europe where he and his wife find a whole new set of values and relationships. The film has many things going for it, including an intelligent script, breathtaking cinematography, and excellent acting. Wyler uses the camera to expand upon the viewpoint and generally enhance the basically rich theme. Critics responded favorably to the film at the time of its release, praising its performances and its dialogue and its rare dignity and power. Even though it may strike modern audiences as somewhat stilted, *Dodsworth* is a superior film about common people with uncommon emotions.

Awards: New York Film Critics Circle Award: Best Actor (Huston); Academy Award: Best Interior Decoration (Richard Day); Academy Award Nominations: Best Picture, Director, Actor (Huston), Supporting Actress (Ouspenskaya), Screenplay (Howard), Sound.

Selected Bibliography

Anderegg, Michael A. *William Wyler*. Boston: Twayne, 1979.
Vermilye, Jerry. *The Films of the Thirties*. New York: Citadel Press, 1990.

DONEN, STANLEY. Director. Born on April 13, 1924, in Columbia, South Carolina. Educated at the University of South Carolina. Donen started out as a dancer and made his Broadway debut in 1940 as a chorus boy in *Pal Joey*, starring Gene Kelly. The next year he collaborated with Kelly on the choreography of *Best Foot Forward* and also appeared in the chorus. In 1943, when the film version of the musical was made, he was again co-choreographer and chorus boy. He subsequently choreographed or co-choreographed many other films, including *Cover Girl, Holiday in Mexico, No Leave No Love, This Time for Keeps, Big City, A Date with Judy*, and *Take Me Out to the Ball Game*. Donen made his directorial debut as Kelly's co-director of *On the Town*. He later co-directed with Kelly several acclaimed MGM musicals and on his own directed other musicals and light films. While his nonmusicals may be charming but forgettable, he will always be remembered for such classic musicals as *Singin' in the Rain* and *Funny Face*. He was fresh, creative, original, taking the musical outdoors (*Seven Brides for Seven Brothers, Pajama Game*) and always able to inspire superior performances from actors he loved and respected. In the 1960s, he worked mostly in Europe, where he directed *Charade*, his first and very successful venture into the suspense genre. He was less successful with *Arabesque*, but when he returned to light romance with *Two for the Road*, he proved he still had the touch. He married actress Yvette Mimieux in 1972.

Filmography: On the Town [co-dir. with Gene Kelly] (1949); Royal Wedding (1951); Singin' in the Rain [co-dir., co-chor. with Kelly], Love Is Better Than Ever, Fearless Fagan (1952); Give a Girl a Break [also co-chor.] (1953); Seven Brides for Seven Brothers, Deep in My Heart (1954); It's Always Fair Weather [co-dir., co-chor. with Kelly] (1955); Funny Face, The Pajama Game [co-dir., co-prod. with George Abbott], Kiss Them for Me (1957); Indiscreet [also prod.], Damn Yankees [co-dir., co-prod. with Abbott] (1958); Once More with Feeling, Surprise Package, The Grass Is Greener [all also prod.] (1960); Charade [also prod.] (1963); Arabesque [also prod.] (1966); Two for the Road, Bedazzled [both also prod.] (1967); Staircase [also prod.] (1969); The Little Prince [also prod.] (1974); Lucky Lady (1975); Movie Movie [also prod.] (1978); Saturn 3 [prod. only] (1980); Blame It on Rio (1984); Academy Award: Special Award (1997).

Honors: Los Angeles Film Critics Association: Life Achievement Award (1989).

Selected Bibliography

Casper, Joseph Andrew. *Stanley Donen*. Metuchen, NJ: Scarecrow Press, 1983.
Silverman, Stephen M. *Dancing on the Ceiling: Stanley Donen and His Movies*. New York: Knopf, 1996.

DOUBLE INDEMNITY (1944), drama. Directed by Billy Wilder; with Barbara Stanwyck, Fred MacMurray, Edward G. Robinson, Porter Hall, Fortunio Bonanova, and Jean Heather; screenplay by Billy Wilder and Raymond Chandler.

This is probably the most famous, certainly the most praised, and possibly the best movie of the film noir genre. In it Billy Wilder pulls out all the stops—and the tricks—to give this story the gritty feel of human depravity in both high and unexpected places. To begin with, he knows how to use black and white filming to exude the aroma of stealth and menace. Then he pulls a switch with his leads, turning the often tough but rarely nasty Barbara Stanwyck into brassy blond with a heart of stone. But most surprising and convincing of all is the spin he puts on Fred MacMurray's nice-guy persona, turning him into an easily manipulated wimp with a weakness for blonds and money. We may hate what he does, but we have trouble hating *him*. It's easier to blame her for taking advantage of his lack of character. Edward G. Robinson supplies the moral center in this grim tale ostensibly based on a sensational real-life case. The story is told in flashback with MacMurray supplying the weary voiceover, an element always compelling in a film noir melodrama. It is generally considered to be one of the darkest thrillers of its time, devoid of any trace of pity or love. Although time has turned this picture into a period piece, it survives as a classic because, while it evokes the sordid spirit of a time gone by, it is unflinching in its probing of the malice ever present in the dark side of the human soul.

Awards: Academy Award Nominations: Best Picture, Director, Actress (Stanwyck), Screenplay, B&W Cinematography, Score of a Dramatic Picture, Sound.

Selected Bibliography

Dickens, Homer. *The Films of Barbara Stanwyck*. Secaucus, NJ: Citadel Press, 1984.
Silver, Alain, and Elizabeth Ward, eds. *Film Noir: An Encyclopedic Reference to the American Style*. Woodstock, NY: Overlook Press, 1979.
Tuska, Jon. *Dark Cinema*. Westport, CT: Greenwood Press, 1984.

DOUGLAS, KIRK. Actor. Born Issur Danielovitch (later changed to Isidore Demsky) on December 9, 1916, in Amsterdam, New York, to illiterate Russian Jewish peasant immigrants. Educated at St. Lawrence University, where he excelled in wrestling and dabbled in school dramatics, and the American Academy of Dramatic Arts. Douglas made his Broadway debut in 1941, but after two minor successes, he left for World War II service in the navy. In 1945 he returned to Broadway in bigger parts and also did some radio work before embarking on a screen career the following year. After two or three relatively good parts, he hit it big in 1949 with an outstanding performance as an unscrupulous boxer punching his way to the top in *Champion*. It set the standard for the type of role he played best and most often in ensuing films—brash, aggressive, and self-centered. There is an intensity about Douglas that is unique and infuses all his performances, whether he is slave or viking, artist or detective, cowboy or war hero. Something basic, something blue-collar (some say something Slavic) comes through in every performance and turns Douglas into a loose-cannon sort of loner/everyman. Like so many icons of the silver screen, Douglas never received an Academy Award even though he made many films that have become classics. He was very convincing as the legendary trumpet player Bix Beiderbeck in *Young Man with a Horn* (1950), as the "gentleman caller" in *The Glass Menagerie* (1950), and as the tormented artist Van Gogh in *Lust for Life* (1956). He could be ruthless (*The Bad and the Beautiful*, 1952); he could be ambitious (*Ace in the Hole*, 1951); he could be heroic (*Ulysses*, 1955). Whether cowboy (*The Big Sky*, 1952) or colonel (*Paths of Glory*, 1957), Douglas took on challenging roles in everything from the classic noir film *Out of the Past* (1947) to the classic epic *Spartacus* (1960), his most ambitious film and the one he is likely to be remembered for longest. Douglas formed his own company, Bryna Productions, in 1955 and later formed another company, Joel Productions. In his later years, although he has remained remarkably active in film acting and production, he has involved himself tirelessly in humanitarian causes, for which he has received numerous awards. He is the father of actor-producer Michael Douglas. In addition to his autobiography, *The Ragman's Son*, he has published two novels: *Dance with the Devil* (1990) and *The Secret* (1992).

Filmography: The Strange Love of Martha Ivers (1946); Mourning Becomes Electra, Out of the Past (1947); I Walk Alone, The Walls of Jericho, My Dear Secretary (1948); A Letter to Three Wives, Champion (1949); Young Man with a Horn, The Glass Menagerie (1950); Along the Great Divide, The Big Carnival [originally titled Ace in the Hole], Detective Story (1951); The Big Trees, The Big Sky, The Bad and the Beautiful (1952); The Story of Three Loves, The Juggler (1953); Act of Love, 20,000 Leagues under the Sea (1954); The Racers, Ulisse/Ulysses [title role; It.], Man without a Star, The Indian Fighter (1955); Lust for Life [as Vincent Van Gogh] (1956); Top Secret Affair, Gunfight at the O.K. Corral [as Doc Holliday] (1957); Paths of Glory, The Vikings (1958); Last Train from Gun Hill, The Devil's Disciple (1959); Strangers When We Meet, Spartacus [title role; also exec. prod.] (1960); The Last Sunset, Town without Pity (1961); Lonely Are the Brave, Two Weeks in Another Town (1962); The Hook, The List of Adrian Messenger, For Love or Money (1963); Seven Days in May (1964); In Harm's Way, The Heroes of Telemark (1965); Cast a Giant Shadow, Is Paris Burning? [as General Patton] (1966); The Way West, The War Wagon (1967); A Lovely Way to Die, The Brotherhood (1968); The Arrangement (1969); There Was a Crooked Man (1970); Summertree [prod. only], The Light at the Edge of the World [also prod.], A Gunfight, Catch Me a Spy (1971); Un Uomo da Rispettare/The Master Touch [It.] (1972); Scalawag [also dir.] (1973); Once Is Not Enough, Posse [also dir., prod.] (1975); Holocaust 2000/The Chosen (1977); The Fury (1978); The Villain, Home Movies (1979); Saturn 3, The Final Countdown (1980); The Man from Snowy River (1982); Eddie Macon's Run (1983); Amos (TVM [TV movie], 1985); Tough Guys [also credit as Issur Danielovitch, creative consultant] (1986); Queenie (TVM, 1987); Oscar (1991); Welcome to Veraz (1992); Greedy (1994).

Honors: Academy Award Nomination: Best Actor (*Champion*, 1949); Academy Award Nomination: Best Actor (*The Bad and the Beautiful*, 1952); Golden Globe Award, New York Film Critics Circle Award, Academy Award Nomination: Best Actor (*Lust for Life*, 1956); Golden Globes: Cecil B. DeMille Award (1967); Presidential Medal of Freedom (1981); Jefferson Award for Public Service as Private Citizen (1983); American Cinema Award (1985); Chevalier of the Legion of Honor, France, for his Contribution to the Arts (1987); German Golden Kamera Award (1988); National Board of Review's Career

Achievement Award (1989); American Film Institute Lifetime Achievement Award (1991).

Selected Bibliography

Douglas, Kirk. *The Ragman's Son: An Autobiography*. New York: Simon and Schuster, 1988.

Munn, Michael. *Kirk Douglas*. New York: St. Martin's Press, 1985.

Thomas, Tony. *The Films of Kirk Douglas*. Secaucus, NJ: Citadel Press, 1972.

DOUGLAS, MELVYN. Actor. Born Melvyn Edouard Hesselberg on April 5, 1901, in Macon, Georgia; died on August 4, 1981. Douglas became interested in acting in high school and, after serving as a medic during World War I, made his stage debut in Chicago in 1919. After several years of touring with various companies, Douglas eventually made his Broadway debut in 1928 playing a gangster in *A Free Soul*. Other Broadway roles followed, but the turning point for him came with his success in *Tonight or Never*. Gloria Swanson asked for him to play opposite her in the film version, and other roles quickly followed including one as Greta Garbo's leading man in *As You Desire Me*. Dissatisfied with the way his film career was going, Douglas returned to Broadway as both actor and director. His film career revived, however, when he displayed a flair for comedy in *She Married Her Boss*, playing opposite Claudette Colbert. Douglas, the epitome of the word *dapper*, was perfect for romantic comedies, playing the suave, sophisticated leading man of such stars as Garbo, Colbert, Crawford, Dietrich, Loy, and Dunne. He was the man who made Garbo laugh in *Ninotchka*. In 1942 he went to Washington as the director of the Arts Council of the Office of Civilian Defense, and the following year he enlisted as a private in the army. Finding his film career unrewarding after he came back from the war, he returned to Broadway where he won a Tony Award for his portrayal of a presidential candidate in *The Best Man*. Douglas returned to films in the early 1960s as a character actor and was soon either winning awards or being nominated for them. He also began appearing on TV, winning an Emmy Award for *Do Not Go Gentle into That Good Night*.

Filmography: Tonight or Never (1931); Prestige, The Wiser Sex, Broken Wing, As You Desire Me, The Old Dark House (1932); The Vampire Bat, Nagana, Counsellor-at-Law (1933); Woman in the Dark, Dangerous Corner (1934); The People's Enemy, She Married Her Boss, Mary Burns Fugitive, Annie Oakley (1935); The Lone Wolf Returns [title role], And So They Were Married, The Gorgeous Hussy, Theodora Goes Wild (1936); Women of Glamour, Captains Courageous, I Met Him in Paris, Angel, I'll Take Romance (1937); Arsene Lupin Returns [title role], There's Always a Woman, The Toy Wife, Fast Company, That Certain Age, The Shining Hour, There's That Woman Again (1938); Tell No Tales, Good Girls Go to Paris, Ninotchka, The Amazing Mr. Williams (1939); Too Many Husbands, He Stayed for Breakfast, Third Finger Left Hand (1940); This Thing Called Love, That Uncertain Feeling, A Woman's Face, Our Wife, Two-Faced Woman (1941); We Were Dancing, They All Kissed the Bride (1942); Three Hearts for Julia (1943); The Sea of Grass, The Guilt of Janet Ames (1947); Mr. Blandings Builds His Dream House (1948); My Own True Love, A Woman's Secret, The Great Sinner

(1949); My Forbidden Past, On the Loose (1951); Billy Budd (1962); Hud (1963); Advance to the Rear, The Americanization of Emily (1964); Rapture (1965); Hotel (1967); I Never Sang for My Father (1970); One Is a Lonely Number, The Candidate (1972); Le Locataire/The Tenant [Fr.] (1976); Twilight's Last Gleaming (1977); The Seduction of Joe Tynan, Being There (1979); The Changeling, Tell Me a Riddle (1980); Ghost Story (1981).

Honors: Academy Award: Best Supporting Actor, National Board of Review Award: Supporting Actor (*Hud*, 1963); Academy Award Nomination: Best Actor (*I Never Sang for My Father*, 1970); Academy Award, Golden Globe Award, New York Film Critics Circle Award: Best Supporting Actor (*Being There*, 1979); Los Angeles Film Critics Association Award: Supporting Actor (*Being There* and *The Seduction of Joe Tynan*, 1979).

Selected Bibliography

Douglas, Melvyn, and Tom Arthur. *See You at the Movies: The Autobiography of Melvyn Douglas*. Lanham, MD: University Press of America, 1986.

DR. JEKYLL AND MR. HYDE (1932), horror. Directed by Rouben Mamoulian; with Fredric March, Miriam Hopkins, Rose Hobart, Holmes Herbert, and Halliwell Hobbes; screenplay by Samuel Hoffenstein and Percy Heath.

Of the many versions of this Robert Louis Stevenson horror classic, this is generally considered to be the best. Fredric March turns in a bravura performance as he vacillates between the tormented Dr. Jekyll and the malevolent Mr. Hyde. Although director Rouben Mamoulian tends to go too far with the pseudoscience at the beginning of the picture, this preoccupation with claptrap does not ultimately detract from a story that always seems to work at some level or other. This mid-Victorian treatment points up the Victorian fixation with lust and sexual repression and the lure of the gutter. The brutality is unbridled in this shocker, with the accent more on sex than violence. The psychological accuracy of Stevenson's vision becomes startlingly clear as one beholds March one moment as the kindly, genteel Dr. Jekyll, hopelessly pursuing the hand of the unattainable Rose Hobart, and the next moment as the brutal, depraved Mr. Hyde engaging in unbridled passion with the slut Miriam Hopkins. Film scholars still marvel at how Mamoulian and cameraman Karl Struss achieved the transformation scenes. It has been suggested that they used special filters or other techniques, but as yet the secret has never been revealed. This film was made two years before the Hays Office and its Production Codes came into existence. Thus, it contains scenes that were later cut, one ten-minute one showing Hyde abusing Hopkins, a scene that has never been reinstated. In fact, the film languished in obscurity for thirty years after MGM suppressed it in favor of its 1941 version. One can now understand why, since this 1932 version is the true classic, against which all other versions pale in comparison.

Awards: Academy Award: Best Actor (March); Academy Award Nominations: Best Screen Adaptation, Best Cinematography; Venice Film Festival Awards: Most Original and Fantastic Film, Favorite Actor (March).

Selected Bibliography

Milne, Tom. *Rouben Mamoulian*. Bloomington: Indiana University Press, 1970.
Peterson, Deborah C. *Fredric March: Craftsman First, Star Second*. Westport, CT: Greenwood Press, 1996.
Waller, Gregory. *American Horrors*. Urbana: University of Illinois Press, 1987.

DUCK SOUP (1933), comedy. Directed by Leo McCarey; with Groucho, Harpo, Chico, and Zeppo Marx, Margaret Dumont, Louis Calhern, Raquel Torres, Edgar Kennedy, Leonid Kinsky, and Charles Middleton; screenplay by Bert Kalmar, Harry Ruby, Arthur Sheekman, and Nat Perrin.

Duck Soup bombed when it was first released, but today it is considered a satiric masterpiece, the Marx Brothers' most sustained bit of insanity. With enough gags for five movies, the laughs come often, maybe too often, although in this instance, more care than usual seems to have been devoted to the timing. The story is a mythical kingdom burlesque that although it makes no sense on the surface, doesn't interfere with the enjoyment of this madcap romp. After all, it's not the story that counts but what goes on within it, and just about everything imaginable (and unimaginable) does. Critics now praise it as an imaginative spoof of war movie heroics and laud its totally irreverent attitude toward such sacred cows as patriotism, religion, diplomacy, courtroom justice, and anything even vaguely respectable. This film was such a slap at the rising fascists that Mussolini considered it a direct insult and banned the film in Italy. Naturally, the Marx Brothers were thrilled to hear that. It is interesting to note that the screenplay was written by, among others, those popular songwriters Bert Kalmar and Harry Ruby, famous for ''Three Little Words.''

Selected Bibliography

Gehring, Wes D. *The Marx Brothers: A Bio-Bibliography*. Westport, CT: Greenwood Press, 1987.
Lahue, Kalton C. *World of Laughter*. Norman: University of Oklahoma Press, 1966.
McCaffrey, Donald W. *The Golden Age of Sound Comedy: Comic Films and Comedians of the Thirties*. South Brunswick, NJ: A. S. Barnes, 1973.

E

EAST OF EDEN (1955), drama. Directed by Elia Kazan; with James Dean, Julie Harris, Raymond Massey, Jo Van Fleet, Burl Ives, Richard Davalos, and Albert Dekker; screenplay by Paul Osborn.

James Dean made his stunning screen debut in this haunting adaptation of John Steinbeck's novel about two brothers' rivalry for the love of their father. Critics reacted to it initially as if they had been jabbed with a cattle prod, twitching in all directions in their efforts to come to terms with a film they tried to hate but couldn't and a new talent they tried to ignore but couldn't take their eyes off. Overblown, overdone, overwrought they said of the film's lush musical score and heavy melodrama. Some called Dean a Brando copycat, but beneath all reviews of him, good or bad, it was clear that all found his performance riveting. It is equally clear that Dean is the incandescent center of this film, radiating powerful emotion in all directions, devastating amateurs who get too close (Davidson, the brother), and either inspiring great performances from good actors (Julie Harris) or superior performances from legendary figures (Raymond Massey). Massey despised Dean and his "method acting," and the intensity of Massey's animosity informs his impassioned performance, especially when it is clear that newcomer Dean is doing more than simply holding his own against a seasoned veteran. Jo Van Fleet was an accomplished actress, but maybe she got that edge that won her the Oscar by crossing swords with Dean. Certainly the two probe every nuance of Oedipal fever. If it's true, as some critics think, that the picture is as long-winded and bloated with biblical allegory as the book, it is nevertheless a film of great performances, of wondrous photography, and a very real sense of time and place. There is admittedly a feverish, high-strung quality to the movie, dotted with moments of violence and scenes that lack coherence, but this very intensity gives the film its neurotic momentum. And it's been said about Dean that although his father doesn't love him, the camera does. Again and again we see loving closeups of a young man overcome with romantic desperation. It is a strange movie—but never a dull one. It is also an unforgettable one, one that has become a staple on the American Movie Channel and a cult favorite among Dean fans.

Awards: Academy Award: Best Supporting Actress (Jo Van Fleet); Golden Globe Awards: Best Picture (Drama), Best Dramatic Actor [Posthumous Award] (Dean), Outstanding Directorial Achievement; National Board of Review Award: Best American Film; Cannes Film Festival Award: Best Dramatic Film; Academy Award Nominations: Best Director, Actor (Dean), Screenplay.

Selected Bibliography

Pauly, Thomas H. *An American Odyssey: Elia Kazan and American Culture.* Philadelphia: Temple University Press, 1983.
Whitman, Mark. *The Films of James Dean.* London: Barnden Castell Williams Ltd., 1974.

EDDY, NELSON. Singer, actor. Born on June 29, 1901, in Providence, Rhode Island; died on March 6, 1967. Eddy started out singing in church choirs as a boy soprano. In his teens he moved to Philadelphia, where he worked at various jobs before winning a competition in 1922 to join the Philadelphia Civic Opera. In 1924 he sang the role of Tonio in *Pagliacci* at the New York Metropolitan Opera. A very successful concert tour and several radio appearances during the 1930s led to a movie contract with MGM. When the studio teamed him with Jeanette MacDonald, the duo enjoyed tremendous popularity throughout the 1930s, mostly in silly but charming operettas beginning with *Naughty Marietta* in 1935. They were billed as ''America's Sweethearts'' or the ''Singing Sweethearts'' and occupy a place in the cinema of that day that, in its own way, rivals the popularity of Astaire and Rogers. The decade of their greatest popularity was one during which audiences yearned for escape, and one way to escape was to remember the age of the great operettas that had flourished up until the end of the 1920s. Film allowed this beloved genre to be carried to the remotest corners of the nation and to sustain its appeal beyond its decline on the stage. Eddy was faulted for being wooden, but many of his roles called for manly sobriety, and anyway, he was doing the gentlemanly thing by deflecting attention to his co-star, a courtesy Mario Lanza never learned. When his partnership with MacDonald ended in 1942 with *I Married an Angel*, Eddy's film career was effectively over. He continued to appear in concerts and nightclubs, performing right up to the end when in 1967, while touring Australia, he collapsed on stage and died of a stroke.

Filmography: Broadway to Hollywood, Dancing Lady (1933); Student Tour (1934); Naughty Marietta (1935); Rose Marie (1936); Maytime, Rosalie (1937); The Girl of the Golden West, Sweethearts (1938); Let Freedom Ring!, Balalaika (1939); New Moon, Bitter Sweet (1940); The Chocolate Soldier (1941); I Married an Angel (1942); The

Phantom of the Opera (1943); Knickerbocker Holiday (1944): Make Mine Music [voice only] (1946); Northwest Outpost (1947).

Selected Bibliography

Castanza, Philip. *The Films of Jeanette MacDonald and Nelson Eddy*. Secaucus, NJ: Citadel Press, 1981.
Kiner, Larry F. *Nelson Eddy: A Bio-Discography*. Metuchen, NJ: Scarecrow Press, 1992.
Rich, Sharon. *Sweethearts: The Timeless Love Affair—on Screen and off—between Jeanette MacDonald and Nelson Eddy*. New York: Donald I. Fine, 1994.

EDGE OF THE CITY (1957), drama. Directed by Martin Ritt; with John Cassavetes, Sidney Poitier, Jack Warden, Ruby Dee, Kathleen Maguire, and Ruth White; screenplay by Robert Alan Aurthur.

This somber account of New York City waterfront life and corruption has echoes of *On the Waterfront* in it, especially in its gritty realism and its absolute sincerity. The friendship between a white army deserter and a black dock worker, both of whom are in conflict with a union racketeer, provides the basis for sober reflections on integration and integrity, especially at the lower rung of society. The acting lifts the film above propaganda, and Ritt's debut as director is very impressive. In addition to Ritt, producer David Susskind and writer Robert Alan Arthur were also making their first film venture, their roots having been in television. This was an early example of the new influence of TV on film, and it woke up a lot of people. It is to the film's credit that it does not present itself as a message movie about race relations. The black-white component is there almost by accident, the focus being on Poitier's befriending Cassavetes, a disturbed loner who feels he doesn't belong with anybody. The race issue surfaces when their boss resents their friendship. Although generally praised, perhaps too highly precisely because of the sensitive race issue, some critics do express thoughtful reservations. Some think it as artificial as an MGM musical (closer to *On the Town* than *On the Waterfront*) and point out, along the way, that the Leonard Rosenman score is an assault on the audience's ears. Others find the Poitier character whiter than white. However, given its time period and its bold message, *Edge of the City* is a provocative milestone in socially sensitive filmmaking.

Selected Bibliography

Carney, Raymond. *The Films of John Cassavetes: Pragmatism, Modernism, and the Movies*. New York: Cambridge University Press, 1994.
Jackson, Carlton. *Picking Up the Tab: The Life and Movies of Martin Ritt*. Bowling Green, OH: Bowling Green State University Popular Press, 1994.
Keyser, Lester J. *The Cinema of Sidney Poitier: The Black Man's Changing Role on the American Screen*. South Brunswick, NJ: A. S. Barnes, 1980.

EDWARDS, BLAKE. Director, producer, screenwriter, former actor. Born William Blake McEdwards on July 26, 1922, in Tulsa, Oklahoma. Edwards got into films in the early 1940s as an actor, appearing in minor roles in such pictures as *A Guy Named Joe* and *The Best Years of Our Lives*. He was more interested in screenwriting and directing than in acting, and after a few years as a screenwriter, he made his debut as a film director in 1955 with *My Sister Eileen*. Edwards worked in both film and television where his flamboyant style and vitality led to a string of successes throughout the late 1950s and early 1960s. Among his television successes were the highly popular *Peter Gunn* and *Mr. Lucky*. The movies he directed during that time were varied and included the farcical *Operation Petticoat*, the romantic *Breakfast at Tiffany's*, the suspenseful *Experiment in Terror*, the bleak *Days of Wine and Roses*, and the hilarious Inspector Clouseau spoofs, *The Pink Panther* and *A Shot in the Dark*. The failure at the box office of his slapstick extravaganza *The Great Race* precipitated a decade-long decline, culminating in his self-exile to England, where he managed a remarkable comeback with the first of several sequels to *The Pink Panther*. After that he had three straight hits including *Victor/Victoria*, the film most critics consider his best. Julie Andrews, his wife since 1969, starred in the film and also played the lead in the stage version of this musical in the mid-1990s.

Filmography: [as screenwriter, alone or in collaboration]: Panhandle [also co-prod., act.), Leather Gloves [also act.] (1948); Stampede [also co-prod.] (1949); Sound Off, Rainbow 'Round My Shoulder (1952); All Ashore, Cruisin' Down the River (1953); Drive a Crooked Road, The Atomic Kid [story only] (1954); My Sister Eileen (1955); Operation Mad Ball (1957); The Couch [story only], Walk on the Wild Side [additional scenes only, uncredited], The Notorious Landlady (1962); Soldier in the Rain (1963); Inspector Clouseau (1968). [as director]: Bring Your Smile Along [also co-story, sc.] (1955); He Laughed Last [also co-story, sc.] (1956); Mister Cory [also sc.] (1957); This Happy Feeling [also sc.] (1958); The Perfect Furlough, Operation Petticoat (1959); High Time (1960); Breakfast at Tiffany's (1961); Experiment in Terror [also prod.] (1962); Days of Wine and Roses (1963); The Pink Panther [also co-sc.], A Shot in the Dark [also prod., co-sc.] (1964); The Great Race [also co-story] (1965); What Did You Do in the War Daddy? [also prod., co-story] (1966); Gunn [also story, co-sc.] (1967); The Party [also prod., story, co-sc.] (1968); Darling Lili [also prod., co-sc.] (1970); Wild Rovers [also co-prod., sc.] (1971); The Carey Treatment (1972); The Tamarind Seed [also sc.] (1974); The Return of the Pink Panther [also prod., co-sc.] (1975); The Pink Panther Strikes Again [also prod., co-sc.] (1976); Revenge of the Pink Panther [also prod., story, co-sc.] (1978); 10 [also prod., sc.] (1979); S.O.B. [also co-prod., sc.] (1981); Victor/Victoria [also co-prod., sc.], Trail of the Pink Panther [also co-prod., co-sc.] (1982); Curse of the Pink Panther [also co-prod., co-sc.], The Man Who Loved Women [also co-prod., co-sc.] (1983); Micki and Maude (1984); A Fine Mess, That's Life! [also co-sc.] (1986); Blind Date (1987); Sunset [also sc.] (1988); Skin Deep [also sc.] (1989); Switch [also sc.] (1991); Son of the Pink Panther [also sc.] (1993).

Honors: French César Award: Best Foreign Film, Italian David Di Donatello Award: Best Foreign Film (*Victor/Victoria*, 1982); Los Angeles Film Critics Association Life Achievement Award (1990).

Selected Bibliography

Lehman, Peter, and William Luhr. *Blake Edwards*. Athens: Ohio University Press, 1981.
Sennett, Ted. *Great Movie Directors*. New York: Harry N. Abrams, 1986.

F

FATHER OF THE BRIDE (1950), comedy. Directed by Vincente Minnelli; with Spencer Tracy, Elizabeth Taylor, Don Taylor, Joan Bennett, Billie Burke, Leo G. Carroll, and Rusty (Russ) Tamblyn; screenplay by Frances Goodrich and Albert Hackett.

"The bride gets the thrills! Father gets the bills!" went the blurb for this thoroughly enchanting comedy about the trials and tribulations a middle-aged family man faces when the daughter he dotes on decides to get married. Some critics find the film fascinating for the dark undercurrents coursing beneath the comedy, pointing especially to the father's obvious jealousy, insecurity, and fears about getting old. Others are mildly offended by its sit-com qualities and its conventional middle-class view of normal romance and marriage among the waspy prosperous people in their waspy suburban homes. Whatever its faults in hindsight, it is a classic piece of MGM fluff with an uncannily accurate eye for what the audiences wanted. It is not a "film" or a "motion picture," nor was it intended to be. What it is, is a Movie, and as with all real Movies, it dazzles the eye with lavish sets, choreographed action (remember, Minnelli directed musicals), and the presence of superstars like Spencer Tracy and Elizabeth Taylor. And let's not forget Joan Bennett, a leading lady in her own right who looks like she could really be Taylor's mother. In context, this one is a winner. Updating it, as the 1991 version tried to do, only smothers it with clumsiness. Spencer Tracy's exasperation as the frustrated father is not a matter of scripting or even of acting but of becoming the character in a way no method actor could ever hope to approach.

Awards: Academy Award Nominations: Best Picture, Actor (Tracy), Screenplay.

Selected Bibliography

Deschner, Donald. *The Films of Spencer Tracy*. New York: Citadel Press, 1968.
Minnelli, Vincente. *I Remember It Well*. London: Angus and Robertson, 1975.
Vermilye, Jerry. *The Films of Elizabeth Taylor*. New York: Beaufort Books, 1982.

FAYE, ALICE. Actress. Born Alice Jeanne Leppert on May 5, 1912, in New York City; died on May 9, 1998. By the time she was fourteen, Faye was already dancing and singing professionally. In 1931 Rudy Vallee picked her out of the chorus line of Broadway's *George White's Scandals* and signed her to tour with his band as a singer. Later it was Vallee who insisted that Fox give her a part in the film version of *George White's Scandals* (1934). When Lillian Harvey, the intended star, walked off the set, Faye was given the lead, in spite of George White's objections. Soon she was signed to a Fox contract and cast as a bleached blond in the Harlow mold. However, she quickly distinguished herself from the other bleachers in the crowd with her distinctive husky speaking voice and contralto singing, and she soon found herself a leading star of light musical films. Because she was always fighting with studio boss Darryl F. Zanuck, Zanuck hired Betty Grable in 1940 deliberately to challenge Faye's position. It worked, and it was not long before Grable took Faye's place as Fox's top musical star, even surpassing her in popularity. In 1945, after an unfortunate appearance in the drama *Fallen Angel,* Faye walked out on her contract and retired from the screen. She returned in 1962 for an isolated appearance as Pat Boone's mother in *State Fair* (1962), but she was miscast, and the movie bombed. In 1973–1974 she was reunited with former screen partner John Payne in a stage revival of the musical *Good News*. She made her last appearance on the screen in 1978 in *Every Girl Should Have One* and *The Magic of Lassie.* In her best films, Faye exudes the aura of a tarnished but tough girl with a heart of gold who's been around and is now down on her luck. If the studio had capitalized on that offbeat image, Faye might have enjoyed greater success. She fits best in a saloon, not at a state fair. To think of 20th Century–Fox playing dominoes with Faye, bumping her in favor of Grable, then bumping Grable in favor of Monroe, is oddly reminiscent of Fox's own *All about Eve* with its scenario of a younger star waiting in the wings to take over from an older star the minute she gets a chance.

Filmography: George White's Scandals, Now I'll Tell, She Learned About Sailors, 365 Nights in Hollywood (1934); George White's 1935 Scandals, Every Night at Eight, Music Is Magic (1935); King of Burlesque, Poor Little Rich Girl, Sing Baby Sing, Stowaway (1936); On the Avenue, Wake Up and Live, You Can't Have Everything, You're a Sweetheart (1937); In Old Chicago, Sally Irene and Mary, Alexander's Ragtime Band (1938); Tail Spin, Rose of Washington Square, Hollywood Cavalcade, Barricade (1939); Little Old New York, Lillian Russell [title role], Tin Pan Alley (1940); That Night in Rio, The Great American Broadcast, Weekend in Havana (1941); Hello Frisco Hello, The Gang's All Here (1943); Four Jills in a Jeep [cameo] (1944); Fallen Angel (1945); State Fair (1962); Won Ton Ton—The Dog Who Saved Hollywood [cameo] (1976); Every Girl Should Have One, The Magic of Lassie (1978).

Selected Bibliography

Moshier, W. Franklyn. *The Alice Faye Movie Book*. Harrisburg, PA: Stackpole, 1974.

Rivadue, Barry. *Alice Faye: A Bio-Bibliography*. Westport, CT: Greenwood Press, 1990.

FIELDS, W. C. Actor, screenwriter. Born William Claude Dukenfield on February 10, 1879, in Philadelphia; died on December 25, 1946. Fields ran away from home at age eleven, and for several months thereafter, he almost starved and was reduced to stealing when he could not find work. Street life was extremely rough, and Fields was routinely beaten in street brawls, one of which resulted in his grotesquely bulbous nose. He also spent many nights in jail. Later, when he was an adult, it was these bitter childhood experiences that resulted in the gleeful misanthropy that characterized Fields's personality on and off screen. Hired as juggler at an amusement park when he was fourteen, he went on to become a vaudeville headliner before he was twenty. In 1905 he appeared in his first Broadway play, *The Ham Tree*, and in 1915 made his film debut, an isolated screen appearance in a short called *Pool Sharks*. It was ten years before he made his next film. Meanwhile, Fields worked hard to secure his position as a stage star, appearing in every version of the *Ziegfeld Follies* from 1915 to 1921, as well as in *George White's Scandals*. In 1923 he starred in the hit Broadway musical comedy *Poppy*. Two years later he appeared in the film version of that play, retitled *Sally of the Sawdust* and directed by D. W. Griffith. Fields appeared in a number of silent films, but he was not really in his element until sound arrived and his inimitable raspy voice could put the final spin on his comic characterizations. Although he is best remembered for his many comedy roles, Fields gave one of his best performances as Mr. Micawber in *David Copperfield* (1935). Fields wrote the screenplays for many of his films, using such weird pseudonyms as Otis J. Criblecoblis and Mahatma Kane Jeeves. In this way he could incorporate his biases into his films. He was not exactly a lovable figure, but the men in his audiences came to identify with him, sharing many of his own gripes, so much so that his popularity continues to this day, and he has become something of a cult personality. Fields was portrayed by Rod Steiger in the film biography *W. C. Fields and Me* (1976).

Filmography: Pool Sharks [short] (1915); Janice Meredith (1924); Sally of the Sawdust (1925); That Royle Girl, It's the Old Army Game, So's Your Old Man (1926); The Potters, Running Wild, Two Flaming Youths (1927); Tillie's Punctured Romance, Fools for Luck (1928); The Golf Specialist [short] (1930); Her Majesty Love (1931); The Dentist [short; also sc.], Million Dollar Legs, If I Had a Million (1932); The Fatal Glass of Beer [also sc.], The Pharmacist [short; also sc.], The Barber Shop [short; also sc.], International House, Tillie and Gus, Alice in Wonderland [as Humpty-Dumpty] (1933); Six of a Kind, You're Telling Me, The Old-Fashioned Way [also story under pseudonym Charles Bogle], Mrs. Wiggs of the Cabbage Patch, It's a Gift [also story under pseudonym Charles Bogle] (1934); David Copperfield [as Micawber], Mississippi, The Man on the Flying Trapeze [also story under pseudonym Charles Bogle] (1935); Poppy (1936); The Big Broadcast of 1938 (1938); You Can't Cheat an Honest Man [also story under pseudonym Charles Bogle] (1939); My Little Chicadee [also co-sc. with Mae West], The Bank Dick [also story under pseudonym Mahatma Kane Jeeves] (1940); Never Give a Sucker an Even Break [also story under pseudonym Otis Criblecoblis] (1941); Tales of Manhattan [a 20-minute episode that was eliminated from the final release print of the film but can be found in some private collections] (1942); Follow the Boys [cameo, in billiard routine], Song of the Open Road [as himself], Sensations [cameo] (1944).

Selected Bibliography

Fields, Ronald J. *W. C. Fields: A Life on Film*. New York: St. Martin's Press, 1984.
Gehring, Wes D. *W. C. Fields: A Bio-Bibliography*. Westport, CT: Greenwood Press, 1984.
Rocks, David T. *W. C. Fields: An Annotated Guide*. Jefferson, NC: McFarland, 1993.

FLYNN, ERROL. Actor. Born on June 20, 1909, in Hobart, Tasmania; died on October 14, 1959. Flynn at his peak during the 1930s and early 1940s was the essence of gallantry and derring-do, a cheerful adventurer with astounding skills but a self-deprecating wit who became everybody's idea of what a buccaneer or a swordsman or a Robin Hood should look and act like. From the start, Flynn marched to a different drummer. The son of a distinguished Australian marine biologist and zoologist, he attended many good schools in Australia and England and was expelled from most of them. At fifteen he began clerking for a Sydney shipping company, and at sixteen he sailed to New Guinea to enter government service, but his restless spirit sidetracked him and he embarked on a search for gold. In 1930 he returned to Sydney, purchased a boat, which he christened *Sirocco*, and sailed back to New Guinea with three friends. He later described this seven-month sea voyage in his first of three books, *Beam Ends* (1937). In New Guinea he became manager of a tobacco plantation while at the same time writing a newspaper column for the Sydney *Bulletin*. Once again in Australia, he was offered the role of Fletcher Christian in a semidocumentary feature-length film, *In the Wake of the Bounty*. In 1933 he went to England, where he joined the Northampton Repertory Company. This exposure led to the leading role in a low-budget mystery film produced by Warner's London branch, and out of this came a Hollywood contract. Flynn arrived in Hollywood in 1935 and became an overnight sensation as the star of *Captain Blood*. Flynn proved to be ideally cast as a dashing swashbuckler. He was tall and athletic and exceptionally handsome. These qualities along with his engaging personality made huge successes of the movies that followed, such as *The Charge of the Light Brigade*, *The Adventures of Robin Hood*, and *The Sea Hawk*. His image as a fearless fighter for justice and a noble leader of men gained him a large and enthusiastic following. But Flynn was equally adept at other action roles such as a gunfighter in epic westerns beginning with *Dodge City* and a soldier in a number of World War II films, most notably *Objective Burma!* As Jack L. Warner noted in his autobiography, *My First Hundred Years in Hollywood*, ''To the Walter Mittys of the world he was all the heroes in one magnificent, sexy, animal package.'' Much to his chagrin, Flynn was barred from the armed services because of a heart defect, recurrent malaria, and latent tuberculosis. Flynn owed much of his sustained popularity to the brilliance of two directors: Michael Curtiz (*Captain Blood*, etc.), from 1935 to 1941, and Raoul Walsh (*Desperate Journey*, etc.), from 1942 to 1945. He also paired well with Alan Hale as his burly sidekick and with Olivia de Havilland, who was his leading lady in several films including *Robin Hood* and *They Died with Their Boots On*, a historically inaccurate film but a wonderfully moving and exciting movie. Flynn's popularity began to slip in the late 1940s, and he added drugs to his heavy smoking and drinking. In 1952 Flynn gave up on Hollywood and went to Europe to try to put his career back together, but the series of flops he made there only worsened his condition. He finally lost everything on *William Tell*, a movie that was never completed. He returned to Hollywood in 1956, and the following year, he received surprisingly good reviews for his performance as a drunken wastrel in *The Sun Also Rises*. He went on to play drunks in his next two films as well, *Too Much Too Soon* (as John Barrymore) and *The Roots of Heaven*. His last picture, *Cuban Rebel Girls*, is a ridiculous semidocumentary tribute to Fidel Castro, which Flynn also wrote, narrated, and co-produced. Flynn died of a heart attack on October 14, 1959, in Vancouver, Canada, at the age of fifty. In a sensational 1980 biography, *Errol Flynn, the Untold Story*, Charles Higham suggested that Flynn had been a Nazi agent working for the Gestapo and a bisexual who had affairs with several male celebrities, among them, by his own admission, Truman Capote.

Filmography: In the Wake of the Bounty [as Fletcher Christian] (1933); Murder at Monte Carlo, The Case of the Curious Bride, Don't Bet on Blondes, Captain Blood [title role] (1935); The Charge of the Light Brigade (1936); Green Light, The Prince and the Pauper [as Miles Hendon], Another Dawn, The Perfect Specimen (1937); The Adventures of Robin Hood [as Robin Hood], Four's a Crowd, The Sisters, The Dawn Patrol (1938); Dodge City, The Private Lives of Elizabeth and Essex [as the Earl of Essex] (1939); Virginia City, The Sea Hawk, Santa Fe Trail (1940); Footsteps in the Dark, Dive Bomber (1941); They Died with Their Boots On [as General Custer], Desperate Journey, Gentleman Jim [as boxer James J. Corbett] (1942); Edge of Darkness, Thank Your Lucky Stars [cameo], Northern Pursuit (1943); Uncertain Glory (1944); Objective Burma!, San Antonio, Never Say Goodbye (1946); Cry Wolf, Escape Me Never (1947); Silver River (1948); Adventures of Don Juan [as Don Juan], It's a Great Feeling [cameo], That Forsyte Woman [as Soames Forsyte] (1949); Montana, Rocky Mountain (1950); Kim [as Mahbub Ali], Hello God [semidocumentary feature], Adventures of Captain Fabian [also sc.] (1951); Mara Maru, Against All Flags, Cruise of the Zaca [color two-reeler record of Flynn's 1946 cruise to the South Seas; also dir. and narr.], Deep-Sea Fishing [one reel] (1952); The Master of Ballantrae (1953); Il Maestro di Don Giovanni/Crossed Swords, William Tell [title role; unfinished], Lilacs in the Spring/Let's Make Up (1954); The Dark Avenger/The Warriors [as Prince Edward], King's Rhapsody (1955); Istanbul (1956); The Big Boodle, The Sun Also Rises [as Mike Campbell] (1957); Too Much Too Soon [as John Barrymore], The Roots of Heaven (1958); Cuban Rebel Girls [also sc., co-prod., narr.] (1959).

Selected Bibliography

Higham, Charles. *Errol Flynn: The Untold Story*. Garden City, NY: Doubleday, 1980.
Thomas, Tony, Rudy Behlmer, and Clifford McCarty. *The Films of Errol Flynn*. New York: Citadel Press, 1969.
Valenti, Peter. *Errol Flynn: A Bio-Bibliography*. Westport, CT: Greenwood Press, 1984.

FOLLOW THE FLEET (1936), musical. Directed by Mark Sandrich; with Fred Astaire, Ginger Rogers, Randolph Scott, Harriet Hilliard (Nelson), Astrid Allwyn, and Betty Grable; screenplay by Dwight Taylor and Allan Scott.

Follow the Fleet is one of those classic, inimitable, Astaire-Rogers 1930s diversions that mix shamelessly silly plots with brilliant music and marvelous dance routines. Most savvy critics are ready to excuse the imperfections in a movie like this as long as they are confined to the story because that's the way musicals are (or used to be before they got ''serious'' and starting spouting messages and flaunting concepts and trying eventually to become opera—and thus respectable). In this delightful film, the story never detracts from the important element—the Astaire-Rogers musical routines. There are seven songs, all by the dean of American popular music, Irving Berlin, the most memorable being ''Let's Face the Music and Dance,'' a haunting melody that manages to be both somber and carefree, a reflection, so it seems, of the contemporary depression mood. The film seems overlong to some critics and uneven to others, but most of them focus on what the audience has come for: the Astaire-Rogers magic. This is the dancing duo at their most buoyant.

Selected Bibliography

Croce, Arlene. *The Fred Astaire & Ginger Rogers Book*. New York: Outerbridge & Lazard, 1972.
Feuer, Jane. *The Hollywood Musical*. Bloomington: Indiana University Press, 1982.
Mueller, John E. *Astaire Dancing: The Musical Films*. New York: Knopf, 1985.

FONDA, HENRY. Actor. Born on May 16, 1905, in Grand Island, Nebraska; died on August 12, 1982. Educated at the University of Minnesota (journalism). Fonda dropped out of college halfway through his studies and became an office boy at an Omaha credit company. In 1925, a friend of the family (who just happened to be the mother of then one-year-old Marlon Brando) asked Fonda to play the leading role in an amateur production at the Omaha Community Playhouse. He jumped at the chance, quit his office boy job, and stayed with the company for three years, receiving a small salary for doubling as the manager's assistant. In 1928, he was playing a lead in New England summer stock when he got in with a group of young theater hopefuls who were forming their own company, the University Players. The group included Joshua Logan, Myron McCormick, Margaret Sullavan, Mildred Natwick, and James Stewart. Fonda did a walk-on in a Broadway play in 1929 and later some other bit parts, but it was with the University Players that he honed his acting style. In 1934, Fonda got rave reviews for the title role in *The Farmer Takes a Wife*, a part he then repeated with enormous success in Hollywood. By the end of the decade he was known and admired all over the world. Fonda is generally considered to be the quintessential American midwestern male with just a hint of a whine in his voice, a touch of homespun in his demeanor, a streak of stubbornness in his attitude, and a whole lot of grit and integrity in his upright behavior. His most representative portrayal remains that of Tom Joad, the young idealistic everyman of *Grapes of Wrath*. He is so sincere, so determined, so brave in the face of overwhelming odds that you never doubt that justice has to be on his side. These same qualities also highlight his performance as the quietly stubborn holdout juror in *12 Angry Men*. In 1942, Fonda enlisted in the navy, eventually earning a commission and several medals. After the war, Fonda made several excellent John Ford westerns before returning to the stage to play *Mister Roberts*, a role he repeated in the film version. He also appeared in *The Caine Mutiny Court-Martial*, and from the mid-1950s on, he alternated between the screen and the stage, meanwhile finding time for two TV series and several TV specials. Fonda was gravely ill during the production of his last film, *On Golden Pond* (1981), for which he received an Oscar just months before his death in 1982.

Filmography: The Farmer Takes a Wife, Way Down East, I Dream Too Much (1935); The Trail of the Lonesome Pine, The Moon's Our Home, Spendthrift (1936); You Only Live Once, Wings of the Morning, Slim, That Certain Woman (1937); I Met My Love Again, Jezebel, Blockade, Spawn of the North, The Mad Miss Manton (1938); Jesse James [as Frank James], Let Us Live, The Story of Alexander Graham Bell [as Bell's associate Thomas Augustus Watson], Young Mr. Lincoln [as Abraham Lincoln], Drums along the Mohawk (1939); The Grapes of Wrath [as Tom Joad], Lillian Russell, The Return of Frank James [again as Frank James], Chad Hanna (1940); The Lady Eve, Wild Geese Calling, You Belong to Me (1941); The Male Animal, Rings on Her Fingers, The Magnificent Dope, Tales of Manhattan, The Big Street (1942); The Immortal Sergeant, The Ox-Bow Incident (1943); My Darling Clementine [as Wyatt Earp] (1946); The Long Night, The Fugitive, Daisy Kenyon (1947); A Miracle Can Happen/On Our Merry Way, Fort Apache (1948); Jigsaw [cameo] (1949); Mister Roberts [title role] (1955); War and Peace [as Pierre] (1956); The Wrong Man, 12 Angry Men [also co-prod.], The Tin Star (1957); Stage Struck (1958); Warlock, The Man Who Understood Women (1959); Advise and Consent, The Longest Day [as Brig. Gen. Theodore Roosevelt, Jr.], How the West Was Won (1962); Spencer's Mountain (1963); The Best Man, Fail Safe [as "The President"], Sex and the Single Girl (1964); The Rounders, In Harm's Way, Battle of the Bulge, Guerre secrète/The Dirty Game (1965); A Big Hand for the Little Lady (1966); Welcome to Hard Times, Stranger on the Run (1967); Firecreek, Madigan, Yours Mine and Ours, The Boston Strangler, C'era una volta il West/Once Upon a Time in the West (1969); The Cheyenne Social Club, There Was a Crooked Man . . . , Too Late the Hero (1970); Sometimes a Great Notion/Never Give an Inch (1971); Le Serpent/The Serpent, Il Mio Nome e Messuno/My Name Is Nobody, Ash Wednesday (1973); Mussolini Ultimo Atto/Mussolini The Last Act/Mussolini The Last Four Days (1974); Midway [as Admiral Chester W. Nimitz], The Last of the Cowboys/The Great Smokey Roadblock (1976); Tentacoli/Tentacles, il Grande Attaco/La Battaglia di Mareth/The Biggest Battle, Roller-coaster (1977); The Swarm, Fedora [cameo] (1978); Meteor, City on Fire, Wanda Nevada (1979); On Golden Pond (1981).

Honors: Academy Award Nomination: Best Actor (*The Grapes of Wrath*, 1940); British Academy Award: Best Actor/Foreign (*12 Angry Men*, 1957); American Film Institute Lifetime Achievement Award (1978); Golden Globes: Cecil B. DeMille Award (1979); Academy Award: Special Award (The consummate actor, in recognition of his brilliant accomplishments and enduring contribution to the art of motion pictures; winner presented a statuette, 1980); Academy Award, Golden Globe Award, National Board of Review Award: Best Actor (*On Golden Pond*, 1981).

Selected Bibliography

Roberts, Allen, and Max Goldstein. *Henry Fonda: A Biography*. Jefferson, NC: McFarland, 1984.

Sweeney, Kevin. *Henry Fonda: A Bio-Bibliography*. Westport, CT: Greenwood Press, 1992.

Thomas, Tony. *The Films of Henry Fonda*. Secaucus, NJ: Citadel Press, 1983.

FONTAINE, JOAN. Actress. Born Joan de Beauvoir de Havilland on October 22, 1917, in Tokyo to British parents. Fontaine, the sister of Olivia de Havilland, trailed behind de Havilland early in her career, but when she did catch up, she surpassed her and wound up winning an Oscar nomination at the age of twenty-three and the Oscar itself at twenty-four. She made her screen debut in 1935 under the name of Joan Burfield in a minor part in the Joan Crawford film *No More Ladies*, but she didn't begin appearing regularly in films until 1937. Except for *A Damsel in Distress* opposite Fred Astaire and *Gunga Din* opposite Douglas Fairbanks, most of her films were B pictures. It was not until the early 1940s that her career took off, thanks to leads in two Hitchcock films. She was nominated for an Oscar for *Rebecca* and *The Constant Nymph* and won the Academy Award, as well as the New York Film Critics Award, for her performance in *Suspicion* in 1941. Fontaine subsequently starred in many films with mixed success. Her image as shy and simpering clung to her after *Rebecca, Suspicion,* and *Jane Eyre*, an image many viewers found cloying. However, it worked particularly well for her in a neglected movie of the late 1940s, *Letter from an Unknown Woman*, in which she plays the romantic heroine of this Stefan Zweig tragedy to perfection. Later she worked hard to reinvent herself as a sophisticated but often bitchy and scheming woman of the world. In the 1940s and 1950s, gossip columnists prattled about the feuds between the sisters, but it seems likely that, beyond normal professional rivalry, most of the rumors were the work of publicity agents. In the 1957 film *Island in the Sun*, Fontaine became one of the first leading ladies to engage in an interracial romance, in this case with Harry Belafonte.

Filmography: [as Joan Burfield]: No More Ladies (1935). [as Joan Fontaine]: Quality Street, The Man Who Found Himself, You Can't Beat Love, Music for Madame, A Damsel in Distress, A Million to One (1937); Maid's Night Out, Blonde Cheat, Sky Giant, The Duke of West Point (1938); Gunga Din, Man of Conquest, The Women (1939); Rebecca (1940); Suspicion (1941); This Above All (1942); The Constant Nymph (1943); Jane Eyre [title role], Frenchman's Creek (1944); The Affairs of Susan (1945);

From This Day Forward (1946); Ivy (1947); The Emperor Waltz, Kiss the Blood Off My Hands, Letter from an Unknown Woman, You Gotta Stay Happy (1948); Born to Be Bad (1950); September Affair, Darling How Could You! (1951); Something to Live For, Ivanhoe [as Lady Rowena] (1952); Decameron Nights, Flight to Tangier, The Bigamist (1953); Casanova's Big Night (1954); Othello [extra] (1955); Serenade, Beyond a Reasonable Doubt (1956); Island in the Sun, Until They Sail (1957); South Pacific [extra], A Certain Smile (1958); Voyage to the Bottom of the Sea (1961); Tender Is the Night (1962); The Witches/The Devil's Own (1966).

Honors: Academy Award Nomination: Best Actress (*Rebecca*, 1940); Academy Award, New York Film Critics Circle Award: Best Actress (*Suspicion*, 1941); Academy Award Nomination: Best Actress (*The Constant Nymph*, 1943).

Selected Bibliography

Beeman, Marsha Lynn. *Joan Fontaine: A Bio-Bibliography*. Westport, CT: Greenwood Press, 1994.
Fontaine, Joan. *No Bed of Roses*. New York: Morrow, 1978.
Higham, Charles. *Sisters: The Story of Olivia de Havilland and Joan Fontaine*. New York: Coward-McCann, 1984.

FORD, GLENN. Actor. Born Gwyllyn Samuel Newton Ford on May 1, 1916, in Quebec. Ford came with his family to California at the age of eight. As a student at Santa Monica High School, he took part in many theatricals, and after graduation he played juvenile supporting parts and eventually leads with various companies along the West Coast. In 1939 he was tested and signed by Columbia Pictures, but just as his career was gaining momentum, the war came along and he felt compelled to join the marines. Once he was back from the war, Ford's popularity soared, especially when he played opposite such stars as Rita Hayworth (*Gilda)* and Bette Davis (*A Stolen Life*). He worked steadily throughout the 1940s and 1950s, always a reliable player even in films of lesser quality. He played a variety of parts, demonstrating equal skill at playing drama (*The Blackboard Jungle, Trial*), comedy (*The Teahouse of the August Moon, The Gazebo*), westerns (*The Cowboy*), even a comedy-western (*The Rounders*). He teamed up with Bette Davis a second time in *A Pocketful of Miracles* for which he won a Golden Globe Award. Ford usually comes across as amiable and easygoing but tough and introspective. In 1971–1972 he starred in the TV series *Cade's County*. He later appeared in a number of miniseries and occasional films. Ford is a highly underrated actor, one of those actors (like Robert Mitchum) whose acting is so natural that he doesn't seem to be acting and thus gets overlooked when awards are handed out. But he has his own distinctive style. It just isn't showy.

Filmography: Heaven with a Barbed Wire Fence, My Son Is Guilty (1939); Convicted Woman, Men without Souls, Babies for Sale, Blondie Plays Cupid, The Lady in Question (1940); So Ends Our Night, Texas, Go West Young Lady (1941); The Adventures of Martin Eden, Flight Lieutenant (1942); The Desperadoes, Destroyer (1943); Gilda, A Stolen Life, Gallant Journey (1946); Framed (1947); The Mating of Millie, The Loves of Carmen, The Return of October, The Man from Colorado (1948); The Undercover Man, Lust for Gold, Mr. Soft Touch, The Doctor and the Girl (1949); The White Tower, Convicted, The Flying Missile (1950); Follow the Sun, The Redhead and the Cowboy, The Secret of Convict Lake (1951); The Green Glove, Young Man with Ideas, Affair in Trinidad (1952); Terror on a Train/Time Bomb, Plunder of the Sun, The Man from the Alamo, The Big Heat, Appointment in Honduras (1953); Human Desire (1954); The Americano, The Violent Men, The Blackboard Jungle, Interrupted Melody, Trial (1955); Ransom, Jubal, The Fastest Gun Alive, The Teahouse of the August Moon (1956); 3:10 to Yuma, Don't Go Near the Water (1957); Cowboy, The Sheepman, Imitation General, Torpedo Run (1958); It Started with a Kiss (1959); The Gazebo (1960); Cimarron, Cry for Happy, A Pocketful of Miracles (1961); The Four Horsemen of the Apocalypse, Experiment in Terror (1962); The Courtship of Eddie's Father, Love Is a Ball (1963); Advance to the Rear, Fate Is the Hunter (1964); Dear Heart, The Rounders (1965); El Mal/Rage, The Money Trap, Is Paris Burning? (1966); A Time for Killing, The Last Challenge (1967); Day of the Evil Gun (1968); Smith!, Heaven with a Gun (1969); Santee (1973); Midway (1976); Goodbye and Amen, Superman (1978); The Visitor (1979); Virus (1980); Happy Birthday to Me (1981); Raw Nerve (1991).

Honors: Golden Globe Award: Best Actor, Comedy/Musical (*A Pocketful of Miracles*, 1961).

Selected Bibliography

Ford, Glenn, and Margaret Redfield. *Glenn Ford, RFD Beverly Hills*. Old Tappan, NJ: Hewitt House, 1970.

FORD, JOHN. Director. Born Sean Aloysius O'Feeney (O'Fearna) on February 1, 1895, in Cape Elizabeth, Maine; died on August 31,1973. After graduating from high school in 1913, Ford went to Hollywood to join his brother, Francis Ford, a director-writer-actor at Universal, who had changed his surname while an actor on Broadway. Ford began his Hollywood career as a set laborer and assistant propman, occasionally working as a stuntman or doubling for his older brother, whom he closely resembled. According to an interview with Peter Bogdanovich, Ford appeared as an extra, one of the hooded Ku Klux Klan riders, in Griffith's *The Birth of a Nation* in 1915. Later that year he became assistant director and featured player in his brother's films. Beginning in 1917, Ford directed more than thirty films, mostly westerns starring Harry Carey, before moving from Universal to Fox in 1920. Ford directed two important silent films, *The Iron Horse* and *Four Sons*, but his reputation as one of the great directors of the American cinema rests on his forty-year sound-film period, when he directed such screen classics as *The Informer, Stagecoach, The Grapes of Wrath, How Green Was My Valley, My Darling Clementine, She Wore a Yellow Ribbon, The Quiet Man, The Searchers,* and *The Man Who Shot Liberty Valance*. He worked in a variety of genres, including westerns, comedies, stage adaptations, historical dramas, and war movies. Of all American directors, Ford is generally considered to have had the clearest personal vision and the most consistent visual style. His ideas and his characters are deceptively simple. Repeated viewings reveal the typical Ford film to be a meditation on the conflict between rugged frontier individualism and inevitable, and perhaps necessary, civilization. While focusing on the conflicts between the individual and society, Ford also celebrated the virtue of the group when it gathers to champion a moral cause. During World War II, Ford was appointed chief of the Field Photographic Branch of the Office of Strategic Services with the rank of lieutenant commander in the navy. As part of his duties, he directed a number of propaganda documentaries. He was later promoted to rear admiral. Initially, Ford's postwar films were not as well received by the critics as his earlier works. But by the 1960s, French and American auteurist critics pioneered a critical reevaluation of Ford, viewing him as a great artist of the screen. Ford was among the most durable creative directors of the American cinema, with over fifty years of continual high-quality work to his credit, all of it stamped with his unmistakable signature. When Orson Welles was asked in a *Playboy* interview which American directors he liked best, he replied, "The old masters. . . . By which I mean John Ford, John Ford, and John Ford."

Filmography: [as Jack Ford]: The Tornado [also sc., act.], The Scrapper [also sc., act.], The Soul Herder, Cheyenne's Pal [also story; all preceding are shorts], Straight Shooting, The Secret Man, A Marked Man [also story], Bucking Broadway (1917); The Phantom Riders, Wild Women, Thieves' Gold, The Scarlet Drop [also story], Hell Bent [also co-sc.], A Woman's Fool, Three Mounted Men (1918); Roped, The Fighting Brothers [short], A Fight for Love, By Indian Post [short], The Rustlers [short], Bare Fists [short], Gun Law [short], The Gun Packer [short], Riders of Vengeance, The Last Outlaw [short], The Outcasts of Poker Flat, The Ace of the Saddle, The Rider of the Law, A Gun Fightin' Gentleman [also co-story], Marked Men (1919); The Prince of Avenue A, The Girl in No. 29, Hitchin' Posts, Just Pals (1920); The Big Punch [also co-sc.], The Freeze Out [also co-sc.], The Wallop, Desperate Trails, Action, Sure Fire, Jackie (1921); Little Miss Smiles, Silver Wings [dir. the Prologue sequences], The Village Blacksmith (1922); The Face on the Barroom Floor, Three Jumps Ahead [also sc.] 1923. [as John Ford]: Cameo Kirby, North of Hudson Bay, Hoodman Blind (1923); The Iron Horse, Hearts of Oak (1924); Lightnin', Kentucky Pride, The Fighting Heart, Thank You (1925); The Shamrock Handicap, Three Bad Men [also co-sc.], The Blue Eagle (1926); Upstream (1927); Mother Machree, Four Songs, Hangman's House, Napoleon's Barber [short], Riley the Cop (1928); Strong Boy, The Black Watch, Salute (1929); Men without Women [also co-story], Born Reckless, Up the River (1930); Seas Beneath, The Brat, Arrowsmith (1931); Air Mail, Flesh (1932); Pilgrimage, Dr. Bull (1933); The Lost Patrol, The World Moves On, Judge Priest (1934); The Whole Town's Talking, The Informer, Steamboat 'Round the Bend (1935); The Prisoner of Shark Island, Mary of Scotland, The Plough and the Stars (1936); Wee Willie Winkie, The Hurricane, The Adventures of Marco Polo [dir. of some action sequences only], Four Men and a Prayer, Submarine Patrol (1938); Stagecoach [also prod.], Young Mr. Lincoln, Drums along the Mohawk (1939); The Grapes of Wrath, The Long Voyage Home (1940); Tobacco Road, Sex Hygiene [army doc.], How Green Was My Valley (1941); The Battle of Midway [navy doc.; also co-phot., co-edit., co-narr.], Torpedo Squadron [Navy doc.] (1942); December 7th [Navy doc.; co-dir. with Gregg Toland], We Sail at Midnight [Navy doc.] (1943); They Were Expendable [also prod.] (1945); My Darling Clementine (1946); The Fugitive [also co-prod.] (1948); Fort Apache [also co-prod.] (1948); Three Godfathers [also co-prod.]

(1950); This Is Korea! [navy doc.] (1951); What Price Glory, The Quiet Man [also co-prod.] (1952); The Sun Shines Bright [also co-prod.], Mogambo (1953); The Long Gray Line, Mister Roberts [completed by Mervyn LeRoy when Ford became ill]; The Bamboo Cross [TV drama], Rookie of the Year [TV drama] (1955); The Searchers (1956); The Wings of Eagles, The Rising of the Moon (1957); So Alone [short], The Last Hurrah [also prod.] (1958); Gideon's Day/Gideon of Scotland Yard, Korea [Dept. of Defense doc.; also co-prod.], The Horse Soldiers (1959); The Colter Craven Story [TV film], Sergeant Rutledge (1960); Two Rode Together, Flashing Spikes [TV film], The Man Who Shot Liberty Valance, How the West Was Won ["Civil War" Episode] (1962); Donovan's Reef [also prod.] (1963); Cheyenne Autumn (1964); Young Cassidy [co-dir. with Jack Cardiff who received sole screen credit] (1965); Seven Women (1966); Chesty [doc.; orig. made for TV; release delayed from 1970] (1976).

Honors: Academy Award, New York Film Critics Circle Award: Best Director (*The Informer*, 1935); New York Film Critics Circle Award, Academy Award Nomination: Best Director (*Stagecoach*, 1939); Academy Award: Best Director (*The Grapes of Wrath*, 1940); New York Film Critics Circle Award: Best Director (*The Grapes of Wrath* and *The Long Voyage Home*, 1940); Academy Award, New York Film Critics Circle Award: Best Director (*How Green Was My Valley*, 1941); Venice Film Festival Award: International Prize (*The Fugitive*, 1948); Academy Award, Directors Guild of America (Quarterly Award and Annual Award), Venice Film Festival Award: International Prize (*The Quiet Man*, 1952); Directors Guild of America: D. W. Griffith Award for Outstanding Directorial Achievement (1953); Golden Globes: Pioneer Award (1954); Directors Guild of America: Outstanding Directorial Achievement [with Mervyn LeRoy] (*Mister Roberts*, 1955); National Board of Review Award: Best Director (*The Last Hurrah*, 1958); American Film Institute Life Achievement Award (1973).

Selected Bibliography

Davis, Ronald L. *John Ford: Hollywood's Old Master*. Norman: University of Oklahoma, 1995.
Gallagher, Tag. *John Ford: The Man and His Films*. Berkeley: University of California Press, 1986.
Sinclair, Andrew. *John Ford: A Biography*. New York: Lorrimer Publishing, 1984.

FOREIGN CORRESPONDENT (1940), mystery/thriller. Directed by Alfred Hitchcock; with Joel McCrea, Laraine Day, Herbert Marshall, George Sanders, Albert Basserman, Robert Benchley, Edmund Gwenn, Eduardo Cianelli, Harry Davenport, and Martin Kosleck; screenplay by Charles Bennett and Joan Harrison (dialogue by James Hilton and Robert Benchley).

This film is vintage Hitchcock, filled with his famous tricks and showpieces, and therein lies the problem. Time has robbed the film of much of its surprise, and the Hitchcock legend has turned viewers into players of trivial pursuit. This essentially old-fashioned cops-and-robbers romp is set against a background of international political intrigue of proportions later preempted by the likes of James Bond and company. In spite of the now rather embarrassing propagandistic finale, understandable given the time and theme of the film, most critics rank *Foreign Correspondent* among Hitchcock's most memorable set pieces.

Some of them, calling it intermittently first-rate, even go so far as to equate watching Hitchcock work to listening to music and insist that those who want to know how to make a movie should see this movie over and over again and study it. Maybe it was fitting that Joseph Goebbels called the film "a masterpiece of propaganda." He ought to know.

Awards: Academy Award Nominations: Best Picture, Supporting Actor (Albert Basserman), Original Screenplay, B&W Cinematography, B&W Art Direction, Special Effects.

Selected Bibliography

Harris, Robert A., and Michael S. Lasky. *The Complete Films of Alfred Hitchcock*. Secaucus, NJ: Carol Publishing, 1993.

42ND STREET (1933), musical. Directed by Lloyd Bacon and Busby Berkeley; with Warner Baxter, Ruby Keeler, George Brent, Bebe Daniels, Dick Powell, Guy Kibbee, Una Merkel, Ginger Rogers, Ned Sparks, and George E. Stone; screenplay by James Seymour and Rian James.

"Sawyer, you're going out a youngster, but you've got to come back a star!" This classic line, a beloved cliché of backstage musicals, comes from what today is considered to be the definitive backstage musical. It's filled with memorable tunes and bright, imaginative production numbers, and even when the acting has an amateurish quality to it, it is charming and fun and sort of reminiscent of the best of spirited regional theater. Ruby Keeler, as the unknown who comes through and registers a hit, is utterly convincing partly because she has the talent to play hammy with sincerity. Even though Keeler's singing ability is limited and her tapping is not tops, she is the epitome of the Broadway novice, while Dick Powell has the voice and the presence forever associated with the tuxedoed tenors surrounded by a bevy of lookalike starlet wannabes. *42nd Street* is generally considered a masterpiece, and while it may be thin on plot and characterization, what musical isn't? The choreography by Berkeley brings this film to masterpiece level, with absolutely astounding numbers in which Berkeley pulls out all the stops, shooting his routines from angles no one ever thought of before. Of course, a huge debt is owed to Al Dubin and Harry Warren (who, incidentally, play themselves in the film) for their terrific score filled with songs that are still fresh today ("42nd. Street," "Shuffle Off to Buffalo," "You're Getting to Be a Habit with Me"). There is no discernible external or internal logic for the variations in Busby Berkeley's kaleidoscopic dance numbers. Apparently Berkeley devised his choreographic spectacles on his own, without reference to the script, and without worrying about whether they would pass as parts of one musical. The director and the editors couldn't figure out how to insert them strategically, and so at the end, there are three big numbers, one right after another. The result is sheer magic.

Awards: Academy Award Nominations: Best Picture, Best Sound.

Selected Bibliography

Feuer, Jane. *The Hollywood Musical*. Bloomington: Indiana University Press, 1982.
Fordin, Hugh. *The World of Entertainment!: Hollywood's Greatest Musicals*. Garden City, NY: Doubleday, 1975.
Thomas, Tony. *Harry Warren and the Hollywood Musical*. Secaucus, NJ: Citadel, 1975.

FRANKENSTEIN (1931), horror. Directed by James Whale; with Colin Clive, Mae Clarke, Boris Karloff, John Boles, Edward Van Sloan, Dwight Frye, Frederick Kerr, and Lionel Belmore; screenplay by Garrett Fort and Francis Edwards Faragoh.

This first (and highly original) telling of Mary Shelley's classic tale is creaky at times and cries out for a musical score, but it's still impressive. Long-censored footage, restored in 1987, enhances the impact of several key scenes, including the drowning of a little girl. Boris Karloff, in the role that made him famous, gives one of the great performances of all time as the monster whose mutation from simple honesty to bone-chilling savagery is mirrored in his expressive eyes. The film's great imaginative coup is to show the monster "growing up" in all-too-human terms. *Frankenstein* is an impressively stylish film unfairly overshadowed by Whales's later deliriously witty *Bride of Frankenstein*. The film also has a certain avant-garde quality, for this is the only time Whales plays the horror absolutely straight, thus giving the film a weird fairy-tale beauty not matched until Cocteau's *La Belle et la Bête*.

Selected Bibliography

Anobile, Richard J., ed. *Frankenstein*. New York: Avon Books, 1974.
Forry, Steven Earl. *Hideous Progenies: Dramatizations of Frankenstein from Mary Shelley to the Present*. Philadelphia: University of Pennsylvania Press, 1989.
Glut, Donald F. *The Frankenstein Legend: A Tribute to Mary Shelley and Boris Karloff*. Metuchen, NJ: Scarecrow Press, 1973.

FRIENDLY PERSUASION (1956), drama. Directed by William Wyler; with Gary Cooper, Dorothy McGuire, Marjorie Main, Anthony Perkins, Richard Eyer, Robert Middleton, Mark Richman, Walter Catlett, and William Schallert; screenplay by Michael Wilson (see note under Awards).

This is a charming, heartwarming story of an Indiana Quaker family whose principles are put to the test during the Civil War. Although it is a simple story, it unfolds with generous portions of action and suspense—and even comedy. The central conflict has to do with the Quaker belief that it is wrong to bear arms against your fellow man. Gary Cooper is perfectly cast as the laconic father, a man of quiet humor and inner strength, and Anthony Perkins in his debut film is well cast as the anguished and unworldly son vainly pursued by Marjorie Main's three formidable daughters. Some critics find its homespun quality not particularly engrossing and consider the film simplistic and predictable. Those who like it do so hesitantly, calling it a film that's hard to like but harder to condemn. It's not a film for all tastes, and its bucolic quality has dated it unfairly, but Wyler's confident direction infuses it with humor and charm and a feeling for fundamental values that may embarrass modern audiences but that still give the Quakers their enviable inner strength. It's hard to condemn excessive gentleness in a world that embraces excessive violence.

Awards: Academy Award Nominations: Best Picture, Director, Supporting Actor (Perkins), Adapted Screenplay (nominee unnamed because of blacklist), Song, Sound.

Selected Bibliography

Kaminsky, Stuart M. *Coop: The Life and Legend of Gary Cooper*. New York: St. Martin's Press, 1980.

Kern, Sharon. *William Wyler: A Guide to References and Resources*. Boston: G. K. Hall, 1984.

Winecoff, Charles. *Split Image: The Life of Anthony Perkins*. New York: Dutton, 1996.

FROM HERE TO ETERNITY (1953), drama. Directed by Fred Zinnemann; with Burt Lancaster, Montgomery Clift, Deborah Kerr, Donna Reed, Frank Sinatra, Philip Ober, Ernest Borgnine, Mickey Shaughnessy, Jack Warden, Claude Akins, and George Reeves; screenplay by Daniel Taradash.

"The Boldest Book of Our Time . . . Honestly, Fearlessly on the Screen!" screamed the blurb for this remarkably faithful adaptation of the James Jones blockbuster novel. At the time of its filming, feelings about it resembled those that had accompanied *Gone with the Wind*, with many wondering if Hollywood could bring it off. Fortunately, Zinnemann selected a superb cast, all of whom seemed meant for the parts they played, including surprise performances by Deborah Kerr, usually a governess, as a sluttish American wife, Donna Reed (the perfect wife) as a prostitute, Ernest Borgnine (Marty?) as a sadist, and Frank Sinatra (the skinny, crooning heartthrob of the 1940s) as feisty Angelo Maggio, a part that won him an Academy Award and heralded his big comeback from near oblivion. It is interesting to note that when it was made, codes were strict about what could be spoken or shown on the screen. Thus, there could be none of the graphic vulgarity of army life or the explicit bawdiness of brothels. Miraculously, Zinnemann manages to transcend these limitations and present a movie that focuses more on the characters themselves than on external trappings. By having to "clean up" the novel, he was forced to probe more deeply into motivation. The movie succeeds because of Fred Zinnemann's sure-handed direction and because the cast is first-rate, especially Montgomery Clift, who manages to make the hardheaded Prewitt an intensely appealing young man. Clift was so good at seducing an audience without ever stepping out of character that his performance was almost overlooked in the general rush to praise Sinatra and Lancaster.

Awards: Academy Awards: Best Picture, Director, Supporting Actor (Sinatra), Supporting Actress (Donna Reed), Screenplay, B&W Cinematography (Burnett Guffy), Sound Recording, Editing (William Lyon); Academy Award Nominations: Best Actor (Lancaster, Clift), Actress (Kerr), B&W Costume Design, Scoring of a Dramatic Picture; Directors Guild of America: Most Outstanding Directorial Achievement (Zinnemann); New York Film Critics Award: Best Picture; *Photoplay* Gold Medal Awards: Gold Medal.

Selected Bibliography

Kalfatovic, Mary C. *Montgomery Clift: A Bio-Bibliography*. Westport, CT: Greenwood Press, 1994.

Peary, Danny. *Alternate Oscars*. New York: Delta, 1993.

Ringgold, Gene, and Clifford McCarty. *The Films of Frank Sinatra*. New York: Citadel Press, 1971.

Sennett, Ted. *Great Movie Directors*. New York: Harry N. Abrams, 1986.

G

GABLE, CLARK. Actor. Born William Clark Gable on February 1, 1901, in Cadiz, Ohio; died on November 16, 1960. Gable dropped out of school and left home at fourteen to work in a tire factory in nearby Akron. It was there that he had his first encounter with the theater. He was just beginning to get somewhere when his father took him with him to the oil fields of Oklahoma. When he was twenty-one, he left his father and joined a traveling troupe. Stranded in Oregon, he did odd jobs until he found another traveling company to join, this one run by Josephine Dillon, a woman fourteen years his senior, who took him to Hollywood where he found work as a film extra. When he was not getting anywhere in movies, Gable headed for Broadway, where he co-starred in a number of successful plays. Lionel Barrymore arranged for a screen test at MGM, but Gable was turned down by that studio, as well as by Warner Bros., where producer Darryl F. Zanuck said, "His ears are too big. He looks like an ape." In 1931, he managed to get cast in a William Boyd Western, *The Painted Desert*, and was then offered an MGM contract. After a number of supporting parts, he appeared in *A Free Soul*. It was not a leading part, but audiences loved the way he pushed Norma Shearer around, and he was on his way to stardom. Soon he was appearing opposite Greta Garbo and Joan Crawford and making one successful movie after another. When he complained about being typecast as a villain, Louis B. Mayer loaned him to Columbia for Frank Capra's *It Happened One Night*. Because it was supposed to be a minor project, Gable accepted the role reluctantly, as did his co-star, Claudette Colbert. To everybody's surprise, including theirs and director Frank Capra's, they all won Academy Awards, and the film was voted best picture of the year. Another part Gable resisted was that of Rhett Butler in *Gone with the Wind*; but all America insisted, Gable gave in, and the rest is history. Gable joined the Army Air Force in World War II, rose in rank from lieutenant to major, and received the Distinguished Flying Cross and Air Medal for flying several bombing missions over Germany. His return to the screen in *Adventure* was announced by MGM as: "Gable's Back, and Garson's Got Him." But the film was a disappointment, as were most of Gable's postwar movies. Gable suffered the fate of those who outlive their glory. He did not age well, he gained weight, and he began drinking heavily. When his contract expired in 1954, MGM didn't renew it. He began freelancing and made an unsuccessful attempt at independent production, but the old Hollywood was dying around him, and there was no longer a place for "The King." Ironically enough, he gave one of the best performances of his life in his last film, John Huston's *The Misfits*, but he died too soon to see the good reviews. Some blame his "difficult" co-stars, Marilyn Monroe and Montgomery Clift, for his early demise. He also did not live to see his first and only child, John Clark, born to Kay Gable shortly after his death.

Filmography: [as extra]: Forbidden Paradise, White Man (1924); Declasée/The Social Exile, The Peacemakers [serial], The Merry Widow, The Plastic Age (1925); North Star, The Johnstown Flood (1926). [as actor]: The Painted Desert, The Easiest Way, Dance Fools Dance, The Secret Six, The Finger Points, Laughing Sinners, A Free Soul, Night Nurse, Sporting Blood, Susan Lenox: Her Fall and Rise, Possessed, Hell Divers (1931); Polly of the Circus, Red Dust, Strange Interlude, No Man of Her Own (1932); The White Sister, Hold Your Man, Night Flight, Dancing Lady (1933); It Happened One Night, Men in White, Manhattan Melodrama, Chained, Forsaking All Others (1934); After Office Hours, The Call of the Wild, China Seas, Mutiny on the Bounty [as Fletcher Christian] (1935); Wife vs. Secretary, San Francisco, Cain and Mabel, Love on the Run (1936); Parnell [title role], Saratoga (1937); Test Pilot, Too Hot to Handle (1938); Idiot's Delight, Gone with the Wind [as Rhett Butler] (1939); Strange Cargo, Boom Town, Comrade X (1940); They Met in Bombay, Honky Tonk (1941); Somewhere I'll Find You (1942); Adventure (1945); The Hucksters (1947); Homecoming, Command Decision (1948); Any Number Can Play (1949); Key to the City, To Please a Lady (1950); Across the Wide Missouri, Callaway Went That-away [cameo] (1951); Lone Star (1952); Never Let Me Go, Mogambo [remake of Red Dust] (1953); Betrayed (1954); Soldier of Fortune, The Tall Men (1955); The King and Four Queens (1956); Band of Angels (1957); Run Silent Run Deep, Teacher's Pet (1958); But Not for Me (1959); It Started in Naples (1960); The Misfits (1961).

Honors: Academy Award: Best Actor (*It Happened One Night*, 1934); Academy Award Nomination: Best Actor (*Mutiny on the Bounty*, 1935); Academy Award Nomination: Best Actor (*Gone with the Wind*, 1939).

Selected Bibliography

Essoe, Gabe. *The Complete Films of Clark Gable*. Secaucus, NJ: Citadel Press, 1970.

Lewis, Judy. *Uncommon Knowledge*. New York: Pocket Books, 1994.

Wayne, Jane Ellen. *Clark Gable: Portrait of a Misfit*. New York: St. Martin's Press, 1993.

GARBO, GRETA. Actress. Born Greta Louisa Gustafsson on September 18, 1905, in Stockholm; died on April 15, 1990. Educated at the Royal Dramatic

Theater training school. Garbo grew up in Sweden in poverty, and after her father died, she began work as a lather girl in a barbershop. She next took a job as a salesgirl in a department store. Because of her looks, she was chosen to appear in a short publicity film sponsored by the store. This led to another publicity short, this one for a bakery, and later that year to the lead in a slapstick comedy film, *Peter the Tramp*. Encouraged by her modest success, she applied for and won a scholarship to the Royal Dramatic Theater training school and soon began playing small roles on the stage as part of her training. It was at the school that she was discovered by Mauritz Stiller, who coached her and eventually took charge of her personal affairs. Friends called them Pygmalion and Galatea, Beauty and the Beast, or Svengali and Trilby. Years later Stiller revealed, "I immediately noticed how easily one could dominate her by looking straight into her eyes." When Louis B. Mayer offered Stiller a contract to work in Hollywood, Stiller insisted on bringing Garbo along. Mayer wasn't happy about that. He thought she was too fat, and others found her uncommunicative. MGM studio publicity could not figure out what kind of image they were supposed to give Garbo. No one expected much from this sullen, reclusive, and rather big woman. But all this changed when they saw the daily rushes of Garbo's first MGM film, *The Torrent*. The moment the camera rolled, this big, awkward, lethargic girl with the stooped shoulders and droopy eyes would suddenly come to life, electrifying the entire production crew with her magnetic personality. Even before the film was finished, Mayer offered her a revised contract at a higher salary. When the film was released, in February 1926, it was both a critical and a popular success. She continued to make a succession of mostly successful films, each enhancing the legend of the "I-want-to-be-alone" girl to the point where she was in danger of self-parody. Perhaps fearing this, she took advantage of the failure of her last film, *Two-Faced Woman*, and retired in 1941 at the height of her career. Until her death in 1990, there was occasional talk of a projected comeback, but nothing ever materialized. Perhaps Garbo did not dare take the risk. Perhaps she saw *Sunset Boulevard* and feared the fate of Norma Desmond. Whatever the motive behind her reclusiveness, Garbo knew a secret that a lot of wannabes could profit from: The more aloof you remain, the more popular you become. It's the old "hard to get" routine applied to stardom. Like Dietrich, she invented a persona and palmed it off on a public maddened by curiosity. By remaining inaccessible, she preserved the illusion that she was special, that she really *was* that glamorous, tragic heroine shining down from the silver screen. And by retiring at the height of her career, she did what James Dean had to die to do: keep them wanting more. What she left was the legacy of a legend whose reputation exceeds her accomplishments. She was not always *that* good, but the camera loved her face, the sound track loved her voice, and she frequently had an air of sophisticated ennui that appealed to depression audiences. Put it this way: She would *never* have appeared on a talk show or allowed herself to be interviewed by Barbara Walters, let alone Geraldo. More than fifty years after her last film, the Greta Garbo mystique remains intact. New audiences have discovered her on television and in special film festivals. Clarence Brown, one of her directors, once said that "without having made a film since 1940, she is still the greatest. She is the prototype of all stars."

Filmography: Luffar Peter/Peter the Tramp (1922); Gösta Berling's Saga/The Legend of Gösta Berling/The Story of Gösta Berling/The Atonement of Gösta Berling (1924); Die freudlose Gasse/The Street of Sorrow/The Joyless Street (1925); The Torrent/Ibanez' Torrent, The Temptress (1926); Flesh and the Devil, Love [as Anna Karenina] (1927); The Divine Woman, The Mysterious Lady, A Woman of Affairs (1928); Wild Orchids, A Man's Man [cameo], The Single Standard, The Kiss (1929); Anna Christie [title role; also Ger. version], Romance (1930); Inspiration, Susan Lenox: Her Fall and Rise, Mata Hari [title role] (1931); Grand Hotel, As You Desire Me (1932); Queen Christina [title role] (1933); The Painted Veil (1934); Anna Karenina [title role] (1935); Camille [title role], Conquest [as Napoleon's mistress Maria], *Walewska* (1937); *Ninotchka* (1939); *Two-Faced Woman* (1941).

Honors: Academy Award Nomination: Best Actress (*Anna Christie* and *Romance*, 1930); New York Film Critics Circle Award: Best Actress (*Anna Karenina*, 1935); New York Film Critics Circle Award, Academy Award Nomination: Best Actress (*Camille*, 1937); Academy Award Nomination: Best Actress (*Ninotchka*, 1939); Academy Award: Special Award, ["for her unforgettable screen performances"] (1954).

Selected Bibliography

Conway, Michael, Dion McGregor, and Mark Ricci. *The Films of Greta Garbo*. New York: Bonanza Books, 1963.
Gronowicz, Antoni. *Garbo*. New York: Simon & Schuster, 1990.
Paris, Barry. *Garbo: A Biography*. New York: Knopf, 1994.

GARDNER, AVA. Actress. Born on December 24, 1922, in Grabton (near Smithfield), North Carolina; died on January 25, 1990, in London. Educated at the Atlantic Christian College, Wilson, North Carolina (secretarial studies). Ava Gardner was one of six children of a dirt-poor tenant farmer in rural North Carolina. While she was visiting her married sister in New York in her late teens, her brother-in-law, a professional photographer, took a picture of her that somehow found its way to MGM's casting department. A screen test was arranged in New York, and Gardner was placed in a grooming program that was standard for promising but inexperienced starlets. It was a long time before she got a chance to play even minor roles, but her marriage in 1942 to Mickey Rooney did much to further her career. Although she and Rooney divorced the following year, Gardner had already gained enough publicity to encourage the studio to star her in *The Killers* in 1946, her breakthrough movie. After this the studio promoted her image as a sensuous, husky-voiced beauty who exuded sexuality, and before long, Gardner became the movie's leading love goddess in the decade between the fading of Rita Hayworth and the blossoming of Marilyn Monroe. Gardner's busy love life made headlines. First she married the oft-married Artie Shaw (1945–1947), then Frank Sinatra (1951–1957). Then

Gardner left Hollywood to hobnob with the international set in Madrid, where she wallowed in the company of playboys and matadors and assorted gigolos, much in the style of Lady Brett, a part she was to play to perfection in *The Sun Also Rises*. She returned to Hollywood three years later and made a successful comeback. Gardner's beauty was also a burden, for she was too often cast for her looks rather than her acting talent. Given the chance, however, she could surprise critics and audiences alike with strong performances, such as in *Show Boat*, where she played Julie, the mulatto girl. In the 1980s, she appeared on TV in various series and made-for-TV movies. In 1990, she had just finished supplying a collaborator with material for an autobiography when she died of pneumonia in London at age sixty-seven.

Filmography: H. M. Pulham Esq. (1941); We Were Dancing, Joe Smith American, Sunday Punch, This Time for Keeps, Calling Dr. Gillespie, Kid Glove Killer (1942); Pilot No. 5, Hitler's Madman, Ghosts on the Loose, Reunion in France, Du Barry Was a Lady, Young Ideas, Lost Angel (1943); Swing Fever, Music for Millions, Three Men in White, Blonde Fever, Maisie Goes to Reno, Two Girls and a Sailor (1944); She Went to the Races (1945); Whistle Stop, The Killers (1946); The Hucksters, Singapore (1947); One Touch of Venus [as the goddess Venus] (1948); The Bribe, The Great Sinner, East Side West Side (1949); My Forbidden Past, Show Boat [as Julie Laverne], Pandora and the Flying Dutchman [as Pandora] (1951); Lone Star, The Snows of Kilimanjaro (1952); Ride Vaquero!, The Band Wagon [cameo], Mogambo (1953); Knights of the Round Table [as Guinevere], The Barefoot Contessa (1954); Bhowani Junction (1956); The Little Hut, The Sun Also Rises (1957); La Maja Desnuda/The Naked Maja, On the Beach (1959); La Sposa Bella/The Angel Wore Red (1960); 55 Days at Peking (1963); Seven Days in May, The Night of the Iguana (1964); La Bibbia/The Bible [as Sarah] (1966); Mayerling [as Empress Elizabeth] (1968); The Devil's Widow/Tam Lin (1971); The Life and Times of Judge Roy Bean [as famed actress Lily Langtry] (1972); Earthquake (1974); Vollmacht zum Mord/Permission to Kill (1975); The Blue Bird [as Luxury] (1976); The Cassandra Crossing, The Sentinel (1977); City on Fire, The Kidnapping of the President (1980); Priest of Love (1981); Regina (1982).

Honors: Academy Award Nomination: Best Actress (*Mogambo*, 1953).

Selected Bibliography

Flamini, Roland. *Ava: A Biography*. New York: Coward, McCann & Geoghegan, 1983.
Fowler, Karin J. *Ava Gardner: A Bio-Bibliography*. Westport, CT: Greenwood Press, 1990.
Gardner, Ava. *Ava: My Story*. New York: Bantam Books, 1990.

GARFIELD, JOHN. Actor. Born Julius Garfinkle on March 4, 1913, in New York City; died on May 21, 1952. Garfield became best known for his tough, rebellious image, the result of growing up on New York's Lower East Side where he flirted with juvenile delinquency. When he entered a state debating contest sponsored by the *New York Times* and won a scholarship, he used the money to enroll in the Ouspenskaya Drama School, after which he served an apprenticeship with Eva Le Gallienne's Civic Repertory Theatre. During the depression he bummed around the country, riding the rails and generally playing hobo. Eventually, he went back to New York, joined the Group Theatre, and before long wound up on Broadway. In 1938 he was signed by Warner Bros. to star in the film *Four Daughters*. Warner saw in Garfield the qualities that had gained stardom for James Cagney, a feisty, short-tempered rebel with a hint of something tender beneath the tough exterior. It was that sensitive undercurrent that helped win him an Academy Award nomination as Best Supporting Actor for *Four Daughters* and Best Actor for *Body and Soul*. In the mid-1940s, after a brilliant performance in *Humoresque* as a gifted violinist in the clutches of a possessive patroness (Joan Crawford), Garfield left Warners and tried his hand at running his own production company while he also freelanced for various studios. Then early in the 1950s his career ended abruptly as a result of the House Un-American Activities Committee investigation. Although he wasn't accused of anything in particular, he was tainted with the suspicion of left-wing sympathies (a holdover from his Group Theatre days) and blacklisted for refusing to name names. When he died of a heart attack in 1952, those close to him said it was the blacklisting that really killed him. Rumors persisted for years that the actor actually had taken his own life.

Filmography: Four Daughters (1938); They Made Me a Criminal, Blackwell's Island, Juarez, Daughters Courageous, Four Wives, Dust Be My Destiny (1939); Castle on the Hudson, Saturday's Children, Flowing Gold, East of the River (1940); The Sea Wolf [as George Leach], Out of the Fog (1941); Dangerously They Live, Tortilla Flat (1942); Air Force, The Fallen Sparrow, Thank Your Lucky Stars (1943); Destination Tokyo, Between Two Worlds, Hollywood Canteen (1944); Pride of the Marines (1945); The Postman Always Rings Twice, Nobody Lives Forever, Humoresque (1946); Body and Soul, Gentleman's Agreement (1947); Force of Evil (1948); We Were Strangers (1949); Under My Skin, The Breaking Point (1950); He Ran All the Way (1951).

Honors: Academy Award Nomination: Best Supporting Actor (*Four Daughters*, 1938); Academy Award Nomination: Best Actor (*Body and Soul*, 1947).

Selected Bibliography

Beaver, James N. *John Garfield: His Life and Films*. South Brunswick, NJ: A. S. Barnes, 1978.

Gelman, Howard. *The Films of John Garfield*. Secaucus, NJ: Citadel Press, 1975.

Swindell, Larry. *Body and Soul: The Story of John Garfield*. New York: Morrow, 1975.

GARLAND, JUDY. Actress, singer. Born Frances Gumm on June 10, 1922, in Grand Rapids, Minnesota; died on June 22, 1969, in London. Garland, who was "born in a trunk," made her stage debut at the age of three. By the time she was five, she was performing with her two older sisters in the "Gumm Sisters Kiddie Act," on stage as well as in short films in which she was billed as "the little girl with the great big voice." When she was nine, the girls changed their stage name to Garland, and soon thereafter Frances changed her name to Judy. After the trio broke up, thirteen-year-old Judy auditioned for Louis B. Mayer himself who, on the strength of her voice alone, signed her to a contract without even bothering with a screen test. After a two-reel short, *Every Sunday*, and a loan-out to Fox for her first feature, *Pigskin Parade*, Judy returned to MGM and scored a hit in *Broadway Melody of 1938*, singing "Dear Mr. Gable" to a photograph of the star. In *Thoroughbreds Don't Cry* she appeared in the first of nine films opposite Mickey Rooney. In 1939 she landed the part of Dorothy in *The Wizard of Oz* and was literally an overnight sensation. "Over the Rainbow," a song that was almost cut from the picture, became her theme song and will forever be associated with her. Judy was still a teenager when she began having a problem with her weight and her nerves, and soon she was on a rollercoaster drug regimen, alternating sleeping pills at night with pep pills during the day. By the time she was twenty-one she was under psychiatric care. Between 1941 and 1951 Garland was married and divorced twice. Her second husband was Vincente Minnelli, who had directed her in the classic musical *Meet Me in St. Louis* and who was the father of Liza Minnelli. Unable to cope with all the pressures of her life, Garland was frequently absent from the set, a chronic situation that led, after repeated suspensions, to her being fired from MGM in 1950 soon after starting work on *Annie Get Your Gun*. Recovery took its time, but eventually, after marrying Sid Luft, she played a very successful engagement at the London Palladium, followed by a triumphant comeback at New York's Palace Theater, playing a record-breaking nineteen-week engagement. In 1954, she returned to the screen in *A Star Is Born*, a role many think her best and one for which she was nominated for an Oscar. Some speculate that if she had won, her career would have risen to new heights and she would have lived out her life on a high note. As it was, she became more and more involved in lawsuits and breakdowns, and in spite of her TV show and concert engagements, her career continued to founder. One bright spot was the small but brilliant part in Stanley Kramer's *Judgment at Nuremberg*, for which she was nominated for an Oscar as Best Supporting Actress. This was followed by an equally strong performance in *A Child Is Waiting*. Her TV show on CBS in 1963 got poor ratings and was canceled before the end of its scheduled run. Garland then divorced Luft and married Mark Herron, a minor actor seven years her junior, whom she divorced in 1967. Then the role she expected to get in the film *Valley of the Dolls* was given to Susan Hayward. Early in 1968, Judy went to London, where she married her fifth husband, a thirty-five-year-old discotheque manager named Mickey Deans. A three-week engagement at a London cabaret turned out to be the worst nightmare of her life. Not only was she habitually late for performances, but her voice frequently cracked, and she constantly forgot her lines. Angered audiences booed, jeered, and tossed trash on the stage. But she seemed to be recovering from the effects of this fiasco and planning yet another comeback when sometime during the night of June 22, 1969, she stumbled in the bathroom of her London apartment. She was found dead in the morning by Deans. The official coroner's verdict attributed her death to an accidental overdose of sleeping pills. But actor-dancer Ray Bolger, Dorothy's Scarecrow friend in *The Wizard of Oz*, commented: "She just plain wore out."

Filmography: [shorts]: The Meglin Kiddie Revue (1929); Holiday in Storyland, The Wedding of Jack and Jill (1930); The Old Lady and the Shoe (1931); La Fiesta de Santa Barbara (1935); Every Sunday (1936). [features]: Pigskin Parade (1936); Broadway Melody of 1938, Thoroughbreds Don't Cry (1937); Everybody Sing, Love Finds Andy Hardy, Listen Darling (1938); The Wizard of Oz, Babes in Arms (1939); Andy Hardy Meets Debutante, Strike Up the Band, Little Nellie Kelly (1940); Meet the Stars No. 4 [short], Cavalcade of the Academy Awards [short], Ziegfeld Girl, Life Begins for Andy Hardy (1941); Babes on Broadway, We Must Have Music [short], For Me and My Gal (1942); Presenting Lily Mars, Thousands Cheer, Girl Crazy (1943); Meet Me in St. Louis (1944); The Clock (1945); The Harvey Girls, Ziegfeld Follies, Till The Clouds Roll By (1946); The Pirate, Easter Parade, Words and Music (1948); In the Good Old Summertime (1949); Summer Stock (1950); A Star Is Born (1954); Pepe [cameo] (1960); Judgment at Nuremberg (1961); Gay Purr-ee [voice only] (1962); A Child Is Waiting, I Could Go on Singing (1963).

Honors: Academy Award: Special Award (Screen Juvenile, 1939); Golden Globe Award, Academy Award Nomination: Best Actress (*A Star Is Born*, 1954); Academy Awards Nomination: Best Supporting Actress (*Judgment at Nuremberg*, 1961); Golden Globes: Cecil B. DeMille Award (1961).

Selected Bibliography

Edwards, Anne. *Judy Garland: A Biography*. New York: Simon & Schuster, 1975.

Fricke, J. *Judy Garland: World's Greatest Entertainer*. New York: Holt, 1992.

Morella, Joe, and Edward Z. Epstein. *Judy: The Complete Films and Career of Judy Garland*. Secaucus, NJ: Citadel Press, 1986.

Shipman, David. *Judy Garland: The Secret Life of an American Legend*. New York: Hyperion, 1993.

Watson, Thomas, and Bill Chapman. *Judy: Portrait of an American Legend*. New York: McGraw-Hill, 1986.

GARSON, GREER. Actress. Born on September 29, 1908 (or 1903), in County Down, Ireland; died on April 6, 1996. Educated at the University of London. Garson dabbled in amateur dramatics for a while before making her professional debut with the Birmingham Repertory Theatre in 1932. A few years later she was appearing in a play in London when Louis B. Mayer spotted her and signed her to an MGM contract. She arrived in Hollywood at a moment when MGM needed someone of her caliber to take the place of Greta Garbo and Norma Shearer, who were retiring. At the height of her popularity in the 1940s Greer Garson was the epitome of the MGM star. Poised, charming, with patrician looks and a warm personality, she seemed cut out to play heroines who were courageous, independent, and self-assured yet tender and compassionate. Her first film, *Goodbye, Mr. Chips*, for which she received an Academy Award nomination, was enormously successful and launched her career as MGM's leading lady of the decade. She made a series of successful films after that, but the one that really put her at the top was *Mrs. Miniver* in which she became the symbol of the courage and gallantry of the British housewife during the Blitz. She won the Best Actress Academy Award for the role. For several years thereafter,

Garson was typecast in Mrs. Miniver–type roles, frequently co-starring with Walter Pidgeon. Later, when she played a wider range of dramatic, even comic, roles, the pictures were of lesser quality, and her popularity began to wane. In the mid-1950s she retired from the screen, except for *Sunrise at Campobello* (in which she played, of all people, Eleanor Roosevelt) and occasional bit parts and TV specials. In 1958 she replaced Rosalind Russell in *Auntie Mame* on Broadway. In later life, she received numerous awards for environmental and other civic and benevolent activities.

Filmography: Goodbye Mr. Chips, Remember? (1939); Pride and Prejudice [as Elizabeth Bennet] (1940); Blossoms in the Dust, When Ladies Meet (1941); Mrs. Miniver [title role], Random Harvest (1942); The Youngest Profession, Madame Curie [as Marie Curie] (1943); Mrs. Parkington [title role] (1944); The Valley of Decision (1945); Adventure (1946); Desire Me (1947); Julia Misbehaves (1948); That Forsyte Woman/The Forsyte Saga [as Irene Forsyte] (1949); The Miniver Story (1950); The Law and the Lady (1951); Julius Caesar [as Calpurnia], Scandal at Scourie (1953); Her Twelve Men (1954); Strange Lady in Town (1955); Sunrise at Campobello [as Eleanor Roosevelt], Pepe (1960); The Singing Nun (1966); The Happiest Millionaire (1967).

Honors: Academy Award Nomination: Best Actress (*Goodbye, Mr. Chips*, 1939); Academy Award Nomination: Best Actress (Blossoms in the Dust, 1941); Academy Award: Best Actress (*Mrs. Miniver*, 1942); Academy Award Nomination: Best Actress (*Madame Curie*, 1943); *Photoplay* Gold Medal Award: Most Popular Female Star (1944); Academy Award Nomination: Best Actress (*The Valley of Decision*, 1945); *Photoplay* Gold Medal Award: Most Popular Female Star (1945); Golden Globe Award, National Board of Review Award, Academy Award Nomination: Best Actress (*Sunrise at Campobello*, 1960).

GASLIGHT (1944), drama. Directed by George Cukor; with Ingrid Bergman, Charles Boyer, Joseph Cotten, Dame May Whitty, Angela Lansbury, and Terry Moore; screenplay by John Van Druten, Walter Reisch, and John L. Balderston.

"A melodrama of a strange love!" "This is love . . . clouded by evil . . . darkened by a secret no one dared to guess! The strange drama of a captive sweetheart!" Thus ran the blurbs for this classic Victorian melodrama. Like *Psycho*, this movie has become a cinematic cliché so that the verb *to gaslight* someone has an instant association. Also the fact that this film is compared, sometimes unfavorably, with previous productions works to lessen the impact of what, objectively, is a classic chiller about a man trying to drive his wife insane. The production is lush, the flavor authentically Victorian, and the performances by the three leads exceptionally compelling. Melodramatic as it is, it is so unapologetically a period piece that the theatrics are appropriate and only serve to heighten the film's suspense. Director George Cukor, famous for lavish productions and a keen sense of the dramatic, paces the film evenly. Critical opinion is sharply divided about this film, many critics preferring the 1939 British production, possibly because the studio went to such great pains to suppress it. They feel that the earlier version had a much surer sense of background, and they are unanimous in the praise of Anton Walbrook's performance with its chilling psychotic edge. Supporters of the newer version credit Cukor with skillful direction, particularly in the way he insinuates a vague sense of unease into the romantic Italian honeymoon scenes and then relentlessly increases the tension until it reaches a climax of suffocating terror in the claustrophobic house in fogbound London where Boyer is methodically driving Bergman insane. In addition to fine performances by Bergman and Boyer, much mention has been made of Angela Lansbury's debut in the role of the insolent parlormaid Boyer uses to add insult to his wife's injury. Perhaps what gives this film its edge is the presence of two cinematic superstars in the leading roles. Walbrook (in the earlier version) may have given the better performance, but Boyer was the matinee idol; and Bergman at her peak was simply unsurpassed. The two of them are what "movie stars" are all about, and together they are what "movies" are all about.

Awards: Academy Awards: Best Actress (Bergman), B&W Art Decoration (Cedric Gibbons, William Ferrari); Golden Globe Award: Best Actress (Bergman); Academy Award Nominations: Best Picture, Script, Photography, Actor (Boyer), Supporting Actress (Lansbury).

Selected Bibliography

Levy, Emanuel. *George Cukor: Master of Elegance: Hollywood's Legendary Director and His Stars*. New York: Morrow, 1994.

Quirk, Lawrence J. *The Complete Films of Ingrid Bergman*. New York: Carol Communications, 1989.

Swindell, Larry. *Charles Boyer: The Reluctant Lover*. Garden City, NY: Doubleday, 1983.

GIANT (1956), drama. Directed by George Stevens; with Elizabeth Taylor, Rock Hudson, James Dean, Carroll Baker, Jane Withers, Chill Wills, Mercedes McCambridge, Dennis Hopper, Sal Mineo, Rodney (Rod) Taylor, and Earl Holliman; screenplay by Fred Guiol and Ivan Moffat.

While the film captures the look and feel of Texas and penetrates something of the Texan ego and narrow-mindedness, it is generally faulted for its pretensions. *Giant* has the sprawl but not the epic sweep of, say, *Gone with the Wind*, a movie comparable in length and ambition. By dragging out the story, Stevens makes it easier to see its flaws. But he also makes it easier to enjoy some unusual performances, especially the one given by James Dean. In itself, it is a tour de force, a mesmerizing intrusion of method acting into a Texas outback dominated by tradition more stifling because it is of such recent origin. Dean ages not well but magnificently; that is, he gives an uncannily convincing portrait of a middle-aged man, yet he still manages to seduce the audience with what has come to be the James Dean repertoire of moody-rebellious-teen tricks: the sidelong glance, the crooked smile, the squint, the slouch, the lope. Add to this the tragic note that the movie was released after Dean's death in an automobile accident, and his performance takes on a special significance, further enhanced by his ever-increasing status as a cult figure. Thus, every frame is cherished by his fans. Elizabeth Taylor's performance has often been called one of her best, and Rock Hudson, as the rock of Texan prejudice, intrigues viewers nowadays because of what they know about his nontraditional lifestyle. Add to this the curious career of George Stevens, who moved from frothy to serious in his long and illustrious career, this being one of his possibly too-serious attempts, and you have a film that, like so many classic films, is interesting for reasons that may far outweigh either its intentions or its pretensions. There is also the added pleasure of seeing Carroll Baker do herself proud in her first important role and of watching the relish with which Mercedes McCambridge takes on Elizabeth Taylor after having previously battled just as viciously—and vainly—with Joan Crawford in *Johnny Guitar*. There is an honesty in her hatred that is scary to watch. Still others get a kick out of seeing a young Dennis Hopper as Rock Hudson's son. Although the film was a box office hit and has been highly praised by many leading critics, those who have reservations have a point. They complain that Stevens seems to be trying so hard to make a serious statement that the film tends to drag—and the mind to wander. It is still hard to see the film objectively, for it carries with it assorted emotional baggage, foremost of which is the fact that this was James Dean's last film. This fact adds inestimable poignancy to his scenes, many of which are simply unforgettable. Add to this the circumstances of Rock Hudson's tragic death, the feud between Mercedes McCambridge and Elizabeth Taylor, not to mention the electrifying presence of Taylor herself (often labeled "the last movie star"), and it is not easy to see clearly just what exactly is going on in the movie. *Giant* has become one of those films that can often be more fun to read about than to watch. Whatever you think of it, it's a film that's hard to ignore.

Awards: Academy Award: Best Director; *Photoplay* Gold Medal Award: Best Picture; Academy Award Nominations: Best Picture, Actor (Dean, Hudson), Supporting Actress (McCambridge), Adapted Screenplay, Color Costume, Design, Color Art Direction, Editing, Scoring of a Dramatic Picture.

Selected Bibliography

Petri, Bruce Humleker. *A Theory of American Film: The Films and Techniques of George Stevens*. New York: Garland, 1987.

Vermilye, Jerry, and Mark Ricci. *The Films of Elizabeth Taylor*. Secaucus, NJ: Citadel Press, 1976.

Whitman, Mark. *The Films of James Dean*. London: Barnden Castell Williams Ltd., 1974.

GIGI (1958), musical. Directed by Vincente Minnelli; with Leslie Caron, Maurice Chevalier, Louis Jourdan, Hermione Gingold, Jacques Bergerac, and Eva Gabor; screenplay by Alan Jay Lerner.

Gigi is another gem from the past that is hard to evaluate other than on its own terms. On those terms, it is a colorful, tuneful, intriguing peek into the musical-beds life of fin de siècle Paris, which serves as a backdrop for the comparatively innocent blossoming of romance between Louis Jourdan and Leslie Caron. True to tradition, however, it cannot help revealing the naughtiness that underlies Gigi's naïveté. In other words, it is another tale of "virtue rewarded," but done with such charm that it is hard to fault. Today it may seem a bit cloying. Teaming Vincente Minnelli and Cecil Beaton, two visual elitists, results in too much dessert and not enough meat and potatoes. Some critics complained that the sets are too cluttered and claustrophobic and that the cast tries to out-French the French, especially Chevalier, who had by that time become something of a "professional Frenchman." (His rendition of "Thank Heaven for Little Girls" has given some viewers pause.) Hermione Gingold has been praised for giving her unique spin to her performance, but to some she seems even more affected than usual. Miraculously, however, these faults seem to be transformed into virtues within the context of the film. The actors are sophisticated, and the material is well suited to their talents. It's hard to imagine anyone but the inimitable Leslie Caron in the starring role, and Louis Jourdan was born to play roles like the one he plays with such aplomb in this film. One reviewer said you would have to search *Roget's Thesaurus* for new words to describe the wonderment of *Gigi*. And despite some critics' objections that Frederick Loewe and Alan Jay Lerner simply reworked *My Fair Lady*, others insist that *Gigi* can more than stand on its own. One critic even went so far as to say that *Gigi* is as perfect a film musical as you can ever expect to see. Whatever the ultimate verdict, there is no doubt that *Gigi* is a feast for eye and ear.

Awards: Academy Awards: Best Picture, Director, Adapted Screenplay, Cinematography (Joseph Ruttenberg), Costumes (Cecil Beaton), Song ("Gigi"), Scoring (Andre Previn); Chevalier received an honorary Oscar for his career achievement; Golden Globe Award: Best Picture/Musical; Directors Guild of America: Grand Award for Direction (Minnelli); *Photoplay* Gold Medal Award: Best Picture.

Selected Bibliography

Fordin, Hugh. *The World of Entertainment!: Hollywood's Greatest Musicals*. Garden City, NY: Doubleday, 1975.
Minnelli, Vincente. *I Remember It Well*. Garden City, NY: Doubleday, 1974.

GOING MY WAY (1944), drama. Directed by Leo McCarey; with Bing Crosby, Barry Fitzgerald, Rise Stevens, Gene Lockhart, Frank McHugh, James Brown, Jean Heather, Stanley Clements, Carl Switzer, and Porter Hall; screenplay by Frank Butler and Frank Cavett.

Going My Way is a movie that can only be taken in context. It appeared near the end of World War II when audiences were war-weary and just a little blitzed on either escapist comedies or home-fires-burning dramas or war-heroics epics and ready for a retreat into a mostly imaginary world of quaint, ethnic charm of a sort unknown to most Americans but apparently coveted by all. (No one bothered to remind anyone that Ireland remained neutral during World War II. Somehow leprechauns and blarney stones always win the American heart.) This was also, of course, a tailor-made vehicle for Bing Crosby, whose laid-back personality and ease with a song had become a reliable soother of World War II nerves. Add Barry Fitzgerald, professional Irishman, and you had enough sweetener to end the sugar shortage. Crosby plays an idealistic young priest interested in athletics (and, of course, music) who is assigned as assistant to crusty old Fitzgerald in a slum church saddled with a burdensome mortgage about to be foreclosed by grasping Gene Lockhart. Forward-looking youth and backward-looking oldster clash continually, but Crosby gradually wins Fitzgerald over. McCarey manages such treacle by his episodic way of handling the proceedings so that a certain element of surprise remains in what is a patently predictable plot. In short: good, clean, innocent fun, with a nice wartime dash of moral uplift.

Awards: Academy Awards: Best Actor (Crosby), Supporting Actor (Fitzgerald), Best Picture, Original Story (McCarey), Screenplay (Butler, Cavett), Best Song ("Swinging on a Star"); Golden Globe Awards: Best Picture, Supporting Actor (Fitzgerald); *Photoplay* Gold Medal Awards: Gold Medal; Academy Award Nominations: Best Actor (Fitzgerald), B&W Cinematography, Editing.

Selected Bibliography

Osterholm, J. Roger. *Bing Crosby: A Bio-Bibliography*. Westport, CT: Greenwood Press, 1994.
Peary, Danny. *Alternate Oscars*. New York: Delta, 1993.
Thomas, Tony. *The Films of the Forties*. Secaucus, NJ: Citadel Press, 1975.

GOLD DIGGERS OF 1933 (1933), musical. Directed by Mervyn LeRoy; with Joan Blondell, Ruby Keeler, Aline MacMahon, Dick Powell, Guy Kibbee, Warren William, Ned Sparks, Ginger Rogers, and Sterling Holloway; screenplay by Erwin Gelskey, James Seymour, David Boehm, and Ben Markson.

This is the second of the archetypal backstage musicals from Warners (the first was the enormously successful *42nd Street*). It is memorable chiefly because Busby Berkeley created an idiosyncratic geometry of kaleidoscopic chorines in big, vulgar, yet innocent numbers that are infinitely more entertaining than the pretentious ballet finales of 1950s musicals like *An American in Paris*. No one mistook this picture for art—and certainly not for life. What it is, is pure Hollywood hokum, doing what only movies can do in a way that continues to define the essence of that medium. It is also a shining example of the way Hollywood quickly learned to attract and use top musical talent. In this case, it was Harry Warren and Al Dubin, fresh from their *42nd Street* success, who wrote the score, which included the Oscar-winning "Lullaby of Broadway." It helped, too, to assemble a good cast, a script loose and loony enough to allow for improvisation, and a sense of desperate fun, desperate because lurking just outside every movie theater was the Great Depression waiting to snatch people back into grim, humorless anxiety. The result is a film that defines what is meant by "pure thirties."

Awards: Academy Award Nomination: Best Sound.

Selected Bibliography

Fordin, Hugh. *The World of Entertainment!: Hollywood's Greatest Musicals.* Garden City, NY: Doubleday, 1975.

Rubin, Martin. *Showstoppers: Busby Berkeley and the Tradition of Spectacle.* New York: Columbia University Press, 1993.

Thomas, Tony. *Harry Warren and the Hollywood Musical.* Secaucus, NJ: Citadel Press, 1975.

GONE WITH THE WIND (1939), historical drama. Directed by Victor Fleming [George Cukor, Sam Wood, B. Reeves Eason]; with Clark Gable, Vivien Leigh, Leslie Howard, Olivia de Havilland, Thomas Mitchell, Barbara O'Neil, Victory Jory, Laura Hope Crews, Hattie McDaniel, Ona Munson, Harry Davenport, Ann Rutherford, Evelyn Keyes, Carroll Nye, Paul Hurst, Isabel Jewell, Cliff Edwards, Ward Bond, Butterfly McQueen, Rand Brooks, Eddie Anderson, Oscar Polk, Jane Darwell, William Bakewell, Violet Kemble-Cooper, Eric Linden, and George Reeves; screenplay by Sidney Howard. Although final credit for the screenplay went solely to Howard, other writers who worked, or were reputed to have worked, on the screenplay include John Balderston, F. Scott Fitzgerald, Michael Foster, Oliver H. P. Garrett, Ben Hecht, Barbara Keon, Wilbur G. Kurtz, Val Lewton, Charles MacArthur, John Lee Mahin, Edwin Justus Mayer, Winston Miller, Donald Ogden Stewart, Jo Swerling, John Van Druten—and David O. Selznick himself who supervised all revisions and whose handiwork can be detected in the finished script.

"Forget it, Louis, no Civil War picture ever made a nickel," said Irving Thalberg to Louis B. Mayer in 1936 when Mayer was contemplating buying the rights to Margaret Mitchell's blockbuster best-seller. When he took Thalberg's advice and decided not to, it was eventually David O. Selznick who took the gamble. The rest, as they say, is history. *GWTW* (as it has come to be known) is indisputably one of the greatest examples of storytelling on film, maintaining interest for nearly four hours by using every trick known to the moviemaking trade. It is so well made that pictures after it have always suffered by comparison. Time may have improved technology and allowed for increased mobility and sophisticated editing, but the timing and momentum and excitement of *GWTW* are the result of good, old-fashioned know-how. No "auteur" was here trying to leave his stamp on the film, no upstaging upstart (or veteran, for that matter) was around to intrude on the integrity of the story, and the special effects are there to serve a clear purpose. As in the book, the most memorable incidents of this saga of the conquered South deal with human conflict set against the backdrop of the war, and this conflict is always given more importance than the history lesson or epic sweep that can so easily distract a director from telling the story. Director Victor Fleming never wastes a frame, never succumbs to the temptation to linger over a sunset or dwell on a face. In short, he avoids the tendency of some veteran directors either to bury the story beneath the spectacle (DeMille) or to favor photography over narrative (David Lean). Vivien Leigh's

Scarlett is a flawless portrayal. Risking her own sanity, Leigh "becomes" Scarlett the way she later "becomes" Blanche du Bois in *A Streetcar Named Desire*—and suffered for it. Gable, who resisted the role of Rhett Butler and was literally drafted to play it, is perfect in the part. And Hattie McDaniel, the first black person ever to win an Oscar, is a miracle as Mammy, a part she seems born to play. But, then, there *are* no weak performances in this incredible cast. They all shine, none brighter than Butterfly McQueen as the unforgettable Prissy who "ain't never birthed a baby." And underscoring it all is the inspired background music by Max Steiner. Seen in contemporary terms, it is racist, sexist, and reactionary—but supremely entertaining. Whole books have been written about it. It is a cinematic milestone, partly because it remains one of the greatest products of the much-maligned but miracle-making studio system. David O. Selznick was determined to make it the pinnacle of his career. He succeeded.

Awards: Academy Awards: Best Picture, Director, Actress (Leigh), Supporting Actress (McDaniel), Screenplay, Color Cinematography (Ernest Haller, Ray Rennahan, Wilfrid M. Cline), Art Direction (Lyle Wheeler, William Cameron Menzies), Editing (Hal C. Kern, James E. Newcom), Special Awards (use of color design, and use of coordinated equipment); *Photoplay* Medal of Honor; Academy Award Nominations: Best Actor (Gable), Supporting Actress (Olivia de Havilland), Original Score (Steiner), Sound, Special Effects.

Selected Bibliography

Bridges, Herb. *The Filming of "Gone with the Wind."* Macon, GA: Mercer University Press, 1984.
Cameron, Judy, and Paul J. Christman. *The Art of "Gone with the Wind": The Making of a Legend.* New York: Prentice-Hall Editions, 1989.
Hauer, Ronald. *David O. Selznick's "Gone with the Wind."* New York: Bonanza Books, 1986.
Lambert, Gavin. *GWTW: The Making of Gone with the Wind.* Boston: Little, Brown, 1973.
Molt, Cynthia Marylee. *"Gone with the Wind" on Film: A Complete Reference.* Jefferson, NC: McFarland & Co., 1990.

GOODBYE, MR. CHIPS (1939), drama. Directed by Sam Wood; with Robert Donat, Greer Garson, Paul von Hernried (Paul Henreid), Terry Kilburn, and John Mills; screenplay by R. C. Sherriff, Claudine West, and Eric Maschwitz.

James Hilton, one of the most popular authors of the 1930s and 1940s (*Lost Horizon, Random Harvest*), wrote this gentle tribute to his schoolmaster father in just a few hours. It was then published in an English newspaper where Alexander Woollcott discovered it and, as rumor has it, "went quietly mad." He read the story aloud over the radio, and it became an immediate best-seller and was quickly snatched by Hollywood. This unassuming movie is a charming account of the life of a schoolteacher, remarkably well acted by Robert Donat, who won an Oscar for his performance. Donat ages fifty years in the movie, beginning as a callow youth and advancing through middle age to a slightly doddering old man. The romance between the schoolteacher and the girl he meets (Garson) is fascinatingly developed. Greer Garson is Katherine, who becomes Donat's wife, only to die all too soon, leaving the schoolmaster nothing but his desire to go forward with his work and with the boys he tutors. Although the movie is something of a museum piece, it is a deeply affecting one. It was a very popular film, and no less a literary figure than Graham Greene has said that it is wrong to despise popularity in the cinema.

Awards: Academy Award: Best Actor (Donat); Academy Award Nominations: Best Picture, Director, Actress, Screenplay, Sound, Editing.

Selected Bibliography

Barrow, Kenneth. *Mr. Chips: The Life of Robert Donat.* London: Methuen, 1985.
Peary, Danny. *Alternate Oscars.* New York: Delta, 1993.
Sennett, Ted. *Hollywood's Golden Year, 1939.* New York: St. Martin's Press, 1989.

GOOD EARTH, THE (1937), drama. Directed by Sidney Franklin; with Paul Muni, Luise Rainer, Walter Connolly, Charley Grapewin, Jessie Ralph, Tilly Losch, Keye Luke, and Harold Huber; screenplay by Talbot Jennings, Tess Slesinger, and Claudine West.

"To the memory of Irving Grant Thalberg we dedicate this picture—his last great achievement!" Inserting this in the credits was Louis B. Mayer's way of acknowledging Thalberg's superior wisdom about the making of this picture, for at the time Thalberg was first considering it, Mayer had quipped: "Who wants to see a picture about Chinese farmers?" It was an echo of Thalberg's sneer at *Gone with the Wind*: "Forget it, Louis, no Civil War picture ever made a nickel." *The Good Earth* has not aged well, but at the time it was considered a masterful job of adaptation, of filming, of special effects, and particularly of acting. This story of greed ruining the lives of a simple Chinese farming couple is inflated and cumbersome, but it is saved by Rainer's genuinely moving portrayal of a Chinese peasant—and by a spectacular storm of locusts, a gimmick still dear to producers of blockbuster disaster movies. Although critics generally find the film well meaning but artificial and unconvincing, they credit the film with being historically valuable as a Hollywood prestige production of the 1930s. It is admittedly dated, but *The Good Earth* remains one of the superb visual adventures of the period—a sort of Chinese *Grapes of Wrath*.

Awards: Academy Awards: Best Actress (Rainer), Cinematography (Karl Freund); Academy Award Nominations: Best Picture, Director, Editing.

Selected Bibliography

Dooley, Roger. *From Scarface to Scarlett: American Films in the 1930s.* New York: Harcourt Brace Jovanovich, 1981.
Vermilye, Jerry. *The Films of the Thirties.* New York: Citadel Press, 1990.

GRABLE, BETTY. Actress. Born Elizabeth Ruth Grable on December 18, 1916, in St. Louis, Missouri; died on July 2, 1973. Grable was trained from age twelve at the Hollywood Professional School, and she began singing and dancing in the chorus line of Hollywood musicals before she was fourteen. In 1931 Sam Goldwyn signed her to a contract, changed her name to Frances Dean, and cast her in bit parts in several of his films, hoping to develop her into a star. The following year, her contract was picked up by RKO, where her name was changed back to Grable and she was given leads in B musicals and comedies as well as bit parts in better pictures. Still a starlet, she moved to Paramount in 1937 and married former child star Jackie Coogan. They divorced in 1940, the same year Darryl F. Zanuck brought her to Fox to use her as a threat to the uncooperative Alice Faye. It worked, and before long, Grable dominated the studio and was a top box office attraction. She had a fresh beauty and shapely legs that are one of the most remembered icons of World War II when she became the number-one "pin-up girl" of the GIs. Fox publicity insured her famous legs with Lloyds of London for a million dollars, and she became the industry's highest-paid star. In 1943 she married trumpeter-bandleader Harry James. They divorced in 1965. Her popularity began to decline in the early 1950s, as did the popularity of the film musical itself, and by the mid-1950s her screen career was over. She went on to appear in nightclubs and occasional stage musicals and was one of the rotation of stars heading the cast in Broadway's *Hello, Dolly!* She died at fifty-six of lung cancer.

Filmography: Happy Days, Let's Go Places, New Movietone Follies of 1930, Whoopee! (1930); Kiki, Palmy Days (1931); The Greeks Had a Word for Them, The Kid from Spain, Probation, Hold'Em Jail (1932); Child of Manhattan, The Sweetheart of Sigma Chi, Cavalcade, Melody Cruise, What Price Innocence? (1933); By Your Leave, Student Tour, The Gay Divorcee (1934); The Nitwits, Old Man Rhythm, Collegiate (1935); Follow the Fleet, Pigskin Parade, Don't Turn 'Em Loose (1936); This Way Please, Thrill of a Lifetime (1937); College Swing, Give Me a Sailor, Campus Confessions (1938); Man about Town, Million Dollar Legs, The Day the Bookies Wept (1939); Down Argentine Way, Tin Pan Alley (1940); Moon over Miami, A Yank in the R.A.F., I Wake Up Screaming (1941); Footlight Serenade, Song of the Islands, Springtime in the Rockies (1942); Coney Island, Sweet Rosie O'Grady (1943); Four Jills in a Jeep, Pin-up Girl (1944); Diamond Horseshoe, The Dolly Sisters (1945); Do You Love Me? [cameo] (1946); The Shocking Miss Pilgrim, Mother Wore Tights (1947); That Lady in Ermine, When My Baby Smiles at Me (1948); The Beautiful Blonde from Bashful Bend (1949); Wabash Avenue, My Blue Heaven (1950); Call Me Mister, Meet Me After the Show (1951); The Farmer Takes a Wife, How to Marry a Millionaire (1953); Three for the Show, How to Be Very Very Popular (1955).

Selected Bibliography

Billman, Larry. *Betty Grable: A Bio-Bibliography*. Westport, CT: Greenwood Press, 1993.

Pastos, Spero. *Pin-up: The Tragedy of Betty Grable*. New York: Putnam, 1986.

Warren, Doug. *Betty Grable, the Reluctant Movie Queen*. New York: St. Martin's Press, 1981.

GRAND HOTEL (1932), drama. Directed by Edmund Goulding; with Greta Garbo, John Barrymore, Joan Crawford, Wallace Beery, Lionel Barrymore,

Lewis Stone, Jean Hersholt, Ferdinand Gottschalk, Tully Marshall, and Mary Carlisle; screenplay by William A. Drake.

"The greatest cast in stage or screen history!" screamed the blurb for this film, and it is undoubtedly the cast that accounts for *Grand Hotel*'s curious place in film history. This film is a classic for being a classic; that is, it is so well known for its concept (the comings and goings of strangers under one roof), for its snatches of dialogue (a hotel where "nothing ever happens"; "I want to be alone"), for its bevy of stars (Garbo, Crawford, two Barrymores, Wallace Beery, et al.), and for its spin-offs (two or three movies, a couple of musicals, and a TV series all based loosely on Vicki Baum's best-selling *Menschen im Hotel*) that serious criticism of it seems irrelevant. It has been called the *Nashville* of its day, a picture with an inflated reputation that is interesting now only as an example of what screen glamour used to be and what "stars" were. The backstage problems are almost more interesting than the storyline of the movie. The director, Edmund Goulding, was known as the "lion tamer" because of his ability to handle difficult actresses, and he had his hands full with Garbo and Crawford, two rival actresses whose shared scenes had to be shot separately and then spliced. Other members of this large, talented cast also clashed or caused problems. Apparently, scene stealing was the sport of choice. But with all its problems, the film was an enormous success, partly because it was promoted with a great deal of publicity hokum that made audiences eager to see the finished product.

Awards: Academy Award: Best Picture.

Selected Bibliography

Conway, Michael, Dion McGregor, and Mark Ricci. *The Films of Greta Garbo*. New York: Bonanza Books, 1963.
Dooley, Roger. *From Scarface to Scarlett: American Films in the 1930s*. New York: Harcourt Brace Jovanovich, 1981.
Vermilye, Jerry. *The Films of the Thirties*. New York: Citadel Press, 1990.

GRANT, CARY. Actor. Born Archibald Alexander Leach on January 18, 1904, in Bristol, England; died on November 29, 1986. The name Cary Grant is synonymous with the golden age of Hollywood. He was an actor whose name tops the list of just about everybody's favorite film star immortals—and another legendary figure who won almost no awards yet captured audiences of every kind with his effortless charm, humor, and modesty. Never did Grant seem to be aware of his own charisma or his incredible good looks, and never did he fail to light up the screen. On top of all this, he was wonderfully versatile, adept at everything from light comedy (at which he excelled) to suspense (Hitchcock adored him), even melodrama (*None But the Lonely Heart*). David Thomson calls him simply "the best and most important actor in the history of the cinema," ascribing his brilliance to the fact that he can reveal both the light and dark sides of human nature simultaneously, "without fraud, disguise, or exaggeration [and] take part in a fantasy without being deceived by it.'' As Archie Leach, Grant grew up poor in a Bristol slum and ran away from home at thirteen to join a traveling acrobatic troupe as song-and-dance man and occasional juggler. When the troupe toured America in 1920, Grant came along, staying to work as a Coney Island lifeguard during the summer and carrying advertising signs about on stilts during the winter. He returned to England in 1923, where he began appearing in musical comedies. Arthur Hammerstein noticed him and brought him back to New York to appear in the musical *Golden Dawn*. This was followed by other Broadway musicals and a summer engagement in St. Louis, where he played and sang in twelve operettas. He continued to Hollywood and signed a Paramount contract. After a series of good supporting roles, he was given the lead opposite Marlene Dietrich in Von Sternberg's *Blonde Venus*. Mae West then chose him as her co-star in *She Done Him Wrong*. (''Why don't you come up sometime 'n see me?'') Before long, Grant was established as a romantic leading man, but toward the end of the decade, he was given the chance to display his flair for screwball comedy in such films as *Topper*, *The Awful Truth*, *Bringing Up Baby*, and *Holiday*, and it was this image of a sophisticated, debonair rebel in a world gone mad that made him a box office favorite for three decades. Grant himself once said: ''I play myself to perfection.'' He died of a stroke at eighty-two.

Filmography: This Is the Night, Sinners in the Sun, Merrily We Go to Hell, The Devil and the Deep, Blonde Venus, Hot Saturday, Madame Butterfly [as Lt. Pinkerton] (1932); She Done Him Wrong, The Woman Accused, The Eagle and the Hawk, Gambling Ship, I'm No Angel, Alice in Wonderland [as the Mock Turtle] (1933); Thirty-Day Princess, Born to Be Bad, Kiss and Make Up, Ladies Should Listen (1934); Enter Madame, Wings in the Dark, The Last Outpost (1935); Sylvia Scarlett, Big Brown Eyes, Suzy, Wedding Present, The Amazing Quest of Ernest Bliss/Romance and Riches/Amazing Adventure (1936); When You're in Love, Topper, The Toast of New York, The Awful Truth (1937); Bringing Up Baby, Holiday (1938); Gunga Din, Only Angels Have Wings, In Name Only (1939); His Girl Friday, My Favorite Wife, The Howards of Virginia (1940); The Philadelphia Story, Penny Serenade, Suspicion (1941); The Talk of the Town, Once upon a Honeymoon (1942); Mr. Lucky (1943); Destination Tokyo, Once upon a Time, None But the Lonely Heart, Arsenic and Old Lace (1944); Without Reservations [cameo], Night and Day [as Cole Porter], Notorious (1946); The Bachelor and the Bobby-Soxer, The Bishop's Wife (1947); Mr. Blandings Builds His Dream House, Every Girl Should Be Married (1948); I Was a Male War Bride (1949); Crisis (1950); People Will Talk (1951); Room for One More, Monkey Business (1952); Dream Wife (1953); To Catch a Thief (1955); The Pride and the Passion, An Affair to Remember, Kiss Them for Me (1957); Indiscreet, Houseboat (1958); North by Northwest, Operation Petticoat (1959); The Grass Is Greener (1961); That Touch of Mink (1962); Charade (1963); Father Goose (1964); Walk Don't Run (1966).

Honors: Academy Award Nomination: Best Actor (*Penny Serenade*, 1941); Academy Award Nomination: Best Actor (*None But the Lonely Heart*, 1944); Special Academy Award (for his cumulative contribution to films, 1969).

Selected Bibliography

Buehrer, Beverley Bare. *Cary Grant: A Bio-Bibliography*. Westport, CT: Greenwood Press, 1990.

Deschner, Donald. *The Complete Films of Cary Grant*. Secaucus, NJ: Citadel Press, 1991.

Highman, Charles, and Roy Moseley. *Cary Grant: The Lonely Heart*. San Diego: Harcourt Brace Jovanovich, 1989.

Trescott, Pamela. *Cary Grant: His Movies and His Life*. Washington, D.C.: Acropolis Books, 1987.

Wansell, Geoffrey. *Haunted Idol: The Story of the Real Cary Grant*. New York: Quill, 1992.

GRAPES OF WRATH, THE (1940), drama. Directed by John Ford; with Henry Fonda, Jane Darwell, John Carradine, Charley Grapewin, Dorris Bowden, Russell Simpson, and John Qualen; screenplay by Nunnally Johnson.

The Grapes of Wrath is one of the few films that truly deserves to be called a classic. It is a totally remarkable film in every way—scenery, cinematography, acting, mood, message, and its mythical realism. It is larger than life, transforming the plight of Oklahoma farmers fleeing westward for survival into the epic struggle of mankind everywhere at any time battling overwhelming odds. It is a film that could so easily have failed. At any point and in lesser hands than Ford's, it could have become maudlin, silly, overblown, could have leaned too far toward socialist propaganda or too close to the Beverly Hillbillies. Instead, it transcends all easy labels with its warmth and sincerity, its nobility and humanity, defying anyone to attach a political label to it. Henry Fonda, that most genuinely American of actors, brings passion to the role of Tom Joad, while Jane Darwell as Ma Joad is earth mother incarnate, the sturdy mainstay of the Joad clan. And in the more than half a century since it came out, *The Grapes of Wrath* has not lost one whit of its power to move.

Awards: Academy Awards: Best Director (Ford), Supporting Actress (Darwell); New York City Film Critics Circle Award, National Board of Review Award: Best Picture; Academy Award Nominations: Best Picture, Actor (Fonda), Screenplay, Editing, Sound.

Selected Bibliography

Gallagher, Tag. *John Ford: The Man and His Films*. Berkeley: University of California Press, 1986.

Peary, Danny. *Alternate Oscars*. New York: Delta, 1993.

Thomas, Tony. *The Films of Henry Fonda*. Secaucus, NJ: Citadel Press, 1983.

GREAT ESCAPE, THE (1963), adventure drama. Directed by John Sturges; with Steve McQueen, James Garner, Richard Attenborough, Charles Bronson, James Coburn, David McCallum, Donald Pleasence, James Donald, Gordon Jackson, and John Leyton; screenplay by James Clavell and W. R. Burnett.

The Great Escape is a perfect "escape" film, masterfully directed and written, with an infectious undercurrent of wry humor. Based on a true story, this account of an attempt at a massive escape from a German prisoner-of-war camp was beautifully photographed by Daniel Fapp on location in Germany. In the hands of producer-director John Sturges, this film manages to tell a serious story without ever skimping on excitement, emotion, and pure entertainment. Early scenes showing the escape plan being formulated are played largely for laughs—sometimes at the expense of reality. But American servicemen are famous for their sense of humor under pressure, a sort of cocky glibness that helps conceal the worry underneath. Sometimes, though, it seems as if the inmates are running the asylum, so lax are the prison authorities. There are some exceptional performances, the most provocative being that of Steve McQueen as a dauntless Yank pilot. James Garner is engaging as usual as the compound's ''scrounger,'' a traditional type in the *Stalag 17* breed of war-prison film. Charles Bronson and James Coburn also turn in impressive performances. But it is the British actors who give some of the finest performances in the picture. Richard Attenborough, as the man who orchestrates the escape, is especially convincing. And Donald Pleasence gives a moving portrayal of a prisoner losing his eyesight. In the background is a rich, sonorous score by Elmer Bernstein whose martial theme is particularly stirring. And the final half hour, with Steve McQueen on a motorcycle heading for the Swiss border, is surely one of the most exciting escape sequences ever filmed. *The Great Escape* has come to be considered one of the very best accounts of an actual wartime escape attempt ever dramatized on film.

Awards: Academy Award Nomination: Best Editing (Ferris Webster).

Selected Bibliography

Guttmacher, Peter. *Legendary War Movies*. New York: MetroBooks, 1996.
Quirk, Lawrence J. *The Great War Films: From ''The Birth of a Nation'' to Today*. Secaucus, NJ: Carol Publishers, 1994.

GREAT MCGINTY, THE (1940), comedy/drama. Directed by Preston Sturges; with Brian Donlevy, Muriel Angelus, Akim Tamiroff, Allyn Joslyn, William Demarest, Louis Jean Heydt, and Arthur Hoyt; screenplay by Preston Sturges.

After a long stretch as a film scenarist, Preston Sturges initiated his career as a director with this film, for which he also wrote the screenplay. Some say this film is not up to his later works, but what makes it important is the fact that in it Sturges displays the originality that sets him apart from other directors. Primarily what makes Sturges unique is his deft blend of comedy and drama and his sharp dialogue. His genius lay in his ability to maintain momentum and still shift mood gears. Sturges's story, as in all his films, departs radically from accepted formula. In this case, his central character leads a life of unrelieved crookedness until suddenly he does one honest thing and immediately becomes a fugitive from justice. No good deed goes unpunished, as the saying goes. Critics praised this film for its satire of the American political system and welcomed Sturges as a director as adroit and inventive as any in the business. The movie opens like a race horse bursting from the starting gate, and the pace never slackens until its surprise conclusion. The irreverent Sturges was Frank Capra's dark side, flinging societal pieties like the success ethic into the face of the audience. In fact, it became Sturges's trademark to burlesque the revered Horatio Alger success stories. Imperfect as it may be, *The Great McGinty* remains a film to be reckoned with.

Awards: Academy Award: Best Original Screenplay (Sturges).

Selected Bibliography

Cywinski, Ray. *Preston Sturges: A Guide to References and Resources*. Boston: G. K. Hall, 1984.

Siegel, Scott, and Barbara Siegel. *American Film Comedy: From Abbott & Costello to Jerry Zucker*. Englewood Cliffs, NJ: Prentice-Hall, 1994.

GREAT ZIEGFELD, THE (1936), musical. Directed by Robert Z. Leonard; with William Powell, Myrna Loy, Luise Rainer, Frank Morgan, Fanny Brice, Virginia Bruce, Reginald Owen, Ray Bolger, and Stanley Morner (Dennis Morgan); screenplay by William Anthony McGuire.

This big, spectacular bonanza of a movie either excites or bores critics, mostly depending on their tolerance for long musicals, for long it is, just ten minutes short of three hours. Ultimately, it's hard to be judgmental about a film that is so representative of the film musical of the 1930s. It is also pure Hollywood hokum biography, in this case the biography of Mr. Broadway himself, Florenz Ziegfeld, a name still to be reckoned with in the annals of entertainment. William Powell is perfectly cast as "Ziggy," and Luise Rainer won an Academy Award for her stunning performance as his second wife, Anna Held. The whole cast is excellent, though, and the musical numbers (e.g., "A Pretty Girl Is Like a Melody") are what Hollywood legend is made of. While most critics find it interesting in the context of its time, others find it inexcusably tedious. Musical taste is so subject to the vagaries of whim that it is difficult to give this movie an objective assessment. Suffice it to say that it chronicles a legendary period and a legendary personality with integrity and verve, and as such, it deserves to be taken on its own terms. And on those terms, it is a fascinating insight into a bygone (but unforgettable) period in American popular musical history.

Awards: Academy Awards: Best Picture, Actress (Rainer), Dance Direction; Academy Award Nominations: Best Director, Original Story, Art Direction, Editing.

Selected Bibliography

Fordin, Hugh. *The World of Entertainment!: Hollywood's Greatest Musicals*. Garden City, NY: Doubleday, 1975.

GUADALCANAL DIARY (1943), war drama. Directed by Lewis Seiler; with Preston Foster, Lloyd Nolan, William Bendix, Richard Conte, Anthony Quinn, and Richard Jaeckel; screenplay by Lamar Trotti.

20th Century–Fox lost no time in bringing the U.S. Marines' successful Solomon Islands campaign to the screen. It was the first important victory of the

Pacific war, and *Guadalcanal Diary* is generally considered to be one of the best World War II war movies. It is a film that manages to be both eloquent and entertaining, avoiding flag waving in favor of understated heroism. Although the deeds of the men are heroic, the men themselves reveal no self-consciousness of heroism. With minor exceptions, *Guadalcanal Diary* is skillfully produced. Of the cast, William Bendix stands out in a seriocomic part as a tough but soft taxi driver from Brooklyn, while Preston Foster and Lloyd Nolan give effective performances in the other principal leads. The film was respected at the time for its authenticity, but now it seems dated in that it features the cliched cross section of acceptable American types. Critics who note contrivances or synthetic touches must remember that making a war film during wartime itself and trying to duplicate contemporary history pose real problems for moviemakers. Despite the difficulties, this film is impressively staged, with location filming actually done at Camp Pendleton, California. It is unapologetically propagandistic—as were all wartime war films—but it is also great storytelling.

Selected Bibliography

Basinger, Jeanine. *The World War II Combat Film: Anatomy of a Genre*. New York: Columbia University Press, 1986.
Guttmacher, Peter. *Legendary War Movies*. New York: MetroBooks, 1996.

GUN CRAZY (1949), crime drama. Directed by Joseph H. Lewis; with Peggy Cummins, John Dall, Berry Kroeger, Morris Carnovsky, Anabel Shaw, Harry Lewis, Nedrick Young, and Rusty (Russ) Tamblyn; screenplay by MacKinlay Kantor and Millard Kaufman (fronting for blacklisted writer Dalton Trumbo).

This "sleeper" has become something of a cult film. Part of its attraction is the surprise of having grit and style mixed so skillfully in what was supposed to be a B movie. Another reason, however, is its innovative filming, including some groundbreaking long shots that are still shown in film classes as examples of inspired cinematography. Peggy Cummins, originally imported from England to play the lead in *Forever Amber* (the part went to Linda Darnell when Cummins was considered too unknown), plays the femme fatale, baby doll with an ice pick, Bonnie type of wicked woman who leads gun-crazy John Dall into a life of crime. Part of their sleazy charm is that they both look like honeymooners, not natural-born killers. Thus, they were among the first of the screen figures to challenge the stereotype of the gum-chewing moll linked with the cigar-chomping ex-con. The film starts off slowly, as if teasing the viewer to dismiss it as inferior. But the pace gradually quickens, and the momentum never abates. It's not a pleasant story, nor was it intended to be. Any sympathy for Dall is a matter of audience stereotyping (innocent-looking young men only go astray when some hard-hearted blond is around). He is as unregenerate as she and proves that if all it takes is for someone to bring it out of you, then it was in there festering all the time. Rotten is rotten, and no external lure can be blamed for its manifestation. Film scholars still cite the opening long shot, a lengthy uninterrupted take (shot from inside a car) of a small-town heist, and the finale, shot in a misty swamp (to avoid the need for extras), as prime examples of cinematic art, and critics still find it superior to *Bonnie and Clyde* and most of its other imitations. Dalton Trumbo, who was blacklisted at the time, later revealed that he wrote the script and persuaded Kaufman to let his name be used.

Selected Bibliography

Rosow, Eugene. *Born to Lose: The Gangster Film in America*. New York: Oxford University Press, 1978.

GUNFIGHT AT THE O.K. CORRAL (1957), western. Directed by John Sturges; with Burt Lancaster, Kirk Douglas, Rhonda Fleming, Jo Van Fleet, John Ireland, Lee Van Cleef, Frank Faylen, Kenneth Tobey, DeForest Kelley, Earl Holliman, Dennis Hopper, Martin Milner, and Olive Carey; screenplay by Leon Uris.

This classic western is generally considered to be a landmark film, superbly produced on all levels, one that lifted the concept of the horse opera into the realm of cinematic respectability. The film recounts the historic confrontation between Wyatt Earp, his brothers, and Doc Holliday and the Clanton gang at the O.K. Corral in Tombstone, Arizona. Burt Lancaster and Kirk Douglas are in top form as Earp and Holliday. Many critics consider this a classic western, masterfully directed by John Sturges, already well known for his *The Magnificent Seven*, a film that this film resembles, as it does *High Noon*. However, the film does have its detractors. Some critics registered a certain indifference to the film, finding it neither particularly interesting nor uninteresting, arguing that it lacks passion and that the climactic shootout comes almost as anticlimax in a western that is really set in a small town. Others find it disappointing, saying that although it is lavishly mounted and carefully executed, it becomes overlong and overwrought. However, the gunfight has become one of those mythical occurrences in the saga of the Old West that take on an aura that continues to fascinate audiences.

Awards: Academy Award Nominations: Best Editing, Sound.

Selected Bibliography

Buscombe, Ed. *The BFI Companion to the Western*. London: Andre Deutsch, 1988.
Hardy, Phil, ed. *The Overlook Film Encyclopedia: The Western*. Woodstock, NY: Overlook Press, 1994.

GUNFIGHTER, THE (1950), western. Directed by Henry King; with Gregory Peck, Helen Westcott, Millard Mitchell, Jean Parker, Karl Malden, Skip Homeier, Verna Felton, Ellen Corby, Richard Jaeckel, and Alan Hale, Jr.; screenplay by William Bowers and William Sellers.

''His only friend was his gun—his only refuge, a woman's heart!'' went the silly blurb for this downbeat, small-scale, but very careful adult western. *The Gunfighter* is a superb western, almost classical in its observance of the unities of time, setting, and action. In this respect it resembles *High Noon*, although it's bleaker and unrelenting. It broke new ground in its day with Peck's characterization of the notorious gunfighter Jimmy Ringo, who's just about over the hill and haunted by his reputation, lonely and fearful of dying at the hands of some young, new quick-draw artist who is unintimidated. Henry King does a magnificent job of directing, and there is excellent acting not only from Peck but from the entire cast. Most critics are favorably inclined toward this film, admiring the classical sense of fate that gives it the dimensions of tragedy. They also comment on the muted quality of the photography that suggests those faded photographs of the nineteenth-century West.

Selected Bibliography

Buscombe, Ed. *The BFI Companion to the Western*. London: Andre Deutsch, 1988.
Griggs, John. *The Films of Gregory Peck*. Secaucus, NJ: Citadel Press, 1984.

GUNGA DIN (1939), adventure drama. Directed by George Stevens; with Cary Grant, Victor McLaglen, Douglas Fairbanks, Jr., Joan Fontaine, Sam Jaffe, Eduardo Ciannelli, Montagu Love, Abner Biberman, and Robert Coote; screenplay by Joel Sayre and Fred Guiol.

This rousing adventure has just about everything: humor, suspense, spectacle, action. This is why it remains one of the all-time great adventure films, even more popular today, at least with film buffs, than it was at the time of its initial release. The story is based vaguely on Rudyard Kipling's famous poem about three soldier-comrades in nineteenth-century India who divide their time between quelling native uprisings and getting into trouble with their superior officers. *Gunga Din* is pure adventure, and it comes vividly alive under the careful direction of George Stevens. Although great liberties were taken with history, the performances by all the principals are so delightful and the action so exciting that all the film's little sins can be forgiven. While modern audiences may wince a bit at the film's smug colonialist attitudes, it is still a captivating adventure yarn filled with well-staged fights, fine performances, and a general sense of rowdy camaraderie. The finale is very exciting and wonderfully satisfying. In short, it's a movie for kids of all ages.

Selected Bibliography

Sennett, Ted. *Hollywood's Golden Year, 1939*. New York: St. Martin's Press, 1989.
Vermilye, Jerry. *The Films of the Thirties*. New York: Citadel Press, 1990.

GUNS OF NAVARONE, THE (1961), war drama. Directed by J. Lee Thompson; with Gregory Peck, David Niven, Anthony Quinn, Stanley Baker, Anthony Quayle, James Darren, Irene Papas, Gia Scala, James Robertson Justice, Richard Harris, Albert Lieven, Bryan Forbes, and Walter Gotell; screenplay by Carl Foreman.

This gripping film about Allied commandos during World War II plotting to destroy German guns is high adventure throughout. In this story, adapted from Alistair MacLean's novel, the Axis countries have virtually overrun Greece and the islands, except for Crete and the tiny island of Kheros. The only chance for the exhausted garrison of 2,000 men is evacuation by sea, through a channel that is guarded by a couple of huge, radar-controlled guns on Navarone. A small band of saboteurs is dispatched to render these guns inoperable. The gang consists of Peck, Niven, Quinn, Baker, Quayle, and Darren. They all turn in creditable performances. Two women have been written into the story, Greek partisans played well by Irene Papas and Gia Scala. The picture has some great edge-of-the-seat scenes including a harrowing cliff-scaling sequence, a scene when the saboteurs are rounded up by the enemy, a spectacular storm segment, and a whopper of a grand finale. This is the sort of movie where you go out for popcorn during the philosophical debates and forget to eat it when the tension mounts. A director who alternates between discussion and destruction is perhaps saying something unsettling about the use of war to settle—or at least stifle—debate.

Awards: Academy Award: Best Special Effects; Academy Award Nominations: Best Picture, Director, Adapted Screenplay, Editing, Score of a Dramatic Picture, Sound.

Selected Bibliography

Griggs, John. *The Films of Gregory Peck*. Secaucus, NJ: Citadel Press, 1984.
Guttmacher, Peter. *Legendary War Movies*. New York: MetroBooks, 1996.

H

HAIL THE CONQUERING HERO (1944), comedy. Directed by Preston Sturges; with Eddie Bracken, Ella Raines, Raymond Walburn, William Demarest, Bill Edwards, Elizabeth Patterson, Jimmy Conlin, Franklin Pangborn, Jack Norton, Paul Porcasi, and Al Bridge; screenplay by Preston Sturges.

It is generally agreed that of all the brilliant Sturges films this one is his best. Eddie Bracken plays a marine who is discharged after one month of service because of hay fever. Buddies carry him back to his hometown where he is mistakenly welcomed as a hero. This gem of a film has been called a wonderful satire on small-town jingoism, a bold undertaking considering that it was made during World War II. Every middle-class American sacred cow is skewered in this uproarious mix of satire, slapstick, and comedy of manners. In addition, it contains dazzling dialogue, made up mostly of mind-boggling non sequiturs, delivered with zany clarity by an incredible gang of crazy characters. Some critics have found its ending a bit sentimental, but given its wartime context, such sentiment is not unexceptional. Most critics liked the film, finding it irresistible in spite of (or maybe because of) its irreverence and its slapstick. What endears it to audiences and critics alike, ultimately, is the humanity shimmering just beneath its seemingly brittle surface, for it is human frailty and goodness of heart that can be perceived beneath what seems like a frantic but futile effort to conceal it.

Awards: Academy Award Nomination: Best Original Screenplay (Sturges).

Selected Bibliography

Cywinski, Ray. *Preston Sturges: A Guide to References and Resources*. Boston: G. K. Hall, 1984.

Levy, Emanuel. *Small-Town America in Film: The Decline and Fall of Community*. New York: Continuum, 1991.

Ursini, James. *The Fabulous Life and Times of Preston Sturges*. New York: Curtis Books, 1973.

HARLOW, JEAN. Actress. Born Harlean Carpenter, on March 3, 1911, in Kansas City, Missouri; died on June 7, 1937. It's hard now to understand what all the fuss was about concerning Harlow. To comprehend her magnetic appeal, you really have to immerse yourself in the 1930s, for surely she symbolizes the 1930s as Marilyn Monroe does the 1950s. Harlow is art deco incarnate. Her stylized platinum-blond hair, her thin, penciled eyebrows, the angular cut of her face, her earthy speech, her exaggerated motions all cry 1930s escapism, sophistication, glamour, and the emergence of a new kind of woman, aggressively made up, decked out, and behaved. She wasn't really beautiful, and she wasn't really talented, but she had a sense of humor and of self-parody that, like Monroe, she knew how to manipulate. Although Harlow's early career was far from spectacular, the public began responding to her vulgar platinum-blond glamour in such films as *The Public Enemy* and *Platinum Blonde*. The turning point in her career came when she signed with MGM, underwent their star-grooming treatment, and soon was transformed from what one critic described as a "coarse, flashy, whorish sexpot" into an actress of some subtlety with a natural flair for comedy. Cast opposite such macho male stars as Clark Gable and Spencer Tracy, Harlow soon became a superstar. She fell ill with uremic poisoning during the filming of *Saratoga* in 1937. She died on June 7 of that year, of a cerebral edema, at age twenty-six.

Filmography: The Saturday Night Kid (1929); Hell's Angels (1930); The Secret Six, The Iron Man, The Public Enemy, Goldie, Platinum Blonde (1931); Three Wise Girls, The Best of the City, Red-Headed Woman, Red Dust (1932); Hold Your Man, Bombshell (1933); Dinner at Eight, The Girl from Missouri (1934); Reckless, China Seas (1935); Riffraff, Wife vs. Secretary, Suzy, Libeled Lady (1936); Personal Property, Saratoga (1937).

Selected Bibliography

Brown, Curtis F. *Jean Harlow*. New York: Pyramid Publications, 1977.

Golden, Eve. *Platinum Girl: The Life and Legends of Jean Harlow*. New York: Abbeville Press, 1991.

Stenn, David. *Bombshell: The Life and Death of Jean Harlow*. New York: Doubleday, 1993.

HATHAWAY, HENRY. Director. Born Henri Leopold de Fiennes on March 13, 1898, in Sacramento, California; died on February 11, 1985. Hathaway may not have the reputation of John Ford or Howard Hawks, but he spent more than forty years turning out westerns and thrillers of considerable quality, many of which have become classics. Hathaway entered films at age ten as a child actor. Following military service in World War I, he became an assistant director, and then after several years both before and behind the camera, he got a chance to direct in 1932 and was an established director of prestige pictures by 1936. At both Paramount and Fox, he acquired a reputation as a skilled craftsman who went about his business without fuss or affectation. He was famous for making do with whatever he had, for staying within budget, and for bringing the film in on schedule. With the right material, he made such superior films as *The Lives of a Bengal Lancer*, *Kiss of Death*, and *The Desert Fox*. In the mid-1940s he pioneered the postwar trend of shooting features on actual exterior locations in a semidocumentary style. He was at ease in any genre, but he was best at action films, particularly westerns and crime dramas. Hathaway wore many hats during his career, but whatever his role, he was always the consummate Hollywood professional, and like so many of Hollywood's top talents, Hathaway never won an award.

Filmography: Heritage of the Desert, Wild Horse Mesa (1932); Under the Tono Rim, Sunset Pass, Man of the Forest, To the Last Man, The Thundering Herd (1933); The Last Round-Up, Come on Marines!, The Witching Hour, Now and Forever (1934); The Lives of a Bengal Lancer, Peter Ibbetson (1935); The Trail of the Lonesome Pine, Go West Young Man (1936); Souls at Sea [also prod.] (1937); Spawn of the North (1938); The Real Glory (1939); Johnny Apollo, Brigham Young, Frontiersman (1940); The Shepherd of the Hills, Sundown (1941); Ten Gentlemen from West Point (1942); China Girl (1943); Home in Indiana, Wing and a Prayer (1944); Nob Hill, The House on 92nd Street (1945); The Dark Corner (1946); 13 Rue Madeleine, Kiss of Death (1947); Call Northside 777 (1948); Down to the Sea in Ships (1949); The Black Rose (1950); You're in the Navy Now/USS Teakettle, Fourteen Hours, Rawhide, The Desert Fox (1951); Red Skies of Montana [dir. some scenes, uncredited], Diplomatic Courier, O Henry's Full House ["The Clarion Call" episode] (1952); Niagara, White Witch Doctor (1953); Prince Valiant, Garden of Evil (1954); The Racers (1955); The Bottom of the Bottle, 23 Paces to Baker Street (1956); The Wayward Bus [directed part, uncredited], Legend of the Lost [also prod.] (1957); From Hell to Texas (1958); Woman Obsessed (1959); Seven Thieves, North to Alaska [also prod.] (1960); How the West Was Won ["The Rivers," "The Plains," "The Outlaws" episodes] (1962); Rampage [dir. some scenes, uncredited] (1963); Of Human Bondage [started, uncredited], Circus World (1964); The Sons of Katie Elder (1965); Nevada Smith [also prod.] (1966); The Last Safari (1967); 5 Card Stud (1968); True Grit (1969); Airport [temporarily replaced ailing George Seaton, uncredited] (1970); Raid on Rommel, Shootout (1971); Hangup/Superdude (1974).

Honors: Academy Award Nomination: Best Director (*The Lives of a Bengal Lancer*, 1935).

Selected Bibliography

Finler, Joel W. *The Movie Directors Story*. London: Octopus Books, 1985.
Sarris, Andrew. *The American Cinema: Directors and Directions 1929–1968*. New York: E. P. Dutton, 1968.

HAWKS, HOWARD. Director, producer, screenwriter. Born Howard Winchester Hawks on May 30, 1896, in Goshen, Indiana; died on December 26, 1977. Educated at Cornell University (mechanical engineering). Hawks is widely recognized as one of the greatest American filmmakers. His long and illustrious career virtually spans the Hollywood studio era. Hawks had his first encounter with the movies in 1916–1917 when he worked in the props department of Famous Players–Lasky. Later he independently produced several films for director Allan Dwan and took a job with the script department of Famous Players–Lasky, where he did a lot of uncredited work on the scripts of dozens of movies. (He also worked uncredited on the screenplays of all the films he directed.) Although he made several films during the silent era, Hawks hit his stride with the coming of sound. His trademark became the machine-gun tempo of the dialogue in his films, with characters frequently delivering their lines at an unnaturally rapid pace, contributing to the madcap momentum of his comedies. Probably the best example of this style is Cary Grant's performance in *His Girl Friday*. Hawks got along well with actors, who liked his method of letting the camera dwell on them rather than using it to intrude upon their performances. Hawks once defined a good director as "someone who doesn't annoy you." He liked to position his camera at eye level in order to capture gestures that were often more eloquent than words in revealing character. Katharine Hepburn, Rosalind Russell, and Ann Sheridan gave some of their best performances in Hawks comedies, as did Cary Grant. Hawks worked in virtually every genre: gangster films, war films, westerns, films noirs, musicals, epics, and science fiction, and his movies celebrate such values as warmth, openness, and a sense of humor. While critics continue to differ on just what Hawks was up to, all agree that he has left us a breathtaking variety of memorable films to enjoy.

Filmography: [many of these were uncredited]: A Little Princess (1917); Quicksands (1923); Tiger Love (1924); The Dressmaker from Paris, The Road to Glory (1925); Fig Leaves, Honesty—The Best Policy (1926); The Cradle Snatchers, Paid to Love, Underworld (1927); The Air Circus, Fazil, A Girl in Every Port (1928); Trent's Last Case (1929); The Dawn Patrol/Flight Commander (1930); The Criminal Code (1931); The Crowd Roars, Red Dust, Scarface, Tiger Shark (1932); Today We Live (1933); Twentieth Century, Viva Villa! (1934); Barbary Coast, Ceiling Zero (1935); Come and Get It/Roaring Timber, The Road to Glory, Sutter's Gold (1936); Captains Courageous (1937); Bringing Up Baby, Test Pilot (1938); Gone with the Wind, Gunga Din, Indianapolis Speedway, Only Angels Have Wings (1939); His Girl Friday (1940); Ball of Fire, Sergeant York (1941); Air Force, Corvette K-225, The Outlaw (1943); To Have and Have Not (1944); The Big Sleep (1946); Red River, A Song Is Born (1948); I Was a Male War Bride (1949); The Thing (1951); The Big Sky, Monkey Business, O. Henry's Full House (1952); Gentlemen Prefer Blondes (1953); Land of the Pharaohs (1955); Rio Bravo (1959); Hatari (1962); Man's Favorite Sport? (1964); Red Line 7000 (1965); El Dorado (1967); Rio Lobo (1970).

Honors: Venice Film Festival Award: Political/Social Film (*The Road to Glory*, 1936); Academy Award Nomination: Best Director (*Sergeant York*, 1941); Directors Guild of America: Quarterly Award (*Red River*, 1948); Academy Award: Special Award: A Master American Filmmaker (1974).

Selected Bibliography

Mast, Gerald. *Howard Hawks, Storyteller*. New York: Oxford University Press, 1982.
McBride, Joseph. *Hawks on Hawks*. Berkeley: University of California Press, 1982.
Poague, Leland A. *Howard Hawks*. Boston: Twayne Publishers, 1982.

HAYWARD, SUSAN. Actress. Born Edythe Marrener on June 30, 1918, in Brooklyn, NY; died on March 14, 1975. Hayward came to Hollywood in 1937 as one of the hundreds of candidates for the role of Scarlett O'Hara in *Gone with the Wind*. She was not ready for the part, but ten years later she starred in a *GWTW* imitation called *Tap Roots*. In between she went from forgettable minor roles to roles in some of the most unforgettable movies of the decade. Like so many of her fellow actresses, Hayward had to work hard to get to the top and stay there. Fortunately, she had not only spunk but talent—and sexy good looks. She stayed at the top throughout the 1950s, but in the 1960s she made a string of embarrassing tearjerkers that led her to retirement in 1964, returning thereafter only occasionally. She attempted suicide in 1955 following a bitter courtroom battle with her first husband, Jess Barker, over the custody of their twins. She died of a brain tumor at the age of fifty-six. Years after her death, it came to light that an alarming number of members of the cast and crew who had worked on *The Conqueror* had died of cancer, including John Wayne. The movie was shot near an atomic testing site in St. George, Utah. Susan Hayward had a special star quality: the cute but determined face, the husky voice with just a trace of southern in it, the breathtaking versatility. One has only to think of *I'll Cry Tomorrow*, *I Want to Live*, and *Smash-Up*, not to mention *With a Song in My Heart*, *The President's Lady*, and *David and Bathsheba*—all biographical roles—to appreciate a talent that perhaps never quite had its fulfilling moment.

Filmography: Hollywood Hotel (1937); The Sisters, Comet over Broadway, Girls on Probation (1938); Our Leading Citizen, Beau Geste, $1,000 a Touchdown (1939); Adam Had Four Sons, Sis Hopkins, Among the Living (1941); Reap the Wild Wind, The Forest Rangers, I Married a Witch, Star Spangled Rhythm (1942); Hit Parade of 1943, Young and Willing, Jack London (1943); The Fighting Seabees, The Hairy Ape, And Now Tomorrow (1944); Deadline at Dawn, Canyon Passage (1946); Smash-Up, the Story of a Woman, They Won't Believe Me, The Lost Moment (1947); Tap Roots, The Saxon Charm (1948); Tulsa, House of Strangers (1949); My Foolish Heart (1950); I'd Climb the Highest Mountain, Rawhide, I Can Get It for You Wholesale, David and Bathsheba [as Bathsheba] (1951); With a Song in My Heart [as singer Jane Froman], The Snows of Kilimanjaro, The Lusty Men (1952); The President's Lady [as Rachel Jackson], White Witch Doctor (1953); Demetrius and the Gladiators [as Messalina], Garden of Evil (1954); Untamed, Soldier of Fortune (1955); I'll Cry Tomorrow [as Lillian Roth] (1955), The Conqueror (1956); Top Secret Affair (1957); I Want to Live (1958); Woman Obsessed, Thunder in the Sun (1959); The Marriage-Go-Round, Ada, Back Street (1961); I Thank a Fool (1962); Stolen Hours (1963); Where Love Has Gone (1964); The Honey Pot, Valley of the Dolls (1967); The Revengers (1972).

Honors: Academy Award Nomination: Best Actress (*Smash-Up, the Story of a Woman*, 1947); Academy Award Nomination: Best Actress (*My Foolish Heart*, 1949); Golden Globe Award, *Photoplay*: Most Popular Female Star, Academy Award Nomination: Best Actress (*With a Song in My Heart*, 1952); Academy Award Nomination: Best Actress (*I'll Cry Tomorrow*, 1955); Cannes Film Festival Award: Best Performance (*I'll Cry*

Tomorrow, 1956); Academy Award, Golden Globe Award, New York Film Critics Award: Best Actress (*I Want to Live*, 1958).

Selected Bibliography

LaGuardia, Robert, and Gene Arceri. *Red: The Tempestuous Life of Susan Hayward.* New York: Macmillan, 1985.

Linet, Beverly. *Susan Hayward: Portrait of a Survivor.* New York: Berkley, 1981.

Moreno, Eduardo. *The Films of Susan Hayward.* Secaucus, NJ: Citadel Press, 1979.

HAYWORTH, RITA. Actress. Born Margarita Carmen Cansino on October 17, 1918, in Brooklyn, New York; died on May 4, 1987. Hayworth, daughter of a Spanish-born dancer and his ''Ziegfeld Follies'' partner, was thirteen and dancing at Mexican night spots in Tijuana and Agua Caliente when she was spotted by a Fox production boss. She made her screen debut in 1935 under her real name, playing bit parts, and was just beginning to get leads in minor pictures when Fox merged with 20th Century and Hayworth was fired. She was back playing bit parts in minor films when she married Edward Judson, a shrewd businessman twenty-two years her senior, who gave up car sales to manage her career. In rapid succession, he got her a seven-year contract with Columbia, changed her name and her hair color, hired a press agent, and saw to it that she was seen at all important Hollywood premieres and social functions. Even so, it was a while before she got a break, but she finally did land a good role as the philandering wife in Howard Hawks's *Only Angels Have Wings* in 1939, and by the early 1940s, she was emerging as a glamorous star. She played a stunning temptress in *Blood and Sand* opposite Tyrone Power, followed by two films in which she danced with Fred Astaire (*You'll Never Get Rich* and *You Were Never Lovelier*) and one in which she danced with Gene Kelly (*Cover Girl*). The film that confirmed Rita's position as Hollywood's ''Love Goddess'' of the era was *Gilda* opposite Glenn Ford. During the time she was reigning queen at Columbia, Hayworth was giving the studio heads headaches with her roller-coaster love life. She had affairs with (and sometimes married) such men as Victor Mature, Orson Welles, Aly Khan, and Dick Haymes. Her reputation became so tarnished that even when Columbia took her back, she never regained her earlier popularity. Meanwhile, Marilyn Monroe had replaced her as the current sexpot. Hayworth returned to the screen in 1957 playing aging beauties, most notably in *Separate Tables* (whose producer she married—and then divorced). In 1981, afflicted with Alzheimer's, she was put in the care of her second daughter, Yasmin Aga Khan. She died at sixty-eight, a ghostly reminder of the glamour queen she had once been.

Filmography: [as Rita Cansino]: Under the Pampas Moon, Charlie Chan in Egypt, Dante's Inferno, Paddy O'Day (1935); Human Cargo, Meet Nero Wolfe, Rebellion (1936); Trouble in Texas, Old Louisiana, Hit the Saddle (1937). [as Rita Hayworth]: Girls Can Play, The Game That Kills, Criminals of the Air, Paid to Dance, The Shadow (1937); Who Killed Gail Preston?, There's Always a Woman, Convicted, Juvenile Court (1938); Homicide Bureau, The Renegade Ranger, The Lone Wolf Spy Hunt, Only Angels

Have Wings, Special Inspector (1939); Music in My Heart, Blondie on a Budget, Susan and God, The Lady in Question, Angels over Broadway (1940); The Strawberry Blonde, Affectionately Yours, Blood and Sand, You'll Never Get Rich (1941); My Gal Sal, Tales of Manhattan, You Were Never Lovelier (1942); Cover Girl (1944); Tonight and Every Night (1945); Gilda (1946); Down to Earth [in dual role] (1947); The Lady from Shanghai, The Loves of Carmen [as Carmen] (1948); Champagne Safari [doc.], Affair in Trinidad (1952); Salome [title role], Miss Sadie Thompson (1953); Fire Down Below, Pal Joey (1957); Separate Tables (1958); They Came to Cordura (1959); The Story on Page One (1960); The Happy Thieves [also prod.] (1962); Circus World (1964); The Money Trap, The Poppy Is Also a Flower (1966); L'Avventura/The Rover (1967); I Bastardi/ Sons of Satan (1969); Sur la Route de Salina/The Road to Salina (1970); The Naked Zoo/The Grove (1971); The Wrath of God (1972).

Selected Bibliography

Leaming, Barbara. *If This Was Happiness: A Biography of Rita Hayworth*. New York: Viking, 1989.

Morella, Joe, and Edward Z. Epstein. *Rita: The Life of Rita Hayworth*. New York: Dell, 1984.

Ringgold, Gene. *The Films of Rita Hayworth: The Legend and Career of a Love Goddess*. Secaucus, NJ: Citadel Press, 1974.

HEIRESS, THE (1949), drama. Directed by William Wyler; with Olivia de Havilland, Ralph Richardson, Montgomery Clift, Miriam Hopkins, Vanessa Brown, Mona Freeman, Ray Collins, and Selena Royle; screenplay by Ruth Goetz and Augustus Goetz.

"She was taught to love and hate—by masters!" Thus went the blurb for this magnificent piece of cinematic literature. Well, at least the blurb is half true. Catherine Sloper was certainly taught to *hate* by masters, but the love she felt was deeply and spontaneously her own. And the strangulation of this love by an overbearing father and a dissembling suitor is what propels this drama to one of the most riveting climaxes ever filmed. Henry James's novel *Washington Square* receives superlative screen treatment in this film version adapted by Ruth and Augustus Goetz from their stage play about spinster de Havilland wooed by fortune-hunter Clift in nineteenth-century New York City. Although some critics consider it a museum piece, all highly professional and heartless, others find that the staginess of the film allows the subtleties of the story to manifest themselves without distraction, for Wyler is the rare sort of director who can take a thoroughly theatrical drama like this and transplant it to film without ever permitting the theatricality of the piece to dominate the screen. *The Heiress* is probably the best film adaptation of Henry James, for it captures his sense of the claustrophobic confinement of Catherine Sloper while constantly reminding the viewer of the world outside that she has renounced after it rejected her. Renunciation is Henry James's great theme, and nowhere is it more tellingly presented than in this flawless film. *The Heiress* is so well orchestrated that, like *Casablanca*, *Rebecca*, or *Brief Encounter*, it "improves" with every viewing as one eagerly anticipates favorite scenes.

Awards: Academy Awards: Best Actress (de Havilland), B&W Art Direction (John Meehan, Harry Horner), Scoring of a Dramatic Picture (Aaron Copland), B&W Costume Design (Edith Head); Golden Globe Award, New York Film Critics Circle Award: Best Actress (de Havilland); National Board of Review Award: Best Actor (Richardson); Academy Award Nominations: Best Picture, Director, Actor (Ralph Richardson), Photography.

Selected Bibliography

Kern, Sharon. *William Wyler: A Guide to References and Resources*. Boston: G. K. Hall, 1984.

Peary, Danny. *Alternate Oscars*. New York: Delta, 1993.

Thomas, Tony. *The Films of Olivia de Havilland*. Secaucus, NJ: Citadel Press, 1983.

HENREID, PAUL. Actor, director. Born either Paul Georg Julius von Hernried or Paul Hernried Ritter von Wasel-Waldingau (depending on your source) on January 10, 1908, in Trieste; died on March 29, 1992. The son of a Viennese baron banker, Henreid began his working career in publishing. In 1933 he was discovered by Otto Preminger, then managing director for Max Reinhardt, and became a leading player with the latter's Vienna theater. In England from 1935, he appeared on stage and in films, then immigrated to the United States in 1940 and became an American citizen. As a Hollywood star he was soon the object of the admiration of American women as a prototype of the Continental lover, aristocratic, elegant, and gallant, memorably opposite Bette Davis in *Now, Voyager* and Ingrid Bergman in *Casablanca*. In the 1950s he began doubling as director and directed a number of films (notably *Dead Ringer* with former co-star Bette Davis) and TV movies before his death in 1992. Paul Henreid was another in that stable of Hollywood leading men whose main function seemed to be to make their co-stars look good. Suave and sophisticated, he was the perfect escort, a Viennese version of George Brent or Herbert Marshall, gentlemen who could be trusted never to upstage whatever "film fatale" they were playing opposite. Before you underestimate him, don't forget that he's the one who got the girl in *Casablanca*.

Filmography: [in Morocco]: Baroud/Love in Morocco (1933). [in Austria]: Morgenrot/Dawn (1933); Hohe Schule/Das Geheimnis des Carlo Cavelli/High School/The Secrets of Cavellie (1934); Nur ein Komödiant/Only a Comedian, Eva (1935). [in the United Kingdom]: Victoria the Great (1937); Goodbye Mr. Chips, An Englishman's Home/Madmen of Europe (1939); Night Train to Munich/Night Train, Under Your Hat (1940). [in the United States]: Joan of Paris, Now Voyager (1942); Casablanca (1943); In Our Time, Between Two Worlds, The Conspirators, Hollywood Canteen (1944); The Spanish Main (1945); Devotion [filmed 1943], Of Human Bondage [as Philip Carey], Deception (1946); Song of Love [as Robert Schumann] (1947); Hollow Triumph/The Scar [also prod.] (1948); Rope of Sand (1949); So Young So Bad, Last of the Buccaneers [as Jean Lafitte] (1950); Pardon My French (1951); For Men Only [also dir., prod.], Thief of Damascus (1952); Siren of Bagdad (1953); Deep in My Heart (1954); Pirates of Tripoli (1955); A Woman's Devotion [also dir.], Meet Me in Las Vegas (1956); Ten Thousand Bedrooms (1957); Girls on the Loose, Live Fast Die Young [both dir. only] (1958);

Holiday for Lovers, Never So Few (1959); The Four Horsemen of the Apocalypse (1962); Dead Ringer [dir. only] (1964); Operation Crossbow, Ballad in Blue/Blues for Lovers [dir., co-story only] (1965); The Madwoman of Chaillot (1969); Exorcist II: The Heretic (1977).

Selected Bibliography

Henreid, Paul, with Julius Fast. *Ladies' Man: An Autobiography*. New York: St. Martin's Press, 1984.

HEPBURN, AUDREY. Actress. Born Edna Hepburn-Ruston on May 4, 1929, near Brussels, Belgium; died on January 20, 1993. Educated at the Arnhem Conservatory (ballet). Hepburn, the daughter of an English banker and a Dutch baroness, was sent to a girls' school near London after her parents' divorce. She was vacationing with her mother in Arnhem, Holland, when World War II broke out and spent the war years in the Nazi-occupied town. After the war, she went to London on a ballet scholarship and soon began modeling for fashion photographers. In the early 1950s she joined Felix Aylmer's acting classes and began playing bit parts in British movies. While filming *Monte Carlo Baby* on the French Riviera, in 1951, she met Colette, the French novelist, who insisted that Hepburn play the lead in the forthcoming Broadway adaptation of her play *Gigi*. Hepburn's success in the play led to a starring part opposite Gregory Peck in *Roman Holiday*, for which she won an Oscar. That same year, she also won the Tony Award for her performance in the Broadway play *Ondine*. Hepburn was fortunate to be given many good roles and to receive many Oscar nominations. Films like *Sabrina*, *Funny Face*, *Love in the Afternoon*, *The Nun's Story*, *Breakfast at Tiffany's*, and *Charade* were all both critical and commercial successes, and one could say she reached her peak in *My Fair Lady*, a film she told Julie Andrews she "didn't have the guts to turn down." And lucky she didn't, for she was born to play Eliza Doolittle. Her career tapered off after that, as she was increasingly drawn to philanthropic causes. She was named a Special Ambassador for UNICEF (United Nations International Children's Emergency Fund) and devoted much of her free time to charity. Shortly after a 1992 mission of mercy to Somalia, Hepburn was diagnosed with colon cancer and died at age sixty-three. Mourning for her death was universal and sincere, for she endeared herself to all as the essence of style, elegance, dignity, high humor, and deep compassion.

Filmography: One Wild Oat, Young Wives' Tale, Laughter in Paradise, The Lavender Hill Mob, Nous irons à Monte Carlo/Monte Carlo Baby (1951); The Secret People (1952); Roman Holiday (1953); Sabrina (1954); War and Peace [as Natasha] (1956); Funny Face, Love in the Afternoon (1957); Green Mansions, The Nun's Story (1959); The Unforgiven (1960); Breakfast at Tiffany's (1961); The Children's Hour (1962); Charade (1963); Paris When It Sizzles, My Fair Lady [as Eliza Doolittle] (1964); How to Steal a Million (1966); Two for the Road, Wait Until Dark (1967); Robin and Marian [as Maid Marian] (1976); Bloodline/Sidney Sheldon's Bloodline (1979); They All Laughed (1981); Always (1989).

Honors: Academy Award, Golden Globe Award, New York Critics Circle Award, British Academy Award: Best Actress (*Roman Holiday*, 1953); Golden Globe Award: World Film Favorite (1954); Academy Award Nomination: Best Actress (*Sabrina*, 1954); New York Film Critics Circle Award, British Academy Award, Academy Award Nomination: Best Actress (*The Nun's Story*, 1959); Academy Award Nomination: Best Actress (*Breakfast at Tiffany's*, 1961); British Academy Award: Best Actress (*My Fair Lady*, 1964); Academy Award Nomination: Best Actress (*Wait Until Dark*, 1967); Golden Globes: Cecil B. DeMille Award (1989); British Academy Award: Special Award (1991); Film Society of Lincoln Center Tribute (1991); Academy Award: Jean Hersholt Humanitarian Award (1992).

Selected Bibliography

Harris, Warren G. *Audrey Hepburn: A Biography*. New York: Simon & Schuster, 1994.

Hofstede, David. *Audrey Hepburn: A Bio-Bibliography*. Westport, CT: Greenwood Press, 1994.

Karney, Robyn. *Audrey Hepburn: A Star Danced*. New York: Arcade, 1995.

Maychick, Diana. *Audrey Hepburn: An Intimate Portrait*. Secaucus, NJ: Carol Press, 1993.

Walker, Alexander. *Audrey: Her Real Story*. New York: St. Martin's Press, 1995.

HEPBURN, KATHARINE. Actress. Born on May 12, 1907, in Hartford, Connecticut. Educated at Bryn Mawr. Katharine Hepburn has become such a national monument that it has rendered her virtually untouchable. Although her long career has had its troubled moments, she is generally regarded as off limits to criticism. With eight Academy Award nominations and four Oscars to her credit, she resides on a level all her own. The truth about Katharine Hepburn is that there have been several Katharine Hepburns during a career spanning more than six decades, from the high-strung society girl of her early films to the wise but eccentric older woman of some of her last films. In between she has played an astonishing variety of roles, proving herself as much an accomplished comedienne as a dramatic actress. Each decade brought forth a new Katharine Hepburn. The shy, chattering young woman of the 1930s gave way to the assertive, wisecracking professional woman of the 1940s. In the 1950s she was the middle-aged but still desirable spinster struggling against shyness in her longing for love. In the 1960s she was a confident, mature, sometimes contentious older woman, a style she maintained thereafter as she played a variety of classic roles. Some find Hepburn's mannerisms affected and her Boston Brahmin finishing-school voice and accent irritating. And, admittedly, she does occasionally lapse into self-parody. But such is the price of survival. Hepburn's well-known feisty and independent personality had its roots in a childhood spent in an atmosphere of complete spiritual freedom and Spartan physical discipline. When she arrived in Hollywood in 1932 to star in the movie that launched her career, *A Bill of Divorcement* opposite John Barrymore, she made herself noticed by flaunting Hollywood conventions of all sorts, from wearing slacks around town to avoiding the social life always considered critical to the advancement of a budding actor. The more she snubbed Hollywood, the more it courted her—

and even awarded her an Oscar within a year. But later in the decade her popularity slipped, and by 1938, she was being labeled "box office poison." So she wangled exclusive rights to the play *The Philadelphia Story* and returned to Broadway to star in it. When the play became a huge success, the movies bid for it, and Hepburn, owning the rights, was able to finagle a deal that included herself in the lead in the movie version and gave her the right to choose her co-stars, which she did wisely, for she chose Cary Grant and James Stewart, two superstars guaranteed to bring people in even if they disliked Hepburn. But audiences liked Hepburn, and the film was a huge success, garnering Oscar nominations all around (and an award for Stewart). After that, Hepburn continued on a winning streak that did not flag for five more decades, although she did take time out now and then for an occasional stage part, even a musical (*Coco*) in 1969. Hepburn met Spencer Tracy while filming *Woman of the Year* in 1942, and the ensuing Tracy-Hepburn relationship (he always insisted on first billing) became the stuff of Hollywood legend. In the way that opposites will attract—and often give off sparks—they performed as a highly successful team in nine popular movies. Their love affair lasted twenty-five years, an open secret that few knew any details about and that the press ignored in deference to the respected couple. Tracy died shortly after the two completed their last film together (*Guess Who's Coming to Dinner?* 1967).

Filmography: A Bill of Divorcement (1932); Christopher Strong, Morning Glory, Little Women (1933); Spitfire, The Little Minister (1934); Break of Hearts, Alice Adams (1935); Sylvia Scarlett, Mary of Scotland, A Woman Rebels (1936); Quality Street, Stage Door (1937); Bringing Up Baby, Holiday (1938); The Philadelphia Story (1940); Woman of the Year, Keeper of the Flame (1942); Stage Door Canteen (1943); Dragon Seed (1944); Without Love (1945); Undercurrent (1946); The Sea of Grass, Song of Love (1947); State of the Union (1948); Adam's Rib (1949); The African Queen (1951); Pat and Mike (1952); Summertime (1955); The Rainmaker, The Iron Petticoat (1956); Desk Set (1957); Suddenly Last Summer (1959); Long Day's Journey into Night (1962); Guess Who's Coming to Dinner? (1967); The Lion in Winter (1968); The Madwoman of Chaillot (1969); The Trojan Women (1972); A Delicate Balance (1973); Love Among the Ruins (TVM, 1975); Rooster Cogburn (1976); Olly Olly Oxen Free (1978); The Corn Is Green (TVM, 1979); On Golden Pond (1981); George Stevens: A Filmmaker's Journey (1984); The Ultimate Solution of Grace Quigley/Grace Quigley (1984); Mrs. Delafield Wants to Marry (TVM, 1986); Laura Lansing Slept Here (TVM, 1988); The Man Upstairs (TVM, 1992); This Can't Be Love (TVM, 1994); Love Affair (1994).

Honors: Academy Award: Best Actress (*Morning Glory*, 1933); Venice Film Festival Award: Best Actress (*Little Women*, 1934); Academy Award Nomination: Best Actress (*Alice Adams*, 1935); New York Film Critics Circle Award, Academy Award Nomination: Best Actress (*The Philadelphia Story*, 1940); Academy Award Nomination: Best Actress (*Woman of the Year*, 1942); Academy Award Nomination: Best Actress (*The African Queen*, 1951); Academy Award Nomination: Best Actress (*Summertime*, 1955); Academy Award Nomination: Best Actress (*Suddenly Last Summer*, 1959); Cannes Film Festival Award, Academy Award Nomination: Best Actress (*Long Day's Journey into Night*, 1962); Academy Award: Best Actress (*Guess Who's Coming to Dinner?* 1967);

Academy Award, British Academy Award: Best Actress (*The Lion in Winter*, 1968); People's Choice Award: Favorite Movie Actress (1975); Academy Award: Best Actress (*On Golden Pond*, 1981); Academy Award: Best Actress (*On Golden Pond*, 1981); People's Choice Award: Favorite Movie Actress (1982).

Selected Bibliography

Bryson, John. *The Private World of Katharine Hepburn*. Boston: Little, Brown, 1990.

Edwards, Anne. *A Remarkable Woman: A Biography of Katharine Hepburn*. New York: Morrow, 1985.

Latham, Caroline. *Katharine Hepburn: Her Films & Stage Career*. New York: Proteus, 1982.

Leaming, Barbara. *Katharine Hepburn*. New York: Crown Publishers, 1995.

Spada, James. *Hepburn: Her Life in Pictures*. Garden City, NY: Doubleday, 1984.

HESTON, CHARLTON. Actor. Born Charles Carter on October 4, 1924, in Evanston, Illinois. Educated at Northwestern University (speech and drama). Heston made his stage debut in stock and his first Broadway appearance as a member of the cast of Katharine Cornell's production of *Anthony and Cleopatra* in 1947. He then began gaining national notice in a succession of TV specials, playing such roles as Antony in *Julius Caesar*, Heathcliff in *Wuthering Heights*, and Petruchio in *The Taming of the Shrew*. He appeared as Mark Antony in an amateur film production of *Julius Caesar* (1949) before making his professional film debut in 1950. Because he was tall, muscular, with a square jaw and a patrician face, he soon developed into Hollywood's most durable epic hero, playing larger-than-life characters from Moses to Michelangelo in a string of spectacular movies. He served six terms as president of the Screen Actors Guild and went on to become chairman of the American Film Institute. He tried his hand at directing in 1982 with *Mother Lode*. His son Fraser Heston (who portrayed the infant Moses in *The Ten Commandments*) is a film director. Heston has a unique place in cinematic history. He could seem rather wooden in some roles, even when he was called upon to be forceful (*Ruby Gentry*, *The Naked Jungle*), but when he was properly cast in imperial roles that called upon him to be noble and majestic (*The Ten Commandments*, *Ben-Hur*), he could rise to the occasion with extraordinary authority.

Filmography: Peer Gynt (1941); Julius Caesar (1949); Dark City (1950); The Greatest Show on Earth, Ruby Gentry, The Savage (1952); Arrowhead, Bad for Each Other, Pony Express, The President's Lady (1953); The Naked Jungle, The Secret of the Incas (1954); The Far Horizons, Lucy Gallant, The Private War of Major Benson (1955); The Ten Commandments, Three Violent People (1956); The Big Country, The Buccaneer, Touch of Evil (1958); Ben-Hur, The Wreck of the Mary Deare (1959); El Cid (1961); Diamond Head, The Pigeon That Took Rome (1962); 55 Days at Peking (1963); The Agony and the Ecstasy, The Greatest Story Ever Told, Major Dundee, The War Lord (1965); Khartoum (1966); All about People (1967); Counterpoint, Planet of the Apes, Will Penny (1968); The Festival Game, Number One (1969); Beneath the Planet of the Apes, The Hawaiians, Julius Caesar, King: A Filmed Record . . . Montgomery to Memphis (1970); The Omega Man, Vietnam! Vietnam! (1971); Call of the Wild, Skyjacked/Sky Terror

(1972); Antony and Cleopatra, Solyent Green (1973); Airport 1975, Earthquake, The Three Musketeers (1974); The Four Musketeers (1975); America at the Movies, The Last Hard Men, Midway, Two Minute Warning (1976); Crossed Swords/Prince and the Pauper, Gray Lady Down (1978); The Awakening, The Mountain Men (1980); Mother Lode/ Search for the Mother Lode; The Last Great Treasure (1982); Directed by William Wyler, The Fantasy Film World of George Pal (1986); Call from Space (1989); Solar Crisis, Treasure Island (1990); Tombstone, Wayne's World 2 (1993).

Honors: Academy Award: Best Actor (*Ben-Hur*, 1959); Golden Globe Award: World Film Favorite (1961); Golden Globes: Cecil B. DeMille Award (1966); Academy Award: Jean Hersholt Humanitarian Award (1977).

Selected Bibliography

Crowther, Bruce. *Charlton Heston: The Epic Presence*. London: Columbus Books, 1986.
Heston, Charlton. *In the Arena: An Autobiography*. New York: Simon & Schuster, 1995.
Rovin, Jeff. *The Films of Charlton Heston*. Secaucus, NJ: Citadel Press, 1977.

HIGH NOON (1952), western. Directed by Fred Zinnemann; with Gary Cooper, Grace Kelly, Lloyd Bridges, Thomas Mitchell, Katy Jurado, Otto Kruger, and Lon Chaney; screenplay by Carl Foreman.

"When the hands point up . . . the excitement starts!" promised the blurb for this classic western. The "hands," of course, are on the grandfather's clock counting down the time to the showdown at high noon in a movie edited to unfold in "real time." The clock is also ticking out the time until Sheriff Cooper either retires or is gunned down in the shootout with the notorious gunfighter who has been terrorizing the town. Zinnemann increases the tension in this suspenseful film through imaginative editing, alternating long shots and close-ups in rapid succession in a way that gives the movie a sort of agitated momentum. Most critics agree that this western is superior to the ordinary outdoor action feature. The tensions and conflicts are clearly defined while Dimitri Tiomkin's award-winning score underscores the sheriff's anguish as he is torn between retiring and thus avoiding a showdown or facing it head on for an ungrateful town. *High Noon* has an old-fashioned quality about it in its depiction of the cowboy as a mythological hero. Already, at the time of the film's release, this myth had begun to sour. Thus, this reincarnation is really a touching good-bye to the myth, a myth that would lie dormant until attempts forty years later by such filmmakers as Kevin Costner and Clint Eastwood to revive it. Thus, it is fitting that Gary Cooper should look tired and alone, the last of a dying breed. Although some critics are embarrassed by its transparent civics lesson (a town wants law and order without having to pay for it), the film has had more than its share of defenders. Some rate it up there with *Stagecoach* for the all-time championship, while others call it a landmark western, superbly directed and masterfully acted, the first so-called adult western.

Awards: Academy Awards: Best Actor (Cooper), Song ("High Noon"), Scoring of a Dramatic Picture (Dimitri Tiomkin), Editing (Harry Gerstad, Elmo Williams); Academy Award Nominations: Best Picture, Director, Screenplay.

Selected Bibliography

Dickens, Homer. *The Films of Gary Cooper*. New York: Citadel Press, 1970.
Gameaux, Josi, ed. *The Grace Kelly Story*. New York: Almanac Publications, 1957.
Hardy, Phil, ed. *The Overlook Film Encyclopedia: The Western*. Woodstock, NY: Overlook Press, 1994.

HIS GIRL FRIDAY (1940), comedy. Directed by Howard Hawks; with Cary Grant, Rosalind Russell, Ralph Bellamy, Gene Lockhart, Helen Mack, Ernest Truex, Clarence Kolb, Porter Hall, Roscoe Karns, Abner Biberman, Cliff Edwards, John Qualen, Frank Jenks, and Billy Gilbert; screenplay by Charles Lederer.

His Girl Friday has been called perhaps the funniest, certainly the fastest, movie ever filmed. Less enthusiastic critics find the machine-gun dialogue nerve-racking and the whirlwind pace simply too frenetic—as if the film were run at a speed a few notches too high. As a matter of fact, the dialogue delivery has been timed at twice the normal conversational speed, and Hawks not only had the actors move twice as fast as normal, but he placed four microphones around the newsroom to pick up overlapping dialogue in the background. It's hard to believe that Rosalind Russell was not the first choice for the part of Hildy, that, in fact, the part had been turned down by Katharine Hepburn, Jean Arthur, Margaret Sullivan, Ginger Rogers, Claudette Colbert, Carole Lombard, and Irene Dunne. Today, no one can remember an actress capable of Russell's rapid-fire delivery along with her great looks and comedic talent. In one of his greatest comedic roles, Grant demonstrates his astonishing versatility, this time both crazy and in control as he manipulates everything and everyone around him. For those weaned on fast-forward, this movie may be just the thing.

Selected Bibliography

Deschner, Donald. *The Complete Films of Cary Grant*. Secaucus, NJ: Citadel Press, 1991.
Mast, Gerald. *Howard Hawks, Storyteller*. New York: Oxford University Press, 1982.
Sennett, Ted. *Lunatics and Lovers: A Tribute to the Giddy and Glittering Era of the Screen's "Screwball" and Romantic Comedies*. New Rochelle, NY: Arlington House, 1973.
Yanni, Nicholas. *Rosalind Russell*. New York: Pyramid Publications, 1975.

HITCHCOCK, ALFRED. Director. Born on August 13, 1899, in Leytonstone, England; died on April 28, 1980. Educated at St. Ignatius College in London as a child; later he attended the School of Engineering and Navigation, where he studied mechanics, electricity, acoustics, and navigation. Hitchcock is one of the few directors whose name routinely appeared above the title of his movies, a name that attracted audiences because it was synonymous with a unique blend of sophistication and terror. Hitchcock made some amazingly innovative films on limited budgets in England before coming to the United States to direct *Rebecca* and launch a new career that only grew in stature as he gained increasing access to all the equipment and support the well-oiled studio system had to offer. Hitchcock was brilliant at casting, often pairing Cary Grant (beneath whose light side was a thinly veiled dark side Hitchcock found fascinating) with a vulnerable, fair-haired heroine such as Joan Fontaine, Ingrid Bergman, Eva Marie Saint, or Grace Kelly. Hitchcock liked blonds for his leading ladies, often surprising audiences as he did when he cast bubbly songstress Doris Day opposite James Stewart in *The Man Who Knew Too Much* and exposed some dark shadows beneath her sunny facade. Perhaps his coup was in casting Janet Leigh as Marian Crane in *Psycho*. Leigh was both bland and beautiful at the same time, and she sent mixed sexual signals. Hitchcock capitalized on these opposites to create tension in the early scenes of the movie and then to have his heroine brutally murdered a third of the way into the film. This continues to shock viewers, even those who have watched the film repeatedly, and much of that sustained shock value is the result of his casting Janet Leigh in the part. The movie continues to dominate discussions of Hitchcock, perhaps unfairly, but there's no reason to think he didn't know exactly what he was doing. If nothing else, it was a brilliant career move, for his glossy thrillers of the 1950s had begun to fade, and he still had a decade and a half's worth of movies left to direct. Hitchcock is one of the most imitated directors of all time. One of his hallmarks is the sudden-shock effect and the lurking of sinister jeopardy beneath a surface of commonplace serenity. Another hallmark of his films is the use of humor, often gallows humor, that works as comic relief to heighten the impact of the horror that follows. In one film, for example, someone comments that the murderer always rapes his victims first, to which a wag replies: "Every cloud has a silver lining." Research into the labyrinth of sexual ambiguity present in his films is only now beginning to be undertaken. Meanwhile, this master of fanciful mystery remains a man of infinite mystery.

Filmography: [in the United Kingdom]: The Lodger/The Case of Jonathan Drew (1926); Downhill/When Boys Leave Home, Easy Virtue, The Ring (1927); The Farmer's Wife, Champagne (1928); Harmony Heaven [co-dir.], The Manxman, Blackmail (1929); Elstree Calling [co-dir.], Juno and the Paycock, Murder (1930); The Skin Game (1931); Rich and Strange/East of Shanghai, Number Seventeen (1932); Waltzes from Vienna/Strauss's Great Waltz (1933); The Man Who Knew Too Much (1934); The 39 Steps (1935); The Secret Agent (1936); Sabotage/The Woman Alone, Young and Innocent/The Girl Was Young (1937); The Lady Vanishes (1938); Jamaica Inn (1939). [in the United States]: Rebecca, Foreign Correspondent (1940); Mr. and Mrs. Smith, Suspicion (1941); Saboteur (1942); Shadow of a Doubt (1943); Lifeboat (1944); Spellbound (1945); Notorious (1946); The Paradine Case, Rope (1948); Under Capricorn [U.K.] (1949); Stage Fright (1950); Strangers on a Train (1951); I Confess (1953); Dial M for Murder, Rear Window (1954); To Catch a Thief, The Trouble with Harry (1955); The Man Who Knew Too Much (1956); The Wrong Man (1957); Vertigo (1958); North by Northwest (1959); Psycho (1960); The Birds (1963); Marnie (1964); Torn Curtain (1966); Topaz (1969); Frenzy [U.K.] (1972); Family Plot (1976).

Honors: New York Film Critics Circle Award: Best Director (*The Lady Vanishes*, 1938); Academy Award Nomination: Best Director (*Rebecca*, 1940); Academy Award Nomination: Best Director (*Spellbound*, 1945); Directors Guild of America Award:

Outstanding Directorial Achievement (*Strangers on a Train*, 1951); Directors Guild of America Award: Outstanding Directorial Achievement, Academy Award Nomination: Best Director (*Rear Window*, 1954); Academy Award Nomination: Best Director (*Psycho*, 1960); Academy Award: Irving G. Thalberg Award (1967); Directors Guild of America (D. W. Griffith Award, 1967); National Board of Review Award: Best Director (*Topaz*, 1969); Golden Globes: Cecil B. DeMille Award (1971); British Academy Award: Academy Fellow (1971); Film Society of Lincoln Center Tribute (1974); American Film Institute Lifetime Achievement Award (1979).

Selected Bibliography

Boyd, David. *Perspectives on Alfred Hitchcock*. New York: G. K. Hall, 1995.

Harris, Robert A., and Michael S. Lasky. *The Complete Films of Alfred Hitchcock*. Secaucus, NJ: Carol Publishing Group, 1993.

Humphries, Patrick. *The Films of Alfred Hitchcock*. New York: Crescent, 1994.

Kapsis, Robert E. *Hitchcock: The Making of a Reputation*. Chicago: University of Chicago Press, 1992.

Sloan, Jane. *Alfred Hitchcock: A Guide to References and Resources*. New York: G. K. Hall, 1993.

HOLDEN, WILLIAM. Actor. Born William Franklin Beedle, Jr., on April 17, 1918, in O'Fallon, Illinois; died on November 16, 1981. Educated at Pasadena Junior College. Holden became a star with his very first real screen role, as the boxer-violinist hero of *Golden Boy*, one of the few real overnight successes in the history of Hollywood. With his clean-cut good looks and pleasant manners, he was quickly typecast in boy-next-door roles, but when he returned from serving in the army in World War II, he had matured to the point where being cast against type as a psychotic killer in *The Dark Past* worked for him and gave his career the boost it needed. Two choice roles followed: one, the writer-gigolo in *Sunset Boulevard*; the other, Judy Holliday's tutor in *Born Yesterday*. But the high point of his career was the role of the tough maverick hero of *Stalag 17*, a role that won him an Oscar. Throughout the 1950s he remained one of Hollywood's most dependable stars, able to couple his still-boyish good looks with a dangerous sexuality, most notably as the hunk in *Picnic*. He moved to Switzerland in later years and traveled extensively in Africa.

Filmography: Prisons Farm [extra] (1938); Million Dollar Legs [bit], Golden Boy (1939); Invisible Stripes, Our Town, Those Were the Days, Arizona (1940); I Wanted Wings, Texas (1941); The Remarkable Andrew, The Fleet's In, Meet the Stewarts (1942); Young and Willing (1943); Blaze of Noon, Dear Ruth, Variety Girl [cameo] (1947); Rachel and the Stranger, Apartment for Peggy, The Man from Colorado (1948); The Dark Past, Streets of Laredo, Miss Grant Takes Richmond (1949); Dear Wife, Father Is a Bachelor, Sunset Boulevard, Union Station (1950); Born Yesterday, Force of Arms, Submarine Command (1951); Boots Malone, The Turning Point (1952); Stalag 17, The Moon Is Blue, Escape from Fort Bravo (1953); Forever Female, Executive Suite, Sabrina (1954); The Country Girl, The Bridges at Toko-Ri, Love Is a Many-Splendored Thing (1955); Picnic, The Proud and the Profane, Toward the Unknown (1956); The Bridge on the River Kwai (1957); The Key (1958); The Horse Soldiers (1959); The World of Suzie

Wong (1960); Satan Never Sleeps, The Counterfeit Traitor, The Lion (1962); Paris When It Sizzles, The 7th Dawn (1964); Alvarez Kelly (1966); Casino Royale (1967); The Devil's Brigade (1968); The Wild Bunch, L'Arbre de Noël/The Christmas Tree (1969); Wild Rovers (1971); The Revengers (1972); Breezy (1973); Open Season, The Towering Inferno (1974); Network (1976); Damien—Omen II, Fedora (1978); Ashanti (1979); When Time Ran Out, The Earthling (1980); S.O.B. (1981).

Honors: Academy Award Nomination: Best Actor (*Sunset Boulevard*, 1950); Academy Award: Best Actor (*Stalag 17*, 1953); *Photoplay* Gold Medal Award: Most Popular Male Star (1954); *Photoplay* Gold Medal Award: Most Popular Male Star (1955); Academy Award Nomination: Best Actor (*Network*, 1976).

Selected Bibliography

Holtzman, William. *William Holden*. New York: Pyramid Publications, 1976.
Quirk, Lawrence J. *The Complete Films of William Holden*. Secaucus, NJ: Citadel Press, 1986.
Thomas, Bob. *Golden Boy: The Untold Story of William Holden*. New York: St. Martin's Press, 1983.

HOPE, BOB. Actor. Born Leslie Townes Hope on May 29, 1903, in Eltham, England. Hope came to the United States at the age of four and grew up in Cleveland, where he won a Chaplin-imitation contest at age ten. In his teens he tried his hand at various odd jobs until his amateur-show act led to vaudeville, where he added comedy routines to his singing and dancing. He had a good part in the Broadway musical *Roberta* in 1933, and for a year or two, he made a number of comedy shorts filmed in New York, but it was his success on radio that got him to Hollywood to appear in *The Big Broadcast of 1938*. It was in this film that he sang what was to become his theme song, ''Thanks for the Memory.'' His first popular screen hit was the superb comedy/thriller *The Cat and the Canary*, but he reached the top with *Road to Singapore*, the first of seven highly successful ''Road'' pictures he made with Bing Crosby and Dorothy Lamour. Hope's style of screen comedy, a mix of quips and wisecracks, thrived through the 1940s, but during the 1950s and 1960s audiences found his films less entertaining. As luck would have it, television came to his rescue, and *Bob Hope Specials* became a TV staple. Throughout his career, Hope traveled widely, entertaining American troops wherever they might be serving, in wars from World War II to Operation Desert Storm. He frequently hosted the Oscar ceremonies, winning ''Special'' awards five times for humanitarian service and contributions to the industry. His numerous awards and citations for humanitarian endeavors include the Presidential Medal of Freedom. Hope authored several humorous books about his career and travels, some in collaboration: *They Got Me Covered* (1941), *I Never Left Home* (1944), *So This Is Peace* (1946), *Have Tux, Will Travel* (1954), *I Owe Russia $1,200* (1963), *Five Women I Love: Obit Hope's Vietnam Story* (1966), *The Last Christmas Show* (1974), *The Road to Hollywood: My 40-Year Love Affair with the Movies* (1977), *Confessions of a*

Hooker: My Life-long Love Affair with Golf (1985), and *Don't Shoot, It's Only Me* (1990).

Filmography: The Big Broadcast of 1938, College Swing, Give Me a Sailor, Thanks for the Memory (1938); Never Say Die, Some Like It Hot, The Cat and the Canary (1939); Road to Singapore, The Ghostbreakers (1940); Road to Zanzibar, Caught in the Draft, Nothing But the Truth, Louisiana Purchase (1941); My Favorite Blonde, Road to Morocco, Star Spangled Rhythm (1942); They Got Me Covered, Let's Face It (1943); The Princess and the Pirate (1944); Road to Utopia, Monsieur Beaucaire (1946); My Favorite Brunette, Where There's Life, Variety Girl [cameo] (1947); Road to Rio, The Paleface (1948); Sorrowful Jones, The Great Lover (1949); Fancy Pants (1950); The Lemon Drop Kid, My Favorite Spy (1951); The Greatest Show on Earth [cameo], Son of Paleface (1952); Road to Bali, Off Limits, Scared Stiff [cameo], Here Come the Girls (1953); Casanova's Big Night (1954); The Seven Little Foys (1955); That Certain Feeling, The Iron Petticoat (1956); Beau James (1957); Paris Holiday (1958); The Five Pennies [cameo], Alias Jesse James (1959); The Facts of Life (1960); Bachelor in Paradise (1961); The Road to Hong Kong (1962); I'll Take Sweden (1965); The Oscar [cameo], Not with My Wife You Don't [cameo], Boy Did I Get the Wrong Number, The Bob Hope Vietnam Christmas Show (1966); Eight on the Lam (1967); The Private Navy of Sgt. O'Farrell (1968); How to Commit Marriage (1969); Cancel My Reservation (1972); The Muppet Movie [cameo] (1979); Spies Like Us [cameo] 1985.

Honors: Academy Award: Special Award (1940); Academy Award: Special Award [for his many services to the academy], (1944); Academy Award: Special Award [for his contribution to the laughter of the world, his service to the motion picture industry, and his devotion to the American premise] (1952); Golden Globe Award: Ambassador of Good Will (1957); Academy Award: Jean Hersholt Humanitarian Award (1959); Golden Globes: Cecil B. DeMille Award (1962); Academy Award: Special Award (1965); Film Society of Lincoln Center Tribute (1979).

Selected Bibliography

Faith, William Robert. *Bob Hope: A Life in Comedy*. New York: Putnam, 1982.
Marx, Arthur. *The Secret Life of Bob Hope*. New York: Barricade Books, 1993.
Thompson, Charles. *Bob Hope: Portrait of a Superstar*. New York: St. Martin's Press, 1981.

HOW GREEN WAS MY VALLEY (1941), drama. Directed by John Ford; with Walter Pidgeon, Maureen O'Hara, Donald Crisp, Anna Lee, Roddy McDowall, John Loder, Sara Allgood, Barry Fitzgerald, Patric Knowles, Rhys Williams, Arthur Shields, Ann Todd, Mae Marsh, U.S. version narrated by Irving Pichel, U.K. version narrated by Rhys Williams; screenplay by Philip Dunne.

"Rich is their humor! Deep are their passions! Reckless are their lives! Mighty is their story!" went one blurb for this fragile and sentimental tale of a way of life in disintegration. Another shouted: " 'What are you? A man or a saint? I don't want him, I want you.' Her desire scorched both their lives with the vicious breath of scandal!" Such was the ballyhoo (apparently considered essential) for this very moving, very human slice of Welsh life. *How Green Was My Valley* is generally considered to be one of director John Ford's undisputed masterpieces, a film that has withstood the test of time. The story, set in a mining area in South Wales and concerning the lives of its hardworking miners and their families, is seen through the eyes of Roddy McDowall, the youngest of seven children in a family called Morgan, headed by Donald Crisp and Sara Allgood. It is a beautiful film, lovingly directed, a film filled to the brim with every facet of human emotion, from disappointment to tragedy to romance. In spite of its acknowledged charm, some critics find fault with the obvious back-lot set and the mixture of accents and think it suffers from Hollywood gloss. Such criticisms seemed small-minded in the face of what today still comes across as a very honest attempt to make life in a world remote to most viewers seem personal and meaningful. In disliking the movie for all the wrong reasons, it is all too easy to overlook its simple virtues, for it has scenes that resonate in the mind long after the lights have gone up. There's alchemy here that cannot be denied.

Awards: Academy Awards: Best Picture, Director, Supporting Actor (Crisp), B&W Cinematography (Arthur Miller), B&W Interior Decoration (Richard Day, Nathan Juran); New York Film Critics Circle Award: Best Director; Academy Award Nominations: Best Supporting Actress (Allgood), Screenplay, Editing, Scoring of a Dramatic Picture, Sound.

Selected Bibliography

Gallagher, Tag. *John Ford: The Man and His Films.* Berkeley: University of California Press, 1986.
Place, Janey Ann. *The Non-Western Films of John Ford.* Secaucus, NJ: Citadel Press, 1979.
Thomas, Tony. *The Films of the Forties.* Secaucus, NJ: Citadel Press, 1975.

HUD (1963), drama. Directed by Martin Ritt; with Paul Newman, Patricia Neal, Melvyn Douglas, Brandon de Wilde, and John Ashley; screenplay by Irving Ravetch and Harriet Frank, Jr.

This film version of McMurtry's bitter novel *Horseman, Pass By* is the story of the moral decay of the modern American West and its decline from a land dominated by the pioneer ethic to a land scourged by mercenaries whose only link with their ancestors is their "rugged independence," a term interchangeable with "ruthless greed." The picture has a number of rewarding elements, not the least of which are the performances by the four leads. Newman is both virile and vicious, although his classic looks make it hard for audiences to dislike him. Melvyn Douglas captures marvelously the characteristics of old age even though it is never quite clear why he holds such a grudge against his son. Thus, his rigid moralizing makes it hard for audiences not to dislike him. Brandon de Wilde is memorable as the nephew, another well-played part in this young actor's tragically brief career. But it is Patricia Neal who steals the show (and the Oscar) with a rich and powerful performance as the housekeeper Newman assaults. Some critics objected to the film's transparent attempt to attain the status of Greek tragedy, but most critics agree that this is some of the finest work director Martin Ritt has ever done.

Awards: Academy Awards: Best Actress (Neal), Supporting Actor (Douglas), B&W Cinematography (James Wong Howe); New York Film Critics Circle Award, National Board of Review Award, British Academy Award: Best Actress (Neal); New York Film Critics Circle Award: Screenplay; Academy Award Nominations: Best Director, Actor (Newman), Adapted Screenplay, B&W Art Direction.

Selected Bibliography

Godfrey, Lionel. *Paul Newman, Superstar: A Critical Biography*. New York: St. Martin's Press, 1979.

Kael, Pauline. *I Lost It at the Movies*. Boston: Little, Brown, 1965.

Neal, Patricia, with Richard DeNeut. *As I Am: An Autobiography*. New York: Simon and Schuster, 1988.

HUDSON, ROCK. Born Roy Harold Scherer, Jr., on November 17, 1925, in Winnetka, Illinois; died on October 2, 1985. With hard work and determination, Rock Hudson mastered the art of seemingly effortless acting and, after a bumpy beginning, went on to prove himself in everything from serious drama to frothy comedy. Blessed with a commanding presence, he made an impact on audiences, both male and female. He was strong, rugged, and classically good looking and possessed a deep baritone voice and killer smile that charmed everyone. Thus his death from AIDS at the age of sixty and the revelation that he had led a carefully closeted double life all along shocked everyone and, more than any other single event, sounded the death knell of the sexual revolution—at least at its most excessive. Although Hudson will probably be remembered for the way he died, objective viewers can still delight in his screen presence, especially in films as varied as *Battle Hymn*, *Giant*, *Seconds*, and *Pillow Talk*. Oddly enough, Hudson had real trouble at the outset. It was one thing to change his name (from Roy Fitzgerald, his stepfather's name), cap his teeth, and coach him in acting, singing, dancing, fencing, and riding; another to get him to deliver his lines properly. But he learned on the job, requiring no fewer than thirty-eight takes before he could successfully complete one line in his first picture, *Fighter Squadron* (1948). But Hudson prevailed, and by the mid-1950s, after *Magnificent Obsession*, he was among the leading stars on the Universal lot. Later he made a successful series of comedies opposite Doris Day, and then in the 1970s he starred on TV in the popular light police series *McMillan and Wife*. He started another series, *The Devlin Connection*, in 1981, but its production was suspended for a year while Hudson was recovering from quintuple-bypass heart surgery. In 1984–1985 he played a recurring role in *Dynasty*.

Filmography: Fighter Squadron (1948); Undertow (1949); I Was a Shoplifter, One Way Street, Winchester '73, Peggy, The Desert Hawk, Shakedown, Double Crossbones (1950); Tomahawk, Air Cadet, The Fat Man, The Iron Man, Bright Victory (1951); Here Come the Nelsons, Bend of the River, Scarlet Angel, Has Anybody Seen My Gal?, Horizons West (1952); The Lawless Breed, Seminole, Sea Devils, The Golden Blade, Gun Fury, Back to God's Country (1953); Taza Son of Cochise, Magnificent Obsession, Bengal Brigade (1954); Captain Lightfoot, One Desire (1955); All That Heaven Allows,

Never Say Goodbye, Giant (1956); Written on the Wind, Battle Hymn, Something of Value, A Farewell to Arms (1957); The Tarnished Angels, Twilight for the Gods (1958); This Earth Is Mine, Pillow Talk (1959); The Last Sunset, Come September (1961); Lover Come Back, The Spiral Road (1962); Marilyn, A Gathering of Eagles (1963); Man's Favorite Sport?, Send Me No Flowers (1964); Strange Bedfellows, A Very Special Favor (1965); Blindfold, Seconds (1966); Tobruk (1967); Ice Station Zebra (1968); Ruba al Prossimo Tuo/A Fine Pair, The Undefeated (1969); The Hornet's Nest, Darling Lili (1970); Pretty Maids All in a Row (1971); Showdown (1973); Embryo (1976); Avalanche (1978); The Mirror Crack'd (1980); The Ambassador (1984).

Honors: Academy Award Nomination: Best Actor (*Giant*, 1956); *Photoplay* Gold Medal Award: Most Popular Male Star (1957); Golden Globe Award: World Film Favorite (1958); Golden Globe Award: World Film Favorite (1959); *Photoplay* Gold Medal Award: Most Popular Male Star (1959); Golden Globe Award: World Film Favorite (1960); Golden Globe Award: World Film Favorite (1962).

Selected Bibliography

Bego, Mark. *Rock Hudson, Public and Private: An Unauthorized Biography*. New York: New American Library, 1986.

Hudson, Rock, and Sara Davidson. *Rock Hudson: His Story*. New York: Morrow, 1986.

Oppenheimer, Jerry, and Jack Vitek. *Idol Rock Hudson: The True Story of an American Film Hero*. New York: Villard Books, 1986.

Royce, Brenda Scott. *Rock Hudson: A Bio-Bibliography*. Westport, CT: Greenwood Press, 1995.

HUSTLER, THE (1961), drama. Directed by Robert Rossen; with Paul Newman, Jackie Gleason, Piper Laurie, George C. Scott, Myron McCormick, Murray Hamilton, Michael Constantine, Jake LaMotta, and Vincent Gardenia; screenplay by Robert Rossen and Sidney Carroll.

This story of a disillusioned drifter and pool hustler, played to perfection by Newman, who challenges legendary Minnesota Fats, also played to perfection by Jackie Gleason, reeks of dingy pool-hall atmosphere and the dread that motivates drifters and gamblers. Although not for all tastes, this movie, when taken on its own terms, is a minor masterpiece, a tribute to the last true era when men of substance played pool with a vengeance. The characters are thoroughly unpleasant, but the actors who portray them are so uniformly good that the strength of the movie finally rests on its acting talent. Director Rossen was very proud of this film, calling it the best film he had ever made, and the critical consensus is that, in spite of its faults, *The Hustler* is the most likeable of Rossen's movies.

Awards: Academy Awards: Best B&W Cinematography (Eugen Schufftan), B&W Art Direction (Harry Horner, Albert Brenner); New York Film Critics Circle Award: Best Director; National Board of Review Award: Best Supporting Actor (Gleason); British Academy Award: Best Actor/Foreign (Newman); Academy Award Nominations: Best Picture, Director, Actor (Newman), Actress (Laurie), Supporting Actor (Gleason, Scott who refused nomination), Adapted Screenplay.

Selected Bibliography

Casty, Alan. *The Films of Robert Rossen*. New York: Museum of Modern Art, 1969. [distributed by New York Graphic Society, Greenwich, CT]

Godfrey, Lionel. *Paul Newman, Superstar: A Criticial Biography*. New York: St. Martin's Press, 1979.

Peary, Danny. *Alternate Oscars*. New York: Delta, 1993.

HUSTON, JOHN. Director, screenwriter, actor. Born on August 5, 1906, in Nevada, Missouri; died on August 28, 1987. John Huston was the son of renowned actor Walter Huston. His early life had all the variety and drama of young Indiana Jones, for Huston dabbled in acting, boxing, riding, writing, and painting—including a stint in the Mexican cavalry, singing on street corners in London, sketching tourists in Paris—before settling in Hollywood where he did everything from playing bit parts to writing screenplays to finally directing some of the most outstanding films in cinema history. His early screenplays include *Jezebel, Juarez, High Sierra*, and *Sergeant York*. His directorial debut was *The Maltese Falcon*, a movie that was a huge success and has since become a cult classic but one that also sparked a controversy that dogged Huston's career ever after. Were his successes due to his directing ability or his casting ability? For he could assemble brilliant ensembles of actors who played off against each other brilliantly. He was also accused of being "arty" in his use of the camera and his choice of seemingly daring but really safe stories to film. But over his long—and truly illustrious—career, Huston tried his hand at too great a variety of films to be easily dismissed or readily understood. Certainly there is eccentricity in his films as well as irreverence and sentimentality and both high and low humor. He seemed constantly to be searching for a voice, and although it can be argued that his distinctive voice recurs regularly during his career, it is probably—and ironically—to be found most perfectly revealed in his last film, *The Dead*, a haunting, lovely film, both a celebration of life and a meditation on its transience, much of which overflowed from Huston's powerful feelings about Ireland, his adopted home for many years. Huston may be loved and hated, scorned and imitated—but he can never be ignored.

Filmography: [as actor only]: The Shakedown, Two Americans (1929); Hell's Heroes, The Storm (1930); The Cardinal (1963); Candy, The Rocky Road to Dublin (1968); De Sade (1969); Myra Breckinridge (1970); The Bridge in the Jungle, Man in the Wilderness, The Deserter (1971); Battle for the Planet of the Apes (1973); Chinatown (1974); Breakout, The Wind and the Lion (1975); Tentacles, Il Grande Attacco/The Biggest Battle (1977); The Bermuda Triangle (1978); The Visitor, Jaguar Lives, Winter Kills (1979); Head On, Agee [interview] (1980); Cannery Row [narr. only] (1982); Lovesick, A Minor Miracle/Young Giants (1983); George Stevens: A Filmmaker's Journey [interview] (1985). [as screenwriter, in collaboration]: A House Divided (1931), Law and Order, Murders in the Rue Morgue (1932); Death Drives Through, It Happened in Paris (1935); Jezebel, The Amazing Dr. Clitterhouse (1938); Juarez (1939); Dr. Ehrlich's Magic Bullet (1940); High Sierra, Sergeant York (1941); The Killers, The Stranger [both not credited], Three Strangers (1946); Mr. North (1988). [as director]: The Maltese Falcon [also sc.] (1941); In This Our Life [also co-sc., uncredited], Across the Pacific (1942); Report from the Aleutians [also sc., narr.; doc.] (1943); The Battle of San Pietro [also sc., narr.; doc.] (1945); Let There Be Light [also co-sc., co-plot, narr.; doc.] (1946); The

Treasure of the Sierra Madre [also sc., act.], Key Largo [also co-sc.] (1948); We Were Strangers [also co-sc.] (1949); The Asphalt Jungle [also prod., co-sc.] (1950); The Red Badge of Courage [also sc.], The African Queen [also co-sc.] (1951); Moulin Rouge [also co-sc.] (1952); Beat the Devil [also prod., co-sc.] (1954); Moby Dick [also prod., co-sc.] (1956); Heaven Knows Mr. Allison [also co-sc.] (1957); The Barbarian and the Geisha, The Roots of Heaven (1958); The Unforgiven (1960); The Misfits (1961); The List of Adrian Messenger [also act.] (1963); The Night of the Iguana [also co-sc.] (1964); The Bible . . . In the Beginning [also act. as Noah] (1966); Casino Royale [co-dir., also act.]; Reflections in a Golden Eye (1967); Sinful Davey, A Walk with Love and Death [also act.] (1969); The Kremlin Letter [also co-sc., act.] (1970); Fat City, The Life and Times of Judge Roy Bean [also act.] (1972); The Mackintosh Man (1973); The Man Who Would Be King [also co-sc.] (1975); Independence (1976); Wise Blood [also act.] (1979); Phobia (1980); Victory (1981); Annie (1982); Under the Volcano (1984); Prizzi's Honor (1985); The Dead (1987).

Honors: Academy Award, Golden Globe Award, New York Film Critics Circle Award: Best Director (*The Treasure of the Sierra Madre*, 1948); Directors Guild of America Award, National Board of Review Award, Academy Award Nomination: Best Director (*The Asphalt Jungle*, 1950); Academy Award Nomination: Best Director (*The African Queen*, 1951); Academy Award Nomination: Best Director (*Moulin Rouge*, 1952); Venice Film Festival Silver Lion Award (*Moulin Rouge*, 1953); New York Film Critics Circle Award, National Board of Review Award: Best Director (*Moby Dick*, 1956); Golden Globe Award, Academy Award Nomination: Best Supporting Actor (*The Cardinal*, 1963); British Academy Award: Academy Fellow, Film Society of Lincoln Center Tribute (1980); Directors Guild of America: D. W. Griffith Award (1982); American Film Institute Lifetime Achievement (1983); Cannes Film Festival Award: Special Prize (1984); Golden Globe Award, New York Film Critics Circle Award, National Society of Film Critics Award, Academy Award Nomination: Best Director (*Prizzi's Honor*, 1985); Venice Film Festival: Special Golden Lion/Career Award (1985); Independent Spirit Award: Director (*The Dead*, 1987).

Selected Bibliography

Cooper, Stephen, ed. *Perspectives on John Huston*. New York: G. K. Hall, 1994.
Hammen, Scott. *John Huston*. Boston: Twayne, 1985.
Huston, John. *An Open Book*. New York: Knopf, 1980.
McCarty, John. *The Films of John Huston*. Secaucus, NJ: Citadel Press, 1987.

I

I AM A FUGITIVE FROM A CHAIN GANG (1932), drama. Directed by Mervyn LeRoy; with Paul Muni, Glenda Farrell, Helen Vinson, Preston Foster, Edward Ellis, and Allen Jenkins; screenplay by Sheridan Gibney and Brown Holmes. ''Six sticks of dynamite that blasted his way to freedom . . . and awoke America's conscience!'' went the blurb for this unvarnished look at the criminal justice system in the early days of the depression. Even though some of the social commentary may seem a little heavy-handed today, the film still packs a hefty punch after all these years. It is a horrifying story told in a semidocumentary style and is generally considered to be a milestone in Hollywood history. Critics have praised it highly for its courage, its artistic sincerity, and its social message, none of which detracts from its high entertainment value. Even though it has been called one of the toughest movies ever made, one that assaults the viewer with its uncompromising look at inhuman conditions in a Georgia penal system, its realism is so riveting that audiences leave the theater having experienced the sort of catharsis usually associated with Greek tragedy. This film, which haunted a generation, remains a reminder that the lowest depths of inhumanity and injustice can be found in one's own backyard.

Awards: Academy Award Nominations: Best Picture, Actor (Muni), Sound.

Selected Bibliography

Dooley, Roger. *From Scarface to Scarlett: American Films in the 1930s*. New York: Harcourt Brace Jovanovich, 1981.

Druxman, Michael B. *Paul Muni: His Life and His Films*. South Brunswick, NJ: A. S. Barnes, 1974.

LeRoy, Mervyn, as told to Dick Kleiner. *Mervyn LeRoy: Take One*. New York: Hawthorn Books, 1974.

INFORMER, THE (1935), drama. Directed by John Ford; with Victor Mc-Laglen, Heather Angel, Preston Foster, Margot Grahame, Wallace Ford, Una O'Connor, and Joseph Sawyer; screenplay by Dudley Nichols.

This much-acclaimed film is the story of a hard-drinking rebel (McLaglen) who informs on a friend to collect the reward during the Irish Rebellion. What makes the picture powerful is its merciless examination of the corruptibility of human nature as revealed in the characterization of McLaglen. Under John Ford's guidance, McLaglen emerges as a blundering, pathetic fool who is not basically vicious yet is guilty of a truly foul betrayal. Although generally praised for its honesty and drama, some critics have reservations. Some marvel at the fact that John Ford got the best reviews of his career for a film they perceived as heavy-handed, humorless, and patronizing, while others fault it for having the look of a silent film without the benefit of titles. However, more charitable critics feel that while the film may have a tedious plot, it succeeds on the basis of strong acting and highly stylized yet brilliantly effective atmospheric sets that never attempt to be realistic. It is through this mythic setting that Ford steers his characters stoically to their grim fates. Critical opinion now ranks this film among John Ford's finest.

Awards: Academy Awards: Best Actor (McLaglen), Director, Music (Steiner), Screenplay; New York Film Critics Circle Awards: Best Film, Best Director (Ford); National Board of Review Award: Best American Film; Venice Film Festival Award: Best Screenplay; Academy Award Nominations: Best Picture, Editing.

Selected Bibliography

Dooley, Roger. *From Scarface to Scarlett: American Films in the 1930s*. New York: Harcourt Brace Jovanovich, 1981.

Place, Janey Ann. *The Non-Western Films of John Ford*. Secaucus, NJ: Citadel Press, 1979.

INVASION OF THE BODY SNATCHERS (1956), science fiction. Directed by Don Siegel; with Kevin McCarthy, Dana Wynter, Larry Gates, King Donovan, and Carolyn Jones; screenplay by Daniel Mainwaring.

"The world as they knew it was slipping away from them. Time was running out for the human race. And there was nothing to hold on to—except each other!" So ran the ads for this classic piece of 1950s sci-fi that tells the chilling story of small-town residents on whom a sort of plant life has descended from the "alien" skies. This plant life then ripens into great pods from each of which emerge "blanks" that become physical shells of each man, woman, and child in the town. While the people are asleep, the blank drains them of all but their impulse to survive. This is a masterpiece of sci-fi cinema, which in spite of its 1978 remake remains a classic. Critics in general find it a persuasive and satisfying film done with understatement and intelligence, a film that not surprisingly later became one of the classic cult films of the sci-fi genre. As a result, probably too much has been read into this story, from a not-so-subtle attack on McCarthyism and the political witch-hunts of the era to an anti-Communist indictment of the Big Brother bureaucracy. Whatever its deeper meanings, it remains a quick-paced chiller that hooks and holds every audience.

Selected Bibliography

Brosnan, John. *Future Tense: The Cinema of Science Fiction*. New York: St. Martin's Press, 1978.

Menville, Douglas Alver. *A Historical and Critical Survey of the Science Fiction Film*. New York: Arno Press, 1975.

Parish, James Robert, and Michael Pitts. *The Great Science Fiction Pictures*. Metuchen, NJ: Scarecrow Press, 1977.

IT HAPPENED ONE NIGHT (1934), comedy. Directed by Frank Capra; with Clark Gable, Claudette Colbert, Walter Connolly, Roscoe Karns, Alan Hale, and Ward Bond; screenplay by Robert Riskin.

"Together for the first time!" boasted the blurb for a film neither Gable nor Colbert wanted to appear in. Or so they said. A few years later when Gable allegedly balked at playing Rhett Butler, audiences began to be skeptical of such protests, chalking them up to Hollywood hype. Whether Gable and Colbert wanted to play these parts or not, the result is that sort of chemistry that explains a phenomenon, for this film was phenomenally successful, drawing in millions of eager viewers who were utterly charmed by the story of a spoiled and snobbish rich girl who falls in love with (and learns middle-class values from) a poor but honest boy. In trying to explain the film's magic, critics have argued that it appealed to depression audiences with its moral cliché about the miserable rich and the happy poor. Some critics dismiss it as "Capracorn," while others find in it the balance between timeliness and timelessness that is the hallmark of a film classic. While part of its charm lies in its reflection of an age, much more is to be found in its use of the picaresque convention: on-the-road episodes of comedy, some of it so scatterbrained that this movie is now considered to be the one that launched the screwball comedy genre of the 1930s. It is all too easy for critics to overlook the essential ingredient that distinguishes a "movie" from other art forms: the visual. Movies are the most transparent of all the arts. They are mostly surface. Audiences respond instantly and primarily to what they see, and when they saw Gable and Colbert sparring and flirting and moving inevitably toward a romantic climax, they liked what they saw. Many of the famous images from the film are still familiar to film buffs: the "walls of Jericho" scene, the hitchhiking scene, and particularly the scene in which Gable removes his shirt and reveals he doesn't wear an undershirt (causing the undershirt industry, so it is said, to go bust). This is a visceral response to two powerful screen presences. Place them against the backdrop of a depression-era cross-country trek, throw in a classic conflict, and you have the ingredients that made this film an enormous success in spite of everything.

Awards: Academy Awards: Best Picture, Director, Actor (Gable), Actress (Colbert), Adaptation (Robert Riskin); National Board of Review: Best American Film.

Selected Bibliography

Essoe, Gabe. *The Complete Films of Clark Gable*. Secaucus, NJ: Citadel Press, 1970.

Scherle, Victor, and William Turner Levy, eds. *The Complete Films of Frank Capra*. New York: Carol Publishing Group, 1992.

Sikov, Ed. *Screwball: Hollywood's Madcap Romantic Comedies*. New York: Crown, 1989.

IT'S A WONDERFUL LIFE (1946), drama. Directed by Frank Capra; with James Stewart, Donna Reed, Lionel Barrymore, Thomas Mitchell, Henry Travers, Beulah Bondi, Frank Faylen, Ward Bond, Gloria Grahame, H. B. Warner, Frank Albertson, Todd Karns, Samuel S. Hinds, Mary Treen, Sheldon Leonard, and Ellen Corby; screenplay by Robert Riskin.

In the wrong hands and with the wrong actors, this film could easily have degenerated into maudlin sentimentality. Instead, Frank Capra, the undisputed master of the genre, managed to mix into this sentimental stew the right ingredients in the right proportion and produce an undisputed classic. Like Dickens's *A Christmas Carol*, *It's a Wonderful Life* is a great story because it is simultaneously timely and timeless. It perfectly reflects the determined optimism of people just emerging from a depression and a war. It celebrates the spirit of the survivor who has hit rock bottom, reversed his course, and returned to rejoice. The survivor in this case is James Stewart, a young husband and father who has reached the end of his rope and, convinced that the world would have been better off had he never been born, attempts suicide. He is rescued by an "angel" in the form of crusty old Henry Travers whose dry wit and earthiness make him all the more believable. To earn his wings, Travers has to rescue Stewart and convince him his life has been worthwhile. He succeeds, and in the process, we revisit earlier scenes and see the contrast between a town without Stewart and a town with. Meanwhile, curmudgeonly old Lionel Barrymore, in his inimitable Scrooge-like impersonation, has bought and corrupted the town and spread gloom and misery everywhere. Barrymore was Capra's one and only choice, and he is excellent. During the 1940s Barrymore read *A Christmas Carol* over the radio every Christmas Eve, throwing himself into the part of Ebeneezer Scrooge so thoroughly that a generation grew up thinking he *was* Scrooge. Barrymore clearly relished his role in *It's a Wonderful Life*, as did all the characters in this flawless film. Stewart has said it was his favorite role, but all of the actors give inspired performances. It was Capra's favorite film, too. He thought it was not only the greatest film he ever made but the greatest film anybody ever made. Critics have now come to agree with the opinion of audiences who have made the viewing of this film an annual Christmas event. This film, which lost money and went relatively unnoticed when it first came out, is now among the top ten most popular movies ever made. No other movie so clearly celebrates middle-class American morals and values. Americans have always idealized the poor and derided the rich, and they have always sided with the underdog. Americans are generous and abhor greed. And above all, they believe in a sense of community and in the idea that "no man is an island." Thus, at the end of the movie, when the story turns treacly, no eyes are dry enough to tell—or care. Like *Casablanca* or *The Third Man*, it is an ageless movie that only improves with age.

Awards: Golden Globe Awards: Best Picture, Director; Academy Award Nominations: Best Picture, Director, Actor (Stewart), Editing, Sound.

Selected Bibliography

Coon, James T. "Frank Capra and 'It's a Wonderful Life': A Burkean Cluster Analysis of a Rhetorically Self-Expressive Film." Master's thesis, Bowling Green State University (no. 5215), 1989.

Hawkins, Jimmy. *"It's a Wonderful Life": The 50th Anniversary Scrapbook*. New York: HarperCollins, 1996.

Levy, Emanuel. *Small-Town America in Film: The Decline and Fall of Community*. New York: Continuum, 1991.

J

JEZEBEL (1938), drama. Directed by William Wyler; with Bette Davis, Henry Fonda, George Brent, Margaret Lindsay, Donald Crisp, Fay Bainter, Spring Byington, Richard Cromwell, and Henry O'Neill; screenplay by Clements Ripley, Abem Finkel, and John Huston.

"DARLING OF DIXIE! . . . Meanest when she's lovin' most!" ran the silly blurb for this impressive and absorbing Civil War drama. *Jezebel* was Bette Davis's compensation for Scarlett O'Hara, a part she desperately wanted but that she turned down when Warners refused to loan her to Selznick unless Selznick also accepted Errol Flynn as Rhett Butler. Bette Davis won her second Academy Award playing a tempestuous southern belle in a bravura performance that many credit to her determination to show Tallulah Bankhead that a Yankee really could play a convincing southerner. Whatever accounted for it, Davis's performance lends plausibility to a plot that stretches credulity when at the end vixen Davis develops an oversized conscience and, at the height of a cholera plague, rides nobly on top a wagon carting corpses to the funeral pyres on the outskirts of New Orleans. Although it met with mixed reviews, most critics agreed that Davis (and Fay Bainter) saved the picture.

Awards: Academy Awards: Best Actress (Davis), Supporting Actress (Fay Bainter); Academy Award Nominations: Best Picture, Score, Cinematography.

Selected Bibliography

Anderegg, Michael A. *William Wyler*. Boston: Twayne, 1979.

Miller, Frank. *Movies We Love: 100 Collectible Classics*. Atlanta, GA: Turner Publishing, 1996.

Ringgold, Gene. *The Films of Bette Davis*. New York: Cadillac, 1966.

Thomas, Tony. *The Films of Henry Fonda*. Secaucus, NJ: Citadel Press, 1983.

JOHNSON, VAN. Actor. Born on August 25, 1916, in Newport, Rhode Island. Johnson was a former Broadway chorus boy who skyrocketed to Hollywood popularity during World War II, captivating audiences with his air of innocent charm. Fans found his blond, blue-eyed, boy-next-door look appealing and thronged to see his movies. Throughout the 1940s he was idolized by hordes of screaming and swooning bobby-soxers, a phenomenon that earned him the label ''The Voiceless Sinatra.'' From time to time, Johnson attempted serious acting, but both audiences and critics remained blinded by his song-and-dance image. He remained with MGM through the mid-1950s, then freelanced with various studios and occasionally worked in Europe. He was only sporadically active in films in the 1960s and hardly at all in the 1970s and 1980s, preferring to appear on the stage, mainly on the dinner theater circuit, and in TV movies. In 1985 he returned to Broadway, replacing Gene Barry in the hit musical *La Cage aux Folles*. Johnson deserves to be remembered—and honored—because he is one of those marvelously versatile actors (like Glenn Ford or Dana Andrews) who tend to slip between the cracks. When you compare the Johnson of *Three Girls and a Sailor* or *Easy to Wed* with the Johnson of *Thirty Seconds over Tokyo*, *Battleground*, *The Caine Mutiny*, *The Last Time I Saw Paris*, or *The End of the Affair*, you can begin to appreciate his impressive talent.

Filmography: Too Many Girls, Murder in the Big House, Somewhere I'll Find You, The War against Mrs. Hadley, Dr. Gillespie's New Assistant (1942); The Human Comedy, Pilot No. 5, Madame Curie, A Guy Named Joe (1943); The White Cliffs of Dover, Three Men in White, Two Girls and a Sailor, Thirty Seconds over Tokyo (1944); Between Two Women, Thrill of a Romance, Weekend at the Waldorf (1945); Ziegfeld Follies, Easy to Wed, No Leave No Love, 'Till the Clouds Roll By (1946); High Barbaree, The Romance of Rosy Ridge (1947); State of the Union, The Bride Goes Wild (1948); Command Decision, Mother Is a Freshman, Scene of the Crime, In the Good Old Summertime, Battleground (1949); The Big Hangover, Duchess of Idaho (1950); Grounds for Marriage, Three Guys Named Mike, Go for Broke, Too Young to Kiss (1951); It's a Big Country, Invitation, When in Rome, Washington Story, Plymouth Adventure (1952); Confidentially Connie, Remains to Be Seen, Easy to Love (1953); The Siege at Red River, Men of the Fighting Lady, The Caine Mutiny, Brigadoon, The Last Time I Saw Paris (1954); The End of the Affair (1955); The Brass Bottle, Miracle in the Rain, 23 Paces to Baker Street (1956); Slander, Kelly and Me, Action of the Tiger (1957); The Last Blitzkrieg, Subway in the Sky, Beyond This Place/Web of Evidence (1959); The Enemy General (1960); The Pied Piper of Hamelin (1961); Wives and Lovers (1963); Divorce American Style (1967); Yours Mine and Ours, Where Angels Go . . . Trouble Follows (1968); Battle Squadron/Eagle over London, The Price of Power (1969); Company of Killers (1970); The Eye of the Spider (1971); The Kidnapping of the President (1980); The Purple Rose of Cairo (1985); Laggiu Nella Giungla (1988); Escape from Paradise, Delta Force Commando 2 (1990).

Selected Bibliography

Beecher, Elizabeth. *Van Johnson: The Luckiest Guy in the World*. Racine, WI: Whitman Publishing, 1947.

JONES, JENNIFER. Actress. Born Phyllis Isley on March 2, 1919, in Tulsa, Oklahoma. In 1939 Jones met actor Robert Walker while both were attending the American Academy of Dramatic Arts in New York. They married and headed for Hollywood, where Jones began her screen career in minor action films under her real name. She caught the attention of David O. Selznick, who saw her potential and set about grooming her for stardom. He changed her name to Jennifer Jones and signed her to a long-term contract. Then, after three years of preparation, he introduced his new discovery to the public in a role carefully selected to make the best use of her wistful, ethereal nature. The film was *The Song of Bernadette*, for which she won an Oscar. After that, in roles carefully selected by Selznick (whom she married after divorcing Walker), she starred in many other high-budget productions, most of which focused on that elusive, fey quality of hers that set her apart from most movie stars. Perhaps it was precisely because she did not fit into a category that Jones made her mark capitalizing on her own special blend of fragile beauty, a trace of a lisp, and a waiflike charm. Unfortunately, these qualities did not wear well as she grew older. Nevertheless, during her short career (scarcely fifteen years), she starred in a surprising number of quality films and was nominated for an Academy Award four times after *Bernadette*. Given the right vehicle, she could give a spellbinding performance, which she did as the mentally disturbed young woman in *Love Letters* or the haunted little girl in *Portrait of Jennie*. Even when critics panned the films, they could find no fault with Jones (except for those who just didn't like her style of acting). Although she resisted typecasting, the image that remains of her is closer to the young French girl who saw the Virgin Mary than to the sultry half-breed who dies in a gun battle with her lover in *Duel in the Sun*. She was particularly memorable as the hapless heroine in *Madame Bovary*.

Filmography: [as Phyllis Isley]: New Frontier, Dick Tracy's G-Men [serial] (1939). [as Jennifer Jones]: The Song of Bernadette (1943), Since You Went Away (1944); Love Letters (1945); Cluny Brown, Duel in the Sun (1946); Portrait of Jennie (1948); We Were Strangers, Madame Bovary (1949); Gone to Earth/The Wild Heart (1950); Carrie, Ruby Gentry (1952); Indiscretion of an American Wife (1953); Beat the Devil (1954); Love Is a Many-Splendored Thing, Good Morning Miss Dove (1955); The Man in the Gray Flannel Suit (1956); The Barretts of Wimpole Street, A Farewell to Arms (1957); Tender Is the Night (1962); The Idol (1966); Angel Angel Down We Go/Cult of the Damned (1969); The Towering Inferno (1974).

Honors: Academy Award, Golden Globe Award: Best Actress (*Song of Bernadette*, 1943); Academy Award Nomination: Best Supporting Actress (*Since You Went Away*, 1944); Academy Award Nomination: Best Actress (*Love Letters*, 1945); Academy Award Nomination: Best Actress (*Duel in the Sun*, 1946); *Photoplay* Gold Medal Award: Most Popular Female Star (1955); Academy Award Nomination: Best Actress (*Love Is a Many-Splendored Thing*, 1955).

Selected Bibliography

Carrier, Jeffrey L. *Jennifer Jones: A Bio-Bibliography*. Westport, CT: Greenwood Press, 1990.

Epstein, Edward Z. *Portrait of Jennifer: A Biography of Jennifer Jones*. New York: Simon & Schuster, 1995.

Linet, Beverly. *Star-crossed: The Story of Robert Walker and Jennifer Jones*. New York: Putnam, 1986.

JUDGMENT AT NUREMBERG (1961), drama. Directed by Stanley Kramer; with Spencer Tracy, Burt Lancaster, Richard Widmark, Marlene Dietrich, Judy Garland, Maximilian Schell, Montgomery Clift, and William Shatner; screenplay by Abby Mann.

''The things you'll see and the things you'll feel are the things that will be part of you as long as you live!'' Those who find this film bleak and static would do well to take this promotional blurb to heart. This intense courtroom drama has been criticized for its length, but considering the supreme importance of its subject matter, length is precisely what the film needs to build to its shattering conclusion. If evil is banal, then its prosecution can also seem banal unless the crimes that are being judged make themselves felt. In this film, they do, because there is such a wondrous fusion of screenplay, performance, and atmosphere. The actors playing the central roles stand out in their well-etched characterizations. Tracy is wise, American levelheadedness at its best, while Lancaster perfectly captures the conflict within a military man loathe to find blame within himself but finally courageous enough to do so, even though he falls short of complete self-knowledge. Marlene Dietrich perfectly embodies the persistent snobbery of the Prussian mentality that thinks it is above politics and incapable of war crimes. Although Judy Garland and Montgomery Clift have been faulted for simply being too famous for their parts, their very fame helps make their brief performances riveting. Seeing in frumpy, hysterical Garland the shadow of Dorothy reminds the viewer of what the Nazis would so blithely have thrown away had Garland's ancestors remained in Europe. And Clift is overwhelming. Perhaps his deteriorating physical condition did lend itself to the part, but one senses that beneath this accidental facade is a tormented soul that sees a horrifying reflection of himself in the castrated half-wit he is portraying. And Maximilian Schell is nothing short of superb in the demanding and unsympathetic role of defense attorney for the accused war criminals. His arguments, his rationalizations, his pleading and outcries are like expressions of the anguished soul of the German people, desperately casting themselves as victims, unable to come to terms with the enormity of the evil they allowed to engulf them and bring them to the brink of extinction.

Awards: Academy Awards: Best Supporting Actor (Schell), Best Adapted Screenplay (Abby Mann); Golden Globe Awards: Best Actor/Drama (Schell), Director, Score; New York Film Critics Circle Awards: Best Actor (Schell), Screenplay; Academy Award Nominations: Best Picture, Actor (Tracy), Supporting Actress (Garland), Supporting Actor (Clift), Cinematography, Art Direction, Film Editing, Costume Design.

Selected Bibliography

Deschner, Donald. *The Complete Films of Spencer Tracy*. New York: Citadel Press, 1968.
Kalfatovic, Mary C. *Montgomery Clift: A Bio-Bibliography*. Westport, CT: Greenwood Press, 1994.
Morella, Joe, and Edward Z. Epstein. *Judy: The Complete Films and Career of Judy Garland*. Secaucus, NJ: Citadel Press, 1986.
Spoto, Donald. *Stanley Kramer: Film Maker*. New York: Putnam, 1978.

K

KAYE, DANNY. Actor, comedian. Born David Daniel Kaminski on January 18, 1913, in Brooklyn, New York; died on March 3, 1987. Kaye dropped out of school when he was thirteen to become a clowning busboy on the "Borscht Circuit" in New York's Catskill Mountains. After that he worked at various jobs including soda jerk and insurance agent while he plugged along in vaudeville and nightclubs, slowly making a name for himself as a singer-dancer-entertainer. From the beginning, it was hard to pin down exactly what Kaye did since he wore so many hats and wore them well. This all led to a long and successful career in pictures, but so much of what he did now seems either dated or downright silly that it takes a little doing to realize what a unique contribution he made to motion pictures. One has only to look at a later film like *Me and the Colonel* to realize Kaye's depths and his piquant talent. He made his Broadway debut in 1939 in *The Straw Hat Revue*, with Imogene Coca. Then, early in 1941, while appearing in Broadway's *Lady in the Dark*, he wowed audiences with a showstopper called "Tchaikovsky," in which he reeled off the names of fifty-four Russian composers, real and imagined, in thirty-eight seconds. Such staccato delivery of tongue-twisting lyrics became his trademark throughout his career. In 1943 he was signed by producer Samuel Goldwyn to star in *Up in Arms*, the first of a string of highly successful technicolor Goldwyn comedies tailor-made to display Kaye's versatility. This versatility was never so well expressed as in *The Secret Life of Walter Mitty* (1947), a film that gave him the opportunity to portray a stunning array of diverse personalities. Kaye also was enormously popular in Britain where *The Court Jester* ("the vessel with the pestle"), his hilarious spoof of swashbucklers, was enthusiastically received. In the late 1950s, when the public taste for his style of comedy started to wane, Kaye began devoting more and more of his time to worldwide travel on behalf of UNICEF (United Nations International Children's Emergency Fund), entertaining children in developing countries. Kaye made only sporadic film appearances after 1960.

Filmography: Up in Arms (1944); Wonder Man (1945); The Kid from Brooklyn (1946); The Secret Life of Walter Mitty (1947); A Song Is Born (1948); It's a Great Feeling [unbilled cameo], The Inspector General (1949); On the Riviera (1951); Hans Christian Andersen (1952); Knock on Wood, White Christmas (1954); The Court Jester (1956); Merry Andrew, Me and the Colonel (1958); The Five Pennies (1959); On the Double (1961); The Man from the Diners' Club (1963); The Madwoman of Chaillot (1969).

Honors: Golden Globe Award: Best Actor in a Comedy/Musical (*On the Riviera*, 1951); Academy Award: Special Award (1954); Golden Globe Award: Best Actor in a Comedy/Musical (*Me and the Colonel*, 1958); Academy Award: Jean Hersholt Humanitarian Award (1981).

Selected Bibliography

Freedland, Michael. *The Secret Life of Danny Kaye*. New York: St. Martin's Press, 1985.
Gottfried, Martin. *Nobody's Fool: The Lives of Danny Kaye*. New York: Simon & Schuster, 1994.
Singer, Kurt D. *The Danny Kaye Story*. New York: T. Nelson, 1958.

KAZAN, ELIA. Director. Born Elia Kazanjoglou on September 7, 1909, in Constantinople (now Istanbul); died in 1994. Educated at Williams College and Yale (drama). Kazan's parents emigrated from Greece when Kazan was four and settled in New York City. In 1932 Kazan joined the Group Theater as an actor and assistant stage manager. He directed his first play in 1935, and from then until 1950, he worked almost exclusively in the theater, establishing a reputation as one of Broadway's finest directors with such successes as *The Skin of Our Teeth*, *A Streetcar Named Desire*, and *Death of a Salesman*. Kazan's theater training had both good and bad effects on his later career as a film director. On the one hand, he had an instinct for quality material, and he was a genius at drawing powerful performances out of his actors. On the other hand, his films often looked stagy, almost liked filmed plays, a characteristic that worked to his disadvantage in scenes of high emotional conflict or sexual tension. His film career really took off with the highly acclaimed *A Tree Grows in Brooklyn* in 1945, followed by *Gentleman's Agreement* and *Pinky*, both controversial films dealing with race and prejudice. In the 1950s Kazan brought some incandescent personalities to the screen, most notably Marlon Brando in *A Streetcar Named Desire*, *Viva Zapata!*, and *On the Waterfront*. He also introduced James Dean to the screen in *East of Eden*, the film that catapulted Dean to fame in a performance that turned a somewhat cerebral story movie into an electrifying visceral experience. During that same decade Kazan both staged and filmed works by such challenging American playwrights as Tennessee Williams, William Inge, and Arthur Miller. His film about his own roots, *America, America*, was a critical success, but audiences found it tedious. Somehow the momentum Kazan could sustain to energize other people's works was beyond him in dealing with his own. His second personal film, *The Arrangement*, fared even worse. While the book it was based on was a success, the movie was a failure. In the 1960s and 1970s Kazan devoted most of his time to writing, turning out six novels and an autobiography. Kazan has left an indelible mark on American film history.

Filmography: The People of the Cumberland (1937); It's Up to You (1941); A Tree Grows in Brooklyn (1945); The Sea of Grass, Boomerang, Gentleman's Agreement (1947); Pinky (1949); Panic in the Streets (1950); A Streetcar Named Desire (1951); Viva Zapata! (1952); Man on a Tightrope (1953); On the Waterfront (1954); East of Eden (1955); Baby Doll (1956); A Face in the Crowd (1957); Wild River (1960); Splendor in the Grass (1961); America America (1963); The Arrangement (1969); The Visitors (1972); The Last Tycoon (1976).

Honors: Academy Award, Golden Globe Award, New York Film Critics Award, National Board of Review Award: Best Director (*Gentleman's Agreement*, 1947); Venice Film Festival Award: International Prize (*Panic in the Streets*, 1950); New York Film Critics Circle Award, Venice Film Festival Award, Academy Award Nomination: Best Director (*A Streetcar Named Desire*, 1951); Berlin Film Festival Award: International Delegate-Jury Prize of the Berlin Senate (*Man on a Tightrope*, 1953); Academy Award, Golden Globe Award, Directors Guild of America Award, New York Film Critics Circle Award, Venice Film Festival Award: Best Director (*On the Waterfront*, 1954); Academy Award Nomination: Best Director, Directors Guild of America Award: Outstanding Directorial Achievement; Cannes Film Festival Award: Best Dramatic Film (*East of Eden*, 1955); Golden Globe Award: Best Director (*Baby Doll*, 1956); Golden Globe Award, Academy Award Nomination: Best Director (*America, America,* 1963); Directors Guild of America: Honorary Lifetime Member (1982); Directors Guild of America: (D. W. Griffith Award (1986).

Selected Bibliography

Kazan, Elia, with Michel Ciment. *Kazan on Kazan*. New York: Viking Press, 1974.
Michaels, Lloyd. *Elia Kazan: A Guide to References and Resources*. Boston: G. K. Hall, 1985.
Pauly, Thomas H. *An American Odyssey: Elia Kazan and American Culture*. Philadelphia: Temple University Press, 1983.

KELLY, GENE. Actor, dancer. Born Eugene Curran Kelly on August 23, 1912, in Pittsburgh, Pennsylvania; died on February 2, 1996. Educated at Penn State and the University of Pittsburgh (economics). Kelly worked at various jobs including dance instructor, gas station attendant, and ditch digger before he made it to Broadway in the chorus of *Leave It to Me* in 1938. Two years later he choreographed *Billy Rose's Diamond Horseshoe* and got the starring part in *Pal Joey*. In 1941 he choreographed *Best Foot Forward* and the following year made his screen debut opposite Judy Garland in *For Me and My Gal*. With an easygoing personality and an acrobatic dancing style, Kelly became increasingly popular in the 1940s in mostly MGM musicals. He was nominated for a Best Actor Oscar for *Anchors Aweigh*. In 1949 he made *On the Town* with Frank Sinatra, the first musical to be shot entirely on location. Its energetic production numbers set against a romantic New York skyline continue to enchant film musical buffs. In 1951 he received a Special Academy Award. This was the year of *An American in Paris*, perhaps the most ambitious musical before *Hello, Dolly!*, which Kelly directed in 1969. The relationship between the two films is interesting in that *An American in Paris*, much heralded at the time, suffered from the sort of excess that finally sank *Hello, Dolly!* Far more interesting to fans of movie musicals was the smaller-scale *Singin' in the Rain* of 1952, an absolutely charming film with an inspired story line, a talented cast, and some exciting production numbers, including Kelly's legendary dancing to the title song. In 1956, Kelly's *Invitation to the Dance*, a musical with no dialogue, won the Grand Prize at the West Berlin Film Festival, but generally it was politely ignored. For the next thirty years, he appeared in a number of nonmusical parts. Kelly suffered a stroke in 1994 and died two years later at the age of eighty-three.

Filmography: For Me and My Gal (1942); Pilot No. 5, Du Barry Was a Lady, Thousands Cheer, The Cross of Lorraine (1943); Cover Girl, Christmas Holiday (1944); Anchors Aweigh (1945); Ziegfeld Follies (1946); Living in a Big Way (1947); The Pirate, The Three Musketeers, Words and Music (1948); Take Me Out to the Ball Game, On the Town (1949); Black Hand, Summer Stock (1950); An American in Paris (1951); It's a Big Country, Singin' in the Rain, The Devil Makes Three (1952); Brigadoon, Seagulls over Sorrento/Crest of the Wave, Deep in My Heart (1954); It's Always Fair Weather (1955); Invitation to the Dance (1956); The Happy Road, Les Girls (1957); Marjorie Morningstar, Tunnel of Love [dir. only] (1958); Let's Make Love [cameo], Inherit the Wind (1960); Gigot [dir. only] (1962); What a Way to Go (1964); Les Demoiselles de Rochefort/The Young Girls of Rochefort, A Guide for the Married Man [dir. only] (1967); Hello Dolly! [dir. only] (1969); The Cheyenne Social Club [dir., prod. only] (1970); 40 Carats (1973); That's Entertainment (1974); That's Entertainment Part II (1976); Viva Knievel! (1977); Xanadu (1980); Reporters (1981); That's Dancing! (1985).

Honors: Academy Award Nomination: Best Actor (*Anchors Aweigh*, 1945); Academy Award: Special Award [in appreciation of his versatility and specifically for his brilliant achievements in choreography on film] (1951); Berlin Film Festival: Golden Bear Award (*Invitation to the Dance*, 1956); Chevalier of the Legion of Honor [by the French government for choreographing the ballet *Pas de Deux* for the Paris Opera] (1960); Golden Globes: Cecil B. DeMille Award (1980); Kennedy Center: Life Achievement Award (1982); American Film Institute: Life Achievement Award (1985).

Selected Bibliography

Basinger, Jeanine. *Gene Kelly*. New York: Pyramid Publications, 1976.
Burrows, Michael. *Gene Kelly—Versatility Personified*. St. Austell, England: Primestyle, 1972.
Hirschhorn, Clive. *Gene Kelly: A Biography*. Chicago: Henry Regnery Co., 1975.
Thomas, Tony. *Song and Dance Man: The Films of Gene Kelly*. Secaucus, NJ: Citadel Press, 1974.

KERR, DEBORAH. Actress. Born Deborah J. Kerr-Trimmer on September 30, 1921, in Helensburgh, Scotland. Trained as a dancer at her aunt's drama school in Bristol, England, and at Sadler's Wells ballet school. At seventeen Kerr made her London debut in the corps de ballet of *Prometheus*. However, she preferred drama and soon was playing bits and walk-ons in various Shakespearean productions. She made her British film debut in the early 1940s in *Major Barbara*, following it with roles usually as a lady of reserve and refinement. After her brilliant performance in *Black Narcissus*, she was brought to Hollywood by MGM in 1947 to play the lead opposite Clark Gable in *The Hucksters*. Although she was well received, her American screen career never really took off until she made everybody sit up and stare with her sensual performance as a neurotic adulteress in *From Here to Eternity*. Her erotic beach scene with Burt Lancaster remains one of the screen's unforgettable moments. After that she played a wider range of roles, receiving in the process six Academy Award nominations but never an Oscar until 1993 when she was given a Special Award. Being overlooked for an Oscar was probably just one of those ironies of the awards process, but it is easy to scowl at an academy that can rush to give one to Grace Kelly or Anna Magnani or Shirley Booth and overlook an actress as intelligent and talented and versatile as Deborah Kerr. Her work in *The Innocents* alone is deserving of special recognition, not to mention her brilliant performance in the incomparable *The King and I*. And imitations have only added luster to *An Affair to Remember*. Perhaps there's consolation in the fact that her co-star in that memorable film, Cary Grant, was also routinely overlooked at Oscar time.

Filmography: Major Barbara, Love on the Dole, Penn of Pennsylvania/Courageous Mr. Penn, Hatter's Castle (1941); The Day Will Dawn/The Avengers (1942); The Life and Death of Colonel Blimp (1943); Perfect Strangers/Vacation from Marriage (1945); I See a Dark Stranger/The Adventuress (1946); Black Narcissus, The Hucksters (1947); If Winter Comes (1948); Edward My Son (1949); Please Believe Me, King Solomon's Mines (1950); Quo Vadis (1951); The Prisoner of Zenda (1952); Thunder in the East, Young Bess, Julius Caesar, Dream Wife, From Here to Eternity (1953); The End of the Affair (1955); The Proud and the Profane, The King and I, Tea and Sympathy (1956); Heaven Knows Mr. Allison, An Affair to Remember (1957); Bonjour Tristesse, Separate Tables (1958); The Journey, Count Your Blessings, Beloved Infidel (1959); The Sundowners, The Grass Is Greener (1960); The Naked Edge, The Innocents (1961); The Chalk Garden (1963); The Night of the Iguana (1964); Marriage on the Rocks (1965); Eye of the Devil, Casino Royale (1967); Prudence and the Pill (1968); The Gypsy Moths, The Arrangement (1969); The Assam Garden (1985).

Honors: New York Film Critics Circle Award: Best Actress (*Black Narcissus, The Adventuress*, 1946); Academy Award Nomination: Best Actress (*Edward, My Son*, 1949); Academy Award Nomination: Best Actress (*From Here to Eternity*, 1953); Golden Globe Award: Best Actress in a Comedy/Musical, Academy Award Nomination: Best Actress (*The King and I*, 1956); New York Film Critics Circle Award, Academy Award Nomination: Best Actress (*Heaven Knows, Mr. Allison*, 1957); *Photoplay* Gold Medal Award: Most Popular Female Star (1957); Golden Globe Award: World Film Favorite (1958); Academy Award Nomination: Best Actress (*Separate Tables*, 1958); New York Film Critics Circle Award, Academy Award Nomination: Best Actress (*The Sundowners*, 1960); Academy Award: Special Award (1993).

Selected Bibliography

Braun, Eric. *Deborah Kerr*. New York: St. Martin's Press, 1978.

KILLERS, THE (1946), drama. Directed by Robert Siodmak; with Burt Lancaster, Ava Gardner, Edmond O'Brien, Albert Dekker, Sam Levene, Virginia Christine, William Conrad, and Charles McGraw; screenplay by Anthony Veiller (and uncredited John Huston).

The Killers is based on a Hemingway short story, and most of the film is an elaboration on the bare bones of that story. Hemingway, however, did have a hand in the elaboration (as did John Huston, who also contributed considerably to the screenplay), and critics generally agree that the entire movie has that Hemingway feel to it in addition to being a prime piece of film noir. Some critics even go so far as to claim this film as *the* definitive example of 1940s film noir for a number of reasons including its superb cast, its musical score, and its underlying current of cynicism and pessimism. Burt Lancaster is outstanding in this, his debut role, and Ava Gardner, in her first leading role, was happy to get the chance to act for a change instead of just slinking around looking sultry. The film employs a seamless flashback technique that works in this case to heighten the suspense as the film builds toward a shattering conclusion. Miklos Rozsa's background music, which adds immensely to the drama and suspense of the film, also enjoyed a long second life as the familiar theme music for TV's *Dragnet* (dum-da-dum-dum). In spite of its general critical acclaim, there is a superficiality to the movie that is more apparent in an age that does not worship Hemingway the way Americans did at midcentury. Energy combined with attention to form and detail plus a Hemingway story, a superb cast, great cinematography, and a top-notch score all add up to a certain aura that obscures the essential slickness of the film.

Awards: Academy Award Nominations: Best Director, Screenplay, Editing, Scoring of a Dramatic Picture.

Selected Bibliography

Fury, David. *The Cinema History of Burt Lancaster*. Minneapolis, MN: Artist's Press, 1989.
Hirsch, Foster. *Film Noir*. New York: DaCapo, 1981.
Thomas, Tony. *The Films of the Forties*. Secaucus, NJ: Citadel Press, 1975.

KING KONG (1933), fantasy/horror. Directed by Merian C. Cooper and Ernest B. Schoedsack; with Fay Wray, Robert Armstrong, Bruce Cabot, Frank Reicher, Sam Hardy, Noble Johnson, and James Flavin; screenplay by James Creelman, Ruth Rose, and Merian C. Cooper.

"The Eighth Wonder of the World!" is the way this classic film was ballyhooed, and in this case, it was no exaggeration. *King Kong* is generally considered to be the greatest monster movie of them all, a miracle of trick photography, special effects, and pure, gripping storytelling. As one of a handful of films that have become enduring icons of American popular culture, its influence cannot be overstated. Its influence has reverberated through moviemaking ever since, and yet it has never been surpassed or even equaled in its flawless blend of action, music, narrative, and character. Even after they know how it was filmed, audiences consistently suspend all disbelief as they sit in awe of the final scene atop the Empire State building. If this film has lost none of its power to stir, excite, and ultimately sadden, it is largely due to the remarkable technical achievements of Willis O'Brien's animation work. But the heart of the film lies in the creation of the semihuman Kong himself, a brilliant tribute to Hollywood's ability to create a fearsome creature that turns out to be more "civilized" than those who would shackle him and humiliate him and rob him of his dignity. Not again until E.T. has such a feat been so skillfully and compellingly accomplished. Detractors may make a passing swipe or two at the film's "hokeyness," but even they have to admit to being completely won over by the film's innocent charm, its total lack of irony, an element long missing in this day of self-conscious filmmaking and unavoidable self-parody. That said, one does have to wonder, as one critic asked, why the natives built a door big enough to let the monster through if they wanted to keep him on the other side of the wall. The answer is not ignorance; it's innocence.

Awards: Not taken seriously when it was released, *King Kong* was not even considered for any awards, respectable or otherwise.

Selected Bibliography

Goldner, Orville, and George E. Turner. *The Making of "King Kong": The Story Behind a Film Classic*. South Brunswick, NJ: A. S. Barnes, 1975.

Gottesman, Ronald, and Harry Geduld, eds. *The Girl in the Hairy Paw: "King Kong" as Myth, Movie, and Monster*. New York: Avon Books, 1976.

Pascall, Jeremy. *The "King Kong" Story*. Secaucus, NJ: Chartwell Books, 1977.

Thorne, Ian. *King Kong*. Mankato, MN: Crestwood House, 1977.

KINGS ROW (1942), drama. Directed by Sam Wood; with Ann Sheridan, Robert Cummings, Ronald Reagan, Betty Field, Charles Coburn, and Claude Rains; screenplay by Casey Robinson.

"Kings Row . . . The town they talk of in whispers!" Some have called this the forerunner of *Peyton Place*, but there is a big difference. Whereas *Peyton Place* capitalizes on the secrets its inhabitants try to conceal for fear of social disapproval, people in Kings Row know that everybody is a hypocrite and that nobody has a monopoly on human fallibility. This film is well directed and well acted throughout, but it will probably be remembered longest as being the best role then-actor Ronald Reagan ever played. His cry of horror ("Where's the rest of me?") when he discovers that his legs have been amputated by a sadistic doctor (Coburn) has become one of those rare moments in screen history. It's easy today to talk about this film being the typical nostalgic view of American small-town life turned inside out (*Our Town* as *Sour Town*), that instead of sweetness and health we get fear, sanctimoniousness, sadism, and madness—

but the fact is that dissection of small-town life had only just recently become
a national pastime with book clubs falling all over themselves to hawk such
novels as *Before the Sun Goes Down* and *A Woman of Property*, novels of
small-town American life, particularly midwestern life, ripe for exploitation.
Curiously enough, this film, which tranquilly accepts the many varieties of psychopathic behavior as the simple facts of life, has its own kind of sentimental
glow. Director Sam Wood gets some remarkably well-defined performances
from this remarkable cast. Ann Sheridan is radiant in the role of a girl from the
wrong side of the tracks, and Betty Field's frightened, passionate Cassie is a
memorable vignette. Charles Coburn and Claude Rains are the town's weird
doctors; Coburn likes to perform amputations without anesthetics, and Rains
keeps his daughter locked up in his house for his own sick purposes.

Selected Bibliography

Finler, Joel W. *The Movie Directors Story*. London: Octopus Books, 1985.

Levy, Emanuel. *Small-Town America in Film: The Decline and Fall of Community*. New
York: Continuum, 1991.

Reagan, Ronald, with Richard G. Huble. *"Where's the Rest of Me?"* New York: Duell,
Sloan and Pearce, 1965.

KRAMER, STANLEY. Producer, director. Born on September 23, 1913, in New
York City. Educated at New York University. Kramer started in films in the
mid-1930s as researcher, film editor, and writer and worked his way up to the
position of associate producer by the early 1940s. After World War II he formed
his own independent motion picture company and produced a string of powerful
films including *Champion*, *Home of the Brave*, *The Men*, *Death of a Salesman*,
High Noon, *The Wild One*, and *The Caine Mutiny*. Kramer acquired a reputation
for producing (and later directing) "message" films that critics labeled simplistic, shallow, even pretentious. Kramer himself admitted that he was not entirely
sure why he was motivated to deliver a message, but it had something to do
with using the medium of film to do more than amuse and divert. Later criticism
has been kinder to Kramer, recognizing the range of a talent that can deliver
everything from *On the Beach* and *Inherit the Wind* to *It's a Mad Mad Mad
Mad World*. He is also appreciated for having bucked the Hollywood system as
an independent producer long before others were willing to take the risk. Aware
of the prevailing critical opinion that has typed many of his films as shallow
and pretentious, Kramer once confessed in an interview: "I feel a tremendous
shortcoming in myself in terms of expression in films. . . . I've been saddled
with the idea of the 'message film' although I don't even know the meaning of
that myself. . . . The theme has dominated to too great an extent everything in
which I have been involved. . . . I would like to express myself a little more
simply and, if you will, artistically." His "artistic" record notwithstanding,
Kramer's sincerity cannot be questioned, and he deserves recognition for taking
a stand and sticking to it. When he received the Irving G. Thalberg Award in
1961, it was for "consistently high quality in filmmaking."

Filmography: [as producer]: So Ends Our Night (1941); The Moon and Sixpence (1942); So This Is New York (1948); Champion, Home of the Brave (1949); The Men, Cyrano de Bergerac (1950); Death of a Salesman (1951); The Sniper, High Noon, The Happy Time, My Six Convicts (1952); The Four Poster, Eight Iron Men, The Juggler, The 5,000 Fingers of Dr. T (1953); The Wild One, The Caine Mutiny (1954). [as producer-director]: Not as a Stranger (1955); The Pride and the Passion (1957); The Defiant Ones (1958); On the Beach (1959); Inherit the Wind (1960); Judgment at Nuremberg (1961); Pressure Point (1962); A Child Is Waiting, It's a Mad Mad Mad Mad World (1963); Guess Who's Coming to Dinner? (1967); The Secret of Santa Vittoria (1969); R.P.M. (1970); Bless the Beasts and the Children (1971); Oklahoma Crude (1973); The Domino Principle (1977); The Runner Stumbles (1979).

Honors: New York Film Critics Circle Award, Academy Award Nomination: Best Director (*The Defiant Ones*, 1958); Golden Globes: Special Award for Artistic Integrity (1960); Golden Globe Award, Academy Award Nomination: Best Director (*Judgment at Nuremberg*, 1961); Academy Award: Irving G. Thalberg Award (1961); Academy Award Nomination: Best Director (*Guess Who's Coming to Dinner?* 1967).

Selected Bibliography

Finler, Joel W. *The Movie Directors Story*. London: Octopus Books, 1985.
Sennett, Ted. *Great Movie Directors*. New York: Harry N. Abrams, 1986.
Spoto, Donald. *Stanley Kramer: Film Maker*. New York: Putnam, 1978.

KUBRICK, STANLEY. Director. Born on July 26, 1928, in the Bronx, New York. Kubrick made his debut as a feature director in 1953 with *Fear and Desire*, a low-budget film he financed with money he had borrowed from relatives and friends. It was virtually a one-man show in which Kubrick did just about everything but the acting. He made his second feature, *Killer's Kiss*, in much the same way. In 1954, Kubrick formed a production company with producer James B. Harris. Their first film was *The Killing*, a tense film noir that was both a critical success and a cult favorite. He followed this with *Paths of Glory*, a powerful antiwar film whose somber, satirical tone was to become increasingly insistent in Kubrick's later works. These films were not commercial successes, and for two years Kubrick was out of work. Then Kirk Douglas, who admired Kubrick's work, asked him to direct *Spartacus*, a superior spectacle that Douglas was producing and starring in. Kubrick did a superb job, but his clashes with Douglas during the filming were so unpleasant that he moved to England where he stayed until he was lured back to direct the controversial *Lolita*, a film that Kubrick liberally laced with the cynicism and black humor that had become and would remain his trademark. These ingredients find their most memorable expression in *Dr. Strangelove or How I Learned to Stop Worrying and Love the Bomb*, a bitterly comic satire in which he treats the possibility of nuclear catastrophe as a grim joke. His next film, *2001: A Space Odyssey*, continues to polarize criticism. Where some find it overblown, tedious, pretentious, and confusing, others consider it a mind-blowing, psychedelic experience not unlike an acid "trip." Still others interpret the film as a sobering indictment of a society hell-bent on committing technological suicide. *A Clockwork Orange* is even bleaker in its scathing view of a violence-obsessed society not only courting its own destruction but wallowing in it. To Kubrick, the future the story portrays is really today's reality barely concealed beneath a veneer of shameless hypocrisy. Kubrick is known to be a notorious perfectionist who can take years to prepare a single film. Often the result is visually stunning but shallow, as was the case with both *Barry Lyndon* and *The Shining*. In *Full Metal Jacket*, Kubrick gives vent to his darkest view of the human race and his rejection of it. It is no wonder, then, that Kubrick has divided critical opinion, with his detractors calling him pretentious, fussy, unfeeling, and self-indulgent, while his loyal followers revere him as a unique artist with personal vision and brilliant visual style, one of the outstanding talents of today's cinema.

Filmography: Day of the Fight (1950); Flying Padre (1951); Fear and Desire (1953); Killer's Kiss (1955); The Killing (1956); Paths of Glory (1957); Spartacus (1960); Lolita (1962); Dr. Strangelove or How I Learned to Stop Worrying and Love the Bomb (1964); 2001: A Space Odyssey (1968); A Clockwork Orange (1971); Barry Lyndon (1975); The Shining (1980); Full Metal Jacket (1987).

Honors: New York Film Critics Circle Award, Academy Award Nomination: Best Director (*Dr. Strangelove*, 1964); Academy Award Nomination: Best Director (*2001: A Space Odyssey*, 1968); New York Film Critics Circle Award, Academy Award Nomination, Best Director (*A Clockwork Orange*, 1971); National Board of Review Award, British Academy Award, Academy Award Nomination: Best Director (*Barry Lyndon*, 1975).

Selected Bibliography

Coyle, Wallace. *Stanley Kubrick: A Guide to References and Sources*. Boston: G. K. Hall, 1980.

Falsetto, Mario. *Stanley Kubrick: A Narrative and Stylistic Analysis*. Westport, CT: Praeger Publishers, 1994.

Kagan, Norman. *The Cinema of Stanley Kubrick*. New York: Holt, Rinehart and Winston, 1972.

L

LADD, ALAN. Actor. Born on September 3, 1913, in Hot Springs, Arkansas; died on November 7, 1964. Short (five foot five) and expressionless, Ladd seemed an unlikely candidate for film stardom back when he was just starting out, and today he seems just as unlikely, but for different reasons. What ultimately worked for him back then was precisely a face so devoid of emotion that it reeked of both menace and mystery, a combination the camera revealed as surely as it could conceal his height. Today, however, Ladd is likely to look like someone trying to imitate what a bad guy ought to look like. In fact, it is just this sort of self-parody Ladd pulls in *Star Spangled Rhythm* in a scene in which, never once cracking a smile, he reaches inside his coat and, instead of a hand gun, pulls out a tiny bow and arrow. His climb to the top did, in fact, take longer because of his perceived blandness, and he spent several years playing minor parts, including a brief appearance as a reporter in *Citizen Kane*. However, his wife, former actress Sue Carol, was an agent, and she worked tirelessly to find him better roles. He got his big break as a paid killer in *This Gun for Hire* in which his stolid, icy-eyed, blond good looks matched so perfectly with the provocative coolness of that film's female star, Veronica Lake, that the studio teamed them in a number of other productions. With the exception of *Shane*, Ladd's later work was largely undistinguished. He was cast in a number of action-packed formula films in which his shortcomings as an actor were not so visible. In 1962, he tried to take his own life. Two years later, at fifty-one, he was found dead from an overdose of sedatives and alcohol, an apparent suicide. It has been suggested that his last role, that of an aging, washed-up movie star in *The Carpetbaggers*, was too close to the mark for comfort.

Filmography: Once in a Lifetime (1932); Pigskin Parade (1936); Last Train from Madrid, Souls at Sea, Hold 'Em Navy, Born to the West (1937); The Goldwyn Follies, Come on Leathernecks, Freshman Year (1938); Beasts of Berlin/Goose Step, Rulers of the Sea (1939); The Green Hornet [serial], Light of the Western Stars, Gangs of Chicago, In Old Missouri, The Howards of Virginia, Those Were the Days, Captain Caution, Wildcat Bus, Meet the Missus, Her First Romance (1940); Great Guns, Citizen Kane, Cadet Girl, Petticoat Politics, The Black Cat, The Reluctant Dragon, Paper Bullets/Gangs, Inc. (1941); Joan of Paris, This Gun for Hire, The Glass Key, Lucky Jordan, Star Spangled Rhythm [cameo] (1942); China (1943); And Now Tomorrow (1944); Salty O'Rourke, Duffy's Tavern [cameo] (1945); The Blue Dahlia, O.S.S., Two Years before the Mast (1946); Calcutta, Variety Girl [cameo] (1947); Saigon, Beyond Glory, Whispering Smith (1948); The Great Gatsby [title role], Chicago Deadline (1949); Captain Carey U.S.A. (1950); Branded, Appointment with Danger (1951); Red Mountain, The Iron Mistress [as Jim Bowie] (1952); Thunder in the East, Desert Legion, Shane, Botany Bay (1953); The Red Beret/Paratrooper, The Black Knight, Saskatchewan, Hell below Zero, Drum Beat (1954); The McConnell Story, Hell on Frisco Bay (1955); Santiago (1956); The Big Land, Boy on a Dolphin (1957); The Deep Six, The Proud Rebel, The Badlanders (1958); The Man in the Net (1959); Guns of the Timberland, All the Young Men, One Foot in Hell (1960); Duel of Champions (1961); 13 West Street (1962); The Carpetbaggers (1964).

Honors: Golden Globe Award: World Film Favorite (1953); *Photoplay* Gold Medal Award: Most Popular Male Star (1953).

Selected Bibliography

Henry, Marilyn, and Ron DeSourdis. *The Films of Alan Ladd*. Secaucus, NJ: Citadel Press, 1981.

Linet, Beverly. *Ladd: The Life, the Legend, the Legacy of Alan Ladd: A Biography*. New York: Arbor House, 1979.

LAKE, VERONICA. Actress. Born Constance Frances Marie Ockelman on November 14, 1919, in Brooklyn, New York; died on July 7, 1973. Lake entered films in 1939 as Constance Keane (her stepfather's surname), changing her name to Veronica Lake in 1941, the year that marked the beginning of her meteoric but brief career. During 1941–1942 she did six films plus a cameo self-parody in *Star Spangled Rhythm*. Of the six, four were unusually striking. First there was the Preston Sturges masterpiece *Sullivan's Travels*. This was followed by two hits opposite Alan Ladd: *This Gun for Hire* and *The Glass Key*. And finally there was the offbeat comedy *I Married a Witch*. By the end of 1942 Veronica Lake was a household name and an established star. She was also a threat to the defense industry. Her hairstyle, known as the "peekaboo bang," was so popular that factory workers who wore it were in danger of getting their long hair caught in the machinery. The government stepped in and banned the hairstyle, and Lake graciously agreed to change hers to something shorter. In 1943 she turned in an impressive performance in *So Proudly We Hail* as a tormented army nurse who sacrifices her life to save her coworkers. Unfortunately, from then on, her career began to fade, and her fame barely survived the war. For one thing, she lacked the sort of career management that might have redefined her in the way Lana Turner or Joan Crawford redefined themselves to accommodate new times and trends. For another, Lake began to catch the eye of such men as Aristotle Onassis and Howard Hughes. In the early 1950s, shortly after she and director André De Toth, her first husband, filed for bankruptcy, she disappeared from view, her name appearing in the papers only on those occasions when she would be arrested for public drunkenness. In the 1960s she was discovered working as a barmaid in a downtown New York hotel. She tried then to revive her career, working off Broadway, in stock, and in rare low-budget films and eventually settled in England. She died at fifty-three of hepatitis.

Filmography: [as Constance Keane]: All Women Have Secrets, Sorority House Dancing Co-Ed (1939); Young as You Feel, Forty Little Mothers (1940). [as Veronica Lake]: I Wanted Wings, Hold Back the Dawn (1941); Sullivan's Travels, This Gun for Hire, The Glass Key, I Married a Witch, Star Spangled Rhythm [cameo] (1942); So Proudly We Hail (1943); The Hour before Dawn (1944); Bring on the Girls, Out of This World, Duffy's Tavern [cameo], Hold That Blonde (1945); Miss Susie Slagle's, The Blue Dahlia (1946); Ramrod, Variety Girl [cameo] (1947); Saigon, The Sainted Sisters, Isn't It Romantic? (1948); Slattery's Hurricane (1949); Stronghold (1952); Footsteps in the Snow (1966); Flesh Feast (1970).

Selected Bibliography

Lake, Veronica, with Donald Bain. *Veronica*. New York: Citadel Press, 1971.
Lenburg, Jeff. *Peekaboo: The Story of Veronica Lake*. New York: St. Martin's Press, 1983.

LAMARR, HEDY. Actress. Born Hedwig Eva Maria Kiesler on November 9, 1913, in Vienna. Lamarr was more a screen personality than a screen actress, astonishingly beautiful but with limited talents. If Lamarr had been smarter, she would have done as Elizabeth Taylor did and projected the image of seductress mixed with ingenue. But Lamarr had too much going against her. For one thing, her accent and looks limited her to exotic parts in which any attempt to "act" only looked forced. For another, she could never live down the stigma of the notorious film *Ecstasy* in which she had a ten-minute nude swimming scene. Ironically, this film, which made her famous, was also the one that sullied her reputation in a way Taylor never suffered in spite of her notoriety. Taylor, of course, had *National Velvet* and *Lassie* and thus started off at least with a wholesome image, the gradual tarnishing of which only added to her mystique. And Taylor also knew how to parody herself, whereas Lamarr took herself seriously. Lamarr's 1940s films were enormously popular, but her most successful film, *Samson and Delilah*, came just as her career was about to decline rapidly. By the early 1950s, her screen career was almost nonexistent. In 1967, bankrupt and desperate, she published her autobiography, *"Ecstasy" and Me*, a blatant attempt to cash in on her notoriety. The book was in such bad taste that Lamarr actually sued her collaborators (for $21 million) for misrepresentation. Regardless of her faded reputation, Lamarr's name still conjures up an image of sultry beauty and exotic mystery. In 1997 it was revealed that during World War II Lamarr had been instrumental in formulating the concept of "frequency hopping," a method of evading enemy interference in radio frequencies used on submarines to guide torpedoes to their destination.

Filmography: [United States only]: Algiers (1938); Lady of the Tropics (1939); I Take This Woman, Boom Town, Comrade X (1940); Come Live with Me, Ziegfeld Girl, H. M. Pulham Esq. (1941); Tortilla Flat, Crossroads, White Cargo (1942); The Heavenly Body, The Conspirators, Experiment Perilous (1944); Her Highness and the Bellboy (1945); The Strange Woman (1946); Dishonored Lady (1947); Let's Live a Little (1948); Samson and Delilah (1949); A Lady without a Passport, Copper Canyon (1950); My Favorite Spy (1951); Love of Three Queens/The Face That Launched a Thousand Ships (1954); The Story of Mankind [as Joan of Arc] (1957); The Female Animal (1958); Instant Karma (1990).

Selected Bibliography

Lamarr, Hedy. *"Ecstasy" and Me: My Life as a Woman*. Greenwich, CT: Fawcett, 1967.
Young, Christopher. *The Films of Hedy Lamarr*. Secaucus, NJ: Citadel Press, 1978.

LANCASTER, BURT. Actor. Born Burton Stephen Lancaster on November 2, 1913, in New York City; died on October 22, 1994. After years of eking out a living touring with circuses and appearing in nightclubs as part of an acrobatic act—and after seeing World War II action in North Africa and Italy with Special Services—Lancaster was reportedly discovered in an elevator by a stage producer who mistook him for an actor and asked him to read for a Broadway part. He got the part, but the play, *The Sound of Hunting* (1945), ran for only three weeks. However, it was just long enough for him to be noticed by Hollywood scouts. The following year, he made his memorable screen debut as Swede in *The Killers*. Immediately established as a star, Lancaster rapidly revealed a sensitive interior beneath his athletic prowess. As early as 1948 he was among the first film actors to become an independent producer, forming the Hecht-Lancaster company with his agent Harold Hecht. Later they were joined by producer James Hill. In the 1950s, Lancaster demonstrated his remarkable versatility by alternating acrobatic portrayals in adventure films with sensitive, sincere performances in such dramas as *Come Back Little Sheba*, *From Here to Eternity*, *The Rose Tattoo*, and *The Sweet Smell of Success*. He also directed one film, *The Kentuckian*, starring himself. His company produced several notable films of the 1950s, including *Marty*. Lancaster extended his career successfully into the 1980s, despite quadruple bypass open-heart surgery in 1983. Late in 1990 he was hospitalized for a stroke that left him partially paralyzed until his death in 1994.

Filmography: The Killers (1946); Variety Girl [cameo], Brute Force, Desert Fury (1947); I Walk Alone, All My Sons, Sorry Wrong Number, Kiss the Blood Off My Hands (1948); Criss Cross, Rope of Sand (1949); The Flame and the Arrow, Mister 880 (1950); Vengeance Valley, Jim Thorpe—All American [title role], Ten Tall Men (1951); The

Crimson Pirate, Come Back Little Sheba (1952); South Sea Woman, From Here to Eternity (1953); His Majesty O'Keefe, Apache, Vera Cruz (1954); The Kentuckian [also dir.], The Rose Tattoo (1955); Trapeze, The Rainmaker (1956); Gunfight at the O.K. Corral [as Wyatt Earp], Sweet Smell of Success (1957); Run Silent Run Deep, Separate Tables (1958); The Devil's Disciple (1959); The Unforgiven, Elmer Gantry (1960); The Young Savages, Judgment at Nuremberg (1961); Birdman of Alcatraz (1962); A Child Is Waiting, The List of Adrian Messenger, The Leopard (1963); Seven Days in May, The Train (1964); The Hallelujah Trail (1965); The Professionals (1966); The Scalphunters, The Swimmer (1968); Castle Keep, The Gypsy Moths (1969); King [doc.], Airport (1970); Lawman, Valdez Is Coming (1971); Ulzana's Raid (1972); Scorpio, Executive Action (1973); The Midnight Man [also co-dir., co-prod., co-sc.] (1974); Conversation Piece (1975); Moses, 1900, Buffalo Bill and the Indians (1976); The Cassandra Crossing, Twilight's Last Gleaming, The Island of Dr. Moreau (1977); Go Tell the Spartans (1978); Zulu Dawn, Arthur Miller on Home Ground [doc.] (1979); Atlantic City, Cattle Annie and Little Britches, The Skin (1981); Local Hero, The Osterman Weekend (1983); Little Treasure (1985); Tough Guys (1986); Il Giorno prima [It.] (1987); Rocket Gibraltar (1988); La Boutique de l'Orfèvre [Fr.], Field of Dreams (1989); The Jeweller's Shop [U.K.; adapted from a short story written by Karol Wojtyla, Pope John Paul II] (1990).

Honors: New York Film Critics Circle Award, Academy Award Nomination: Best Actor (*From Here to Eternity*, 1953); Berlin Film Festival Award: Best Actor (*Trapeze*, 1956); Academy Award, Golden Globe Award, New York Film Critics Circle Award: Best Actor (*Elmer Gantry*, 1960); British Academy Award, Venice Film Festival Award, Academy Award Nomination: Best Actor (*Birdman of Alcatraz*, 1962); New York Film Critics Circle Award, National Society of Film Critics Award, Los Angeles Film Critics Association Award, British Academy Award, Italy's David Di Donatello Award, Academy Award Nomination: Best Actor (*Atlantic City*, 1981).

Selected Bibliography

Crowther, Bruce. *Burt Lancaster: A Life in Films*. London: Robert Hale, 1991.
Fury, David. *The Cinema History of Burt Lancaster*. Minneapolis: Artist's Press, 1989.
Hunter, Allan. *Burt Lancaster: The Man and His Movies*. Edinburgh: Paul Harris Publishing, 1984.

LANG, FRITZ. Director. Born Friedrich Christian Anton Lang on December 5, 1890, in Vienna; died on August 2, 1976. Educated at the Technische Hochshule (architecture); Vienna Academy of Graphic Arts (art); School of Arts and Crafts, Munich (art); and Academie Julien, Paris. After a spectacular career in German films in the 1920s and 1930s, during which he directed the masterpiece *Metropolis*, Lang traveled to Paris, where he made one film, and then on to the United States where he spent the next twenty years turning out many highly original and highly acclaimed American films in a variety of genres, mainly thrillers: *Man Hunt, Scarlet Street, While the City Sleeps*, and some outstanding westerns: *The Return of Frank James, Rancho Notorious*. Of all the continental refugees, Lang adapted most naturally to America. His American films are among his greatest because he found the studio system better organized and more adept at narrative genres. Tired of fighting insensitive producers, Lang went to India in the mid-1950s to make a film, then returned to Germany for his last set of films. Throughout his films there is a nightmarish quality of victims trapped in bizarre conspiracies. According to film scholar David Thomson, "No other director so convinces us that melodramatic threat of extinction in the crime movie is the metaphor of a much greater danger." He maintains tension, says Thomson, in his "relentless narrative pace and in the undeflected observation of fear, anger, joy, and action eating into nerves and morality." Within Lang's works there is often a disarming simplicity in the truths that lurk beneath his murky surfaces.

Filmography: [U.S. films only]: Fury (1936); You Only Live Once (1937); You and Me (1938); The Return of Frank James (1940); Western Union, Man Hunt (1941); Hangmen Also Die (1943); The Woman in the Window, Ministry of Fear (1944); Scarlet Street (1945); Cloak and Dagger (1946); Secret beyond the Door (1948); House by the River, American Guerrilla in the Philippines (1950); Rancho Notorious, Clash by Night (1952); The Blue Gardenia, The Big Heat (1953); Human Desire (1954); Moonfleet (1955); While the City Sleeps, Beyond a Reasonable Doubt (1956).

Honors: Venice Film Festival Award: Special Mention (*Hangmen Also Die*, 1946).

Selected Bibliography

Humphries, Reynold. *Fritz Lang: Genre and Representation in His American Films*. Baltimore: Johns Hopkins University Press, 1989.

Kaplan, E. Ann. *Fritz Lang: A Guide to References and Resources*. Boston: G. K. Hall, 1981.

Ott, Frederick W. *The Films of Fritz Lang*. Secaucus, NJ: Citadel Press, 1979.

LAUGHTON, CHARLES. Actor. Born on July 1, 1899, in Scarborough, England; died on December 15, 1962. Educated at Stonyhurst College and the Royal Academy of Dramatic Art. Laughton made his professional debut on London's West End in 1926, and in 1928 he co-starred with Elsa Lanchester, whom he married the following year, the same year he made his film debut. The Laughtons came to New York in 1931 with the play *Payment Deferred*, and the following year Laughton launched his long and illustrious career as a Hollywood character star. Although Laughton gave some of his finest performances in British films (*The Private Life of Henry VIII*, for which he won an Oscar, and *Rembrandt*), most of his films were made in the United States, and in 1950 he became an American citizen. Rotund and boisterous, Laughton was a brilliant performer with an astonishing range. Given his fish face, thick lips, and droopy eyes, he seemed destined to be typecast. However, he refused to limit himself, and during his career he played sadists, butlers, heads of state, murderers, lawyers, bohemians, Milquetoasts—all with great flair and obvious relish. He could be a shameless ham when he wanted to, especially when playing a minor role in a trivial film. The year 1935 was his annus mirabilis, the year during which he played three of his most memorable roles: Ruggles in *Ruggles of Red Gap*, Javert in *Les Misérables*, and Captain Bligh in *Mutiny on the Bounty*. Other memorable film appearances were in *The Hunchback of Notre Dame* (as Quasimodo), *The Canterville Ghost*, *The Big Clock*, *Witness for the Prosecution*, and his last, *Advise and Consent*. In 1955 Laughton directed *The Night of the Hunter*, a visually striking and dramatically gripping production that showed much promise for a new career as a filmmaker. But he never made another. Instead, he spent much of his later years touring with highly acclaimed readings of Shaw's *Don Juan in Hell*, Stephen Vincent Benét's *John Brown's Body*, and selections from the Bible. He also appeared frequently on radio and TV.

Filmography: Bluebottles [short], Day Dreams [short] (1928); Picadilly (1929); Comets, Wolves/Wanted Men (1930); Down River (1931); Devil and the Deep, The Old Dark House, Payment Deferred, The Sign of the Cross, If I Had a Million, Island of Lost Souls (1932); The Private Life of Henry VIII, White Woman (1933); The Barretts of Wimpole Street (1934); Ruggles of Red Gap, Les Misérables, Mutiny on the Bounty (1935); Rembrandt (1936); I Claudius (1937); Vessel of Wrath/The Beachcomber, St. Martin's Lane/Sidewalks of London (1938); Jamaica Inn, The Hunchback of Notre Dame (1939); They Knew What They Wanted (1940); It Started with Eve (1941); The Tuttles of Tahiti, Tales of Manhattan, Stand by for Action (1942); Forever and a Day, This Land Is Mine, The Man from Down Under (1943); The Canterville Ghost (1944); The Suspect, Captain Kidd (1945); Because of Him (1946); The Paradine Cast, Arch of Triumph, The Big Clock, The Girl from Manhattan (1948); The Bribe (1949); The Man on the Eiffel Tower (1950); The Blue Veil, The Strange Door (1951); O. Henry's Full House, Abbott and Costello Meet Captain Kidd (1952); Salome, Young Bess (1953); Hobson's Choice (1954), The Night of the Hunter [dir. only] (1955); Witness for the Prosecution (1957); Under Ten Flags, Spartacus (1960); Advise and Consent (1962).

Honors: Academy Award: Best Actor (*The Private Life of Henry VIII*, 1932–1933); New York Film Critics Circle Award: Best Actor (*Mutiny on the Bounty* and *Ruggles of Red Gap*, 1935); Academy Award Nomination: Best Actor (*Mutiny on the Bounty*, 1935); Academy Award Nomination: Best Actor (*Witness for the Prosecution*, 1957).

Selected Bibliography

Callow, Simon. *Charles Laughton: A Difficult Actor*. New York: Grove Press, 1988.

Higham, Charles. *Charles Laughton: An Intimate Biography*. Garden City, NY: Doubleday, 1976.

Lanchester, Elsa. *Charles Laughton and I*. New York: Harcourt, Brace and Company, 1993.

LAURA (1944), mystery/drama. Directed by Otto Preminger (took over from Rouben Mamoulian); with Gene Tierney, Dana Andrews, Clifton Webb, Vincent Price, Judith Anderson, Grant Mitchell, Lane Chandler, and Dorothy Adams; screenplay by Jay Dratler, Samuel Hoffenstein, and Betty Reinhardt.

It is hard to judge *Laura* on its own merits. Like *Double Indemnity*, or even *Sunset Boulevard*, this film, at least for later viewers, comes with too much hype to live up to. That it is not as good as its admirers claim is probably true, just as it is probably better than it seems to a viewer primed to see a "classic." What's good about it is both technical and thematic. Technically, it is beautifully photographed and sumptuously laid out, its dialogue is witty, and its music haunting. Thematically, it flirts boldly with necrophilia as the hard-boiled detective finds himself seduced by the portrait and legend of the beautiful Laura, now presumed dead. Presumed, because the face of the woman found dead in Laura's apartment was rendered unrecognizable by the shotgun blast that killed her. Forensically sophisticated modern audiences have a problem with this, since they know that (1) there are many other ways of identifying a corpse and (2) the likelihood of the Laura and the real victim resembling each other so closely in every other way as to be indistinguishable seriously damages the film's credibility. Much has been made of the film's deceptively leisurely pace that builds without the audience really being aware of it. They may not be aware of it precisely because it isn't really there. The pace is slow, and no one is surprised when the faceless corpse turns out not to be Laura, or when Laura returns "from vacation" somewhere without a telephone or access to the news. And why hasn't the real victim been declared a missing person? While *Laura* contains all the clichés of film noir (not to mention voyeurism and necrophilia), its special charm lies in the fact that it does not, like most, take place in back alleys, shabby dives, and seedy hotel rooms. Instead, it is a high-society thriller reeking of money and class and refined decadence. Who can forget Clifton Webb, flawless as an effete sophisticate, typing his society column while bathing in a marble tub and welcoming Dana Andrews to his posh penthouse with a dismissive wave of the hand and this remark: "It's lavish, but I call it home."

Awards: Academy Award: Best B&W Cinematography (Joseph LaShelle); Academy Award Nominations: Best Director, Supporting Actor (Webb), Screenplay, B&W Art Direction.

Selected Bibliography

Pratley, Gerald. *The Cinema of Otto Preminger*. New York: A. S. Barnes, 1971.
Silver, Alain, and Elizabeth Ward, eds. *Film Noir: An Encyclopedic Reference to the American Style*. Woodstock, NY: Overlook Press, 1979.
Thomas, Tony. *The Films of the Forties*. Secaucus, NJ: Citadel Press, 1975.

LAUREL AND HARDY. Actors, comedians. Stan Laurel was born Arthur Stanley Jefferson on June 16, 1890, in Ulverston, England; he died on February 23, 1965. Oliver Hardy was born on January 18, 1892, in Harlem, Georgia; he died on August 7, 1957. Laurel and Hardy were the most successful comedy team in screen history. They started out in silent films and were enormously popular. They then moved smoothly to talkies where, if anything, they became even more popular, partly because their voices (and the dialogue given them) fit their images and personalities. They first teamed up in 1926, and over the next thirty years, they appeared in more than 100 films, 27 of them features. The plots of most of these films were deceptively simple, usually based on the exploitation of a single idea on which the two could improvise endlessly and brilliantly, almost as if Robin Williams were pitted against his alter ego. Theirs was quintessential situation comedy, the situation usually being one that the audience could easily feel superior to while the two buffoons behaved with incredible stupidity. They would begin by getting into trouble as a result of some witless act, usually on the part of Laurel, and then get involved in an increasingly complicated mess that got worse the more they tried to extricate themselves. Along the way they would hurl insults at each other and commit frustrated acts of destruction. Shy, skinny Laurel and pudgy, pushy Hardy perfectly complemented each other. Laurel was constantly perplexed by the simplest things, while Hardy, who had a short fuse, would lord it over Laurel, ridiculing him until something would happen to deflate Hardy whose embarrassment would then be doubly humiliating. Meanwhile, they always sported derby hats, to indicate that they were gentlemen, and they were always careful to refer to each other as Mr. Laurel and Mr. Hardy. After they severed their ties with Hal Roach in 1940, their films were not as good, and in 1945, they stopped making them and went on tour. In 1950 they returned to the screen in a French-Italian bomb called *Atoll K*, which was released in the United States as *Robinson Crusoe-Land* and later as *Utopia*. In 1954, they planned a comeback with a series of color films, but plans came to an abrupt end when Hardy suffered a stroke from which he never recovered. When Hardy died in 1957, Laurel resolved never to perform again, but he continued writing comedy material until his own death in 1965. Laurel and Hardy belong to a rich heritage of classic film comedy teams (Three Stooges, The Marx Brothers, Our Gang) that live on because they have become TV staples.

Filmography: [only the films they made together] [shorts]: Lucky Dog (1917); 45 Minutes from Hollywood (1926); Duck Soup, Slipping Wives, Love'Em and Weep, Why Girls Love Sailors, With Love and Hisses, Sugar Daddies, Sailors Beware,The Second Hundred Years, Call of the Cuckoos, Hats Off, Do Detectives Think?, Putting Pants on Philip, The Battle of the Century (1927); Leave'Em Laughing, Flying Elephants, The Finishing Touch, From Soup to Nuts, You're Darn Tootin', Their Purple Moment, Should Married Men Go Home?, Two Tars, Habeas Corpus, We Faw Down (1928); Liberty, Wrong Again, That's My Wife, Big Business, Unaccustomed as We Are [first talkie], Double Whoopee, Berth Marks, Men o'War, Perfect Day, They Go Boom, Bacon Grabbers, The Hoose-Gow, Angora Love (1929); Night Owls, Blotto, Brats, Beldow Zero, Hog Wild, The Laurel-Hardy Murder Case, Another Fine Mess (1930); Be Big, Chickens Come Home, The Stolen Jools, Laughing Gravy, Our Wife, Come Clean, One Good Turn, Beau Hunks, On the Loose (1931); Helpmates, Any Old Port, The Music Box, The Chimp, County Hospital, Scram!, Their First Mistake, Towed in a Hole (1932); Twice Two, Me and My Pal, The Midnight Patrol, Busy Bodies, Wild Poses, Dirty Work (1933); Oliver the Eighth, Going Bye-Bye, Them Thar Hills, The Live Ghost (1934); Tit for Tat, The Fixer-Uppers, Thicker Than Water (1935); On the Wrong Trek (1936); The Tree in a Test Tube [doc.] (1943). [features]: Hollywood Revue of 1929 (1929); The Rogue Song (1930); Pardon Us (1931); Pack Up Your Troubles (1932); The Devil's Brother, Sons of the Desert (1933); Hollywood Party, Babes in Toyland (1934); Bonnie Scotland (1935); The Bohemian Girl, Our Relations (1936); Way Out West, Pick a Star (1937); Swiss Miss, Block-Heads (1938); The Flying Deuces (1939); A Chump at Oxford, Saps at Sea (1940); Great Guns (1941); A-Haunting We Will Go (1942); Air Raid

Wardens, Jitterbugs, The Dancing Masters (1943); The Big Noise (1944); Nothing But Trouble, The Bullfighters (1945); Atoll K/Robinson Crusoe-Land/Utopia (1950).

Honors: Academy Award: Short/Comedy (*The Music Box*, 1932); Academy Award: Special Award for [Stan Laurel] (1960).

Selected Bibliography

Crowther, Bruce. *Laurel and Hardy: Clown Princes of Comedy*. London: Columbus Books, 1987.
Everson, William K. *The Complete Films of Laurel & Hardy*. New York: Carol, 1967.
Gehring, Wes D. *Laurel and Hardy: A Bio-Bibliography*. Westport, CT: Greenwood Press, 1990.
Maltin, Leonard, ed. *The Laurel & Hardy Book*. New York: Curtis, 1973.
Skretvedt, Randy. *Laurel and Hardy: The Magic behind the Movies*. Beverly Hills, CA: Moonstone Press, 1987.

LEIGH, JANET. Actress. Born Jeanette Helen Morrison on July 6, 1927, in Merced, California. Educated at the College of the Pacific, Stockton, California (music, psychology). Try to imagine either Marilyn Monroe or Elizabeth Taylor as Marian Crane in *Psycho* and you know why Janet Leigh was Hitchcock's perfect choice. He needed a familiar name and a pretty face, but not someone who would detract from the subtler things that were going on in this dark, intensely interesting movie. As it turned out, in a role that might have paralyzed another actress's career, Janet Leigh has only benefited from her association with *Psycho*. For hers was the kind of charming, perky, sultry innocence that did not dominate a film. Thus, although she made a slew of films over many years, she is best (maybe only) remembered for three, and even in these she was not really the "star." Besides *Psycho*, there was *Touch of Evil* and *The Manchurian Candidate*. Even the way she was discovered explains part of the elusive appeal of this lovely actress. Norma Shearer saw a photograph of her when Leigh was only nineteen and showed it to Louis B. Mayer, who immediately signed her to a contract, changed her name, and starred her opposite Van Johnson in *The Romance of Rosy Ridge* where her fresh, innocent prettiness fit perfectly her character as a mountaineer's daughter. She was twenty. By the time she was twenty-four, she had married Tony Curtis, and the two of them became Hollywood's "adorable couple." Her film career waned in the 1960s, and she turned to TV, where she was active as a mature lead or in strong secondary roles.

Filmography: If Winter Comes, The Romance of Rosy Ridge (1947); Hills of Home, Words and Music (1948); Act of Violence, The Doctor and the Girl, Holiday Affair, Little Women, The Red Danube, That Forsyte Woman (1949); Angels in the Outfield, It's a Big Country, Strictly Dishonorable, Two Tickets to Broadway (1951); Fearless Fagan, Just This Once, Scaramouch (1952); Confidentially Connie, Houdini, The Naked Spur, Walking My Baby Back Home (1953); The Black Shield of Falworth, Living It Up, Prince Valiant, Rogue Cop (1954); My Sister Eileen, Pete Kelly's Blues (1955); Safari (1956); Jet Pilot (1957); The Perfect Furlough, Touch of Evil, The Vikings (1958);

Pepe, Psycho, Who Was That Lady? (1960); The Manchurian Candidate (1962): Bye Bye Birdie, Wives and Lovers (1963); An American Dream, Harper, Kid Rodelo, The Spy in the Green Hat, Three on a Couch (1966); Grand Slam/Adogni Coso (1968); Hello Down There/Sub-a-Dub-Dub (1969); Night of the Lepus, One Is a Lonely Number (1972); Boardwalk (1979); The Fog (1980); Hitchcock, Il Brivido del Genio/The Thrill of Genius (1985); The Fantasy Film World of George Pal (1986).

Honors: Golden Globe Award, Academy Award Nomination: Best Supporting Actress (*Psycho*, 1960).

Selected Bibliography

Leigh, Janet, with Christopher Nickens. *Behind the Scenes of ''Psycho,'' the Classic Thriller*. New York: Harmony Books, 1995.

LEROY, MERVYN. Director, producer. Born on October 15, 1900, in San Francisco; died on September 13, 1987. LeRoy arrived in Hollywood in 1919 with a letter of recommendation from a cousin, producer Jesse L. Lasky, and got his first job there in the wardrobe department of Famous Players–Lasky. Before long, LeRoy was working in the lab, then was promoted to assistant cameraman. At the same time, he began appearing in films, at first as an extra bit player, then as a featured player. LeRoy became a director in 1927, and during the 1930s he established his reputation when he directed several powerful social dramas, notably *Little Caesar* and *I Am a Fugitive from a Chain Gang*. But LeRoy was also adept at other genres as demonstrated in musicals like *Gold Diggers of 1933* and comedies like *Tugboat Annie*. In 1938 he joined MGM, where, during the 1940s, he directed romantic films such as *Waterloo Bridge* and *Random Harvest* and the exciting and very moving World War II action drama *Thirty Seconds over Tokyo*. He was also responsible for the lavish costume spectacle *Quo Vadis* in 1951. As a producer LeRoy was responsible for *The Wizard of Oz*. He also produced several of the films he directed. LeRoy's reputation declined somewhat after World War II, when he turned out a string of mediocre films for MGM, but it revived when he returned to Warners in the mid-1950s and directed several quality films, among them the controversial *The Bad Seed*. He retired in the mid-1960s, content to know that he had turned out an impressive number of commercial and critical successes.

Filmography: No Place to Go/Her Primitive Mate (1927); Flying Romeos, Harold Teen, Oh Kay! (1928); Naughty Baby, Hot Stuff, Broadway Babies, Little Johnny Jones (1929); Playing Around, Showgirl in Hollywood, Numbered Men, Top Speed (1930); Little Caesar, Gentleman's Fate, Too Young to Marry, Broad Minded, Five Star Final, Local Boy Makes Good, Tonight or Never (1936); The King and the Chorus Girl, They Won't Forget, The Great Garrick (1937); Fools for Scandal, Dramatic School (1938); Stand Up and Fight, The Wizard of Oz [prod. only], At the Circus (1939); Waterloo Bridge, Escape (1940); Blossoms in the Dust, Unholy Partners (1941); Johnny Eager, Random Harvest (1942); Madame Curie (1943); Thirty Seconds over Tokyo (1944); The House I Live In (1945); Without Reservations (1946); Home-coming (1948); Little Women, Any Number Can Play (1949); East Side West Side (1950); Quo Vadis (1951); Lovely to Look At,

Million Dollar Mermaid (1952); Latin Lovers (1953); Rose Marie (1954); Strange Lady in Town, Mister Roberts [completed for ailing John Ford] (1955); The Bad Seed, Toward the Unknown (1956); No Time for Sergeants, Home before Dark (1958); The FBI Story (1959); Wake me When It's Over (1960); The Devil at 4 O'Clock (1961); A Majority of One, Gypsy (1962); Mary Mary (1963); Moment to Moment (1965).

Honors: Academy Award Nomination: Best Director (*Random Harvest*, 1942); Academy Award: Special Award, Producer/Director (*The House I Live In*, 1945); Directors Guild of America: Outstanding Directorial Achievement [with John Ford] (*Mister Roberts*, 1955); Golden Globes: Cecil B. DeMille Award (1956); Academy Award: Irving G. Thalberg Memorial Award (1975).

Selected Bibliography

Finler, Joel W. *The Movie Directors Story*. London: Octopus Books, 1985.
LeRoy, Mervyn, as told to Dick Kleiner. *Mervyn LeRoy: Take One*. New York: Hawthorne Books, 1974.
Sennett, Ted. *Great Movie Directors*. New York: Harry N. Abrams, 1986.

LETTER, THE (1940), drama. Directed by William Wyler; with Bette Davis, Herbert Marshall, James Stephenson, Frieda Inescort, and Gale Sondergaard; screenplay by Howard Koch.

Bette Davis is in top form in this classic Somerset Maugham melodrama about a woman scorned and the fury that provokes murder and is then hidden beneath a veneer of icy hypocrisy. Until, that is, a letter is discovered that unravels her web of deceit. The entire production coalesces into a satisfying whole because of the attention paid to its individual ingredients. Not only is the casting excellent (Herbert Marshall and James Stephenson are particularly good), but the setting evokes the smoldering passions aroused by the exotic East. Some quarrel with Max Steiner's score, finding it uninspired and intrusive, too busy underlining the action. Perhaps there are moments when understatement would have better served the cinematic purpose, but there are other moments when the music is perfect punctuation, creating and holding a mood, as well as pointing up the drama. The only actress to reach the top playing largely unsympathetic roles, Davis is so good at being bad that viewers find themselves rooting for her even as they await her final comeuppance. No one knew better than William Wyler how to exploit this tension within both star and audience. Some find it unfortunate that her fate had to conform to contemporary censorship standards and did not follow the Maugham story, but the way it comes about in the film is so close to classic poetic justice that it's hard to fault.

Awards: Academy Award Nominations: Best Picture, Director, Actress (Davis), Supporting Actor (Stephenson), B&W Cinematography, Editing, Original Score.

Selected Bibliography

Anderegg, Michael A. *William Wyler*. Boston: Twayne, 1979.
Ringgold, Gene. *The Films of Bette Davis*. New York: Cadillac, 1966.

LETTER FROM AN UNKNOWN WOMAN (1948), drama. Directed by Max Ophüls; with Joan Fontaine, Louis Jourdan, Mady Christians, Marcel Journet, and Art Smith; screenplay by Howard Koch.

"The story that will live . . . as long as there is love!" This blurb is about the only cliché in this superb, exquisitely rendered adaptation of Stefan Zweig's haunting novella. Director Max Ophüls lovingly re-creates the Vienna of his memory as his camera circles around the sets and the characters, subtly revealing the fragile connections that ultimately are not strong enough to hold people together. Joan Fontaine is an adoring young girl whose love for a pianist's music blinds her to his shallowness, while Louis Jourdan, the pianist, sees women as mirrors into which he can gaze narcissistically. That he will seduce a girl and forget her is more believable by far than that he should remember and regret. They are obviously wrong for each other, and yet her obsession with him promises sometimes to conquer all. Astute critics accurately assess this movie as being a "woman's picture" in the best sense of the word; that is, it succeeds where the routine woman's picture never quite measures up. At the time of its release, its special qualities went unnoticed, and the movie was generally patronized and dismissed. Now there is high praise for Max Ophüls's sensitive direction and for Joan Fontaine's exquisite performance. The overall atmosphere of the film, a film that conjures up the evanescent charm of turn-of-the-century Vienna, contributes consistently to the sense of cherished illusions and innocent heartbreak. This film is reminiscent of *A Portrait of Jennie* in the way it maintains a consistent mood that so brilliantly evokes a bygone day. Those who unabashedly surrender themselves to this film come away feeling as if they had just experienced a haunting journey in time.

Selected Bibliography

Beeman, Marsha Lynn. *Joan Fontaine: A Bio-Bibliography*. Westport, CT: Greenwood Press, 1994.

Willemen, Paul, ed. *Ophüls*. New York: Zoetrope, 1978.

LETTER TO THREE WIVES, A (1949), drama. Directed by Joseph L. Mankiewicz; with Jeanne Crain, Linda Darnell, Ann Sothern, Kirk Douglas, Paul Douglas, Jeffrey Lynn, Barbara Lawrence, Connie Gilchrist, Florence Bates, and Thelma Ritter; screenplay by Joseph L. Mankiewicz.

A Letter to Three Wives focuses on the anxieties of three wives who believe they are soon to lose their husbands to another woman. This cleverly constructed film is generally considered one of the best movies ever made about marriage. While the picture is impressive in every aspect, two main factors contribute to its overall quality. One is the unique story of three young housewives in Westchester, New York, who are all jealous of the same woman. This "other woman" sends a letter to all three wives explaining that she has run away with one of their spouses but without identifying which one. The audience is then given a chance to figure out which one it is, before a surprise denouement explains all.

The other factor contributing to the film's success is the performance of Paul Douglas, a well-known stage actor of the day who was making his debut in pictures. The ensemble cast is generally outstanding in a movie that has more than its share of memorable scenes. It was the film that established Mankiewicz as a major writer/director talent (he was soon to do *All about Eve*), and he was credited with saving Fox from bankruptcy. (A decade later he was accused of bankrupting Fox when he did *Cleopatra*.) It's inevitable that a social comedy should date, but there is still plenty of bite in this story, and it is interesting precisely because it saves and savors a piece of the past. The selection of Celeste Holm as narrator of the film, the vixen Addie Ross, has been singled out for special praise, some calling it a stroke of genius on Mankiewicz's part; for she had the perfect voice for such a role, sweet and sour, kind and bitchy. It is equally brilliant of Mankiewicz never to let us see her.

Awards: Academy Awards: Best Director, Screenplay (Joseph Mankiewicz); Academy Award Nomination: Best Picture.

Selected Bibliography

Greist, Kenneth. *Pictures Will Talk: The Life and Films of Joseph L. Mankiewicz*. New York: Scribner, 1978.
Thomas, Tony. *The Films of the Forties*. Secaucus, NJ: Citadel Press, 1975.

LIBELED LADY (1936), drama. Directed by Jack Conway; with Jean Harlow, William Powell, Myrna Loy, Spencer Tracy, Walter Connolly, Charley Grapewin, and Cora Witherspoon; screenplay by Maurine Watkins, Howard Emmett Rogers, and George Oppenheimer.

Even though *Libeled Lady* has a somewhat convoluted plot, its madcap situations and excellent ensemble acting make a tangled plot part of the fun. This is a classic depression-era comedy with an unbeatable cast made even better in concert. Powell and Loy had already proved themselves a winning team as Mr. and Mrs. North in the Thin Man movies, and the chemistry between Tracy and Harlow is pure magic. This is a vintage 1930s story about a newspaperman who tries to frame a young Park Avenue millionairess in order to get her to drop her $5 million libel suit and winds up falling in love with her. Critics at the time praised the production values of this film as well as its costumes, script, and direction. Contemporary critics have been less kind, finding the picture charmless and stamped out. Obviously it's a movie that has to be taken on its own terms and within its own time frame—when, as someone put it, old man trouble was at both your front *and* back door. Take Jean Harlow, for example. Modern audiences find it difficult to understand her appeal, yet critics of this movie praised her for her scene-stealing performance. Her style would never have survived the 1930s, while it is easy to see how it was that Loy's, Tracy's, and Powell's did.

Awards: Academy Award Nomination: Best Picture.

Selected Bibliography

Conway, Michael, and Mark Ricci. *The Films of Jean Harlow*. New York: Citadel Press, 1965.

McCaffrey, Donald W. *The Golden Age of Sound Comedy: Comic Films and Comedians of the 30s*. South Brunswick, NJ: A. S. Barnes, 1973.

Peary, Danny. *Alternate Oscars*. New York: Delta, 1993.

LIFE WITH FATHER (1947), comedy/drama. Directed by Michael Curtiz; with Irene Dunne, William Powell, Edmund Gwenn, ZaSu Pitts, Elizabeth Taylor, Jimmy Lydon, and Martin Milner; screenplay by Donald Ogden Stewart.

"Take your cookie to see the picture that takes the cake for laughs" went the overly cute and somewhat tasteless blurb for the screen version of *Life with Father*, a play by Howard Lindsay and Russell Crouse, based on Clarence Day's autobiographical book of the same name. The play enjoyed a record-breaking run on Broadway of 3,224 performances before being brought to the screen. The story revolves around the eccentricities of Father and the tireless attempts by Mother to placate him. Elizabeth Taylor was still sweetly feminine and demure when she played the visitor to the Day household. Critical opinion is mixed about this film. While some critics praise Curtiz, Powell, and the whole production, others, while finding no fault with Powell, find the movie too much of a period piece. But a movie does not always have to be timeless to be worthwhile. Some have to be taken in the spirit of the times, for they set out to be nothing more than a re-creation of those times. During the 1940s there was a great nostalgia for turn-of-the-century drama: *Easter Parade*, *Meet Me in St. Louis*, *My Gal Sal*, *Yankee Doodle Dandy*—the list goes on. Since then it has become increasingly difficult for audiences to relate to a past that seems more unreal to them than the future. Even the screen version of *Hello, Dolly* didn't survive the eclipse. It's interesting, by the way, to note that eight years after Clark Gable was permitted to say "Frankly, my dear, I don't give a damn" in *Gone with the Wind*, censors still clipped Father's famous last line: "I'm going to be baptized, damn it!"

Awards:
Academy Award Nominations: Best Actor (Powell), Color Cinematography, Color Art Direction, Scoring of a Dramatic Picture.

Selected Bibliography

Kinnard, Roy, and R. J. Vitone. *The American Films of Michael Curtiz*. Metuchen, NJ: Scarecrow Press, 1986.

Thomas, Tony. *The Films of the Forties*. Secaucus, NJ: Citadel Press, 1975.

LITTLE CAESAR (1930), crime drama. Directed by Mervyn LeRoy; with Edward G. Robinson, Douglas Fairbanks, Jr., Glenda Farrell, Stanley Fields, Sidney Blackmer, Ralph Ince, and George E. Stone; screenplay by Francis Edward Faragoh.

''This game ain't for guys that's soft!'' Edward G. Robinson was elevated to stardom on the basis of his mesmerizing performance as Caesar Enrico Bandello, a character based on Al Capone from the best-selling novel by W. R. Burnett, who wrote the book in four hectic weeks after hearing live on radio a gangster raid of a club in Chicago where a friend of his who played in the band was shot dead. Robinson's fame had its downside, though. It took him years to transcend his image as a tough, unredeemable villain, a fate that galled him all the more because in real life he was a mild-mannered man with a taste for art and other refinements. *Little Caesar* also initiated a cycle of gangster films that were rougher and meaner than what had previously been filmed. The only mitigating factor in these depression tales of evil was the pervasive awareness that these were tough times that triggered all manner of antisocial behavior. After Jack Warner rejected Clark Gable as Robinson's sidekick because his ears stuck out, Douglas Fairbanks played the part and did a great job. That the movie looks somewhat dated now is understandable given the fact that Prohibition-style gangsterism seems so old-fashioned these days and the gangsters themselves such silly stereotypes. But the movie's influence on future crime films is undeniable. The totally unrepentant ganster-hero would surface again and again, most notably perhaps in James Cagney's riveting performance in *White Heat*. And it was a stock component of film noir. Although its pace may seem a bit sluggish today and its violence more implied than explicit, *Little Caesar* compensates with a unique blend of grim humor and pervasive menace.

Awards: Academy Award Nomination: Best Adapted Screenplay.

Selected Bibliography

Marill, Alvin H. *The Complete Films of Edward G. Robinson*. Secaucus, NJ: Carol, 1990.
Peary, Danny. *Alternate Oscars*. New York: Delta, 1993.
Rosow, Eugene. *Born to Lose: The Gangster Film in America*. New York: Oxford University Press, 1978.

LITTLE FOXES, THE (1941), drama. Directed by William Wyler; with Bette Davis, Herbert Marshall, Teresa Wright, Richard Carlson, Patricia Collinge, Dan Duryea, and Charles Dingle; screenplay by Lillian Hellman.

This is an outstanding adaptation of Lillian Hellman's story of greed and corruption within a southern family on the verge of financial ruin. Everyone from the imperious Bette Davis on down turns in a virtually flawless performance. Davis's ''murder-by-neglect'' of her sick husband (Marshall) is certainly one of the most brilliant but harrowing scenes in film history. Davis is furious because he won't finance her brothers' get-rich-quick scheme. They argue, and suddenly Marshall is stricken with a heart attack and accidentally breaks the bottle of medicine that will save him. Davis knows another bottle is upstairs, but she doesn't budge. Instead, she sits by and watches him struggle, her face frozen in midframe. The camera pans as Marshall (out of focus) crawls to the staircase and then tries to pull himself up, only to collapse and die. Meanwhile, the audience is forced to watch the unblinking Davis whose face is a mask of utter heartlessness. Although the movie now creaks, critics today find it an intriguing artifact of bygone moviemaking, pointing to such things as Gregg Toland's deep-focus camera work, Wyler's somber direction, the film's sumptuous production values, and the galvanizing performances of its stars. In the vicious center of this cast of intense overactors is the feline Davis, her face a chalky mask, her mouth spewing venom as only she can spew it. She is obviously relishing the role, motivated by her determination to outshine Tallulah Bankhead, who had created the role on Broadway and who had vied with Davis for the screen part.

Awards: Academy Award Nominations: Best Picture, Actress (Davis), Supporting Actress (Collinge, Wright), Screenplay, B&W Art Direction, Editing, Scoring of a Dramatic Picture.

Selected Bibliography

Anderegg, Michael A. *William Wyler*. Boston: Twayne, 1979.
Falk, Doris V. *Lillian Hellman*. New York: Ungar, 1978.
Ringgold, Gene. *The Films of Bette Davis*. New York: Cadillac, 1966.

LIVES OF A BENGAL LANCER, THE (1935), adventure/drama. Directed by Henry Hathaway; with Gary Cooper, Franchot Tone, Richard Cromwell, Sir Guy Standing, C. Aubrey Smith, Monte Blue, Kathleen Burke, Noble Johnson, Lumsden Hare, Akim Tamiroff, J. Carrol Naish, and Douglass Dumbrille; screenplay by Waldemar Young, John L. Balderston, Achmed Abdullah, Grover Jones, and W. S. McNutt.

"1750 to 11. Always outnumbered! Never outfought!" With its nonstop action, *Lives of a Bengal Lancer* remains one of the great adventure films. Hathaway maintains a fast pace in this rousing film, his first significant film as a director and one that became immensely popular with the public. Hathaway insisted on casting Cooper in the film, declaring that he was determined to build Cooper into one of America's great film heroes. In theme and locale, *Lancer* is of the *Beau Geste* school, a sweeping military narrative in Britain's desert badlands. This picture is an adolescent fantasy, but it is so infectious that viewers of all ages feel pride in the heroism of the Lancers as they prevail against impossible odds. It has been suggested that there is an underlying homoeroticism in this movie, especially evident in the comic camaraderie between Cooper and Tone. More likely, this is a Freudian reading of the natural bonding of adolescents, a characteristic common to men (or women) who prolong their adolescence by doing such things as joining the marines or the foreign legion—or the Bengal Lancers.

Awards: Academy Awards: Best Assistant Directors (Clem Beauchamp, Paul Wing); Academy Award Nominations: Best Picture, Director, Screenplay, Art Direction, Editing, Sound.

Selected Bibliography

Dickens, Homer. *The Films of Gary Cooper*. New York: Citadel Press, 1970.
Dooley, Roger. *From Scarface to Scarlett: American Films in the 1930s*. New York:
    Harcourt Brace Jovanovich, 1981.
Finler, Joel W. *Movie Directors Story*. London: Octopus Books, 1985.

LOGAN, JOSHUA. Director, playwright. Born on October 5, 1908, in Texarkana, Texas; died on July 12, 1988. Educated at Princeton, where he played football, boxed, and became active in school dramatics. Logan is perhaps best known for his spectacular success in the theater, having produced and directed some of the classics of the midcentury American stage. However, since films outlast theater performances, his small but distinguished filmography is destined to make him better remembered as a director of several films that appear on everyone's best films list. Early in his career he had a nose for talent, and already in the late 1920s he organized the University Players, a summer stock group (in Cape Cod) that launched the careers of such future stars as James Stewart, Henry Fonda, and Margaret Sullavan. Logan next received a scholarship to the Moscow Art Theater and studied under Stanislavsky. In 1932 he returned to the United States, whereupon he directed and acted in many Broadway plays. He was also dialogue director in Hollywood on such films as *The Garden of Allah* and *History Is Made at Night*. He then co-directed the film *I Met My Love Again*. That same year, he scored his first major hit as a Broadway director with *On Borrowed Time*. This was followed by such a prolific output that by early 1940 he was suffering so badly from exhaustion and insomnia that he had himself committed to a psychiatric hospital for more than a year. After World War II service with the Air Force Combat Intelligence, he returned to Broadway, where he scored a succession of hits as the director of such plays and musicals as *Annie Get Your Gun*, *Mister Roberts* (also co-author), *South Pacific* (also co-author), and *Picnic*. It wasn't until 1955 that Logan turned seriously to the making of films. His first two productions, *Picnic* and *Bus Stop*, were unanimously acclaimed, and many consider Marilyn Monroe's performance in the latter the best of her career. Although critics largely remained cool to much of Logan's later film work, possibly because of their skepticism about stage directors who dabble in film, they did praise *Sayonara*, and two or three of the musicals he filmed turn up regularly in film retrospectives. Like Grace Kelly's and James Dean's, Logan's film work was limited but memorable.

Filmography: I Met My Love Again [co-dir. with Arthur Ripley] (1938); Higher and Higher [co-play basis only] (1944); Mister Roberts [co-sc. from co-play only] (1955); Picnic, Bus Stop (1956); Sayonara (1957); South Pacific (1958); Tall Story (1960); Fanny (1961); Ensign Pulver [co-sc.] (1964); Camelot (1967); Paint Your Wagon (1969).

Honors: Directors Guild of America: Outstanding Directorial Achievement, Golden Globe Award: Director, Academy Award Nomination: Best Director (*Picnic*, 1955); Directors Guild of America: Outstanding Directorial Achievement, Academy Award Nomination: Best Director (*Sayonara*, 1957).

Selected Bibliography

Logan, Josh. *Josh: My Up-and-Down In-and-Out Life*. New York: Delacorte, 1976.
————. *Movie Stars, Real People, and Me*. New York: Delacorte, 1978.

LOLITA (1962), drama. Directed by Stanley Kubrick; with James Mason, Shelley Winters, Peter Sellers, Sue Lyon, Marianne Stone, and Diana Decker; screenplay by Vladimir Nabokov.

"How did they ever make a movie of Lolita?" As much controversy surrounded the filming of this book as the publishing of it. Publishers lined up to reject Nabokov's bold romance between a middle-aged professor and a sexually precocious twelve-year-old girl. Finally, Olympia Press of Paris agreed to publish it, and it became an instant best-seller with sales soaring as word of its scandalous contents spread. Kubrick had to fight to be allowed to film it, but he finally won after getting Nabokov himself to agree to write the script—and tone down the story. After several attempts, an acceptable script was produced, and Kubrick managed to distill the essence of the film without damage to its salacious subtext. Actually, one might argue that his success, like the success of other hot properties tailored to pacify the censors, was due in large part to the fact that accommodating censorship only served to hone his creativity. By not being explicit, Kubrick was able, by using gesture, innuendo, and camera tricks, to suggest things that could not be verbalized. Because film is the most visual (and visceral) of media, it can insinuate, with the arch of an eyebrow or the narrowing of an eye, what words are forced to spell out. Kubrick's choice of cast was inspired. The ever-underrated James Mason is perfect as the lascivious Humbert Humbert, complete with a wicked sense of humor that Mason's throaty diction only enhances. No one knows better than Mason how to mix the paternal, the pathetic, and the prurient into one wicked brew. Sue Lyon, whose career never took off, seems born to the role. She was barely fourteen when she played the fifteen-year-old (moved up from the book's twelve-) Dolores Haze, not even old enough to see herself in the movie that was restricted to people over eighteen. Shelley Winters is almost too good as Lyon's sex-starved mother, a part it seems she could play in her sleep. There is a rich undercurrent of exquisite black comedy in this film, an element that is wonderfully realized, especially by Peter Sellers, who gives an inspired performance as Quilty, Humbert Humbert's nemesis. If there is any fault to be found with the film, aside from its tameness, it is its length. It seems that Nabokov tried to cram his whole book into the screenplay, the result being not only excessive length but, in some ways, an entirely different text. When you realize that only a few years later films like *Who's Afraid of Virginia Woolf?* and *Midnight Cowboy* could be released without "censorship," it's easy to see what a revolutionary decade the 1960s really was.

Awards: Academy Award Nomination: Best Screenplay.

Selected Bibliography

Kael, Pauline. *I Lost It at the Movies*. Boston: Little, Brown, 1965.
Kagan, Norman. *The Cinema of Stanley Kubrick*. New York: Holt, Rinehart and Winston, 1972.

LOMBARD, CAROLE. Actress. Born Jane Alice Peters on October 6, 1908, in Fort Wayne, Indiana; died on January 19, 1942, in a plane crash. Lombard played her first screen role at twelve in Allan Dwan's *A Perfect Crime*. After completing junior high school, she returned to films in 1925 as an ingenue under a contract with Fox where she played the stereotypical blond heroine in several routine films before her contract was terminated by the studio. She then signed with Mack Sennett and in 1927–1928 appeared in more than a dozen two-reel slapstick comedies. Returning to feature films, she found herself once again stuck in routine roles until she was cast opposite John Barrymore in Howard Hawks's *Twentieth Century* in 1934. It was the first of several hilarious screwball comedies that made good use of her special comedic talent. This was followed by such outstanding successes as *My Man Godfrey, Nothing Sacred*, and *To Be or Not to Be*, her last film. Lombard was at the peak of her career when she was killed in a plane crash in January 1942 while returning to California from a U.S. Bond–selling tour of the Midwest. Her sudden death shocked her fans and devastated her second husband, Clark Gable. President Franklin D. Roosevelt expressed the feeling of many in his condolence telegram to Gable: "She brought great joy to all who knew her and to millions who knew her only as a great artist. She gave unselfishly of time and talent to serve her government in peace and war. She loved her country. She is and always will be a star, one we shall never forget nor cease to be grateful to." Lombard will be remembered as one of Hollywood's most talented and glamorous stars of the 1930s, a sophisticated comedienne who infused her screen roles with wit and charm and the warmth of her personality. She was, in a way, the blond counterpart of raven-haired Rosalind Russell, both of them blessed with beauty, brains, and astonishing talent for sophisticated comedy.

Filmography: A Perfect Crime (1921); Marriage in Transit, Hearts and Spurs, Durand of the Badlands (1925); The Road to Glory [bit] (1926); The Divine Sinner, Power, Show Folks, Ned McCobb's Daughter (1928); High Voltage, Big News, The Racketeer (1929); The Arizona Kid, Safety in Numbers, Fast and Loose (1930); It Pays to Advertise, Man of the World, Ladies' Man, Up Pops the Devil, I Take This Woman (1931); No One Man, Sinners in the Sun, Virtue, No More Orchids, No Man of Her Own (1932); From Hell to Heaven, Supernatural, The Eagle and the Hawk, Brief Moment, White Woman (1933); Bolero, We're Not Dressing, Twentieth Century, Now and Forever, Lady by Choice, The Gay Bride (1934); Rumba, Hands across the Table (1935); Love before Breakfast, The Princess Comes Across, My Man Godfrey (1936); Swing High Swing Low, Nothing Sacred, True Confession (1937); Fools for Scandal (1938); Made for Each Other, In Name Only (1939); Vigil in the Night, They Knew What They Wanted (1940); Mr. and Mrs. Smith (1941); To Be or Not to Be (1942).

Honors: Academy Award Nomination: Best Actress (*My Man Godfrey*, 1936).

Selected Bibliography

Matzen, Robert D. *Carole Lombard: A Bio-Bibliography*. Westport, CT: Greenwood Press, 1988.
Ott, Frederick W. *The Films of Carole Lombard*. Secaucus, NJ: Citadel Press, 1972.
Swindell, Larry. *Screwball: The Life of Carole Lombard*. New York: Morrow, 1975.

LONGEST DAY, THE (1962), war drama. Directed by Ken Annakin, Andrew Marton, and Bernhard Wicki; with John Wayne, Rod Steiger, Robert Ryan, Peter Lawford, Henry Fonda, Robert Mitchum, Richard Todd, Richard Burton, Richard Beymer, Jeffrey Hunter, Sal Mineo, Roddy McDowall, Eddie Albert, Curt Jurgens, Gert Frobe, Sean Connery, Robert Wagner, Red Buttons, Mel Ferrer, and many others; screenplay by Cornelius Ryan, Romain Gary, James Jones, David Pursall, and Jack Seddon.

This is one of the great epic World War II films. It is a brilliant and moving re-creation of the Allied invasion of Normandy on June 6, 1944, and it features an all-star international cast plus Oscar-winning special effects and cinematography. Much of its impact lies in its relentless buildup of events from the trivial to the grand that culminate in the greatest invasion force in history. Because it is filmed in semidocumentary style, the scale and scope of the film never overwhelm the ugly little realities, the moments of raw courage, the incredible sacrifices that portray war not as grand and noble but as savage but sometimes necessary. The film comes about as close as a film can to revealing the unfathomable heroism of ordinary foot soldiers. Understated but ever present is the reminder that this invasion was undertaken for liberation, not conquest. The members of the international cast are so collectively good that they themselves operate like a well-oiled combat unit. In fact, it is pointless to single anyone out for special praise, since they achieve such an uncanny group dynamic. The marvel of this film is that it avoids extremes of either recruitment jingoism or pacifist propaganda. Its ultimate effect is to overwhelm the audience with a sense of wonder and awe and gratitude and total admiration in the presence of something at once so awful and yet so grand.

Honors: Academy Award: Special Effects; Academy Award, Golden Globe Award: Best B&W Cinematography (Jean Bourgoin, Henri Persin, Walter Wottitz); Academy Award Nomination: Best Picture.

Selected Bibliography

Basinger, Jeanine. *The World War II Combat Film: Anatomy of a Genre*. New York: Columbia University Press, 1986.
Kagan, Norman. *The War Film*. New York: Pyramid, 1974.
Suid, Lawrence H. *Guts and Glory: Great American War Movies*. Reading, MA: Addison-Wesley Publishing Company, 1978.

LOST HORIZON (1937), fantasy/drama. Directed by Frank Capra; with Ronald Colman, Jane Wyatt, John Howard, Edward Everett Horton, Margo, Sam Jaffe, H. B. Warner, Isabel Jewell, and Thomas Mitchell; screenplay by Robert Riskin.

Although *Lost Horizon* has the quality of other Frank Capra masterpieces, it is also unlike any other film he made. In this one he eschews his usual middle-class milieu for a world of exotic adventure and fantasy. The film is based on James Hilton's classic novel (the first paperback and still in print) about five people stranded in a remote Tibetan land where health, peace, and longevity reign. The ingredients are so skillfully blended that skepticism is overwhelmed by the Hollywood sleight of hand that can concoct this kind of depression-era escape film. Hilton had created a world so appealing in its goodness, simplicity, and promise that the very name "Shangri-La" has entered the vocabulary as a synonym for paradise, and Capra's re-creation of this paradise did much to make the name stick. In the film, Ronald Colman is everyman, gradually accommo-dating himself to life in the Valley of the Blue Moon and learning to appreciate its wisdom and recipe for fulfillment. Sam Jaffe is a marvel as the ancient Belgian priest who first founded Shangri-La some 300 years before—a Methu-selah who is still alive, thanks to the Utopian philosophy of the community he has nurtured. When H. B. Warner, who plays the venerable Chang, the oldest disciple of the High Lama, explains the peaceful valley's philosophy of mod-eration in everything, it was a message that depression-weary audiences seemed eager to hear. Detractors, like Graham Greene, felt that Shangri-La looked too much like Beverly Hills; others thought the set design pure Ziegfeld. The film does pose an interesting question, one similar to the mystery of the wall in *King Kong* and why in the world, then, natives would build a door in it big enough to let the monster through if they wanted to keep him on the other side. As for *Lost Horizon*, the question is how, using only a pickaxe and a rope, they got the grand piano along a footpath on which persons must walk single file and with a sheer drop of 3,000 feet or so. Might as well ask how a beautiful young woman of twenty can age in a few seconds to a shriveled sixty. In Shangri-La anything is possible. What *isn't* possible is to lift the film (and the story) out of its context. An attempt at a musical remake in 1973 was a disaster.

Awards: Academy Awards: Best Interior Decoration (Stephen Goosson), Editing (Gene Havlick, Gene Milford); Academy Award Nominations: Best Picture, Music, Supporting Actor (Warner).

Selected Bibliography

Dooley, Roger. *From Scarface to Scarlett: American Films in the 1930s*. New York: Harcourt Brace Jovanovich, 1981.
Quirk, Lawrence J. *The Films of Ronald Colman*. Secaucus, NJ: Citadel Press, 1977.
Scherle, Victor, and William Turner Levy, eds. *The Complete Films of Frank Capra*. New York: Carol Publishing Group, 1992.

LOST PATROL, THE (1934), adventure/drama. Directed by John Ford; with Victor McLaglen, Boris Karloff, Wallace Ford, Reginald Denny, Alan Hale, J. M. Kerrigan, and Billy Bevan; screenplay by Dudley Nichols.

"Boiling passions in the burning sands!" screamed the blurb for this fast-paced, action-filled classic. The story takes place in the Mesopotamian desert during the campaign of the English against militant Arabs in 1917. Besides the bleak desert, the only other setting in the entire picture is the oasis that a patrol, lost after the commanding officer has been killed, discovers. The story is about a small British military group lost in the Mesopotamian desert and under repeated attack from Arabs as the unit dwindles. The essential plot has been reworked many times since in such films as *Bad Lands*, *Sahara*, *Bataan*, *The Last of the Comanches*, and *Escape from Fort Bravo*. Although there's not a woman in the cast—and not that much to the story—the suspense, the dialogue, and the excellent direction make *Lost Patrol* a very satisfying piece of pure entertainment. John Ford demonstrates in this early film all the promise he was to fulfill in a lifetime of exceptional films. Even though it has been much imitated, this original version of the "lost patrol" theme retains many powerful moments.

Awards: Academy Award Nomination: Best Score (Max Steiner).

Selected Bibliography

Dooley, Roger. *From Scarface to Scarlett: American Films in the 1930s*. New York: Harcourt Brace Jovanovich, 1981.
Gallagher, Tag. *John Ford: The Man and His Films*. Berkeley: University of California Press, 1986.

LOST WEEKEND, THE (1945), drama. Directed by Billy Wilder; with Ray Milland, Jane Wyman, Philip Terry, Howard da Silva, Doris Dowling, Frank Faylen, and Mary Young; screenplay by Billy Wilder and Charles Brackett.

"From the bestseller that was talked about in whispers!" and "The picture that dares to bare a man's soul!" ran the blurbs for this chilling slice-of-life about the pathetic disintegration of an alcoholic. Billy Wilder defied convention when he undertook to film this unrelenting drama of alcoholism. Actually, postwar Hollywood was already experimenting with mature, realistic "problem" themes such as bigotry and perversion, and although studios still felt nervous about it, they relented when their top directors proposed taking a risk. In this case, the risk paid off. *The Lost Weekend* marked a particularly outstanding achievement, for it was both an honest portrayal and a box office success. *The Lost Weekend* is the story of a would-be writer who has not yet gotten around to putting anything much down on paper. He talks about writing incessantly, but just as he is about to get down to business, he heads for the bottle to prime the pump and is soon too drunk to think straight, let alone write straight. His drunks usually last for days, and invariably he winds up hocking his typewriter at the local pawnshop. Ray Milland, more noted for his role in light comedy, gives a surprisingly strong performance, but it came as no surprise that he got the Oscar for it. The Academy has always admired (and sometimes rewarded) actors who play against type, especially when they play drunks, like Burt Lancaster in *Come Back, Little Sheba*, Bing Crosby in *The Country Girl*, James Mason in *A Star Is Born*, and Susan Hayward in *I'll Cry Tomorrow*—not to mention Lee Remick and Jack Lemmon in *Days of Wine and Roses*. Treat it as a sickness rather than a weakness, and you have a surefire winner. The point has been made that Milland's performance is so powerful, it never elicited the laughter with which drunks are usually greeted. The truth is that before background music was added (originally it was believed that the film would be more realistic without it), preview audiences howled when, in the throes of a DT (delirium tremens) hallucination, Milland watches bats attacking a mouse. The music is necessary to focus the scene and frighten the audience, and it works. The same is true of the setting, for what makes the film so gripping is the brilliance with which Wilder uses John F. Seitz's camera work to range from an unvarnished portrait of New York, brutally stripped of all glamour, to an almost Wellesian evocation of the alcoholic's inner world. There is much that is surrealistic in Wilder's approach and much that has been imitated. (Incidentally, powerful lobbyists for the liquor industry offered as much as $5 million for the negative of the film so it could be destroyed.)

Awards: Academy Awards: Best Picture, Director, Actor (Milland), Screenplay; New York Film Critics Circle Awards: Best Picture, Actor (Milland), Director; National Board of Review Award: Actor (Milland).

Selected Bibliography

Dick, Bernard. *Billy Wilder*. Boston: Twayne, 1980.
Milland, Ray. *Wide-eyed in Babylon: An Autobiography*. New York: Morrow, 1974.
Thomas, Tony. *The Films of the Forties*. Secaucus, NJ: Citadel Press, 1975.

LOY, MYRNA. Actress. Born Myrna Adele Williams on August 2, 1905, in Raidersburg, near Helena, Montana; died on December 15, 1993. Myrna Loy had a long, illustrious, but underrated career as an accomplished actress in dozens of films spanning seven decades. She was possessed of a pert but somewhat plain beauty that made her versatile to cast but that also kept redefining her image. She came to Los Angeles in 1918, where she attended high school and occasionally taught dancing. At eighteen she joined the chorus line in the pre-feature live show at Grauman's Chinese Theater in Hollywood and began making the rounds of studio casting departments. Valentino gave her a screen test, but it was unsuccessful. Soon after, however, she began getting bit parts in films. Before long she was typecast as an exotic vamp, often Oriental, always mysterious. For nearly ten years, in more than sixty films, she rarely stepped out of character. Then, when she stumbled into the Nora half of the incredibly successful team of Nick and Nora in the "Thin Man" detective series, she became enormously popular as a smart, wisecracking, sophisticated woman. Later, as she grew into more mature roles, she could be a slightly "vague" mother or a doting wife (*Mr. Blandings Builds His Dream House, Cheaper by the Dozen*). The transition to talkies in the late 1920s had been problematic at first, for she had a thin, slightly reedy voice, but she soon mastered the technique of projecting her voice for the microphones, and before long, it became a voice that seemed to fit perfectly the frail charm of this endearing actress. In 1937 Walter Winchell crowned her the ''Queen'' of Hollywood; Clark Gable the ''King.'' She surprised everyone with her strong performance in *The Best Years of Our Lives*, playing the compassionate wife of a troubled returning serviceman in a way all American wives could relate to. It was the role that proved what an accomplished and versatile actress she really was.

Filmography: Pretty Ladies (1925); Ben-Hur, The Cave Man, The Gilded Highway, Across the Pacific, Why Girls Go Back Home, Don Juan, The Exquisite Sinner, So This Is Paris (1926); Finger Prints, Ham and Eggs at the Front, Bitter Apples, The Heart of Maryland, The Jazz Singer, If I Were Single, The Climbers, Simple Sis, A Sailor's Sweetheart, The Girl from Chicago (1927); What Price Beauty, Beware of Married Men, Turn Back the Hours, The Crimson City, Pay as You Enter, State Street Sadie, The Midnight Taxi (1928); Noah's Ark, Fancy Baggage, The Desert Song, The Black Watch, The Squall, Hardboiled Rose, Evidence, The Show of Shows, The Great Divide (1929); Cameo Kirby, Isle of Escape, Under a Texas Moon, Cock o' the Walk, Bridge of the Regiment, Last of the Duanes, Renegades, The Jazz Cinderella, The Truth about Youth, The Devil to Pay, Rogue of the Rio Grande (1930); Body and Soul, The Naughty Flirt, A Connecticut Yankee, Hush Money, Transatlantic, Rebound, Skyline, Consolation Marriage, Arrowsmith (1931); Emma, The Wet Parade, Vanity Fair, The Woman in Room 13, New Morals for Old, Love Me Tonight, Thirteen Women, The Mask of Fu Manchu, The Animal Kingdom (1932); Topaze, The Barbarian, When Ladies Meet, Penthouse, Night Flight, The Prizefighter and the Lady (1933); Men in White, Manhattan Melodrama, The Thin Man, Stamboul Quest, Evelyn Prentice, Broadway Bill (1934); Wings in the Dark, Whipsaw (1935); Wife vs. Secretary, Petticoat Fever, The Great Ziegfeld, To Mary—With Love, Libeled Lady, After the Thin Man (1936); Parnell, Double Wedding (1937); Man-Proof, Test Pilot, Too Hot to Handle (1938); Lucky Night, The Rains Came, Another Thin Man (1939); I Love You Again, Third Finger Left Hand (1940); Love Crazy, Shadow of the Thin Man (1941); The Thin Man Goes Home (1944); So Goes My Love, The Best Years of Our Lives; The Bachelor and the Bobby-Soxer, The Senator Was Indiscreet, Song of the Thin Man (1947); Mr. Blandings Builds His Dream House (1948); The Red Pony, That Dangerous Age/If This Be Sin (1949); Cheaper by the Dozen (1950); Belles on Their Toes (1952); The Ambassador's Daughter (1956); Lonelyhearts (1958); From the Terrace, Midnight Lace (1960); The April Fools (1969); Airport 1975 (1974); The End (1978); Just Tell Me What You Want (1980).

Honors: Motion Picture Academy New York City gala events (1985, 1987); Theater named after her in her hometown of Helena, Montana (1987); John F. Kennedy Center for the Performing Arts Lifetime Achievement Award (1988); Academy Award: Special Award (1990).

Selected Bibliography

Kay, Karyn. *Myrna Loy*. New York: Pyramid Publications, 1977.
Kotsilibas-Davis, James. *Myrna Loy: Being and Becoming*. New York: Knopf, 1987.
Quirk, Lawrence J. *The Films of Myrna Loy*. Secaucus, NJ: Citadel Press, 1980.

LUBITSCH, ERNST. Director. Born on January 28, 1892, in Berlin; died on November 30, 1947. Lubitsch became interested in the stage while acting in high school plays. After a few years of part-time music hall performance, he joined Max Reinhardt's famous Deutsches Theater, where he rapidly advanced from bit parts to character leads. The following year, he began appearing in a series of film comedies and soon began writing and directing his own films. In 1918 he made his mark as a serious director with *Die Augen der Mummie/The Eyes of the Mummy*, a tragic drama starring Pola Negri. That same year, he scored an international box office hit with *Carmen/Gypsy Blood*, also starring Negri. But these early achievements could not compare with his great triumph of 1919, *Die Austernprinzessin/The Oyster Princess*, a sparkling satire caricaturing American manners. In this film, he demonstrated for the first time the subtle humor and the ingenious wit that would eventually come to be known as ''the Lubitsch Touch.'' His reputation as a leading figure in international motion pictures reached a new peak in *Madame Du Barry/Passion* and *Anna Boleyn/Deception*. After a brief visit to America in 1921, Lubitsch returned the following year at the request of Mary Pickford. The one film he directed her in, *Rosita*, was a critical success, but the public (and Pickford) disliked it. In his American films, Lubitsch focused his satire on two main themes—sex and money—depicting sex as a game rich people play to kill time. Lubitsch enjoyed phenomenal success in Hollywood. He surpassed his European triumphs by directing an uninterrupted string of hits. As his influence spread, he became widely imitated—but never surpassed. With the advent of sound, Lubitsch moved to Paramount where, in 1935, he became production manager. In 1939, he moved to MGM to direct one of the greatest triumphs of his career, *Ninotchka*, starring Greta Garbo. A few years later he moved to 20th Century–Fox, but by then his health had begun to fail, and after two or three false starts and one completed film, he died of a heart attack in 1947. At his funeral, when Billy Wilder shook his head and said, ''No more Lubitsch,'' William Wyler replied. ''Worse than that—no more Lubitsch films.''

Filmography: [in the United States]: Rosita (1923); The Marriage Circle, Three Women, Forbidden Paradise (1924); Kiss Me Again, Lady Windemere's Fan (1925); So This Is Paris (1926); The Student Prince/The Student Prince in Old Heidelberg (1927); The Patriot (1928); Eternal Love, The Love Parade (1929); Paramount on Parade (co-dir. with ten others), Monte Carlo (1930); The Smiling Lieutenant (1931); The Man I Killed/Broken Lullaby, One Hour with You, Trouble in Paradise, If I Had a Million [one episode] (1932); Design for Living (1933); The Merry Widow (1934); Desire (1936); Angel (1937); Bluebeard's Eighth Wife (1938); Ninotchka (1939); The Shop around the Corner (1940); That Uncertain Feeling (1941); To Be or Not to Be (1942); Heaven Can Wait (1943); A Royal Scandal [prod. only] (1945); Cluny Brown (1946); That Lady in Ermine [completed by Otto Preminger] (1948).

Honors: Academy Award Nomination: Best Director (*The Patriot*, 1928–1929); Academy Award Nomination: Best Director (*The Love Parade*, 1929–1930); Academy Award: Special Award [for his ''25-year contribution to motion pictures''] (1937); French Legion of Honor [for his contribution to motion pictures] (1938); Academy Award Nomination: Best Director (*Heaven Can Wait*, 1943); Academy Award: Special Award [for his distinguished contributions to the art of the motion picture] (1946).

Selected Bibliography

Carringer, Robert L., and Barry Sabath. *Ernst Lubitsch: A Guide to References and Resources*. Boston: G. K. Hall, 1978.

Eyman, Scott. *Ernst Lubitsch: Laughter in Paradise*. New York: Simon & Schuster, 1993.

Weinberg, Herman G. *The Lubitsch Touch: A Critical Study*. New York: Dover, 1977.

LUPINO, IDA. Actress, director, screenwriter. Born on February 4, 1918, in London; died on August 4, 1995. Educated at the Royal Academy of Dramatic Arts. Lupino was the daughter of the well-known British comedian Stanley Lupino and actress Connie Emerald, descending from a theatrical family that dated back to the seventeenth century. An American director discovered her while he was in England looking for a Lolita type to star in his first British film, *Her First Affaire* (1933). She appeared in a number of other British films that same year and then went to Hollywood on a Paramount contract. After some routine minor parts, she landed a strong role in *The Light That Failed* in 1940 and was signed by Warners, where she typically portrayed hardened, often vulgar or ambitious women. She considered her Hollywood acting career a failure and once referred to herself as a ''poor man's Bette Davis.'' Be that as it may, Lupino gave one of her strongest performances in *Devotion*, the story of the Brontës, in which she played the part of Emily Brontë with great depth of feeling. For some reason, the film, made in 1943, was not released until 1946, and it has yet to be released on video or laserdisc. In the early 1950s, Lupino turned to writing, directing, and producing motion pictures and TV series and movies. Her first venture as co-producer and co-screenwriter was *Not Wanted* in 1949. When the film's director Elmer Clifton suffered a heart attack three days into shooting, Lupino took over and did a creditable job but got no screen credit for it. She did get credit on her next film, *Never Fear*, but it was not a success in spite of some powerful dramatic passages and documentarylike sequences. Lupino had her biggest success, both critical and commercial, with *The Hitch-Hiker*, a harrowing fact-based story of a psychopathic killer. She also drew admiration for *The Bigamist*, a compassionate exposition of the fuzzy roots of a dual marital affair. Lupino's creative contribution to American film far exceeded her nominal role as virtually the only woman director working in Hollywood during the 1950s. Later in the decade she returned to acting, venturing into directing only once more in 1966 with *The Trouble with Angels* in which she cast Rosalind Russell (Auntie Mame) as a mother superior (!).

Filmography: [as actress]: Her First Affaire, Money for Speed, High Finance, Prince of Arcadia, The Ghost Camera, I Lived with You (1933); Search for Beauty, Come on Marines, Ready for Love (1934); Paris in Spring, Smart Girl, Peter Ibbetson (1935); Anything Goes, One Rainy Afternoon, Yours for the Asking, The Gay Desperado (1936); Sea Devils, Let's Get Married, Artists and Models, Fight for Your Lady (1937); The Lone Wolf Spy Hunt, The Lady and the Mob, The Adventures of Sherlock Holmes (1939); The Light That Failed, They Drive by Night (1940); High Sierra, The Sea Wolf,

Out of the Fog, Ladies in Retirement (1941); Moontide, Life Begins at Eight-Thirty (1942); The Hard Way, Forever and a Day, Thank Your Lucky Stars (1943); In Our Time, Hollywood Canteen (1944); Pillow to Post (1945); Devotion (filmed 1943; released 1946); The Man I Love, Deep Valley, Escape Me Never (1947); Road House (1948); Lust for Gold (1949); Woman in Hiding (1950); On Dangerous Ground, Beware My Lovely (1952); Jennifer (1953); Private Hell 36 (1954); Women's Prison, The Big Knife (1955); While the City Sleeps, Strange Intruder (1956); Backtrack (1969); Junior Bonner (1972); The Devil's Rain (1975); The Food of the Gods (1976); My Boys Are Good Boys (1978); Deadhead Miles (1982). [as producer]: *Not Wanted* [co-prod., co-sc., also co-dir.; uncredited] (1949). [as director/co-producer]: Never Fear/The Young Lovers [also co-sc.], Outrage [also co-sc.] (1950); Hard Fast and Beautiful (1951); The Hitch-Hiker [also co-sc.], The Bigamist [also act.] (1953); The Trouble with Angels (1966).

Honors: New York Film Critics Circle Award: Best Actress (*The Hard Way*, 1943).

Selected Bibliography

Kuhn, Annette, ed. *Queen of the B's: Ida Lupino behind the Camera*. Westport, CT: Praeger Publishers, 1995.
Stewart, Lucy Ann Liggett. *Ida Lupino as a Film Director, 1949–1953: An Auteur Approach*. New York: Arno Press, 1980.
Vermilye, Jerry. *Ida Lupino*. New York: Pyramid Publications, 1977.

LUST FOR LIFE (1956), biographical drama. Directed by Vincente Minnelli; with Kirk Douglas, Anthony Quinn, James Donald, Pamela Brown, Everett Sloane, Niall MacGinnis, Noel Purcell, Henry Daniell, Hill Bennett, Lionel Jeffries, and Eric Pohlmann; screenplay by Norman Corwin.

"It Happens in Bright Sunlight" went the puzzling ad for this bold film adaptation of Irving Stone's celebrated biography of the tormented Dutch artist Vincent van Gogh (Kirk Douglas) and his stormy relationship with Gauguin (Anthony Quinn). Unlike the usual Hollywood lives of artists, *Lust for Life* is thoughtful, ambitious, and generally unembarrassing. But it is precisely its fidelity to facts that has made some critics feel that something is missing. While they praise the acting, the script, the photography, and the direction, they wonder if the trees obscure a clear view of the forest. While some critics toss about adjectives like "exquisite" and "brilliant" and "shattering," others find it "faithful but slow moving," "uninspiring," "less exciting than it should be," and "lacking the entertainment of the Stone novel" and complain that Kirk Douglas, competent as he is, does not get as close to the audience as, say, Jose Ferrer does as Toulouse-Lautrec in *Moulin Rouge*. It is interesting to note, by the way, that Anthony Quinn got his Oscar for only eight minutes of screen time in a two-hour movie.

Awards: Academy Award: Best Supporting Actor (Anthony Quinn); Golden Globe Award, New York Film Critics Circle Award: Best Actor (Kirk Douglas); Academy Award Nominations: Best Actor (Kirk Douglas), Adapted Screenplay, Color Art Direction.

Selected Bibliography

Marrill, Alvin H. *The Films of Anthony Quinn*. Secaucus, NJ: Citadel Press, 1975.
Minnelli, Vincente. *I Remember It Well*. Garden City, NY: Doubleday, 1974.
Thomas, Tony. *The Films of Kirk Douglas*. Secaucus, NJ: Citadel Press, 1972.

M

MACDONALD, JEANETTE. Actress, singer. Born on June 18, 1901, in Philadelphia; died on January 14, 1965. MacDonald started as a Broadway chorus girl in the early 1920s but was soon picked to play leads in stage musicals and operettas. Richard Dix saw her perform and talked Paramount into giving her a screen test. Ernst Lubitsch saw the test and chose her to star in *The Love Parade* and then in one or two other sophisticated screen musicals opposite Maurice Chevalier. She signed with MGM in 1933, and after that, she became increasingly popular as a singing star, especially after she teamed up with Nelson Eddy in the most successful singing partnership in musical film history. At the height of their popularity, in the late 1930s, the two were known as "America's Sweethearts," and their string of saccharine screen musicals brought millions of American and European customers to the box office. Wartime audiences, however, were less appreciative of musicals set in distant European fantasy lands, and in 1942, MGM terminated MacDonald's contract. She returned to the screen in a cameo and in two mother roles, then retired from films to seek a new career in concert halls and on the stage. Although they have long been held up to ridicule by cynics and stand-up comics for such schmaltzy numbers as "Indian Love Call," the Eddy-MacDonald musicals have now come to enjoy the status of "high camp." What the duo did was bridge a gap between the secure, if imaginary, turn-of-the-century world of privilege and pastiche and innocence and the modern world of (apparent) realism and deprivation.

Filmography: The Love Parade (1929); The Vagabond King, Monte Carlo, Let's Go Native, The Lottery Bride, Oh for a Man! (1930); Don't Bet on Women, Annabelle's Affairs (1931); One Hour with You, Love Me Tonight (1932); The Cat and the Fiddle, The Merry Widow (1934); Naughty Marietta (1935); Rose Marie, San Francisco (1936); Maytime, The Firefly (1937); The Girl of the Golden West, Sweethearts (1938); Broadway Serenade (1939); New Moon, Bitter Sweet (1940); Smilin' Through (1941); I Married an Angel, Cairo (1942); Follow the Boys [cameo] (1944); Three Daring Daughters (1948); The Sun Comes Up (1949).

Selected Bibliography

Parish, James Robert. *The Jeanette MacDonald Story*. New York: Mason/Charter, 1976.
Rich, Sharon. *Sweethearts: The Timeless Love Affair—On Screen and Off—Between Jeanette MacDonald and Nelson Eddy*. New York: Donald I. Fine, 1994.
Stern, Lee Edward. *Jeanette MacDonald*. New York: Jove Publications, 1977.

MACMURRAY, FRED. Actor. Born on August 30, 1908, in Kankakee, Illinois; died on November 5, 1991. MacMurray started out as a band saxophonist and vocalist to pay his way through Carroll College in Wisconsin. While performing in California, he appeared as an extra in a few films in the late 1920s. In 1930 he appeared in a Broadway revue with the Californian Collegians and three years later performed with the same group in the Broadway musical *Roberta*. He was then signed by Paramount and was put into films of all genres until gradually he began to make his mark in comedies, from the subtle to the farcical. Although he departed from this stereotype to play a heel in such movies as *Double Indemnity* (1944) and *The Apartment* (1960), comedy was where he was most comfortable and where he finished out his career. Throughout his long career, he proved himself one of Hollywood's most enduring stars. He became well known for his amiable, easygoing attitude, his sense of self-irony, and his very expressive double takes. His flagging popularity revived in the 1960s, thanks to the long-running TV series *My Three Sons* (1960–1972) and to a string of successful Disney family films in which he played the lead. It has been rumored that his face provided the model for the comic-strip hero Captain Marvel. He was married from 1954 until his death in 1991 to actress June Haver. Like Ray Milland, who played against type in *The Lost Weekend*, MacMurray will probably be remembered for *Double Indemnity* long after his comedy roles have been forgotten. In comedy, he and Claudette Colbert worked well together and could have made a great team, but fate decreed otherwise, and they went their separate ways.

Filmography: Girls Go Wild, Glad Rag Doll, Tiger Rose, Friends of Mr. Sweeney (1934); Grand Old Girl, The Gilded Lily, Car 99, Men without Names, Alice Adams, Hands across the Table, The Bride Comes Home (1935); The Trail of the Lonesome Pine, 13 Hours by Air, The Princess Comes Across, The Texas Rangers (1936); Champagne Waltz, Maid of Salem, Swing High—Swing Low, Exclusive, True Confession (1937); Cocoanut Grove, Sing You Sinners, Men with Wings (1938); Cafe Society, Invitation to Happiness, Honeymoon in Bali (1939); Remember the Night, Little Old New York, Too Many Husbands, Rangers of Fortune (1940); Virginia, One Night in Lisbon, Dive Bomber, New York Town (1941); The Lady Is Willing, Take a Letter Darling, The Forest Rangers, Star Spangled Rhythm (1942); Flight for Freedom, Above Suspicion, No Time for Love (1943); Standing Room Only, And the Angels Sing, Double Indemnity (1944); Practically Yours, Where Do We Go From Here?, Murder He Says, Captain Eddie (1945); Pardon My Past, Smoky (1946); Suddenly It's Spring, The Egg and I, Singapore (1947); On Our Merry Way/A Miracle Can Happen, The Miracle of the Bells, Don't Trust Your Husband/An Innocent Affair (1948); Family Honeymoon, Father Was a Fullback (1949); Borderline, Never a Dull Moment (1950); A Millionaire for Christy, Callaway Went Thataway (1951); Fair Wind to Java, The Moonlighter (1953); The Caine Mutiny, Pushover, Woman's World (1954); The Far Horizons, The Rains of Ranchipur, At Gunpoint (1955); There's Always Tomorrow (1956); Guns for a Coward, Quantez (1957); Day of the Badman (1958); Good Day for Hanging, The Shaggy Dog, Face of a Fugitive, The Oregon Trail (1959); The Apartment (1960); The Absent-Minded Professor (1961); Bon Voyage! (1962); Son of Flubber (1963); Kisses for My President (1964); Follow Me Boys! (1966); The Happiest Millionaire (1967); Charley and the Angel (1973); The Swarm (1978).

MAGNIFICENT AMBERSONS, THE (1942), drama. Directed by Orson Welles; with Tim Holt, Joseph Cotten, Dolores Costello, Anne Baxter, Agnes Moorehead, Ray Collins, Richard Bennett, and Erskine Sanford; screenplay by Orson Welles.

"Real life screened more daringly than it's ever been before!" promised the blurb for Welles's second feature film, a film considered by many to be his second masterpiece. However, this film has had a highly controversial history, and the verdict is not in yet. Those who defend its brilliance argue that it has never really been seen in its entirety—certainly not as Welles wanted it. Others say that in spite of its surface brilliance, it remains shrill, self-conscious, overdone—and ultimately overrated. Most rate it below *Citizen Kane*, and even when they call it brilliant, they defend its flaws by blaming them on the fact that the film was taken out of Welles's hands, then recut and reshot by others. Some bold critics, less susceptible to Welles's formidable reputation, have expressed serious reservations about this film. To them it seems that Welles devoted reels and reels of film to chronicling the foibles of a spoiled brat who grows up to be a spiteful young man. They bemoan the absence of contrast in the film, seeing it as one long tale of woe without a trace of sentimentality. Herein lies the problem. The movie is a technical marvel, with sets, cinematography, costumes, and characters all performing magnificently, but when all is said and done, there is something contrived, something artificial, something shrill about it. If anything sums up the hysteria level of this film it is Agnes Moorehead's shrill performance as the long-suffering, repressed, spinster aunt who gives new meaning to "chewing the scenery." Anyone who remembers her as Mirilly, the housekeeper opposite Lionel Barrymore in radio's *Mayor of the Town*, or as the invalid wife in imminent peril in radio's most frenetic drama *Sorry, Wrong Number* will see (and hear) the same over-the-top acting that was once a staple of dramatic schools but has never been in vogue in motion pictures. Fortunately, the central character is Tim Holt, who is portrayed first as the spoiled, curly-haired darling of the town's richest family, then for the major portion as a conceited, power-conscious, insufferable youth. Since he gives a performance everyone marveled at (and few have forgiven him for), he counterbalances some of Moorehead's histrionics. Modern audiences can easily be sidetracked by Welles's loving re-creation of a bygone day, a day that probably never was. Shooting a sleighing scene over twelve days in a studio freezer is indication enough of his devotion to a mythical past in which even cars are maligned as threats to progress. In spite of the film's indictment of the age's hypocrisy, the loving evocation of the times suggests that the quality of life in a gossip-ridden but orderly society far outweighs the advantages of technology. When a preview audience in Pomona saw the film, viewers talked back to the characters on the screen, laughed at what was going on, even made jokes. Their response so terrified George J. Schaefer, president of RKO, that he left the theater red-faced, believing that Welles had presented him with a financial disaster. Perhaps the overriding problem with this film is that it is so rich in innovative technique that it would take several viewings to absorb even the most essential elements. This is the point at which a "movie" crosses the line and becomes a "film." The Welles touch is there in every frame regardless of what his defenders say. For example, there is his famous use of overlapping dialogue, a technique designed to give a natural feel to the words spoken but that can also become an irritating distraction. What happens is that the volume of the words diminishes as characters recede from the camera and increases as the camera picks them up. Meanwhile, street sounds and the voices of townspeople can be heard in the background. Whatever you may think of *The Magnificent Ambersons*, it is not a film that can easily be ignored.

Awards: New York Film Critics Circle Award: Best Actress (Moorehead); Academy Award Nominations: Best Picture, Supporting Actress (Moorehead), B&W Cinematography, B&W Art Direction.

Selected Bibliography

Cowie, Peter. *The Cinema of Orson Welles*. London: A. Zwemmer, 1965.

Higham, Charles. *The Films of Orson Welles*. Berkeley: University of California Press, 1970.

Levy, Emanuel. *Small-Town America in Film: The Decline and Fall of Community*. New York: Continuum, 1991.

MALTESE FALCON, THE (1941), mystery/drama. Directed by John Huston; with Humphrey Bogart, Mary Astor, Peter Lorre, Sydney Greenstreet, Ward Bond, Gladys George, Barton MacLane, Elisha Cook, Jr., Lee Patrick, and Jerome Cowan; screenplay by John Huston.

"A guy without a conscience! A dame without a heart!" "He's as fast on the draw as he is in the drawing room!" Thus ran the blurbs for this film noir classic that set standards in the crime genre for decades to come. It was John Huston's first time up as director and has the distinction of being a huge critical and popular success as well as a cult classic. Critics praised this film as one of the best examples of melodramatic storytelling in cinematic form, commenting on the excellence of the mystery story itself and praising the outstanding writing, direction, acting, and editing. What makes it a prototype film noir is the vein of unease missing from the two earlier versions of Hammett's novel. Filmed almost entirely in interiors, it presents a claustrophobic world in which betrayal, deception, and perversion reveal the corruption at its core. Critics continue to find this movie a fresh and entertaining experience, a movie that still contains surprises and still manages to deliver a few curious emotional punches. It also continues to baffle anyone trying to tie up the loose strings of the plot. But fans of this film disdain any search for logic in it. Like the works of British playwright Harold Pinter, this film is praised for its incoherence. One wonders where the line is drawn between films that are either condemned or esteemed for the very same thing. It probably has something to do with the presence of an all-star cast. Caught in a debate with a fan bemoaning the colorization of *The Maltese Falcon*, one baffled viewer declared, "Even in color, I can't figure it out"—a comment worthy of Harold Pinter (or Gracie Allen).

Awards: Academy Award Nominations: Best Picture, Supporting Actor (Greenstreet), Screenplay.

Selected Bibliography

Anobile, Richard J., ed. *The Maltese Falcon*. New York: Avon Books, 1974.
McCarty, John. *The Films of John Huston*. Secaucus, NJ: Citadel Press, 1987.
Silver, Alain, and Elizabeth Ward, eds. *Film Noir: An Encyclopedic Reference to the American Style*. Woodstock, NY: Overlook Press, 1979.

MANKIEWICZ, JOSEPH L. Director, producer, screenwriter. Born on February 11, 1909, in Wilkes-Barre, Pennsylvania; died on February 5, 1993. Educated at Columbia University. While working in Berlin as an assistant correspondent for the Chicago *Tribune*, Mankiewicz had his first experience with films as a translator into English of titles for UFA (Universum Film Aktiengesellschaft). He returned to the United States in 1929, the same year he played a reporter in *Woman Trap*. In 1936 he became a producer, first at Paramount, then at Fox, but it was ten years before he would get a chance to direct. As it so happened, Ernst Lubitsch fell ill on the set of *Dragonwyck*, and Mankiewicz was called in as a last-minute replacement. From then on, he turned out to be one of Hollywood's most literate directors. Although there were some complaints about the "talkiness" of his films, all had to agree that what was said on the screen was usually superior dialogue laced with wit and intelligence, the sort that often inspired actors to greater heights. Two prime examples are *A Letter to Three Wives* and *All about Eve*. Mankiewicz's adaptation of *Julius Caesar* is considered by many to be one of the most successful transformations to the screen of a Shakespearean play. The film bristles with tension and suspense, the timing is perfect, and the performances are uniformly excellent. In spite of Marlon Brando's peevish comments about being miscast, he is electrifying as Marc Antony, his funeral oration ("Friends, Romans, countrymen . . .") being one of the best renditions within memory. Unfortunately, Mankiewicz's *Cleopatra*, the direction of which he took over from Rouben Mamoulian, was a monumental disaster, owing very much to circumstances way beyond his control (e.g., Elizabeth Taylor's near-fatal illness and the Taylor-Burton very public love affair). At the 1991 special tribute to Mankiewicz by the Motion Picture Academy, actor Michael Caine called him "the most civilized man I ever met in the cinema."

Filmography: [as screenwriter]: Slightly Scarlet, Paramount on Parade [uncredited], The Social Lion, The Sap from Syracuse [uncredited], Only Saps Work (1930); The Gang Buster, Finn and Hattie, June Moon, Skippy, Dude Ranch [uncredited], Touchdown [uncredited], Sooky (1931); This Reckless Age, Sky Bride, Million Dollar Legs, If I Had a Million (1932); Diplomaniacs, Emergency Call, Too Much Harmony, Alice in Wonderland (1933); Manhattan Melodrama, Our Daily Bread, Forsaking All Others (1934); I Live My Life (1935). [as producer]: The Three Godfathers, Fury, The Gorgeous Hussy, Love on the Run (1936); The Bride Wore Red, Double Wedding (1937); Mannequin, Three Comrades, The Shopworn Angel, The Shining Hour, A Christmas Carol (1938); The Adventures of Huckleberry Finn (1939); Strange Cargo, The Philadelphia Story (1940); The Wild Man of Borneo, The Feminine Touch (1941); Woman of the Year, Reunion in France (1942); The Keys of the Kingdom [also co-sc.] (1945). [as director]: Dragonwyck [also sc.], Somewhere in the Night [also co-sc.] (1946); The Late George Apley, The Ghost and Mrs. Muir (1947); Escape (1948); A Letter to Three Wives [also sc.]; House of Strangers (1949); No Way Out [also co-sc.], All About Eve [also sc.] (1950); People Will Talk [also sc.] (1951); Five Fingers (1952); Julius Caesar [also sc.] (1953); The Barefoot Contessa [also exec. prod., sc.] (1954); Guys and Dolls [also sc.] (1955); The Quiet American [also prod., sc.] (1958); Suddenly Last Summer (1959); Cleopatra [also co-sc.] (1963); The Honey Pot/It Comes Up Murder [also co-prod., sc.] (1967); King: A Filmed Record . . . Montgomery to Memphis [doc.; co-dir. with Sidney Lumet], There Was a Crooked Man [also prod.] (1970); Sleuth (1972).

Honors: Directors Guild of America: Quarterly Award, Academy Awards: Best Director, Screenplay (*A Letter to Three Wives*, 1949); Academy Awards: Best Director, Screenplay, Golden Globe Award: Screenplay, Directors Guild of America: Quarterly Award and Annual Award, New York Film Critics Circle Award: Best Director (*All about Eve*, 1950); Cannes Film Festival Award: Special Jury Prize (*All about Eve*, 1951); Directors Guild of America: Quarterly Award, Academy Award Nomination: Best Picture (*Five Fingers*, 1952); Academy Award Nomination: Best Director (*Sleuth*, 1972); Directors Guild of America: Honorary Life Member (1980); Directors Guild of America: D. W. Griffith Award (1985); Venice Film Festival: Career Award (1987).

Selected Bibliography

Dick, Bernard F. *Joseph L. Mankiewicz*. Boston: Twayne, 1983.

Geist, Kenneth L. *Pictures Will Talk: The Life and Films of Joseph L. Mankiewicz*. New York: Scribner, 1978.

Taylor, John Russell. *Joseph L. Mankiewicz: An Index to His Work*. London: British Film Institute, 1960.

MANN, ANTHONY. Director. Born Emil Anton Bundmann on June 30, 1906, in Port Loma, near San Diego, California; died on April 29, 1967, in Berlin. Mann began performing as a child in San Diego, then in New York, where the family moved around 1917. He quit high school in 1923 to work a night shift at Westinghouse and spent his days hunting for acting jobs. Soon he was playing bit parts, then larger roles in off-Broadway and Broadway productions. In the early 1930s he began directing for the stage, and in 1938, he left Broadway and joined the Selznick company as a casting director, talent scout, and supervisor of screen tests. The following year he moved over to Paramount as an assistant director and worked in that capacity on Preston Sturges's *Sullivan's Travels* (1941), among other films. Known now as Anthony Mann, he began directing low- to medium-budget films for such studios as RKO and Republic in 1942. His first major production was Universal's *Winchester'73* (1950), a western starring James Stewart, which had been originally assigned to Fritz Lang. The western became Mann's favorite genre and James Stewart his favorite star. In his best films, Mann acquired a reputation for meticulous craftsmanship and for spectacular outdoor cinematography. He also seemed intuitively able to portray inner tensions through visual expression. He died of a heart attack on location in Berlin during the production of *A Dandy in Aspic*. The film was completed by its star, Laurence Harvey, and released posthumously in 1968.

Filmography: Dr. Broadway, Moonlight in Havana (1942); Nobody's Darling (1943); My Best Gal, Strangers in the Night (1944); The Great Flamarion, Two O'Clock Courage, Sing Your Way Home (1945); Strange Impersonation, The Bamboo Blonde (1946); Desperate, Railroaded (1947); T-Men, Raw Deal (1948); Follow Me Quietly, Reign of Terror/The Black Book, Border Incident (1949); Side Street, Winchester'73, The Furies, Devil's Doorway (1950); The Tall Target (1951); Bend of the River (1952); The Naked Spur, Thunder Bay (1953); The Glenn Miller Story (1954); The Far Country, Strategic Air Command, The Man from Laramie, The Last Frontier (1955); Serenade (1956); Men in War, The Tin Star (1957); God's Little Acre, Man of the West (1958); Cimarron (1960); El Cid (1961); The Fall of the Roman Empire (1964); The Heroes of Telemark (1965); A Dandy in Aspic (1968).

Selected Bibliography

Basinger, Jeanine. *Anthony Mann*. Boston: Twayne, 1979.
Kitses, Demetrius John. *Horizons West: Anthony Mann, Budd Boetticher, Sam Peckinpah: Studies of Authorship within the Western*. Bloomington: Indiana University Press, 1970.

MANN, DELBERT. Director. Born on January 30, 1920, in Lawrence, Kansas. Mann was one of the first directors to start out in television and then move to film. He got his start during the so-called golden age of television—the 1950s—when live drama challenged directors to combine theatrical techniques with cinematic ones. Mann took to it instinctively, and when the Paddy Chayefsky's TV play *Marty* became a hit, Mann transferred it to the screen, where it won four Academy Awards. Following that success, he directed two more Chayefsky scripts (*The Bachelor Party* and *The Middle of the Night*), after which he tried his hand at other theatrical adaptations such as *Desire under the Elms*, *Separate Tables*, and *The Dark at the Top of the Stairs*. Later in the decade, when the taste for adapted stage plays and Marty-style realism gave way to epics and glamour, Mann proved himself adept at light fare with two Doris Day comedies (*Lover Come Back* and *That Touch of Mink*) as well as romances and adventures. In the 1970s Mann returned to television where he piloted many impressive movies and even staged a live revival of *The Member of the Wedding* in 1982.

Filmography: Marty (1955); The Bachelor Party (1957); Desire under the Elms, Separate Tables (1958); Middle of the Night (1959); The Dark at the Top of the Stairs (1960); Love Come Back, The Outsider (1961); That Touch of Mink (1962); A Gathering of Eagles (1963); Dear Heart (1964); Quick Before It Melts [also co-prod.] (1965); Mister Buddwing [also co-prod.] (1966); Fitzwilly (1967); The Pink Jungle (1968); Kidnapped (1971); Birch Interval (1976); Night Crossing (1982); Brontë (1983).

Honors: Academy Award: Best Director, Directors Guild of America Award: Most Outstanding Directorial Achievement, Cannes Film Festival Award: Palme d'Or (*Marty*, 1955).

Selected Bibliography

Harwell, Sara, ed. *The Papers of Delbert Mann*. Nashville: Vanderbilt University (The Jean and Alexander Heart Library), 1993.

Sarris, Andrew. *The American Cinema: Directors and Directions 1929–1968*. New York: E. P. Dutton, 1968.

MAN WHO SHOT LIBERTY VALANCE, THE (1962), western. Directed by John Ford; with James Stewart, John Wayne, Vera Miles, Lee Marvin, Edmond O'Brien, Andy Devine, Woody Strode, Jeanette Nolan, Ken Murray, John Qualen, Strother Martin, Lee Van Cleef, John Carradine, and Carleton Young; screenplay by James Warner Bellah and Willis Goldbeck.

This film was panned and patronized when it was first released, but it has now come to be regarded as an American classic, especially by Ford scholars. The truth is that while it is an enjoyable film, it does fall short of its innate story potential. The trouble is that John Ford and his writers have overplayed their hands, taking a simple premise, developing it skillfully to its natural conclusion, and then running it into the ground, thus destroying the very simplicity they strived for. Defenders of this film call it Ford's purest and most sustained expression of the familiar themes of the passing of the Old West, while dissenters consider it a clumsy, obvious western with the director overindulging himself. Others criticize it for being shot too much indoors or on a sound stage, a circumstance that gives it a curiously claustrophobic feeling, especially for what is supposed to be a western. Nevertheless, the film has acquired a cult following, part of the reason being the teaming of veterans Stewart and Wayne and the virtuoso performance of Lee Marvin as Liberty Valance.

Awards: Academy Award Nomination: Best B&W Costume Design.

Selected Bibliography

Hardy, Phil, ed. *The Overlook Film Encyclopedia: The Western*. Woodstock, NY: Overlook Press, 1994.

Pickard, Roy. *Jimmy Stewart: A Life in Film*. New York: St. Martin's Press, 1993.

Place, Janey Ann. *The Western Films of John Ford*. Secaucus, NJ: Citadel Press, 1974.
Zmijewsky, Steve, Boris Zmijewsky, and Mark Ricci. *The Complete Films of John Wayne*. Secaucus, NJ: Citadel Press, 1983.

MARCH, FREDRIC. Actor. Born Ernest Frederick McIntyre Bickel on August 31, 1897, in Racine, Wisconsin; died on April 14, 1975. Educated at the University of Wisconsin. March's studies were interrupted by World War I, but when he returned, he began to take part in college dramatics. In 1920 he went to New York intending to become a banker but soon surrendered to the temptation to become an actor. Although his stage career was slow to take off, he did find work as an extra in the many films being shot in the New York area. His first Broadway lead was in *The Devil in the Cheese* in 1926 where he met Florence Eldridge, whom he married and with whom he occasionally starred in both plays and films. During his early days in Hollywood, March played mostly romantic roles, but gradually he became recognized as an actor of considerable range and one who seemed to understand intuitively the art of screen acting. Throughout his film career, he played a variety of roles, from comedy to adventure, winning his first Oscar for the challenging dual role in *Dr. Jekyll and Mr. Hyde* and a second as the troubled returning war veteran in *The Best Years of Our Lives*. Another of his most memorable screen roles was the lead in *The Adventures of Mark Twain* in which he portrayed the revered writer from youth to old age with a real feeling for the part. Other memorable screen roles include his role as Norman Maine in the original *A Star Is Born*, as Willy Loman in *Death of a Salesman*, and as William Jennings Bryan in *Inherit the Wind*.

Filmography: The Dummy, The Wild Party, The Studio Murder Mystery, Jealousy, Paris Bound, Footlights and Fools, The Marriage Playground (1929); Sarah and Son, Ladies Love Brutes, True to the Navy, Paramount on Parade, Manslaughter, Laughter (1930); The Royal Family of Broadway, Honor among Lovers, The Night Angel, My Sin (1931); Dr. Jekyll and Mr. Hyde, Strangers in Love, Merrily We Go to Hell, Make Me a Star, Smilin' Through, The Sign of the Cross (1932); Tonight Is Ours, The Eagle and the Hawk, Design for Living (1933); All of Me, Death Takes a Holiday, Good Dame, The Affairs of Cellini, The Barretts of Wimpole Street, We Live Again (1934); Les Miserables, Anna Karenina, The Dark Angel, Mary of Scotland, The Road to Glory, Anthony Adverse (1936); A Star Is Born, Nothing Sacred (1937); The Buccaneer, There Goes My Heart (1938); Trade Winds (1939); Susan and God, Victory (1940); So Ends Our Night, One Foot in Heaven, Bedtime Story (1941); I Married a Witch (1942); The Adventures of Mark Twain, Tomorrow the World (1944); The Best Years of Our Lives (1946); Another Part of the Forest, An Act of Murder/Live Today for Tomorrow (1948); Christopher Columbus (1949); Death of a Salesman (1951); It's a Big Country (1952); Man on a Tightrope (1953); Executive Suite (1954); The Bridges at Toko-Ri, The Desperate Hours (1955); Alexander the Great, The Man in the Gray Flannel Suit (1956); Middle of the Night (1959); Inherit the Wind (1960); The Young Doctors (1961); The Condemned of Altona (1962); Seven Days in May (1964); Hombre (1967); Tick Tick Tick (1970); The Iceman Cometh (1973).

Honors: Academy Award Nomination: Best Actor (*The Royal Family of Broadway*, 1930–1931); Academy Award, Venice Film Festival Award: Best Actor (*Dr. Jekyll and*

Mr. Hyde, 1931–1932); Academy Award Nomination: Best Actor (*A Star Is Born*, 1937); Academy Award: Best Actor (*The Best Years of Our Lives*, 1946); Golden Globe Award, Academy Award Nomination: Best Actor (*Death of a Salesman*, 1951); Venice Film Festival Award: Best Actor (*Death of a Salesman*, 1952); Berlin Film Festival Award: Best Actor (*Inherit the Wind*, 1960).

Selected Bibliography

Peterson, Deborah C. *Fredric March: Craftsman First, Star Second.* Westport, CT: Greenwood Press, 1996.
Quirk, Lawrence J. *The Films of Fredric March.* New York: Citadel Press, 1971.

MARX BROTHERS. Comedy team. Chico (born Leonard, on March 26, 1886; died on October 11, 1961), Harpo (born Adolph but known as Arthur, on November 21, 1888; died on September 28, 1964), Groucho (born Julius Henry, on October 2, 1890; died on August 19, 1977), and Zeppo (born Herbert, on February 25, 1901; died on November 30, 1979). The Marx Brothers became one of the most popular movie comedy teams of all time, even though they made only a dozen films together. Their off-the-wall style, perfected over the years, was not immediately welcomed by the depression-weary public, but before long, audiences began to respond more and more favorably to their unique style until they achieved a kind of show-biz immortality so that even today they are a concept (and Groucho has been immortalized in caricature as the cigar-chomping, wisecracking, eyebrow-twitching lecher he so popularized in his later years, especially on television). It was the Marx Brothers' mother, Minna Schoenberg (immortalized in the early 1970s in the Broadway musical *Minnie's Boys*), who recognized her children's talents and started them in show business. Minnie got her boys started in vaudeville as a musical team that evolved through various combinations, some featuring even a fifth brother, others using a different tag to identify their act. But it wasn't until the act turned from music to comedy that the Marx Brothers began to catch on. Even so, success eluded them until their Broadway hits *The Cocoanuts* in 1925 and *Animal Crackers* in 1928. By this time they had honed their inimitable comedy style and developed distinctive personal characteristics that later lit up the screen in their zany, anarchic films of the 1930s. Except for a brief appearance by Harpo in the silent film *Too Many Kisses*, the Marx Brothers made their screen debut in 1929 in the film version of *The Cocoanuts*. Despite the indifferent direction, the silly plots, and the intrusive music that plagued most of their films, the almost surrealist quality of the Marx Brothers' absurdist style appealed equally to intellectuals and lowbrows. The Marx Brothers' screen comedy reached a peak of brilliance in their last film for Paramount, *Duck Soup*, directed by Leo McCarey, and their first film for MGM, *A Night at the Opera*, a great box office success directed by Sam Wood under the guidance of Irving Thalberg. The films that followed were increasingly inferior, but devotees find moments worth the trouble in even their worst films. The Marx Brothers made their last appearance as a team in *Love Happy* in 1950. All three appeared in Irwin Allen's *The Story of Mankind* but in unrelated episodes (with Harpo peculiarly cast as Sir Isaac Newton), and they were reunited on TV in a *General Electric Theater* comedy, *The Incredible Jewel Robbery*. Other than that they went their separate ways. Chico retired early and spent his last years relaxing with cards and friends. Harpo, who after several weeks of shooting was replaced by Alan Young in the title role of the film *Androcles and the Lion* in 1952, made a number of guest appearances on TV and published his memoirs—*Harpo Speaks!*—in 1961. Groucho, the youngest of the three, remained the most active, appearing in occasional films and hosting the TV comedy-quiz show *You Bet Your Life*. He was still ready with a quip and an insult in infrequent guest appearances on TV in the early 1970s. In 1972, at the age of eighty-two, he returned to the New York stage after an absence of forty-three years with a one-man show at Carnegie Hall.

Filmography: The Cocoanuts (1929); Animal Crackers (1930); Monkey Business (1931); Horse Feathers (1932); Duck Soup (1933); A Night at the Opera (1935); A Day at the Races (1937); Room Service (1938); At the Circus (1939); Go West (1940); The Big Store (1941); A Night in Casablanca (1946); The Story of Mankind (1957).

Honors: Cannes Film Festival: Special Award [to Groucho Marx] (1972); Academy Award: Special Award [to Groucho Marx] (1973).

Selected Bibliography

Gehring, Wes D. *The Marx Brothers: A Bio-Bibliography*. Westport, CT: Greenwood Press, 1987.
Marx, Arthur, and Robert Fisher. *Groucho: A Life in Revue*. New York: S. French, 1988.
Marx, Harpo, with Roland Barber. *Harpo Speaks!* New York: Limelight, 1985.
Marx, Maxine. *Growing Up with Chico*. Englewood Cliffs, NJ: Prentice-Hall, 1980.

MASSEY, RAYMOND. Actor. Born on August 30, 1896, in Toronto; died on July 29, 1983. Educated at Oxford. Massey made his film debut in 1931. Although he played Abraham Lincoln in only two films, *Abe Lincoln in Illinois* and *How the West Was Won*, he has become closely identified with that role, partly because he also played it on the stage. More often he was likely to be cast as a moralist, an evildoer, or a fanatic. In *The Fountainhead*, for example, he played the complex role of a newspaper tycoon who starts out as an insensitive opportunist but who eventually has the guts to take a stand on the side of artistic integrity even when it spells his ruin. In the early 1960s he portrayed Dr. Gillespie in the *Dr. Kildare* TV series. It's all too easy to underestimate Massey because he happened to be one of those actors who immerse themselves so thoroughly in their roles that their own personalities get submerged. With some actors like, say, James Cagney, the personality shines through both tough guy and hoofer, but with actors like Massey, even though there is a recognizable gaunt presence, there is also such consummate acting that one forgets who that striking figure was in *The Forty-ninth Parallel*, *The Fountainhead*, or *East of Eden*. In the latter, his highly charged confrontations with the unpredictable James Dean enhanced both their performances while also presenting a textbook example of the clash of not just generations but generational acting styles. Massey had a tendency to overact, but he knew this, and that is probably why he preferred roles as wide-eyed zealots or sadistic Nazis or out-of-control villains.

Filmography: The Crooked Billet/International Spy (1929); The Speckled Band, The Face at the Window, The Old Dark House (1932); The Scarlet Pimpernel (1935); Things to Come (1936); Fire over England, Dreaming Lips, Under the Red Robe, The Prisoner of Zenda, The Hurricane (1937); The Drum/Drums, Black Limelight (1938); Abe Lincoln in Illinois, Santa Fe Trail (1940); 49th Parallel/The Invaders (1941); Reap the Wild Wind, Dangerously They Live, Desperate Journey (1942); Action in the North Atlantic (1943); Arsenic and Old Lace, The Woman in the Window (1944); Hotel Berlin, God Is My Co-Pilot (1945); A Matter of Life and Death/Stairway to Heaven (1946); Possessed, Mourning Becomes Electra (1947); The Fountainhead, Roseanna McCoy (1949); Chain Lightning, Barricade, Dallas (1950); Sugarfoot, David and Bathsheba, Come Fill the Cup (1951); Carson City (1952); The Desert Song (1953); Prince of Players, Battle Cry, East of Eden, Seven Angry Men (1955); Omar Khayyam (1957); The Naked and the Dead (1958); The Great Impostor, The Queen's Guards, The Fiercest Heart (1961); How the West Was Won (1962); Mackenna's Gold (1969).

Honors: Academy Award Nomination: Best Actor (*Abe Lincoln in Illinois*, 1940).

Selected Bibliography

Massey, Raymond. *A Hundred Different Lives: An Autobiography*. Boston: Little, Brown, 1979.

———. *When I Was Young*. Boston: Little, Brown, 1976.

MCCAREY, LEO. Director, producer, screenwriter. Born on October 3, 1898, in Los Angeles; died on July 5, 1969. Educated at the University of Southern California School of Law. McCarey started out in films as assistant director to Tod Browning on *The Virgin of Stamboul* in 1920. Later he gained valuable experience working at the Hal Roach studio, where he wrote the stories for most of the Laurel and Hardy silent shorts and directed four of them. In 1929, McCarey turned to feature films in which he imposed his own style of madcap comedy on such noted comedians as Eddie Cantor, the Marx Brothers, W. C. Fields, Mae West, and Harold Lloyd. McCarey's trademark blend of broad humor and unabashed sentimentality resulted in such comedy classics as *Ruggles of Red Gap* and *The Awful Truth*, on the one hand, and such maudlin gems as *Make Way for Tomorrow* and *Going My Way*, on the other. From 1937 on, he produced practically all his own films and wrote the stories or screenplays for most of them.

Filmography: [as director, features only]: Society Secrets (1921); The Sophomore, Red Hot Rhythm (1929); Wild Company, Let's Go Native, Part Time Wife/The Shepper—Newfounder (1930); Indiscreet (1931); The Kid from Spain (1932); Duck Soup (1933); Six of a Kind, Belle of the Nineties (1934); Ruggles of Red Gap (1935); The Milky Way (1936); Make Way for Tomorrow, The Awful Truth (1937); Love Affair (1939); Once Upon a Honeymoon (1942); Going My Way (1944); The Bells of St. Mary's (1945); Good Sam (1948); My Son John (1952); An Affair to Remember [remake of Love Affair] (1957); Rally 'Round the Flag Boys! (1958); Satan Never Sleeps/The Devil Never Sleeps (1962).

Honors: Academy Award: Best Director (*The Awful Truth*, 1937); Academy Award Nomination: Best Original Screenplay *(Love Affair*, 1939); Academy Award Nomination: Best Original Screenplay (*My Favorite Wife*, 1940); Academy Awards: Best Director, Original Story, New York Film Critics Circle Award: Best Director (*Going My Way*, 1944); Academy Award Nomination: Best Director (*The Bells of St. Mary's*, 1945).

Selected Bibliography

Finler, Joel W. *Movie Directors Story*. London: Octopus Books, 1985.
Gehring, Wes D. *Leo McCarey and the Comic Anti-hero in American Film*. New York: Arno Press, 1980.

MEET ME IN ST. LOUIS (1944), musical. Directed by Vincente Minnelli; with Judy Garland, Margaret O'Brien, Lucille Bremer, Tom Drake, Mary Astor, Leon Ames, Marjorie Main, June Lockhart, Harry Davenport, Joan Carroll, and Hugh Marlowe; screenplay by Irving Brecher and Fred F. Finkelhoffe.

This film has everything a romantic musical should have. For many critics and for a vast number of fans, *Meet Me in St. Louis* is undoubtedly the best period musical ever made. It is a movie that is utterly American and one that evokes powerful feelings of nostalgia, patriotism, love for the family that seems so real, regret for the passing of an age, and longing for something elusive but essential that seems to bind this family into a strong, devoted unit. It is a movie filled with excellent performances and brimming with wonderful music. Judy Garland never looked or performed better, and Marjorie Main adds enough salt to the soup to keep it from cloying. But stealing every scene she's in is the inimitable Margaret O'Brien, arguably the greatest child actor in film history. This captivating musical remains fresh through successive viewings; in fact, this charming bit of romantic nostalgia seems to get better and better the farther away we move from the now magical/mythical world of turn-of-the-century America—a world of innocence and love, of decency and high humor. Perhaps the secret to the magic of this film lies in the tremors of dismay that threaten to uproot this happy family, foreshadowing the end of an era when such wholesome and uncomplicated happiness could exist. Minnelli manages all this old-fashioned sentiment without being banal or mawkish. Particularly appropriate is the music, all of it memorable, with certain numbers having become standards such as the wistful "Boy Next Door," the spirited "Trolley Song," and the yuletide classic "Have Yourself a Merry Little Christmas."

Awards: Academy Award: Special Award (Margaret O'Brien: Outstanding Child Actress of the Year); Academy Award Nominations: Screenplay, Cinematography, Score, Song ("The Trolley Song").

Selected Bibliography

Altman, Rick. *The American Film Musical*. Bloomington: Indiana University Press, 1987.
Minnelli, Vincente. *I Remember It Well*. Garden City, NY: Doubleday, 1974.
Morella, Joe, and Edward Z. Epstein. *Judy: The Complete Films and Career of Judy Garland*. Secaucus, NJ: Citadel Press, 1986.

MILDRED PIERCE (1945), drama. Directed by Michael Curtiz; with Joan Crawford, Jack Carson, Zachary Scott, Eve Arden, Bruce Bennett, Ann Blyth, and Butterfly McQueen; screenplay by Ranald MacDougall.

"The kind of woman most men want and shouldn't have!" screamed this misleading blurb for one of the all-time great film soapers. Arguments have raged ever since its release about the appropriateness of an Oscar for Crawford and the quality of the picture, some saying both Crawford and the picture are overrated, others claiming that *Mildred Pierce* is what movies are all about: larger-than-life suffering, revenge, and redemption. And in this case, whatever sleaze may have been in the James M. Cain novel has been deftly purged by the writers, while Crawford rises above the whole sordid mess with a tough but tender portrayal of a woman who plays the hand she's been dealt in the best way she knows how. Crawford, one of the screen's durables, beat all the odds with this surprising performance in which she reinvented herself (not for the first time in her career) as a no-nonsense, independent, courageous woman-against-the-world postwar heroine. Ranald MacDougall deserves much credit for a script that remains realistic and adult without ever crossing the line into what at the time was forbidden territory. Ann Blyth does a remarkable job in playing against type. Audiences used to her sweet smile and lovely singing voice were shocked to see her as the baby-faced Daughter from Hell. And Eve Arden adds just the right dash of vinegar as the wisecracking friend. This is a classic "woman's picture," and it set the pace for similar Crawford vehicles to follow. It's matinee magic, all glossy and moody with a glamorous star suffering in luxury on behalf of "daughter dearest."

Awards: Academy Award, National Board of Review: Best Actress (Crawford); Academy Award Nominations: Best Picture, Supporting Actress (Arden, Blyth), Screenplay, B&W Cinematography.

Selected Bibliography

Kinnard, Roy, and R. J. Vitone. *The American Films of Michael Curtiz*. Metuchen, NJ: Scarecrow Press, 1986.

Quirk, Lawrence J. *The Complete Films of Joan Crawford*. Secaucus, NJ: Citadel Press, 1988.

Thomas, Tony. *The Films of the Forties*. Secaucus, NJ: Citadel Press, 1975.

MILLAND, RAY. Actor, director. Born Reginald Truscott-Jones on January 3, 1907 (per birth certificate; most sources give 1905), in Neath, Wales; died on March 10, 1986. Educated at the University of Wales. After three years of service as a guardsman with the Royal Household Cavalry in London, Milland entered British films in 1929 using the name Spike Milland, but soon changed it to Raymond Milland. He arrived in Hollywood in 1930 and for several years thereafter played mostly second leads, graduating to leads in the mid-1930s. He played suave, debonair leading men in many drawing room comedies and an occasional mystery or adventure. Although he was a very good actor, he seemed so at ease in the light parts he played that it wasn't until he played the part of an alcoholic in *The Lost Weekend* that audiences (and critics) sat up and took notice. He won an Oscar for that performance, but parts that good or better were not forthcoming, and he turned to directing in 1955 with indifferent success. After a return to the screen in *Love Story* in 1970, he turned to playing leads in low-budget horror films and TV serials.

Filmography: The Playing, The Informer, The Flying Scotsman, The Lady from the Sea/ Goodwin Sands (1929); Way for a Sailor, Passion Flower (1930); The Bachelor Father, Just a Gigolo, Bought, Ambassador Bill, Blonde Crazy (1931); The Man Who Played God, Polly of the Circus, Payment Deferred (1932); Orders Is Orders, This Is the Life (1933); Bolero, We're Not Dressing, Many Happy Returns, Charlie Chan in London, Menace (1934); One Hour Late, The Gilded Lily, Four Hours to Kill, The Glass Key, Alias Mary Dow (1935); Next Time We Love, The Return of Sophie Lang, The Big Broadcast of 1937, The Jungle Princess, Three Smart Girls (1936); Bulldog Drummond Escapes, Wings over Honolulu, Easy Living, Ebb Tide, Wise Girl (1937); Her Jungle Love, Tropic Holiday, Men with Wings, Say It in French (1938); French without Tears, Hotel Imperial, Beau Geste, Everything Happens at Night (1939); Irene, The Doctor Takes a Wife, Untamed, Arise My Love (1940); I Wanted Wings, Skylark (1941); The Lady Has Plans, Reap the Wild Wind, Are Husbands Necessary?, The Major and the Minor, Star Spangled Rhythm (1942); The Crystal Ball, Forever and a Day (1943); The Uninvited, Lady in the Dark, Till We Meet Again, Ministry of Fear (1944); The Lost Weekend (1945); Kitty, The Well Groomed Bride (1946); California, The Imperfect Lady, The Trouble with Women, Variety Girl, Golden Earrings (1947); The Big Clock, So Evil My Love, Miss Tatlock's Millions, Sealed Verdict (1948); Alias Nick Beal, It Happens Every Spring (1949); A Woman of Distinction, A Life of Her Own, Copper Canyon (1950); Circle of Danger, Night into Morning, Rhubarb, Close to My Heart (1951); Bugles in the Afternoon, Something to Live For, The Thief (1952); Jamaica Run, Let's Do It Again (1953); Dial M for Murder (1954); The Girl in the Red Velvet Swing, A Man Alone (1955); Lisbon, Three Brave Men, The River's Edge, High Flight (1957); The Safecracker (1958); Premature Burial, Panic in the Year Zero! (1962); X—The Man with the X-Ray Eyes (1963); The Confession/Quick Let's Get Married (1965); Hostile Witness (1967); Rose Rosse per il Fuhrer (1968); Company of Killers/The Protectors, Love Story (1970); The Big Game, Frogs, The Thing with Two Heads, Embassy (1972); The House in Nightmare Park/Crazy House, Terror in the Wax Museum (1973); Gold (1974); Escape to Witch Mountain (1975); Aces High, The Last Tycoon (1976); Slavers, Oil, The Swiss Conspiracy, The Uncanny (1977); The Girl in the Yellow Pajamas, Black-out, Oliver's Story (1978); Battlestar Gallactica, Game for Vultures (1979); The Attic, Survival Run (1980); The Sea Serpent (1986).

Honors: Academy Award, Golden Globe Award, New York Film Critics Circle Award, National Board of Review Award: Best Actor (*The Lost Weekend*, 1945); Cannes Film Festival Award: International Jury Prize/Actor (*The Lost Weekend*, 1946).

Selected Bibliography

Brown, Mary Wale. "Ray Milland: Actor, Welsh Fusilier, 1979–83." In *Reel Life on Hollywood Movie Sets*. Riverside, CA: Ariadne Press, 1995. 159–164.

Milland, Ray. *Wide-eyed in Babylon: An Autobiography*. New York: Morrow, 1974.

MILLER, ANN. Actress, dancer. Born Lucille Ann Collier on April 12, 1919, in Chireno, Texas. A professional dancer from childhood, Ann Miller broke into films at fifteen in a bit part in *Anne of Green Gables*. She then signed with RKO and was named one of the *New Faces of 1937*. During three years at RKO she was in mostly forgettable films except for *Room Service*, in which she was manhandled by the Marx Brothers, and *You Can't Take It with You*, in which she was one of the zany family members. She then moved on to Republic, playing her first lead in *Melody Ranch* opposite Gene Autry. After her very visible tapping in *Hit Parade of 1941*, Miller was signed by Columbia, where for the next few years she made a string of low-budget B musical comedies, the most memorable being as a disc jockey in *Reveille with Beverly*, a bright, wartime musical that featured five famous big bands. By the time she reached the big league of MGM's glossy productions in the late 1940s, she was thirty and typically cast in comic or bitchy second leads, most memorably in *On the Town*, in which she stole the show with a frenzied cave-woman dance, and *Kiss Me Kate* (1953), in which she appeared in peak form in the role of Bianca. A thorough professional, Miller never gave a poor performance in any picture she was in, and often she was the best thing in it. After her film career ended in the mid-1950s, she appeared in nightclubs and occasional stage and TV productions. In 1969–1970 she inherited the lead role in the musical *Mame* from Angela Lansbury, and in the 1980s she enjoyed a tremendous success opposite Mickey Rooney in the burlesque musical pastiche *Sugar Babies*.

Filmography: The Devil on Horseback (1936); New Faces of 1937, Stage Door, The Life of the Party (1937); Radio City Revels, Having Wonderful Time, You Can't Take It with You, Room Service, Tarnished Angel (1938); Too Many Girls, Hit Parade of 1941, Melody Ranch (1940); Time Out for Rhythm, Go West Young Lady (1941); True to the Army, Priorities on Parade (1942); Reveille with Beverly, What's Buzzin' Cousin? (1943); Jam Session, Hey Rookie, Carolina Blues (1944); Eve Knew Her Apples, Eadie Was a Lady (1945); The Thrill of Brazil (1946); The Kissing Bandit, Easter Parade (1948); On the Town (1949); Watch the Birdie (1950); Texas Carnival, Two Tickets to Broadway (1951); Lovely to Look At (1952); Small Town Girl, Kiss Me Kate (1953); Deep in My Heart (1954); Hit the Deck (1955); The Opposite Sex, The Great American Pastime (1956); Won Ton Ton—The Dog Who Saved Hollywood [cameo] (1976); That's Entertainment III (1994).

Selected Bibliography

Connor, Jim. *Ann Miller, Tops in Taps: An Authorized Pictorial History*. New York: Watts, 1981.

Miller, Ann, with Norma Lee Browning. *Miller's High Life*. Garden City, NY: Doubleday, 1972.

MINNELLI, VINCENTE. Director. Born on February 28, 1903, in Chicago; died on July 25, 1986. Minnelli left school at sixteen and soon thereafter joined Chicago's Balaban and Katz motion picture theater chain as an assistant stage manager and costume designer for its live prefeature program. From there he went to New York's Paramount Theater as set and costume designer. In 1932 he created the decor and costumes for the operetta *Du Barry* at the request of its star, Grace Moore, and the following year he was appointed art director of New York's Radio City Music Hall. After a checkered career as everything from billboard painter to art director of New York's Radio City Music Hall, Minnelli turned director in 1935 when he staged several very successful Broadway musicals including *Ziegfeld Follies* and *Very Warm for May*. He was invited to Hollywood by MGM producer Arthur Freed in 1940, and after two years of intensive training in film technique, he was allowed to film isolated musical numbers for Judy Garland in Busby Berkeley's *Strike Up the Band* and *Babes on Broadway*. With all this experience behind him, Minnelli became a highly successful film director right from the start, and before long, he came to be recognized as an outstanding director of such lavish musicals as *Meet Me in St. Louis* and *The Pirate*, as well as the drama *The Clock*, starring Judy Garland, whom he married in 1945. The following year, their daughter, Liza Minnelli, was born. They divorced in 1951. Minnelli's musicals have a style all their own, especially in the controlled way he uses color and in the way he so adroitly integrates musical numbers with film narrative. His successes of the 1950s include *An American in Paris*, *The Band Wagon*, and *Gigi*, all of which won awards. Although Minnelli is identified mostly with screen musicals, he also did fine work in other genres. In fact, most of his films were actually nonmusicals, some of the best of them being such varied efforts as *Father of the Bride*, *The Bad and the Beautiful*, and *Lust for Life*. Minnelli's reputation faded somewhat as interest in musicals declined and his own touch faltered. However, for all his successes, he has earned a place in the pantheon of superior film directors.

Filmography: Cabin in the Sky, I Dood It (1943); Meet Me in St. Louis (1944); The Clock, Yolanda and the Thief (1945); Ziegfeld Follies, Undercurrent, Till the Clouds Roll By [three Judy Garland numbers only] (1946); The Pirate (1948); Madame Bovary (1949); Father of the Bride (1950); Father's Little Dividend, An American in Paris (1951); The Bad and the Beautiful (1952); The Story of Three Loves ["Mademoiselle" episode], The Band Wagon (1953); The Long Long Trailer, Brigadoon (1954); The Cobweb, Kismet (1955); Lust for Life, Tea and Sympathy (1956); Designing Woman, The Seventh Sin (co-dir. with Ronald Neame; uncredited) (1957); Gigi, The Reluctant Debutante (1958); Some Came Running (1959); Home From the Hill, Bells Are Ringing (1960); The Four Horsemen of the Apocalypse, Two Weeks in Another Town (1962); The Courtship of Eddie's Father (1963); Goodbye Charlie (1964); The Sandpiper (1965); On a Clear Day You Can See Forever (1970); A Matter of Time (1976).

Honors: Cannes Film Festival Award: Best Director/Musical Comedy (*Ziegfeld Follies*, 1947); Directors Guild of America: Quarterly Award (*Father's Little Dividend*, 1951); Academy Award Nomination: Best Director (*An American in Paris*, 1951); Academy Award, Golden Globe Award: Best Director, Directors Guild of America: Grand Award for Direction (*Gigi*, 1958).

Selected Bibliography

Fordin, Hugh. *The World of Entertainment!: Hollywood's Greatest Musicals*. Garden City, NY: Doubleday, 1975.

Minnelli, Vincente. *I Remember It Well*. Garden City, NY: Doubleday, 1974.

Sennett, Ted. *Great Movie Directors*. New York: Harry N. Abrams, 1986.

MIRACLE OF MORGAN'S CREEK, THE (1944), comedy. Directed by Preston Sturges; with Eddie Bracken, Betty Hutton, William Demarest, Diana Lynn, Brian Donlevy, Akim Tamiroff, Porter Hall, Almira Sessions, and Jimmy Conlin; screenplay by Preston Sturges.

Morgan's Creek is the name of the town where the action in this movie takes place, and the miracle, as director Preston Sturges terms it, is the birth to Eddie Bracken and Betty Hutton of a set of sextuplets. The scandal surrounding it, though, is what sets things going, beginning with the fact that Betty attends an all-night party, gets pregnant, and can't remember who the father is. Actually, in good old Hollywood style, she and Bracken did get married first, but they can't remember what each other looks like, only that they didn't give their right names. It's all typical Sturges—frenetic blend of satire and slapstick, full of wild dialogue and a healthy irreverence for all things deemed respectable. Many say that the "miracle" of *The Miracle of Morgan's Creek* is how the film ever got made in the first place. This diatribe—against American morals, against the wartime romances of servicemen, against just about everything that the country held sacred during World War II—is reckless, exaggerated, and very funny. Sturges is at his irreverent best with his screenplay and direction of this most unlikely story. This is one of Preston Sturges's surreal comedies, a picture that was held up a year because of censorship problems. See it and you'll know why.

Awards: Academy Award Nomination: Best Original Screenplay.

Selected Bibliography

Jacobs, Diane. *Christmas in July: The Life and Art of Preston Sturges*. Berkeley: University of California Press, 1992.

Siegel, Scott, and Barbara Siegel. *American Film Comedy: From Abbott & Costello to Jerry Zucker*. Englewood Cliffs, NJ: Prentice-Hall, 1994.

MIRACLE ON 34TH STREET (1947), comedy-fantasy. Directed by George Seaton; with Maureen O'Hara, John Payne, Edmund Gwenn, Thelma Ritter, Gene Lockhart, Natalie Wood, Porter Hall, and William Frawley; screenplay by George Seaton.

This holiday classic is an actor's holiday, filled with choice parts that these particular cast members obviously relish. It's a charming real-life fairy tale of a Macy's Santa Claus (played to perfection by Gwenn) encountering a skeptical child (Wood) and going to court to prove he really is Santa. What gives Gwenn's performance its punch is the fact that his character, an inmate of an old people's home, really does believe he is Santa and is therefore puzzled by all the fuss. Gene Lockhart is perfect as the judge, and Porter Hall lends just the right touch to the role of a neurotic personnel director for Macy's. Natalie Wood, who was to go on to full adult stardom, surprised everyone with her charming skepticism. This film marked the debut of Thelma Ritter, who was to become a legendary screen character actress and comedienne. As with all good grown-up myths, what keeps the cream from curdling is the salty humor and the lack of cloying sentimentality. But the film also has excellent plotting, with the elements of Santa Claus's trial so skillfully manipulated that the verdict declaring him the real thing—absurd as it may be—seems the only right one. This is suspension of disbelief at its greatest and a real testament to the magic of storytelling.

Awards: Academy Awards: Best Supporting Actor (Gwenn), Original Story (Valentine Davies), Adapted Screenplay (Seaton); Golden Globe Awards: Best Supporting Actor (Gwenn), Screenplay (Seaton); Academy Award Nomination: Best Picture.

Selected Bibliography

Byron, Stuart, and Elisabeth Weis, eds. *The National Society of Film Critics on Movie Comedy*. New York: Grossman Publishers, 1977.
Thomas, Tony. *The Films of the Forties*. Secaucus, NJ: Citadel Press, 1975.

MISTER ROBERTS (1955), comedy/drama. Directed by John Ford and Mervyn LeRoy; with Henry Fonda, James Cagney, William Powell, Jack Lemmon, Betsy Palmer, Ward Bond, Nick Adams, Philip Carey, Harry Carey, Jr., and Ken Curtis; screenplay by Frank Nugent and Joshua Logan.

As a play, *Mr. Roberts* became something of a minor classic, making a screen adaptation more challenging to accomplish. Criticism is mixed about the results, but it is generally felt that the play's humor and sentimentality are transferred intact to the screen. The story concerns a World War II supply ship, its martinet captain, and the junior officer who finally takes command when the crew's frustration with the captain creates unbearable tension. Henry Fonda repeats his stage role as the cargo officer who resents not having seen action in the Pacific during World War II. James Cagney gives another of his superb performances, this time as the tyrannical captain of the ship. William Powell's laid-back ship's doctor is a standout, and Jack Lemmon corners the comedy of the film as Ensign Pulver. In spite of some very negative critical response, audiences warmed to this film. As is so often the case with movies of this kind, however, it is the famous faces that people go to see. Put Fonda, Cagney, and Lemmon together, and they could be reading the phone book. In *Mr. Roberts* they do considerably more than that.

Awards: Academy Award: Best Supporting Actor (Lemmon); Academy Award Nominations: Best Picture, Sound.

Selected Bibliography

LeRoy, Mervyn, as told to Dick Kleiner. *Mervyn LeRoy: Take One*. New York: Hawthorne Books, 1974.
Place, Janey Ann. *The Non-Western Films of John Ford*. Secaucus, NJ: Citadel Press, 1979.
Thomas, Tony. *The Films of Henry Fonda*. Secaucus, NJ: Citadel Press, 1983.

MITCHUM, ROBERT. Actor. Born on August 6, 1917, in Bridgeport, Connecticut; died on July 2, 1997. Mitchum had a long and ironic career. In his early days, he turned in one good performance after another, but it all seemed so effortless that he was easily underrated and taken for granted. Later, as he aged, his popularity increased, and he was given good roles to play. The trouble was that he had more and more trouble taking himself or his profession seriously, and thus he became what he had always been accused of: apathetic, listless, expressionless. Fortunately, this laid-back super cool coincided with a trend among leading men so that he simply seemed ahead of his times. Whatever the verdict, Mitchum was a talent to reckon with. And over the years he emerged as a personality as distinctive as Gable, Cooper, Cagney, Grant, Stewart, or any of the other immediately recognizable screen personalities. Part of his stone-faced, tough-guy approach came naturally as the result of a rather adventurous youth including an arrest for vagrancy at sixteen, a stretch on a Georgia chain gang, and jobs as an engine wiper on a freighter, a nightclub bouncer, and a promoter for a California astrologer. After his marriage to his high school sweetheart in 1940 and the birth of a son, Mitchum decided to settle down and took a job at Lockheed Aircraft as a drop hammer operator. In 1942 he joined the Long Beach Theater Guild, where he gained experience acting in its productions. He entered movies in 1943, appearing in no fewer than eighteen productions in that year alone, among them war films, comedies, dramas, and the first of many "Hopalong Cassidy" westerns. Mitchum's big break came in 1945 with *The Story of G.I. Joe*, for which he was nominated for a Best Supporting Actor Oscar. Following a stint in the army just at the end of the war, Mitchum resumed his screen career in 1946 as a star. In 1948–1949 he was arrested for possession of marijuana and spent fifty days in jail. Instead of hurting his reputation, the shocking charge only enhanced his reputation as Hollywood's Bad Boy, an image he used to advantage in many films over the next four decades. His film portrait gallery ranged from loner heroes to unscrupulous villains. He attributed his sleepy eyes to a combination of chronic insomnia and a boxing injury. And the I-don't-care attitude that characterized his screen personality is very much part of the real Mitchum. Even though he continued to make films into the 1980s and 1990s, he also found time to star in three extremely successful TV miniseries: *The Winds of War*, *North and South*, and *War and Remembrance*.

Filmography: Hoppy Serves a Writ, The Leather Burners, Border Patrol, Follow the Band, Colt Comrades, The Human Comedy, We've Never Been Licked, Beyond the Last Frontier, Bar 20, Doughboys in Ireland, Corvette K-225, Aerial Gunner, Lone Star Trail, False Colors, The Dancing Masters, Riders of the Deadline, Cry Havoc, Gung Ho! (1943); Johnny Doesn't Live Here Any More, When Strangers Marry, The Girl Rush, Thirty Seconds over Tokyo, Nevada (1944); West of the Pecos, The Story of G.I. Joe (1945); Till the End of Time, Undercurrent, The Locket (1946); Pursued, Crossfire, Desire Me, Out of the Past (1947); Rachel and the Stranger, Blood on the Moon (1948); The Red Pony, The Big Steal, Holiday Affair (1949); Where Danger Lives (1950); My Forbidden Past, His Kind of Woman, The Racket (1951); Macao, One Minute to Zero, The Lusty Men (1952); Second Chance, Angel Face, White Witch Doctor (1953); She Couldn't Say No, River of No Return, Track of the Cat (1954); Not as a Stranger, The

Night of the Hunter, Man with the Gun (1955); Foreign Intrigue, Bandido (1956); Heaven Knows Mr. Allison, Fire Down Below, The Enemy Below (1957); Thunder Road, The Hunters (1958); The Angry Hills, The Wonderful Country (1959); Home From the Hill, The Sundowners, The Night Fighters, The Grass Is Greener (1960); The Last Time I Saw Archie (1961); Cape Fear, The Longest Day, Two for the Seesaw (1962); The List of Adrian Messenger, Rampage (1963); Man in the Middle, What a Way to Go! (1964); Mister Moses (1965); The Way West, El Dorado (1967); Villa Rides, Anzio, 5 Card Stud, Secret Ceremony (1968); Young Billy Young, The Good Guys and the Bad Guys (1969); Ryan's Daughter (1970); Going Home (1971); The Wrath of God (1972); The Friends of Eddie Coyle (1973); The Yakuza, Farewell My Lovely (1975); Midway, The Last Tycoon (1976); The Amsterdam Kill (1977); Matilda, The Big Sleep (1978); Sergeant Steiner/Breakthrough (1979); Agency (1981); That Championship Season (1982); The Ambassador, Maria's Lovers (1985); Mr. North, Scrooged (1988); Cape Fear [remake] (1991); Tombstone (1993).

Honors: Academy Award Nomination: Best Supporting Actor (*The Story of G.I. Joe*, 1945).

Selected Bibliography

Malcolm, Derek. *Robert Mitchum*. New York: Hippocrene Books, 1984.
Marill, Alvin H. *Robert Mitchum on the Screen*. South Brunswick, NJ: A. S. Barnes, 1978.
Roberts, J. W. *Robert Mitchum: A Bio-Bibliography*. Westport, CT: Greenwood Press, 1992.

MODERN TIMES (1936), comedy. Directed by Charlie Chaplin; with Charlie Chaplin, Paulette Goddard, Henry Bergman, Chester Conklin, and Stanley "Tiny" Sandford; screenplay by Charlie Chaplin.

"You'll never laugh as long and as loud again as long as you live!" boasted the blurb for this silent comedy produced well into the sound period. It was Chaplin's last silent film and a good example of his disenchantment with so-called technical advances in filmmaking. In this film, Chaplin attacks the machine age and satirizes social ills by telling the sad story of a machine worker who suffers temporary derangement, the result of tightening bolts on a factory treadmill with clocklike precision. This derangement creates numerous situations in which Chaplin finds himself the victim of circumstances. *Modern Times* is all Chaplin, and it was his last appearance as the tramp. This film, the last of the great silent feature pictures, truly marked the passing of an era. And although it is about the social disorders of the 1930s, it is actually one of Chaplin's happiest and most lighthearted pictures.

Selected Bibliography

Gehring, Wes D. *Charlie Chaplin: A Bio-Bibliography*. Westport, CT: Greenwood Press, 1983.
Maland, Charles J. *Chaplin and American Culture: The Evolution of a Star Image*. Princeton, NJ: Princeton University Press, 1989.

MONROE, MARILYN. Actress. Born Norma Jean Mortenson on June 1, 1926, in Los Angeles; died on August 5, 1962. The more that is written, documented, or speculated about Marilyn Monroe, the more the mystery deepens, not just the mystery surrounding her death but the mystery of her talent, her legacy, her legend. As with all authentic myths, the mythical qualities are polished, not probed, by analysis. And like Elvis Presley and James Dean, she has a reputation that has flourished long after her death to the point where her fame has actually increased (witness her face on a postage stamp thirty-five years after her death). Monroe had a great, natural talent, so spontaneous it seemed accidental. Sensing this, she tried to "learn" how to act, and this only made her self-conscious and awkward. That she was able, with great effort, to overcome this self-imposed restraint testifies to the superiority of real talent over acquired technique. But this conflict between the instinctive and the adopted disabled her psychologically and emotionally to the point where she could no longer take the strain. She listened to her detractors who thought her a "dumb blond" instead of listening to her instincts. But the attentive viewer is always aware of the moment on screen when she drops all artifice and relies solely upon instinct. At that point, all the creative complexities of her personality result in a performance that can only be called riveting (e.g., *The Seven Year Itch*). Too bad it has taken so long for Marilyn Monroe to be appreciated. It's quite possible that she will someday be regarded as the supreme film actress of the century.

Filmography: Scudda-Hoo! Scudda-Hay! [bit], Dangerous Years [bit], Ladies of the Chorus (1948); Love Happy, A Ticket to Tomahawk, The Asphalt Jungle, All About Eve, Right Cross, The Fireball (1950); Hometown Story, As Young as You Feel, Love Nest, Let's Make It Legal (1951); Clash by Night, We're Not Married, Don't Bother to Knock, Monkey Business, O. Henry's Full House (1952); Niagara, Gentlemen Prefer Blondes, How to Marry a Millionaire (1953); River of No Return, There's No Business Like Show Business (1954); The Seven Year Itch (1955); Bus Stop (1956); The Prince and the Showgirl (1957); Some Like It Hot (1959); Let's Make Love (1960); The Misfits (1961).

Honors: *Photoplay*: Gold Medal Special Award (1952); Golden Globe Award: World Film Favorite (1953); *Photoplay* Gold Medal Award: Most Popular Female Star (1953); Golden Globe Award: Best Actress, Comedy/Musical (*Some Like It Hot*, 1959); Golden Globe Award: World Film Favorite (1961).

Selected Bibliography

Note: More than fifty books have been written about Marilyn Monroe since her death in 1962, and the output shows no signs of diminishing. Many of them have to do with her tumultuous life and mysterious death. Here I have listed only a handful of books from those dealing with her career rather than her private life. The ones I have chosen are of a very general nature, but they are a starting place.

Brown, Peter Harry, and Patte B. Barham. *Marilyn: The Last Take*. New York: Dutton, 1992.

Conway, Michael, and Mark Ricci. *The Complete Films of Marilyn Monroe*. Secaucus, NJ: Citadel Press, 1964.

Haspier, James. *Marilyn: The Ultimate Look at the Legend*. New York: Holt, 1991.

Kobal, John, ed. *Marilyn Monroe: A Life on Film.* New York: Hamlyn, 1974.
Riese, Randall, and Neal Hitchens. *The Unabridged Marilyn: Her Life from A to Z.* New
        York: Congdon & Weed, 1987.

MR. DEEDS GOES TO TOWN (1936), comedy. Directed by Frank Capra; with
Gary Cooper, Jean Arthur, George Bancroft, Lionel Stander, Douglass Dumbrille, Mayo Methot, Raymond Walburn, Walter Catlett, and H. B. Warner;
screenplay by Robert Riskin.

Critics in general often find it tricky to know just how to deal with Frank
Capra, who could be shamelessly sentimental (producing what wags called
"Capra-corn") or delightfully illogical and still manage somehow to make his
excesses work. Critics who thought Capra was better taken in small doses and
that *Deeds* was overlong admit that it's hard to deny one's enjoyment in this
fairy tale illustrating the triumph of small-town values over big-city cynicism.
The story has Gary Cooper as Longfellow Deeds, a greeting-card poet from
New England, meet Jean Arthur, a wiseacre newspaperwoman who begins by
making a public joke of him and ends up falling in love with him. It's formula
Capra: a simple story with a populist point of view, told with such charm and
acted so well by Gary Cooper and Jean Arthur that it has become another Frank
Capra classic. Cooper's hesitant, stumbling style is perfectly suited to the part
of Deeds. The surprise was newcomer Arthur who, in spite of a bad case of
nerves before each scene, displayed that endearing pixiness that was to be her
trademark for years to come.

Awards: Academy Award: Best Director; New York Film Critics Circle Award, National
Board of Review Award: Best Picture; Academy Award Nominations: Best Picture, Actor
(Cooper), Screenplay, Sound.

Selected Bibliography

Dickens, Homer. *The Films of Gary Cooper.* Secaucus, NJ: Citadel Press, 1970.
Dooley, Roger. *From Scarface to Scarlett: American Films in the 1930s.* New York:
        Harcourt Brace Jovanovich, 1981.
Scherle, Victor, and William Turner Levy, eds. *The Complete Films of Frank Capra.*
        New York: Carol Publishing Group, 1992.

MRS. MINIVER (1942), drama/war. Directed by William Wyler; with Greer
Garson, Walter Pidgeon, Dame May Whitty, Teresa Wright, Reginald Owen,
Henry Travers, Richard Ney, Henry Wilcoxon, Helmut Dantine, and Peter Law-
ford; screenplay by Arthur Wimperis, George Froeschel, James Hilton, and
Claudine West.

It is still possible for a sentimental person to enjoy this saga of fortitude in
the face of war if only for its bravery and romance and wholesomeness; but at
the time it came out, even the hard of heart found it irresistible, for it is sheer,
shameless, and superb wartime propaganda about an English family during the
infamous Blitz. As such, it brought the war home, especially to Americans just
entering it and just beginning to realize how vulnerable everyone was to the

threat of rapacious evil. Greer Garson was thereafter forever identified with the heroine she portrayed so perfectly—brave, courteous, resourceful, controlled, and unutterably noble. She may seem a bit over the top to jaded, modern audiences, but moments of crisis have always been known to bring into sharper relief latent personality traits that prompt one to "rise to the occasion." In this respect, Garson epitomizes the vast majority of hardworking, long-suffering English housewives whose patriotism and deep determination became a palpable defense in the bitter struggle against Nazi Germany. Her inner strength inspires others to tap their own secret depths.

Awards: Academy Awards: Best Actress (Garson), Supporting Actress (Wright), Director, Cinematography (Joseph Ruttenberg), Screenplay; Irving G. Thalberg Memorial Award (Producer Sidney Franklin); Academy Award Nominations: Best Actor (Pidgeon), Supporting Actor (Travers), Sound, Editing, Special Effects.

Selected Bibliography

Anderegg, Michael A. *William Wyler*. Boston: Twayne, 1979.
Guttmacher, Peter. *Legendary War Movies*. New York: MetroBooks, 1996.

MR. SMITH GOES TO WASHINGTON (1939), drama. Directed by Frank Capra; with James Stewart, Jean Arthur, Claude Rains, Edward Arnold, Guy Kibbee, Thomas Mitchell, Eugene Pallette, Beulah Bondi, Harry Carey, H. B. Warner, Charles Lane, Porter Hall, and Jack Carson; screenplay by Sidney Buchman.

"Stirring—in the seeing! Precious—in the remembering!" went the blurb for this classic Capra drama. Although the word *cornball* was used to describe this picture, critics cannot really bring themselves to find too much fault with a movie that ingratiates itself the way this one does. It's an adult fairy tale with a noble young hero in the Senate lion's den filibustering himself to death for the sake of honor and justice. In this film Frank Capra capitalized on his success with *Mr. Deeds Goes to Town*, again with Jean Arthur as a hard-boiled dame, but this time employing the talents of the stammering James Stewart rather than the stammering Gary Cooper as her foil. Somehow stammering in Capra always denotes an honest shyness rather than a guilty conscience. At any rate, Stewart is the youthful idealist who finds nothing but corruption in the U.S. Senate. As he combats corruption, the comedy spins along so smoothly and rapidly that the audience doesn't have time to be bothered by the sentiment, for Capra always knows when to add salt to the dialogue and pepper to the action. And while leading critics might hail it as the great American picture, Joseph P. Kennedy, then American ambassador to Great Britain, failed to see what an expression of democracy in the making of such a movie it was. "I feel that to show this film in foreign countries will do inestimable harm to American prestige all over the world," he said. But the film was distributed internationally and to great acclaim. It was obvious to the "common man" that the fact that such a film can be made and can be popular is the very essence of democratic freedom. In fact, what makes this film work is its universal theme that all that is necessary for the triumph of evil is the inaction of good men. With Stewart's magnificent performance as its inspiring center, the film is packed with emotion in every scene as it chronicles the great American values.

Awards: Academy Award: Best Original Story (Lewis R. Foster); New York Film Critics Circle Award: Best Actor (Stewart); Academy Award Nominations: Best Picture, Director, Actor (Stewart), Supporting Actor (Carey), Screenplay, Art Direction, Editing, Score, Sound.

Selected Bibliography

Jones, Ken D., Arthur F. McClure, and Alfred E. Twomey. *The Films of James Stewart*. New York: Castle Books, 1970.
Scherle, Victor, and William Turner Levy, eds. *The Complete Films of Frank Capra*. New York: Carol Publishing Group, 1992.
Sennett, Ted. *Hollywood's Golden Year, 1939*. New York: St. Martin's Press, 1989.

MUNI, PAUL. Actor. Born Muni Weisenfreund on September 22, 1895, in Lemberg, Austria-Hungary (later Lwow, Poland; now Lvov, Ukraine); died on August 25, 1967. Muni was the sort of film personality who was enormously popular in his heyday but whose star quickly faded. Although he was a consummate actor, his acting is largely of the old school: theatrical, mannered, stylized. He appeared as the "great actor" whose performances impressed many moviegoers while putting off those who were inclined toward the newer, cinematic, relaxed style of acting. However, in his best pictures, of which there were quite a few, he is worth remembering for some of the screen's most memorable performances. Muni was the son of an itinerant actor and actress, and he appeared with them on stage from early childhood. The family immigrated to the United States when Muni was seven and continued its theatrical activity on the Yiddish stage, joining the Yiddish Art Theater company in 1918. He was thirty-one when he made his English-language stage debut in the 1926 Broadway production of *We Americans*, and in 1929, he was signed by Fox, winning an Oscar nomination for his very first role, in *The Valiant*. But after another season on Broadway, Muni returned to the screen to star in two successive personal triumphs, *Scarface* and *I Am a Fugitive from a Chain Gang*, winning an Oscar nomination for the latter. Muni then signed a long-term contract with Warners and quickly became the studio's most distinguished actor, scoring his biggest success with a string of portrayals of famous people in the Warners biofilms of the 1930s (*The Story of Louis Pasteur*, *The Life of Emile Zola*, and *Juarez*). Then disagreements over subsequent roles led to a mutual termination of his contract, and from then on, Muni alternated between stage and screen. He appeared in few films after that, but each film was greeted with enthusiasm by both critics and public, so entrenched was his reputation. His last movie role was in the film *The Last Angry Man* in 1959. Deteriorating health and advancing blindness kept him virtually inactive until his death of a heart ailment in 1967 at the age of seventy-one. Muni's bravura style of acting is no longer fashionable, but what endures is his indomitable spirit that transcended popularity in the true tradition of thespianism.

Filmography: The Valiant, Seven Faces (1929); Scarface, I Am a Fugitive from a Chain Gang (1932); The World Changes (1933); Hi Nellie! (1934); Bordertown, Black Fury, Dr. Socrates (1935); The Story of Louis Pasteur (1936); The Good Earth, The Woman I Love, The Life of Emile Zola (1937); Juarez, We Are Not Alone (1939); Hudson's Bay (1941); The Commandos Strike at Dawn, Stage Door Canteen [cameo] (1943); A Song to Remember, Counter-Attack (1945); Angel on My Shoulder (1946); Stranger on the Prowl (1952); The Last Angry Man (1959).

Honors: Academy Award Nomination: Best Actor (*The Valiant*, 1928–1929); Academy Award Nomination: Best Actor (I *Am a Fugitive from a Chain Gang*, 1932–1933); Academy Award, Venice Film Festival Award: Best Actor (*The Story of Louis Pasteur*, 1936); New York Film Critics Circle Award, Academy Award Nomination: Best Actor (*The Life of Emile Zola*, 1937); Academy Award Nomination: Best Actor (*The Last Angry Man*, 1959).

Selected Bibliography

Druxman, Michael B. *Paul Muni: His Life and His Films*. South Brunswick, NJ: A. S. Barnes, 1974.
Lawrence, Jerome. *Actor: The Life and Times of Paul Muni*. New York: Putnam, 1974.

MUTINY ON THE BOUNTY (1935), adventure drama. Directed by Frank Lloyd; with Charles Laughton, Clark Gable, Franchot Tone, Herbert Mundin, Eddie Quillan, Dudley Digges, Donald Crisp, Movita, Henry Stephenson, and Spring Byington; screenplay by Talbot Jennings, Jules Furthman, and Carey Wilson.

This original version of the Nordhoff and Hall classic tale of mutiny on the high seas set the standard for adventure epics with its excitement, drama, thrills, and the classic confrontation of good against evil. Critics generally agree that this is a truly great film in every important respect. It was enormously successful at the box office, it established Clark Gable as the epitome of manliness, and it made Charles Laughton the villain you love to hate. The film was also helped by the fact that it was based on an actual mutiny. In addition to its state-of-the-art special effects and its epic proportions, this picture is blessed with several excellent performances. Charles Laughton is outstanding as Captain Bligh, and although some critics have thought it a one-note performance, Laughton makes Bligh such a total tyrant that no actor since has been able to erase the public's identification of Laughton with the part. Some of this has to do with the fact that this first version concentrates on Bligh's incredible 4,000-mile voyage in an open boat and the succeeding court trial in which Laughton gets to turn the courtroom into a theater. Many see the corrupt, sadistic Bligh as the strongest person on the screen, a great villain, pompous, self-righteous, completely mad— like Hitler, someone you can't just laugh off.

Awards: Academy Award: Best Picture; Academy Award Nominations: Best Director, Actor (Gable, Laughton, Tone), Screenplay, Editing, Score.

Selected Bibliography

Callow, Simon. *Charles Laughton: A Difficult Actor*. New York: Grove Press, 1988.
Dooley, Roger. *From Scarface to Scarlett: American Films in the 1930s*. New York: Harcourt Brace Jovanovich, 1981.
Essoe, Gabe. *The Complete Films of Clark Gable*. Secaucus, NJ: Citadel Press, 1970.

MY DARLING CLEMENTINE (1946), western. Directed by John Ford; with Henry Fonda, Linda Darnell, Victor Mature, Walter Brennan, Cathy Downs, Tim Holt, Ward Bond, Alan Mowbray, John Ireland, and Jane Darwell; screenplay by Samuel G. Engel and Winston Miller.

Perhaps it was John Ford's reluctance to direct this film that motivated him to turn it into a cinematic poem. Every scene is the product of a keen and sensitive, one might even say poetic, eye. It is an unquestionably beautiful film, with Ford taking advantage of the spectacular Monument Valley location he prized so much. He also attempts to be as faithful as possible to the actual events that transpired that fateful day of the shootout at the O.K. Corral. This is, of course, a man's film and one of Ford's best among his fifty-four westerns. Some critics have criticized the pacing of the film, faulting Ford for preferring style over movement, but others see this film as an archetypal western mood piece, a nostalgic tribute to a bygone day and thus necessarily moody and measured. What keeps the film going is Henry Fonda's simple, sincere performance. Counterpoint to Fonda's directness is Victor Mature's turn as a Boston aristocrat turned gambler and killer. For viewers, what makes the film enjoyable is not the accuracy of the final shootout but the series of incidents leading up to it that give the shootout meaning.

Selected Bibliography

Hardy, Phil, ed. *The Overlook Film Encyclopedia: The Western*. Woodstock, NY: Overlook Press, 1994.
Place, Janey Ann. *The Western Films of John Ford*. Secaucus, NJ: Citadel Press, 1974.

N

NATIONAL VELVET (1944), drama. Directed by Clarence Brown; with Mickey Rooney, Elizabeth Taylor, Donald Crisp, Anne Revere, Angela Lansbury, Reginald Owen, Norma Varden, Jackie "Butch" Jenkins, and Terry Kilburn; screenplay by Theodore Reeves and Helen Deutsch.

National Velvet is one of the most likable movies of all time. It may be schmaltzy, dated, corny, whatever the going putdown term may be, but it is still irresistible, mostly because a very young Elizabeth Taylor is enchanting and Mickey Rooney was never better, not to mention Anne Revere, a venerable character actress, who won an Oscar for Best Supporting Actress as Taylor's mother. Set in England, it is the story of a former jockey (Rooney) who's become embittered and plans to steal from a family that befriends him, but the family's eleven-year-old daughter, Velvet, softens him. At this point Velvet (Taylor) becomes the dominant character in the story. She's crazy about horses, and when a neighbor raffles off a horse he can't handle, she wins it on tickets paid for by Rooney. Over the objections of both Rooney and her father, the horse is entered in the greatest race in England, the Grand National Sweepstakes. It is a story told with warmth and understanding. Fortunately, for Taylor's career, this proved to be a most important picture because it left an indelible impression in the minds of audiences of a sweet, young, virginal girl interested only in horses and wholesomeness, an impression that it took fifteen to twenty years to tarnish, by which time Taylor had reinvented herself as an icon of a different dimension. The road from *National Velvet* and *Lassie* to *Butterfield 8*, *Cat on a Hot Tin Roof*, and *Who's Afraid of Virginia Woolf?* is a gradual slope, softened by the memory of *Father of the Bride*, *Father's Little Dividend*, and *A Place in the Sun*, all movies that reinforced the innocent image well before the tarnished one emerged. And by the time it did, audiences were ready for a bit of threadbare velvet.

Awards: Academy Awards: Best Supporting Actress (Ann Revere), Editing (Robert J. Kern); Academy Award Nominations: Best Director, Cinematography, Art, Color Art Decoration.

Selected Bibliography

Miller, Frank. *Movies We Love: 100 Collectible Classics.* Atlanta, GA: Turner Publishing, 1996.

Rooney, Mickey. *I.E.: An Autobiography.* New York: Putnam, 1965.

Vermilye, Jerry, and Mark Ricci. *The Films of Elizabeth Taylor.* Secaucus, NJ: Citadel Press, 1976.

NEAL, PATRICIA. Actress. Born on January 20, 1926, in Packard, Kentucky. Educated at Northwestern University (drama). Neal's film career got an auspicious start. On the one hand, she was given a starring part opposite veteran actor Gary Cooper in her very first movie, *The Fountainhead*, based on Ayn Rand's controversial novel. On the other hand, her affair with Cooper created such a backlash that she ended up suffering a nervous breakdown, from which she never really recovered. In 1953 she married writer Roald Dahl and was away from the screen until 1957 when she appeared in Elia Kazan's *A Face in the Crowd*. Neal's career was interrupted again by a series of strokes in the mid-1960s, but her comeback appearance in *The Subject Was Roses* in 1968 earned her an Oscar nomination. In 1981 a TV movie recounting her strokes and her amazing recovery had Glenda Jackson playing the role of Patricia Neal. Since then she has continued to make occasional appearances in films. Neal is a fascinating actress to watch and to listen to. Her features are classic and her voice tinged with a slightly husky drawl. But from the start it was clear that she was in danger of becoming a parody of herself before she had a chance to stretch her talents. Fortunately, she managed to get some challenging roles before her health accelerated her decline.

Filmography: The Fountainhead, The Hasty Heart, It's a Great Feeling, John Loves Mary (1949); The Breaking Point, Bright Leaf, Three Secrets (1950); The Day the Earth Stood Still, Operation Pacific, Raton Pass, Weekend with Father (1951); Diplomatic Courier, Something for the Birds, Washington Story (1952); A Face in the Crowd (1957); Breakfast at Tiffany's (1961); Hud (1963); Psyche '59 (1964); In Harm's Way (1965); The Subject Was Roses (1968); The Night Digger (1971); Baxter, Happy Mother's Day—Love George/Run Stranger Run (1973); Widow's Nest (1977); The Passage (1979); Ghost Story (1981).

Honors: Academy Award, New York Film Critics Circle Award, National Board of Review Award, British Academy Award: Best Actress (*Hud*, 1963); British Academy Award: Best Actress/Foreign (*In Harm's Way*, 1965); Academy Award Nomination: Best Actress (*The Subject Was Roses*, 1968).

Selected Bibliography

Neal, Patricia, with Richard DeNeut. *As I Am: An Autobiography.* New York: Simon & Schuster, 1988.

NEGULESCO, JEAN. Director. Born on February 26, 1900, in Craiova, Rumania; died on July 18, 1993, in Marbella, Spain. Negulesco began his professional career in Paris in the 1920s as a painter and stage decorator. When he came to New York in 1927 to exhibit his works, he decided to remain. He entered films in the early 1930s as an assistant producer, then second-unit director and associate director. In addition to collaborating on several screenplays for some minor films, he also directed a number of two-reel shorts and other series. He began his career as a director of feature films in 1941 with *Singapore Woman* but was removed in midproduction. However, he retained sole screen credit as the film's director. Negulesco had better luck with his next feature, *The Mask of Dimitrios*, a quirky thriller with an outstanding performance by Peter Lorre. He went on to direct several tough, noirish, black-and-white melodramas for Warners, notably *Humoresque* with Joan Crawford, and he reached his peak with *Johnny Belinda*, an offbeat drama about the rape of a deaf-mute girl that earned an Oscar for Jane Wyman plus seven Oscar nominations, including Best Picture and Best Director. Negulesco then moved to 20th Century–Fox where he distinguished himself with such movies as *Road House* and *Three Came Home*, the latter an unusually moving World War II drama about life in a Japanese prison camp for women, starring Claudette Colbert. Negulesco skillfully made the transition from black and white to color and CinemaScope in the 1950s with such lavish entertainments as *How to Marry a Millionaire* and *Three Coins in the Fountain*. Critics sneered at these films, but the public loved them, and they continue to be favorites on movie channels.

Filmography: Singapore Woman (1941); The Mask of Dimitrios, The Conspirators (1944); Three Strangers, Nobody Lives Forever, Humoresque (1946); Deep Valley (1947); Johnny Belinda, Road House (1948); Brittania Mews/The Forbidden Street (1949); Under My Skin, Three Came Home, The Mudlark (1950); Take Care of My Little Girl (1951); Phone Call from a Stranger, Lydia Bailey, Lure of the Wilderness, O. Henry's Full House [The "Last Leaf" episode] (1952); Titanic, How to Marry a Millionaire, Scandal at Scourie (1953); Three Coins in the Fountain, Woman's World (1954); Daddy Long Legs, The Rains of Ranchipur (1955); Boy on a Dolphin (1957); The Gift of Love, A Certain Smile (1958); Count Your Blessings, The Best of Everything (1959); Jessica (1962); The Pleasure Seekers (1964); The Heroes/The Invincible Sex (1969); Hello-Goodbye (1970).

Honors: Academy Award Nomination: Director (*Johnny Belinda*, 1948); Nine-day New York retrospective coinciding with his eighty-fourth birthday at which he was hailed "The Prince of Melodrama" (1984).

Selected Bibliography

Negulesco, Jean. *Things I Did and Things I Think I Did*. New York: Linden Press/Simon & Schuster, 1984.

Sennett, Ted. *Great Movie Directors*. New York: Harry N. Abrams, 1986.

NIGHT AT THE OPERA, A (1935), comedy. Directed by Sam Wood; with Groucho Marx, Chico Marx, Harpo Marx, Kitty Carlisle, Allan Jones, Walter

Woolf King, Margaret Dumont, and Sigfried Rumann; screenplay by George S. Kaufman and Morrie Ryskind.

Critics are divided on whether or not this is the Marx Brothers' best film, but it certainly was their most popular and the one that has more memorable moments in it (and some eminently forgettable ones). It is a rather serious grand opera satire in which the comics conspire to get a pair of Italian singers a break in the United States. Its virtues outweigh its vices—its virtues being the inimitable Marx Brothers at the top of their form, its vices being the romantic leads who become more unbearable as time goes by. Some think, though, that the syrupy musical interludes only make the salty comedy look that much better.

Selected Bibliography

Gehring, Wes D. *The Marx Brothers: A Bio-Bibliography*. Westport, CT: Greenwood Press, 1987.

Miller, Frank. *Movies We Love: 100 Collectible Classics*. Atlanta, GA: Turner Publishing, 1996.

NIGHTMARE ALLEY (1947), melodrama. Directed by Edmund Goulding; with Tyrone Power, Joan Blondell, Coleen Gray, Helen Walker, Taylor Holmes, Mike Mazurki, Ian Keith, and Julia Dean; screenplay by Jules Furthman.

Nightmare Alley is the morbid but fascinating story of a carnival heel (Power) entangled with a mind reader (Blondell) in a blackmail scam involving assorted weirdos in this highly original melodrama. It is a harsh, brutal story that deals with the darkest side of carnival life. Power is a reform school graduate who works his way up through the ranks of sleazy carnival life, using women to further his advancement and stepping on them as he climbs. The most vivid of these is Joan Blondell, the girl he manipulates in order to extract from her the secrets of the mind-reading act. Some critics feel that the film tries too hard to be respectable, tries to downplay its tawdriness a little too much. However, even they agree that this is still a harsh, moody, and quite extraordinary melodrama. Power turns in an excellent performance as the fairground huckster who becomes famous as a fake spiritualist, only to slip back into the notoriety of a boozed-up, live-chicken-eating geek. It is unlike Hollywood to undertake such an oddball film and more unusual to feature matinee idol Power as the star of this thoroughly unpleasant drama. But it worked, and the movie remains interesting and well done, not least because Power proves that he was more than just a pretty face. Power, who persuaded 20th Century–Fox to let him play the double-crossing charlata.., puts his black-Irish good looks to marvelously ambivalent effect. Playing against his star-image type, he unsettles viewers who hope at any moment to see Mr. Good Guy emerge from within this ugly facade. With this movie Power joined the ranks of actors like Ray Milland and Fred MacMurray who have so stunningly played against type.

Selected Bibliography

Belafonte, Dennis, with Alvin H. Marill. *The Films of Tyrone Power*. Secaucus, NJ: Citadel Press, 1979.

Finler, Joel W. *The Movie Directors Story*. London: Octopus Books, 1985.

NIGHT OF THE HUNTER, THE (1955), melodrama. Directed by Charles Laughton; with Robert Mitchum, Shelley Winters, Lillian Gish, Evelyn Barden, Peter Graves, James Gleason, Billy Chapin, and Sally Jane Bruce; screenplay by James Agee.

The Night of the Hunter is one of the most frightening movies ever made, an atmospheric allegory of innocence, evil, and hypocrisy, with psychotic religious fanatic Mitchum chasing homeless children for money stolen by their father. This was Charles Laughton's first and only foray into directing, and although critics are mixed in their responses, history has come down on the side of this bold study of good versus evil, and audiences have turned it into a cult film. Mitchum is marvelously sinister, making much of his celebrated stony expression to suggest a mask hiding real villainy. And Lillian Gish, legendary film actress from the silent days, is excellent as the matron who takes in the kids Mitchum is stalking. This offbeat film, with Mitchum as the psychopathic preacher with ''Love'' and ''Hate'' tattooed on his knuckles, unfolds within a stunning series of images, from idyllic riverside exteriors to menacing, expressionistic interiors. The style of this unique film reaches its pitch in the extraordinary moonlight flight of the two children as they glide silently downriver, watched over by animals seen in huge close-up. Most critics praise the work as a genuinely sinister work, singling out for special notice its startling sound effects, camera angles, and shadowy lighting. Laughton himself called the film a nightmarish sort of Mother Goose tale and felt that Mitchum was the only one who could really project the homicidal religious crackpot. The sadistic, vicious-minded character the actor so chillingly projected was to haunt Mitchum later, and according to some reports, he was reluctant to discuss the part for many years afterward.

Selected Bibliography

Higham, Charles. *Charles Laughton: An Intimate Biography*. Garden City, NY: Doubleday, 1976.

Roberts, J. W. *Robert Mitchum: A Bio-Bibliography*. Westport, CT: Greenwood Press, 1992.

Winters, Shelley. *Shelley: Also Known as Shirley*. New York: Ballantine, 1980.

NINOTCHKA (1939), comedy. Directed by Ernst Lubitsch; with Greta Garbo, Melvyn Douglas, Ina Claire, Bela Lugosi, Sig Ruman, Felix Bressart, Alexander Granach, and Richard Carle; screenplay by Billy Wilder, Charles Brackett, and Walter Reisch.

''Garbo laughs!'' howled the blurb for this Garbo film, the first time since 1934 that she had been seen in a movie that takes place in the twentieth century and the first time ever that her material was predominantly comic. Although her character still had an icy aura, at least at the outset, she brings her incredible sensual abandon to the role of a glum, scientifically trained Bolshevik envoy who succumbs to Parisian freedom and to the twin temptations of Melvyn Douglas and champagne. The film includes a historic encounter, when the great instinctual artist of the screen meets the great stylist and technician of the stage— Ina Claire, as a Russian grand duchess. The fur flies exquisitely. Directed by Ernst Lubitsch, this light, satirical comedy has the nonchalance and the sophistication that was his trademark. Garbo, playing a Russian comrade staying in Paris on government business, could have had no better director than the inimitable Lubitsch, who presents a mirthful, delightful farce that pokes fun at the Soviets and Stalin-dominated Russia. Garbo is magnificent and so is the film. Looking back upon this film, contemporary critics do not find it quite the delight it was cracked up to be. However, they find it consistently amusing and admire the way Garbo throws herself into the part. *Ninotchka* was the basis for the musical and the film *Silk Stockings* and for *The Iron Petticoat* in which Katharine Hepburn in the starring role affects a Russian accent that is more Boston Brahmin with a Slavic spin.

Awards: Academy Award Nominations: Best Actress (Garbo), Picture, Original Story, Screenplay.

Selected Bibliography

Conway, Michael, Dion McGregor, and Mark Ricci. *The Films of Greta Garbo*. New York: Bonanza Books, 1963.
Poague, Leland A. *The Cinema of Ernst Lubitsch*. South Brunswick, NJ: A. S. Barnes, 1978.
Sennett, Ted. *Hollywood's Golden Year, 1939*. New York: St. Martin's Press, 1989.

NIVEN, DAVID. Actor. Born James David Graham Niven on March 1, 1909, in Kirriemuir, Scotland; died on July 29, 1983. Niven was a durable star of Hollywood and British films, well known for his urbane wit and dapper charm. He attended the Sandhurst military school and served with the Highland Light Infantry in Malta before becoming a drifter, working at such odd jobs as lumberman, laundry messenger, news reporter, gunnery instructor to Cuban revolutionists, representative of a London wine firm to the United States, bartender, and by his own account, a promoter and petty criminal. His travels finally took him to Los Angeles, where he entered films as an extra in 1934, soon becoming a reliable leading man and second lead. At the outbreak of World War II he was among the first Hollywood stars to join the war effort, entering the British army as a lieutenant with the commandos. He was discharged as a colonel. Although he was typically seen in urbane comedy roles, he proved himself on several occasions to be an accomplished dramatic actor. In the 1950s and 1960s he enjoyed a very successful career in television, as both producer and actor. Niven wrote two novels, *Round and Rugged Rocks* (in the United States, *Once*

Over Lightly) and *Go Slowly, Come Back Quickly*, and two witty autobiographical volumes, *The Moon Is a Balloon* and *Bring on the Empty Horses*, both
republished in 1985 under one cover, entitled *Niven*.

Filmography: Mutiny on the Bounty [extra], Barbary Coast, Without Regret, A Feather
in Her Hat, Splendor (1935); Rose Marie, Palm Springs, Thank You Jeeves, Dodsworth,
The Charge of the Light Brigade, Beloved Enemy (1936); We Have Our Moments, The
Prisoner of Zenda, Dinner at the Ritz (1937); Bluebeard's Eighth Wife, Four Men and
a Prayer, Three Blind Mice, Dawn Patrol (1938); Wuthering Heights, Bachelor Mother,
The Real Glory, Eternally Yours (1939); Raffles (1940); The First of the Few/Spitfire
(1942); The Way Ahead (1944); A Matter of Life and Death/Stairway to Heaven, Mag-
nificent Doll (1946); The Perfect Marriage, The Other Love, The Bishop's Wife (1947);
Bonnie Prince Charlie, Enchantment (1948); A Kiss in the Dark (1949); The Elusive
Pimpernel/The Fighting Pimpernel, A Kiss for Corliss, The Toast of New Orleans (1950);
Soldiers Three, Happy Go Lovely, Appointment with Venus/Island Rescue (1951); The
Lady Says No (1952); The Moon Is Blue (1953); The Love Lottery, Happy Ever After/
Tonight's the Night (1954); Carrington V.C./Court Martial, The King's Thief (1955);
The Birds and the Bees, Around the World in 80 Days (1956); Oh Men! Oh Women!,
The Little Hut, My Man Godfrey, The Silken Affair (1957); Bonjour Tristesse, Separate
Tables (1958); Ask Any Girl, Happy Anniversary (1959); Please Don't Eat the Daisies
(1960); The Guns of Navarone, The Best of Enemies (1961); The Road to Hong Kong,
Guns of Darkness, Conquered City (1962); 55 Days at Peking (1963); The Pink Panther,
Bedtime Story (1964); Lady L (1965); Where the Spies Are (1966); Casino Royale, Eye
of the Devil (1967); Prudence and the Pill, The Impossible Years (1968); The Extraor-
dinary Seaman, Before Winter Comes, The Brain (1969); The Statue (1971); King Queen
Knave (1972); Old Dracula (1974); Paper Tiger (1975); No Deposit—No Return, Murder
by Death (1976); Candleshoe, Death on the Nile (1978); Escape to Athena, A Nightingale
Sang in Berkeley Square (1979); Rough Cut, The Sea Wolves (1980); The Trail of the
Pink Panther, Better Late Than Never (1982); Curse of the Pink Panther (1983).

Honors: Golden Globe Award: Best Actor Comedy/Musical (*The Moon Is Blue*, 1953);
Academy Award, New York Film Critics Circle Award, Golden Globe Award: Best Actor
(*Separate Tables*, 1958).

Selected Bibliography

Fowler, Karin J. *David Niven: A Bio-Bibliography*. Westport, CT: Greenwood Press,
    1995.
Garrett, Gerard. *The Films of David Niven*. Secaucus, NJ: Citadel Press, 1976.
Hutchinson, Tom. *Niven's Hollywood*. London: Macmillan, 1984.

NORTH BY NORTHWEST (1959), mystery. Directed by Alfred Hitchcock; with
Cary Grant, Eva Marie Saint, James Mason, Leo G. Carroll, Martin Landau,
Jessie Royce Landis, Philip Ober, Adam Williams, Josephine Hutchinson, and
Edward Platt; screenplay by Ernest Lehman.

North by Northwest is a prime example of why Hitchcock's reputation for
poking around in the dark recesses of human nature while maintaining a dia-
bolically ironic sunniness on the surface continues to grow. When Hitchcock
once tried to calm a tense Ingrid Bergman by reminding her, "It's only a movie,

Ingrid,'' he meant it—at least in the sense that movies must first be ''movies,'' dazzling sequences of visual sleight of hand that carry audiences along without giving them time to realize that what they are thoroughly enjoying may often be something that would repulse them in real life. While he is revealing the dark side of human nature with one hand, he is patting us on the head reassuringly with the other. In this film, he mixes suspense, intrigue, comedy, and humor into a witch's brew that leaves audiences both disarmed and disturbed. This film treads a bizarre tightrope between sex and repression, nightmarish thriller and sophisticated. It is a film that invites readings on many different levels and from many different angles. For example, some see it as a paranoid Freudian nightmare in which mothers, lovers, gays, and cops all conspire against a man. Others see it as a parable on modern America in which final escape must be made down the treacherous face of Mount Rushmore. Perhaps it is the improbable classic some critics have called it, but one could say that about most, if not all, classics including *Moby Dick*, *The Nutcracker*, *Les Miserables*, and *It's a Wonderful Life*. In this film, Hitchcock is working within the convention that the star cannot possibly come to harm. Once this dawns on you, you begin to appreciate Hitchcock's tongue-in-cheek approach, for the presence of a star sends signals no script alone can achieve. Hitchcock liked working with Cary Grant because Grant's mere presence could provide the viewer with the mix of unease and reassurance so necessary to the story. The year after *North by Northwest* was released, Hitchcock would pull a dirty trick in *Psycho* and kill off the leading lady in the second reel, an event that was especially shocking because it violated the trust he had heretofore established between himself and the viewer. *North by Northwest* is one of Hitchcock's trickiest films, ranking along with *Vertigo* and *Rear Window* in its disturbing blend of the macabre, the salacious, and the darkly humorous all done with style and class.

Awards: Academy Award Nominations: Best Story and Screenplay, Art Direction, Film Editing.

Selected Bibliography

Arginteanu, Judy. *The Movies of Alfred Hitchcock*. Minneapolis: Lerner, 1994.
Deschner, Donald. *The Complete Films of Cary Grant*. Secaucus, NJ: Citadel Press, 1991.
Miller, Frank. *Movies We Love: 100 Collectible Classics*. Atlanta, GA: Turner Publishing, 1996.

NOTHING SACRED (1937), comedy. Directed by William Wellman; with Carole Lombard, Fredric March, Walter Connolly, Charles Winninger, Sig Rumann, and Frank Fay; screenplay by Ben Hecht.

Although this comedy teeters sometimes uneasily between satire and screwball comedy, it remains a triumph of caustic film comedy that continues to cheer the hearts of those for whom it provides a welcome antidote to ''Capra-corn'' in its view of small towns as hellholes to be ''got out of'' rather than the last refuge of solid middle-class values. This film features a fine performance by

Lombard, by then christened "the Duse of daffy comedy," as a small town girl, supposedly dying of radium poisoning, who takes advantage of a publicity stunt when a newspaper brings her to New York for one last fling. It has generally been perceived as one of Hollywood's most bitter and hilarious satires, full of crazy comedy elements and superb wisecracks. Some have even called it the pinnacle of screen comedy. While its comedy has admittedly lost some of its edge, its dark view of the newspaper world has not. Because it does hold up a mirror, albeit a distorted one, to a very real world of hoopla and cheap sensationalism, it entertains at a level above the commonplace kind of comedy. In 1953 it was made into the stage musical *Hazel Flagg* with music by Jule Styne. This in turn became the Dean Martin and Jerry Lewis comedy *Living It Up* (with Lewis in the Lombard role!).

Selected Bibliography

Levy, Emanuel. *Small-Town America in Film: The Decline and Fall of Community*. New York: Continuum, 1991.

McCaffrey, Donald W. *The Golden Age of Sound Comedy: Comic Films and Comedians of the 30s*. South Brunswick, NJ: A. S. Barnes, 1973.

Ott, Frederick W. *The Films of Carole Lombard*. Secaucus, NJ: Citadel Press, 1972.

NOTORIOUS (1946), thriller. Directed by Alfred Hitchcock; with Cary Grant, Ingrid Bergman, Claude Rains, Louis Calhern, Reinhold Schunzel, and Moroni Olsen; screenplay by Ben Hecht.

This brilliant film combines romance and suspense, mystery and action, in another Hitchcock brew that audiences find surprising and disturbing but ultimately satisfying. Grant and Bergman bring their "movie star" luminosity to this dark thriller with Bergman as the daughter of a Nazi, a shady lady who trades secrets and all sorts of things with American agent Cary Grant. The suspense is terrific. Part of Hitchcock's magic formula is to create the illusion that all you see is surface when actually what you "feel" is the tension, not only the sexual tension between the stars but the international tension present in any tale of espionage. Passionate love scenes and nerve-racking suspense are the twin poles between which Hitchcock routinely stretches his peculiar morality tales. Critics have called it both great trash and great fun, including it among Hitchcock's finest films of the 1940s. Certainly it invites multiple interpretations in the manner of so much of Hitchcock's best work. In this case, what is intriguing is the *sense* that beneath its surface, sizzling with passion and suspense, lies a sickening tangle of self-sacrifice, exploitation, suspicion, and emotional dependence. Grant, oddly enough, is the least sympathetic character, a side he could get away with without losing audience sympathy. In its misanthropic portrait of manipulation, this deceptive "wartime romance" anticipates *Vertigo*.

Awards: Academy Award Nominations: Best Supporting Actor (Rains), Original Screenplay.

Selected Bibliography

Arginteanu, Judy. *The Movies of Alfred Hitchcock*. Minneapolis, MN: Lerner, 1994.

Deschner, Donald. *The Complete Films of Cary Grant*. Secaucus, NJ: Citadel Press, 1991.

Quirk, Lawrence J. *The Complete Films of Ingrid Bergman*. New York: Carol Communications, 1989.

NOVAK, KIM. Born Marilyn Pauline Novak on February 13, 1933, in Chicago. Kim Novak has never received the recognition she deserves, most likely because she got lost among the sex symbols that Hollywood was so intent on promoting in the 1950s and early 1960s. It is true that she had all the prerequisites for a sex symbol: a certain icy aloofness (à la Grace Kelly) plus an earthy sensuality (à la Jayne Mansfield) and a sense of humor (à la Marilyn Monroe), but perhaps what she lacked was the faux innocence necessary then to get away with it. As it was, she did not fit into any easy category and thus found herself in a variety of roles that never succeeded in establishing her at the top. She got her start playing a bit part in a Jane Russell vehicle, *The French Line*, in 1954. That same year, she was signed by Columbia and groomed to stardom by studio chief Harry Cohn as a possible replacement for Rita Hayworth, who was becoming increasingly uncooperative. Although she was uncomfortable in front of the camera, Novak quickly developed into a popular star, again mostly because she was reminiscent of other blond sexpots of the time. By 1956 she was voted America's number-one box office attraction, but her popularity faded by the early 1960s despite her increasing dramatic skills, particularly because the critics refused to take her seriously. During her heyday as a star, Novak's name appeared frequently in the newspapers, romantically linked to such celebrities as Frank Sinatra, Cary Grant, and Aly Khan. She made the headlines in 1958 when an expensive sports car given to her by the playboy son of Dominican dictator Rafael Trujillo became a subject of discussion in the U.S. Congress. She was briefly (1965–1966) married to English actor Richard Johnson, her co-star in *The Amorous Adventures of Moll Flanders*. In 1976 she married a veterinarian and a few years later retired from the screen to devote herself to breeding horses and raising llamas in Oregon and Carmel, California. She returned to film acting in the late 1980s, in the process of a sobering attempt to sum up her career for an autobiography. If ever there was a true victim of the sexpot hysteria of the 1950s it was Kim Novak. Grace Kelly got out famously, Marilyn infamously, Jayne Mansfield ghoulishly. Others folded their bosoms and stole away. But Kim Novak, who at another time could have reigned supreme, was discarded the moment the granny look took over and pretty faces were dumped. Watch her in *Picnic* and in *Vertigo* to see the makings of an actress another age might have appreciated.

Filmography: The French Line [bit], Pushover, Phffft (1954); Son of Sinbad [bit], Five against the House, The Man with the Golden Arm (1955); Picnic, The Eddy Duchin Story (1956); Jeanne Eagels, Pal Joey (1957); Vertigo, Bell Book and Candle (1958); Middle of the Night (1959); Strangers When We Meet, Pepe (1960); Boys' Night Out,

The Notorious Landlady (1962); Of Human Bondage, Kiss Me Stupid (1964); The Amorous Adventures of Moll Flanders (1965); The Legend of Lylah Clare (1968); The Great Bank Robbery (1969); Tales That Witness Madness (1973); The White Buffalo (1977); Just a Gigolo (1979); The Mirror Crack'd (1980); Es hat mir sehr gefreut (1987); The Children (1990); Libestraum (1991).

Honors: Golden Globe Award: Most Promising Newcomer (1954); *Photoplay* Gold Medal Award: Most Popular Female Star (1956).

Selected Bibliography

Brown, Peter. *Kim Novak: Reluctant Goddess*. New York: St. Martin's Press, 1986.
Kleno, Larry. *Kim Novak on Camera*. San Diego: A. S. Barnes, 1980.

NOW, VOYAGER (1942), melodrama. Directed by Irving Rapper; with Bette Davis, Paul Henreid, Claude Rains, Gladys Cooper, Bonita Granville, John Loder, Ilka Chase, Lee Patrick, Mary Wickes, and Janis Wilson; screenplay by Casey Robinson.

This movie offered Bette Davis every opportunity to display her dramatic range, and she took full advantage of the situation. First, she's the ugly duckling who takes off her glasses and is transformed into a glamorous woman. Second, she has a domineering mother (in a marvelous turn by Gladys Cooper) who has driven her into well nigh terminal neurosis. Fortunately, with the help of a kindly psychiatrist (Claude Rains), she conquers her fears and finds the love of her life. Unfortunately, that love (Paul Henreid, in a polished, understated performance) is already married and, what's worse, has an emotionally disturbed daughter. At this point Davis becomes the soap-opera heroine par excellence when she befriends the girl and, after a brief bittersweet shipboard romance with Henreid, retreats into the shadows, long-suffering but magnificently noble. The Max Steiner score, justifiably admired, adds a lush background to the emotional turmoil on screen. *Now, Voyager* has been called a "crummy classic," a "campy tearjerker variation on the Cinderella story," "high kitsch," "a glorification of female sacrifice," a "schlock classic," but what matters is less the story than the fact that it is Bette Davis we're watching. She's been called a living acting school because her performances, brilliant as they are, always call attention to themselves. That is why she was so easy to impersonate and why she ended up impersonating herself. This made her the quintessential movie actress, a point too many aspiring actors ignore at their peril. *Now, Voyager* is a Movie, in every sense of the word.

Awards: Academy Award: Best Score for a Dramatic Picture (Max Steiner); Academy Award Nominations: Best Actress (Davis); Supporting Actress (Cooper).

Selected Bibliography

Henreid, Paul, with Julius Fast. *Ladies' Man: An Autobiography*. New York: St. Martin's Press, 1984.
Ringgold, Gene. *Bette Davis: Her Films and Career*. Secaucus, NJ: Citadel Press, 1985.
Thomas, Tony. *The Films of the Forties*. Secaucus, NJ: Citadel Press, 1975.

O

O'CONNOR, DONALD. Actor/dancer. Born on August 28, 1925, in Chicago. The son of circus performers turned vaudevillians, O'Connor joined the family act as an infant and was eleven years old when he made his film debut performing a specialty routine with two of his brothers in *Melody for Two* in 1937. He was then signed by Paramount and played adolescent roles in several films, including Huckleberry Finn in *Tom Sawyer—Detective* and Beau as a child [who grew up to be Gary Cooper!] in *Beau Geste*. O'Connor paid his dues playing the juvenile lead in several minor Universal musicals in the 1940s (usually opposite Peggy Ryan but also Gloria Jean and Ann Blyth) before sharing top billing with Gene Kelly and Debbie Reynolds in *Singin' in the Rain* in 1952. After that, his career took a different—many would say a downward—turn when he appeared in a series of pictures featuring Francis, the Talking Mule. During the 1950s he also co-starred in several major musical films (*Call Me Madame* with Ethel Merman; *There's No Business Like Show Business*, also with Ethel Merman but more importantly with Marilyn Monroe as O'Connor's love interest), and in 1953, he won an Emmy for *The Colgate Comedy Hour*, which he hosted on a rotating basis for three years. In 1954–1955 he starred in *The Donald O'Connor Texaco Show*. In 1957 he portrayed screen comedian Buster Keaton in the film biography *The Buster Keaton Story*. Thereafter, he appeared in only a few films, concentrating instead on composing music for the concert hall. In 1956 he conducted the Los Angeles Philharmonic in the premier performance of his first symphony, *Reflections d'un Comique*. An album of his music was later recorded in Europe by the Brussels Symphony Orchestra. O'Connor has remained busy making cameo appearances in films into the 1990s. Also in the 1990s he released tap dancing/exercise videos.

Filmography: Melody for Two (1937); Men with Wings, Sing You Sinners, Sons of the Legion, Tom Sawyer—Detective (1938); Beau Geste, Death of a Champion, Million Dollar Legs, Night Work, On Your Toes, Unmarried (1939); Give Out, Sisters, Private Buckaroo, When Johnny Comes Marching Home (1942); It Comes Up Love, Mister Big, Top Man (1943); Bowery to Broadway, Chip Off the Old Block, Follow the Boys, Get Hep to Love, The Merry Monahans, This Is the Life (1944); Patrick the Great (1945); Something in the Wind (1947); Are You with It?, Feudin' Fussin' and a-Fightin' (1948); Francis, Yes Sir That's My Baby (1949); Curtain Call at Cactus Creek, The Milkman (1950); Double Crossbones, Francis Goes to the Races (1951); Francis Goes to West Point, Singin' in the Rain (1952); Call Me Madam, Francis Covers the Big Town, I Love Melvin, Walking My Baby Back Home (1953); Francis Joins the Wacs, There's No Business Like Show Business (1954); Francis in the Navy (1955); Anything Goes (1956); The Buster Keaton Story (1957); Cry for Happy, The Wonders of Aladdin (1961); That Funny Feeling (1965); That's Entertainment (1974); The Big Fix (1978); Ragtime (1981); Pandemonium (1982); A Time to Remember (1990); Toys (1992); That's Entertainment III (1994).

Honors: Golden Globe Award: Best Actor Comedy/Musical (*Singin' in the Rain*, 1952).

Selected Bibliography

Feuer, Jane. *The Hollywood Musical*. Bloomington: Indiana University Press, 1982.

OF MICE AND MEN (1939), drama. Directed by Lewis Milestone; with Lon Chaney, Jr., Burgess Meredith, Betty Field, Charles Bickford, Bob Steele, and Noah Beery, Jr.; screenplay by Eugene Solow.

"The picture Hollywood said could never be made!" Says who? Indeed, Hollywood has filmed *Of Mice and Men* three times, and it continues to maintain its hold on audiences, especially when it is done as skillfully as in this 1939 version. Although it was released in 1940, it belongs with those dozen or more classic films that mark 1939 as the golden year of Hollywood cinema. It is a simple story, and some attribute its success to this simplicity. It can be looked at from various interesting angles, however, each contributing something toward explaining its inexplicable appeal. In 1940 it appealed to the same audiences who were attracted to *The Grapes of Wrath*, another unlikely box office success with the same tragic, depression-era grittiness. With the depression rapidly receding and the world at war, audiences could look back at an era too painful to contemplate at the time. This is another Steinbeck morality tale, and for most of his career, admirers were charmed by his naive social philosophy. And then there is the strange bonding between two unlike friends, the small, bedraggled, intelligent George and the simpleminded hulk Lennie. It heralded such odd couples as Rizzo (Dustin Hoffman) and Starbuck (Jon Voigt) in *Midnight Cowboy*, *Butch Cassidy and the Sundance Kid*, the autistic Dustin Hoffman and the brash Tom Cruise of *Rainman*, not to mention assorted other buddy movies. Chaney gives the best performance of his career as feebleminded Lennie who, with migrant-worker Meredith, tries to live peacefully on a ranch. Under the skillful direction of Lewis Milestone, the picture retains all of the forceful and poignant drama of John Steinbeck's original play and novel. Betty Field, a brilliant, underrated actress, is excellent as the bored young farmer's wife who provokes tragedy by playing the sex kitten. Burgess Meredith, a real pro, shines as Lennie's friend and keeper who is forced to turn executioner rather than let society's notions of justice loose on his charge. This film also made a dubious contribution to the style of filmmaking. The opening scene, of George and Lennie fleeing from a posse, is shown before the main title credits appear—an innovation for 1939 that has become commonplace in filmmaking ever since, even when there seems to be no good reason for it.

Awards: Academy Award Nominations: Best Picture, Original Score, Sound.

Selected Bibliography

Dooley, Roger. *From Scarface to Scarlett: American Films in the 1930s*. New York: Harcourt Brace Jovanovich, 1981.
Thomas, Tony. *The Films of the Forties*. Secaucus, NJ: Citadel Press, 1975.

O'HARA, MAUREEN. Actress. Born Maureen Fitzsimons on August 17, 1920, in Millwall, near Dublin, Ireland. Educated at the Abbey School in Dublin. O'Hara performed on radio before making her film debut in London in 1938. The following year she signed a contract with the partnership of Erich Pommer and Charles Laughton and left with Laughton for Hollywood, where she first played the role of Esmeralda in *The Hunchback of Notre Dame*. O'Hara was at her liveliest and most appealing in a number of John Ford films, notably *How Green Was My Valley* and *The Quiet Man* in which she played John Wayne's Irish wife and sparring partner. O'Hara photographed particularly well in color and was much in demand for films where she could be displayed to best advantage. She virtually retired from films after 1971's *Big Jake* when she moved with her third husband, aviation pioneer Charles F. Blair, to St. Croix and helped him run his commuter airline until his death, after which O'Hara took full control of the company's operations. O'Hara returned to the screen to play the domineering mother of John Candy in the 1991 comedy *Only the Lonely*.

Filmography: The Hunchback of Notre Dame, Jamaica Inn (1939); A Bill of Divorcement, Dance Girl Dance (1940); How Green Was My Valley, They Met in Argentina (1941); The Black Swan, Ten Gentlemen from West Point, To the Shores of Tripoli (1942); The Fallen Sparrow, The Immortal Sergeant, This Land Is Mine (1943); Buffalo Bill (1944); The Spanish Main (1945); Do You Love Me?, Sentimental Journey (1946); The Foxes of Harrow, The Homestretch, Miracle on 34th Street, Sinbad the Sailor (1947); Sitting Pretty (1948); Baghdad, Father Was a Fullback, The Forbidden Street, A Woman's Secret (1949); Comanche Territory, Rio Grande, Tripoli (1950); Flame of Araby (1951); Against All Flags, At Sword's Point, Kangaroo, The Quiet Man, The Redhead from Wyoming (1952); War Arrow (1953); Lady Godiva, The Long Gray Line, The Magnificent Matador (1955); Everything But the Truth, Lisbon (1956); The Wings of Eagles (1957); Malaga, Our Man in Havana (1960); The Deadly Companions, The Parent Trap (1961); Mr. Hobbs Takes a Vacation (1962); McClintock!, Spencer's Moun-

tain (1963); The Battle of the Villa Fiorita (1965); The Rare Breed (1966); How Do I
Love Thee? (1971); Big Jake (1971); Only the Lonely (1991).

ON THE TOWN (1949), musical. Directed by Gene Kelly and Stanley Donen;
with Gene Kelly, Frank Sinatra, Vera-Ellen, Betty Garrett, Ann Miller, Jules
Munshin, Alice Pearce, and Florence Bates; screenplay by Adolph Green and
Betty Comden.

This energetic Betty Comden–Adolph Green–Leonard Bernstein musical (inspired by Jerome Robbins's ballet *Fancy Free*) is about three sailors on leave
for one day in New York City. This was Kelly and Donen's first full directing
assignment, and they made screen history by actually shooting on location, not
an easy thing where musicals are involved. It was a wise gamble, though, for
this Cook's tour of New York is itself so colorful and exciting that it helps a
rather silly story and some exaggerated production numbers seem spontaneous
and, therefore, forgivable. Critics remain divided about its merits, but that's
always been the case where musicals are concerned. Most admire the film's
momentum and high-voltage performers. However, many who think the film so
exuberant that it threatens at moments to bounce right off the screen also find
it just a bit unlikable. What they find unlikable, depending on the critic, are
such things as the serious ballet toward the end, which tends to dampen the
high spirits; the exaggerated love of New York, which seems forced; and production numbers, which are both hearty and uninspired. But the movie has so
many charming moments and is so much a part of its time that, taken in context,
it shines, if for no better reason than to see Sinatra at his swooner-crooner peak
and realize how tricky it was to film on location and risk letting him be mobbed
by bobby-soxers. It may be an overrated film, but it has its irresistible charms.

Selected Bibliography

Fordin, Hugh. *The World of Entertainment!: Hollywood's Greatest Musicals*. Garden
    City, NY: Doubleday, 1975.
Ringgold, Gene, and Clifford McCarty. *The Films of Frank Sinatra*. New York: Citadel
    Press, 1971.
Thomas, Tony. *Song and Dance Man: The Films of Gene Kelly*. Secaucus, NJ: Citadel
    Press, 1974.

ON THE WATERFRONT (1954), drama. Directed by Elia Kazan; with Marlon
Brando, Karl Malden, Lee J. Cobb, Rod Steiger, Pat Henning, Eva Marie Saint,
Leif Erickson, Tony Galento, John Hamilton, and Nehemiah Persoff; screenplay
by Budd Schulberg.

On the Waterfront is a gritty drama about corruption on the New York docks,
particularly when it comes to the power of the unions over the dock workers.
Marlon Brando gives a multifaceted performance as the uneducated dock hand
who is tough on the outside but a softie on the inside, and Lee J. Cobb plays
his part as a union boss with his own special brand of arrogant authority. Rod
Steiger has been praised for his role as Brando's brother even though he seems

at times to be mimicking Brando's trademark hesitant manner of speaking. This film has been unduly praised for its "realism," used here as a synonym for anything ugly, seedy, dingy, and grim. In this picture it has been applied to everything from the dialogue ("poetic in its simplicity") to the rundown tenements and clammy docks meant to evoke a pitiless, colorless, humorless world where surviving means losing one's illusions. The film is an emotionally draining experience from beginning to end, intensified by the gritty documentary approach of cinematographer Boris Kaufman. It is also an extremely violent film. Some critics find the impact of the film undermined both by the religious symbolism and by the embarrassing special pleading on behalf of informers, a jarring element that stems most likely from the fact that Kazan and Schulberg named names during the McCarthy witch-hunts. Critics who hated the film thought it mere pastiche of ingredients dredged up from the gangland pictures of the 1930s and given a contemporary spin. However, the consensus among viewers and critics at the time was that this film was an extraordinarily powerful, exciting, and imaginative work of cinematic art created by a gathering of truly gifted professionals.

Awards: Academy Awards: Best Picture, Director, Actor (Brando), Supporting Actress (Saint), Story & Screenplay, Cinematography (Boris Kaufman), Art Direction–Set Decoration (Richard Day), Editing (Gene Milford); Golden Globe Awards: Best Picture (Drama), Actor (Brando), Director, B&W Cinematography (Boris Kaufman); Directors Guild of America Award: Most Outstanding Directorial Achievement (Kazan); New York Film Critics Circle Awards: Best Picture, Actor (Brando), Director; National Board of Review: Best American Film; British Academy Award: Best Actor/Foreign (Brando); Venice Film Festival Award: Silver Prize Winner (Kazan); Italian Critics Prize: Best Picture.

Selected Bibliography

Carey, Gary. *Marlon Brando: The Only Contender*. New York: St. Martin's Press, 1985.
Michaels, Lloyd. *Elia Kazan: A Guide to References and Resources*. Boston: G. K. Hall, 1985.
Peary, Danny. *Alternate Oscars*. New York: Delta, 1993.

OUT OF THE PAST (1947), Mystery. Directed by Jacques Tourneur; with Robert Mitchum, Jane Greer, Kirk Douglas, Rhonda Fleming, Richard Webb, Steve Brodie, Virginia Huston, Paul Valentine, and Dickie Moore; screenplay by Geoffrey Homes (Daniel Mainwaring).

This superbly crafted B movie classic is the definitive example of film noir. Its seedy sets and sleazy characters live out their doomed lives in the shadowed frenzy of greed and treachery and murder. It might be trash, as some critics labeled it, but it's hard to take your eyes off it. It is as fraught with demonic irony and inexorable fate as a Greek tragedy and even more irresistible because watching commoners self-destruct is a lot closer to home than watching aristocrats. In the winter of 1946, RKO happened to have an ensemble of "B movie poets" whose efforts combined to give this film its polish and turn it into a cult classic. Sympathetic critics eschewed the "trash" label in favor of "superbly crafted pulp." Indeed, Daniel Mainwaring (*Invasion of the Body Snatchers*) was already well known for his brooding novels and screenplays, while the down-beat, tragic otherworldliness of director Jacques Tourneur is realized in the abstract lighting patterns of cinematographer Nick Musuraca (*The Spiral Staircase*). This film has been called one of the most bewildering and beautiful films ever made, and indeed, like *Laura*, the more closely you pay attention to the plot, the more confused you become. A film like this has to be absorbed, not analyzed. The cast rounds out the circle of B movie poets with Mitchum at his somnolent, sexy, droopy-eyed best and Jane Greer as the baby-faced, charming killer. The movie was remade in 1984 as *Against All Odds* with Greer in a maturer role. But it would be hard to surpass the original with its fascinating vision of a doomed and perversely corrupt world inhabited by obsessed people intensely destined to bring themselves and everyone around them down.

Selected Bibliography

Marill, Alvin H. *Robert Mitchum on the Screen*. South Brunswick, NJ: A. S. Barnes, 1978.

Shadoian, Jack. *Dreams and Dead Ends: The American Gangster/Crime Film*. Cambridge: MIT Press, 1977.

Silver, Alain, and Elizabeth Ward, eds. *Film Noir: An Encyclopedic Reference to the American Style*. Woodstock, NY: Overlook Press, 1979.

OX-BOW INCIDENT, THE (1943), western. Directed by William Wellman; with Henry Fonda, Dana Andrews, Mary Beth Hughes, Anthony Quinn, William Eythe, Henry Morgan, Jane Darwell, Frank Conroy, and Harry Davenport; screenplay by Lamar Trotti.

This film version of the novel by Walter Van Tilburg Clark could be called a western film noir because Fox's decision to cut costs by shooting it entirely on a studio set served, ironically enough, to darken the mood of claustrophobic tension. Indeed, its relationship to film noir can be detected not just in the dark shadowy photography but also in its gallery of the grotesque characters. Some critics take issue with the violence of the theme, arguing that too much time is spent on the single hanging incident of the novel at the expense of other action. Others find a political spin to the film, calling it a simplistically liberal western in which three drifters, lynched as rustlers on the flimsiest of evidence, are posthumously proven innocent by good-guy Fonda. Still other critics feel the film takes itself too seriously, tries too hard to be respectable, to make a statement. And, indeed, it does suffer from the sort of staginess and stuffiness that works brilliantly in a claustrophobic drama like *A Streetcar Named Desire* but works against a "concept" film, especially one that tries too hard not to be a western. This flaw is insinuated in the sort of praise that says of this powerful portrait of mob violence that it rises to the level of Greek tragedy. *The Ox-Bow Incident*, like its short-story source, is tied to its period, its style, and its context and, more so than many of its contemporaries, can only be truly appreciated when that is understood and accepted.

Awards: Academy Award Nomination: Best Picture.

Selected Bibliography

Hardy, Phil. *The Western: The Complete Film Sourcebook.* New York: William Morrow, 1983.
Thomas, Tony. *The Films of Henry Fonda.* Secaucus, NJ: Citadel Press, 1983.

P

PATHS OF GLORY (1957), war. Directed by Stanley Kubrick; with Kirk Douglas, Ralph Meeker, Adolphe Menjou, George Macready, Wayne Morris, Richard Anderson, Timothy Carey, Suzanne Christian, and Bert Freed; screenplay by Stanley Kubrick, Calder Willingham, and Jim Thompson.

During World War I, a French general orders his men on a futile mission; then, when it fails, he picks three soldiers to be tried and executed for cowardice. This shocking antiwar movie, based on fact, has become something of a cult favorite in spite of its unpleasant and highly controversial subject matter. Some critics rank it with Lewis Milestone's *All Quiet on the Western Front* (1930) and consider it one of the greatest antiwar films ever made, while others feel that it is less an antiwar movie than an attack on the military mind. The story is also about the class structure within the French army, from aristocratic generals at the top in their sunny, spacious châteaus to dogface soldiers in dark trenches. Caught in between is Kirk Douglas who sympathizes with the men but is powerless to do anything for them. It ultimately falls to Douglas to try the three hapless soldiers for cowardice. This is a film full of anger and restless energy, and although set in France (where it was banned for years), it is obviously intended to apply to all armies everywhere. If there is anything wrong with the film, it is that it suffers from an excess of moral superiority. In the end, there is no way out, not even for a sympathetic viewer. It is as if God came to earth and decided to spare no one, to forgive no one, to condemn all without mercy. In storytelling, there is an unwritten law that the audience must feel safe in the hands of the author. This film forgets that and thus becomes propaganda—but powerful propaganda. If its moral tone is a flaw, then it is a magnificent one, and the film deserves attention precisely because it tries nobly to accomplish the impossible.

Selected Bibliography

Guttmacher, Peter. *Legendary War Movies*. New York: MetroBooks, 1996.
Kagan, Norman. *The Cinema of Stanley Kubrick*. New York: Holt, Rinehart and Winston, 1972.
Peary, Danny. *Alternate Oscars*. New York: Delta, 1993.

PECK, GREGORY. Actor. Born Eldred Gregory Peck on April 15, 1916, in La Jolla, California. Educated at San Diego State College, the University of California at Berkeley (premed, English), and the Neighborhood Playhouse School of Dramatics. After seeing Vera Zorina in *I Married an Angel* in New York, Peck dropped premed and joined a small campus theater group. He returned to New York City in 1939 where he won a scholarship to the prestigious Neighborhood Playhouse School of Dramatics. Soon he was appearing in a number of plays that, while not very successful, nevertheless brought Peck good reviews and attracted the attention of Hollywood. During the war, there was a shortage of leading men, and Peck, exempted from military service because of a spinal injury, was able to help fill the gap. He was so much in demand that at the outset of his career he was under contract to four studios: RKO, 20th Century–Fox, Selznick Productions, and MGM. It was Peck's second film, *The Keys of the Kingdom*, that made him a star. In it he established his reputation as a man of quiet dignity and authority, a persona he exhibited thereafter in such films as *The Yearling*, *Gentleman's Agreement*, and especially, *To Kill a Mockingbird*. But there was also a dark side to Peck's persona, that of a man deeply troubled by demons that threatened to push him to the brink of madness, as in *Spellbound*, *Duel in the Sun*, and *Twelve O'Clock High*. After his award-winning performance in *To Kill a Mockingbird*, Peck made a number of forgettable potboilers including the embarrassment *The Boys from Brazil*. As his film career faded, Peck turned his efforts to philanthropic efforts in support of arts organizations. He was one of the founders of the American Film Institute, served as three-term president of the Academy of Motion Picture Arts and Sciences, and was a member of the National Council of Arts. Actor and philanthropist merged in the 1982 television production of *The Blue and the Grey*, with Peck playing Abraham Lincoln.

Filmography: Days of Glory, The Keys of the Kingdom (1944); Spellbound, The Valley of Decision (1945); Duel in the Sun, The Yearling (1946); Gentleman's Agreement, The Macomber Affair (1947); The Paradine Case, Yellow Sky (1948); The Great Sinner, Twelve O'Clock High (1949); The Gunfighter (1950); Captain Horatio Hornblower, David and Bathsheba, Only the Valiant (1951); The Snows of Kilimanjaro, The World in His Arms (1952); Roman Holiday (1953); Man with a Million/The Million Pound Note, Night People, The Purple Plain (1954); The Man in the Gray Flannel Suit, Moby Dick (1956); Designing Woman (1957); The Big Country [also co-prod.], The Bravados (1958); Beloved Infidel, On the Beach, Pork Chop Hill [also exec. prod.] (1959); The Guns of Navarone (1961); Cape Fear, How the West Was Won, To Kill a Mockingbird (1962); Captain Newman, M.D. (1963); Behold a Pale Horse (1964); Mirage (1965);

Arabesque (1966); The Chairman/Most Dangerous Man in the World, MacKenna's Gold, Marooned, The Stalking Moon (1969); I Walk the Line (1970); Shootout (1971); The Trial of the Catonsville Nine (1972); Billy Two Hats/Lady and the Outlaw, The Dove (1974); The Omen (1976); MacArthur (1977); The Boys from Brazil (1978); The Sea Wolves (1980); The Blue and the Grey [TV] (1982); Directed by William Wyler (1986); Amazing Grace and Chuck (1987); Old Gringo (1989); Cape Fear, Other People's Money (1991).

Honors: Academy Award Nomination: Best Actor (*The Keys of the Kingdom*, 1945); Golden Globe Award, Academy Award Nomination: Best Actor (*The Yearling*, 1946); Academy Award Nomination: Best Actor (*Gentleman's Agreement*, 1947); Academy Award Nomination: Best Actor (*Twelve O'Clock High*, 1949); Golden Globe Award: World Film Favorite, New York Film Critics Circle Award: Best Actor (*Twelve O'Clock High*, 1950); Golden Globe Award: World Film Favorite (1954); Academy Award, Golden Globe Award: Best Actor (*To Kill a Mockingbird*, 1962); Academy Award: Jean Hersholt Humanitarian Award (1967); Golden Globes: Cecil B. DeMille Award (1968); American Film Institute Life Achievement Award (1989); Film Society of Lincoln Center Tribute (1992).

Selected Bibliography

Freedland, Michael. *Gregory Peck: A Biography*. New York: William Morrow, 1980.
Griggs, John. *The Films of Gregory Peck*. Secaucus, NJ: Citadel Press, 1984.
Thomas, Tony. *Gregory Peck*. New York: Pyramid Publications, 1977.

PHILADELPHIA STORY, THE (1940), comedy. Directed by George Cukor; with Cary Grant, Katharine Hepburn, James Stewart, Ruth Hussey, John Howard, Roland Young, John Halliday, Virginia Weidler, Mary Nash, Henry Daniell, and Hillary Brooke; screenplay by Donald Ogden Stewart.

At the time of its release, this was an extremely popular and critically acclaimed film, but it has dated, and today it seems stilted and often slow moving. Its place in film history owes much to its stellar cast, especially James Stewart in an offbeat turn that won him an Oscar. The film is also well known as the one that saved Hepburn's movie career. Once branded "box office poison," Hepburn fled to New York where she was a hit in the stage version of *The Philadelphia Story*, a play written especially to accommodate her talents. She then bought the rights, which she sold to Hollywood with the provision that she star in it, along with the leading men of her choice. The gamble paid off, and Hepburn remained a top Hollywood star for the next four decades. Critics now find the film flawed by tedious interludes of cloying philosophizing along the lines that "poor men aren't all noble and rich men not all cads," a point few would bother to argue. Some critics find Hepburn's final acceptance of her disreputable father puzzling and her constant agonizing over what she wants out of life tiresome. But looked at for its "movieness," it remains interesting, for Hepburn wisely plays off her own public personality—the snooty, priggish phony—then allows herself to get her comeuppance. For all its flaws, this movie is irresistibly entertaining. Although it is not brilliantly witty or spontaneous, it is well crafted so that the surface bubbles with a consistent humor. In the eyes of one critic, the movie is like a faux gem that has more sparkle than the real thing.

Awards: Academy Awards: Best Actor (Stewart), Screenplay; Academy Award Nominations: Best Picture, Actress (Hepburn), Supporting Actress (Hussey), Director.

Selected Bibliography

Deschner, Donald. *The Complete Films of Cary Grant*. Secaucus, NJ: Citadel Press, 1991.
Latham, Caroline. *Katharine Hepburn: Her Films & Stage Career*. New York: Proteus, 1982.
Pickard, Roy. *Jimmy Stewart: A Life in Film*. New York: St. Martin's Press, 1993.

PICNIC (1955), drama. Directed by Joshua Logan; with William Holden, Rosalind Russell, Kim Novak, Betty Field, Cliff Robertson, Arthur O'Connell, Verna Felton, Susan Strasberg, Nick Adams, Phyllis Newman, and Elizabeth W. Wilson; screenplay by Daniel Taradash.

This film is based on the William Inge play about a drifter (Holden) who stops over in a Kansas town to visit an old buddy (Robertson) and steals his buddy's girlfriend (Novak). It is a film rich in characterization and subtle overtones. On the surface the characters seem two-dimensional: Holden the hunk, Robertson the good-guy friend, Novak the impatient virgin, Field the wise and worried mother, Russell the spinster schoolmarm, O'Connell the set-in-his-ways bachelor, and so on. Beneath the surface, however, there are rumblings of another sort, barely concealed hints of sexual tension that many critics of the time failed to see. Those critics expected the sunny simplicity of *State Fair* or *Pajama Game*, not the dark ambiguities of *Brideshead Revisited* or *The Comfort of Strangers*. So what they thought was the same old eternal triangle is really a twisted triangle with Novak not as a prize but as a pawn between two men whose friendship has homoerotic overtones. Holden is presented as a shirtless stud who is more hustler than Hud, and Novak trembles like a butterfly caught in a shutter, not perceiving that the two men are using her to play games with each other. At the other end of the sexual spectrum are Russell and O'Connell. If Holden is Inge's Stanley Kowalski, Russell is Inge's cat on a hot tin roof. O'Connell, as the man who prefers TV to sex, is Inge's version of the boorish American male. Somewhere in between is Betty Field, suddenly realizing that she is seeing her life in the rearview mirror ("One day you're 21," she tells Novak, "the next you're 40"). Seen from this angle, the film's bright technicolor and wide-screen Cinemascope provide an ironic backdrop to a drama of shadowy passions and repressed desire. *Picnic* is clearly no picnic.

Awards: Academy Awards: Best Color Art Direction, Editing (Charles Nelson, William A. Lyon); Academy Award Nominations: Best Picture, Supporting Actor (Arthur O'Connell), Director, Scoring of a Dramatic Picture.

Selected Bibliography

Kleno, Larry. *Kim Novak on Camera*. San Diego, CA: A. S. Barnes, 1980.
Levy, Emanuel. *Small-Town America in Film: The Decline and Fall of Community*. New York: Continuum, 1991.

Quirk, Lawrence J. *The Complete Films of William Holden*. Secaucus, NJ: Citadel Press, 1986.

PICTURE OF DORIAN GRAY, THE (1945), drama. Directed by Albert Lewin; with George Sanders, Hurd Hatfield, Donna Reed, Angela Lansbury, Peter Lawford, and Lowell Gilmore; narrated by Cedric Hardwicke; screenplay by Albert Lewin.

This film is a sadly underrated version of Oscar Wilde's Faustian tale about a young Victorian gentleman who sells his soul to retain his youth. Narcissistically enchanted by his own portrait, Dorian Gray expresses a desire to look like that forever. He gets his wish, and as he embarks on a life of total depravity, his portrait reveals all the consequences of debauchery and evil to the point where it is too hideous even for Dorian to behold. Hatfield has been accused of looking too perfect ("glacéed" as one critic put it). But it is precisely that look of unreal youth that gives the character its edge. Whereas we in the audience who are in on what's happening realize that he is not truly "young" in the sense of the freshness of youth, those around him, who marvel at his agelessness, can only sense that something is wrong that they cannot put their finger on. Hatfield—cool, beautiful, imperturbable—effortlessly suggests the corruptibility of Dorian's dark soul. So perfect is his whole persona that it seemed to put a curse on Hatfield's career, which never really went anywhere after this picture. When Hatfield surfaced more than forty years later on an episode of *Murder, She Wrote*, audiences who remembered him were disappointed to see—even though he had aged well—that he had aged at all. And what irony it was to see him appearing with Angela Lansbury, the Sybil Vane of *Dorian Gray*, the delicate young singer Dorian drove to suicide—the first of many heinous crimes. Also excellent in the film is George Sanders, perfectly cast as the cynical, epigrammatic Lord Henry Wotton, the mentor who leads Dorian into temptation. The stylized sets, fine black-and-white photography, and even pacing make this a fine example of film adaptation of a celebrated work of art. The use of color at the moment when the hideous portrait is at last revealed to the audience has lost some of its shock value, but it remains an ingenious touch. Unfortunately, director Lewin has been as underrated as this classic film.

Awards: Academy Award: B&W Cinematography (Harry Stradling); Golden Globe Award, Academy Award Nomination: Best Supporting Actress (Angela Lansbury).

Selected Bibliography

Thomas, Tony. *The Films of the Forties*. Secaucus, NJ: Citadel Press, 1975.
Van Der Beets, Richard. *George Sanders: An Exhausted Life*. Lanham, MD: Madison Books, 1990.

PINOCCHIO (1940), children's/fantasy/animated. Directed by Ben Sharpsteen and Hamilton Luske; with voices of Dickie Jones, Christian Rub, Cliff Edwards, Evelyn Venable, Walter Catlett, and Frankie Darro; screenplay by Ted Sears,

Webb Smith, Joseph Sabo, Otto Englander, William Cottrell, Erdman Penner, and Aurelius Battaglia.

This movie, made in 1940 and carefully restored for the 1992 rerelease, comes from the era of full animation, before Disney and all the other animators started cutting corners. New films like *The Little Mermaid, Beauty and the Beast*, and *Anastasia* have returned to this tradition, thanks to labor-saving help from computers, but in 1940 real human artists lovingly illustrated every frame of this movie and weren't afraid to take pains with the details, like the waves on the ocean that curl back in horror at the approach of Monstro the Whale. This was Walt Disney's second full-length animated feature, and it remains one of his greatest classics, brilliantly (and, in some scenes, terrifyingly) created, with awesome detail and images so startling that one generation of children after another has been enthralled by the gripping and unforgettable tale. *Pinocchio* is a technical masterpiece far exceeding most of what Disney did before or after. Everything about this film is wonderful. Disney and scores of artists labored several years to produce *Pinocchio*, and their effort shows. The incredible detail of this animated feature (its sharp dimensions achieved by a multiplane camera setup) is everywhere in evidence. Disney characters, at least in this best of all eras for the company, move not only their heads and mouths but their eyes, ears, arms, legs, and noses; backgrounds are replete with constant movement (leaves swaying in the breeze, water rippling), movement so sadly lacking in the flat and uninspired animation of today. The movie looks great, it contains memorable songs (including the enchanting "When You Wish Upon a Star"), and the story is scary in a way kids can identify with. Pinocchio is without a doubt the most passive and simpleminded of the Disney cartoon heroes, but he's surrounded by a colorful gallery of villains and connivers, including the evil Stromboli, who thinks there is money to be made from a wooden puppet who can walk and talk. The beauty of *Pinocchio* is that what happens to Pinocchio seems plausible to the average child—unlike what happens, say, to the Little Mermaid. Children may not understand falling in love with a prince, but they understand not listening to your father, being a bad boy, and running away and getting into real trouble. The movie is genuinely exciting and romantic, and it is great to look at in this wonderfully restored version, its colors fresh and sparkling, the story timeless.

Selected Bibliography

Jackson, Kathy Merlock. *Disney: A Bio-Bibliography*. Westport, CT: Greenwood Press, 1993.
Maltin, Leonard. *The Disney Films*. New York: Crown Publishers, 1984.

PLACE IN THE SUN, A (1951), drama. Directed by George Stevens; with Montgomery Clift, Elizabeth Taylor, Shelley Winters, Keefe Brasselle, Raymond Burr, and Anne Revere; screenplay by Michael Wilson and Harry Brown.

This provocative film by George Stevens manages to explore depths that Dreiser's powerful novel (*An American Tragedy*) only hinted at. It derives most of its power from Clift's brilliant performance, a performance almost matched by Winters as a plain girl who loses him to glamorous Taylor. If the film seems somewhat dated, it's because the time it's set in (the 1950s) now seems dated. That decade was really the end of an era, and the movie must be taken on its own terms. One has to remember that this is, first and foremost, a "movie" and that it depends very much on the glamour and deception and melodrama that characterize movies. Clift's execution is made to seem doubly tragic when Taylor, a vision in black, appears at his cell to say goodbye, and he (and we) realize that losing Liz is a punishment worse than death. Likewise, when we behold a sniveling Winters whining about "the three of us" and promising to scrimp and save while visions of Taylor dance in Clift's head, we can only agree with critic Pauline Kael's wickedly apt comment that what Clift does to Winters is not murder; it's euthanasia. The telephone scene between Clift and his mother, Anne Revere, speaks volumes in a few agonizing minutes, and we immediately understand the background he is coming from and how doomed he really is in a world too dazzling and deceptive for him ever to survive in. Critics who dismiss the movie for whatever reason often fail to realize the depths beneath its realistic surface. The cumulative impact of the Stevens film is overwhelming; the dark psychological overtones, the eerie cry of a loon, the overlapping dissolves, the shadowy landscapes, all combine to affect you emotionally without your conscious awareness. Although some critics find this sort of treatment mannered and pretentious, the consensus is that this is a very impressive film.

Awards: Academy Awards: Best Director, Screenplay, B&W Cinematography (William C. Mellor), Score (Franz Waxman), B&W Costumes (Edith Head), Editing (William Hornbeck); Academy Award Nominations: Best Picture, Actor (Clift), Actress (Winters).

Selected Bibliography

Kalfatovic, Mary C. *Montgomery Clift: A Bio-Bibliography*. Westport, CT: Greenwood Press, 1994.

Petri, Bruce Humleker. *A Theory of American Film: The Films and Techniques of George Stevens*. New York: Garland, 1987.

Vermilye, Jerry, and Mark Ricci. *The Films of Elizabeth Taylor*. Secaucus, NJ: Citadel Press, 1976.

Winters, Shelley. *Shelley: Also Known as Shirley*. New York: Ballantine, 1980.

POSTMAN ALWAYS RINGS TWICE, THE (1946), crime. Directed by Tay Garnett; with Lana Turner, John Garfield, Cecil Kellaway, Hume Cronyn, Audrey Totter, Leon Ames, and Alan Reed; screenplay by Harry Ruskin and Niven Busch.

This James M. Cain novel of passion and murder, like his equally powerful *Double Indemnity*, is made menacingly realistic by director Tay Garnett. Garfield and Turner sizzle in this sordid drama of lovers whose problems just begin when they murder her husband (Kellaway). Despite changes in James M. Cain's original story (mostly for censorship purposes), the film is more shocking by implication than the exaggerated and explicit 1981 remake. Cain's stories always deal with sleazy love triangles and repressed sexuality, a theme that is brilliantly exploited in this film. Turner gives one of her best performances as an itchy, oversexed woman married to an unattractive and domineering older man. She was reluctant to make the film at first, worrying that it made her look too much of a slut, but Garnett convinced her that it would do wonders for her career by showing that she was, above all else, a serious dramatic actress. So impressed was Cain with Turner's performance that he presented her with a leather-bound first edition of the novel, inscribing it: "For my dear Lana, thank you for giving a performance that was even finer than I expected." It is interesting to note that Lana Turner's Cora is dressed in impeccable white, once a symbol of virtue but here, as in *Heart of Darkness* and *Suddenly, Last Summer*, a symbol of corruption, depravity, and evil. The film is admittedly dated, but that is part of its charm, for it reveals in so many touches a verisimilitude no historic re-creation can ever quite achieve.

Selected Bibliography

Gelman, Howard. *The Films of John Garfield*. Secaucus, NJ: Citadel Press, 1975.
Silver, Alain, and Elizabeth Ward, eds. *Film Noir: An Encyclopedic Reference to the American Style*. Woodstock, NY: Overlook Press, 1979.
Valentino, Lou. *The Films of Lana Turner*. Secaucus, NJ: Citadel Press, 1978.

POWELL, DICK. Actor, director, producer. Born Richard E. Powell on November 14, 1904, in Mountain View, Arkansas; died on January 2, 1963. Powell started out as a crooner in Warner Bros. musicals in the 1930s, often opposite Ruby Keeler, and was a big hit with his choir-boy face and cheerful personality. For over a decade he made a succession of frothy musicals and comedies while he grew increasingly restless to do better things. His big chance came in 1944 when he was offered the role of Philip Marlowe in *Murder, My Sweet*, the film version of Raymond Chandler's *Farewell, My Lovely*. It was a startling transition for Powell, but he made it work. By now his cherubic face was showing just enough age to make it seem a transparent mask for the tough guy underneath— anticipating, in a way, Audie Murphy as Billy the Kid. In the early 1950s he entered yet another phase of his colorful career, this time as producer-director of films and as president of the prosperous Four Star TV production company. He hosted (and occasionally acted in) "Four Star Playhouse" (1952–1956), "Dick Powell's Zane Grey Theatre" (1956–1962), and "The Dick Powell Show" (1961–1963), while supervising a number of other shows produced by the company. Directing *The Conquerors* on location in Utah, near an atomic testing site, may have hastened his death from cancer. A startling number of persons involved in that project died of cancer within the next few years, including John Wayne and Susan Hayward. Powell's second wife (1936–1945) was Joan Blondell, with whom he appeared in a number of those 1930s comedies; his widow is June Allyson. He was impersonated on the screen by his son, Dick Powell, Jr., in John Schlesinger's *The Day of the Locust* (1975).

Filmography: [as performer, except where noted]: Blessed Event, Too Busy to Work (1932); 42nd Street, College Coach, Convention City, Footlight Parade, Gold Diggers of 1933, The King's Vacation (1933); Dames, Flirtation Walk, Happiness Ahead, Twenty Million Sweethearts, Wonder Bar (1934); Broadway Gondolier, Gold Diggers of 1935, A Midsummer Night's Dream, Page Miss Glory, Shipmates Forever, Thanks a Million (1935); Colleen, Gold Diggers of 1937, Hearts Divided, Stage Struck (1936); Hollywood Hotel, On the Avenue, The Singing Marine, Varsity Show (1937); The Cowboy from Brooklyn, Going Places, Hard to Get (1938); Naughty But Nice (1939); Christmas in July, I Want a Divorce (1940); Abbott and Costello in the Navy, Model Wife (1941); Star Spangled Rhythm (1942); Happy Go Lucky, Riding High, True to Life (1943); It Happened Tomorrow, Meet the People, Murder My Sweet (1944); Cornered (1945); Johnny O'Clock (1947); The Pitfall, Rogue's Regiment, Station West, To the Ends of the Earth (1948); Mrs. Mike (1949); The Reformer and the Redhead, Right Cross (1950); Cry Danger, The Tall Target, You Never Can Tell (1951); The Bad and the Beautiful (1952); Split Second [dir., prod.] (1953); Susan Slept Here, The Conqueror [dir., prod.], You Can't Run Away from It [dir., prod.] (1956); The Enemy Below [dir., prod.] (1957); The Hunters [dir., prod.] (1958).

Selected Bibliography

Thomas, Tony. *The Dick Powell Story*. Burbank, CA: Riverwood Press, 1993.

POWER, TYRONE. Born Tyrone Edmund Power, Jr., on May 5, 1913, in Cincinnati, Ohio; died on November 15, 1958. The son of matinee idol Tyrone Power (Sr.), Power went on stage in his teens and played bit parts in films and plays of the early 1930s. Blessed with extreme good looks, a pleasantly sincere personality, and some acting ability, he became a major box office draw at 20th Century–Fox until World War II service interrupted his career. After the war, he attempted more serious projects, the most impressive being *Nightmare Alley*, a shocking film in which he sinks to the lowest levels of depravity with the help of an assortment of carnival freaks. He was excellent as Larry Darrel in Somerset Maugham's *The Razor's Edge*, revealing hidden depths that added a rare dimension to the film. Critics had trouble accepting depth from either Maugham or Power, and many of them failed to see how complex both the novel and its hero could be. Maugham, always the gentleman, observes Larry obliquely, allowing us to accept the fact that this seemingly shallow young man could go off to Tibet in search of his soul. Since shallowness was the impression Tyrone Power conveyed in real life, he demonstrated skill in taking viewers along on his spiritual search. After this, he did more swashbucklers (*Captain from Castile*, *Prince of Foxes*, *The Black Rose*), but his popularity was on the wane as the public taste for such fare declined. He did more theater work in the 1950s but was back filming another epic, *Solomon and Sheba*, in Madrid, when he died suddenly of a heart attack at the age of forty-five.

Filmography: Tom Brown of Culver (1932); Flirtation Walk (1934); Girls' Dormitory, Ladies in Love, Lloyd's of London (1936); Cafe Metropole, Love Is News, Second Honeymoon, Thin Ice (1937); Alexander's Ragtime Band, In Old Chicago, Marie Antoinette, Suez (1938); Day-Time Wife, Jesse James, The Rains Came, Rose of Washing-

ton Square, Second Fiddle (1939); Brigham Young—Frontiersman, Johnny Apollo, The
Mark of Zorro (1940); Blood and Sand, A Yank in the RAF (1941); The Black Swan,
Son of Fury, This Above All (1942); Crash Dive, Daredevils of the West (1943); The
Razor's Edge (1946); Captain from Castile, Nightmare Alley (1947); The Luck of the
Irish, That Wonderful Urge (1948); Prince of Foxes (1949); American Guerilla in the
Philippines, The Black Rose (1950); I'll Never Forget You/The House in the Square,
Rawhide/Desperate Siege (1951); Diplomatic Courier, Pony Soldier (1952); King of the
Khyber Rifles, Mississippi Gambler (1953); The Long Gray Line, Untamed (1955); The
Eddy Duchin Story (1956); Abandon Ship!/Seven Waves Away, The Rising of the Moon,
The Sun Also Rises (1957); Witness for the Prosecution (1957).

Selected Bibliography

Arce, Hector. *The Secret Life of Tyrone Power*. New York: Morrow, 1979.

Belafonte, Dennis, with Alvin H. Marill. *The Films of Tyrone Power*. Secaucus, NJ:
    Citadel Press, 1979.

Guiles, Fred Lawrence. *Tyrone Power: The Last Idol*. Garden City, NY: Doubleday,
    1979.

PREMINGER, OTTO. Director, producer, actor. Born Otto Ludwig Preminger
on December 5, 1906, in Vienna; died on April 23, 1986, in New York. Educated at the University of Vienna (law). Preminger started out as an assistant to
German stage producer Max Reinhardt and began his directing career with the
1935 Broadway melodrama "Libel." After directing a couple of B films at 20th
Century–Fox, he got into a dispute with Darryl Zanuck, which brought his brief
directorial career to a halt. However, he soon found himself in demand as an
actor—often playing the part of a Nazi since he looked and sounded like one.
It was in this way that he finagled his way back to directing. Preminger made
his breakthrough with the critical and commercial success *Laura* in 1944, a film
he took over from Rouben Mamoulian. When his subsequent work at Fox
proved disappointing, he turned to independently producing his own films and
soon gained a reputation for turning out controversial works dealing with hith-
erto taboo subjects such as drug addiction (*The Man with the Golden Arm*).
Critics accused Preminger of not being an auteur, that is, of not having a discernible style—a signature—but he nevertheless turned out a series of polished
successes such as *Anatomy of a Murder*, *Exodus*, and *Advise and Consent*.

Filmography: [director, unless otherwise noted]: Die grosse Liebe (1932); Under Your
Spell (1936); Danger—Love at Work (1937); The Pied Piper [per.] (1942); Margin for
Error [also per.], They Got Me Covered (1943); In the Meantime, Darling [also prod.],
Laura [also prod.] (1944); Fallen Angel [also prod.], A Royal Scandal, Where Do We
Go From Here? [perf.] (1945); Centennial Summer [also prod.] (1946); Daisy Kenyon
[also prod.]; Forever Amber (1947); The Fan [also prod.], Whirlpool [also prod.] (1949);
Where the Sidewalk Ends [also prod.] (1950); The 13th Letter [also prod.] (1951); Angel
Face [also prod.], The Moon Is Blue [also prod.], Stalag 17 [perf.] (1953); Carmen Jones
[also prod.], River of No Return (1954); The Court-Martial of Billy Mitchell, The Man
with the Golden Arm [also prod.] (1955); Saint Joan [also prod.] (1957); Bonjour Tristesse [also prod.] (1958); Anatomy of a Murder [also prod.], Porgy and Bess (1959);

Exodus [also prod.] (1960); Advise and Consent [also prod.] (1962); The Cardinal [also prod.] (1963); Bunny Lake Is Missing [also prod.], In Harm's Way [also prod.] (1965); Hurry Sundown [also prod.] (1967); Skidoo [also prod.] (1968); Tell Me That You Love Me, Junie Moon [also prod.] (1970); Such Good Friends [also prod.] (1971); Rosebud [also prod.] (1975); Hollywood on Trial [per.] (1976); The Human Factor [also prod.] (1979).

Honors: Berlin Film Festival: Bronze Bear Award (*Carmen Jones*, 1955); Academy Award Nomination: Best Director (*The Cardinal*, 1963).

Selected Bibliography

Frischauer, Willi. *Behind the Scenes of Otto Preminger: An Unauthorized Biography*. London: Michael Joseph, 1973.

Pratley, Gerald. *The Cinema of Otto Preminger*. New York: A. S. Barnes, 1971.

Preminger, Otto. *Preminger: An Autobiography*. Garden City, NY: Doubleday, 1977.

PRICE, VINCENT. Born on May 27, 1911, in St. Louis, Missouri; died on October 25, 1993, in Los Angeles, California. Educated at Yale (art history, English), the University of London (fine arts), and Nuremberg University. Price initially gained attention in England where his debonair manner and mellifluous voice made him a popular stage star. He made his Hollywood debut in 1938 and appeared in a series of costume dramas, but he later played effete villains in several films and turned in strong performances in straight dramas—notably, Otto Preminger's *Laura* and Anatole Litvak's *The Long Night*. It was the irony of fate that Price soon became associated almost exclusively with the horror genre, primarily as the result of playing the revenge-driven sculptor in the 3-D classic of the macabre *House of Wax*. In the early 1960s Price began appearing in movies produced by American International Pictures, a studio that specialized in cheap teen genre fare for drive-ins. He often worked with director Roger Corman, starring in a series of low-budget Gothic chillers loosely based on the stories of Edgar Allan Poe. Sometimes he appeared with such aging Hollywood icons as Peter Lorre, Boris Karloff, and Basil Rathbone. Price cheerfully accepted the stereotyped roles fate had dealt him, never hesitating to spoof his onscreen image as the "Master of Menace," playing Egghead on the TV series *Batman*, supplying the rap narration for Michael Jackson's landmark song and video "Thriller," and serving for eight years as the urbane but mildly sinister host of the PBS series "Mystery." Price provided the voice for the diabolical Professor Ratigan in the Disney animated feature *The Great Mouse Detective*. His last major role in a feature was as Mr. Maranov, the transplanted Russian nobleman who charms Bette Davis and Lillian Gish in Lindsay Anderson's *The Whales of August*. Price was a significant influence on quirky genre filmmaker Tim Burton, who cast him as the kindly old inventor who creates *Edward Scissorhands*. This charming cameo was Price's final film appearance.

Filmography: Service De Luxe (1938); The Private Lives of Elizabeth and Essex/Elizabeth the Queen, The Tower of London (1939); Brigham Young—Frontiersman, Green Hell, The House of Seven Gables, Hudson's Bay, The Invisible Man Returns (1940);

The Eve of St. Mark, The Keys of the Kingdom, Laura, Wilson (1944); A Royal Scandal (1945); Dragonwyck, Shock (1946); The Long Night, Moss Rose, The Web (1947); Rogue's Regiment, The Three Musketeers, Up in Central Park (1948); Baghdad, The Bribe (1949); The Baron of Arizona, Champagne for Caesar, Curtain Call at Cactus Creek (1950); Adventures of Captain Fabian, His Kind of Woman (1951); The Las Vegas Story (1952); House of Wax (1953); Dangerous Mission, Casanova's Big Night, The Mad Magician (1954); Son of Sinbad (1955); Serenade, The Ten Commandments, While the City Sleeps (1956); The Story of Mankind (1957); The Fly, House on Haunted Hill (1958); The Bat, The Big Circus, The Return of the Fly, The Tingler (1959); House of Usher/Fall of the House of Usher (1960); Master of the World, The Pit and the Pendulum (1961); Confessions of an Opium Eater/Souls for Sale, Convicts Four/Reprieve, Tales of Terror, Tower of London (1962); Beach Party, Diary of a Madman, The Haunted Palace, The Raven, Twice-Told Tales (1963); The Comedy of Terrors/Graveside Story, The Last Man on Earth, The Masque of the Red Death (1964); Tomb of Ligeia, War Gods of the Deep/City under the Sea (1965); Dr. Goldfoot and the Bikini Machine (1966); The Jackals (1967); The Conqueror Worm/Witchfinder General (1968); More Dead Than Alive, The Oblong Box, The Trouble with Girls (1969); Cry of the Banshee, Scream and Scream Again (1970); The Abominable Dr. Phibes (1971); Dr. Phibes Rises Again (1972); Theatre of Blood (1973); It's Not the Size That Counts/Percy's Progress, Madhouse (1974); Journey into Fear (1975); Scavenger Hunt (1979); The Monster Club (1980); House of the Long Shadows, Making Michael Jackson's Thriller [narr.—''Thriller''] (1983); Bloodbath at the House of Death (1984); The Great Mouse Detective, The Offspring/From a Whisper to a Scream (1986); The Whales of August (1987); Dead Heat (1988); Backtrack (1989); Edward Scissorhands (1990).

Honors: Los Angeles Film Critics Association: Life Achievement (1991).

Selected Bibliography

Levinson, Gary J. *Vincent Price: Pictorial Tribute*. Miami: Movie-House Publications, 1972.
McAsh, Iain F. *The Films of Vincent Price*. London: Barnden Castell Williams, 1974.
Parish, James Robert, with Steven Whitney. *Vincent Price Unmasked*. New York: Drake Publishers, 1974.

PRIDE AND PREJUDICE (1940), drama. Directed by Robert Z. Leonard; with Greer Garson, Laurence Olivier, Edna May Oliver, Edmund Gwenn, Mary Boland, Maureen O'Sullivan, Karen Morley, Melville Cooper, E .E. Clive, Ann Rutherford, and Marsha Hunt; screenplay by Aldous Huxley and Jane Murfin.

Aldous Huxley, famous for *Brave New World*, seems an unlikely choice to adapt a comedy of manners about the self-assured and self-contained world of late eighteenth-century rural England in which, while Napoleon plunders Europe across the Channel, the chief concern of the Bennet family is to see that their five daughters are properly married. However, the screenplay is a winner, preserving the wit and elegance as well as the wisdom of the Jane Austen classic. Olivier, fresh from the success of *Wuthering Heights* and *Rebecca*, was an obvious choice for the role of the proud Mr. Darcy. Some critics think that he looks unhappy in the role because Vivien Leigh was not chosen as his co-star.

In fact, he was puzzled that the film was such a success without her. Greer Garson, appearing here before she was stigmatized as unbearably noble following her appearance in *Mrs. Miniver*, is well suited to play a spirited young lady, fully the match of a Mr. Darcy. There was worry about the heavy hand of MGM on such fragile material, but the studio did a creditable job of retaining the elegance of the original.

Awards: Academy Award: Best Interior Decoration/B&W.

Selected Bibliography

Miller, Frank. *Movies We Love: 100 Collectible Classics*. Atlanta, GA: Turner Publishing, 1996.
Thomas, Tony. *The Films of the Forties*. Secaucus, NJ: Citadel Press, 1975.

PRIDE OF THE YANKEES, THE (1942), biography/sports. Directed by Sam Wood; with Gary Cooper, Teresa Wright, Babe Ruth, Walter Brennan, Dan Duryea, Ludwig Stossel, Addison Richards, and Hardie Albright; screenplay by Jo Swerling and Herman J. Mankiewicz.

Every once in a while Hollywood comes out with a baseball picture that is as appealing to nonfans as it is to fans. Pictures like *The Stratton Story*, *The Jackie Robinson Story*, *The Winning Team*, *The Natural*, and *Field of Dreams* come to mind. But the granddaddy of them all is this superb biography of baseball star Lou Gehrig. In this picture Samuel Goldwyn produced a stirring epitaph on Lou Gehrig, the New York kid who rose to the baseball heights and later met such a tragic end. To the credit of the screenwriters (and to Paul Gallico who wrote the original), Gehrig is depicted for what he was, a quiet, plodding personality who strived for and achieved perfection in his profession. Cooper is excellent in the lead, performing in that unique style of his that seems artless, almost accidental, and yet convinces us that we are not really watching the familiar blink and stammer of Gary Cooper but the unassuming innate gentleness and strength of character of this baseball great himself, a man whose name will be forever linked to the disease that took his life.

Awards: Academy Award: Editing (Daniel Mandell); Academy Award Nominations: Best Picture, Actor (Cooper), Actress (Teresa Wright).

Selected Bibliography

Swindell, Larry. *The Last Hero: A Biography of Gary Cooper*. Garden City, NY: Doubleday, 1980.

PSYCHO (1960), horror/thriller. Directed by Alfred Hitchcock; with Anthony Perkins, Janet Leigh, Vera Miles, John Gavin, Martin Balsam, John McIntire, Simon Oakland, John Anderson, Frank Albertson, and Patricia Hitchcock; screenplay by Joseph Stefano.

Critics have called *Psycho* everything from a very black comedy to a stunning, if sadistic, two-hour joke. It is all of this and more, for it disturbs and pleases on various levels, and while one may agree with Hitchcock's claim that he was merely having fun, one can also feel discomfort with, as one blurb put it, Hitchcock's descent "into the icy blackness of the unexplained." For it was not just humorless people who vilified the film when it first came out and were offended by its graphic violence. Astute critics who "got" the joke still wondered about its tastelessness, wondering if the film wasn't a reflection of a very unpleasant mind. The final verdict is not yet in and probably never will be. Challenges to taste are always highly controversial because they raise the question of motive, with the motives of those eager to defend tastelessness as questionable as the motives of those eager to decry it. Meanwhile, the film continues to demand a disproportionate amount of attention from students of film. It is very hard to take the film out of its context and still appreciate it. For one thing, Hitchcock knew that an audience accustomed to his glossy color entertainments of the 1950s would be unsettled by the film's gritty, film noirish tone and style. On the one hand, they might take comfort initially in Hitchcock's use of some horror flick clichés: thief on the run, grabbing financial happiness while she can, runs into creature from the lagoon (where she ends up) with an Addams family–style haunted house in the background—and the living dead in the fruit cellar. On the other hand, this blond isn't on the run in designer clothes and fancy cars, zipping up a sunny California highway to stay at the Marriott. She's in cheap clothes and a cheap used car, driving through pelting rain to stop at a run-down motel where she is the only guest. And when the leading lady is murdered in the second reel, audiences are deprived of the assurance of the director that all would end well. They have walked a plank, and now they don't know what to expect or where to look. The film's excessive violence was also something new to film, and the trick photography of the shower scene demonstrated techniques for creating optical illusions that were more terrifying than the real thing. The whole hokey psychoanalytical ending is just so much nonsense, but viewers who had "enjoyed" the film's violence needed to have something to believe in, in order to justify their own voyeurism. (Hitchcock, incidentally, had pioneered pop-psychological thrillers in his notorious *Spellbound*.) Many books and articles have been written about this landmark film, all of them challenging, none of them totally satisfying. The movie had a strange effect on the careers of its stars. Only Janet Leigh survived intact, and even she has had to carry around the baggage of the shower scene the rest of her life. She is totally identified with that role, a role she claims to have relished but one she might not have chosen had she known what was to come, for Hitchcock was banking on her "starlet" status. Both Vera Miles and John Gavin never went on to do very much in pictures. Most perversely affected, though, was Anthony Perkins, who continued to make sequel after sequel the more his career faded, until he finally became a grotesque caricature of himself.

Awards: Academy Award Nominations: Best Director, Supporting Actress (Leigh), Cinematography, Art Direction.

Selected Bibliography

Leigh, Janet, with Christopher Nickens. *Behind the Scenes of "Psycho," the Classic Thriller.* New York: Harmony Books, 1995.

Rebello, Stephen. *Alfred Hitchcock and the Making of "Psycho."* New York: Dembner Books, 1990.

Winecoff, Charles. *Split Image: The Life of Anthony Perkins.* New York: Dutton, 1996.

PUBLIC ENEMY, THE (1931), crime. Directed by William Wellman; with James Cagney, Jean Harlow, Eddie Woods, Beryl Mercer, Donald Cook, Joan Blondell, and Mae Clarke; screenplay by Harvey Thew.

Where *Little Caesar* had its share of violence, this film portrays the underworld in even seedier terms, taking on the most gruesome situations and portraying sex and violence graphically, even for its time. (*The Public Enemy* was made before the Hays Office established its rigid codes.) A postscript said that the producers wanted to "depict honestly an environment that exists today in certain strata of American life, rather than glorify the hoodlum or the criminal." The film had a different effect: Cagney was playful and dynamic and so much more appealing than the characters opposed to him that audiences rooted for him in spite of themselves. This part made Cagney famous and deservedly so, for he makes up for the film's occasional flaws and dated notions. It's a raw and brutal film with some repulsive scenes: Cagney pushing a grapefruit into Mae Clarke's face, socking another "moll" on the chin for persuading him to take her in for the night while he's drunk, and spitting a mouthful of beer into the face of a speakeasy proprietor for using a rival's product. Discerning critics located the real power of *The Public Enemy* in its brutal assault on the nerves and in the virtuoso performance by James Cagney. This was one of the earliest films to (1) acknowledge that crime could be, at least in part, the product of poor social conditions, (2) reveal liquor as the basis for the Mob's illegal income, and (3) base events and characters on real-life events and gangsters to create myth from fact. This early gangster film was very influential in the development of the urban American crime film.

Awards: Academy Award Nomination: Best Original Story.

Selected Bibliography

Conway, Michael, and Mark Ricci. *The Films of Jean Harlow.* New York: Citadel Press, 1965.

Dickens, Homer. *The Complete Films of James Cagney.* Secaucus, NJ: Carol, 1989.

Rosow, Eugene. *Born to Lose: The Gangster Film in America.* New York: Oxford University Press, 1978.

Q

QUEEN CHRISTINA (1933), historical/romance. Directed by Rouben Mamoulian; with Greta Garbo, John Gilbert, Ian Keith, Lewis Stone, C. Aubrey Smith, Gustav von Seyffertitz, Reginald Owen, and Elizabeth Young; screenplay by S. N. Behrman, Salka Viertel, and H. M. Harwood.

This is arguably Garbo's finest film, silent or sound. Her own personality and that of the character she is playing are one, even though this is a highly romanticized conception of the seventeenth-century monarch. The real Queen Christina of Sweden was a great lover, all right—but one who loved women, not men. She was also short, fat, and unattractive, thrived on smutty stories, and hated to bathe. Garbo's Christina is a sanitized queen with more human passion than obsession with power, one who decides to control her own destiny, no matter how tragic, rather than be controlled by the fate a throne may decree. This is the quintessential Garbo film in which the actress encompasses what seems to be every human passion, revealing in gripping scenes her strength, sorrow, weaknesses, and joy in an extraordinary performance. Even so, the film was not an immediate success and took years to earn back its investment. It has been speculated that some of the Garbo allure might have worn thin with the public. For all the praise heaped on it by critics dazzled by the famous Garbo mystique, the film suffers from lethargy. Nevertheless, as is so often true of "movies," it is that elusive thing called "star quality" that wins the day.

Selected Bibliography

Conway, Michael, Dion McGregor, and Mark Ricci. *The Films of Greta Garbo*. New York: Bonanza Books, 1963.
Milne, Tom. *Rouben Mamoulian*. London: Thames & Hudson, 1969.
Peary, Danny. *Alternate Oscars*. New York: Delta, 1993.

QUIET MAN, THE (1952), romance/comedy. Directed by John Ford; with John Wayne, Maureen O'Hara, Barry Fitzgerald, Victor McLaglen, Mildred Natwick, Arthur Shields, Ward Bond, Ken Curtis, Mae Marsh, Jack MacGowran, Sean McClory, and Francis Ford; screenplay by Frank S. Nugent.

The Quiet Man is director John Ford's sentimental journey into Ireland's past and back to his own Irish roots. In what is generally thought to be one of Ford's greatest films, John Wayne (always Ford's actor of choice) becomes Ford's alter ego as Wayne battles bullies from Ford's childhood and courts the girl Ford let get away. It is a colorful, vibrant, full-blooded film filled with action and passion and a richness only a labor of love can ultimately bestow. The film contains some of the most visually extraordinary scenes ever filmed, some done in muted, diffused tones that give them an unearthly luminosity. Against this backdrop, the characters shine through as both very human and inescapably symbolic— almost mythical. Admirable as this film is, it can seem shamelessly excessive, with Ford throwing in everything but leprechauns and the blarney stone. One is left, ultimately, with the riddle of the Irish mentality still unsolved. How is it, one asks, in a land so poor, with a church so harsh, and opportunity so scarce, where fathers who can't support their overly large families are driven to drink and unmarried pregnant girls are driven to suicide, that even those forced to flee the country dissolve in tears at the sound of its name and yearn to return if only to be buried there? Maybe the answer is somewhere in this extraordinary picture after all.

Awards: Academy Awards: Best Director, Cinematography/Color; Directors Guild of America: Quarterly Award; Academy Award Nominations: Best Picture, Best Supporting Actor (McLaglen), Best Screenplay, Best Art Direction/Set Decoration.

Selected Bibliography

Peary, Danny. *Alternate Oscars*. New York: Delta, 1993.

Place, Janey Ann. *The Non-Western Films of John Ford*. Secaucus, NJ: Citadel Press, 1979.

Zmijewsky, Steve, Boris Zmijewsky, and Mark Ricci. *The Complete Films of John Wayne*. Secaucus, NJ: Citadel Press, 1983.

QUINN, ANTHONY. Actor. Born on April 21, 1915, in Chihuahua, Mexico. Quinn began his film career in 1936 and played heavies throughout the 1940s before hitting it big in two memorable roles, one as Zapata's (Marlon Brando's) brother in *Viva Zapata!* in 1952, the other as Gauguin, opposite Kirk Douglas's van Gogh, in *Lust for Life* in 1956. He gave other outstanding performances as the vicious circus performer in Fellini's *La Strada* and the opportunistic Bedouin, Auda Abu Tayi, in David Lean's *Lawrence of Arabia*. But he is perhaps best known for the title role in *Zorba the Greek*, a part he seemed born to play. Quinn has had a record run as an actor and continues to appear in movies as well as on TV. Although Quinn always turns in a good performance, much of his value lies in his ability to impersonate almost any nationality. He is a sort of cinematic chameleon, able to adapt to whatever script. He has played, among other roles, the part of an Indian, a Mexican, a Greek, an Italian, an Arab, a Frenchman, an Asian, an Irishman—the list goes on.

Filmography: Parole, The Plainsman (1936); Daughter of Shanghai, The Last Train from Madrid, Partners in Crime, Swing High Swing Low, Waikiki Wedding (1937); The Buccaneer, Bulldog Drummond in Africa, Dangerous to Know, Hunted Men, King of Alcatraz, Tip-Off Girls (1938); Island of Lost Men, King of Chinatown, Television Spy, Union Pacific (1939); City for Conquest, Emergency Squad, The Ghost Breakers, Parole Fixer, Road to Singapore, Texas Rangers Ride Again (1940); Blood and Sand, Bullets for O'Hara, Knockout, Manpower, The Perfect Snob, They Died with Their Boots On, Thieves Fall Out (1941); The Black Swan, Larceny Inc., Road to Morocco (1942); Guadalcanal Diary, The Ox-Bow Incident (1943); Buffalo Bill, Irish Eyes Are Smiling, Ladies of Washington, Roger Touhy—Gangster (1944); Back to Bataan, China Sky, Where Do We Go From Here? (1945); California (1946); Black Gold, The Imperfect Lady, Sinbad the Sailor, Tycoon (1947); The Brave Bulls, Mask of the Avenger (1951); Against All Flags, The Brigand, Viva Zapata!, The World in His Arms (1952); Blowing Wild, City beneath the Sea, East of Sumatra, Ride Vaquero, Seminole (1953); Attila, La Strada, The Long Wait (1954); The Beachcomber, The Magnificent Matador, The Naked Street, Seven Cities of Gold, Ulysses (1955); Angels of Darkness/Donne proibite, The Last Man to Hang, Lust for Life [as Gauguin], Man from Del Rio, The Wild Party (1956); The Hunchback of Notre Dame/Notre-dame de Paris, The Ride Back, The Rising of the Moon, The River's Edge, The Story of Esther Costello, Wild Is the Wind (1957); The Buccaneer, Hot Spell (1958); Alive and Kicking, The Black Orchid, Last Train from Gun Hill, The Savage Innocents, Warlock (1959); Heller in Pink Tights, Portrait in Black (1960); A Circle of Deception, The Guns of Navarone (1961); Barabbas/Barabba, Lawrence of Arabia, Requiem for a Heavyweight (1962); Behold a Pale Horse, Zorba the Greek [also assoc. prod.] (1964); A High Wind in Jamaica (1965); Lost Command (1966); The Happening (1967); Guns for San Sebastian/La bataille de San Sebastian, The Magus, The Shoes of the Fisherman (1968); A Dream of Kings, The Secret of Santa Vittoria (1969); Flap, R.P.M., Walk in the Spring Rain (1970); Across 110th Street [also exec. prod.], Arruza (1972); Deaf Smith and Johnny Ears/Los Amigos, The Don Is Dead/Beautiful But Deadly (1973); The Destructors/Marseilles Contract (1974); The Inheritance/Eredita ferramonti, Target of an Assassin/Tigers Don't Cry/The Long Shot (1976); Mohammad, Messenger of God/The Message (1977); Caravans, The Children of Sanchez, The Greek Tycoon (1978); The Passage (1979); High Risk, Lion of the Desert, The Salamander (1981); Valentina/1919 (1982); Circle of Power/Mystique/Naked Weekend/Brainwash [exec. prod.] (1983); Ingrid (1985); Pasion de hombre/A Man of Passion, Stradivari (1989); Ghosts Can't Do It, Revenge (1990); A Star for Two, Jungle Fever, Mobsters, Only the Lonely (1991); Last Action Hero (1993).

Honors: Academy Award: Best Supporting Actor (*Viva Zapata!*, 1952); Academy Award: Best Supporting Actor (*Lust for Life*, 1956); Academy Award Nomination: Best Actor (*Wild Is the Wind*, 1957); National Board of Review, Academy Award Nomination: Best Actor (*Zorba the Greek*, 1964); Golden Globes: Cecil B. DeMille Award (1986).

Selected Bibliography

Marill, Alvin H. *The Films of Anthony Quinn*. Secaucus, NJ: Citadel Press, 1975.
Quinn, Anthony, *The Original Sin: A Self-Portrait*. Boston: Little, Brown, 1972.
Quinn, Anthony, with Daniel Paisner. *One Man Tango*. New York: HarperCollins, 1995.

R

RAINS, CLAUDE. Actor. Born William Claude Rains on November 10, 1889, in London; died on May 30, 1967. Rains was one of the most accomplished, persuasive, and durable character actors on the screen for almost forty years. He had a suave demeanor and a superbly controlled sardonic manner that made him charming even when playing villains, which he was called upon to do frequently on the screen. He started out on the London stage at age eleven, first toured the United States in 1914, and became a leading player of the Theatre Guild in 1926. He was a middle-aged man by the time he got into films in 1933. Rains gained the attention of the studios because of his stage reputation and his expressive face, but ironically enough, his face was completely hidden behind bandages in his motion picture debut, the title role in *The Invisible Man* (1933). Thereafter, however, Rains's face, as well as his distinctive voice and manner, enhanced a long string of films at Warners and other studios in which he played with subtlety a wide range of character leads and supporting roles. He was nominated for Oscars four times but never won an Academy Award. He was particularly effective in a number of appearances opposite Bette Davis, particularly *Mr. Skeffington* and *Deception*. Rains's one big starring part was in *The Phantom of the Opera* in which he played the leading role so sympathetically that he has never been surpassed, not even in the musical versions. The 1940s was his decade of prime achievement, a time when he played such varying roles as the French police officer in *Casablanca*, the incestuous doctor in *Kings Row*, the corrupt senior senator in *Mr. Smith Goes to Washington*, and the neurotic composer in *Deception*. And his role in *Lawrence of Arabia* as Dryden, deftly underplayed, is a minor gem.

Filmography: The Invisible Man (1933); The Clairvoyant, Crime without Passion, The Man Who Reclaimed His Head (1934); The Last Outpost, The Mystery of Edwin Drood

(1935); Anthony Adverse, Hearts Divided, Stolen Holiday (1936); The Prince and the Pauper, They Won't Forget (1937); The Adventures of Robin Hood, Four Daughters, Gold Is Where You Find It, White Banners (1938); Daughters Courageous, Four Wives, Juarez, Mr. Smith Goes to Washington, They Made Me a Criminal (1939); The Lady with Red Hair, Saturday's Children, The Sea Hawk (1940); Four Mothers, Here Comes Mr. Jordan, The Wolf Man (1941); Casablanca, Kings Row, Moontide, Now Voyager, Strange Holiday (1942); Forever and a Day, Phantom of the Opera (1943); Mr. Skeffington, Passage to Marseille (1944); This Love of Ours (1945); Angel on My Shoulder, Caesar and Cleopatra, Deception, Notorious (1946); The Unsuspected (1947); The Passionate Friends, Rope of Sand, Song of Surrender (1949); Where Danger Lives, The White Tower (1950); Sealed Cargo (1951); The Paris Express (1953); Lisbon (1956); Pied Piper of Hamelin (1957); This Earth Is Mine (1959); The Lost World (1960); The Battle of the Worlds (1961); Lawrence of Arabia (1962); Twilight of Honor (1963); The Greatest Story Ever Told (1965).

Honors: Academy Award Nomination: Best Supporting Actor (*Mr. Smith Goes to Washington*, 1939); Academy Award Nomination: Best Supporting Actor (*Casablanca*, 1943); Academy Award Nomination: Best Supporting Actor (*Notorious*, 1946).

Selected Bibliography

Harmetz, Aljean. *Round up the Usual Suspects: The Making of Casablanca: Bogart, Bergman, and World War II*. New York: Hyperion, 1992.

RAY, NICHOLAS. Director. Born Raymond Nicholas Kienzle on August 7, 1911, in Galesville, Wisconsin; died on June 16, 1979. Educated at the University of Chicago and the University of Wisconsin. Before he became a film director, Ray studied architecture with Frank Lloyd Wright. After that he worked with Elia Kazan and John Houseman on various stage projects. He made his film debut with *They Live by Night*, a well-told story of lovers on the run from the law. His first important film was *Knock on Any Door*, a movie that made a forceful social statement about juvenile delinquency but sacrificed dramatic emphasis in favor of polemics. The film starred Humphrey Bogart, who also appeared in Ray's next project, *In a Lonely Place*, a film that is among the best work either man ever did. By this time Ray was revealing his interest in disaffected loners, troubled individuals who either by chance or by choice find themselves incapable of conforming to society's demands. As an asocial screenwriter suspected of murder, Bogart gave one of his most passionate performances. Not only is it one of the best movies about Hollywood; it is also a bitter comment on the postwar condition. *On Dangerous Ground* starred the gifted Robert Ryan as a disillusioned city cop who becomes infected with the violence all around him. Ray used a restless, fluid camera technique that suggested the uncertainties of modern city life. Ray's most famous film is *Rebel without a Cause*, the movie that made James Dean an overnight sensation and has remained a cult classic ever since it appeared in the mid-1950s. Because he was an outsider, Ray was often accused of being an overgrown teenager, but his real theme was not so much rebellious teenagers but disaffected people in general at the mercy of a society that demands conformity and saps individuality. The only choices within such a framework are either capitulation or destruction. He pursued this theme on an adult level in *Bigger Than Life*, the story of a man whose addiction to cortisone leads to emotional disturbances that cause him to challenge the hypocrisy of contemporary social standards. In these latter two movies, Ray demonstrated a skill in the use of CinemaScope that few directors achieved. This achievement was due in part to his apprenticeship with Frank Lloyd Wright from whom he acquired a keen sense of space and horizontal line. Largely taken for granted at home, Ray was lionized by the French and became something of a cult figure. Strangely enough, just as the Ray cult was catching on in the United States, Ray turned to directing epics that lacked the intensity of his more compact works. Ray subsequently abandoned Hollywood for Europe, returning to the States in the late 1960s to teach film at New York State University at Binghamton. His deteriorating health limited his activities to occasional cameo appearances in films of other directors. He himself was the subject of *Lightning over Water*, which he directed in collaboration with Wim Wenders. The film chronicled the final months of Ray's bout with cancer.

Filmography: [as director, unless otherwise noted]: A Tree Grows in Brooklyn [asst. dir.] (1945); Knock on Any Door, They Live by Night [also adaptation], A Woman's Secret (1949); Born to Be Bad, In a Lonely Place (1950); Flying Leathernecks, On Dangerous Ground (1951); The Lusty Men (1952); Johnny Guitar (1954); Rebel without a Cause [also story], Run for Cover (1955); Bigger Than Life, Hot Blood (1956); Bitter Victory/Amere Victoire [also sc.], The True Story of Jesse James (1957); Party Girl, Wind across the Everglades (1958); The Savage Innocents [also sc.] (1959); King of Kings (1961); 55 Days at Peking [also per.] (1963); Circus World [co-story] (1964); You Can't Go Home Again (1973); I'm a Stranger Here Myself [per.] (1974); The American Friend/Der Amerikanische Freund [per.] (1977); Hair [per.] (1979); Lightning over Water [per., co-dir.] (1980); Crystal Gazing [per.] (1982).

Selected Bibliography

Andrew, Geoff. *The Films of Nicholas Ray: The Poet of Nightfall*. London: Letts, 1991.
Blaine, Allan. *Nicholas Ray: A Guide to References and Resources*. Boston: G. K. Hall, 1984.
Eisenschitz, Bernard. *Nicholas Ray: An American Journey*. Trans. Tom Milne. Boston: Faber and Faber, 1993.

REAR WINDOW (1954), thriller. Directed by Alfred Hitchcock; with James Stewart, Grace Kelly, Wendell Corey, Thelma Ritter, and Raymond Burr; screenplay by John Michael Hayes.

"If you do not experience delicious terror when you see *Rear Window* , then pinch yourself—you are most probably dead." Thus went the blurb for this, one of Hitchcock's most stylish thrillers and one of the director's top two favorites (the other was *Shadow of a Doubt*). *Rear Window* stars one of Hitchcock's favorite actors, James Stewart, in a role tailor-made for him. Since this is a movie about voyeurism, viewers have to have someone they can still respect, maybe even identify with, someone like Stewart who allows them to satisfy their curiosity without excessive guilt. Grace Kelly, another Hitchcock favorite, provides the class and style necessary to contrast with the sordid things going on in the backyard of Stewart's apartment building. Hitchcock welcomed the challenge of a restricted set, managing not to lose a second of suspense. He also pulls off a neat trick (one he later uses in *Psycho*) of involving the audience by turning it into a bunch of voyeurs watching a voyeur watch others. Filled with suspense and excitement, this film is a superb example of how to make a film on a single set and still make the viewer feel free of claustrophobia and totally engrossed. Hitchcock also uses humor to punctuate the suspense and to reveal the characters' own honesty about what they are up to. Even though it's Stewart's job, as a photographer, to watch others, he still has qualms, and Hitchcock does punish him in the end by giving him a second broken leg. In addition to witty lines from Stewart and Kelly ("Previews of coming attractions," she coos as she shows Stewart the peignoir she has brought for staying overnight), it has Thelma Ritter, looking as if she just wandered in from a Rock Hudson–Doris Day movie, making her trademark quips about what's going on. Among some Hitchcock scholars there is the feeling that, of all Hitchcock's films, this is the one that most reveals the man. The violation of intimacy aside, they say, Hitchcock has nowhere else come so close to pure misanthropy, nor given us so disturbing a sense of what it is like to watch the "silent film" of other people's lives, whether across a courtyard or up on a screen.

Awards: New York Film Critics Circle Award, National Board of Review Award: Best Actress (Kelly); Academy Award Nomination: Best Director.

Selected Bibliography

Harris, Robert A., and Michael S. Lasky. *The Complete Films of Alfred Hitchcock*. Secaucus, NJ: Carol Publishing Group, 1993.

Humphries, Patrick. *The Films of Alfred Hitchcock*. New York: Crescent, 1994.

Raubicheck, Walter, and Walter Srebnick, eds. *Hitchcock's Re-released Films: From Rope to Vertigo*. Detroit, MI: Wayne State University Press, 1991.

REBECCA (1940), thriller. Directed by Alfred Hitchcock; with Laurence Olivier, Joan Fontaine, George Sanders, Judith Anderson, Nigel Bruce, Reginald Denny, C. Aubrey Smith, Gladys Cooper, Florence Bates, Leo G. Carroll, and Melville Cooper; screenplay by Robert E. Sherwood and Joan Harrison.

"Riveting and painful—a tale of fear and guilt, class and power," says Helen MacKintosh, one of a handful of critics able to appreciate how much Hitchcock darkened the tones of Daphne du Maurier's classic but slick modern Gothic novel. This was Hitchcock's first American film and one in which, like *The Wrong Man*, the Hitchcock touch is understated. This was such a popular and well-told novel that Hitchcock wisely let the narrative unfold as written, tampering only with the ending because, at the time, the Hollywood code would not permit a murderer to go unpunished regardless of how justifiable his crime might be. This fidelity to the novel was a treat for the millions of readers who knew the book intimately, from its famous opening line (''Last night I dreamt I went to Manderley again'') to its Jane Eyre ending with Mrs. Danvers, eyes glazed with madness, setting fire to Manderley and then perishing in the flames. Olivier is properly circumspect as the man with a sordid secret whose second wife is the exact opposite of his first, the ravishing but corrupt Rebecca. It is interesting that Rebecca, whose name is the title of the book, never actually appears in the novel, while her successor, over whom the spirit of Rebecca hovers, is never given any name except that of Mrs. deWinter, an indication of how overshadowed she is by the personality of a woman she thinks she has to compete with. She is nudged in this direction by the sinister Mrs. Danvers, marvelously played by Judith Anderson, whose idolatry of Rebecca has dark, sexual overtones. George Sanders is impeccable as Rebecca's erstwhile lover who tries to blackmail Olivier. Gladys Cooper and Nigel Bruce round out the excellent cast. Florence Bates is particularly memorable as the rich, obnoxious American woman from whose bullying Fontaine escapes when Olivier proposes marriage. But it is Joan Fontaine who carries the picture in a role tailor-made for her looks and talents. She narrates the story, and it is with her we identify if we have ever felt uncomfortable in a situation where new rules apply and we feel we cannot measure up regardless of how hard we try. Fontaine's shy, simpering ways are saved from being irritating by her innocent charm and an inner strength that gradually reveals itself as her self-confidence grows. Some critics have complained that Olivier seems ill at ease in his part, but it is soon clear that he is a man with a deeply troubled conscience who has also fallen, quite naturally, under the influence of Mrs. Danvers and has good reason to feel ill at ease.

Awards: Academy Awards: Best Picture, B&W Cinematography (George Barnes); Academy Award Nominations: Best Director, Actor (Olivier), Actress (Fontaine), Supporting Actress (Anderson), Screenplay, B&W Art Direction, Editing, Original Score, Special Effects.

Selected Bibliography

Beeman, Marsha Lynn. *Joan Fontaine: A Bio-Bibliography*. Westport, CT: Greenwood Press, 1994.

Sterritt, David. *The Films of Alfred Hitchcock*. Cambridge: Cambridge University Press, 1993.

Thomas, Tony. *The Films of the Forties*. Secaucus, NJ: Citadel Press, 1975.

REBEL WITHOUT A CAUSE (1955), drama. Directed by Nicholas Ray; with James Dean, Natalie Wood, Sal Mineo, Jim Backus, Ann Doran, William Hopper, Rochelle Hudson, Corey Allen, Edward Platt, Dennis Hopper, and Nick Adams; screenplay by Stewart Stern.

This portrait of alienated youth spoke to a whole generation and still retains much of its power in spite of some dated elements. This landmark movie contains all the themes that were to appear in one form or another in youth-oriented films that were a growing genre in the age of emerging identification of teenagers as a distinct segment of the population: the search for self-esteem, the lack of communication with parents, the support of friends, the vague restlessness, elusive disenchantment, and above all, the self-pity that comes from feeling "misunderstood." The word *alienation* was just entering the social vocabulary at this time, after having initially been applied to that original "rebel without a cause," Holden Caulfield in *The Catcher in the Rye*, then the "beats" of the Kerouac generation, and later to Ken Kesey's "Merry Pranksters." But what makes this film special is the presence of James Dean, who is not only perfectly cast as the rebel but whose death even before the film was released created a curious overlapping of film and reality to the point where it seemed he was acting out in real life a sort of sequel to *Rebel* in which this time he really does die in a car crash. Much of the power of the film can be attributed to Nicholas Ray's forceful and compelling direction. His meticulous attention to detail results in a film that is much more than a teenage exploitation film. Although James Dean is a teen rebel, he is also a more mature representation of the alienation that went beyond teenage angst. Dean says time and again in the film that he doesn't want to cause any trouble. He is not out for a rumble, does not run with gangs, is not excessively self-destructive. He's the catcher in the rye who wants to cut through the world's phoniness and connect with life somewhere beneath its stultifying surfaces. Set as it is in upper-middle-class surroundings, this was the first film to suggest that juvenile violence is not necessarily bred in the slums but can also manifest itself in bad boys from good families.

Awards: Academy Award Nominations: Best Actor (Dean), Supporting Actor (Sal Mineo), Supporting Actress (Natalie Wood), Director (Kazan); Golden Globe Awards: Best Picture (Drama), Posthumous Award for Best Dramatic Actor (Dean), Outstanding Directorial Achievement (Kazan); Cannes Film Festival: Best Dramatic Film.

Selected Bibliography

Andrew, Geoff. *The Films of Nicholas Ray: The Poet of Nightfall*. London: Letts, 1991.
Spoto, Donald. *Rebel: The Life and Legend of James Dean*. New York: HarperCollins, 1996.
Whitman, Mark. *The Films of James Dean*. London: Barnden Castell Williams Ltd., 1974.

RED BADGE OF COURAGE, THE (1951), war. Directed by John Huston; with Audie Murphy, Bill Mauldin, Douglas Dick, Royal Dano, John Dierkes, Arthur Hunnicut, Tim Durant, Andy Devine; narrated by James Whitmore; screenplay by John Huston.

Stephen Crane's Civil War novel receives both epic and personal treatment by director Huston in this celebrated screen adaptation written and directed by the incomparable John Huston. Sweeping battle scenes and some truly terrifying Rebel cavalry charges highlight this study of the fine line between cowardice and bravery. The film includes many memorable scenes and many stirring moments. When the picture was first released, reviews were so negative that it was taken back to the cutting room and severely edited. Lillian Ross wrote a fascinating account of this film's troubled production in which she explains how the editors did a hatchet job on the film in their attempt to turn it into a routine war movie. Curiously enough the film took on a life of its own, as if in the process of butchering it, the editors accidentally distilled its essence. Despite its mutilation, this film is still praised among critics for the remarkable delicacy and depth of feeling in the fragments that remain. Visually, the texture of the camera work is reminiscent of the harsh, dustily faded textures of Matthew Brady's Civil War pictures. And then there is the disturbing presence of Audie Murphy himself, the most decorated soldier of World War II, struggling with cowardice in a performance that subtly but compellingly reveals the wrenching ambivalence at the heart of heroism. It's high time the shamefully underrated Audie Murphy was reevaluated, and *The Red Badge of Courage* is a good place to start.

Selected Bibliography

Guttmacher, Peter. *Legendary War Movies*. New York: MetroBooks, 1996.
McCarty, John. *The Films of John Huston*. Secaucus, NJ: Citadel Press, 1987.
Ross, Lillian. *Picture*. New York: Anchor, 1993.

RED RIVER (1948), western. Directed by Howard Hawks; with John Wayne, Montgomery Clift, Walter Brennan, Joanne Dru, John Ireland, Noah Beery, Jr., Paul Fix, Coleen Gray, Harry Carey, Jr., Harry Carey, Sr., Chief Yowlachie, and Hank Worden; screenplay by Borden Chase and Charles Schnee.

There have been many classic westerns, but this Howard Hawks masterpiece certainly ranks among the top ten of the genre. *Red River* is a relentless tale of hard men as rugged as the range they ride, an unforgettable sweeping spectacle with the kind of grandeur few westerns have achieved. One of the greatest American adventures, it is really a western *Mutiny on the Bounty*. Clift (in his first released film) rebels against his tyrannical guardian Wayne during a cattle drive. This was a new turn for Wayne, and those who praised him for playing an unsympathetic role also thought that age had caught up with him, that this role might be his last, and that Clift would take his place. History is nothing if not ironic, and as it turned out, Clift was gone by the early 1960s while Wayne was going strong up until the mid-1970s. This movie has everything going for it, from magnificently photographed vistas, stampedes, and Indian battles to outstanding performances, particularly by Wayne and Clift. This film, delayed by bad weather, sickness, and the threat of lawsuits, succeeded in spite of it all to become both a critical and popular success. Many westerns that claim to be history are merely fiction passing as history, but *Red River* has the feel of history re-created with impressive fidelity. Of course, it owes a lot to the strength of its universal story line: the mythic confrontation between youth and age, authority and rebellion, father and son, past and future.

Awards: Directors Guild of America: Quarterly Award.

Selected Bibliography

Hardy, Phil, ed. *The Overlook Film Encyclopedia: The Western*. Woodstock, NY: Overlook Press, 1994.

Kalfatovic, Mary C. *Montgomery Clift: A Bio-Bibliography*. Westport, CT: Greenwood Press, 1994.

Mast, Gerald. *Howard Hawks, Storyteller*. New York: Oxford University Press, 1982.

Zmijewsky, Steve, Boris Zmijewsky, and Mark Ricci. *The Complete Films of John Wayne*. Secaucus, NJ: Citadel Press, 1983.

RIDE THE HIGH COUNTRY (1962), western. Directed by Sam Peckinpah; with Randolph Scott, Joel McCrea, Mariette Hartley, Ronald Starr, Edgar Buchanan, R. G. Armstrong, Warren Oates, John Anderson, L. Q. Jones, James Drury; screenplay by N. B. Stone, Jr.

This film, Sam Peckinpah's second and some think greatest, is a lyrical, almost mythical, seriocomic tribute to the age of great westerns and to two veteran western actors. It is the story of two old-timers who, while guarding a gold shipment, reflect on the paths their lives have taken. This is a much-loved as well as a critically acclaimed film. Peckinpah's attention to detail, realistic settings, and total understanding of character also make it a many-layered treat that repeated viewings only enhance. The film is a bittersweet farewell not only to the passing of the western and these two stalwarts of the genre but also to the decline of the Old West. Critics were quick to comment on the touching humor in the portrayals of Scott and McCrea as over-the-hill cowboys who achieve an almost biblical grandeur when, suddenly realizing that the world has left them behind, they struggle not to fall from grace when a tempting gold shipment comes between them.

Awards: Cannes Film Festival: First Prize; Brussels Film Festival: Grand Prize; Mexican Film Festival: Silver Goddess for Best Foreign Film.

Selected Bibliography

Butler, Terence. *Crucified Heroes: The Films of Sam Peckinpah*. London: Gordon Fraser, 1979.

Hardy, Phil, ed. *The Overlook Film Encyclopedia: The Western*. Woodstock, NY: Overlook Press, 1994.

Parish, James Robert, and Michael R. Pitts. *The Great Western Pictures*. Metuchen, NJ: Scarecrow Press, 1976.

ROBINSON, EDWARD G. Actor. Born Emmanuel Goldenberg on December 12, 1893, in Bucharest, Romania; died on February 26, 1973. Educated at the American Academy of Dramatic Arts. Over a long and distinguished career, mostly in movies, but also on TV and the stage, Robinson imbued his many different roles with the indelible stamp of his forceful and authoritative personality. Unattractive in a curiously attractive way, Robinson could play everything from a hardened, unregenerate gangster to a kindly old Norwegian immigrant farmer. He began appearing in stock in 1913 and made it to Broadway in 1915, where he remained for the next fifteen years, making only one film appearance during the silent era. After the advent of sound, Robinson began to be seen regularly in movies. After his great success with *Little Caesar* (1930), a performance that became a prototype for screen gangster portrayals, Robinson was typecast for several years in similar roles, but he gradually broadened his range and proved himself a highly skilled actor in a great variety of parts. He gave memorable performances in two screen biographies: *Dr. Ehrlich's Magic Bullet*, the story of the German scientist who developed a cure for venereal disease, and *A Dispatch from Reuters*, the story of the man who pioneered the telegraphic news agency. Some of his best portrayals were in psychological dramas of the 1940s, notably *Flesh and Fantasy*, *Double Indemnity*, *The Woman in the Window*, and *Scarlet Street*. Although on the screen he often appeared aggressive and unpolished, in his private life he was an art connoisseur with quite an impressive collection. This keen interest of his led the Academy of Dramatic Arts to label him as a Renaissance man when they gave him a Special Academy Award in 1973, just a month after his death.

Filmography: The Bright Shawl (1923); A Hole in the Wall (1929); East Is West, A Lady to Love, Little Caesar, Night Ride, Outside the Law, The Widow from Chicago (1930); Five Star Final, Smart Money (1931); The Hatchet Man, Silver Dollar, Tiger Shark, Two Seconds (1932); I Loved a Woman, The Little Giant (1933); Dark Hazard, The Man with Two Faces (1934); Barbary Coast, The Whole Town's Talking [dual roles] (1935); Bullets or Ballots (1936); Kid Galahad/Battling Bellhop, The Last Gangster, Thunder in the City (1937); The Amazing Doctor Clitterhouse, I Am the Law, A Slight Case of Murder (1938); Blackmail, Confessions of a Nazi Spy (1939); Brother Orchid, A Dispatch from Reuters, Dr. Ehrlich's Magic Bullet (1940); Manpower, The Sea Wolf, Unholy Partners (1941); Larceny Inc., Tales of Manhattan (1942); Destroyer, Flesh and Fantasy (1943); Double Indemnity, Mr. Winkle Goes to War, Tampico, The Woman in the Window (1944); Journey Together [RAF propaganda film; U.K.], Our Vines Have Tender Grapes, Scarlet Street (1945); The Stranger (1946); The Red House (1947); All My Sons, Key Largo, Night Has a Thousand Eyes (1948); House of Strangers, It's a Great Feeling [cameo] (1949); Operation X/My Daughter Joy (1950); Actors and Sin (1952); Big Leaguer, The Glass Web, Vice Squad (1953); Black Tuesday, A Bullet for Joey, Hell on Frisco Bay, Illegal, Tight Spot, The Violent Men (1955); Nightmare, The Ten Commandments (1956); A Hole in the Head (1959); Pepe [cameo], Seven Thieves (1960); My Geisha, Two Weeks in Another Town (1962); A Boy Ten Feet Tall/Sammy Going South, The Prize (1963); Cheyenne Autumn, Good Neighbor Sam, The Outrage, Robin and the Seven Hoods [cameo] (1964); The Cincinnati Kid, Peking Blonde/La blonde de Pekin/The Blonde from Peking (1967); The Biggest Bundle of Them All, Grand Slam/Adogni Costo, It's Your Move/Uno scacco tutto matt/Mad Checkmate, Never a Dull Moment, Operation St. Peter's (1968); MacKenna's Gold (1969); Song of Norway (1970); Neither by Day or Night, Solyent Green (1973).

Honors: Cannes Film Festival Award: Best Actor (*House of Strangers*, 1949); Academy Award: Special Award (Renaissance Man, 1972).

Selected Bibliography

Hirsch, Foster. *Edward G. Robinson*. New York: Pyramid Publications, 1975.
Marill, Alvin H. *The Complete Films of Edward G. Robinson*. Secaucus, NJ: Carol, 1990.

Robinson, Edward G., with Leonard Spigelgass. *All My Yesterdays: An Autobiography.* New York: Hawthorn Books, 1973.

ROGERS, GINGER. Actress. Born Virginia Katherine McMath on July 16, 1911, in Independence, Missouri; died on April 26, 1995. Ginger Rogers was a versatile star of Hollywood films of the 1930s, 1940s, and 1950s, alternating between comedy, musicals, and melodramas. Her stage mother groomed her from early childhood for a show business career, but when at age six she was offered a film contract, her mother decided that her daughter was not yet ready for a career after all. Rogers finally made her professional debut at fourteen, filling in for a week as a dancer with Eddie Foy's vaudeville troupe at Fort Worth, Texas. The following year, she won a Charleston contest and began singing and dancing on the vaudeville circuit, sometimes with her own act, sometimes with her first husband, Jack Pepper. During that period she appeared in several shorts, including the three-reeler *Campus Sweethearts*, opposite Rudy Vallee. The turning point in Rogers's career came late in 1929, when she was picked for the second female lead in the Kalmar and Ruby Broadway musical *Top Speed*. During the run of that show and her next Broadway musical, George Gershwin's *Girl Crazy*, she began her film career in minor Paramount features that were shot at the studio's East Coast facilities in Astoria, Queens. In 1931 she went to Hollywood on a contract with Pathé. After appearing in several B films, she freelanced with various companies until she finally settled at RKO. It was here that she became Fred Astaire's dancing partner in a string of popular romantic screen musicals. Their success was phenomenal, and viewers still thrill to the on-screen chemistry between these two charming professionals—not to mention their superb dancing. During the 1940s, Rogers proved her versatility in both comic and dramatic roles. In 1940 she won a Best Actress Oscar for her dramatic performance in *Kitty Foyle* and two years later enchanted audiences with her comedic talents in *The Major and the Minor*. Although she alternated between comedy and drama in the 1950s, she devoted more and more time to the stage. In 1965 she made a successful comeback on Broadway when she took over the lead role in the musical *Hello Dolly!* from Carol Channing, and in 1969, she scored a hit as the star of the London production of *Mame*. Although she suffered poor health in her later years, she still made a number of public appearances and was often interviewed about the golden age of Hollywood and her important part in it.

Filmography: Young Man of Manhattan, Queen High, The Sap from Syracuse, Follow the Leader (1930); Honor among Lovers, The Tip Off, Suicide Fleet (1931); Carnival Boat, The Tenderfoot, The Thirteenth Guest, Hat Check Girl, You Said a Mouthful (1932); 42nd Street, Broadway Bad, Gold Diggers of 1933, Professional Sweetheart, A Shriek in the Night, Don't Bet on Love, Sitting Pretty, Flying Down to Rio, Chance at Heaven (1933); Rafter Romance, Finishing School, 20 Million Sweethearts, Change of Heart, Upper World, The Gay Divorcee, Romance in Manhattan (1934); Roberta, Star of Midnight, Top Hat, In Person (1935); Follow the Fleet, Swing Time (1936); Shall

We Dance, Stage Door (1937); Having Wonderful Time, Vivacious Lady, Carefree (1938); The Story of Vernon and Irene Castle, Bachelor Mother, Fifth Avenue Girl (1939); Primrose Path, Lucky Partners, Kitty Foyle (1940); Tom Dick and Harry (1941); Roxie Hart, Tales of Manhattan, The Major and the Minor, Once Upon a Honeymoon (1942); Tender Comrade (1943); Lady in the Dark, I'll Be Seeing You (1944); Weekend at the Waldorf (1945); Heartbeat, Magnificent Doll [as Dolly Madison] (1946); It Had to Be You (1947); The Barkleys of Broadway (1949); Perfect Strangers, Storm Warning (1950); The Groom Wore Spurs (1951); We're Not Married, Monkey Business, Dreamboat (1952); Forever Female (1953); Black Widow, Beautiful Stranger/Twist of Fate [U.K.] (1954); Tight Spot (1955); The First Traveling Saleslady, Teenage Rebel (1956); Oh Men! Oh Women! (1957); The Confession/Seven Different Ways/Quick Let's Get Married [release delayed until 1971] (1964); Harlow [as Jean Harlow's mother in Carol Lynley version] (1965).

Honors: Academy Award: Best Actress (*Kitty Foyle*, 1940).

Selected Bibliography

Rogers, Ginger. *Ginger, My Story*. New York: HarperCollins, 1991.

ROMAN HOLIDAY (1953), romance/comedy. Directed by William Wyler; with Audrey Hepburn, Gregory Peck, Eddie Albert, and Tullio Carminati; screenplay by Ian McLellan Hunter and John Dighton.

This enchanting modern fairly tale might have been a run-of-the-mill romantic comedy in other hands, but the combination of Wyler's directorial know-how, Peck's and Albert's underplayed romantic paternalism, and Audrey Hepburn's inimitable charm makes this film one of the most charming films of the 1950s. Appearing when it did, it seemed to herald a new age finally emerging from the long, ugly shadow of war. Here was Rome, once the infamous "Open City," now made to look once again like the fabled city of old. In its midst emerges the magic presence of enchanting Audrey Hepburn, playing a lonely princess as if born to the part, a refreshing image of innocence and wistfulness and longing. Perhaps the most symbolic scene in the film is the one in which she has her hair cut short and emerges from the beauty shop into the sunny streets of Rome unencumbered and ready to live. Women everywhere followed suit, and short hair became an early symbol of some sort of as yet unspecified liberation. The sad sweetness of an impossible love affair between Hepburn and Peck may seem quaint by today's standards when a princess and a journalist might try to fool themselves into thinking they could thumb their noses at tradition and get away with it; but the recognition of the reality that underlies their acceptance of duty over passion is mature, moving, and ultimately satisfying. It is the reality that underlies all genuine fairy tales. Since this picture appeared, the world has had more than enough opportunity to see what happens when selfish lovers think they can ignore this reality (the princesses of Monaco; the princes of England). Although this film has inspired several imitations, none has come close to the bittersweet charm of the original.

Awards: Academy Awards: Best Actress (Hepburn), Costumer (Edith Head), Story (Ian McLellan Hunter); Golden Globe Award: Best Actress (Hepburn); Directors Guild of America: Outstanding Directorial Achievement; New York Film Critics Circle Award: Best Actress (Hepburn); British Academy Award: Best Actress—British (Hepburn); Academy Award Nominations: Best Picture, Director, Supporting Actor (Albert), Screenplay, Cinematography (B&W), Art Direction/Set Decoration (B&W), Film Editing.

Selected Bibliography

Hofstede, David. *Audrey Hepburn: A Bio-Bibliography*. Westport, CT: Greenwood Press, 1994.

Kern, Sharon. *William Wyler: A Guide to References and Resources*. Boston: G. K. Hall, 1984.

ROONEY, MICKEY. Actor, singer, dancer. Born Joe Yule, Jr., on September 23, 1920, in Brooklyn, New York. Rooney made his stage debut in his family's vaudeville act at the age of eighteen months and his film debut in 1927 at age six, in the first of some fifty two-reel comedies in the "Mickey McGuire" series. In 1932 he changed his name to "Mickey Rooney" and began appearing in feature films. For ten years he played the title character in the "Andy Hardy" series, during which time he appeared to much acclaim in *Boys Town* and also made a number of enormously popular and successful "backyard" musicals opposite Judy Garland. His roles in *The Human Comedy* and *National Velvet* earned him the title of most popular film star. After the war, Rooney established himself as a versatile character actor in such films as *Baby Face Nelson* and *Breakfast at Tiffany's*. He made a triumphant stage debut in the late 1970s in the glitzy Broadway musical *Sugar Babies*, opposite Ann Miller, and won high praise for his sensitive portrayal of a retarded man in the 1981 TV drama *Bill*. If anyone deserves the title Mr. Hollywood, it is Mickey Rooney, whose career parallels the history of Hollywood from the beginning of sound to the present and who moved smoothly from child star to mature lead to older character actor, singing, dancing, and playing every conceivable role along the path of his phenomenal career.

Filmography: The Beast of the City, Fast Companions, My Pal the King (1932); The Big Cage, The Big Chance, Broadway to Hollywood, The Chief, The Life of Jimmy Dolan (1933); Beloved, Blind Date, Chained, Death on the Diamond, Half a Sinner, Hide-Out, I Like It That Way, The Lost Jungle, Love Birds, Manhattan Melodrama, Upperworld (1934); Ah Wilderness, The County Chairman, The Healer, A Midsummer Night's Dream, Riffraff (1935); The Devil Is a Sissy, Down the Stretch, Little Lord Fauntleroy (1936); Captains Courageous, A Family Affair, Hoosier Schoolboy, Live Love and Learn, Slave Ship, Thoroughbreds Don't Cry (1937); Boys Town, Hold That Kiss, Judge Hardy's Children, Lord Jeff, Love Is a Headache, Out West with the Hardys, Stablemates, You're Only Young Once (1938); Andy Hardy Gets Spring Fever, Babes in Arms, The Hardys Ride High, Huckleberry Finn/Adventures of Huckleberry Finn, Judge Hardy and Son (1939); Andy Hardy Meets Debutante, Strike Up the Band, Young Tom Edison (1940); Andy Hardy's Private Secretary, Babes on Broadway, Life Begins for Andy Hardy, Men of Boys Town (1941); Andy Hardy's Double Life, The Courtship of Andy Hardy, A Yank at Eton (1942); Girl Crazy, The Human Comedy, Thousands Cheer (1943); Andy Hardy's Blonde Trouble, National Velvet (1944); Love Laughs at Andy Hardy (1946); Killer McCoy (1947); Summer Holiday, Words and Music (1948); The Big Wheel (1949); The Fireball, He's a Cockeyed Wonder, Quicksand (1950); My Outlaw Brother, My True Story, The Strip (1951); Sound Off (1952); All Ashore, Off Limits, A Slight Case of Larceny (1953); The Atomic Kid, The Bridges at Toko-Ri, Drive a Crooked Road (1954); The Twinkle in God's Eye [also song composer] (1955); The Bold and the Brave [also song composer], Francis in the Haunted House, Jaguar [assoc. prod.], Magnificent Roughnecks (1956); Baby Face Nelson, Operation Mad Ball (1957); Andy Hardy Comes Home [also song composer], A Nice Little Bank That Should Be Robbed (1958); The Big Operator/Anatomy of a Syndicate, The Last Mile (1959); Platinum High School/Trouble at 16, The Private Lives of Adam and Eve [also dir.] (1960); Breakfast at Tiffany's, Everything's Ducky, King of the Roaring 20's—The Story of Arnold Rothstein (1961); Requiem for a Heavyweight (1962); It's a Mad Mad Mad Mad World (1963); The Secret Invasion (1964); How to Stuff a Wild Bikini (1965); Ambush Bay (1966); The Devil in Love/Il diavolo innamorato, Skidoo (1968); 80 Steps to Jonah, The Comic, The Extraordinary Seaman (1969); Cockeyed Cowboys of Calico County (1970); B. J. Presents (1971); Pulp, Richard (1972); That's Entertainment (1974); Bon Baisers de Hong Kong (1975); The Domino Killings, Pete's Dragon (1977); The Magic of Lassie (1978); Arabian Adventure, The Black Stallion (1979); The Fox and the Hound (1981); La traversee de la Pacific (1982); The Care Bears Movie (1985); Lightning, The White Stallion (1986); Rudolph & Frosty's Christmas in July (1988); Erik the Viking (1989); My Heroes Have Always Been Cowboys, Silent Night Deadly Night 5: The Toymaker (1991); The Legend of Wolf Mountain (1992); La Vida Lactea/ The Milky Life, Sweet Justice (1993); The Adventures of the Red Baron, That's Entertainment III (1994).

Honors: Academy Award: Special Award (Youth Actor, 1938); Academy Award Nomination: Best Actor (*Babes in Arms*, 1939); Academy Award Nomination: Best Actor (*The Human Comedy*, 1943); Academy Award Nomination: Best Supporting Actor (The Bold and the Brave, 1956); Academy Award Nomination: Best Supporting Actor (*The Black Stallion*, 1979); Academy Award: Jean Hersholt Humanitarian Award (1982).

Selected Bibliography

Marx, Arthur. *The Nine Lives of Mickey Rooney*. New York: Stein and Day, 1986.
Rooney, Mickey. *I. E.: An Autobiography*. New York: Putnam, 1965.
———. *Life Is Too Short*. New York: Villard, 1991.

ROSSEN, ROBERT. Director, screenwriter, producer. Born Robert Rosen on March 16, 1908, in New York City; died on February 18, 1966. Educated at New York University. Rossen's early work as a writer and director of socially conscious plays led to a writing contract with Warner Bros. in 1936. During the next seven years, Rossen supplied scripts for such directors as Lloyd Bacon, Mervyn LeRoy, and Lewis Milestone. His writing betrayed his Communist leanings and led to a subpoena from the House Un-American Activities Committee in 1947. It was four years before Rossen was eventually tried and blacklisted, and during that time he established himself as an independent producer and director of notable films such as *Body and Soul* and *All the King's Men*. After

Rossen "named names" in 1953, he was allowed to continue working, but he chose not to return to Hollywood. His film output after that, although uneven, produced such memorable films as *The Hustler* and *Lilith*. The latter, a disturbing story of obsession set in a mental hospital, was denounced by U.S. critics when it was released but has since come to be regarded by many as Rossen's best work.

Filmography: [as director only, except where noted]: Body and Soul, Johnny O'Clock [also sc.] (1947); All the King's Men [also prod., sc.] (1949); The Brave Bulls [also prod.] (1951); Mambo [also sc., story] (1954); Alexander the Great [also prod., sc.] (1956); Island in the Sun (1957); They Came to Cordura [also sc.] (1959); The Hustler [also prod., co-sc.] (1961); The Cool World (1963); Lilith [also prod., sc.] (1964).

Honors: Golden Globe Award: Best Director, Directors Guild of America: Quarterly Award and Annual Award (*All the King's Men*, 1949); New York Film Critics Circle Award, Academy Award Nomination: Best Director (*The Hustler*, 1961).

Selected Bibliography

Casty, Alan. *The Films of Robert Rossen*. New York: MOMA, 1969. (Distributed by New York Graphic Society, Greenwich, CT.)

Sennett, Ted. *Great Movie Directors*. New York: Harry N. Abrams, 1986.

RUSSELL, ROSALIND. Actress. Born June 4, 1908, in Waterbury, Connecticut; died on November 28, 1976. Educated at Marymount College and the American Academy of Dramatic Arts. The daughter of a lawyer and a fashion editor, Russell went on stage in the late 1920s and made her film debut in 1934. She played mostly dramatic parts at first, but in the early 1940s she made a series of bright comedies. Later on, when she returned to dramas, audiences didn't quite know how to take her, and her career went into a decline, although she made a standout appearance as the spinster schoolteacher in *Picnic*. She bounced back in the late 1950s with *Auntie Mame*, a part she was born to play, and won a Golden Globe Award for her leading role in *Gypsy*, a part she was not that good in. After that, she was seen mostly in character parts. In her heyday, Russell defined the image of the modern woman who can compete in a man's world and still maintain her allure. An accomplished comedienne, Russell could hilariously devastate any adversary with a look or a wisecrack—and usually get away with it. But this beautiful actress also had a deep, dramatic side and an intelligence that gave polish to all her performances. Words like *style*, *wit*, *sophistication*, *charm*, *independence* all apply to this gifted actress. The reason she was nominated so often for an Oscar but never got one seems clearly to be a case of Academy members caught in a dilemma: They would nominate her for a dramatic role, then think of her as a comic actress. And comics seldom—if ever—receive prestigious awards (unless they're "special" awards given to the likes of Bob Hope). The fact that Russell also excelled in musicals was still another problem for the Academy. Thus, like Claudette Colbert, this talented woman fell between the cracks. Fortunately, we have her inimitable performances on film—proof that, in addition to entertaining us royally, she deserves a place among the screen's classic beauties. She was married to producer Frederick Brisson.

Filmography: Evelyn Prentice, Forsaking All Others, The President Vanishes (1934); Casino Murder Case, China Seas, The Night Is Young, Reckless, Rendezvous, West Point of the Air (1935); Craig's Wife, It Had to Happen, Trouble for Two, Under Two Flags (1936); Live Love and Learn, Night Must Fall (1937); The Citadel Press, Four's a Crowd, Man-Proof (1938); Fast and Loose, The Women (1939); Hired Wife, His Girl Friday, No Time for Comedy/Guy with a Grin (1940); Design for Scandal, The Feminine Touch, They Met in Bombay, This Thing Called Love (1941); My Sister Eileen, Take a Letter Darling (1942); Flight for Freedom, What a Woman! (1943); Roughly Speaking, She Wouldn't Say Yes (1945); Sister Kenny (1946); The Guilt of Janet Ames, Mourning Becomes Electra (1947); The Velvet Touch (1948); Tell It to the Judge (1949); A Woman of Distinction (1950); Never Wave at a Wac (1952); The Girl Rush, Picnic (1955); Auntie Mame (1958); Five Finger Exercise, Gypsy, A Majority of One (1962); The Trouble with Angels (1966); Oh Dad Poor Dad Mama's Hung You in the Closet and I'm Feeling So Sad, Rosie (1967); Where Angels Go Trouble Follows (1968); Mrs. Pollifax—Spy (1971).

Honors: Academy Award Nomination: Best Actress (*My Sister Eileen*, 1942); Golden Globe Award, Academy Award Nomination: Best Actress (*Sister Kenny*, 1946); Golden Globe Award, Academy Award Nomination: Best Actress (*Mourning Becomes Electra*, 1947); Golden Globe Award, Academy Award Nomination: Best Actress (*Auntie Mame*, 1958); Golden Globe Award: Best Actress—Comedy/Musical (*Auntie Mame*, 1958); Golden Globe Award: Best Actress—Comedy/Musical (*A Majority of One*); Golden Globe Award: Best Actress—Comedy/Musical (*Gypsy*, 1962); Academy Award: Jean Hersholt Humanitarian Award (1972).

Selected Bibliography

Russell, Rosalind, and Chris Chase. *Life Is a Banquet*. New York: Random House, 1977.
Yanni, Nicholas. *Rosalind Russell*. New York: Pyramid Publications, 1975.

RYAN, ROBERT. Actor. Born on November 11, 1909, in Chicago; died on July 11, 1973. Educated at Loyola Academy in Chicago, Dartmouth, and Max Reinhardt Theatrical Workshop in Hollywood. Ryan made his stage debut in 1939, then spent the following year playing minor parts in Paramount films. In 1941–1942 he returned to Broadway in *Clash by Night*, only to head back to Hollywood the year after that with an RKO contract. After he returned from World War II service, he began getting better parts, and his career accelerated. In the late 1940s and early 1950s, he played a number of memorable parts; for example, as Joan Bennett's illicit lover in Jean Renoir's *The Woman on the Beach*, as the anti-Semitic murderer in Edward Dmytryk's *Crossfire*, as the nemesis who menaces Van Heflin in Fred Zinnemann's *Act of Violence*, as the paranoid millionaire husband of Barbara Bel Geddes in Max Ophüls's *Caught*, as a washed-up boxer in Robert Wise's *The Set-Up*, and repeating his stage role from a decade earlier, as the cynical lover in Fritz Lang's *Clash by Night*. He later freelanced, and although he appeared in a lot of films of questionable quality, he always managed to give an excellent performance, either as hero or villain.

He also appeared successfully in occasional stage productions, including the American Shakespeare Festival 1960 production of *Antony and Cleopatra*, in which he played Antony to Katharine Hepburn's Cleopatra; the 1968 Broadway revival of *The Front Page*; and the 1971 off-Broadway revival of *Long Day's Journey into Night*. In contrast to the psychopaths and bigots he often portrayed on the screen, Ryan was in reality a modest man and a committed social activist. He was among the founders of both the UCLA Theatre Group and a nonsectarian private school in California's San Fernando Valley. Ryan has acquired something of a cult following among people who, quite rightly, think he was underrated.

Filmography: Golden Gloves, Northwest Mounted Police, Queen of the Mob, Texas Rangers Ride Again (1940); The Feminine Touch (1941); Behind the Rising Sun, Bombardier, Gangway for Tomorrow, The Iron Major, The Sky's the Limit, Tender Comrade (1943); Marine Raiders (1944); Crossfire, Trail Street, The Woman on the Beach (1947); Berlin Express, The Boy with Green Hair, Return of the Bad Men (1948); Act of Violence, Caught, The Set-Up (1949); Born to Be Bad, I Married a Communist/Woman on Pier 13, The Secret Fury (1950); Best of the Badmen, Flying Leathernecks, On Dangerous Ground, The Racket (1951); Beware My Lovely, Clash by Night, Horizons West (1952); City beneath the Sea, Inferno, The Naked Spur (1953); About Mrs. Leslie, Alaska Seas, Her 12 Men (1954); Bad Day at Black Rock, Escape to Burma, House of Bamboo, The Tall Men (1955); Back from Eternity, The Proud Ones (1956); Men in War (1957); God's Little Acre, Lonelyhearts (1958); Day of the Outlaw, Odds against Tomorrow (1959); Ice Palace (1960); The Canadians, King of Kings (1961); Billy Budd, The Longest Day (1962); Battle of the Bulge, The Crooked Road, The Dirty Game/La Guerre Secrete, The Professionals (1966); The Busy Body, The Dirty Dozen, Hour of the Gun, A Minute to Pray, A Second to Die/Un minuto per pregare un instante per morire/ Escondido (1967); Anzio/The Battle for Anzio, Custer of the West (1968); The Wild Bunch (1969); Captain Nemo and the Underwater City (1970); Lawman, The Love Machine (1971); And Hope to Die/La course du lievre a travers les champs (1972); Executive Action, The Iceman Cometh, Lolly Madonna XXX/Lolly-Madonna War (1973); The Outfit (1974).

Honors: Academy Award Nomination: Best Supporting Actor (*Crossfire*, 1947); National Society of Film Critics: Special Award (posthumous), National Board of Review: Best Actor (*The Iceman Cometh*, 1973).

Selected Bibliography

Jarlett, Franklin. *Robert Ryan: A Biography and Critical Filmography*. Jefferson, NC: McFarland, 1990.

S

SAN FRANCISCO (1936), romance/disaster. Directed by W. S. Van Dyke; with Clark Gable, Jeanette MacDonald, Spencer Tracy, Jack Holt, Jessie Ralph, Ted Healy, Shirley Ross, and Al Shean; screenplay by Anita Loos.

This is top-notch entertainment all wrapped up in a lavish package. MacDonald's belle of San Francisco may seem a bit over the top for modern audiences, but the music, Tracy's performance, and earthquake climax more than compensate for any incidental deficiencies. This film established MGM as the most powerful studio in Hollywood. It had the stars, the story, and the special effects that remain as thrilling as ever. Teaming Gable and Tracy was an inspiration, and it wasn't long after this movie that they were together again in both *Test Pilot* and *Boom Town*. Neither actor wanted to make this film. Gable didn't like MacDonald, and Tracy was uncomfortable playing a priest, the vocation his father had wished for him. But Van Dyke wheedled and begged, and the two relented—and gave stellar performances. Some critics think that *San Francisco* is the greatest film Van Dyke ever directed. Certainly he seems to push the actors to maintain the fast pace of that bawdy era and provides the colorful backdrop for this exciting piece of fictionalized history. The earthquake sequence alone is a true marvel of engineering. It is said that movie pioneer D. W. Griffith visited the set and asked if he might direct a scene. Van Dyke, who had begun his career as an assistant on Griffith's *Intolerance*, was only too glad to oblige. No one knows exactly which scene Griffith directed, but close analysis suggests it was the one during the earthquake that makes use of a spinning wagon wheel that finally stops as the tremors end. This would be a typical Griffith touch. Loos and Robert Hopkins, who did the original story, had long envisioned writing *San Francisco*. They were both natives of the city and were eager to capture the city's vibrant personality, particularly as it had been at the turn of the century, before the Great Earthquake.

Awards: Academy Award: Sound Recording; Academy Award Nominations: Best Picture, Actor (Tracy), Director, Assistant Director, Original Story.

Selected Bibliography

Miller, Frank. *Movies We Love: 100 Collectible Classics*. Atlanta, GA: Turner Publishing, 1996.
Stern, Lee Edward. *Jeanette MacDonald*. New York: Jove Publications, 1977.

SCOTT, RANDOLPH. Actor. Born George Randolph Crane Scott on January 23, 1898, in Orange County, Virginia; died on March 2, 1987, in Los Angeles, California. Educated at the Georgia Institute of Technology in Atlanta, the University of North Carolina, and the Pasadena Playhouse. Scott entered films as a bit player in 1929 with the help of Howard Hughes and proved himself to be a versatile lead throughout the 1930s. During and after World War II he played several military heroes before turning to westerns in which he became extremely popular as a weathered, quiet-talking cowboy. Scott did some of his best work in the late 1950s, when he formed the Ranown Production Company with Harry Joe Brown and starred in a series of mature westerns directed by Budd Boetticher. His last film, *Ride the High Country*, was his swansong. In it he and Joel McCrea play last-of-a-kind cowboys in a movie that was itself the last of its kind. Scott was one of Hollywood's durables, like Glenn Ford and John Wayne, turning in such accomplished, effortless performances that what he did seemed natural and not like acting.

Filmography: The Far Call (1929); Women Men Marry (1931); Heritage of the Desert, Hot Saturday, Wild Horse Mesa (1932); Broken Dreams, Cocktail Hour, Hello Everybody!, Man of the Forest, Murders in the Zoo, Sunset Pass, Supernatural, The Thundering Herd, To the Last Man (1933); The Last Round-Up, Wagon Wheels (1934); Home on the Range, Roberta, Rocky Mountain Mystery, She, So Red the Rose, Village Tale (1935); And Sudden Death, Follow the Fleet, Go West Young Man, The Last of the Mohicans (1936); High Wide and Handsome (1937); Rebecca of Sunnybrook Farm, The Road to Reno, The Texans (1938); Coast Guard, Frontier Marshal, Jesse James (1939); My Favorite Wife, Virginia City, When the Daltons Rode (1940); Belle Starr, Paris Calling, Western Union (1941); Pittsburgh, The Spoilers, To the Shores of Tripoli (1942); The Bombardier, Corvette K-225, The Desperadoes, Gung Ho! (1943); Belle of the Yukon, Follow the Boys (1944); Captain Kidd, China Sky (1945); Abilene Town, Badman's Territory, Home Sweet Homicide (1946); Christmas Eve/Sinner's Holiday, Gunfighters, Trail Street (1947); Albuquerque, Coroner Creek, Return of the Bad Men (1948); Canadian Pacific, The Doolins of Oklahoma, Fighting Man of the Plains, The Walking Hills (1949); Cariboo Trail, Colt .45/Thundercloud, The Nevadan (1950); Fort Worth, Man in the Saddle, Santa Fe, Starlift, Sugarfoot/Swirl of Glory (1951); Carson City, Hangman's Knot, The Man behind the Gun (1952); The Stranger Wore a Gun, Thunder over the Plains (1953); The Bounty Hunter, Riding Shotgun (1954); A Lawless Street [also assoc. prod.], Rage at Dawn, Tall Man Riding, Ten Wanted Men [also assoc. prod.] (1955); Seven Men from Now, Seventh Cavalry [also assoc. prod.] (1956); Decision at Sundown,

Shoot Out at Medicine Bend, The Tall T (1957); Buchanan Rides Alone [also assoc. prod.] (1958); Ride Lonesome [also exec. prod.], Westbound (1959); Comanche Station (1960); Ride the High Country (1962).

Selected Bibliography

Crow, Jefferson Brim. *Randolph Scott: The Gentleman from Virginia: A Film Biography.* Carrollton, TX: Wind River Publishing, 1987.

SEA HAWK, THE (1940), romance/adventure/war. Directed by Michael Curtiz; with Errol Flynn, Brenda Marshall, Claude Rains, Donald Crisp, Flora Robson, Alan Hale, Henry Daniell, Una O'Connor, and Gilbert Roland; screenplay by Howard Koch and Seton I. Miller.

"If you miss it, you will owe yourself an apology!" ran the blurb for this epic film based loosely on the popular Rafael Sabatini novel, here turned into more of a cross between *Robin Hood* and *Captain Blood*. Errol Flynn is at his dashing best in this bold and swashbuckling adventure on the high seas. In this remake of the 1923 version, the screenplay has been expanded to include endless episodes of court intrigue during the reign of Queen Elizabeth. Critics are divided over the film, with some maintaining that a poor script, sluggish pacing, and uninspired direction weigh the film down. Some feel that endless episodes of court intrigue tend to diminish the effect of the epic sweep of the high seas dramatics, while others think the large sets, sweeping sea battles, and armies of extras bring the film up to epic standards and carry the day. Both sides agree, however, that this film is ultimately a hugely enjoyable swashbuckler from the days when "packaging" wasn't such a dirty word—and Jack Warner was master of the art.

Awards: Academy Awards: Best B&W Art Direction (Anton Grot), Score (Erich Wolfgang Korngold), Sound, Special Effects.

Selected Bibliography

Kinnard, Roy, and R. J. Vitone. *The American Films of Michael Curtiz.* Metuchen, NJ: Scarecrow Press, 1986.

Valenti, Peter. *Errol Flynn: A Bio-Bibliography.* Westport, CT: Greenwood Press, 1984.

SEARCH, THE (1948), drama. Directed by Fred Zinnemann; with Montgomery Clift, Ivan Jandl, Aline MacMahon, Jarmila Novotna, and Wendell Corey; screenplay by Richard Schweizer, David Wechsler, and Paul Jarrico.

This is one of the most moving films ever made, a poignant drama of an American soldier (Clift) caring for a concentration camp survivor (Jandl) in postwar Berlin while the boy's mother trudges from one Displaced Persons' Camp to the next, desperately searching for him. Its quasi-documentary style keeps it from becoming overly sentimental and allows the heart-wrenching story itself to unfold with eloquent understatement. The emphasis is on the terrors of the refugee children of World War II, and it emerges as a grim reminder that it was the children who were the most innocent of all victims of Nazi terror. This was Clift's first film, and he brings to it the style of acting he became known for—hesitant, impulsive—yet realistic and engaging. The movie crosscuts between what is happening to the boy and scenes of his persistent Czech mother (played by opera singer Jarmila Novotna) trudging from camp to camp in search of him. This deceptively simple film is set against the stark backdrop of the ruins of a bombed-out German city, a scene of incredible devastation that makes its own mute statement about war and inhumanity. Only four of the actors in the film were professionals, the others having been recruited on the spot. The ending may seem contrived, but the film builds up to it with such honesty and genuine feeling that the ending is fully justified—and thoroughly satisfying. After all that sacrifice and suffering, the characters deserve a happy ending— and so does the audience. The ending went unmatched until *Schindler's List*.

Awards: Academy Awards: Original Story (Richard Schweitzer, David Wechsler), Special Award (Ivan Jandl, for outstanding juvenile performance of 1948); Golden Globe Awards: Screenplay (Richard Schweitzer), Best Film Promoting International Understanding, Special Award to Best Juvenile Actor (Jandl); Academy Award Nomination: Best Actor (Clift).

Selected Bibliography

Kalfatovic, Mary C. *Montgomery Clift: A Bio-Bibliography*. Westport, CT: Greenwood Press, 1994.
Zinnemann, Fred. *A Life in the Movies: An Autobiography*. New York. Charles Scribner's Sons, 1992.

SEARCHERS, THE (1956), western. Directed by John Ford; with John Wayne, Jeffrey Hunter, Vera Miles, Ward Bond, Natalie Wood, John Qualen, Harry Carey, Jr., Olive Carey, Antonio Moreno, Henry Brandon, Hank Worden, Lana Wood, Dorothy Jordan, and Pat Wayne; screenplay by Frank S. Nugent.

This film has acquired something of a cult following, so revered are John Ford and John Wayne for surpassing themselves in this dark, disturbing drama. In it John Wayne relentlessly searches for his niece (Wood), kidnapped by the Indians who killed her family. It is hard to imagine anyone but Ford bringing this magnificent film to the screen. And John Wayne gives one of the greatest performances of his career as the complex, conflicted Ethan Edwards. Ford balances drama and humor in a way that allows wit and irony to temper grim reality. He also relies to a great extent on visual impact, from the close-ups of facial expressions and gestures to the sweeping panoramas of his beloved Monument Valley. Wayne personifies the tragedy of *The Searchers* in that while he has the ruthlessness necessary to tame the West, he cannot participate in the world that has resulted. Throughout the film, he walks a fine line between savagery and civilization. This is best illustrated by the fact that although he relentlessly searches for his niece in order to rescue her from her captors, he is reviled by the belief that her contact with them has irrevocably tainted her. There are no easy answers in this film, nothing as simple as the opposition of good and evil, for we see Anglos and Indians alike as being capable of acts of both compassion and brutality. Those not dazzled by its director and star find the film overlong and repetitious and the humor forced. They also wonder if its weighty theme isn't somewhat too ponderous for a western. Call it the *Shane* syndrome, but in an attempt to elevate the western, movies like this one flirt with pretentiousness. The West is a ready-made myth. It requires no embellishment.

Awards: Academy Award Nominations: Best Editing, Original Musical Score.

Selected Bibliography

Hardy, Phil, ed. *The Overlook Film Encyclopedia: The Western*. Woodstock, NY: Overlook Press, 1994.
Parish, James Robert, and Michael R. Pitts. *The Great Western Pictures*. Metuchen, NJ: Scarecrow Press, 1976.
Zmijewsky, Steve, Boris Zmijewsky, and Mark Ricci. *The Complete Films of John Wayne*. Secaucus, NJ: Citadel Press, 1983.

SEPARATE TABLES (1958), drama. Directed by Delbert Mann; with Burt Lancaster, Rita Hayworth, David Niven, Deborah Kerr, Wendy Hiller, Gladys Cooper, Cathleen Nesbitt, Rod Taylor, and Felix Aylmer; screenplay by Terence Rattigan and John Gay.

Separate Tables is a variation on the Grand Hotel theme, but it's a durable concoction that, when well done, is always justifiable. In this case, it is eminently justifiable since what we have is an adult, intelligent, beautifully acted film filled with exquisite dramatic moments and strong emotional undercurrents. To anyone who knows the play on which it is based, the screen adaptation is a marvel of interweaving that appears to be one ensemble tale rather than two separate stories. The Terence Rattigan play on which this movie is based consists of two separate vignettes that take place at the same English boardinghouse. Much of the appeal of the play is the remarkable change in characterization the actors were able to make as they assume different roles in each of the segments. Although Rattigan and John Gay have masterfully blended the two playlets into one literate and absorbing full-length film, some critics feel that the genteel melodramas seem less convincing on the screen than they did on the stage. Those who see only the film, though, are not troubled by this comparison and can thus enjoy it for what it is, a compelling drama of the loneliness and transiency that threaten to disrupt the most seemingly impregnable happiness.

Awards: Academy Awards, Golden Globe Awards, New York Film Critics Circle Awards: Best Actor (Niven), Supporting Actress (Wendy Hiller); Academy Award Nominations: Best Picture, Actress (Kerr), Adapted Screenplay, B&W Cinematography, Scoring of a Dramatic Picture.

Selected Bibliography

Crowther, Bruce. *Burt Lancaster: A Life in Films*. London: Robert Hale, 1991.
Garrett, Gerard. *The Films of David Niven*. Secaucus, NJ: Citadel Press, 1976.

SEVEN BRIDES FOR SEVEN BROTHERS (1954), musical/dance. Directed by Stanley Donen; with Howard Keel, Jane Powell, Jeff Richards, Russ Tamblyn, Tommy Rall, Virginia Gibson, Julie Newmeyer (Newmar), Ruta Kilmonis (Lee), and Matt Mattox; screenplay by Ålbert Hackett, Frances Goodrich, and Dorothy Kingsley.

"I now pronounce you—men and wives!" Thus ran the blurb for this film based very loosely on the tale of the rape of the Sabine women. It is really more of a dance fest than a traditional musical, a happy, hand-clapping, foot-stomping country type of musical with all the slickness of a Broadway show. Johnny Mercer and Gene de Paul provide the eight production numbers, and Howard Keel's hearty baritone and Jane Powell's sweet soprano give the songs added luster. It is a rollicking film with a breathless pace, well-defined characters, and an incredible vitality under Stanley Donen's direction. A real standout is the acrobatic hoedown staged around a barn-raising shindig, during which six of the title's seven brothers vie in love rivalry with the town boys for the favor of the mountain belles. Although it was a novelty to set a musical in the great outdoors, the fact that the "outdoors" was really a studio backlot led some critics to find it disappointingly studio bound. Even so, many found it a refreshing new direction in musical films, but it was a trend that never really caught on, despite such efforts as *Brigadoon* and *West Side Story*. The later TV version of *Seven Brides for Seven Brothers* only proved how unlikely this style of musical was to succeed. For what it is and what it does, however, it is a landmark film.

Awards: Academy Award: Best Scoring of a Musical Picture (Adolph Deutsch, Saul Chaplin); Academy Award Nominations: Best Picture, Screenplay, Color Cinematography, Editing; National Board of Review: Special Award (Michael Kidd, choreography).

Selected Bibliography

Casper, Joseph Andrew. *Stanley Donen*. Metuchen, NJ: Scarecrow Press, 1983.

Fordin, Hugh. *The World of Entertainment!: Hollywood's Greatest Musicals*. Garden City, NY: Doubleday, 1975.

Taylor, John Russell, and Arthur Jackson. *The Hollywood Musical*. London: Secker & Warburg, 1971.

SHANE (1953), western. Directed by George Stevens; with Alan Ladd, Jean Arthur, Van Heflin, Jack Palance, Brandon de Wilde, Ben Johnson, Edgar Buchanan, Emile Meyer, and Elisha Cook, Jr.; screenplay by A. B. Guthrie, Jr. and Jack Sher.

This story of a former gunfighter who comes to the defense of homesteaders and is idolized by their son is generally considered a classic western. At the time it appeared, the popularity of the western was already on the decline, and many see in this movie a foreshadowing of the end, especially when Alan Ladd, who has long wanted to hang up his guns, rides away at the end while Brandon de Wilde calls after him to come back, a scene that communicates a sense of finality, the end of an era. It was Alan Ladd's last memorable film performance and Jean Arthur's last film. In this film, director Stevens mounts the powerful drama of an old West dying as the new age, the era of the homesteader, takes over the range and settles it. Ladd is excellent as the doomed hero, an outcast looking in on a society that has rejected him, a society he nevertheless tries to embrace. Much of the acclaim the film has received can be attributed to its overriding sense of tragic irony. Shane, a notorious gunfighter, uses his socially scorned ''skills'' to save the very people who scorn him. Some critics find this movie pretentious and overrated and cringe at the film's blatant attempt to create a myth. Others find the film overplanned and uninspired and too self-important and argue that it looks as if it were self-consciously intended as a landmark film right from the start with its slow pace and persistent solemnity. Nevertheless, the film found a wide audience and continues to be included on the short list of classic westerns.

Awards: Academy Award: Best Color Cinematography (Loyal Griggs); Directors Guild of America: Outstanding Directorial Achievement; *Photoplay* Gold Medal Award: Most Popular Male Star (Ladd); Academy Award Nominations: Best Picture, Director, Supporting Actor (de Wilde, Palance), Screenplay.

Selected Bibliography

Hardy, Phil, ed. *The Overlook Film Encyclopedia: The Western.* Woodstock, NY: Overlook Press, 1994.

Henry, Marilyn, and Ron DeSourdis. *The Films of Alan Ladd.* Secaucus, NJ: Citadel Press, 1981.

Petri, Bruce Humleker. *A Theory of American Film: The Films and Techniques of George Stevens.* New York: Garland, 1987.

SHIP OF FOOLS (1965), drama. Directed by Stanley Kramer; with Vivien Leigh, Oskar Werner, Simone Signoret, José Ferrer, Lee Marvin, Jose Greco, George Segal, Elizabeth Ashley, Michael Dunn, Charles Korvin, and Lilia Skala; screenplay by Abby Mann.

Some have called this picture *Grand Hotel* at sea, and so it is, since passengers on an ocean liner are as random as guests at a hotel. But the difference in this case is that, unlike a hotel, a ship can be a floating prison, for there is nowhere to go, nowhere to flee to, in a time of crisis. And this is certainly a time of crisis, for it is 1933, and this is a German ship traveling from Veracruz to Bremerhaven. Katherine Anne Porter explained the title as referring to the ''simple almost universal image of the ship of this world on its voyage to eternity'' (adding, ''I am a passenger on that ship''), but her vessel is more than that. It is also a microcosm of the emerging Nazi world, and the fools are those who do not see what is coming. As screen entertainment, it is intelligent and eminently satisfying most of the time. All of the principals give strong performances, from José Ferrer as a loathsome disciple of the emerging Hitlerian new order to Vivien Leigh as a fading American divorcee who enjoys leading men on and then throwing cold water on their desires. Of equal importance are the contributions of Simone Signoret in the role of La Condesa and Oskar Werner as Dr. Schumann, the ship's doctor. Also impressive are George Segal and Elizabeth Ashley as young lovers whose minds are at war with their passions. Although generally critically acclaimed, there are dissenting voices who find the movie loud and crude and fraught with deformed relationships. Kinder critics, while voicing reservations about its yards and yards of liberal cliché, feel that the superb cast makes it almost watchable. John Simon is even more caustic. More moderate critics view it as a reflection upon the human condition, so subtle an orchestration of the elements of love and hate and so special in its treatment that it is unfair to judge it by the standards of any other film.

Awards: Academy Awards: Best B&W Cinematography, B&W Art Direction; Academy Award Nominations: Best Picture, Actor (Werner), Actress (Signoret), Supporting Actor (Michael Dunn), Adapted Screenplay, B&W Costume Design.

Selected Bibliography

Spoto, Donald. *Stanley Kramer: Film Maker*. New York: Putnam, 1978.

SINATRA, FRANK. Singer, actor. Born Francis Albert Sinatra on December 12, 1915, in Hoboken, New Jersey; died on May 15, 1998. Sinatra was a singer with the Harry James and Tommy Dorsey orchestras when he emerged as a pop idol in the early 1940s. He made his film debut in 1943 and appeared in light comedies and musicals throughout the decade. His first memorable role was in *Anchors Aweigh* with Gene Kelly. They teamed again (along with Jules Munshin) in *On the Town*, a sparkling musical, the first to be filmed on location (in New York) and one that has become a classic. In 1952, hemorrhaged vocal chords brought the first phase of his career to an end, but Sinatra wasn't through even though everyone thought he was. Instead, he departed from singing and comedy for a while, pursuing straight dramatic roles in which he proved himself an accomplished dramatic actor. He made a comeback with a vengeance as Maggio in *From Here to Eternity*, for which he won an Oscar. He did another star turn as a heroin addict in Otto Preminger's *The Man with the Golden Arm*. Perhaps the dramatic role he will be remembered best for was that of Bennett Marco in the political psychodrama *The Manchurian Candidate*, a film that has achieved the status of cult classic. After he regained his vocal powers, Sinatra emerged as a show business institution, turning out pop hits, selling out Vegas nightclubs, and starring in an assortment of international films, including some creditable crime thrillers. His fabled decline and dramatic resurgence allegedly served as the basis for the Johnny Fontane character in *The Godfather* (1972), whose foundering career is put right, thanks to "mob" muscle. In addition to his rumored mob connections, Sinatra led a colorful life in other respects, from his very public romances with glamorous stars like Ava Gardner to his altercations with the paparazzi. Above it all swung Sinatra the singer, a man generally considered to be the best pop singer of the century and the essence of a show business phenomenon. A man who made Grammy Award–winning recordings into his eighties deserves to be called "a legend in his own time."

Filmography: Las Vegas Nights (1941); Ship Ahoy (1942); Higher and Higher, Reveille with Beverly (1943); Step Lively, Anchors Aweigh, The House I Live In [short] (1945); Till the Clouds Roll By (1946); It Happened in Brooklyn (1947); The Kissing Bandit, The Miracle of the Bells (1948); On the Town, Take Me Out to the Ball Game (1949); Double Dynamite (1951); Meet Danny Wilson (1952); From Here to Eternity (1953); Suddenly, Three Coins in the Fountain [song composer], Young at Heart (1954); Guys and Dolls, The Man with the Golden Arm, Not as a Stranger, The Tender Trap (1955); Around the World in 80 Days, High Society, Johnny Concho [also prod.] (1956); The Joker Is Wild/All the Way, Pal Joey, The Pride and the Passion (1957); Kings Go Forth, Some Came Running (1958); A Hole in the Head [also prod., song composer] (1959); Can-Can, Ocean's Eleven, Pepe (1960); The Devil at 4 O'Clock (1961); Advise and Consent [song composer], The Manchurian Candidate (1962); Sergeants 3 [also prod.] (1962); Come Blow Your Horn, Four for Texas, The List of Adrian Messenger (1963); Robin and the Seven Hoods [also prod.] (1964); Marriage on the Rocks, None But the Brave [also dir., prod.], Von Ryan's Express (1965); Assault on a Queen [also exec. prod.], Cast a Giant Shadow (1966); The Naked Runner, Tony Rome (1967); The Detective, Lady in Cement (1968); Dirty Dingus Magee (1970); That's Entertainment! (1974); The First Deadly Sin [exec. prod.] (1980); Cannonball Run II (1984); Who Framed Roger Rabbit? (1988); Entertaining the Troops (1989); Listen Up: The Lives of Quincy Jones (1990).

Honors: Academy Award, Golden Globe Award: Best Supporting Actor (*From Here to Eternity*, 1953); Academy Award Nomination: Best Actor (*The Man with the Golden Arm*, 1955); Golden Globe Award: Best Actor—Comedy/Musical (*Pal Joey*, 1957); Academy Award: Jean Hersholt Humanitarian Award; Golden Globes: Cecil B. DeMille Award (1970).

Selected Bibliography

Dellar, Fred. *Sinatra: His Life and Times*. London: Omnibus, 1995.

Lonstein, Albert, and Vito R. Marino. *The Revised Compleat Sinatra*. Ellenville, NY: S. M. Lonstein, 1979.

Rockwell, John. *Sinatra: An American Classic*. New York: Random House, 1984.

SINGIN' IN THE RAIN (1952), musical. Directed by Gene Kelly and Stanley Donen; with Gene Kelly, Debbie Reynolds, Donald O'Connor, Jean Hagen, Cyd Charisse, Millard Mitchell, Douglas Fowley, Madge Blake, and Rita Moreno; screenplay by Betty Comden and Adolph Green.

Singin' in the Rain is generally considered by critics and audiences alike to be the greatest movie musical of all time. It is funny, bright, tuneful, colorful, imaginative, and thoroughly entertaining. Its spoof of Hollywood at the moment sound was introduced is fraught with comic possibilities, all of which are taken advantage of, along with every sort of in-joke possible when Hollywood is free to make fun of itself. Because it is a spoof of itself, the movie has layers within layers of delightful surprises. A pie in the face is no longer considered very funny (unless you're twelve), but when Jean Hagen gets one—quite by accident—from Debbie Reynolds, it is more than just an eminently satisfying moment; it is a scene that echoes down the halls of classic Hollywood comedy.

The cast is so superbly talented, it's hard to single anyone out for special praise, but Jean Hagen as the shrieking, shrewish Lena Lamont is a sensation in a performance that is pivotal to the success of this film. She's the wicked witch out to exploit innocent Debbie Reynolds, and her undoing makes for one of the most gratifying moments in film history. But it's only one of dozens of satisfying moments in this fast-paced film. A special treat is the appearance of Cyd Charisse in the "Broadway Ballet" sequence. The sequence is so totally gratuitous that while it is mocking Hollywood's disregard for logic, it is making us rejoice over that disregard, if only because it provides an opportunity to see those fabulous Charisse legs in rare form. An added irony is the fact that it was Kelly who was responsible for introducing ballet sequences into musicals, a novelty that quickly wore off. Thus, he is—probably inadvertently in this case—making fun of himself. This film works on several levels, presenting a great musical but also commenting—often unfavorably but always accurately—on the wild personalities and studio machinations that characterized that colorful period. Film buffs are given an extra treat when they realize that Debbie Reynolds is driving Andy Hardy's old jalopy and that Gene Kelly's house is a leftover from the Garbo/Gilbert 1927 silent classic *Flesh and Fantasy*. And, of course, the music is a pastiche of numbers taken from the best of MGM's dazzling musical output since talkies began, all but a few written by Arthur Freed and Nacio Herb Brown.

Awards: Golden Globe Award: Best Actor—Comedy/Musical (O'Connor); Academy Award Nominations: Best Supporting Actress (Hagen), Scoring of a Musical Picture.

Selected Bibliography

Casper, Joseph Andrew. *Stanley Donen*. Metuchen, NJ: Scarecrow Press, 1983.

Fordin, Hugh. *The World of Entertainment!: Hollywood's Greatest Musicals*. Garden City, NY: Doubleday, 1975.

Peary, Danny. *Alternate Oscars*. New York: Delta, 1993.

Thomas, Tony. *Song and Dance Man: The Films of Gene Kelly*. Secaucus, NJ: Citadel Press, 1974.

SOME LIKE IT HOT (1959), comedy. Directed by Billy Wilder; with Jack Lemmon, Tony Curtis, Marilyn Monroe, Joe E. Brown, George Raft, Pat O'Brien, Nehemiah Persoff, Joan Shawlee, and Mike Mazurki; screenplay by Billy Wilder and I. A. L. Diamond.

This is one of the great screen comedies of all time. Basing it on a simple concept, Wilder and Diamond expand on the conceit with hysterical results. But script and direction are only a part of the mix. The catalyst is the cast. Lemmon and Curtis, who just happen to witness the St. Valentine's Day Massacre, make a hilarious team of guys in drag as they try to evade their pursuers by joining an all-girl band. And Marilyn Monroe, in a brilliant bit of self-parody, gives the whole crazy romp its own brand of zany logic. "You have to be orderly to shoot disorder; this was the best disorder we ever had," Wilder jokingly remarked after the often difficult shooting was completed. *Some Like It Hot* is more than fugitives and hanky-panky; it is also a superb send-up of gangster films and sex roles. It has been noted that the film deals with such things as transvestism, impotence, and role confusion, with uproarious innocence. Lemmon and Curtis create believable characters, never once camping up their parts, while Monroe exhibits that special Monroe magic that will forever puzzle audiences who wonder how much is real, how much is accident, how much is parody, how much technique. Who cares? What finally matters is that one finally senses that one is in the presence of a highly original talent, the one-of-a-kind mold that gets cast and then broken only a few times in a generation. Even though it may be true that the movie flogs its central idea to death, it is also true that it then recovers with a smart line or situation. It has, in any case, become a milestone of film comedy. It has been called everything from a black farce to a smart-alecky parody complete with blatant sexist stereotyping, crude one-liners, and unabashed bad taste.

Awards: Academy Award: Best B&W Costume Design (Orry Kelly); Golden Globe Awards: Best Picture, Actor (Lemmon); British Academy Award: Best Foreign Actor (Jack Lemmon); Academy Award Nominations: Best Director, Actor (Lemmon), Adapted Screenplay, B&W Cinematography, B&W Art Direction.

Selected Bibliography

Lahue, Kalton C. *World of Laughter*. Norman: University of Oklahoma Press, 1966.
Peary, Danny. *Alternate Oscars*. New York: Delta, 1993.
Seidman, Steve. *The Film Career of Billy Wilder*. Boston: G. K. Hall, 1977.
Spada, James. *Monroe: Her Life in Pictures*. Garden City, NY: Doubleday, 1982.

SONG OF BERNADETTE (1943), religious/biography. Directed by Henry King; with Jennifer Jones, William Eythe, Charles Bickford, Vincent Price, Lee J. Cobb, Anne Revere, and Gladys Cooper; screenplay by George Seaton.

This is an absorbing, well-made adaptation of Franz Werfel's celebrated novel. The film tackles a difficult and delicate subject—that of an ignorant young peasant girl who is visited by the Virgin Mary—and makes uncanny sense of it. Viewers need not be believers to appreciate the humanity and psychology of these very real characters as they wrestle with a truly terrifying possibility, for to believe or not to believe offers equal risks. Rather than becoming cloying, the story is generously laced with the bitterness of envy, the agony of doubt, and the heartbreak of forsaken love. At every turn Bernadette's credibility is challenged; thus she convinces not by logic but by placid persistence. For all the bullying she takes from her "superiors" alone, she deserves to be a saint. Jennifer Jones, in her first starring role, glows with an innocence and a radiance that put her detractors to shame. Her confrontations with the clergymen/inquisitors (particularly Charles Bickford) convince you that some higher power is inspiring her. Some have complained that the movie is overlong or that it commercializes a religious experience, but these charges seem merely small-minded in the face of a mystical experience that defies refutation. What irritates her detractors, both in real life and her own life, is the unnerving possibility that she has been blessed and they haven't. Gladys Cooper, as the jealous Mother Superior who thinks Bernadette is vain and proud, sums up the resentment of those who envy Bernadette when she wonders aloud why it is not she, after a lifetime of praying until her throat is parched, who is being visited by the Virgin. The way this picture can move even the most stubborn skeptic is, itself, a sort of miracle.

Awards: Academy Awards: Best Actress (Jones), B&W Cinematography, B&W Interior Decoration (James Basevi, William Darling), Score for a Dramatic Picture (Alfred Newman); Golden Globe Awards: Best Picture, Actress (Jones); Academy Award Nominations: Best Picture, Director, Supporting Actor (Bickford), Supporting Actress (Cooper, Revere), Screenplay, Editing, Sound.

Selected Bibliography

Carrier, Jeffrey L. *Jennifer Jones: A Bio-Bibliography*. Westport, CT: Greenwood Press, 1990.

SOUTHERNER, THE (1945), drama. Directed by Jean Renoir; with Zachary Scott, Betty Field, Beulah Bondi, J. Carrol Naish, Norman Lloyd, Bunny Sunshine, Jay Gilpin, Estelle Taylor, Percy Kilbride, and Blanche Yurka; screenplay by Jean Renoir.

Though only French director/writer Jean Renoir is credited with writing the screenplay for this poetic tribute to rural American life, William Faulkner also worked on the script. His touch is evident in the film's realistic depiction of courage and freedom and impressionistic in its view of nature. It is all so vividly rendered that you can almost smell the earth as the plow turns it over and the river after the flood that almost ends the struggle of these dirt-poor tenant farmers. The story is the account of a year in the life of a poor white Texas family and their struggle to work their farm while under the constant threat of poverty and hunger. Zachary Scott, almost unrecognizable as a young tenant farmer (his typical role was the scumbag in *Mildred Pierce*) gives the performance of his career. The underrated Betty Field plays his wife with a marvelous mixture of stoicism and quiet desperation. The picture has moments of power and beauty and a certain solemn mystery that belie the tasteless hype United Artists used to try to promote what they figured would be a loser: "She was his woman . . . and he was her man!" ran the blurb. "That's all they had to fight with—against the world, the flesh, and the devil!" Some critics deplore the relentless bleakness of the film, finding it depressing in its utter hopelessness. Other critics find this a welcome antidote to traditional Hollywood depictions of "real people" and consider it Renoir's most successful American film. It has been compared favorably with *The Grapes of Wrath* with which it shares a certain earthy poetry, even though it lacks the breadth of the latter. In *The Southerner* there is little of the Faulkner whose famous speech upon winning the Nobel Prize spoke of how the human spirit would not only survive but prevail. Nevertheless, it is an achievement of a very special sort and is easily at home amidst the classics of the American cinema.

Awards: Academy Award Nominations: Best Director, Scoring of a Dramatic Picture, Sound.

Selected Bibliography

Braudy, Leo. *Jean Renoir: The World of His Films*. New York: Columbia University Press, 1989.
Durgnat, Raymond. *Jean Renoir*. Berkeley: University of California Press, 1974.

STAGECOACH (1939), western. Directed by John Ford; with Claire Trevor, John Wayne, Andy Devine, John Carradine, Thomas Mitchell, Louise Platt, George Bancroft, Donald Meek, Berton Churchill, Tim Holt, Tom Tyler, Chris-Pin Martin, Francis Ford, and Jack Pennick; screenplay by Joseph Landin.

Stagecoach, sometimes called *Grand Hotel* on wheels, is generally considered to be Ford's greatest epic of the frontier. This film surpassed all previous westerns and vastly influenced those that followed. It is a broad portrait of pioneer life in the untamed Southwest, as well as an in-depth character study of eight people, all diverse in their pursuits and all traveling to separate fates on a journey packed with danger. It was the first western to probe deeply into its characters and to expose the symbolic meanings beneath the surface plot of their life and death struggles. The landscape of the awesome Monument Valley serves as a constant reminder of the freedom of the frontier in conflict with the dangers inherent in enjoying that freedom. There is a constant sense of history running throughout the film, as the characters endure hazards and suffer indignities. Ford manipulates his ensemble of prominent players in a way that elicits top-notch performances from all of them. This is the film that made the public realize that John Wayne could also act, and it permitted Claire Trevor to display the talents that unfortunately would always be underrated. As usual, John Ford wrestles with big themes, like good versus evil and people discovering more nobility within themselves than they ever imagined. Later Ford would lean more toward the puzzling ambiguities that can favor evil and cowardice as well as goodness and bravery. In *Stagecoach* he is dealing with allegory, not ambiguity. Two remakes since have not held up well by comparison, reinforcing the constantly repeated but too often unheeded admonition never to try to remake a classic.

Awards: Academy Awards: Best Score, Supporting Actor (Mitchell); New York Film Critics Award: Director; Academy Award Nominations: Best Picture, Director, B&W Cinematography, Art Direction, Editing.

Selected Bibliography

Parish, James Robert, and Michael R. Pitts. *The Great Western Pictures*. Metuchen, NJ: Scarecrow Press, 1976.
Place, Janey Ann. *The Western Films of John Ford*. Secaucus, NJ: Citadel Press, 1974.
Sennett, Ted. *Hollywood's Golden Year, 1939*. New York: St. Martin's Press, 1989.

STAGE DOOR (1937), comedy/drama. Directed by Gregory La Cava; with Katharine Hepburn, Ginger Rogers, Adolphe Menjou, Andrea Leeds, Gail Patrick,

Constance Collier, Lucille Ball, Eve Arden, Ann Miller, Ralph Forbes, Franklin Pangborn, and Jack Carson; screenplay by Morrie Ryskind and Anthony Veiller.

A theatrical boardinghouse is the setting for this view of aspiring young actresses who vent their bitterness against the economic uncertainties of legitimate employment in sharp, biting dialogue. It is funny in spots, emotionally effective, and generally brisk and entertaining. The cast is headed by Hepburn, who plays a rich girl trying to succeed on her own. Menjou is cast as the lecherous producer and Leeds as a hypersensitive actress. The film also features Lucille Ball, Ann Miller, Eve Arden, and Jack Carson, personalities destined to become stars in their own right. A brilliant script and strong, realistic acting make this film a treat to behold. It is easily one of the most entertaining comedies of the 1930s, and it is still gratifying to see how Rogers holds her own with ease against the formidable Katharine Hepburn as the two trade wisecracks. In general, critics praise the performances in this film and find it a rare example of a film substantially improving on a stage original.

Awards: Academy Award Nominations: Best Picture, Screenplay, Director, Supporting Actress (Leeds).

Selected Bibliography

Peary, Danny. *Alternate Oscars*. New York: Delta, 1993.
Spada, James. *Hepburn: Her Life in Pictures*. Garden City, NY: Doubleday, 1984.
Vermilye, Jerry. *The Films of the Thirties*. New York: Citadel Press, 1990.

STALAG 17 (1953), drama/war. Directed by Billy Wilder; with William Holden, Don Taylor, Otto Preminger, Robert Strauss, Harvey Lembeck, Richard Erdman, Peter Graves, Neville Brand, Sig Ruman, and Ross Bagdasarian; screenplay by Billy Wilder and Edwin Blum.

Stalag 17 is a wonder of a film, alternately funny, scary, cynical, sad, and deeply moving on all levels. Wilder's touch was never more sure nor more deft than in this story of American prisoners of war in a German prison camp, one of whom (Holden) is suspected by his fellow prisoners of being a Nazi spy. Holden was universally praised for turning in a bravura performance as a heel-turned-hero, and director-actor Otto Preminger creates an indelible portrait as the vicious, arrogant camp commandant, the embodiment of sheer sadistic evil, who is ultimately outwitted by the prisoners. The film is hard to classify accurately. On one level it is a lusty comedy full of masculine humor, but the humor is also often dark, giving the film a melodramatic, sometimes tragic, edge. While some critics praise this blend of comedy and melodrama, others feel that the mix is an uneasy one. They see the comedy degenerating into buffoonery and siring such TV sitcoms as *Hogan's Heroes* and *Sergeant Bilko*, while the melodrama anticipates the darkly cynical *King Rat*. The problem is that the two moods aren't properly synthesized. Thus, the bleakness of the settings creates a reality that is jarringly contradicted by the comic opera crew of Germans headed by Preminger. However, taken on its own terms, *Stalag 17* is a rare achievement.

Awards: Academy Award: Best Actor (Holden); Directors Guild of America Award: Outstanding Directorial Achievement; Academy Award Nominations: Best Director, Supporting Actor (Strauss).

Selected Bibliography

Quirk, Lawrence J. *The Complete Films of William Holden.* Secaucus, NJ: Citadel Press, 1986.

Zolotow, Maurice. *Billy Wilder in Hollywood.* New York: G. P. Putnam's Sons, 1977.

STANWYCK, BARBARA. Actress. Born Ruby Stevens on July 16, 1907, in Brooklyn, New York; died on January 20, 1990, in Santa Monica, California. Stanwyck was an enduring, thoroughly professional star who remained at the top for three decades and was considered by many to be the epitome of the film actress. One film scholar has suggested that she was the first actress to understand the uniqueness of film acting and to put it to best advantage. She was not glamorous in the traditional sense, and she frequently played wicked characters, yet she exuded a magnetism on the screen that captured the audience's attention and made her one of the most loved and respected screen personalities. Beneath her toughness she always seemed vulnerable—even when she wasn't, as in *Double Indemnity*; but even in that film she manages to gain a measure of sympathy for a woman who should be despised if only because she seems so tragically caught in her own web, more like Medea than Lady Macbeth. Maybe it's simply that, like Bette Davis, she was so good at being bad that you find yourself rooting for her even when you know she's wrong. Stanwyck started out as a stage and cabaret dancer, moving to Hollywood with her first husband, vaudevillian Frank Fay. She made impressive appearances in her early films, but it was *Stella Dallas* that made her a star—and in a way established her screen persona as the long-suffering heroine in what was then known as a "woman's picture." But she also played in such comedy screen classics as *The Lady Eve* and *Ball of Fire*, showing that, like Colbert and Hepburn, she could play anything. Stanwyck was at her peak in the 1940s, but when her big screen career faltered at the end of the 1950s, she remained popular on such TV shows as *The Barbara Stanwyck Show* (1960–1961) and *Big Valley* (1965–1969), winning Emmys for both. She was lured out of semiretirement in 1983 to co-star in TV's *The Thorn Birds*, for which she won another Emmy, and in the series *Dynasty II: The Colbys* (1985–1986).

Filmography: Broadway Nights (1927); The Locked Door, Mexicali Rose (1929); Ladies of Leisure (1930); Illicit, The Miracle Woman, Night Nurse, Ten Cents a Dance (1931); Forbidden, The Purchase Price, Shopworn, So Big (1932); Baby Face, The Bitter Tea of General Yen, Ever in My Heart, Ladies They Talk About (1933); Gambling Lady, A Lost Lady (1934); Annie Oakley, Red Salute/Her Enlisted Man, The Secret Bride, Woman in Red (1935); Banjo on My Knee, The Bride Walks Out, His Brother's Wife, A Message to Garcia, The Plough and the Stars (1936); Breakfast for Two, Internes Can't Take Money, Stella Dallas, This Is My Affair (1937); Always Goodbye, The Mad Miss Manton (1938); Golden Boy, Union Pacific (1939); Remember the Night (1940);

Ball of Fire, The Lady Eve, Meet John Doe, You Belong to Me (1941); The Gay Sisters, The Great Man's Lady (1942); Flesh and Fantasy, Lady of Burlesque (1943); Double Indemnity, Hollywood Canteen (1944); Christmas in Connecticut (1945); The Bride Wore Boots, California, My Reputation, The Strange Love of Martha Ivers (1946); Cry Wolf, The Other Love, The Two Mrs. Carrolls, Variety Girl (1947); B. F.'s Daughter, Sorry Wrong Number (1948); East Side West Side, The File on Thelma Jordon/Thelma Jordon, The Lady Gambles (1949); The Furies, No Man of Her Own, To Please a Lady (1950); The Man with a Cloak (1951); Clash by Night (1952); All I Desire, Blowing Wild, Jeopardy, The Moonlighter, Titanic (1953); Cattle Queen of Montana, Executive Suite, Witness to Murder (1954); Escape to Burma, The Violent Men (1955); The Maverick Queen, There's Always Tomorrow, These Wilder Years (1956); Crime of Passion, Forty Guns, Trooper Hook (1957); Walk on the Wild Side (1962); The Night Walker, Roustabout (1964); The Thorn Birds (TVM, 1983); Going Hollywood: The War Years (1988).

Honors: Academy Award Nomination: Best Actress (*Stella Dallas*, 1937); Academy Award Nomination: Best Actress (*Ball of Fire*, 1941); Academy Award Nomination: Best Actress (*Sorry, Wrong Number*, 1948); *Photoplay*: Most Popular Female Star (1966); *Photoplay*: Most Popular Female Star (1967); Golden Globes: Cecil B. DeMille Award (1985); American Film Institute Life Achievement Award (1987); Academy Award: Special Award (1991); Los Angeles Film Critics Association: Lifetime Achievement (1991); Film Society of Lincoln Center Tribute (1991).

Selected Bibliography

Dickens, Homer. *The Films of Barbara Stanwyck*. Secaucus, NJ: Citadel Press, 1984.
Madsen, Axel. *Stanwyck*. New York: HarperCollins, 1994.

STAR IS BORN, A (1937), drama. Directed by William Wellman; with Fredric March, Janet Gaynor, Adolphe Menjou, May Robson, Andy Devine, Lionel Stander, and Franklin Pangborn; screenplay by Robert Carson, Dorothy Parker, and Alan Campbell.

Two remakes haven't dimmed the glow of this drama about a self-destructive actor and the young movie hopeful he marries. Fredric March and Janet Gaynor are outstanding in this acerbic profile of Hollywood in the 1930s, he as a fading star and she as a rising one. *A Star Is Born* captures brilliantly the inanity of a Hollywood that insists on redoing Gaynor's face when there is nothing wrong with the face she has. This incident was repeated in the Judy Garland version in 1954 and stands out as one of the film's memorable scenes. While the film presents an unvarnished look at the behind-the-scenes manipulations of people on both sides of the camera, it also shows how it is still possible for someone with real talent and honest drive to make it to the top without selling out. The famous Dorothy Parker black humor is evident in some of the film's venomous dialogue and contributes to the quality of honesty that film scholars admire so much. Some find it self-congratulatory, but films about Hollywood can hardly escape those pitfalls since they deal with the conflict between insecurity and egomania. The more celebrities doubt themselves, the more they need the adoration of others. Contemporary critics tend to consider this original version superior in its unvarnished look at the Hollywood dream factory. They like its caustic edge and the way it keeps its distance from the very dream factory that threatens to engulf it—as it did in the 1976 Barbra Streisand bomb. Some even insist that this is the most accurate study of Hollywood ever put on film. Perhaps, however, it is not entirely fair to compare this original with either of its two remakes, since the remakes are not only both musicals but vehicles showcasing the talents of two of the most formidable musical talents of the twentieth century: Judy Garland and Barbra Streisand. Each version is best judged on its own terms.

Awards: Academy Award: Best Original Story (William Wellman, Robert Carson); Academy Award Nominations: Best Picture, Actor (March), Actress (Gaynor), Director.

Selected Bibliography

Dooley, Roger. *From Scarface to Scarlett: American Films in the 1930s.* New York: Harcourt Brace Jovanovich, 1981.
Wellman, William Augustus. *A Short Time for Insanity: An Autobiography.* New York: Hawthorn Books, 1974.

STAR IS BORN, A (1954), musical. Directed by George Cukor; with Judy Garland, James Mason, Charles Bickford, Jack Carson, and Tom Noonan; screenplay by Moss Hart.

This is an intense, semimusical remake of the 1937 classic about a doomed Hollywood couple, with Judy Garland giving one of her very best performances as the singer whose star rises as her husband's declines. Mason is excellent in the part of the debonair alcoholic who, in the act of discovering Garland, plants the seeds of his own destruction. This version, the second of three, follows the plot of the 1937 version to which musical numbers have been added, numbers that showcase the range of Garland's enormous talent—from "Born in a Trunk," in which she pulls out all the stops in a medley of favorite show biz songs, to "The Man Who Got Away," a heartbreaking blues number written just for her big voice and her ability to belt a song. *A Star Is Born* is one of those rare films that successfully integrate music with drama. Since the story line is so predictable, it becomes melodramatic, but in a way that reminds us that more often than not our lives are clichés. There is no escaping the fact that audiences—certainly contemporary audiences—saw Garland with all the baggage she brings to this role, and it is impossible to watch her without being aware that she is magnificently self-destructive, unfolding her autobiography in every note she sings. It's impossible to separate the singer from the song, and this is what ultimately makes this film a classic. While we watch Mason reaching for the bottle and destroying himself, we nervously wonder when it will be Garland's turn to fall apart—right before our very eyes. It's a great but harrowing example of one of the unique things film can do. This version of *A Star Is Born* has been called a fascinating orgy of self-pity and cynicism overwhelmed by Garland's nakedly intense performance. Looking back, it is now clear that for Garland this was a last-ditch attempt to get back on top and revitalize her career. When the Oscar went to Grace Kelly instead for what most critics consider a dull performance, Garland seemed to slip her moorings and sink deeper and deeper into a private hell from which she never returned.

Awards: Golden Globe Awards, British Academy Awards: Best Actress (Garland), Actor (Mason); Academy Award Nominations: Best Actor (Mason), Actress (Garland), Color Costume Design, Color Art Direction, Scoring of a Musical Picture, Song ("The Man That Got Away").

Selected Bibliography

Fordin, Hugh. *The World of Entertainment!: Hollywood's Greatest Musicals*. Garden City, NY: Doubleday, 1975.

Levy, Emanuel. *George Cukor: Master of Elegance: Hollywood's Legendary Director and His Stars*. New York: Morrow, 1994.

Morella, Joe, and Edward Z. Epstein. *Judy: The Complete Films and Career of Judy Garland*. Secaucus, NJ: Citadel Press, 1986.

Peary, Danny. *Alternate Oscars*. New York: Delta, 1993.

STEVENS, GEORGE. Director. Born on December 18, 1904, in Oakland, California; died on March 8, 1975, in Paris. Stevens, the son of performers, entered films at age seventeen as a cameraman and later worked for the Hal Roach Company where he directed his first shorts. He joined RKO in 1934 and proceeded to churn out a series of formula comedies and light musicals. His first major success was the Katharine Hepburn classic *Alice Adams*, followed by the Astaire-Rogers classic *Swing Time*, the spirited *Gunga Din*, and the first of the legendary Katharine Hepburn–Spencer Tracy comedies, *Woman of the Year*. During World War II Stevens headed the Army Signal Corps Special Motion Picture Unit and brought back the only color films taken of the Normandy Invasion and the subsequent liberation of Europe. Stevens returned to civilian life in 1945 and before long was turning out more memorable films including *I Remember Mama*, *A Place in the Sun*, *Shane*, and *Giant*. Stevens's last film, *The Only Game in Town*, was a return to his earlier, more modest, style. He served as chief of the United States Information Service's motion picture division from 1962 to 1967 and was named the first head of the American Film Institute in 1977. His son George Stevens, Jr., is a producer who made an acclaimed documentary on his father, *George Stevens: A Filmmaker's Journey*, in 1984.

Filmography: [as director, unless otherwise noted]: The Cohens and Kellys in Trouble (1933); Bachelor Bait, Hollywood Party, Kentucky Kernels (1934); Alice Adams, Annie Oakley, Laddie, The Nitwits (1935); Swing Time (1936); A Damsel in Distress, Quality Street (1937); Vivacious Lady [also prod.] (1938); Gunga Din [also prod.] (1939); Vigil in the Night [also prod.] (1940); Penny Serenade [also prod.] (1941); The Talk of the Town [also prod.], Woman of the Year (1942); The More the Merrier [also prod.] (1943); I Remember Mama, On Our Merry Way/A Miracle Can Happen [uncredited direction of Stewart-Fonda segment] (1948); A Place in the Sun [also prod.] (1951); Something to

Live For [also prod.] (1952); Shane [also prod.] (1953); Giant [also prod.] (1956); The Diary of Anne Frank [also prod.] (1959); The Greatest Story Ever Told [prod., sc.] (1965); The Only Game in Town (1970).

Honors: Venice Film Festival: Special Mention Medals (*Vivacious Lady*, 1938); New York Film Critics Circle Award, Academy Award Nomination: Best Director (*The More the Merrier*, 1943); Academy Award: Best Director, Directors Guild of America: Quarterly Award (*A Place in the Sun*, 1951); Academy Award: Irving G. Thalberg Memorial Award (1953); Directors Guild of America Award: Outstanding Directorial Achievement, National Board of Review Award, Academy Award Nomination: Best Director (*Shane*, 1953); Academy Award: Best Director, Directors Guild of America: Most Outstanding Directorial Achievement (*Giant*, 1956); Directors Guild of America: D. W. Griffith Award (1959); Academy Award Nomination: Best Director (*The Diary of Anne Frank*, 1959).

Selected Bibliography

Petri, Bruce Humleker. *A Theory of American Film: The Films and Techniques of George Stevens*. New York: Garland, 1987.
Richie, Donald. *George Stevens: An American Romantic*. New York: MoMA, 1970. (distributed by New York Graphic Society, Greenwich, CT)

STEWART, JAMES. Actor. Born on May 20, 1908, in Indiana, Pennsylvania; died on July 3, 1997. Educated at Princeton (architecture). While at Princeton, Stewart met Joshua Logan, who convinced him to try acting. Stewart did summer stock with the University Players in Falmouth, Massachusetts, along with Henry Fonda and Margaret Sullavan. Although he had only two lines in one play he did, they brought the house down—and brought him to the attention of a New York critic—and of Hedda Hopper, who recommended him for a screen test, which resulted in an MGM contract. From the first, Stewart's performances stood out. They were raw, edgy, full of nervous energy. They also projected innocence and wistfulness and exuberance and hope, qualities that summed up what was good and endearing in the American character. In his later films, Stewart still retained a certain naive charm that made him difficult not to like, even when he was not particularly likable. Stewart got his first big break opposite Eleanor Powell in *Born to Dance* in which he introduced Cole Porter's "Easy to Love." He was no singer, but he did his best, and audiences not only forgave him—they adored him. He has been called the most complete actor-personality in the history of American film. He is undoubtedly the most loved. Alfred Hitchcock saw this and exploited Stewart's eternal good-guy persona in *Rear Window*, where audiences accepted Stewart as a voyeur, even cheered him because if Stewart did it, it must be okay. Stewart belongs with actors like Henry Fonda, Clark Gable, Spencer Tracy, Cary Grant, and John Wayne, actors of astonishing natural talent who endeared themselves to audiences from the 1930s into the 1960s, actors who usually played themselves so well that they seemed inseparable from the characters they were playing, actors whose performances seemed so effortless, they were usually overlooked at awards time. Stewart did receive an Oscar early in his career for *The Philadelphia Story*, but it was in *Mr. Smith Goes to Washington* that he played a part tailor-made for his unique talents, and he went on to give many excellent performances in such pictures as *Destry Rides Again*, *Anatomy of a Murder*, and *It's a Wonderful Life*. The last-named, which has become a Christmas classic, is probably the movie most closely identified with Stewart. In it he is most thoroughly and genuinely himself, playing a character who hits heights and depths that round out the portrait of a man wrestling with all aspects of his humanity, from sinking into despair and wishing for death to returning to save his town, his family, and his own soul. Stewart continued to perform into the 1990s not only in films but also on the stage and on television.

Filmography: Art Trouble (1934); The Murder Man (1935); After the Thin Man, Born to Dance, The Gorgeous Hussy, Next Time We Love, Rose Marie/Indian Love Call, Small Town Girl/One Horse Town, Speed, Wife vs. Secretary (1936); The Last Gangster, Navy Blue and Gold, Seventh Heaven (1937); Of Human Hearts, The Shopworn Angel, Vivacious Lady, You Can't Take It with You (1938); Destry Rides Again, Ice Follies of 1939, It's a Wonderful World, Made for Each Other, Mr. Smith Goes to Washington (1939); The Mortal Storm, No Time for Comedy/Guy with a Gun, The Philadelphia Story, The Shop around the Corner (1940); Come Live with Me, Pot O'Gold, Ziegfeld Girl (1941); It's a Wonderful Life (1946); Magic Town (1947); Call Northside 777, On Our Merry Way/A Miracle Can Happen, Rope, You Gotta Stay Happy (1948); Malaya, The Stratton Story (1949); Broken Arrow, Harvey, The Jackpot, Winchester '73/Montana Winchester (1950); No Highway in the Sky/No Highway (1951); Bend of the River, Carbine Williams, The Greatest Show on Earth (1952); The Naked Spur, Thunder Bay (1953); The Glenn Miller Story, Rear Window (1954); The Far Country, The Man from Laramie, Strategic Air Command (1956); Night Passage, The Spirit of St. Louis (1957); Bell Book and Candle, Vertigo (1958); Anatomy of a Murder, The FBI Story (1959); The Mountain Road (1960); Two Rode Together (1961); How the West Was Won, The Man Who Shot Liberty Valance, Mr. Hobbs Takes a Vacation (1962); Take Her She's Mine (1963); Cheyenne Autumn (1964); Dear Brigitte, Shenandoah (1965); Flight of the Phoenix, The Rare Breed (1966); Bandolero!, Firecreek (1968); The Cheyenne Social Club (1970); Directed by John Ford, Fool's Parade (1971); That's Entertainment! (1974); The Shootist (1976); Airport '77 (1977); The Big Sleep, The Magic of Lassie (1978); Going Hollywood: The War Years (1988).

Honors: New York Film Critics Circle Award, Academy Award Nomination: Best Actor (*Mr. Smith Goes to Washington*, 1939); Academy Award: Best Actor (*The Philadelphia Story*, 1940); Academy Award Nomination: Best Actor (*It's a Wonderful Life*, 1946); Academy Award Nomination: Best Actor (*Harvey*, 1950); New York Film Critics Circle Award, Venice Film Festival Award, Academy Award Nomination: Best Actor (*Anatomy of a Murder*, 1959); Berlin Film Festival Award: Best Actor (*Mr. Hobbs Takes a Vacation*, 1962); American Film Institute Lifetime Achievement Award (1980); Academy Award: Special Award (1984); Cannes Film Festival Career Achievement Award (1985); Film Society of Lincoln Center Tribute [For his fifty years of memorable performances. For his high ideals both on and off the screen. With the respect and affection of his colleagues. Winner presented a Statuette] (1990).

Selected Bibliography:

Coe, Jonathan. *Jimmy Stewart: A Wonderful Life*. New York: Arcade Publishing, 1994.

Dewey, Donald. *James Stewart: A Biography*. Atlanta, GA: Turner Publishing, 1996.

Molyneaux, Gerard. *James Stewart: A Bio-Bibliography*. Westport, CT: Greenwood Press, 1992.

Pickard, Roy. *Jimmy Stewart: A Life in Film*. New York: St. Martin's Press, 1993.

STRANGERS ON A TRAIN (1951), thriller. Directed by Alfred Hitchcock; with Farley Granger, Robert Walker, Ruth Roman, Leo G. Carroll, Patricia Hitchcock, and Marion Lorne; screenplay by Raymond Chandler and Czenzi Ormonde.

Strangers on a Train is one of Hitchcock's most accomplished works, and some consider it the best of his American films. Granger and Walker are excellent as strangers who meet on a train and are soon agreeing to commit murder for each other. Walker is supposed to be the truly evil one, Granger the duped innocent, but it is clear that the two are alter egos who find reinforcement in each other. Walker was another of Hitchcock's ingenious choices, for up until then he had been known as the all-American-boy type, the wide-eyed innocent GI who wooed and married Judy Garland in twenty-four hours in *The Clock*. His surface charm made his evil character all the more menacing. In this film, Walker proposes to get rid of Granger's irritating wife if Granger will get rid of Walker's annoying mother. Walker cheerfully fulfills his end of the bargain, but the horrified Granger cannot reciprocate. The movie builds to a frenzied climax at an amusement park where a carousel whirls out of control and Walker ends up crushed beneath it. The ending triggered imitations that have now given it a clichéd quality, but there is another scene in the movie so original and so representative of Hitchcock that it remains a classic. It is the scene at the tennis match where Granger is one of the players. Walker is in the crowd, staring straight ahead at Granger, his head never moving, while all the others in the crowd wag their heads back and forth as they follow the tennis ball. It's typical of Hitchcock's chilling humor and does much to move the bizarre plot forward. The basic plot has been imitated many times, but no remake has measured up to the macabre magic of the Hitchcock touch. Some scholars are now taking a closer look at elements of homoeroticism in Hitchcock films (e.g., *Rope*, *Psycho*) and find *Strangers on a Train* particularly germane to their studies. It goes a long way toward providing a more believable basis for the friendship that springs up so quickly between these two young men. Those who know the works—and the sexual orientation—of Patricia Highsmith, who wrote the original story, have even more reason to take the possibility seriously.

Awards: Directors Guild of America: Quarterly Award (Hitchcock); Academy Award Nomination: Best B&W Cinematography.

Selected Bibliography

Hurley, Neil P. *Soul in Suspense: Hitchcock's Fright and Delight*. Metuchen, NJ: Scarecrow Press, 1993.

Peary, Danny. *Alternate Oscars*. New York: Delta, 1993.
Sterritt, David. *The Films of Alfred Hitchcock*. Cambridge: Cambridge University Press, 1993.

STREETCAR NAMED DESIRE, A (1951), drama. Directed by Elia Kazan; with Marlon Brando, Vivien Leigh, Kim Hunter, and Karl Malden; screenplay by Oscar Saul.

This is the classic screen version of the Tennessee Williams play that opened on Broadway in 1947 and ran for two years. Marlon Brando reprises his stage role as the brutish Stanley Kowalski and is electrifying. Vivien Leigh, who had been playing Blanche DuBois on the London stage, brings a deeply neurotic edge to her performance that lifts it above the ordinary into a realm beyond mere talent or incentive into something driven and self-destructive. Contemporary audiences could not help seeing Blanche as an aging Scarlett O'Hara (Leigh's famous first Oscar-winning role), and this projection added a dimension to how she was perceived. Just as Scarlett had foolishly put herself at risk and ended up being attacked in *Gone with the Wind*, here is Blanche DuBois, foolishly tempting Stanley, who eventually rapes her. But Scarlett is the tough half of this complex personality. The tender, vulnerable, soft half is Blanche, who bends under the weight of a sordid past. That past includes not only her own nymphomania but also the discovery of her first husband's homosexuality, her upbraiding him about it, and his subsequent suicide. Production codes in effect at the time of the filming precluded any mention of her dead husband's homosexuality. They also stipulated that the movie had to end with Stella preparing to leave Stanley after the rape even though in the play she stays. Most movies do not really suffer from censorship; in fact, censorship has often inspired great creative achievements. However, the withholding of crucial information, such as Blanche's dead husband's homosexuality, seriously distorts this film, for it obscures her darker feelings of guilt and remorse and her twisted desires. She is, after all, a projection of Tennessee Williams himself, just as Emma Bovary was of Flaubert and Hedda Gabler of Ibsen. As a homosexual himself, Williams knew the hypocrisy of gay bashing just as he knew the attraction of rough trade like Stanley Kowalski. It is not absolutely necessary to know this to appreciate this excellent film—it stands on its own, nevertheless—but knowing it rounds out the portrait of a tortured personality driven to madness by unbearable guilt. Even so, when the film was first released, it created a firestorm of controversy. It was immoral, decadent, vulgar, and sinful, its critics cried. And this was after substantial cuts had been made. It is fascinating to compare the cut version with the now-available uncut one. The differences are startling and in some cases do make a considerable difference. The raw power of the movie tends to compensate for the cut version's murky spots, but when they are clarified, the clarity is dazzling. We even begin to suspect that the real object of Mitch's courting is not Blanche but Stanley. Brando holds nothing back in this textbook example of method acting, and Vivien Leigh gives one of those rare performances that can truly be said to evoke pity and terror. We now know that Leigh was descending into madness in her own life at that time, a madness from which she never recovered. At some point in her performance she ceased playing a role and became Blanche. In addition to an inspired use of black and white photography and a claustrophobic set, this film features Alex North's brilliant score, surely one of the best ever written for a movie and one of the few that can truly stand on its own.

Awards: Academy Awards: Best Actress (Leigh), Supporting Actor (Malden), Supporting Actress (Hunter), Art Direction/B&W (Richard Day); Golden Globe Award: Supporting Actress (Hunter); New York Film Critics Circle Awards: Best Picture, Actress (Leigh), Director; Venice Film Festival: Special Jury Prizes: Picture, Actress (Leigh).

Selected Bibliography

Michaels, Lloyd. *Elia Kazan: A Guide to References and Resources*. Boston: G. K. Hall, 1985.
Peary, Danny. *Alternate Oscars*. New York: Delta, 1993.
Thomas, Tony. *The Films of Marlon Brando*. Secaucus, NJ: Citadel Press, 1973.
Walker, Alexander. *Vivien: The Life of Vivien Leigh*. New York: Weidenfeld & Nicolson, 1987.

STURGES, PRESTON. Director, screenwriter. Born Edmund Preston Biden on August 29, 1898, in Chicago, Illinois; died on August 6, 1959, in New York. Educated at the School of Military Aeronautics in Austin, Texas. Sturges is generally considered to be one of the most original directors and writers in screen history. He possessed a rare ability in both his writing and his directing to combine cynicism with sentiment in a way that made him what might be called "a thinking man's Frank Capra." He turned out fresh, biting films full of witty dialogue and fast pacing. His target was the effects of materialism on ordinary people and how it turned them into hypocrites. Ironically enough, while he was condemning popular taste and mass conformity, he was not above using the formulas of popular comedy to convey his message. Sturges had a colorful childhood, and as a young man, he helped his mother with her cosmetics business. But after World War I, he began writing plays, one of which, *Strictly Dishonorable*, was a Broadway hit in 1929. Two years later, he adapted it for the movies and stayed on in Hollywood during the 1930s, working on some fine films, but he didn't find his own distinctive voice, as both writer and director, until *The Great McGinty* in 1940. He then made what most critics agree to be his two best films, *The Lady Eve* and *Sullivan's Travels*, both in 1941. After that he made three screwball satires that were very successful all around but didn't quite measure up to these two. After World War II and these six classic comedies, Sturges's career faded rapidly as he made one embarrassing feature after another. It was as if he had burned himself out turning out six superb features in under five years and had lost his touch. Actually, now that his screenplays have been published, we can appreciate a richer and more extensive career. Nevertheless, six great films, two of them classics, is not a negligible accomplishment. The number of books about him alone testifies to an enormous measure of scholarly respect.

Filmography: [as screenwriter]: The Big Pond [dialogue only], Fast and Loose [additional dialogue] (1930); Strictly Dishonorable [play basis only] (1931); Child of Manhattan [play basis only], The Power and the Glory (1933); Thirty-Day Princess, Imitation of Life [uncredited], We Live Again (1934); Diamond Jim, The Good Fairy (1935); Next Time We Love [uncredited] (1936); One Rainy Afternoon [song composer], Easy Living, Hotel Haywire (1937); If I Were King, Port of Seven Seas (1938); Never Say Die (1939); The Birds and the Bees (1956); Rock-a-Bye Baby [story only] (1958). [as director-screenwriter]: Christmas in July [also prod.], The Great McGinty (1940); The Lady Eve, Sullivan's Travels (1941); The Palm Beach Story (1942); The Miracle of Morgan's Creek, Hail the Conquering Hero, Star Spangled Rhythm [per. only], The Great Moment (1944); Mad Wednesday [also prod.] (1947); Unfaithfully Yours [also prod.] (1948); The Beautiful Blonde from Bashful Bend [also prod.] (1949); Les Carnets du Major Thompson/The French They Are a Funny Race (1955); Paris Holiday [per.], Rock-a-Bye Baby [based loosely on Sturges's *The Miracle of Morgan's Creek*] (1958).

Honors: Academy Award Nomination: Original Screenplay (*The Great McGinty*, 1940).

Selected Bibliography

Cywinski, Raymond J. *Preston Sturges: A Guide to References and Resources*. Boston: G. K. Hall, 1984.
Jacobs, Diane. *Christmas in July: The Life and Art of Preston Sturges*. Berkeley: University of California Press, 1992.
Sturges, Preston. *Preston Sturges*. Ed. Sandy Sturges. New York: Simon and Schuster, 1990.

SULLIVAN'S TRAVELS (1941), comedy/drama. Directed by Preston Sturges; with Joel McCrea, Veronica Lake, Robert Warwick, William Demarest, Eric Blore, Robert Greig, Jimmy Conlin, Al Bridge, Franklin Pangborn, and Porter Hall; screenplay by Preston Sturges.

This brilliant, often devastating look at Hollywood and the real world behind its tinsel is generally considered to be Preston Sturges's greatest film. It is the story of a movie director who tires of making fluff and decides to do a ''serious'' film. He plans to make an art house film entitled *O Brother, Where Art Thou*, in which he intends to probe the meaning of poverty. Dressed as a tramp, he sets out with ten cents in his pocket to experience life in ''the real world.'' What he learns is that the suffering masses do not want to see films about the suffering masses; they want escape. In short, they want fluff. Although the plot may sound a bit contrived, everything in this wonderful film works. *Sullivan's Travels* is a delightful comedy-drama, the unique type of film for which Sturges was noted. Although the film has sometimes been read as a defense of Hollywood escapism, what Sturges is really doing is poking fun at the awful liberal solemnities of problem pictures and movies with a message. Ironically, in trying to satirize films with messages, Sturges could not avoid making a film with one, this one being, as he himself put it, ''to leave the preaching to the preachers.''

One treat for modern audiences is the chance to get inside the 1930s and get a real sense of what the depression decade felt like. Another treat is watching the reaction of the poor, wretched, chain-gang prisoners (and of the downtrodden black congregation) to the showing of a Mickey Mouse cartoon at the Black Baptist church. As the faces of both prisoners and parishioners turn from utter despair to absolute joy, with hysterical laughter rattling the rafters of the church, something happens that is sheer screen magic. And the magician is Preston Sturges, one of the most original directorial talents in cinematic history.

Selected Bibliography

Jacobs, Diane. *Christmas in July: The Life and Art of Preston Sturges.* Berkeley: University of California Press, 1992.

Siegel, Scott, and Barbara Siegel. *American Film Comedy: From Abbott & Costello to Jerry Zucker.* Englewood Cliffs, NJ: Prentice-Hall, 1994.

SUNDOWNERS, THE (1960), drama. Directed by Fred Zinnemann; with Deborah Kerr, Robert Mitchum, Peter Ustinov, Glynis Johns, Dina Merrill, Chips Rafferty, Michael Anderson, Jr., Lola Brooks, Wylie Watson, and Mervyn Johns; screenplay by Isobel Lennart.

This fine film by Zinnemann, a major director, was overlooked when it came out, and it has yet to achieve the reputation it deserves. The story takes place in Australia, and the location filming turns Australia into a palpable character in this epic about the space and emptiness of the country. Robert Mitchum gives a magnificent offbeat performance as a man who doesn't want to stay in one place, and Deborah Kerr, in what some consider her richest performance, is earthy as the wife who keeps moving with him. There are marvelous sequences that leave lasting impressions—for example, one about a race horse, another about a sheep-shearing contest. The story builds slowly but with a steadily increasing momentum that only adds to the latter sequences. Some critics think that Zinnemann's preoccupation with such themes as the indomitable spirit of the human character result in a film that seems overlong and repetitious—and even a bit artificial. However, most critics find Zinnemann's poetic glances into the souls of his characters the very thing that makes the picture the achievement it is.

Awards: New York Film Critics Circle Award: Best Actress (Kerr); Academy Award Nominations: Best Picture, Director, Actress (Kerr), Supporting Actress (Johns), Screenplay Adaptation.

Selected Bibliography

Roberts, J. W. *Robert Mitchum: A Bio-Bibliography.* Westport, CT: Greenwood Press, 1992.

Zinnemann, Fred. *A Life in the Movies: An Autobiography.* New York. Charles Scribner's Sons, 1992.

SUNSET BOULEVARD (1950), drama. Directed by Billy Wilder; with Gloria Swanson, William Holden, Erich von Stroheim, Nancy Olson, Fred Clark, Jack

Webb, Hedda Hopper, Buster Keaton, Cecil B. DeMille, and Anna Q. Nilsson; screenplay by Charles Brackett, Billy Wilder, and D. M. Marshman, Jr.

No other motion picture about Hollywood comes near Billy Wilder's searing, uncompromising, and utterly fascinating portrait of the film community. And beneath it all, vanity, madness, and murder are raging. This black comedy is about faded silent film star Norma Desmond (Swanson), living in the past with her butler (von Stroheim), who shelters hack screenwriter (Holden) as a boyfriend. In *Sunset Boulevard* Wilder captures the tragic, nostalgic longing for a grand Hollywood past that silent stars could never possibly reclaim. The film excels in ordinary and extraordinary passions, and Swanson's Norma provides one of many razor-sharp insights into the whole film when she says: "We didn't need dialogue. We had faces then. They don't have faces anymore, maybe one, Garbo." Some critics consider this film the blackest of all accounts of itself and praise its dark, nightmarish quality, while others are bothered by its cynical lack of faith in humanity. Still others praise its writing, acting, directing, and photography as ingredients so flawlessly blended as to cast a spell over an audience and hold it enthralled to the shattering climax. Today this film is hailed as one of the best examples of film noir, bearing the inimitable stamp of that master of the genre, Billy Wilder, who gave us *Double Indemnity*. It is curiously ironic, as one observer pointed out, that this weird but fascinating film is about an art that, even though it is still relatively new, is already haunted by ghosts.

Awards: Academy Awards: Best Screenplay, B&W Art Direction, Scoring of a Dramatic Picture; Golden Globe Awards: Best Picture, Actress (Swanson), Director, Score (Franz Waxman); Directors Guild of America: Quarterly Award; National Board of Review Award: Best Actress; Academy Award Nominations: Best Picture, Director, Actress (Swanson), Actor (Holden), Supporting Actor (von Stroheim), Supporting Actress (Olson), B&W Cinematography, Editing. In 1989, it was selected by the National Film Registry of the Library of Congress as one of twenty-five landmark films, leading examples of American cinematic art.

Selected Bibliography

Peary, Danny. *Alternate Oscars*. New York: Delta, 1993.

Quirk, Lawrence J. *The Complete Films of William Holden*. Secaucus, NJ: Citadel Press, 1986.

Swanson, Gloria. *Swanson on Swanson*. New York: Random House, 1980.

Zolotow, Maurice. *Billy Wilder in Hollywood*. New York: G. P. Putnam's Sons, 1977.

SWING TIME (1936), musical. Directed by George Stevens; with Fred Astaire, Ginger Rogers, Victor Moore, Helen Broderick, Eric Blore, and Betty Furness; screenplay by Howard Lindsay and Allan Scott.

This is one of the best Astaire-Rogers films all about a dance team whose romance is hampered by Fred's engagement to a girl back home. It's smart, chic, and classy and has great Jerome Kern songs to back it up, including the classic "The Way You Look Tonight." George Stevens directed this musical, one of three he did at RKO, long before he became known for such "important" films as *Shane* and *Giant* and *The Diary of Anne Frank*. Today the movie seems dated and predictable, very much of its time. But taken on its own terms and in its own context, it comes alive as a shimmering piece of depression-era escapism with all those white art deco sets and the silly contrivance of the plot all done to reach that climactic, sensual Astaire-Rogers dance sequence. And when timeless music accompanies incomparable dancing, you have enchanted moments worthy of movie immortality.

Awards: Academy Award: Best Song (''The Way You Look Tonight''; music, Jerome Kern; lyrics, Dorothy Fields); Academy Award Nomination: Best Dance Direction (''Bo Jangles'').

Selected Bibliography

Faris, Jocelyn. *Ginger Rogers: A Bio-Bibliography*. Westport, CT: Greenwood Press, 1994.

Fordin, Hugh. *The World of Entertainment!: Hollywood's Greatest Musicals*. Garden City, NY: Doubleday, 1975.

Mueller, John E. *Astaire Dancing: The Musical Films*. New York: Knopf, 1985.

Petri, Bruce Humleker. *A Theory of American Film: The Films and Techniques of George Stevens*. New York: Garland, 1987.

T

TALE OF TWO CITIES, A (1935), historical. Directed by Jack Conway; with Ronald Colman, Elizabeth Allan, Edna May Oliver, Reginald Owen, Basil Rathbone, Blanche Yurka, Isabel Jewell, Walter Catlett, Henry B. Walthall, H. B. Warner, and Donald Woods; screenplay by W. P. Lipscomb and S. N. Behrman.

This is generally considered to be the best film production of Charles Dickens's classic novel (there have been at least six others), and it is certainly the most popular. This lavish production still holds up well today largely because it is a product of the best of the studio system, a system that guaranteed a troupe of contract players who could usually be counted on to play their parts well. The often overly mannered Ronald Colman gives one of the best performances of his life as the world-weary martyr, a role he had long wanted to play. Equally memorable is Blanche Yurka as the sinister Mme. DeFarge, endlessly cackling as she knits a long scarf and decides who the next victim of the Terror is to be. The story has been simplified so that it can be told very clearly, and the dialogue is quite natural. Critics raved then and continue to rave about the superb production values and the skill of its participants, calling it a screen classic and saying that it is technically about as flawless as possible, a film clearly made with respect and loving care. The film was a huge success and gave producer David O. Selznick the freedom to walk away from MGM (and from his father-in-law, Louis B. Mayer) and set up Selznick International Pictures, a move that allowed him four years later to produce *Gone with the Wind*.

Awards: Academy Award Nominations: Best Picture, Editing.

Selected Bibliography

Dooley, Roger. *From Scarface to Scarlett: American Films in the 1930s*. New York: Harcourt Brace Jovanovich, 1981.

Quirk, Lawrence J. *The Films of Ronald Colman*. Secaucus, NJ: Citadel Press, 1977.
Vermilye, Jerry. *The Films of the Thirties*. New York: Citadel Press, 1990.

TALK OF THE TOWN, THE (1942), comedy. Directed by George Stevens; with Jean Arthur, Ronald Colman, Cary Grant, Glenda Farrell, Edgar Buchanan, Charles Dingle, Rex Ingram, Emma Dunn, Tom Tyler, and Lloyd Bridges; screenplay by Irwin Shaw and Sidney Buchman.

This is an attractive seriocomic tale of civic corruption, with Grant as a factory worker on the run from a trumped-up charge of arson and murder, Arthur as the childhood friend with whom he seeks shelter, and Colman as the stuffy professor already ensconced as her lodger. Grant, Arthur, and Colman are a terrific threesome, playing well off one another in a finely constructed love triangle. Both men want Arthur, yet Colman never lets his desire for her take precedence over the justice that must be done. George Stevens directs his cast well, handling the double-edged story with grace and style. Although it's a rather silly and confusing story, this weakness is offset by the pleasant people in it whose high spirits make it ultimately quite likable. George Stevens's direction is excellent for the most part. The film is an unusual mixture of comedy and drama, and while the transition from serious to slaphappy sometimes is a bit awkward, this is basically solid escapist comedy.

Awards: Academy Award Nominations: Best Picture, Original Story, Screenplay, Cinematography, Art Direction/Set Decoration, Score, Editing.

Selected Bibliography

Deschner, Donald. *The Complete Films of Cary Grant*. Secaucus, NJ: Citadel Press, 1991.
Petri, Bruce Humleker. *A Theory of American Film: The Films and Techniques of George Stevens*. New York: Garland, 1987.
Quirk, Lawrence J. *The Films of Ronald Colman*. Secaucus, NJ: Citadel Press, 1977.

TARZAN, THE APE MAN (1932), adventure/romance. Directed by W. S. Van Dyke; with Johnny Weissmuller, Maureen O'Sullivan, C. Aubrey Smith, Neil Hamilton, and Doris Lloyd; screenplay by Cyril Hume and Ivor Novello.

A legend began when MGM cast Johnny Weissmuller, a twenty-eight-year-old swimming champ from the 1924 and 1928 Olympic Games, as Tarzan in the first sound version of Edgar Rice Burroughs's popular story. The story, which has become a modern myth, concerns the confrontation between British gentry and jungle savagery and what happens when the daughter of an English hunter is captured by Tarzan and decides she prefers his animal charms to those of her wimpy fiance. This original Weissmuller-MGM Tarzan film creaks here and there, but over all, it still holds up, thanks to a plush production and vivid atmosphere (with jungle footage left over from *Trader Horn*, the first film ever to be shot on location in Africa). There is something essentially ludicrous about the predicament of a ladylike young lady abducted by a man who has lived like an ape and who pokes and pummels her with the gestures of an ape. But the silliness is irresistible, and the whole thing great fun, a jungle version of Beauty and the Beast. The picture never pretends to be realistic about jungle life; it's simply an entertaining romantic adventure—lighthearted and agreeable. Its appeal is to that part of us that always longed to build tree houses and rafts and run through the woods or swing from vines, an alternate way of life increasingly attractive in the modern world of gadgets that keep nature at too safe a distance. Although most viewers have become accustomed to (or spoiled by) the technological superiority of *Raiders of the Lost Ark*–type jungle adventures, *Tarzan* still has enough thrills to put most films to shame. The almost nonstop excitement holds up even today, making it one of Hollywood's most memorable adventure films. The movie was filmed previously in 1918 and remade in 1959 and 1981.

Selected Bibliography

Miller, Frank. *Movies We Love: 100 Collectible Classics*. Atlanta, GA: Turner Publishing, 1996.
Onyx, Narda. *Water, World, and Weissmuller: A Biography*. Los Angeles: Vion Publishing, 1964.

TAYLOR, ELIZABETH. Actress. Born on February 17, 1932, in London, England. This strikingly beautiful actress, sometimes called the last true "movie star," has lived so much of her checkered private life in the public eye that it has tended to overshadow her screen personality. In fact, although she was a powerful screen presence from the 1940s through the 1960s, while at the same time making headlines with her many marriages and many illnesses, it is still too early to judge her acting talent without her image as a celebrity getting in the way. Beginning with *National Velvet*, already her fourth picture, made when she was twelve, she was exhibiting a charisma that would soon give her power over men like Louis B. Mayer. She made the transition from child actress to adult actress without a hitch, and by the beginning of the 1950s, she was radiating charm and beauty in *Father of the Bride* and *A Place in the Sun*. In fact, in the latter, it was clear to viewers at the time that Clift's choice was not between a shop girl and a debutante but between Shelley Winters, character actress, and Elizabeth Taylor, movie star. For the condemned Clift, having to give her up was a fate worse than the execution. In spite of a low regard among many critics for her acting talents, Taylor honed a latent but undisciplined talent into Oscar-winning performances in *Butterfield 8* and *Who's Afraid of Virginia Woolf?* and Oscar-nominated ones in three others. Her gripping performance in *Suddenly, Last Summer*—in competition with the formidable Katharine Hepburn—does credit to the demanding Tennessee Williams script. Detractors argued that in her more neurotic roles she was merely playing herself—but when compared to other beautiful faces (Hedy Lamarr, for example, or Jane Russell), it is easy to see how much better Taylor is at revealing a complex personality behind the flawless features. Taylor has continued to perform in semiretirement, appearing in occasional TV and movie roles while promoting her own perfume and cosmetics line. She has also worked tirelessly as a fund-raiser for AIDS research.

Filmography: There's One Born Every Minute (1942); Lassie Come Home (1943); Jane Eyre, National Velvet (1944); Courage of Lassie (1946); Cynthia, Life with Father (1947); A Date with Judy, Julia Misbehaves (1948); Conspirator, Little Women (1949); The Big Hangover, Father of the Bride (1950); Quo Vadis [unbilled cameo], Father's Little Dividend, A Place in the Sun, Callaway Went Thataway [cameo] (1951); Ivanhoe, Love Is Better Than Ever (1952); The Girl Who Had Everything (1953); Beau Brummel, Elephant Walk, The Last Time I Saw Paris, Rhapsody (1954); Giant (1956); Raintree County (1957); Cat on a Hot Tin Roof (1958); Suddenly Last Summer (1959); Scent of Mystery [unbilled cameo], Butterfield 8 (1960); Cleopatra, The V.I.P.s (1963); The Sandpiper (1965); Who's Afraid of Virginia Woolf? (1966); The Comedians, Reflections in a Golden Eye, The Taming of the Shrew, Doctor Faustus [as Helen of Troy] (1967); Boom!, Secret Ceremony (1968); The Only Game in Town (1970); Under Milk Wood (1971); Hammersmith Is Out, X Y and Zee (1972); Ash Wednesday, Night Watch, The Driver's Seat [It.], That's Entertainment! (1974); The Blue Bird, It's Showtime, Victory at Entebbe (1976); A Little Night Music (1978); Winter Kills (1979); The Mirror Crack'd (1980); Genocide [doc.; narr. only] (1981); George Stevens: A Filmmaker's Journey (1984); Young Toscanini/Il Giovane Toscanini (1988); The Flintstones (1994).

Honors: Golden Globes: Special Award for Consistent Performance (1956); Academy Award Nomination: Best Actress (*Raintree County*, 1957); Academy Award Nomination: Best Actress (*Cat on a Hot Tin Roof*, 1958); Golden Globe Award, Academy Award Nomination: Best Actress (*Suddenly, Last Summer*, 1959); Academy Award: Best Actress (*Butterfield 8*, 1960); Academy Award, New York Film Critics Circle Award, National Board of Review Award, British Academy Award: Best Actress (*Who's Afraid of Virginia Woolf?* 1966); Berlin Film Festival Award: Best Actress (*Hammersmith Is Out*, 1972); Golden Globe Award: World Film Favorite (1973); Golden Globes: Cecil B. DeMille Award (1984); Film Society of Lincoln Center Tribute (1986); Academy Award: Jean Hersholt Humanitarian Award (1992); American Film Institute Lifetime Achievement Award (1993).

Selected Bibliography

Heymann, C. David. *Liz: An Intimate Biography of Elizabeth Taylor*. New York: Carol, 1995.

Latham, Caroline, and Jeannie Sakol. *All about Elizabeth: Elizabeth Taylor, Public and Private*. New York: Onyx, 1991.

Spoto, Donald. *A Passion for Life: The Biography of Elizabeth Taylor*. New York: HarperCollins, 1995.

Vermilye, Jerry, and Mark Ricci. *The Films of Elizabeth Taylor*. Secaucus, NJ: Citadel Press, 1976.

Walker, Alexander. *Elizabeth: The Life of Elizabeth Taylor*. New York: G. Weidenfeld, 1991.

TAYLOR, ROBERT. Actor. Born Spangler Arlington Brugh on August 5, 1911, in Filley, Nebraska; died on June 8, 1969. Educated at Doane College in Nebraska (music). He followed his cello teacher to Pomona College in California, where his performance in a college production led to a screen test and a long-term contract with MGM. Billed as "The Man with the Perfect Profile," Taylor had looks that were often described as "pretty." Nevertheless, he was able to project a masculinity that made him the rival of such male stars as Clark Gable and James Stewart as a romantic leading man. His first important role was in *Magnificent Obsession* in 1935, and for the next thirty years he played opposite some of the screen's most glamorous leading ladies, from Garbo and Harlow to Ava Gardner and Elizabeth Taylor. Age did much to rid Taylor of the glamour looks, helping him to develop as an actor by playing parts of greater maturity and deeper character. He also acquired a reputation among directors as a thorough professional who took his work seriously, worked hard at it, and thereby compensated for any deficiencies. During World War II, he served as a flight instructor with the U.S. Navy's Air Transport. He also directed seventeen navy training films and narrated the feature-length documentary *The Fighting Lady*. His personal life was free of scandal. He was married twice, first to Barbara Stanwyck from 1939 to 1951 and then to Ursula Thiess from 1954 until his death of lung cancer in 1969 at the age of fifty-seven.

Filmography: Handy Andy, There's Always Tomorrow, A Wicked Woman (1934); Broadway Melody of 1936, Buried Loot [short], Magnificent Obsession, Murder in the Fleet, Society Doctor, Times Square Lady, West Point of the Air (1935); The Gorgeous Hussy, His Brother's Wife, Private Number, Small Town Girl/One Horse Town (1936); Broadway Melody of 1938, Camille, Lest We Forget, Personal Property, This Is My Affair (1937); The Crowd Roars, Three Comrades, A Yank at Oxford (1938); Lady of the Tropics, Lucky Night, Remember?, Stand Up and Fight (1939); Escape, Flight Command, Waterloo Bridge (1940); Billy the Kid, Johnny Eager, When Ladies Meet/Strange Skirts, Her Cardboard Lover, Stand By for Action (1942); Above Suspicion, Bataan, Song of Russia, The Youngest Profession (1943); The Fighting Lady [doc.; narr.] (1944); Undercurrent (1946); High Wall (1947); Ambush, The Bribe, The Conspirator (1949); Devil's Doorway (1950); Quo Vadis?, Westward the Women (1951); Ivanhoe (1952); All the Brothers Were Valiant, I Love Melvin [cameo], Knights of the Round Table, Ride Vaquero (1953); Rogue Cop, Valley of the Kings (1954); Many Rivers to Cross, Quentin Durward/The Adventures of Quentin Durward (1955); D-Day the Sixth of June, The Last Hunt, The Power and the Prize (1956); Tip on a Dead Jockey (1957); The Law and Jake Wade, Party Girl, Saddle the Wind (1958); The Hangman, The House of the Seven Hawks, Killers of Kilimanjaro (1959); Cattle King, Miracle of the White Stallions (1963); A House Is Not a Home, The Night Walker (1964); Johnny Tiger, Savage Pampas/Pampa Salvaje (1966); The Glass Sphinx/La Sfinge d'Oro, Hondo, Return of the Gunfighter/Wyatt (1967); Where Angels Go Trouble Follows (1968); The Day the Hot Line Got Hot/Hot Line (1969).

Honors: Golden Globe Award: World Film Favorite (1953).

Selected Bibliography

Quirk, Lawrence J. *The Films of Robert Taylor*. Secaucus, NJ: Citadel Press, 1975.
Wayne, Jane Ellen. *The Life of Robert Taylor*. New York: Warner Paperback Library, 1973.
———. *Robert Taylor: The Man with the Perfect Face*. New York: St. Martin's Press, 1989.

TEMPLE, SHIRLEY. Actress. Born on April 23, 1928, in Santa Monica, California. A rare and original talent, Temple entered movies at the age of three, and by the time she was six, she had established herself as a star, first by stealing the show in *Baby Take a Bow* and then in *Stand Up and Cheer*. Her bouncing blond curls, effervescence, and radiant charm helped ease the pain of depression-weary audiences the world over, while she virtually kept 20th Century–Fox afloat with her astounding profitability. Temple earned a Special 1934 Oscar in grateful recognition of her outstanding contribution to screen entertainment. The phenomenon of Shirley Temple still defies analysis. You have but to see one of her 1930s-era pictures to recognize something unique. Part of it is her professionalism. She seems to know exactly what to do and yet avoid the cutesyness and coyness and all the awful affectations that so often afflict child actors. Beyond that, she seems completely without vanity or guile, genuinely interested in her fellow actors and willing to work well in an ensemble. Her young face was unparalleled in its sweetness, intelligence, compassion, and uncanny beauty, helped a great deal by dimples any stage mother would kill for. Of such a piece were her looks and talents that as she grew into adolescence, the magic dissipated and she became a chubby-cheeked teenager with a strain of priggishness that made audiences uncomfortable. In her later films, she might be good, but she was not good enough, her personality having lost its spontaneity. She retired from films in 1949, the same year she divorced her first husband, John Agar. In the late 1960s, as Shirley Temple Black, she entered politics and has served as ambassador to both Ghana and the former Czechoslovakia.

Filmography: The Red Haired Alibi (1932); Baby Take a Bow, Bright Eyes, Change of Heart, Little Miss Marker, Now and Forever, Now I'll Tell, Stand Up and Cheer (1934); Curly Top, The Little Colonel, The Littlest Rebel, Our Little Girl (1935); Captain January, Dimples, Poor Little Rich Girl, Stowaway (1936); Heidi, Wee Willie Winkie (1937); Just Around the Corner, Little Miss Broadway, Rebecca of Sunnybrook Farm (1938); The Little Princess, Susannah of the Mounties (1939); The Blue Bird, Young People (1940); Kathleen (1941); Miss Annie Rooney (1942); I'll Be Seeing You, Since You Went Away (1944); Kiss and Tell (1945); The Bachelor and the Bobby-Soxer, Honeymoon, That Hagen Girl (1947); Fort Apache (1948); Adventure in Baltimore, A Kiss for Corliss/Almost a Bride, Mr. Belvedere Goes to College, The Story of Seabiscuit (1949); Going Hollywood: The War Years (1988).

Honors: Academy Award: Special Award [In grateful recognition of her outstanding contribution to screen entertainment during the year 1934, she was presented a Miniature Statuette] (1934).

Selected Bibliography

Edwards, Anne. *Shirley Temple: American Princess*. New York: William Morrow, 1988.
Lester, David, and Irene David. *The Shirley Temple Story*. New York: Putnam, 1983.
Temple, Shirley. *Child Star: An Autobiography*. New York: McGraw-Hill, 1988.
Windeler, Robert. *The Films of Shirley Temple*. Secaucus, NJ: Citadel Press, 1978.

TEN COMMANDMENTS, THE (1956), religious drama. Directed by Cecil B. DeMille; with Charlton Heston, Yul Brynner, Anne Baxter, Edward G. Robinson, Yvonne De Carlo, Debra Paget, John Derek, Cedric Hardwicke, H. B. Warner, Henry Wilcoxon, Nina Foch, Martha Scott, Judith Anderson, Vincent Price, John Carradine, and Woodrow (Woody) Strode; screenplay by Aeneas MacKenzie, Jesse L. Lasky, Jr., Fredric M. Frank, and Jack Garris.

DeMille pulled out all the stops on this, his last film spectacular, and a spectacle it is. First filmed in 1923, this remake was made when DeMille had at his command all the benefits of the new technology, including CinemaScope, but also the expertise of a stable of actors trained during the heyday of the studio system and able to deliver fine performances. He was also lucky in that during the 1950s Hollywood went all out in its war against television, and its major weapon was the screen epic with its casts of thousands, its triumphant marches, its lavish rituals, its immense battle scenes, and in the case of this film, its ability to make miracles really happen through special effects. This biblical epic follows Moses's life from birth and abandonment through manhood, slavery, and the trials he encountered in leading the Jews out of Egypt. In this film, DeMille brought to life the story of Moses on a scale no other filmmaker ever envisioned. Everything is presented in a grandiose style, yet the fine cast is never overwhelmed by the lavish sweep of this epic. Heston is magnificent as Moses, playing the great prophet as a humble man with a great inner strength. His role is unforgettable, and it is a part with which he will forever be identified. Brynner plays the pharaoh with utmost seriousness. In a cast this large, it was important for DeMille to have a strong ensemble. The supporting players give Heston, Brynner, and their director strength; there is hardly a bad performance in the lot. "To transfer the Bible to the screen you cannot cheat," DeMille said. "You have to believe." DeMille's vision remains a powerful one. This was the culmination of a life's work, with each element in the massive work meticulously scrutinized by the director. The film is a testament to both DeMille's love of his subject and his undeniable talent as the master of the epic cinema. Most reviewers damned it with faint praise, calling the production Hollywood hokum and the script shallow Biblespeak, on the one hand, while admitting that its overwhelming vulgarity ultimately imbues the film with a strange, inexplicable power, proving that DeMille knew exactly what he was up to. Who, after all, can question the seriousness of purpose of a director who took three weeks on the orgy scene alone? Maybe he did throw sex and sand into the moviegoers' eyes longer than anyone else ever dared to. The point is that he pulled it off because he knew movies and moviegoers. After all, he was making movies long before they became "films." Today *The Ten Commandments* is as much an annual holiday staple as *White Christmas* or *The Sound of Music*.

Awards: Academy Award: Special Effects; National Board of Review Award: Best Actor (Brynner); Academy Award Nomination: Best Picture.

Selected Bibliography

Crowther, Bruce. *Charlton Heston: The Epic Presence*. London: Columbus Books, 1986.
Ringgold, Gene, and DeWitt Bodeen. *The Films of Cecil B. DeMille*. New York: Citadel Press, 1969.
Smith, Gary A. *Epic Films: Cast, Credits, and Commentary on Over 250 Historical Spectacular Movies*. Jefferson, NC: McFarland, 1991.

THIN MAN, THE (1934), mystery/comedy. Directed by W. S. Van Dyke; with William Powell, Myrna Loy, Maureen O'Sullivan, Nat Pendleton, Minna Gombell, Cesar Romero, Natalie Moorhead, Edward Ellis, and Porter Hall; screenplay by Albert Hackett and Frances Goodrich.

This first pairing of what was to become one of the movies' great romantic teams was shot in just two weeks and has gone on to become the sophisticated comedy-mystery par excellence, inspiring five sequels as well as countless imitations. Adapted from Dashiell Hammett's novel, this is probably the best-loved detective film ever made and certainly one of the most popular. What makes *The Thin Man* an enduring film is the interplay between Powell and Loy. It started a new cycle in screen entertainment by demonstrating that a murder mystery could also be a sophisticated screwball comedy. And it turned several decades of movies upside down by showing a suave man of the world (Powell) who made love to his own rich, funny, and good-humored wife (Loy). As Nick and Nora Charles, Powell and Loy startled and delighted the country by their heavy drinking (without remorse) and unconventional diversions. Dashiell Hammett's fifth and last novel was something of a departure in that it was less a hard-boiled thriller than a sequence of sophisticated banter in which nobody, least of all Nick and Nora, took the tough guy ethos very seriously. What enchants, really, is the relationship between Nick and Nora as they live an eternal cocktail hour, bewailing hangovers that only another little drink will cure, in a marvelous blend of marital familiarity and constant courtship.

Awards: Academy Award Nominations: Best Picture, Director, Actor (Powell), Writing Adaptation.

Selected Bibliography

Dooley, Roger. *From Scarface to Scarlett: American Films in the 1930s*. New York: Harcourt Brace Jovanovich, 1981.
Miller, Frank. *Movies We Love: 100 Collectible Classics*. Atlanta, GA: Turner Publishing, 1996.
Quirk, Lawrence J. *The Films of Myrna Loy*. Secaucus, NJ: Citadel Press, 1980.

THREE CAME HOME (1950), war. Directed by Jean Negulesco; with Claudette Colbert, Patric Knowles, Florence Desmond, Sessue Hayakawa, Sylvia Andrew, and Phyllis Morris; screenplay by Nunnally Johnson.

Stunning performances by Colbert and Hayakawa make this a first-rate movie of life in a Japanese prison camp for women in Borneo during World War II. This is a true story, taken from the autobiographical account by Agnes Newton

Keith, a well-known writer in the 1930s and 1940s. Critics generally consider this to be a well-made and harrowing war adventure, one that is deeply disturbing on one level and wonderfully heroic on another. *Three Came Home* is a cinematic achievement that the passing of time has not diminished. On the contrary, this film takes on greater meaning in light of the history of the nearly fifty years since it appeared. Agnes Newton Keith has said that her intention was not to open old wounds or rekindle old hatreds. Instead, her purpose was to put the blame on war itself and to show how it dehumanizes all who deal in it or are touched by it. So, even though the Japanese guards are portrayed as brutal and insensitive, they are balanced by the presence of the camp commandant (Hayakawa), a cultured man the audience cannot help sympathizing with. Hayakawa not only befriends Keith and her son but is shown as a tragic victim himself of the war when he learns that his wife and three small children have all perished in the horror of Hiroshima. When he reveals this news to Keith, the two of them are united as parents in a deeply moving scene that underscores Keith's point. No ending on film can surpass the sheer drama of this one as Keith's husband, now crippled from mistreatment and malnutrition, is reunited with his wife and son. This wonderful film has become a staple on the History Channel, allowing newer and younger audiences to appreciate a balanced view of the bestiality of war from the pen of a woman who found compassion in heart when she had every reason to remain bitter. This film also showcases the tremendous range of Claudette Colbert's acting talent. It's hard to imagine that the heroic, middle-aged housewife and mother in *Three Came Home* is played by the temptress who, as Cleopatra, took a nude bath in milk in *The Sign of the Cross* or, as a screwball comedienne in *It Happened One Night*, hitched her skirt to hitch a ride.

Selected Bibliography

Quirk, Lawrence J. *Claudette Colbert: An Illustrated Biography*. New York: Crown, 1985.

TO HAVE AND HAVE NOT (1944), drama. Directed by Howard Hawks; with Humphrey Bogart, Walter Brennan, Lauren Bacall, Hoagy Carmichael, Dan Seymour, Marcel Dalio, Dolores Moran, and Sheldon Leonard; screenplay by Jules Furthman and William Faulkner.

"You know how to whistle, don't you, Steve? You just put your lips together and blow." This Bacall come-on to Bogart has outlasted the memory of a movie made memorable by the incendiary pairing of middle-aged Bogart with nineteen-year-old newcomer Bacall. This Hemingway novel, generally considered to be his worst, forms the basis for Hawks's version of *Casablanca* in which tough skipper-for-hire Bogart reluctantly becomes involved with the French Resistance but less reluctantly woos even tougher Bacall (in her film debut). Their legendary love scenes make the movie, but there are also solid performances, taut action, and a couple of songs. With an eye to the lucrative box office of *Cas-*

ablanca, Warner Bros. turned out another epic of similar genre. There are enough similarities in both films to warrant more than cursory attention, not the least of which is the fact that Humphrey Bogart is starred in each. Warners gave this picture its usually classy production values—including casting, scoring, and direction—but praise for it has been guarded. Whatever the critical verdict, this is a picture that has found a niche somewhere between a cult film and a camp classic.

Selected Bibliography

Mast, Gerald. *Howard Hawks, Storyteller*. New York: Oxford University Press, 1982.

McCarty, Clifford. *The Complete Films of Humphrey Bogart*. Secaucus, NJ: Citadel Press, 1965.

Royce, Brenda Scott. *Lauren Bacall: A Bio-Bibliography*. Westport, CT: Greenwood Press, 1992.

TO KILL A MOCKINGBIRD (1962), drama. Directed by Robert Mulligan; with Gregory Peck, Mary Badham, Phillip Alford, John Megna, Robert Duvall, and Brock Peters; screenplay by Horton Foote.

This moody, nostalgic portrayal of childhood mischief set in the racially divided 1930s town of Macomb County, Alabama, is based on the semiautobiographical, Pulitzer Prize–winning novel of 1960 by Harper Lee. As if by magic, the movie manages to capture the special aura of a small southern town and the people who live there. The children in the movie are particularly good. Badham, who plays the tough little sister, is a nine-year-old who had never acted before, and Alford, also in his first role at age thirteen, turns in an impressive performance in a part not quite as developed as Badham's. (Kim Stanley, as the voice of the grown-up Badham, narrates the story.) The third child in the cast is Megna, whose character Dill is based on author Truman Capote, a childhood friend of Harper Lee's. Adult actors have traditionally been warned not to appear in scenes with children (or animals, for that matter) because they are notorious scene-stealers. However, in this movie, Peck more than holds his own with his laid-back wholesomeness and his rich, mellow voice. So good is he, in fact, that it is easy to see why he won an Oscar for his performance. Peck once said that *Mockingbird* was, without question, his favorite film, that he was able to draw on his own childhood to better relate to the children's characters, through whose eyes the film is seen. The film, which was scripted by Horton Foote, so wonderfully follows the spirit of Lee's novel that it brought high praise from the author herself for what she called a beautiful and moving motion picture. The picture was also warmly received by audiences responding not only to their own nostalgic feelings but to Peck's heroic portrayal of an exemplary citizen and father. A telling indictment of racial prejudice in the Deep South, *To Kill a Mockingbird* is also a charming tale of the emergence of two youngsters from the realm of wild childhood fantasy to the horizon of maturity, responsibility, compassion, and social insight.

Awards: Academy Awards: Best Actor (Peck), Adapted Screenplay (Foote), B&W Art Direction (Golitzen, Bumstead); Golden Globe Awards: Best Actor (Peck), Best Film Promoting International Understanding; Academy Award Nominations: Best Picture, Director, Supporting Actress (Badham), B&W Cinematography, Original Music Score.

Selected Bibliography

Griggs, John. *The Films of Gregory Peck*. Secaucus, NJ: Citadel Press, 1984.

TOUCH OF EVIL (1958), crime. Directed by Orson Welles; with Charlton Heston, Orson Welles, Janet Leigh, Joseph Calleia, Akim Tamiroff, Marlene Dietrich, Dennis Weaver, Valentin de Vargas, Mort Mills, Victor Milian, Joanna Moore, and Zsa Zsa Gabor; screenplay by Orson Welles.

This offbeat, noirish film is generally considered to be one of the top fifty films of all time—for reasons not always easy to understand. The famous opening shot, considered by many to be the greatest single shot ever put on film, is one of the reasons. The picture's choppy editing, done against Welles's wishes and to his utter dismay, was greatly admired by European critics, and Welles even received the international prize at the 1958 Brussels World's Fair. The confusing, complex narrative and structure, while annoying to studio executives, is the sort of puzzle film buffs enjoy. Added to these curiosities is a peculiar cast consisting of characters not usually thought of as appearing on the same screen together, such as Welles and Leigh or Heston and Weaver, not to mention unbilled cameos by the likes of Marlene Dietrich, Zsa Zsa Gabor, Joseph Cotten, Ray Collins, and Mercedes McCambridge. While most critics find this a movie to reckon with, they also express a general discontent with the film's "artiness." At times it seems to flounder in its own brilliance, and while it is studded with good scenes, they do not necessarily add up to a satisfying picture. Some think the movie simply overrated, calling it an atmospheric melodrama that gets bogged down in Wellesian flourishes that some call genius, others pure balderdash. As is the case with *The Magnificent Ambersons*, critical opinion is affected more by the critic's opinion of Orson Welles than of the picture itself.

Awards: Brussels World's Fair: International Prize.

Selected Bibliography

Higham, Charles. *The Films of Orson Welles*. Berkeley: University of California Press, 1970.
Peary, Danny. *Alternate Oscars*. New York: Delta, 1993.
Rovin, Jeff. *The Films of Charlton Heston*. Secaucus, NJ: Citadel Press, 1977.

TRACY, SPENCER. Actor. Born on April 5, 1900, in Milwaukee, Wisconsin; died on June 10, 1967. Educated at the Northwestern Military Academy, Ripon College, and the American Academy of Dramatic Arts in New York. Tracy's early childhood was one of intense rebelliousness, exemplified by the fact that he was expelled from no fewer than fifteen grade schools. By the time he reached high school, however, he had settled down quite a bit and was earning good grades and even thinking seriously of entering the priesthood. But at Ripon College Tracy got involved in college theatrical productions, and it wasn't long before he went off to New York to enroll in the American Academy of Dramatic Arts. It was in *Yellow* in 1926 that he first came to the attention of critics, and audiences loved him in *Baby Cyclone* the following year. But by 1929, three flops in a row had brought his career to a standstill. That same year Tracy appeared in two low-budget short films: as a gangster in *Taxi Talks* and as a World War I veteran in *Hard Guy*; but the films were unexceptional. Tracy went back to the stage and finally made a breakthrough in *The Last Mile* playing killer John Mears. Director John Ford caught one of his performances and persuaded Fox to sign Tracy for Ford's upcoming film *Up the River* in 1930. Although he received critical praise for two or three of the films he made for Fox, most of them were financial failures, and Fox was reluctant to promote him in quality features. Tracy felt caught in a squeeze. He needed better roles to advance his career, yet he couldn't get better roles if the films continued to bomb. Frustrated, Tracy rebelled by drinking heavily, fighting with producers and directors, and disappearing from film sets for days at a time. Finally, Fox did cast him as a ruthless business tycoon in its prestige production of *The Power and the Glory*, but when this film flopped, Tracy was convinced that he was washed up. Even so, and against Louis B. Mayer's wishes, Irving Thalberg brought him to MGM, and within no time, Tracy became the first actor to win back-to-back Oscars (*Captains Courageous*, 1937; *Boys Town*, 1938). His career experienced a further boost when he began appearing in a series of sophisticated comedies opposite Katharine Hepburn. His gruff, down-to-earth manner provided a perfect counterpoint to Hepburn's finishing-school decorum. Tracy continued at MGM until his erratic behavior on the set of *Tribute to a Bad Man* in 1956 caused the production to shut down and forced director Robert Wise to fire him. As his health declined, Tracy became more of a recluse. However, during the last decade of his life, he did form a strong friendship with director Stanley Kramer, who guided him through such superb performances as the Clarence Darrow–inspired lawyer in *Inherit the Wind* and the wise judge in *Judgment at Nuremberg*. Suffering from emphysema, Tracy made his last screen appearance opposite Hepburn in Kramer's *Guess Who's Coming to Dinner?* Tracy died two weeks after filming was completed. Tracy projected an inner strength and self-assurance that used to be a more familiar ingredient among Hollywood actors (Stewart, Peck, Heston, Andrews) but that is in short supply today. Stanley Kramer recalls: ''I was afraid to say, 'Spencer, you're a great actor.' He'd only say, 'Now what the hell kind of thing is that to come out with?' He wanted to know it; he needed to know it. But he didn't want you to say it—just think it. And maybe that was one of the reasons he was a great actor. He thought and listened better than anyone in the history of motion pictures. A silent close-up reaction of Spencer Tracy said it all.'' Tracy's seemingly effortless approach to his vocation earned him the respect of his peers and helped

him become one of the most distinguished and venerated actors of his generation.

Filmography: Up the River (1930); Goldie, Quick Millions, Six Cylinder Love (1931);
Disorderly Conduct, Me and My Gal, The Painted Woman, She Wanted a Millionaire,
Sky Devils, Society Girl, Young America (1932); 20,000 Years in Sing Sing, The Face
in the Sky, The Mad Game, Man's Castle, The Power and the Glory, Shanghai Madness
(1933); Bottoms Up, Looking for Trouble, Marie Galante, Now I'll Tell, The Show-Off
(1934); Dante's Inferno, It's a Small World, The Murder Man, Riffraff, Whipsaw (1935);
Fury, Libeled Lady, San Francisco (1936); The Big City/Skyscraper Wilderness, Captains
Courageous, Mannequin, They Gave Him a Gun (1937); Boys Town, Test Pilot (1938);
Stanley and Livingstone (1939); Boom Town, Edison the Man, I Take This Woman,
Northwest Passage (1940); Dr. Jekyll and Mr. Hyde, Men of Boys Town (1941); Keeper
of the Flame, Tortilla Flat, Woman of the Year (1942); A Guy Named Joe (1943); The
Seventh Cross, Thirty Seconds over Tokyo (1944); Without Love (1945); Cass Timber-
lane, The Sea of Grass (1947); State of the Union (1948); Adam's Rib, Edward My Son,
Malaya (1949); Father of the Bride (1950); Father's Little Dividend, The People against
O'Hara (1951); Pat and Mike, Plymouth Adventure (1952); The Actress (1953); Broken
Lance (1954); Bad Day at Black Rock (1955); The Mountain (1956); Desk Set (1957);
The Last Hurrah, The Old Man and the Sea (1958); Inherit the Wind (1960); The Devil
at 4 O'clock, Judgment at Nuremberg (1961); How the West Was Won (1962); It's a
Mad Mad Mad Mad World (1963); Guess Who's Coming to Dinner? (1967); George
Stevens: A Filmmaker's Journey (1984); Going Hollywood: The War Years (1988).

Honors: Academy Award Nomination: Best Actor (*San Francisco*, 1936); Academy
Award: Best Actor (*Captains Courageous*, 1937); Academy Award: Best Actor (*Boys
Town*, 1938); Academy Award Nomination: Best Actor (*Father of the Bride*, 1950);
Golden Globe Award: Actor/Drama (*The Actress*, 1953); Cannes Film Festival Award,
Academy Award Nomination: Best Actor (*Bad Day at Black Rock*, 1955); National Board
of Review Award: Best Actor (*The Old Man and the Sea* and *The Last Hurrah*, 1958);
Academy Award Nomination: Best Actor (*The Old Man and the Sea*, 1958); Academy
Award Nomination: Best Actor (*Judgment at Nuremberg*, 1961); Academy Award Nom-
ination: Best Actor (*Guess Who's Coming to Dinner?*, 1967); British Academy Award:
Best Actor (*Guess Who's Coming to Dinner?*, 1968).

Selected Bibliography

Davidson, Bill. *Spencer Tracy: Tragic Idol*. London: Sidgwick & Jackson, 1987.
Deschner, Donald. *The Complete Films of Spencer Tracy*. Secaucus, NJ: Citadel Press,
    1968.
Fisher, James. *Spencer Tracy: A Bio-Bibliography*. Westport, CT: Greenwood Press,
    1994.

TREASURE OF THE SIERRA MADRE, THE (1948), adventure. Directed by
John Huston; with Humphrey Bogart, Walter Huston, Tim Holt, Bruce Bennett,
Barton MacLane, and Alfonso Bedoya; screenplay by John Huston.

"Greed, gold and gunplay on a Mexican mountain of malice!" "The nearer
they got to their treasure the further they got from the law!" Maybe it was the
overblown rhetoric of blurbs like these that kept audiences away, but *The Treasure of the Sierra Madre* was not a box office success. Some think that audiences

merely rejected Bogart's evil character—not the Bogart they had come to love and respect throughout the 1940s—and thus they had real trouble accepting his death at the end of the film. However, the film was a critical success and has since been recognized as the classic it is. Bogart gives the performance of a lifetime, one full of humor and humiliation, anger and malice. John Huston produced a number of great films, but this tale of greed, fear, and murder in Mexico is arguably his finest. Huston here creates a classic film, one that relentlessly exposes the destructive nature of greed. With overwhelming irony, he reveals how the soul is corrupted in the ruthless acquisition of riches. Bogart is "everyman" whose initial desire only to have his "fair share" turns into a passion for everyone's share. Walter Huston is the wise voice of experience, able to predict the tragic outcome of this tale but unable to prevent it. Tim Holt, an underrated actor who was allowed to give two or three unforgettable performances in his career, is a fine counterpoint to the aggressive Bogart. This wonderful movie has the simplicity and depth, the clarity and grandeur, of timeless myth.

Awards: Academy Awards: Best Director, Supporting Actor (Walter Huston), Screenplay; Golden Globe Award, New York Film Critics Circle Award: Best Picture; Venice Film Festival Award: Score (Max Steiner); Academy Award Nomination: Best Picture.

Selected Bibliography

McCarty, Clifford. *The Complete Films of Humphrey Bogart*. Secaucus, NJ: Citadel Press, 1965.
McCarty, John. *The Films of John Huston*. Secaucus, NJ: Citadel Press, 1987.
Peary, Danny. *Alternate Oscars*. New York: Delta, 1993.

TREE GROWS IN BROOKLYN, A (1945), drama. Directed by Elia Kazan; with Dorothy McGuire, Joan Blondell, James Dunn, Lloyd Nolan, Peggy Ann Garner, Ted Donaldson, James Gleason, Ruth Nelson, and John Alexander; screenplay by Tess Slesinger and Frank Davis.

This is a sensitive film adaptation of Betty Smith's novel about a bright young girl trying to rise above the hardships of her tenement life in turn-of-the-century Brooklyn, New York. The earthy quality of Brooklyn tenement squalor has been given a literal translation to the screen by Elia Kazan. In this, his directorial debut, Kazan avoids letting the material slip into sit-com comedy or soap opera melodrama, no mean trick when you are dealing with material like this. Peggy Ann Garner is so good as the young girl that she was given a Special Academy Award, and James Dunn, in the role of a lifetime, won the award for Best Supporting Actor. This picture is of interest if for no other reason than that it is a prime example of a superbly detailed studio production of its day, the sort of movie that just isn't made any more. It is strangely reminiscent of the live television drama of the 1950s, those moody, gentle family dramas that usually starred Kim Stanley.

Awards: Academy Awards: Best Supporting Actor (James Dunn), Special Award (Outstanding Child Actress, Peggy Ann Garner); Academy Award Nomination: Best Screenplay.

Selected Bibliography

Pauly, Thomas H. *An American Odyssey: Elia Kazan and American Culture*. Philadelphia: Temple University Press, 1983.

TURNER, LANA. Actress. Born Julia Jean Mildred Frances Turner on February 8, 1920, in Wallace, Idaho; died on June 29, 1995. According to Hollywood legend, Lana Turner was wearing a tight sweater and sipping a soda at Schwab's drugstore when she was spotted by a talent scout, turning that drugstore into a mecca for Turner wannabes. Actually, she was sitting at the counter of an ice cream parlor across from Hollywood High School when she was spotted by a talent scout. She was soon making an impression in run-of-the-mill dramas, finally becoming a star when she was cast opposite such leading men as Spencer Tracy, Clark Gable, and Robert Taylor in a number of early 1940s features, including *Honky Tonk* and *Johnny Eager*. She is probably best remembered for her steamy role in the gritty melodrama *The Postman Always Rings Twice*. Turner got her biggest dramatic break, however, in *Peyton Place* in a role that won her an Academy Award nomination. After that she made a succession of tearjerkers such as *Imitation of Life* and *Madame X*. In her later years, Turner turned up on various TV shows, particularly *Falcon Crest*. She lived a stormy private life, marrying several times and having a longtime affair with mobster Johnny Stompanato, who was stabbed to death by Turner's daughter Cheryl Crane, an incident that inspired Woody Allen's *September* and, to a certain extent, Harold Robbins's *Where Love Has Gone*.

Filmography: The Great Garrick, They Won't Forget (1937); The Adventures of Marco Polo, Dramatic School, Love Finds Andy Hardy, Rich Man Poor Girl (1938); Calling Dr. Kildare, Dancing Co-ed, These Glamour Girls (1939); Two Girls on Broadway, We Who Are Young (1940); Dr. Jekyll and Mr. Hyde, Honky Tonk, Johnny Eager, Ziegfeld Girl (1941); Somewhere I'll Find You (1942); Slightly Dangerous, The Youngest Profession (1943); Marriage Is a Private Affair (1944); Keep Your Powder Dry, Weekend at the Waldorf (1945); The Postman Always Rings Twice (1946); Cass Timberlane, Green Dolphin Street (1947); Homecoming, The Three Musketeers (1948); A Life of Her Own (1950); Mr. Imperium (1951); The Bad and the Beautiful, The Merry Widow (1952); Latin Lovers (1953); Betrayed, The Flame and the Flesh (1954); The Prodigal, The Rains of Ranchipur, The Sea Chase (1955); Diane (1956); Peyton Place (1957); Another Time Another Place [also prod.], The Lady Takes a Flyer (1958); Imitation of Life (1959); Portrait in Black (1960); Bachelor in Paradise, By Love Possessed (1961); Who's Got the Action (1962); Love Has Many Faces (1965); Madame X (1966); The Big Cube (1969); Persecution/The Terror of Sheba/The Graveyard (1974); Bittersweet Love (1976); Witches' Brew (1980); That's Entertainment! III (1994).

Honors: Academy Award Nomination: Best Actress (*Peyton Place*, 1957).

Selected Bibliography

Crane, Cheryl, with Cliff Jahr. *Detour: A Hollywood Story*. New York: Arbor House/
    William Morrow, 1988.
Turner, Lana. *Lana—The Lady, the Legend, the Truth*. New York: Dutton, 1982.
Valentino, Lou. *The Films of Lana Turner*. Secaucus, NJ: Citadel Press, 1978.
Wayne, Jane Ellen. *Lana: The Life and Loves of Lana Turner*. New York: St. Martin's
    Press, 1994.

12 ANGRY MEN (1957), drama. Directed by Sidney Lumet; with Henry Fonda, Lee J. Cobb, Ed Begley, E. G. Marshall, Jack Klugman, Jack Warden, Martin Balsam, John Fiedler, George Voskovec, Robert Webber, Edward Binns, and Joseph Sweeney; screenplay by Reginald Rose.

This film was a landmark film in its day, especially in its use of television techniques being applied to movies and in its innovative use of abrupt changes of camera angles. Today the film has to be taken as a period piece, for it is hopelessly dated. For one thing, the jury consists of twelve white males. For another, without air conditioning, they all suffer from being locked in a stifling room in midsummer, and the heat has a lot to do with their impatience (their ''rush to judgment'') and their frequent outbursts of temper. In making this film, director Sidney Lumet carefully plotted and sketched every visual nuance. As had been his habit with theatrical productions, he also rehearsed his cast for a full two weeks before the actual twenty-day shoot. The resulting real-time drama made film history. Fonda is compelling in a part made to order for his persona as the good guy up against impossible odds. The others in the cast (handpicked by Lumet) were leading stage and television actors whose wonderful work in this film was rewarded in many cases by eventual cinematic stardom. The film is an unsettling one in many ways, as much an indictment as an affirmation of America's jury system. Regardless, it generates a great deal of suspense, thanks to Reginald Rose's script (a reworking of his teleplay) and Sidney Lumet's direction, both of which are so professional that one wonders why the movie was not a hit. While most critics responded favorably to the film, some have speculated that the problem with the film is that it is ultimately contrived, and while it plays well as melodrama, it becomes predictable and clichéd. For the audience it soon becomes a game of who will give in next and how. Although intended as a lesson in the responsibility of citizens to their society, and as encouragement to stand alone against the mob, what it does subliminally is to frighten citizens into worrying about what happens when there are no Henry Fondas on the jury. Critics, happy to witness a message film with momentum, praised it as an absorbing experience with more suspense than most thrillers. Intended originally to extol the virtues of the jury system, the film cannot avoid exposing its weaknesses. Whatever its effect, this is a film deserving of serious attention.

Awards: Directors Guild of America Award: Outstanding Directorial Achievement; Berlin Film Festival Award: Golden Bear; Academy Award Nominations: Best Picture, Director, Screenplay Adaptation.

Selected Bibliography

Bowles, Stephen E. *Sidney Lumet: A Guide to References and Resources*. Boston: G. K. Hall, 1979.
Sweeney, Kevin. *Henry Fonda: A Bio-Bibliography*. Westport, CT: Greenwood Press, 1992.

TWELVE O'CLOCK HIGH (1949), war. Directed by Henry King; with Gregory Peck, Hugh Marlowe, Gary Merrill, Millard Mitchell, Dean Jagger, and Paul Stewart; screenplay by Sy Bartlett and Beirne Lay, Jr.

This was one of the first films to take a realistic look at World War II heroism and reveal its fighting men as vulnerable. Peck's character is entirely human—a man with real emotions, fears, and inadequacies. Jagger gives the film's pivotal performance as an introspective, older military man who has lived through one world war and now holds together the frayed ends of the 918th Bomber Group. In addition to fine acting, this film features some stunning camera work by Leon Shamroy and one of the most riveting aerial attack sequences ever put on film. This picture broke new ground by daring to suggest that officers and men are fundamentally different after all and that the individuality we fight to preserve is the one luxury we cannot afford during wartime. Ironically, those who fight to preserve democracy cannot afford to behave in a democratic way.

Awards: Academy Awards: Best Supporting Actor (Jagger), Sound Recording; Academy Award Nominations: Best Picture, Actor (Peck).

Selected Bibliography

Doherty, Thomas Patrick. *Projection of War: Hollywood, American Culture, and World War II*. New York: Columbia University Press, 1993.
Griggs, John. *The Films of Gregory Peck*. Secaucus, NJ: Citadel Press, 1984.
Manvell, Roger. *Films and the Second World War*. South Brunswick, NJ: A. S. Barnes, 1974.

TWENTIETH CENTURY (1934), comedy. Directed by Howard Hawks; with John Barrymore, Carole Lombard, Walter Connolly, Roscoe Karns, Etienne Girardot, Ralph Forbes, Charles Levison (Lane), and Edgar Kennedy; screenplay by Ben Hecht and Charles MacArthur.

In this classic screwball comedy Barrymore, an ego-driven Broadway producer, transforms Lombard, a lowly shopgirl, into a star. When she walks out on him and heads east on the famous 20th Century Limited, he pursues her, doing everything possible to win her back. Barrymore is at his funniest in this madcap film, playing a part so close to his own personality that he flirts with self-parody. It is interesting to note that the original play on which *Twentieth Century* was based was Bruce Millholland's *Napoleon of Broadway*, a fitting name for such an egomaniac as Jaffe. Ben Hecht and Charles MacArthur adapted their stage version from the Millholland original, then scripted the film from their own play. Later, the play returned to Broadway as the musical *On the Twentieth Century*. It was Carole Lombard's performance, playing "Galatea" to Barrymore's ''Pygmalion,'' that established her as a comedienne, and in her skin-tight satins, she is the incarnation of the giddy glamour of 1930s comedy. Critics compare this picture favorably with Hawks's later triumph *His Girl Friday*.

Selected Bibliography

Mast, Gerald. *Howard Hawks, Storyteller*. New York: Oxford University Press, 1982.
Ott, Frederick W. *The Films of Carole Lombard*. Secaucus, NJ: Citadel Press, 1972.
Sennett, Ted. *Lunatics and Lovers: A Tribute to the Giddy and Glittering Era of the Screen's ''Screwball'' and Romantic Comedies*. New Rochelle, NY: Arlington House, 1973.

20,000 LEAGUES UNDER THE SEA (1954), science fiction/adventure/fantasy. Directed by Richard Fleischer; with Kirk Douglas, James Mason, Paul Lukas, Peter Lorre, Robert J. Wilke, and Carleton Young; screenplay by Earl Fenton.

This was the first live-action movie made by Walt Disney at his own studio, and it turned out to be one of the best science fiction movies ever filmed. Earl Fenton's script sticks very close to Jules Verne's mind-boggling vision in which Douglas and Lukas get involved with power-hungry Captain Nemo (Mason) who operates a futuristic submarine. Memorable action sequences and a fine cast make this film a winner. The story of the ''monster'' ship *Nautilus*, incredible as it may be, is so compellingly developed that viewers have no problem suspending their disbelief and joining this astonishing excursion through Captain Nemo's underseas realm. This is still considered to be one of Disney's most ambitious live-action adaptations. Given the embarrassment of the 1997 television remake, one might safely call this Disney version incomparable.

Awards: Academy Awards: Best Color Art Direction (John Meehan and Emile Kuri), Special Effects; Academy Award Nomination: Best Editing.

Selected Bibliography

Jackson, Kathy Merlock. *Disney: A Bio-Bibliography*. Westport, CT: Greenwood Press, 1993.
Maltin, Leonard. *The Disney Films*. New York: Crown Publishers, 1984.
Thomas, Tony. *The Films of Kirk Douglas*. Secaucus, NJ: Citadel Press, 1972.

V

VERTIGO (1958), thriller. Directed by Alfred Hitchcock; with James Stewart, Kim Novak, Barbara Bel Geddes, Tom Helmore, Henry Jones, Ellen Corby, Raymond Bailey, and Lee Patrick; screenplay by Alec Coppel and Samuel Taylor.

Vertigo got a lukewarm reception from critics when it was first released, but today critical opinion rates it very high in the Hitchcock canon, perhaps at the top, for it is a multilayered film that while satisfying on any level, almost requires more than one viewing to appreciate its ingenious complexity fully. In what is arguably Hitchcock's most intensely personal, self-revealing picture, *Vertigo* is the story of a man who is possessed by the image of a lost love and becomes increasingly compulsive in his desire to re-create that image. *Vertigo*'s story appealed to Hitchcock for reasons that become more apparent in light of the director's own obsessions. Hitchcock tended to become fascinated with the actresses he starred in his films. He chose women whose cool, blond, sophisticated looks played against their sexuality, women like Grace Kelly, Vera Miles, Joan Fontaine, Ingrid Bergman, Tippi Hedren, and in this case, Kim Novak, and carefully molded their appearances and actions to conform to his rigid standards of beauty and sexual appeal. *Vertigo* is about just such attempts to realize an ideal image and to capture an illusion, using its main character's obsessive pathology to convey this theme. When the seemingly normal hero, who has become warped in his desire for a woman who never really existed, screams, "Did he train you? Did he rehearse you? Did he tell you exactly what to do and what to say?" he might easily be referring not to the murderer who set him up but to himself and to Hitchcock—the master who obsessively trained his pupil-actresses. Novak is a woman who feels compelled to deny her own identity and allow herself to be degraded in order to please the men who ask her to play a part. As Hitchcock pointed out, Stewart's pursuit of the image becomes a form of necrophilia. It also makes him, like the character he played in *Rear Window*, a voyeur who observes and imagines rather than acts in the real world. With the rise of the auteur theory and interest in directors' lives and careers (along with a number of books delving into Hitchcock's dark side), fascination with the multifaceted *Vertigo* continues to mount. Some critics are uncomfortable with this bleak, cynical view of human obsession, but even they agree that this is Hitchcock at the very peak of his powers.

Awards: Academy Award Nominations: Best Sound, Art Direction.

Selected Bibliography

Jones, Ken D., Arthur F. McClure, and Alfred E. Twomey. *The Films of James Stewart*. New York: Castle Books, 1970.

Kleno, Larry. *Kim Novak on Camera*. San Diego, CA: A. S. Barnes, 1980.

Raubicheck, Walter, and Walter Srebnick, eds. *Hitchcock's Re-released Films: From Rope to Vertigo*. Detroit, MI: Wayne State University Press, 1991.

VIDOR, KING. Director. Born King Wallis Vidor on February 8, 1894, in Galveston, Texas; died on November 1, 1982. Vidor shot local events for national newsreel companies before forming the Hotex Motion Picture Company in Houston in 1914. He then moved to Hollywood, where he eventually settled at Universal as a writer. His first directing work in Hollywood was independently produced, including *The Turn of the Road*, an extremely successful feature with Vidor's Christian Science beliefs as thematic material. After a series of further successes, the director founded "Vidor Village," a small studio from which he planned to produce independently. The experiment failed, but Vidor found work directing feature films for the Metro and Goldwyn studios in 1922. The merger that created MGM in 1924 also made Vidor a senior director for the company, and his fifth film for the young studio, *The Big Parade*, was a landmark critical and popular success. The film, reportedly one of the most profitable silent films ever produced, vaulted MGM to front-rank studio status and gave Vidor unheard of creative control. Vidor acquired a reputation as a bankable director and went on to make such outstanding features as *Street Scene, Our Daily Bread, The Champ,* and *Stella Dallas*. Vidor walked out in frustration on *The Wizard of Oz* in 1939, and seven years later, he did the same thing with the "adult" western *Duel in the Sun*. Three years later he signed with Warner Bros. to make *The Fountainhead*, a stunning but controversial adaptation of Ayn Rand's radical egoism. This story of an architect's battle with professional and social hypocrisy was among Vidor's most fully realized productions of the postwar period. The film has been viciously attacked by a number of critics, any one of whom could have been an understudy for the role of critic Elsworth Toohey, the arrogant philistine. Although equally striking, *Beyond the Forest* is thematically bizarre. This tale of a small-town doctor's wife (Bette Davis) and her ambitions bombed at the box office and effectively ended Davis's twenty-year career at Warners.

The film has since become a camp cult classic, the one that includes Davis's unforgettable put-down as she surveys a friend's "rec" room: "What a dump!" Vidor's last three features were disappointing epics, among them the misguided *War and Peace*. King Vidor's films range across all genres, but they are unified by a concern with the struggle for selfhood in a pluralistic, mass society.

Filmography: [as director, unless otherwise noted]: The Intrigue [per.] (1916); Better Times [also sc.], The Other Half [also sc.], Poor Relations [also sc.], The Turn in the Road [also sc.] (1919); The Family Honor, The Jack-Knife Man (1920); Love Never Dies [also sc.], The Sky Pilot (1921); Conquering the Woman, Dusk to Dawn, Peg O' My Heart, The Real Adventure (1922); Souls for Sale, Three Wise Fools [also adaptation], The Woman of Bronze (1923); Happiness, His Hour, Wife of the Centaur [also sc.], Wild Oranges [also sc.], Wine of Youth [also prod.] (1924); The Big Parade, Proud Flesh (1925); Bardelys the Magnificent, La Boheme (1926); The Patsy (1927); The Crowd [also sc., story], Show People [also prod.] (1928); Hallelujah [also story] (1929); Billy the Kid/Highwayman Rides [also prod.], Not So Dumb (1930); The Champ [also prod.], Street Scene (1931); Bird of Paradise [also prod.], Cyndara (1932); The Stranger's Return [prod.] (1933); Our Daily Bread [also story] (1934); So Red the Rose, The Wedding Night (1935); The Texas Rangers [also story] (1936); Stella Dallas (1937); The Citadel (1938); Comrade X, Northwest Passage (1940); H. M. Pulham Esq. [also sc.] (1941); An American Romance [also prod., story] (1944); Duel in the Sun (1946); On Our Merry Way/A Miracle Can Happen [co-dir.] (1948); Beyond the Forest, The Fountainhead (1949); Lightning Strikes Twice (1951); Japanese War Bride, Ruby Gentry [also prod.] (1952); Man without a Star (1955); War and Peace [also sc., adaptation] (1956); Solomon and Sheba (1959).

Honors: Academy Award Nomination: Best Director (*The Crowd*, 1927–1928); Academy Award Nomination: Best Director (*Hallelujah*, 1929–1930); Academy Award Nomination: Best Director (*The Champ*, 1931–1932); Venice Film Festival Award: Best Director (*The Wedding Night*, 1935); Academy Award Nomination: Best Director (*The Citadel*, 1938); Directors Guild of America Award: Outstanding Directorial Achievement, Academy Award Nomination: Best Director (*War and Peace*, 1956); Academy Award: Special Award [for his incomparable achievements as cinematic creator and innovator] (1978).

Selected Bibliography

Baxter, John. *King Vidor*. New York: Monarch Press, 1976.
Lang, Robert. *American Film Melodrama: Griffith, Vidor, Minnelli*. Princeton, NJ: Princeton University Press, 1989.
Vidor, King. *King Vidor on Film Making*. New York: McKay, 1972.

VIVA ZAPATA! (1952), biography. Directed by Elia Kazan; with Marlon Brando, Jean Peters, Anthony Quinn, Joseph Wiseman, Margo, and Mildred Dunnock; screenplay by John Steinbeck.

Brando is perfect in the title role of this film about a Mexican peasant's rise to power and eventual presidency. And Quinn is also good in an Oscar-winning performance as Brando's brother. The film remains vivid and meaningful to this day. Kazan directed this exciting biography with great flair for authenticity and period, injecting vitality into almost every frame and graphically capturing a bloody era of the Mexican past. Brando presents an idealized version of Zapata, who was in reality more barbaric and did not hesitate to execute his enemies en masse. The film has been criticized for its 1950s-style liberalism packaged in doubtful folklore and simplistic storytelling, but this is classic Hollywood myth making that is seldom questioned when Disney does it. The tension between straightforward adventure and pessimistic allegory about the corrupting nature of power that some critics consider a major flaw in the film would be a virtue if Zapata were animated and Brando did a voiceover. When it appeared, this film had great appeal to ardent Brando fans, many of whom had sympathies with any Latino rebel and relished Brando (the "wild one") in the part.

Awards: Academy Award: Best Supporting Actor (Quinn); British Academy Award, Cannes Film Festival Award: Best Actor (Brando); Academy Award Nominations: Best Actor (Brando), Story & Screenplay, Art Direction, Scoring of a Dramatic Picture.

Selected Bibliography

Marill, Alvin H. *The Films of Anthony Quinn*. Secaucus, NJ: Citadel Press, 1975.

Michaels, Lloyd. *Elia Kazan: A Guide to References and Resources*. Boston: G. K. Hall, 1985.

Thomas, Tony. *The Films of Marlon Brando*. Secaucus, NJ: Citadel Press, 1973.

W

WAYNE, JOHN. Actor. Born Marion Michael Morrison on May 26, 1907, in Winterset, Iowa; died on June 11, 1979. Educated at the University of Southern California, Los Angeles. John Wayne's image as a rugged individualist and embodiment of the frontier spirit has overshadowed his career to the point that it is virtually impossible to separate Wayne the legend from Wayne the actor. He held several minor jobs at Fox before moving in front of the cameras in the late 1920s in a series of bit roles. Director John Ford took note of him and recommended him for the lead in the 1930 western epic *The Big Trail*, but nothing much came of it, and Wayne spent the 1930s in a series of low-budget westerns that gave him little chance to grow as an actor. John Ford gave Wayne's career another boost in 1939 by casting him as the Ringo Kid in *Stagecoach*, a role that made Wayne a top-ranking box office attraction. Exempted from military service, Wayne compensated by appearing in a succession of war films in which he could be both tough and compassionate. These roles were the beginning of the Wayne legend, and before long he had become larger than life. In the late 1940s he was given a chance to expand his image by appearing in such superior westerns as *Red River*, *Fort Apache*, and *She Wore a Yellow Ribbon*, pictures in which he plumbed depths never before revealed. During the 1950s and 1960s he fluctuated between boilerplate action movies and an occasional superior western under a top director like John Ford, who directed him in *The Searchers*, a classic movie that has become something of a cult film. Wayne, like Gable, Grant, Mitchum, and others, was a victim of his own legend—so natural at what he did and so taken for granted that he was routinely overlooked for awards. When he finally did win a Best Actor Oscar for *True Grit*, it was a classic case of Hollywood catching up with a long overdue honor, for it was not a particularly impressive picture. It is generally conceded that Wayne's best picture in the 1970s was his last, *The Shootist*, in which he played a dying gunman who is just beginning to understand his own life and legend, a fitting elegy for a man who was himself dying of cancer during the filming of the movie.

Filmography: Salute, Words and Music (1929); The Big Trail, Men Are Like That, Men without Women (1930); Arizona, Girls Demand Excitement, Maker of Men, The Range Feud, Three Girls Lost (1931); The Big Stampede, Haunted Gold, The Hurricane Express, Lady and Gent, Ride Him Cowboy, The Shadow of the Eagle, Texas Cyclone, Two Fisted Law (1932); Baby Face, His Private Secretary, The Life of Jimmy Dolan, The Man from Monterey, Riders of Destiny, Sagebrush Trail, Somewhere in Sonora, The Telegraph Trail (1933); 'Neath the Arizona Skies, Blue Steel, The Lucky Texan, The Man from Utah, Randy Rides Alone, The Star Packer, The Trail Beyond, West of the Divide (1934); The Dawn Rider, The Desert Trail, The Lawless Frontier, Lawless Range, The New Frontier, Paradise Canyon, Rainbow Valley, Texas Terror, The Three Musketeers, Westward Ho (1935); Conflict, King of the Pecos, The Lawless Nineties, The Lonely Trail, The Oregon Trail, Sea Spoilers, Winds of the Wasteland (1936); Adventure's End, California Straight Ahead, I Cover the War, Idol of the Crowds (1937); Born to the West, Overland Stage Raiders, Pals of the Saddle, Red River Range, Santa Fe Stampede (1938); Allegheny Uprising, The New Frontier, The Night Riders, Stagecoach, Three Texas Steers, Wyoming Outlaw (1939); Dark Command, The Long Voyage Home, Seven Sinners, Three Faces West (1940); Lady from Louisiana, Shepherd of the Hills (1941); Flying Tigers, In Old California, Lady for a Night, Pittsburgh, Reap the Wild Wind, Reunion in France, The Spoilers (1942); A Lady Takes a Chance, War of the Wildcats/In Old Oklahoma (1943); The Fighting Seabees, Tall in the Saddle (1944); Back to Bataan, Dakota, Flame of Barbary Coast, They Were Expendable (1945); Without Reservations (1946); Angel and the Badman, Tycoon (1947); 3 Godfathers, Fort Apache, Red River, Wake of the Red Witch (1948); The Fighting Kentuckian, Sands of Iwo Jima, She Wore a Yellow Ribbon (1949); Rio Grande (1950); Bullfighter and the Lady, Flying Leathernecks, Operation Pacific (1951); Big Jim McLain, The Quiet Man (1952); Hondo, Island in the Sky, Trouble along the Way (1953); The High and the Mighty (1954); Blood Alley, The Sea Chase (1955); The Conqueror, The Searchers (1956); Jet Pilot, Legend of the Lost/Timbuctu, The Wings of Eagles (1957); The Barbarian and the Geisha, China Doll, I Married a Woman (1958); The Horse Soldiers, Rio Bravo (1959); The Alamo, North to Alaska (1960); The Comancheros (1961); Hatari, How the West Was Won, The Longest Day, The Man Who Shot Liberty Valance (1962); Donovan's Reef, McClintock! (1963); Circus World (1964); The Greatest Story Ever Told, In Harm's Way, The Sons of Katie Elder (1965); Cast a Giant Shadow (1966); El Dorado, The War Wagon (1967); The Green Berets [also co-dir.] (1968); True Grit, The Undefeated (1969); Chisum, Rio Lobo (1970); Big Jake, Directed by John Ford (1971); The Cowboys (1972); Cahill—United States Marshal, The Train Robbers (1973); McQ (1974); Brannigan, Rooster Cogburn (1975); It's Showtime, The Shootist (1976); Going Hollywood: The War Years (1988).

Honors: Academy Award Nomination: Best Actor (*Sands of Iwo Jima*, 1949); *Photoplay* Gold Medal Award: Most Popular Male Star (*Sands of Iwo Jima*, 1950); Golden Globe Award: World Film Favorite (1952); Golden Globes: Cecil B. DeMille Award (1965); Academy Award, Golden Globe Award: Best Actor (*True Grit*, 1969); People's Choice Award: Favorite Movie Actor (1974); People's Choice Award: Favorite Movie Actor

(1975); People's Choice Award: Favorite Movie Actor (1976); People's Choice Award: Favorite Movie Actor (1977).

Selected Bibliography

Riggin, Judith M. *John Wayne: A Bio-Bibliography*. Westport, CT: Greenwood Press, 1992.

Roberts, Randy, and James S. Olson. *John Wayne: American*. New York: Free Press, 1995.

Zmijewsky, Steve, Boris Zmijewsky, and Mark Ricci. *The Complete Films of John Wayne*. Secaucus, NJ: Citadel Press, 1983.

WELLES, ORSON. Director, producer, screenwriter, actor, author. Born George Orson Welles on May 6, 1915, in Kenosha, Wisconsin; died on October 9, 1985. It will be a while before the verdict on Orson Welles is finally in, if indeed it ever is. He was heralded as a wunderkind in the 1930s even before his Mercury Theatre group frightened an entire nation with its eerily realistic broadcast of H. G. Wells's "War of the Worlds" in 1938. The image of Welles as wunderkind was indelibly reinforced with *Citizen Kane*, a film he wrote, directed, and starred in at the age of twenty-four. Many consider this the best film ever made, and it almost always appears on top-ten lists. Those who dare to differ get treated with the contempt usually accorded philistines. Welles had such a roller-coaster career that it is hard to perceive any particular pattern unless it would be one of deliberate disorganization. He dabbled in every genre, but his greatest successes were with contemporary stories such as *Touch of Evil* (like *Kane*, another cult film) and *The Lady from Shanghai*. Welles was brilliantly creative with his innovative camera techniques, but more often than not, they had the effect of calling attention to themselves. A critic of David Lean's later epics once said that when directors get older, they become photographers. In that respect, Welles aged early, for when people talk about his pictures, it is invariably in terms of his cinematic tricks, like the famous scene set in the mirror room of an amusement park's crazy house in *The Lady from Shanghai*. At the time of his death in 1985, he was in the middle of *The Other Side of the Wind*, a film he had been working on since the 1970s. Interestingly enough, it was the story of a famous filmmaker struggling to find financing for a film—and obviously autobiographical. Also interesting is the fact that the man playing the Welles role was John Huston, a director with his own unique style and colorful career. In all probability, Welles will be better known for his influence on filmmaking than for his accomplishments, for he was, when all is said and done, a director's director.

Filmography: The Hearts of Age [per., dir.; short] (1934); Too Much Johnson [dir.; short] (1938); Citizen Kane [per., dir., prod., co-sc.] (1941); It's All True [dir.], Journey into Fear [per., prod.], The Magnificent Ambersons [dir., prod., sc.] (1942); Follow the Boys [per.], Jane Eyre [per.] (1944); The Stranger [per., dir.], Tomorrow Is Forever [per.] (1946); The Lady from Shanghai [per., dir., sc.], Macbeth [per., adaptation, dir., prod.] (1948); Black Magic/Cagliostro [per.], Prince of Foxes [per.], The Third Man [per.]

(1949); The Black Rose [per.] (1950); Othello [per., dir., prod., sc., adaptation], Trent's Last Case [per.] (1952); Trouble in the Glen [per.] (1953); Royal Affairs in Versailles/ Si Versailles m'tait conte/Affairs in Versailles [per.], Three Cases of Murder [per.] (1954); Don Quixote/Don Kikhot [per., dir., sc.], Mr. Arkadin/Confidential Report [per., dir., sc.] (1955); Moby Dick [per.] (1956); Man in the Shadow [per.] (1957); The Long Hot Summer [per.], The Roots of Heaven [per.], South Seas Adventure [per.], Touch of Evil [per., dir., sc.] (1958); Compulsion [per.] (1959); The Battle of Austerlitz/Austerlitz [per.], Crack in the Mirror [per.] (1960); Rogopag [per.], The Tartars/I Tartari [per.] (1962); The Trial [per., dir., sc.], The V.I.P.s [per.] (1963); The Chimes at Midnight/ Falstaff [per., dir., prod., sc., adaptation], A Man for All Seasons [per.] (1966); Casino Royale [per.], I'll Never Forget What's 'is Name [per.], The Sailor from Gibraltar [per.] (1967); The Immortal Story/Histoire Immortelle [per., dir., sc.], Oedipus the King [per.] (1968); Catch-22 [per.], The Kremlin Letter [per.], Start the Revolution without Me [per.], Upon This Rock [per.] (1970); The Battle of Neretva/Bitkia Na Neretvi [per.], Directed by John Ford [per.], A Safe Place [per.], Waterloo [per.] (1971); Get to Know Your Rabbit [per.], Malpertuis: Histoire d'une maison maudite [per.], Necromancy/The Witching [per.], The Other Side of the Wind [dir.], Ten Days Wonder/La decade prodigieuse [per.], Treasure Island [per., sc.] (1972); F for Fake/Verites et mensonges [per., dir., sc., idea, additional photography] (1973); Challenge [per.] (1974); Ten Little Indians/And Then There Were None [per.] (1975); Voyage of the Damned [per.] (1976); Rime of the Ancient Mariner [per.] (1977); Filming Othello [per., dir.], The Late Great Planet Earth [per.] (1978); The Muppet Movie [per.] (1979); Butterfly [per.], Genocide [per.], History of the World—Part 1 [per.], The Man Who Saw Tomorrow [per.] (1981); Orson Welles a la cinematheque [per.] (1982); Almonds and Raisins [per.] (1983); In Our Hands [per.], Slapstick (of Another Kind) [per.], Where Is Parsifal? [per.] (1984); The Transformers [per.] (1986); Someone to Love [per.] (1987); Hot Money [per.] (1989); Hollywood Mavericks [per.] (1990).

Honors: Academy Award: Best Original Screenplay [with Herman J. Mankiewicz] (*Citizen Kane*, 1941); New York Film Critics Circle Award, National Board of Review Award: Best Picture (*Citizen Kane*, 1941); Academy Award Nominations: Best Director, Actor (*Citizen Kane*, (1941); Cannes Film Festival Award: Grand Prize (*Othello*, 1952); Cannes Film Festival Award: Actor [with Dean Stockwell, Bradford Dillman] (*Compulsion*, 1959); Cannes Film Festival: 20th Anniversary Prize [for *The Chimes at Midnight* and for his contribution to world cinema] (1966); Academy Award: Special Award (1970); American Film Institute Life Achievement Award (1975); Directors Guild of America: (D. W. Griffith Award (1983).

Selected Bibliography

Beja, Morris, ed. *Perspectives on Orson Welles*. New York: G. K. Hall, 1995.

Thomson, David. *Rosebud: The Story of Orson Welles*. New York: Alfred A. Knopf, 1996.

Welles, Orson, and Peter Bogdanovich. *This Is Orson Welles*. Ed. Jonathan Rosenbaum. New York: HarperCollins, 1992.

WELLMAN, WILLIAM. Director. Born William Augustus Wellman on February 29, 1896, in Brookline, Massachusetts; died on December 9, 1975. Wellman was a troubled youth who lacked direction and motivation. After a stint in the foreign legion, he became a pilot in World War I and was discharged as a hero after his plane was shot down. He was then transferred to California as a flight instructor, where his old friend Douglas Fairbanks invited him to come to Hollywood. Decked out in his dress uniform, Wellman arrived at Fairbanks's studio and was promptly offered a good-sized part in *Knickerbocker Buckaroo*. To him, being an actor was both unpleasant and unmanly. He decided instead to try his hand at directing, and after a few years in menial jobs, he started directing low-budget westerns. In 1927, however, he got the chance to direct *Wings*, the first film to win an Academy Award. After that, Wellman went on to direct such excellent but diverse films as *The Public Enemy*, *A Star Is Born* (1937 version), *Nothing Sacred*, and *The Ox-Bow Incident*. He also directed two outstanding war films, *The Story of G.I. Joe* and *Battleground*. Like all who worked within the studio system, Wellman did what he was told. Consequently, he directed quite a few mediocre films, and his reputation has suffered at the hands of purists. However, when his triumphs are examined, Wellman ranks unquestionably among the top directors of Hollywood's golden age.

Filmography: The Knickerbocker Buckaroo [only film as per.] (1919); Big Dan, Cupid's Fireman, The Man Who Won, Second Hand Love (1923); The Circus Cowboy, Not a Drum Was Heard, Vagabond Trail (1924); When Husbands Flirt (1925); The Boob, The Cat's Pajamas, You Never Know Women (1926); Wings (1927); Beggars of Life [also prod.], Ladies of the Mob, The Legion of the Condemned (1928); Chinatown Nights, The Man I Love, Woman Trap (1929); Dangerous Paradise, Maybe It's Love, Young Eagles (1930); Night Nurse, Other Men's Women, The Public Enemy, Safe in Hell, Star Witness (1931); The Conquerors, The Hatchet Man, Love Is a Racket, The Purchase Price, So Big (1932); Central Airport, College Coach, Frisco Jenny, Heroes for Sale, Lilly Turner, Midnight Mary, Wild Boys of the Road (1933); Looking for Trouble, The President Vanishes, Stingaree (1934); Call of the Wild (1935); The Robin Hood of El Dorado [also sc.], Small Town Girl/One Horse Town (1936); The Last Gangster, Nothing Sacred, A Star Is Born (1937); Men with Wings (1938); Beau Geste [also prod.], The Light That Failed [also prod.] (1939); Reaching for the Sun [also prod.] (1941); The Great Man's Lady [also prod.], Roxie Hart, Thunder Birds (1942); Lady of Burlesque, The Ox-Bow Incident (1943); Buffalo Bill (1944); The Story of G.I. Joe, This Man's Navy (1945); Gallant Journey [also prod., sc.] (1946); Magic Town (1947); The Iron Curtain/Behind the Iron Curtain, Yellow Sky (1948); Battleground (1949); The Happy Years, The Next Voice You Hear (1950); Across the Wide Missouri, It's a Big Country, Westward the Women (1951); My Man and I (1952); Island in the Sky (1953); The High and the Mighty, Track of the Cat (1954); Blood Alley (1955); Goodbye My Lady (1956); Darby's Rangers (1958); Lafayette Escadrille [also prod., story] (1958).

Honors: Academy Award: Best Original Story [with Robert Carson], Academy Award Nomination: Best Director (*A Star Is Born*, 1937); Academy Award Nomination: Best Director (*Battleground*, 1949); Directors Guild of America Award: Outstanding Directorial Achievement, Academy Award Nomination: Best Director (*The High and the Mighty*, 1954); Directors Guild of America: D. W. Griffith Award (1972).

Selected Bibliography

Thompson, Frank T. *William Wellman*. Metuchen, NJ: Scarecrow Press, 1983.
Wellman, William Augustus. *A Short Time for Insanity: An Autobiography*. New York: Hawthorn Books, 1974.

WEST, MAE. Actress, screenwriter. Born on August 17, 1892, in Brooklyn, New York; died on November 23, 1980. West went on the stage as a vaude-villian at the age of fourteen. Twenty years later she wrote, produced, and directed the 1926 Broadway show *Sex*, which resulted in her being jailed on obscenity charges. The following year, her next play, *Drag*, was banned on Broadway because its subject matter was homosexuality. West's exaggerated style was so over the top that she always did have an aura of the drag queen about her, and her appearance and mannerisms hinted at transvestitism. With *Diamond Lil* (1928), West became the toast of Broadway, and in 1932 she signed with Paramount. Her first film role was in *Night after Night* (1932) in which George Raft said she stole everything but the cameras. The first film to star West was *She Done Him Wrong*, the film version of *Diamond Lil*, and it broke box office records and saved Paramount from selling out to MGM. The Hays office brought in a new censorship code in 1934, largely to restrain West's excesses, but she only cottoned to the challenge and continued to make films that walked a fine line between naughtiness and vulgarity. Her popularity waned in the late 1930s, and after the failure of *The Heat's On* in 1943, the first movie she did not script herself, she returned to the stage. Meanwhile, her fame took a new twist when her name was applied to the inflatable vestlike life preserver distributed to troops during World War II. (Her name is enshrined in *Webster's* and other dictionaries.) West turned down numerous film offers, including *Sunset Boulevard*, but she did finally make a comeback of sorts in the recklessly tasteless *Myra Breckinridge*. Her trademark was the sexual innuendo and the double entendre, and some of her quips have become part of the language. In fact, the title of her 1959 autobiography, *Goodness Had Nothing to Do with It*, is her retort to someone who said to her, "Goodness, what a lovely fur coat." With her nonthreatening self-parody of the blond bombshell sex symbol, West had a Marilyn-like "innocence" and a Marlene-like "irony" about her. She was the living embodiment of Oscar Wilde's quip that "nothing succeeds like excess."

Filmography: [as performer, except where noted]: Night after Night [per.] (1932); I'm No Angel [also sc., story], She Done Him Wrong [from play *Diamond Lil*; per.] (1933); Belle of the Nineties [also sc., story] (1934); Goin' to Town [also sc.] (1935); Go West Young Man [also sc.], Klondike Annie [also sc.] (1936); Every Day's a Holiday [also sc.] (1937); My Little Chicadee [also sc.] (1940); The Heat's On [per.] (1943); Myra Breckinridge [per.] (1970); It's Showtime [per.] (1976); Sextette [from play; per.] (1978).

Selected Bibliography

Hamilton, Marybeth. *"When I'm Bad, I'm Better": Mae West, Sex, and American Popular Entertainment*. New York: HarperCollins, 1995.

Sochen, June. *Mae West: "She Who Laughs, Lasts."* Arlington Heights, IL: H. Davidson, 1992.
Ward, Carol M. *Mae West: A Bio-Bibliography*. Westport, CT: Greenwood Press, 1989.

WEST SIDE STORY (1961), musical. Directed by Robert Wise and Jerome Robbins; with Natalie Wood, Richard Beymer, George Chakiris, Rita Moreno, Russ Tamblyn, Tucker Smith, David Winters, Tony Mordente, Simon Oakland, and John Astin; screenplay by Ernest Lehman.

West Side Story is a triumph of style over substance. It's Romeo and Juliet transplanted to New York's West Side, and while the plot is thin and predictable, the musical score is rich and varied. Wood and Beymer lack the charisma necessary to carry the leads as they should be, but they are surrounded by some outstanding talent, and the musical numbers are staged with excitement and feeling. *West Side Story*, one of the most popular film musicals in history, owed much of its success to its appeal to teenagers. Its attraction to them is its romanticized slice of tough urban life. More critical observers find the blend of fantasy and reality rather strained, particularly when a menacing street gang suddenly starts dancing down a dark alley. While critics generally admire this violent musical and its classic themes of young love and early death, others have reservations about the film's attempt to blend fantasy and reality, arguing that its essentially theatrical conception conflicts with its determinedly realistic settings, making much of it seem rather silly. Which is another way of saying that *West Side Story* can't make up its mind whether it wants to be *On the Waterfront* or *On the Town*.

Awards: Academy Awards: Best Picture, Directors, Supporting Actor (Chakiris), Supporting Actress (Moreno), Color Cinematography (Daniel L. Fapp), Musical Score (Saul Chaplin, Johnny Green, Sid Ramin, Irwin Kostal), Costume Design/Color (Irene Sharaff), Editing, Sound; Golden Globe Award: Best Picture/Musical; Directors Guild of America Award: Director (Wise, Robbins); New York Film Critics Circle Award: Best Picture; Academy Award: Special Award (Robbins, "for his brilliant achievements in the art of choreography on film").

Selected Bibliography

Fordin, Hugh. *The World of Entertainment!: Hollywood's Greatest Musicals*. Garden City, NY: Doubleday, 1975.
Peary, Danny. *Alternate Oscars*. New York: Delta, 1993.
Thompson, Frank T. *Robert Wise: A Bio-Bibliography*. Westport, CT: Greenwood Press, 1995.

WHITE HEAT (1949), crime. Directed by Raoul Walsh; with James Cagney, Virginia Mayo, Edmond O'Brien, Margaret Wycherly, and Steve Cochran; screenplay by Ivan Goff and Ben Roberts.

In this bizarre picture, Cagney returned to gangster films as a psychopathic hood with the mother of all Oedipus complexes. James Cagney plays a tough guy who likes to sit on his mother's lap and who goes berserk in the prison mess hall when he learns of her death. It is one of the most harrowing scenes in movie history, and it was made in one take with Cagney being encouraged to let out all the stops. And he does—emitting a horrible sobbing whine that just keeps coming, while punching out anyone who gets near him. None of James Cagney's great gangster films of the 1930s comes anywhere close to the supercharged production of *White Heat*. Here this great actor reveals the psychotic core of the true gangster. Cagney is a homicidal maniac, and he knows it. Never before was Cagney, as gangster Cody Jarrett, so intense, electrifying, or lethal. This is without a doubt one of the toughest and most explicit crime films ever made. The final scene, with Cagney atop an oil refinery about to be blown up, calling out his warped triumph to his deceased mother, provides one of the most memorable climaxes in film history.

Selected Bibliography

Canham, Kingsley. *The Hollywood Professionals*. New York: A. S. Barnes, 1973.
Dickens, Homer. *The Complete Films of James Cagney*. Secaucus, NJ: Carol, 1989.
Rosow, Eugene. *Born to Lose: The Gangster Film in America*. New York: Oxford University Press, 1978.

WIDMARK, RICHARD. Actor. Born on December 26, 1914, in Sunrise, Michigan. Educated at Lake Forest College (law, drama). Widmark started out on the Broadway stage playing tough guys and heavies. It was an image he transferred with menacing style to the screen in his debut film, *Kiss of Death*, in 1947 in which he played a giggling psychopath who, in one famous scene, pushes a crippled old lady in a wheel chair down a flight of stairs. For this performance, he won an Oscar nomination. In addition to other tough-guy roles, he played noted character roles in *Judgment at Nuremberg* and *The Bedford Incident*, but too often he was typecast as a villain. One unfortunate exception was his role as the dauphin in Otto Preminger's *Saint Joan*, a film in which just about everyone seemed to have been miscast. Widmark has also produced several films, including the spy thriller *The Secret Ways*, which was scripted by his wife, Jean Hazelwood.

Filmography: Kiss of Death (1947); Road House, The Street with No Name, Yellow Sky (1948); Down to the Sea in Ships, Slattery's Hurricane (1949); Halls of Montezuma, Night and the City, No Way Out, Panic in the Streets (1950); The Frogmen (1951); Don't Bother to Knock, My Pal Gus, O. Henry's Full House, Red Skies of Montana/ Smoke Jumpers (1952); Destination Gobi, Pickup on South Street, Take the High Ground (1953); Broken Lance, Garden of Evil, Hell and High Water (1954); The Cobweb, A Prize of Gold (1955); Backlash, The Last Wagon, Run for the Sun (1956); Saint Joan, Time Limit [also co-prod.] (1957); The Law and Jake Wade, The Tunnel of Love (1958); The Trap [also prod.], Warlock (1959); The Alamo (1960); Judgment at Nuremberg, The Secret Ways, Two Rode Together (1961); How the West Was Won (1962); Cheyenne Autumn, Flight from Ashiya (1964); The Bedford Incident [also prod.] (1965); Alvarez Kelly (1966); The Way West (1967); Madigan (1968); Death of a Gunfighter, A Talent for Loving/Gun Crazy (1969); The Moonshine War (1970); When the Legends Die

(1972); Murder on the Orient Express (1974); The Sell Out (1975); To the Devil—A Daughter/Child of Satan (1976); The Domino Killings, Rollercoaster, Twilight's Last Gleaming (1977); Coma, The Swarm (1978); Bear Island (1980); National Lampoon Goes to the Movies/National Lampoon's Movie Madness (1981); The Final Option/Who Dares Wins, Hanky Panky (1982); Against All Odds (1984); True Colors (1991).

Honors: Golden Globe Award: Most Promising Newcomer/Male, Academy Award Nomination: Best Supporting Actor (*Kiss of Death*, 1947).

Selected Bibliography

Holston, Kim R. *Richard Widmark: A Bio-Bibliography.* Westport, CT: Greenwood Press, 1990.

WILDER, BILLY. Director, screenwriter. Born Samuel Wilder, on June 22, 1906, in Vienna, Austria. Educated at the University of Vienna (law). Billy Wilder is one of the most versatile personalities in screen history, writing and directing an astonishing variety of outstanding films including everything from dark, psychotic drama (*Sunset Boulevard*) to cheerfully salacious comedy (*The Seven Year Itch, Some Like It Hot*) to vintage film noir (*Double Indemnity*) to gritty social realism (*The Lost Weekend*). After leaving law school in Vienna and working as a tabloid journalist, Wilder drifted into screenwriting. From 1929 to 1933, he wrote screenplays for a number of important German films in which he began to develop the convoluted but controlled style that came to characterize his best American work. In 1933, after co-directing a film in France, Wilder arrived in Hollywood, part of the large émigré influx of German and Austrian film talent forced out of Europe by the growing tide of anti-Semitism. In 1938 he formed a writing partnership with screenwriter Charles Brackett, and they quickly became one of Hollywood's top teams, writing screenplays for such movies as *Ninotchka* and *Ball of Fire*. *Sunset Boulevard* marked both the end of Wilder's years with Brackett and the high point of his career as a visual stylist. The films after that are never so daringly imaginative in terms of lighting and camera angles as they once had been. In his later films, Wilder preferred to do more with art direction and set design as ways of emphasizing his characters' psychological dilemmas. Wilder's career peaked in the late 1950s and early 1960s with such films as *Witness for the Prosecution*, *The Apartment*, and *One, Two, Three*. After that he suffered a series of setbacks, beginning with the critically lambasted *Kiss Me, Stupid*, with its tasteless humor. Tastelessness was something Wilder always flirted with, but at his best, as in *Some Like It Hot*, he was able to avoid crudeness by maintaining a light touch. Although he never did recover from the downward slide, his earlier reputation as a sharp observer of American mores and manners remains untarnished. Like so many émigré directors of his time, Wilder had a sixth sense for what was essentially and peculiarly American about American culture, an instinct that allowed him to bring to the screen some breathtakingly perceptive insights into American life and character.

Filmography: [as screenwriter]: People on Sunday/Menschen am Sonntag (1929); Der Mann der seinem Morder sucht, Emil and the Detectives/Emil und die Detektive (1931); Adorable [story] (1933); Mauvaise Graine [also dir.], Music in the Air, One Exciting Adventure [story] (1934); The Lottery Lover (1935); Champagne Waltz [story] (1937); Bluebeard's Eighth Wife, That Certain Age (1938); Midnight, Ninotchka, What a Life (1939); Arise My Love, Rhythm on the River [story] (1940); Ball of Fire, Hold Back the Dawn (1941). [as director, screenwriter]: The Major and the Minor (1942); Five Graves to Cairo [dir. only] (1943); Double Indemnity (1944); The Lost Weekend (1945); The Emperor Waltz [also story], A Foreign Affair, A Song Is Born [sc. only, uncredited] (1948); Sunset Boulevard [dir. only] (1950); The Big Carnival/Ace in the Hole [also prod., story] (1951); Stalag 17 [also prod.] (1953); Sabrina [also prod.] (1954); The Seven Year Itch (1955); Love in the Afternoon [also prod.], The Spirit of St. Louis, Witness for the Prosecution (1957); Some Like It Hot [also prod.] (1959); The Apartment [prod.] (1960); One Two Three [prod.] (1961); Irma La Douce [prod.] (1963); Kiss Me Stupid [prod.] (1964); The Fortune Cookie [prod.] (1966); The Private Life of Sherlock Holmes [prod.] (1970); Avanti! [also prod.] (1972); The Front Page (1974); Fedora [also prod.] (1978); Portrait of a 60% Perfect Man [per. only] (1980); Buddy Buddy (1981); Directed by William Wyler [per. only] (1986); The Exiles [per. only] (1989).

Honors: Academy Award Nomination: Best Screenplay (*Ninotchka*, 1939); Academy Award Nomination: Best Screenplay (*Hold Back the Dawn* and *Ball of Fire*, 1941); Academy Award Nomination: Best Screenplay (*Double Indemnity*, 1944); Academy Award, New York Film Critics Circle Award: Best Director, Academy Award Nomination: Best Screenplay (*The Lost Weekend*, 1945); Cannes Film Festival Award: Grand Prize (*The Lost Weekend*, 1946); Academy Award Nomination: Best Screenplay (*A Foreign Affair*, 1948); Academy Award: Best Story and Screenplay, Golden Globe Award, Directors Guild of America Quarterly Award, Academy Award Nomination: Best Director (*Sunset Boulevard*, 1950); Directors Guild of America Award: Outstanding Directorial Achievement, Academy Award Nomination: Best Director (*Stalag 17*, 1953); Golden Globe Award: Best Screenplay, Directors Guild of America Award: Outstanding Directorial Achievement, Academy Award Nominations: Best Director, Screenplay (*Sabrina*, 1954); Directors Guild of America Award: Outstanding Directorial Achievement, Academy Award Nomination: Best Director (*Witness for the Prosecution*, 1957); Academy Award Nominations: Best Director, Screenplay (*Some Like It Hot*, 1959); Academy Awards: Best Director, Original Screenplay, Directors Guild of America Award: Direction, New York Film Critics Circle Award: Best Director (*The Apartment*, 1960); Academy Award Nomination: Best Original Screenplay (*The Fortune Cookie*, 1966); Film Society of Lincoln Center Tribute (1982); Directors Guild of America: D. W. Griffith Award (1984); American Film Institute Life Achievement Award (1986); Academy Award: Irving G. Thalberg Memorial Award (1987); Los Angeles Film Critics Association: Career Achievement Award (1994); British Academy Award: Academy Fellow (1994).

Selected Bibliography

Dick, Bernard F. *Billy Wilder*. Boston: Twayne, 1980.

Seidman, Steve. *The Film Career of Billy Wilder*. Boston: G. K. Hall, 1977.

Zolotow, Maurice. *Billy Wilder in Hollywood*. New York: G. P. Putnam's Sons, 1977.

WINTERS, SHELLEY. Actress. Born Shirley Schrift on August 18, 1922, in St. Louis, Missouri. Educated at Wayne State University, the Dramatic Workshop of the New School for Social Research, and the New York Actors Studio. Winters made her Broadway debut in 1941 and entered films two years later, eventually gaining attention as Ronald Colman's sleazy mistress (and murder victim) in *A Double Life* in 1947. Two years later she gave an overlooked performance as Myrtle, the slatternly wife of the garage owner who shoots Gatsby, in an underappreciated version of *The Great Gatsby*. Initially, Winters played roles that capitalized on her earthy sensuality, but in 1951 she convinced George Stevens she could alter herself to play the drab, whining factory worker who vies with debutante Elizabeth Taylor for Montgomery Clift in *A Place in the Sun*. The role earned Winters her first Oscar nomination and led to a succession of memorable performances. In the late 1950s, Winters made the transition to character roles. She was marvelous as the ignorant, possessive mother in *Lolita* and won Oscars for outstanding performances in *The Diary of Anne Frank, A Patch of Blue*, and *The Poseidon Adventure*. Winters has worked steadily into the 1990s, not only in films and TV but occasionally on stage, turning in straight and camp performances in both obscure and memorable films. Among her cult classics are *What's the Matter with Helen?* and Roger Corman's *Bloody Mama*. She has also become, through her work at the Actors Studio, one of the country's top acting instructors. Winters's two autobiographies recount her numerous liaisons with a host of Hollywood leading men. She was married to Vittorio Gassman from 1952 to 1954 and to Anthony Franciosa from 1957 to 1960.

Filmography: Knickerbocker Holiday, Sailor's Holiday, She's a Soldier Too (1944); A Thousand and One Nights, Tonight and Every Night (1945); A Double Life, The Gangster (1947); Cry of the City, Larceny (1948); The Great Gatsby, Johnny Stool Pigeon, Take One False Step (1949); Frenchie, South Sea Sinner, Winchester '73/Montana Winchester (1950); Behave Yourself, He Ran All the Way, A Place in the Sun, The Raging Tide (1951); Meet Danny Wilson, My Man and I, Phone Call from a Stranger, Untamed Frontier (1952); Executive Suite, Mambo, Playgirl, Saskatchewan, Tennessee Champ (1954); The Big Knife, I Am a Camera, I Died a Thousand Times, The Night of the Hunter, The Treasure of Pancho Villa, The Diary of Anne Frank, Odds against Tomorrow (1959); Let No Man Write My Epitaph (1960); The Young Savages (1961); The Chapman Report, Lolita (1962); The Balcony, Wives and Lovers (1963); A House Is Not a Home, Time of Indifference/Gli Indifferenti (1964); The Greatest Story Ever Told, A Patch of Blue (1965); Alfie, Harper, The Three Sisters (1966); Enter Laughing (1967); Buona Sera, Mrs. Campbell, The Scalphunters, Wild in the Streets (1968); The Mad Room (1969); Bloody Mama, Flap, How Do I Love Thee? (1970); What's the Matter with Helen?, Who Slew Auntie Roo? (1971); The Poseidon Adventure, Something to Hide/Shattered (1972); Blume in Love, Cleopatra Jones (1973); Diamonds, Journey into Fear, Poor Pretty Eddie, That Lucky Touch (1975); Next Stop Greenwich Village, The Tenant/Le Locataire (1976); Pete's Dragon, Tentacles/Tentacoli, Un Borghese Piccolo (1977); King of the Gypsies, City on Fire, The Magician of Lublin, The Visitor (1979); Looping, My Mother My Daughter, S.O.B. (1981); Fanny Hill (1983); Ellie, George Stevens: A Filmmaker's Journey, Over the Brooklyn Bridge/My Darling Shiksa, Witchfire (1984); Deja Vu (1985); The Delta Force, Very Close Quarters (1986); Hello Actors Studio (1987); Purple People Eater, Rudolph & Frosty's Christmas in July (1988); An

Unremarkable Life (1989); Stepping Out, Superstar: The Life and Times of Andy Warhol, Touch of a Stranger (1991); The Pickle (1993); Silence of the Hams (1994); Heavy, Jury Duty (1995); Portrait of a Lady (1996).

Honors: Academy Award Nomination: Best Actress (*A Place in the Sun*, 1951); Academy Award: Best Supporting Actress (*The Diary of Anne Frank*, 1959); Academy Award: Best Supporting Actress (*A Patch of Blue*, 1965); Golden Globe Award, Academy Award Nomination: Best Supporting Actress (*The Poseidon Adventure*, 1972).

Selected Bibliography

Winters, Shelley. *Shelley: Also Known as Shirley*. New York: Ballantine, 1980.
————. *Shelley II: The Middle of My Century*. New York: Simon and Schuster, 1989.

WISE, ROBERT. Director, producer. Born on September 10, 1914, in Winchester, Indiana. Educated at Franklin College in Indiana. Wise is a veteran Hollywood craftsman whose prolific body of work contains a number of startlingly original gems. Before he ever directed a film, Wise made cinematic history at RKO as editor of Orson Welles's *Citizen Kane* and *The Magnificent Ambersons*. Not long thereafter, he made an auspicious directorial debut with the classy horror film *The Curse of the Cat People*. Wise's last film at RKO, the acclaimed boxing film *The Set-up*, established him as a leading Hollywood talent. Through the mid-1960s he directed for various studios and in various genres including the sci-fi classic *The Day the Earth Stood Still*, the submarine drama *Run Silent, Run Deep*, the popular musical *West Side Story*, and the blockbuster musical of all time *The Sound of Music*. Since the 1970s Wise has directed only a handful of films, mostly big-budget spectacles that have fallen short of his earlier achievements.

Filmography: [as director only]: The Curse of the Cat People [co-dir.], Mademoiselle Fifi (1944); The Body Snatcher (1945); Criminal Court, A Game of Death (1946); Born to Kill (1947); Blood on the Moon, Mystery in Mexico (1948); The Set-up (1949); Three Secrets, Two Flags West (1950); The Day the Earth Stood Still, The House on Telegraph Hill (1951); The Captive City, Something for the Birds (1952); The Desert Rats, Destination Gobi, So Big (1953); Executive Suite (1954); Helen of Troy (1955); Somebody Up There Likes Me, Tribute to a Bad Man (1956); This Could Be the Night, Until They Sail (1957); I Want to Live, Run Silent Run Deep (1958); Odds against Tomorrow [also prod.] (1959); West Side Story [also prod.] (1961); Two for the Seesaw, The Haunting [also prod.] (1963); The Sound of Music [also prod.] (1965); The Sand Pebbles [also prod.] (1966); Star! [also prod.] (1968); The Andromeda Strain [also prod.] (1971); Two People [also prod.] (1973); The Hindenburg [also prod.] (1975); Audrey Rose (1977); Star Trek—The Motion Picture (1979); 50 Years of Action, The Fantasy Film World of George Pal (1986); Rooftops (1989).

Honors: Academy Award Nomination: Editing (*Citizen Kane*, 1941); Academy Award Nomination: Best Director (*I Want to Live*, 1958); Academy Award, Directors Guild of America Award: Best Director (*West Side Story*, 1961); Academy Award, Directors Guild of America Award: Best Director (*The Sound of Music*, 1965); Academy Award: Irving G. Thalberg Award (1966); Directors Guild of America: Honorary Lifetime Member (1982); Directors Guild of America: D. W. Griffith Award (1987).

Selected Bibliography

Sennett, Ted. *Great Movie Directors*. New York: Harry N. Abrams, 1986.
Thompson, Frank T. *Robert Wise: A Bio-Bibliography*. Westport, CT: Greenwood Press, 1995.

WITNESS FOR THE PROSECUTION (1957), mystery. Directed by Billy Wilder; with Marlene Dietrich, Tyrone Power, Charles Laughton, Elsa Lanchester, John Williams, Henry Daniell, Una O'Connor, and Ian Wolfe; screenplay by Billy Wilder and Harry Kurnitz.

This film is yet another demonstration of the multifaceted talents of Billy Wilder. In this case, he has adapted one of Agatha Christie's most ingenious mysteries into a courtroom drama that is immensely entertaining and satisfying. The plot, of course, is implausible, but then Christie was the master of the implausible, suspension of disbelief being a prerequisite for reading any classic whodunit. What matters is the nature of the implausibility, and in this case, the gimmick is inspired. Christie merely asks the question behind all good, imaginative fiction—"What if?"—and answers it with great ingenuity. This being a "movie," the primary level of satisfaction must rest in the visual, and Billy Wilder is unsurpassed in his manipulation of sights, scenes, and mise-en-scène. The way Laughton irritates Power by using his monocle to reflect sunlight into Power's eyes and keep him off balance is one example. Dietrich posing as a cockney wench and displaying her scarred face in a pub is another, as is the scene of Dietrich singing a sultry number in a bombed-out basement café in Hamburg. In one reviewer's opinion, the undisputed star of the picture is Alexander Trauner's magnificent re-creation of the Old Bailey. Added to this is Wilder's subtle use of black and white photography, which gives the picture a film noir quality. Above all, however, is the cast Wilder assembled to tell this fascinating story. Laughton is at his scene-stealing best, as is his nurse (and real-life wife) Elsa Lanchester. Dietrich pulls off the neatest trick of all in the pub scene. Power, in his last completed film, is excellent at concealing guilt beneath a layer of charming insincerity.

Awards: Directors Guild of America: Outstanding Directorial Achievement (Wilder); Academy Award Nominations: Best Picture, Director, Actor (Laughton), Supporting Actress (Lanchester), Editing, Sound.

Selected Bibliography

Belafonte, Dennis, with Alvin H. Marill. *The Films of Tyrone Power*. Secaucus, NJ: Citadel Press, 1979.
Callow, Simon. *Charles Laughton: A Difficult Actor*. New York: Grove Press, 1988.
Dick, Bernard F. *Billy Wilder*. Boston: Twayne, 1980.
Dickens, Homer. *The Complete Films of Marlene Dietrich*. Secaucus, NJ: Carol, 1992.

WIZARD OF OZ, THE (1939), musical fantasy. Directed by Victor Fleming; with Judy Garland, Ray Bolger, Bert Lahr, Jack Haley, Frank Morgan, Billie

Burke, Margaret Hamilton, Charley Grapewin, Clara Blandick, and the Singer Midgets; screenplay by Noel Langley, Florence Ryerson and Edgar Allan Woolf.

The Wizard of Oz has become one of the world's most beloved films. It is the film that made the teenage Judy Garland an international star, and it is as fresh today as it was the day it was released. Fresher, perhaps, if you consider that the film was not an immediate success and that many were skeptical about its chances from the first. It didn't help matters that this film appeared in 1939, the annus mirabilis of filmmaking, the year in which *Gone with the Wind* topped the list of a dozen first-rate films and another dozen runners-up. Nevertheless, it attracted a loyal audience, and when it finally was shown on television, it immediately became staple fare, particularly for holiday viewing. It owes much to its excellent cast, all of whom seem inspired choices, even though few of them were first choices. Who can imagine anyone but Frank Morgan as the wizard or Margaret Hamilton as the Wicked Witch? Who can imagine a trio of Dorothy's friends composed of any other than Ray Bolger as the Scarecrow, Bert Lahr as the Cowardly Lion, and Jack Haley as the Tin Woodman? And, of course, the choice of Judy Garland to play Dorothy (after they couldn't get Shirley Temple) is the sort of miracle Hollywood myths are made of. She broke hearts (and still does) singing "Over the Rainbow," the Harold Arlen–"Yip" Harburg song that almost got dropped from the film only to become Judy's theme song and a popular standard. Nor can one forget Billie Burke as Glinda or all those Munchkins—or poor old Toto, Dorothy's faithful dog. But to single out the actors is only to scratch the surface, for this film also owes so much to visual effects and cinematography and imaginative sets—and Victor Fleming's brilliant direction. Like all fairy tales, *The Wizard of Oz* is so beloved that it has taken on a life of its own that defies criticism. Some may find its soggy sentimentality cloying and cringe at the grotesque little Munchkins only to be charmed by comedy that never patronizes and a message that never dates. In short, like all great films, it has acquired the untouchability of myth.

Awards: Academy Award: Best Original Score, Song ("Over the Rainbow"); Academy Award Nominations: Best Picture, Art Direction, Special Effects.

Selected Bibliography

Harmetz, Aljean. *The Making of "The Wizard of Oz."* New York: Alfred A. Knopf, 1977.

McClelland, Doug. *Down the Yellow Brick Road: The Making of "The Wizard of Oz."* New York: Pyramid Publications, 1976.

Morella, Joe, and Edward Z. Epstein. *Judy: The Complete Films and Career of Judy Garland.* Secaucus, NJ: Citadel Press, 1986.

WOOD, NATALIE. Actress. Born Natasha Gurdin on July 20, 1938, in San Francisco; died on November 29, 1981, off Santa Catalina Island. Wood was the daughter of architect and set designer Nicholas Gurdin and ballet dancer Maria Gurdin and the sister of actress Lana Wood. She began as a child actress and is particularly remembered for her role in the Christmas classic *Miracle on*

34th Street. In the mid-1950s she managed the tricky transition to teenage roles and was particularly effective in *Rebel without a Cause*. She hit her stride in the 1960s in *Splendor in the Grass* and *Love with the Proper Stranger* and even appeared in two musicals, *West Side Story* and *Gypsy*, but with less success. Her singing voice had to be dubbed and her dance routines simplified. In *West Side Story* she couldn't manage either the magnetism or the accent of Maria, and in *Gypsy* her diminutive build seemed unsuited for the part of the statuesque Gypsy Rose Lee. She made only intermittent appearances during the 1970s. Then in 1983, just after filming *Brainstorm*, she drowned in a mysterious incident on her own yacht. She was married to actor Robert Wagner (1957–1963), then to British producer Richard Gregson, and then to Wagner for the second time from 1972.

Filmography: The Bride Wore Boots, Tomorrow Is Forever (1946); Driftwood, The Ghost and Mrs. Muir, Miracle on 34th Street (1947); Chicken Every Sunday, Scudda Hoo! Scudda Hay! (1948); Father Was a Fullback, The Green Promise (1949); Jackpot, Never a Dull Moment, No Sad Songs for Me, Our Very Own (1950); The Blue Veil, Dear Brat (1951); Just for You, The Rose Bowl Story, The Star (1952); The Silver Chalice (1954); One Desire, Rebel without a Cause (1955); The Burning Hills, A Cry in the Night, The Girl He Left Behind, The Searchers (1956); Bombers B-52 (1957); Kings Go Forth, Marjorie Morningstar (1958); Cash McCall (1959); All the Fine Young Cannibals (1960); Splendor in the Grass, West Side Story (1961); Gypsy (1962); Love with the Proper Stranger (1963); Sex and the Single Girl (1964); The Great Race, Inside Daisy Clover (1965); Penelope, This Property Is Condemned (1966); Bob & Carol & Ted & Alice (1969); Peeper (1975); Meteor (1979); The Last Married Couple in America, Willie and Phil (1980); Brainstorm (1983).

Honors: Academy Award Nomination: Best Supporting Actress (*Rebel without a Cause*, 1955); Golden Globe Award: Most Promising Newcomer (1956); Academy Award Nomination: Best Actress (*Splendor in the Grass*, 1961); Academy Award Nomination: Best Actress (*Love with the Proper Stranger*, 1963); Golden Globe Award: World Film Favorite (1965).

Selected Bibliography

Harris, Warren G. *Natalie & R. J.: Hollywood's Star-Crossed Lovers*. New York: Doubleday, 1988.

Nickens, Christopher. *Natalie Wood: A Biography in Photographs*. Garden City, NY: Doubleday, 1986.

Wood, Lana. *Natalie: A Memoir by Her Sister*. New York: Putnam's, 1984.

WUTHERING HEIGHTS (1939), romance. Directed by William Wyler; with Merle Oberon, Laurence Olivier, David Niven, Flora Robson, Donald Crisp, Geraldine Fitzgerald, Leo G. Carroll, Cecil Kellaway, Miles Mander, and Hugh Williams; screenplay by Ben Hecht and Charles MacArthur.

Another of the masterworks from 1939, this wildly romantic film makes a praiseworthy attempt at capturing the power of at least the first half of this classic Emily Brontë novel, and in all respects, it is an outstanding production typical of its day, complete with tacked-on "happy ending" and a first-rate cast. Sensitive direction and superb performances make this famous story of doomed love in pre-Victorian England come fully alive. Laurence Olivier once said that in this film director William Wyler taught him how to act on the screen, and there's no doubt that he does an astonishing job of revealing Heathcliff's barely contained passion. This movie is less faithful to the novel and closer to the story that readers with fevered imaginations and a taste for the Gothic prefer to read into Brontë's novel. And why not? Those who liked *Jane Eyre* by Emily's sister Charlotte had every reason to expect something similar from Charlotte's younger sister. And with the promise of a spooky name like *Wuthering Heights* as the title, they were well prepared for a Thornfield Hall revisited. Goldwyn may not have realized all this, but he had a taste for the romantic, and in his notorious demand for a happy ending, he was only following in the tradition of *Jane Eyre*. Daphne du Maurier's *Rebecca* was an enormous best-seller about this time (and was to appear as a Hitchcock movie the following year), complete with all the Gothic trappings—and with a happy ending. Audiences, then, were primed for a "movie," and that is what they got. And for all the carping about Merle Oberon's not being up to the part, she is spirited, beautiful, and vain—just the sort Heathcliff, with his lame leg and festering resentment of his "betters," would idealize. But one must not overlook the striking visuals: Wuthering Heights perched impossibly on the side of a windswept hill in contrast to the classic elegance of Thrushcross Grange nestled in a shady grove, the vastness of the windswept moors, Cathy with her arms laden with heather, Cathy and Heathcliff atop Pennistow Crag pledging their love and vowing to conquer the world, Cathy in the blizzard outside Mr. Lockwood's bedroom window, begging to be let in—and finally, Cathy and Heathcliff, reunited in death, walking hand in hand in the snow. It all adds up to a wonderfully satisfying cinematic experience—and one that demands that the lovers be reunited—even in death. No remake has ever come close, no matter how faithful to the text. There's a lesson in this about the relationship between literature and film.

Awards: Academy Award: Best B&W Cinematography (Gregg Toland); New York Film Critics Circle Award: Best Picture; Academy Award Nominations: Best Picture, Director, Actor (Olivier), Supporting Actress (Fitzgerald), Screenplay, Art Direction, Original Score.

Selected Bibliography

Anderegg, Michael A. *William Wyler*. Boston: Twayne, 1979.
Sennett, Ted. *Hollywood's Golden Year, 1939*. New York: St. Martin's Press, 1989.
Vermilye, Jerry. *The Films of the Thirties*. New York: Citadel Press, 1990.

WYLER, WILLIAM. Director. Born on July 1, 1902, in Mulhouse [Mülhausen], Alsace-Lorraine; died on July 27, 1981. Educated at the Paris Conservatoire (violin). Born of German-Swiss-Jewish parentage, Wyler went to school in Switzerland, preparing for a career as a haberdasher in Paris. While at home with his parents 1920, he met Carl Laemmle, his mother's cousin from America and president of Universal Studios. Laemmle invited Wyler to America, where he worked for Universal, first in New York, and then Hollywood. At first he was given only routine tasks to perform, but in 1925 he was given the chance to try his hand at directing low-budget westerns, and by 1928, he had directed two dozen two-reelers, seven feature-length westerns, and one comedy. Over the next decade, Wyler built a reputation as a director of safe and successful film adaptations of classic literary works and contemporary theater. It was at this time that Wyler teamed up with Gregg Toland, the cameraman who would develop the deep focus technique that would enhance such Wyler films as *The Little Foxes* and *Jezebel*. Wyler's winning streak continued with *Wuthering Heights*, *The Letter*, and *Mrs. Miniver*, for which he won his first Academy Award. During the war, Wyler flew several dangerous missions over Europe, gathering air combat footage, suffering injuries over Italy that left him partially deaf. After the war, he made one last picture for Goldwyn, *The Best Years of Our Lives*, a film for which he won a second Oscar and that proved to be the top box office draw of the decade. In 1948, he and fellow directors Frank Capra, George Stevens, and Samuel Briskin formed their own production company, Liberty Films, which was later taken over by Paramount. Wyler maintained his stride for the next two decades with such quality films as *The Heiress*, *Detective Story*, *Roman Holiday*, *Ben-Hur*, and *Funny Girl*. Few film directors have demonstrated the depth, range, longevity, and sensitivity that William Wyler gave to the American screen. Yet like many of the early Hollywood destiny shapers, Wyler possessed neither a background in the arts nor even an all-American upbringing. Always the outsider, he had an uncanny knack for penetrating the soul of American life and culture.

Filmography: Lazy Lightning, The Stolen Ranch (1926); Blazing Days, The Border Cavalier, Desert Dust, Hard Fists, Straight Shootin' (1927); Anybody Here Seen Kelly?, Thunder Riders (1928); Hell's Heroes, The Love Trap, The Shakedown (1929); The Storm (1930); A House Divided, Tom Brown of Culver (1932); Counsellor-at-Law, Her First Mate (1933); Glamour (1934); The Gay Deception, The Good Fairy (1935); Come and Get It/Roaring Timber, Dodsworth, These Three (1936); Dead End (1937); Jezebel (1938); Wuthering Heights (1939); The Letter, The Westerner (1940); The Little Foxes (1941); Mrs. Miniver (1942); The Fighting Lady (1944); Thunderbolt (1945); The Best Years of Our Lives (1946); The Heiress [also prod.] (1949); Detective Story [also prod.] (1951); Carrie [also prod.] (1952); Roman Holiday [also prod.] (1953); The Desperate Hours [also prod.] (1955); Friendly Persuasion [also prod.] (1956); The Big Country [also prod.] (1958); Ben-Hur (1959); The Children's Hour [also prod.] (1962); The Collector (1965); How to Steal a Million (1966); Funny Girl (1968); The Liberation of L. B. Jones (1970); Directed by William Wyler (1986).

Honors: Academy Award Nomination: Best Director (*Dodsworth*, 1936); Venice Film Festival Award: Special Mention Medal: Artistic Ensemble (*Jezebel*, 1938); Academy Award Nomination: Best Director (*Wuthering Heights*, 1939); Academy Award Nomination: Best Director (*The Letter*, 1940); Academy Award Nomination: Best Director (*The Little Foxes*, 1941); Academy Award: Best Director (*Mrs. Miniver*, 1942); Academy

Award, New York Film Critics Circle Award, National Board of Review Award: Best Director (*The Best Years of Our Lives*, 1946); Academy Award Nomination: Best Director (*The Heiress*, 1949); Academy Award Nomination: Best Director (*Detective Story*, 1951); Directors Guild of America: Outstanding Directorial Achievement, Academy Award Nomination: Best Director (*Roman Holiday*, 1953); National Board of Review Award: Best Director (*The Desperate Hours*, 1955); Directors Guild of America: Outstanding Directorial Achievement, Academy Award Nomination: Best Director (*Friendly Persuasion*, 1956); Cannes Film Festival Award: Palme d'Or (*Friendly Persuasion*, 1957); Academy Award, Golden Globe Award, Directors Guild of America Award: Best Director (*Ben-Hur*, 1959); Academy Award: Irving G. Thalberg Award (1965); Directors Guild of America: (D. W. Griffith Award (1965); Academy Award Nomination: Best Director (*The Collector*, 1965); American Film Institute Life Achievement Award (1976).

Selected Bibliography

Anderegg, Michael A. *William Wyler*. Boston: Twayne, 1979.
Kern, Sharon. *William Wyler: A Guide to References and Resources*. Boston: G. K. Hall, 1984.
Madsen, Axel. *William Wyler: The Authorized Biography*. New York: Crowell, 1973.

WYMAN, JANE. Actress. Born Sarah Jane Fulks on January 4, 1914, in St. Joseph, Missouri. Educated at the University of Missouri. Wyman began her career as a radio singer and entered films in the mid-1930s as a bit player and chorine (using the name Jane Durrell). She was typecast as a pert blond in a string of low-budget films until she finally was recognized for her sensitive performance in Billy Wilder's *The Lost Weekend*, opposite Ray Milland. After that she distinguished herself in several fine dramas, particularly her unsympathetic role as the mother in *The Yearling*, as a deaf-mute rape victim in *Johnny Belinda* (for which she received an Oscar), and as the object of Rock Hudson's *Magnificent Obsession* in the 1954 Douglas Sirk melodrama. Later critics have since pointed to *All That Heaven Allows* as a high point in her career, a landmark film with the radical (for the times) message that suburban mothers should stop worrying about keeping the perfect home and follow their hearts. From 1955 to 1958 Wyman appeared regularly on TV as hostess and star of *Fireside Theatre* (renamed *The Jane Wyman Show* in her honor). Following an absence of several years, she resurfaced in a number of TV movies and emerged as one of America's favorite matriarchs in the popular soap *Falcon Crest* (1981–1990). Wyman was formerly married to actor and future President Ronald Reagan. Wyman's is a curious story and, in a way, a rather sad one. She seems destined to be forgotten or neglected because for some inexplicable reason she never became a "celebrity." If it weren't for her years on *Falcon Crest*, she might easily be lost in the dustbin of cinematic history, yet for a long time she was at the very top, appearing in everything from light musicals to comedies to melodramas to tearjerkers. She starred with many of Hollywood's leading men, was named most popular actress of the year more than once, and was considered, all in all, a high-profile box office draw. Part of her "problem" may be that she was too professional, thereby forgoing a reputation for being chronically late or uncooperative or "difficult." She showed up on time, knew her lines, and gave polished performances. There was no scandal in her life, nothing to put her face on the cover of the tabloids. But one suspects that another part of her problem is the perception that behind the button nose and beneath the mannered exterior lurks a vixen, a person with a nasty, icy core—that she might just after all really be the hard-boiled matriarch she played on *Falcon Crest* or the stern mother in *The Yearling* who seemed just a tad too willing to slaughter her son's pet deer for the sake of the corn.

Filmography: Gold Diggers of 1937, My Man Godfrey, Smart Blonde (1936); The King and the Chorus Girl, Mr. Dodd Takes the Air, Public Wedding, Ready Willing and Able, The Singing Marine, Slim (1937); The Crowd Roars, He Couldn't Say No, International Spy/The Spy Ring, Wide Open Faces (1938); The Kid from Kokomo, Kid Nightingale, Private Detective, Tail Spin, Torchy Plays with Dynamite (1939); An Angel from Texas, Brother Rat and a Baby, Flight Angels, Gambling on the High Seas, My Love Came Back, Tugboat Annie Sails Again (1940); Bad Men of Missouri, The Body Disappears, Honeymoon for Three, You're in the Army Now (1941); Footlight Serenade, Larceny Inc., My Favorite Spy (1942); Princess O'Rourke (1943); Crime by Night, The Doughgirls, Hollywood Canteen, Make Your Own Bed (1944); The Lost Weekend (1945); Night and Day, One More Tomorrow, The Yearling (1946); Cheyenne/Wyoming Kid, Magic Town (1947); Johnny Belinda (1948); It's a Great Feeling, A Kiss in the Dark, The Lady Takes a Sailor (1949); The Glass Menagerie, Stage Fright (1950); The Blue Veil, Here Comes the Groom, Starlift, Three Guys Named Mike (1951); Just For You, The Story of Will Rogers (1952); Let's Do It Again, So Big (1953); Magnificent Obsession (1954); All that Heaven Allows, Lucy Gallant (1955); Miracle in the Rain (1956); Holiday for Lovers (1959); Pollyanna (1960); Bon Voyage (1962); How to Commit Marriage (1969).

Honors: Academy Award Nomination: Best Actress (*The Yearling*, 1946); Academy Award, Golden Globe Award: Best Actress (*Johnny Belinda*, 1948); *Photoplay* Gold Medal Award: Most Popular Female Star (*Johnny Belinda*, 1949); Golden Globe Award: World Film Favorite (1950); Golden Globe Award, Academy Award Nomination: Best Actress (*The Blue Veil*, 1951); Academy Award Nomination: Best Actress (*Magnificent Obsession*, 1954).

Selected Bibliography

Morella, Joe, and Edward Z. Epstein. *Jane Wyman: A Biography*. New York: Delacorte Press, 1985.
Quirk, Lawrence J. *Jane Wyman, the Actress and the Woman: An Illustrated Biography*. New York: Dembner Books, 1986.

Y

YANKEE DOODLE DANDY (1942), musical. Directed by Michael Curtiz; with James Cagney, Joan Leslie, Walter Huston, Irene Manning, Rosemary DeCamp, Richard Whorf, Jeanne Cagney, S. Z. Sakall, Walter Catlett, Frances Langford, Eddie Foy, Jr., and George Tobias; screenplay by Robert Buckner and Edmund Joseph.

The real George M. Cohan, who saw this picture while he was recuperating from a serious operation, had this to say when asked how he liked it: ''My God, what an act to follow!'' This enchanting film, which earned Cagney a well-deserved Oscar for Best Actor, presents not only a portrait of song-and-dance man Cohan but also a portrait of early twentieth-century America. This gem of a film is all Cagney. Director Michael Curtiz took Cagney's advice throughout and let the hoofer have his way with every scene. When Cagney did his dance numbers, he made them up as he went along. This is a film you find fault with at your peril. Made in the early days of war, it is packed with jingoistic Americanism that audiences needed and responded to. And nobody worried about trite plot turns when Cohan's sentimental tunes were being sung and Cagney had his Irish up. As a tribute to America, to show business, and to a great gentleman of the theater, this musical biography has it all. And like all things that are truly a product of their time, this film is a classic, as fresh today as ever—and even more sentimental as you behold the inimitable Cagney at his brilliant best.

Awards: Academy Awards: Best Actor (Cagney), Scoring of a Musical Picture (Ray Heindorf, Heinz Roemheld), Sound Recording; New York Film Critics Circle Award: Best Actor (Cagney); Academy Award Nominations: Best Picture, Director, Supporting Actor (Huston), Original Story, Editing.

Selected Bibliography

Dickens, Homer. *The Complete Films of James Cagney*. Secaucus, NJ: Carol, 1989.
Kinnard, Roy, and R. J. Vitone. *The American Films of Michael Curtiz*. Metuchen, NJ: Scarecrow Press, 1986.
Peary, Danny. *Alternate Oscars*. New York: Delta, 1993.

YEARLING, THE (1946), drama. Directed by Clarence Brown; with Gregory Peck, Jane Wyman, Claude Jarman, Jr., Chill Wills, Margaret Wycherly, Henry Travers, Jeff York, Forrest Tucker, and June Lockhart; screenplay by Paul Osborn.

This deeply moving adaptation of Marjorie Kinnan Rawlings's tale of a boy attached to a young deer was filmed on location in Florida in exquisite Technicolor. In fact, it won an Oscar for Cinematography and Art Direction, not to mention the special Oscar awarded Jarman for this debut performance. Jarman's career did not last long, but if he made only this one film, it would be a career to be proud of. The yearling in the story represents the freedom of the boy's childhood. But when the deer becomes destructive, the boy's mother has no choice but to shoot him. Jane Wyman plays the tough role of the mother and manages to gain the audience's understanding if not always its sympathy. Her choice is the intrusion of reality in a seemingly idyllic world lived in a forest glade. But it's either shoot the deer or lose the corn crop and starve. When the boy ultimately realizes this, he has forever left his childhood behind him. Gregory Peck is flawless as the boy's father, especially with his rich, mellow voice just made, it seems, to wrap itself around those southern slurs and that peculiar grammar. An actor named Donn Gift plays the boy's friend—a strange little creature called Fodderwing who seems to have strayed in from a story by Truman Capote or Harper Lee. It is a movie studded with memorable moments: Jody and Fodderwing together, Jody alone with his yearling, Jody's mother so pleased at her dumb joke that she reveals a streak of humor that catches the viewer off guard, Peck serving as a very uncomfortable mannequin for a dress Wyman is sewing while Jody snickers. It's a movie that captures an atmosphere, as if the camera's eye can see more than is there, and it does it all without sentimentality.

Awards: Academy Award: Cinematography/Color (Charles Rosher, Leonard Smith, Arthur Arling), Interior Decoration/Color (Cedric Gibbons, Paul Groess); Golden Globe Award: Actor (Peck); Academy Award Nominations: Best Picture, Actor (Peck), Actress (Wyman), Director.

Selected Bibliography

Griggs, John. *The Films of Gregory Peck*. Secaucus, NJ: Citadel Press, 1984.
Morella, Joe, and Edward Z. Epstein. *Jane Wyman: A Biography*. New York: Delacorte Press, 1985.

YOUNG, LORETTA. Actress. Born Gretchen Michaela Young on January 6, 1913, in Salt Lake City, Utah. Young actually broke into films at the age of three as a bit player, but that part of her career was short-lived, and she returned to her convent education until she resurfaced at the age of fourteen playing a supporting role in *Naughty But Nice*, a role that earned her a contract with First National. In the mid-1930s Young switched to Fox and was soon one of Hollywood's most prominent leading ladies in a number of mostly mediocre productions. Her career reached its peak during the late 1940s in such acclaimed pictures as *The Farmer's Daughter*, for which she won an Academy Award, and *Come to the Stable*, for which she won an Academy Award nomination. By 1954 Young had retired from the screen in favor of a successful second career as the glamorous hostess, and frequent star, of TV's long-running anthology series *The Loretta Young Show* (1954–1963). Like Jane Wyman, Loretta Young was a thorough professional, always turning in an accomplished performance, always playing by the rules, and destined to be forgotten—or at least neglected. She was enormously well liked during her long career, especially when she reached a vast television audience before whom she could play a variety of challenging roles. Perhaps her image was too pure. She was most respected when she played either a nun or a milkmaid. Nevertheless, film buffs of Hollywood's golden age will find many gems among her many films, one of the most offbeat being her role as the professor who kills a student who sexually attacks her in *The Accused*.

Filmography: Sweet Kitty Bellairs (1916); Naughty But Nice (1927); The Head Man, Laugh Clown Laugh, The Magnificent First, Scarlet Seas, The Whip Woman (1928); The Careless Age, Fast Life, The Forward Pass, The Girl in the Glass Cage, The Show of Shows, The Squall (1929); The Devil to Pay, Loose Ankles, The Man from Blankley's, Road to Paradise, The Second Story Murder/The Second Floor Mystery, The Truth about Youth (1930); Beau Ideal, Big Business Girl, I Like Your Nerve, Kismet, Platinum Blonde, The Right of Way, The Ruling Voice, Three Girls Lost, Too Young to Marry (1931); The Hatchet Man, Life Begins, Play Girl, Taxi!, They Call It Sin, Week-end Marriage (1932); The Devil's in Love, Employees Entrance, Grand Slam, Heroes for Sale, The Life of Jimmy Dolan, Man's Castle, Midnight Mary, She Had to Say Yes, Zoo in Budapest (1933); Born to Be Bad, Bulldog Drummond Strikes Back, Caravan, House of Rothschild, The White Parade (1934); Call of the Wild, Clive of India, The Crusades, Shanghai (1935); Ladies in Love, Private Number, Ramona, The Unguarded Hour (1936); Cafe Metropole, Love Is News, Love under Fire, Second Honeymoon, Wife Doctor and Nurse (1937); Four Men and a Prayer, Kentucky, Suez (1938); Eternally Yours, The Story of Alexander Graham Bell, Wife Husband and Friend (1939); The Doctor Takes a Wife, He Stayed for Breakfast (1940); Bedtime Story, Lady from Cheyenne, The Men in Her Life (1941); China, A Night to Remember (1943); And Now Tomorrow, Ladies Courageous (1944); Along Came Jones (1945); The Perfect Marriage, The Stranger (1946); The Bishop's Wife, The Farmer's Daughter (1947); The Accused, Rachel and the Stranger (1948); Come to the Stable, Mother Is a Freshman (1949); Key to the City (1950); Cause for Alarm, Half Angel (1951); Because of You, Paula (1952); It Happens Every Thursday (1953); Going Hollywood: The War Years (1988).

Honors: Academy Award: Best Actress (*The Farmer's Daughter*, 1947); Academy Award Nomination: Best Actress (*Come to the Stable*, 1949).

Selected Bibliography

Morella, Joe, and Edward Z. Epstein. *Loretta Young: An Extraordinary Life*. New York: Delacorte Press, 1986.

YOUNG MAN WITH A HORN (1950), drama. Directed by Michael Curtiz; with Kirk Douglas, Lauren Bacall, Doris Day, Juano Hernandez, Hoagy Carmichael, and Mary Beth Hughes; screenplay by Carl Foreman and Edmund H. North.

This underrated little gem works superbly on several levels. At one level it is a glimpse of history, a set piece, a re-creation of a time between the wars when great jazz musicians played contemporary music that has now become classic. It was the era of one-night stands and band singers, of dingy hotel rooms and glittering dance halls, of the Roaring Twenties followed by the Great Depression. At another level it is a biography of an artist so dedicated to his music that it becomes the obsession that first thrills and finally kills him. This musician was the great trumpeter Bix Beiderbeck, and through Kirk Douglas's intense portrayal (and Harry James's magnificent trumpet playing) we feel both the loneliness and the sacredness of a singleness of purpose that would brook no compromise. On yet another level, this movie is a twisted romantic triangle, with possessive Lauren Bacall pursuing Douglas for her own dark reasons, sunny Doris Day bewildered by Bacall and no match for her machinations, and Douglas compulsively drawn to his trumpet, the iron mistress that ultimately brings him down. Warners tacked on a happy ending (Day comes to his rescue after Bacall leaves him and he goes on the skids) that doesn't ring true but leaves a lump in the throat. Aside from that, there is a toughness to this story that bears scrutiny, particularly the Bacall role, a role Joan Crawford or Bette Davis would have relished. But Bacall holds her own as the hard-as-nails woman who stops at nothing to get what she wants even though she is not sure why she wants it, then deliberately loses it. There is a curious scene where Douglas returns home late, having missed the party Bacall has thrown for him, just in time to see Bacall saying goodnight to a girlfriend she has known for years. Although the movie stays far away from any overt suggestions, there is an undercurrent here of something amiss, as if Douglas senses more than he immediately realizes about what just might be going on. Seen in this light, Bacall's neurotic behavior suddenly makes perfect sense. Incidentally, the sound track is great, with James at his sweetest and Day in top form.

Selected Bibliography

Baker, Dorothy. *Young Man with a Horn*. Boston: Houghton Mifflin, 1938.
Quirk, Lawrence J. *Lauren Bacall: Her Films and Career*. Secaucus, NJ: Citadel Press, 1986.
Thomas, Tony. *The Films of Kirk Douglas*. Secaucus, NJ: Citadel Press, 1972.
Young, Christopher. *The Films of Doris Day*. Secaucus, NJ: Citadel Press, 1977.

Z

ZINNEMANN, FRED. Director. Born on April 29, 1907, in Vienna, Austria; died on March 14, 1997, in London. Educated at the University of Vienna (law) and the Ecole Technique de Photographie et de Cinématographie in Paris. Fred Zinnemann's career spanned six decades, during which he directed twenty-two features and nineteen short subjects and won four Oscars. He is probably best remembered for such classic films as *High Noon*, *From Here to Eternity*, *A Man for All Seasons*, and *Julia*. Zinnemann's films are all compelling dramas of solitary individuals of high principles tested by tragic events. He is famous for his meticulous attention to detail, a gift for brilliant casting, and a preoccupation with the moral dilemmas of his characters. Zinnemann's penchant for realism and authenticity is evident in *The Search*, one of his finest films. Shot in war-ravaged Germany, the film stars Montgomery Clift in his screen debut as a GI who cares for a lost Czech boy traumatized by the war. The film is a minor classic because in it the blend of atmosphere, narrative, and characterization is in perfect harmony with the heartbreaking humanitarianism at its core. Zinnemann was another of those fabulous European émigrés who seem to be able to do anything. In addition to his poignant dramas chronicling the torments of angst-ridden heroes, he was also able to turn out Rodgers and Hammerstein's *Oklahoma!* using, for the first time, the wide screen format Todd-AO. Add to this *The Nun's Story*, *The Day of the Jackal*, and *The Member of the Wedding*, and his versatility is simply astonishing.

Filmography: [as director unless otherwise noted]: People on Sunday/Menschen am Sonntag [prod. asst.] (1929); All Quiet on the Western Front [per.] (1930); The Wave/Redes/Pescados [co-dir.] (1935); That Mothers Might Live (1938); Eyes in the Night, Kid Glove Killer (1942); The Seventh Cross (1944); Little Mr. Jim, My Brother Talks to Horses (1946); The Search (1948); The Men/Battle Stripe (1950); Benjy [short], Teresa

(1951); High Noon, The Member of the Wedding (1952); From Here to Eternity (1953); Oklahoma! (1955); A Hatful of Rain (1957); The Nun's Story (1959); The Sundowners [also prod.] (1960); Behold a Pale Horse [also prod.] (1964); A Man for All Seasons [also prod.] (1966); The Day of the Jackal (1973); Julia (1977); Five Days One Summer [also prod.] (1983); George Stevens: A Filmmaker's Journey [per.] (1984).

Honors: Academy Award: Director (*That Mothers Might Live* [MGM Miniatures], 1938); Directors Guild of America: Quarterly Award, Academy Award Nomination: Best Director (*The Search*, 1948); Academy Award: Producer (*Benjy* [doc./short], 1951); Directors Guild of America Quarterly Award, New York Film Critics Circle Award, Academy Award Nomination: Best Director (*High Noon*, 1952); Academy Award, Golden Globe Award, New York Film Critics Circle Award, Directors Guild of America Award: Best Director (*From Here to Eternity*, 1953); National Board of Review Award, Academy Award Nomination: Best Director (*The Nun's Story*, 1959); Academy Award Nomination: Best Director (*The Sundowners*, 1960); Academy Award, Golden Globe Award, New York Film Critics Circle Award, National Board of Review Award, Directors Guild of America Award: Best Director (*A Man for All Seasons*, 1966); Academy Award Nomination: Best Director (*Julia*, 1977).

Selected Bibliography

Griffith, Richard. *Fred Zinnemann*. New York: Museum of Modern Art, 1958.
Sennett, Ted. *Great Movie Directors*. New York: Harry N. Abrams, 1986.
Zinnemann, Fred. *A Life in the Movies: An Autobiography*. New York. Charles Scribner's Sons, 1992.

Appendix I
FILM FESTIVALS

Festival Name: **Access Awards**
Festival Location: Encinitas, CA
Info: Awards competition open to the public (especially educational and government access users).
Address: 103 North Highway 101, #2010, Encinitas, CA 92024
Telephone: 619–753–5310

Festival Name: **Athens International Film & Video Festival**
Festival Location: Athens, OH
Info: Looks for works that show a high degree of artistic ability and content. $20,000 in cash and equipment is awarded to the competition winners. Accepted formats include 35mm, 16mm, ¾", and ½".
Address: PO Box 388, Athens, OH 45701
Telephone: 614–593–1330
Fax: 614–593–1328

Festival Name: **Carolina Film & Video Festival**
Festival Location: Greensboro, NC
Info: Now in its fifth year at the University of North Carolina—Greensboro. Works in all genres and categories are accepted, including animations, documentaries, experimental, narrative, and more. $2,500 in awards.
Address: 100 Carmichael Building, Greensboro, NC 27512–5001
Telephone: 910–334–5360

Festival Name: **Charlotte Film & Video Festival**
Festival Location: Charlotte, NC
Info: This is one of the largest independent film festivals in the Southeast. Cash awards are made to the winners.
Address: 2730 Randolph Road, Charlotte, NC 28207

Telephone: 704–337–2109
Fax: 704–337–2101
E-mail: mintfilm@aol.com

Festival Name: **Chicago Latino Film Festival**
Festival Location: Chicago, IL
Info: Films from Portugal, Latin America, and Spain compete for cash prizes.
Address: 600 South Michigan Avenue, Chicago, IL 60605
Telephone: 312–431–1330
Fax: 312–360–0629

Festival Name: **Cine Golden Eagle Film & Video Competition**
Festival Location: Washington, D.C.
Info: Short and documentary films, video, and multimedia productions. Cine enters some
   of the award winners in foreign fests.
Address: 1001 Connecticut Avenue, Suite 638, Washington D.C. 20036
Telephone: 202–785–1136
Fax: 202–785–4114

Festival Name: **Creil International Women's Film Festival**
Festival Location: Creil, France
Info: Oldest fest of films by women.
Address: 24700 McBean Parkway, Valencia, CA 91355
Telephone: 212–473–3400
Fax: 805–254–2088

Festival Name: **Dallas Video Festival**
Festival Location: Dallas Museum of Art, Dallas, TX
Info: The Dallas Video Festival provides a showcase for new works by national, international, and regional independent artists; hands-on workshops for children; screenings
   of groundbreaking work by television's pioneers; demonstrations of the latest tech-
   nologies that are expanding the possibilities of video, and demonstrations of electronic
   media for all independent artists. Entries may be narrative, documentary, animation,
   experimental, computer graphics, works by children, children's programming, music
   videos, etc. The festival is also accepting entries for the interactive zone (CD-ROM,
   CD-I, 3DO, hypertext, etc.). Works will be chosen by the director for the four days
   of curated festival programming, with the exception of two juried programs: (1) The
   Texas Show, which will be compiled and distributed to nontheatrical venues throughout the year; to be included in The Texas Show, the work must be under twenty-five
   minutes and have been produced either in Texas or by a Texas resident; (2) Texas
   Interactive, a sampling of the best interactive multimedia work produced in Texas,
   which will be compiled onto a CD-ROM.
Address: 215A Henry Street, Dallas, TX 75226
Telephone: 214–651–8888
E-mail: vbart@aol.com

Festival Name: **Film and Architecture International Festival**
Festival Location: Graz, Austria
Info: Fest for thematic treatment of the multilayered relations between film and archi-
   tecture.

Address: Reichbauerstrasse 38, A-8010, Graz, Austria
Telephone: 0316–84–24–87
Fax: 0316–82–95–11

Festival Name: **Golden Rose of Montreux**
Festival Location: Montreux, Switzerland
Info: Organized by the Swiss Broadcasting Corporation and the City of Montreux. Annual competition for light entertainment TV programs.
Address: 488 Madison Avenue, Suite 1710, New York, NY 10022
Telephone: 212–223–0044
Fax: 212–223–4531

Festival Name: **Hometown Video Festival**
Festival Location: Sacramento, CA
Info: Sponsored by the Alliance for Community Media, this fest recognizes outstanding local programming.
Address: 3001 J Street, Suite 201, Sacramento, CA 95816
Telephone: 916–441–6277
Fax: 916–441–7670

Festival Name: **Humboldt International Film Festival**
Festival Location: Arcata, CA
Info: This is the oldest student-run film festival in the United States. All genres accepted, but entries must be under sixty minutes and have been completed in the last three years.
Address: Theater Arts Department, Humboldt State University, Arcata, CA 95521
Telephone: 707–826–4113
Fax: 707–826–5494

Festival Name: **International Monitor Awards**
Festival Location: New York, NY
Info: Worldwide competition recognizes excellence in all areas of electronic production and postproduction.
Address: 350 Fifth Avenue, #2400, New York, NY 10118
Telephone: 212–629–3266
Fax: 212–629–3265

Festival Name: **International Wildlife Film Festival**
Festival Location: Missoula, MT
Info: An annual celebration of wildlife, this is the longest-running festival of its kind in the world. Founded by the well-known bear biologist Dr. Charles Jonkel in 1977.
Address: 802 Front Street, Missoula, MT 59801
Telephone: 406–728–9380

Festival Name: **Jewish Video Competition**
Festival Location: Berkeley, CA
Info: Encourages independent video productions and interactive media on Jewish themes.
Address: 2911 Russell Street, Berkeley, CA 94705
Telephone: 510–549–6952

Appendix II
FILM SCHOOLS: INSTITUTIONS OFFERING GRADUATE WORK IN FILM, TELEVISION, AND VIDEO

Additional information about programs listed below may be obtained by consulting *Peterson's Guide to Graduate Programs in the Humanities, Arts, and Social Sciences* or by writing directly to the dean of a graduate school or chair of a department at the address given.

Academy of Art College, Department of Motion Pictures/Video, 79 New Montgomery Street, San Francisco, CA 94105–3410. Awards M.F.A.

American Film Institute Center for Advanced Film and Television Studies, Los Angeles, CA 90027–1657. Offers programs in cinematography (M.F.A.), directing (M.F.A.), editing (M.F.A.), producing (M.F.A.), production design (M.F.A.), screenwriting (M.F.A.).

American University, School of Communication, Graduate Film and Video Program, Washington, D.C. 20016–8001. Offers film and video production (M.A.), including film criticism, scriptwriting. Part-time programs available.

American University, School of Communication, Weekend Programs in Communication, Washington, D.C. 20016–8001. Offerings include producing for film and video (M.A.).

Art Center College of Design, Film Department, Pasadena, CA 91103–1999. Awards M.F.A.

Boston University, College of Communication, School of Broadcasting and Film, Boston, MA 02215. Offerings include film (M.S.).

Brigham Young University, College of Fine Arts and Communications, Department of Theatre and Film, Provo, UT 84602–1001. Offers programs in theater and film (M.A., Ph.D.).

California College of Arts and Crafts, Program in Film/Video/Performance, San Francisco, CA 94107. Awards M.F.A.

California Institute of the Arts, School of Film/Video, Valencia, CA 91355–2430. Offers programs in directing for theater, video, and cinema (M.F.A.); film/video (M.F.A.). M.F.A. (directing for theater, video, and cinema) offered jointly with the School of Theatre.

Central Michigan University, College of Arts and Sciences, Department of Broadcast and Cinematic Arts, Mount Pleasant, MI 48859. Awards M.A., M.S.A

Chapman University, School of Communication Arts, Orange, CA 92866. Program in Film and TV Production awards M.F.A. Program in Film Studies awards M.A.

Claremont Graduate School, Department of Fine Art, Claremont, CA 91711–6163. Offerings include filmmaking (M.A., M.F.A.).

College of Staten Island of the City University of New York, Program in Cinema Studies, Staten Island, NY 10314–6600. Awards M.A. Part-time and evening/weekend programs available.

Columbia College, Department of Film, 600 South Michigan Avenue, Chicago, IL 60605–1997. Offers program in film and video (M.F.A.). Part-time programs available. Department of English offerings include literature and film (M.A.).

Columbia University, Graduate School of Arts and Sciences, Department of Film, New York, NY 10027. Awards Ph.M., Ph.D.

Columbia University, School of the Arts, Division of Film, New York, NY 10027. Offers programs in directing (M.F.A.), history/theory (M.F.A.), and producing and screenwriting (M.F.A.).

Emory University, Graduate School of Arts and Sciences, Department of Film Studies, Atlanta, GA 30322–1100. Awards MA.

Florida State University, School of Motion Picture, Television, and Recording Arts. Tallahassee, FL 32306. Awards M.F.A.

Howard University, School of Communications, Department of Radio, Television and Film, 2400 Sixth Street, NW, Washington, D.C. 20059–0002. Offerings include film (M.F.A.).

Loyola Marymount University, College of Communication and Fine Arts, Department of Communication Arts, Los Angeles, CA 90045-8350. Offers programs in film screenwriting (M.F.A.), television screenwriting (M.F.A.).

New York University, Tisch School of the Arts, Graduate Film Department, New York, NY 10012–1019. Awards M.F.A.

New York University, Tisch School of the Arts and Graduate School of Arts and Science, Department of Cinema Studies, New York, NY 10012–1019, Awards M.A., Ph.D. Part-time programs available.

Northwestern University, School of Speech, Department of Radio/Television/Film, Evanston, IL 60208. Awards M.A., M.F.A., Ph.D.

Ohio University, Graduate Studies, College of Fine Arts, School of Film, Athens, OH 45701–2979. Awards M.A., M.F.A.

San Diego State University, College of Professional Studies and Fine Arts, School of Communication, Department of Telecommunications and Film, San Diego, CA 92182. Awards M.A.

San Francisco Art Institute, Department of Filmmaking, San Francisco, CA 94133–2299. Awards M.F.A.

San Francisco State University, College of Creative Arts, Department of Cinema, San Francisco, CA 94132–1722. Offers programs in cinema (M.F.A.), cinema studies (M.A.).

School of the Art Institute of Chicago, Department of Filmmaking, Chicago, IL 60603–3103. Awards M.F.A.

Southern Illinois University at Carbondale, College of Mass Communication and Media Arts, Department of Cinema and Photography, Carbondale, IL 62901–6806. Offers programs in cinema (M.F.A.), photography (M.F.A.). Part-time programs available.

Stanford University, School of Humanities and Sciences, Department of Communication, Stanford, CA 94305–9991. Offerings include film (A.M.).

Syracuse University, College of Visual and Performing Arts, Department of Drama, Syracuse, NY 13244–0003. Offerings include cinema/drama (M.F.A.), with option in directing/acting.

Syracuse University, College of Visual and Performing Arts, School of Art and Design, Department of Art Media Studies, Syracuse, NY 13244–0003. Offerings include film-art drama (M.F.A.), video research (M.F.A.).

Temple University, School of Communications and Theater, Department of Film and Media Arts, Philadelphia, PA 19012. Awards M.F.A. Part-time programs available.

University of Alabama, College of Communication, Department of Telecommunication and Film, Tuscaloosa, AL 35487. Awards M.A.

University of British Columbia, Faculties of Arts and Graduate Studies, Department of Theatre, Film and Creative Writing, Film Studies Program, Vancouver, BC V6T 1Z1, Canada. Offers film and video production (M.F.A.), film studies (M.A.).

University of California, Los Angeles, School of Theater, Film and Television, Department of Film and Television, Los Angeles, CA 90095. Awards M.A., M.F.A., Ph.D.

University of Iowa, College of Liberal Arts, Program in Film and Video Production, Iowa City, IA 52242. Awards M.F.A.

University of Kansas, College of Liberal Arts and Sciences, Department of Theatre and Film, Lawrence, KS 66045. Awards M.A., Ph.D.

University of Memphis, College of Communication and Fine Arts, Department of Communication, Memphis, TN 38152. Offerings include film and video production (M.A.).

University of Miami, School of Communications, Coral Gables, FL 33124. Offerings include motion pictures (M.F.A.).

University of New Orleans, College of Liberal Arts, Department of Drama and Communication, New Orleans, LA 70148. Offers programs in communications (M.A.), including film, television; creative writing (M.F.A.); drama (M.A.).

University of North Carolina at Greensboro, College of Arts and Sciences, Department of Broadcasting/Cinema and Theatre, Greensboro, NC 27412–2001. Offers program in drama (M.Ed., M.F.A.) including drama (M.F.A.), film and video (M.F.A.).

University of North Texas, College of Arts and Sciences, Department of Radio/Television/Film, Denton, TX 76203–6737. Awards M.A., M.S. Part-time programs available.

University of Southern California, Graduate School, College of Letters, Arts and Sciences, Department of English, Program in Film and Literature, Los Angeles, CA 90089. Awards Ph.D.

University of Southern California, Graduate School, School of Cinema-Television, Program in Critical Studies, Los Angeles, CA 90089. Awards M.A., Ph.D.

University of Southern California, Graduate School, School of Cinema-Television, Program in Film, Literature, and Culture, Los Angeles, CA 90089. Awards Ph.D.

University of Southern California, Graduate School, School of Cinema-Television: Program in Film, Video, and Computer Animation; Program in Motion Picture Producing; Program in Screenwriting, Los Angeles, CA 90089. Awards M.F.A.

University of Texas at Austin, Graduate School, College of Communication, Department of Radio-Television-Film, Austin, TX 78712. Offerings include film production (M.F.A.).

University of Utah, College of Fine Arts, Department of Arts, Salt Lake City, UT 84112. Offerings include film (M.F.A.).

University of Wisconsin at Milwaukee, School of Fine Arts, Interdepartmental Program in Performing Arts, Milwaukee, WI 53201–0413. Offerings include film (M.F.A.).

Virginia Commonwealth University, School of the Arts, Department of Design, Program in Photography/Film, Richmond, VA 23284-9005. Awards M.F.A.

York University, Faculty of Fine Arts, Program in Film and Video, North York, ON M3J 1P3, Canada. Awards M.F.A.

Appendix III
FILM ARCHIVES AND MUSEUMS

Anthology Film Archives
32–34 2nd Avenue
New York, NY 10003
Phone: 212–505–5181
Fax: 212–477–2714
Facilities include: visual and written research library, publications of texts on film and written research library, public screening of films in the collection, and presentation of video works.

Association of Movie Imaging Archivists
c/o National Center for Film and Video Presentation
American Film Institute
2021 North Western Avenue
Box 27999
Los Angeles, CA 90027

Em Gee Film Library
Suite 103, 6924 Canby Avenue
Reseda, CA 91335
Phone: 818–881–8110
Fax: 818–981–5506
Subjects: Public domain, classic films, feature films, comedy, documentaries, westerns, animation
All film formats: VHS, Umatic.NTSC

Hollywood Film Registry
6926 Melrose Avenue
Hollywood, CA 90038
Phone: 213–937–7067
Fax: 213–655–8889

Subjects: Historical archives, stock shots, locations, personalities, Americana, documentaries, and classic films.
16mm, 35mm; most video formats

Imageways
Second Floor
412 West 48th Street
New York, NY 10036
Phone: 212–265–1287
Fax: 212–586–0339
Subjects: Stock shots, newsreels, comedy, animation, classic films, documentaries, industry, educational films, television.
Film: 1" videotape with time-coded ¾" cassettes

John E. Allen
116 North Avenue
Park Ridge, NJ 07656
Phone: 201–391–6335
Fax: 201–391–6335
Subjects: Historical archive, newsreels, war, Russia, industry, transport, classic films, educational films, travelogues.
Mainly film, some video

Original Film Video Library
P.O. Box 3457
Anaheim, CA 92803
Phone: 714–526–4392
Fax: 714–526–4392
Subjects: Classic films, advertising, trailers, television, animation.
16 mm, 35 mm only

Streamline Archives
Suite 1314
432 Park Avenue South
New York, NY 10016
Phone: 212–696–2616
Fax: 212–696–0021
Subjects: Stock shots, newsreels, current affairs, classic films, feature films, educational, industry, sport, TV, advertising, travelogues.
16mm, 35 mm; most video formats; PAC, NTSC, and SECAM

Video Tape Library
Suite 2, 1509 North Crescent Heights Boulevard
Los Angeles, CA 90046
Phone: 213–656–4330
Fax: 213–656–8746
Subjects: Stock shots, current affairs, newsreels, locations, beauty, comedy, classic films, sport, leisure, environmental, medicine, out-takes (newsreels from 1929 to 1967).
20% film, 80% video

Video Yesteryear
Box C
Sandy Hook, CT 06482
Phone: 203–744–2476
Fax: 203–797–0819
Subjects: Historical archive, classic films, TV (large collection of vintage film and TV clips).

Worldview Entertainment
6 East 39th Street
New York, NY 10016
Phone: 212–679–8230
Fax: 212–686–0801
Subjects: historical archives, classic film, newsreels.
16mm, 35mm; all video formats; NTSC

SELECTED BIBLIOGRAPHY

The following bibliography is by no means exhaustive, nor is it intended to be. A complete bibliography would not only fill volumes but could never be up-to-date. Serious scholars of cinema must narrow their research to a particular topic (e.g., genre, person, period, technique, impact) and then locate appropriate sources within works on those topics as these works are uncovered. Thus, one of the purposes of the selected bibliographies at the end of each entry is to give scholars a nod in the right direction. Once you have uncovered two or three books about, say, Bette Davis, you will find, in most cases, that these books will contain bibliographies leading you forward to new discoveries. Therefore, this general bibliography can only serve as a basic source of information about such broad topics as the studio system or the star system or the developing art of moviemaking technique. Also included are some primary works on such film genres as horror, musical, western, comedy, film noir, and so on., and on the history of the major studios. These works contain information of a general sort that provides the curious student with the background necessary to give specific research a credible context. In some cases I have picked older books over more recent books because I preferred books that concentrated on the 1930–1965 time frame almost exclusively.

CAMERAMEN

Higham, Charles. *Hollywood Cameramen*. Bloomington: Indiana University Press, 1970.

COMEDY

Byron, Stuart, and Elisabeth Weis, eds. *The National Society of Film Critics on Movie Comedy*. New York: Grossman Publishers, 1977.
Gehring, Wes D. *Screwball Comedy: Hollywood's Madcap Romantic Comedies*. New York: Crown, 1989.

McCaffrey, Donald W. *The Golden Age of Sound Comedy: Comic Films and Comedians of the 30s.* South Brunswick, NJ: A. S. Barnes, 1973.

Sennett, Ted. *Lunatics and Lovers: A Tribute to the Giddy and Glittering Era of the Screen's "Screwball" and Romantic Comedies.* New Rochelle, NY: Arlington House, 1973.

Siegel, Scott, and Barbara Siegel. *American Film Comedy.* New York: Prentice-Hall, 1994.

Sikov, Ed. *Screwball: Hollywood's Madcap Romantic Comedies.* New York: Crown, 1989.

COMPOSERS

Palmer, Christopher. *The Composer in Hollywood.* New York: Marion Boyars, 1990.

COSTUMES

Perez, Susan. *Film Costume.* Metuchen, NJ: Scarecrow, 1981.

CRITICISM

Ebert, Roger, ed. *Roger Ebert's Book of Film.* W. W. Norton, 1997.

Kael, Pauline. *5001 Nights at the Movies.* New York: Henry Holt, 1991.

———. *I Lost It at the Movies.* Boston: Little, Brown, 1965.

———. *Kiss Kiss, Bang Bang.* New York: Bantam, 1968.

Poteet, G. Howard. *Film Criticism in Popular American Periodicals, 1933–1967: A Computer-assisted Content Analysis.* New York: Revisionist Press Cinema Series, 1977.

DIRECTORS

Andrew, Geoff. *The Film Handbook.* London: Longman, 1989.

Brandy, Leo, and Morris Dickstein. *Great Film Directors.* New York: Oxford University Press, 1978.

Canham, Kingsley. *The Hollywood Professionals.* New York: A. S. Barnes, 1973.

Finler, Joel W. *The Movie Directors Story.* London: Octopus Books, 1985.

Sarris, Andrew. *The American Cinema: Directors and Directions 1929–1968.* New York: E. P. Dutton, 1968.

———. *Interviews with Directors.* New York: Avon, 1969.

EPICS

Smith, Gary A. *Epic Films: Cast, Credits, and Commentary on over 250 Historical Spectacular Movies.* Jefferson, NC: McFarland, 1991.

FILM NOIR

Hirsch, Foster. *Film Noir*. New York: DaCapo, 1981.

Silver, Alain, and Elizabeth Ward, eds. *Film Noir: An Encyclopedic Reference to the American Style*. Woodstock, NY: Overlook Press, 1979.

Tuska, Jon. *Dark Cinema*. Westport, CT: Greenwood Press, 1984.

GANGSTER

Alloway, Lawrence. *Violent America*. New York: Museum of Modern Art, 1971.

McArthur, Colin. *Underworld, U.S.A.* New York: Viking Press, 1972.

Rosow, Eugene. *Born to Lose: The Gangster Film in America*. New York: Oxford University Press, 1978.

GENERAL

Elley, Derek. *Variety Movie Guide*. London: Hamlyn [annual].

Gebert, Michael. *The Encyclopedia of Movie Awards*. New York: St. Martin's Press, 1996.

International Motion Picture Almanac. New York: Quigley Publishing [annual].

Katz, Ephraim. *The Film Encyclopedia*. New York: HarperCollins, 1994.

Levy, Emanuel. *Small-Town America in Film: The Decline and Fall of Community*. New York: Continuum, 1991.

Maltin, Leonard, ed. *Leonard Maltin's Movie and Video Guide*. New York: Plume [annual].

———. *Leonard Maltin's Movie Encyclopedia*. New York: Dutton, 1994.

Miller, Frank. *Movies We Love: 100 Collectible Classics*. Atlanta, GA: Turner Publishing, 1996.

Milne, Tom, ed. *The Time Out Film Guide*. New York: Penguin [biennial].

Peary, Danny. *Alternate Oscars*. New York: Delta, 1993.

Rivkin, Allen, and Laura Kerr. *Hello, Hollywood!: A Book about the Movies by the People Who Make Them*. New York: Doubleday & Co., 1962.

Robertson, Patrick. *Guiness Film Facts and Feats*. New York: Sterling Publishing, 1985.

Thomas, Tony. *The Films of the Forties*. Secaucus, NJ: Citadel Press, 1975.

Thomson, David. *A Biographical Dictionary of Film*. 3rd ed. New York: Knopf, 1994.

Vermilye, Jerry. *The Films of the Thirties*. New York: Citadel Press, 1990.

Walker, John, ed. *Halliwell's Film Guide*. New York: HarperCollins [annual].

GENRES

Altman, Rick, ed. *Genre*. London: Routledge & Kegan Paul, 1981.

Cawelti, John G. *Adventure, Mystery and Romance*. Chicago: University of Chicago Press, 1976.

Gehring, Wes D. *Handbook of American Film Genres*. Westport, CT: Greenwood Press, 1988.

Grant, Barry Keith. *Film Genre Reader*. Austin: University of Texas Press, 1986.

Kaminsky, Stuart. *American Film Genres*. New York: Dell, 1977.

Schatz, Thomas. *Hollywood Genres*. Philadelphia: Temple University Press, 1981.

HISTORY

Allen, Robert C. and Douglas Gomery. *Film History*. New York: Knopf, 1985.

Altman, Diana. *Hollywood East: Louis B. Mayer and the Origins of the Studio System*. Secaucus, NJ: Carol, 1992.

Basinger, Jeanine. *American Cinema: One Hundred Years of Filmmaking*. New York: Rizzoli International Publications, 1994.

Belton, John. *American Cinema, American Culture*. New York: McGraw-Hill, 1994.

Bordwell, David, Janet Staiger, and Kristin Thompson. *The Classical Hollywood Cinema*. New York: Columbia University Press, 1985.

Eyman, Scott. *The Speed of Sound: Hollywood and the Talkie Revolution, 1926–1930*. New York: Simon & Schuster, 1997.

Friedrich, Otto. *City of Nets: A Portrait of Hollywood in the 1940's*. New York: Harper & Row, 1986.

Giannetti, Louis D., and Scott Eyman. *Flashback: A Brief History of Film*. Englewood Cliffs, NJ: Prentice-Hall, 1996.

Gomery, Douglas. *Movie History: A Survey*. Belmont, CA: Wadsworth, 1991.

Nowell-Smith, Geoffrey, ed. *The Oxford History of World Cinema*. New York: Oxford University Press, 1996.

HORROR

Grant, Barry Keith. *Planks of Reason*. Metuchen, NJ: Scarecrow, 1988.

Huss, Roy, and T. J. Ross. *Focus on the Horror Film*. Englewood Cliffs, NJ: Prentice-Hall, 1972.

Waller, Gregory. *American Horrors*. Urbana: University of Illinois Press, 1987.

MAKEUP

Westmore, Frank. *The Westmores of Hollywood*. Philadelphia: J. B. Lippincott, 1974.

MUSICALS

Altman, Rick. *The American Film Musical*. Bloomington: Indiana University Press, 1987.

Barrios, Richard. *A Song in the Dark: The Birth of the Musical Film*. New York: Oxford University Press, 1995.

Feuer, Jane. *The Hollywood Musical*. Bloomington, Indiana University Press, 1982.

Fordin, Hugh. *The World of Entertainment!: Hollywood's Greatest Musicals*. New York: Doubleday, 1975.

SCIENCE FICTION

Brosnan, John. *Future Tense: The Cinema of Science Fiction*. New York: St. Martin's Press, 1978.

Menville, Douglas Alver. *A Historical and Critical Survey of the Science Fiction Film*. New York: Arno Press, 1975.
Parish, James Robert, and Michael Pitts. *The Great Science Fiction Pictures*. Metuchen, NJ: Scarecrow Press, 1977.

SCREENWRITERS

Stempel, Tom. *Framework*. New York: Ungar, 1988.

SET DESIGNERS

Barsacq, Leon. *Caligari's Cabinet and Other Grand Illusions*. New York: New American Library, 1976.

SUSPENSE/THRILLER

Derry, Charles. *The Suspense Thriller*. Jefferson, NC: McFarland, 1988.
Telotte, J. P. *Voices in the Dark*. Urbana: University of Illinois Press, 1989.

WAR

Basinger, Jeanine. *The World War II Combat Film: Anatomy of a Genre*. New York: Columbia University Press, 1986.
Doherty, Thomas Patrick. *Projection of War: Hollywood, American Culture, and World War II*. New York: Columbia University Press, 1993.
Guttmacher, Peter. *Legendary War Movies*. New York: MetroBooks, 1996.
Quirk, Lawrence J. *The Great War Films: From "The Birth of a Nation" to Today*. Secaucus, NJ: Carol Publishers, 1994.

WESTERNS

Buscombe, Ed. *The BFI Companion to the Western*. London: Andre Deutsch, 1988.
Cawelti, John G. *The Six-Gun Mystique*. Bowling Green, OH: Bowling Green University Popular Press, 1971.
Fenin, George and William K. Everson. *The Western*. New York: Grossman, 1973.
Hardy, Phil, ed. *The Overlook Film Encyclopedia: The Western*. Woodstock, NY: Overlook Press, 1994.
Moore, Archie P. *Shooting Stars*. Bloomington: Indiana University Press, 1987.
Nachbar, Jack. *Focus on the Western*. Englewood Cliffs, NJ: Prentice-Hall, 1974.
Parish, James Robert, and Michael R. Pitts. *The Great Western Pictures*. Metuchen, NJ: Scarecrow Press, 1976.
Tuska, Jon. *The Filming of the West*. Garden City, NY: Doubleday, 1976.

INDEX

Note: Boldface numbers indicate location of main entries.

About the Author

THOMAS WHISSEN is Professor Emeritus of English at Wright State University. He has written books on popular culture and fiction, including *Cult Classic Fiction* (trans., Greenwood, 1992) and *The Devil's Advocates* (Greenwood, 1989) and has published articles on mystery writers in *Great American Mystery Writers* (Greenwood, 1994) as well as articles on cartoons and popular writers. He is also the translator of *Inside the Concentration Camps: Eyewitness Accounts of Life in Hitler's Death Camps* (Praeger, 1996).

ISBN 0-313-29487-9

90000>

EAN

9 780313 294877

HARDCOVER BAR CODE